W9-AMB-087

The
Which? Guide
to
Country Pubs

The
Which? Guide
to
Country Pubs

EDITED BY PETER HAYDON

CONSUMERS' ASSOCIATION

Which? Books are commissioned and researched by
Consumers' Association and published by Which? Ltd,
2 Marylebone Road, London NW1 4DF

Distributed by The Penguin Group:
Penguin Books Ltd, 27 Wrights Lane, London W8 5TZ

First edition 1993
Second edition 1995
Third edition 1997
Fourth edition 1999

British Library Cataloguing in Publication Data
A catalogue record for this book is available from the British Library

ISBN 0 85202 748 6

For a full list of Which? books, please write to:
Which? Books, Castlemead, Gascoyne Way,
Hertford X, SG14 1LH
or access our web site at http://www.which.net

Typeset by Saxon Graphics Ltd, Derby
Printed and bound in England by Clays Ltd, St Ives plc

Cover design and photograph by Kyzen
Typographic design by Paul Saunders

Contents

How to use the *Guide*

The *Guide* is divided into two parts. At the front is the main section, which lists country pubs throughout Britain selected for the quality of their food, drink and atmosphere; the selections are based on reports from the general public backed up by independent inspections. Towards the back you will find the 'Out and About' section, which features more than 300 additional pubs which are also well worth a visit. These have been selected less on the basis of the food they offer (some do not offer food at all; in other cases, we have had insufficient feedback to be able to assess cooking), but rather for other qualities that set them apart – perhaps for their superlative beers, hospitality, character, setting, history or other attribute.

Layout

Both parts of the *Guide* are further divided into the following sections: England, Scotland and Wales. Pubs are listed alphabetically by locality; they are put in their true *geographical* location, rather than at their postal address. If a pub is difficult to find, directions are given (after the address and telephone number). It is always worth checking by telephone if you are unsure about the exact location of an out-of-the-way pub.

How to find a pub in a particular area

Go to the full-colour maps at the centre of the book and choose the general area that you want. Towns and villages where pubs in the *Guide* are located are marked with a tankard symbol; turn to that locality in the appropriate section of the book, where you will find details of the pub (or pubs) there.

Awards

🏵🏵 denotes a pub where the quality of the bar food is comparable to that of a 'serious' restaurant – i.e. ingredients are consistently first-class and imagination and style are hallmarks of the kitchen. See the centre of the book for a list of these pubs.

🏵 signifies that the pub offers above-average bar food that shows ambition and good ideas, or simple pub fare prepared particularly well. See the centre of the book for list.

🍺 denotes a pub serving exceptional draught beers. See page 10 for list.

🍷 indicates a pub serving better-than-average wines, with a selection (usually six or more) of decent wines by the glass. See page 12 for list.

Other symbols in entries

▲ indicates a pub which offers accommodation.

[NEW ENTRY] appears after a pub's name if it did not feature in the last edition as a main entry (although it might have featured as an Out and About). See page 14 for list.

LOCAL PRODUCE   '*Flashes*' These highlight a particular point of interest in selected main entries, such as 'cheese', 'setting' or 'whisky', indicating that the pub has something special, perhaps unique, about it. See end of colour section for list of flashes.

Sample dishes

These are listed at the end of each main entry and are examples of typical dishes from the menu. Prices are based on figures provided by the pub licensee; in most cases, prices have been rounded up to the nearest 25 pence. Note that items listed may not always be available (particularly if they are 'specials').

Food and drink

Details of bar food mentioned in the entries are based on all the feedback we have received since the last edition of the *Guide* was published, including official inspections, notes from readers, and information provided by the licensees. Many pubs vary their menus from day to day, so specific items may no longer be in the kitchen's repertoire. If dishes are available in a separate restaurant and not in the bar, we mention that in the entry. Similarly, the range of draught beers may differ from time to time, especially if a pub has guest brews. Any real ciders are also listed. Information about wine is geared to what is generally available in the bar; in some pubs with a separate restaurant, you may need to request to see the full wine list (most pubs will oblige). The number of wines available by the glass is usually given in the text.

Opening hours and other details

The information given in the italics section at the end of each entry has been supplied by the pub and may be subject to change. If you are making a special journey, it is always worthwhile phoning beforehand to check opening and bar food times, and any other details that are important to you, such as restrictions on children or dogs, wheelchair access, etc.

✪ 'Open' times: these are the pub's full licensing hours. (Sunday hours are given separately if different.) Opening times may vary, especially in pubs that rely heavily on seasonal trade; days and times when a pub is closed are also listed.

- Bar food (and restaurant) times: these denote when food is served in the bar (and restaurant, if there is one). L and D are sometimes used to indicated lunch and dinner, to avoid confusion.

- Children: often children are allowed in a family room or eating area of a pub, but not in the main bar area. Any restrictions on children are listed.

- Car park: if a pub has its own car park, this is noted.

- Wheelchair access: this means that the proprietor has confirmed that the entrance to the bar/dining-room is at least 80cm wide and passages at least 120cm across – the Royal Association for Disability and Rehabilitation (RADAR) recommendations. If 'also WC' is given, it means that the proprietor has told us that the toilet facilities are suitable for disabled people.

- Garden/patio: details are based on information provided by the licensee. If a pub has a children's play area or another interesting feature – e.g. a boules pitch – this is mentioned in the text.

- Smoking: restrictions on smoking or special areas designated for non-smokers are noted.

- Music: if background or live music is ever played, or if a pub has a jukebox, this is stated.

- Dogs: any restrictions on dogs *inside* the pub are listed. Most pubs will allow dogs in their gardens. Guide dogs are normally exempt from restrictions, although it is best to check beforehand if you have special requirements.

- Cards: major credit and debit cards are listed if a pub accepts these as a means of payment. Note that this service may apply only to restaurant meals and/or accommodation. If a pub does not accept cards, we note this.

- Accommodation: if a pub offers overnight accommodation, the number of bedrooms and a range of B&B prices – from the lowest you can expect to pay for a single room (or single occupancy of a twin/double) to the most you are likely to pay for a twin/double – are listed. Pub bedrooms have not been officially inspected for this guide. Additional accommodation – e.g. in a self-catering cottage – may be mentioned in the text.

Report forms

At the very back of the book are report forms which you may use to recount your experiences in the pubs already featured in this guide, or in other pubs which you think we should include. The address is FREEPOST, so no stamp is necessary (full details on the report forms). Because *The Which? Guide to Country Pubs*, like its sister publication *The Good Food Guide*, relies to a great extent on unsolicited feedback from readers, your comments are invaluable to us and will form a major part of our research when we prepare future editions.

Pubs serving exceptional draught beers

Most pubs in the *Guide* serve acceptable real ales. This list includes establishments which are making a special effort in that direction. In all of them, the quality of draught beers is exceptional, and this is backed up by knowledgeable cellar work. We have also taken into account the range of styles and strengths available. Pubs that support independent local and regional country breweries have been given preference.

ENGLAND
Berkshire
Bell Inn, Aldworth
Dundas Arms, Kintbury
Pot Kiln, Frilsham
Buckinghamshire
Red Lion, Chenies
Cambridgeshire
Anchor Inn, Sutton Gault
Cheshire
Bhurtpore Inn, Aston
Cornwall
Maltsters Arms, Chapel Amble
Rashleigh, Polkerris
Royal Oak, Lostwithiel
Trengilly Wartha, Constantine
Cumbria
Abbey Bridge, Lanercost
Black Bull, Coniston
Britannia Inn, Elterwater
Drunken Duck Inn, Ambleside
Masons Arms, Cartmel Fell
Queens Head Hotel, Troutbeck
Shepherds Inn, Melmerby
White Horse Inn, Scales
Derbyshire
Three Stags Heads, Wardlow
    Mires
White Horse Inn, Woolley
    Moor
Devon
Castle Inn, Lydford
Church House Inn, Holne
Drewe Arms, Broadhembury
Duke of York, Iddesleigh
Jack in the Green, Rockbeare
Masons Arms, Branscombe
Masons Arms Inn, Knowstone
Nobody Inn, Doddiscombsleigh
Oxenham Arms, South Zeal
Peter Tavy Inn, Peter Tavy

Tower Inn, Slapton
Union Inn, Dolton
Waterman's Arms, Ashprington
Dorset
Bottle Inn, Marshwood
Fox Inn, Corscombe
Langton Arms, Tarrant Monkton
East Sussex
Griffin Inn, Fletching
Jolly Sportsman, East Chiltington
Old Oak, Arlington
Ypres Castle, Rye
Essex
Bell Inn, Horndon on the Hill
White Horse, Ridgewell
Gloucestershire
Kings Head, Bledington
New Inn, Coln St Aldwyns
Hampshire
Flower Pots Inn, Cheriton
Hawkley Inn, Hawkley
Peat Spade Inn, Longstock
Red House, Whitchurch
Sun, Bentworth
White Horse Inn, Priors Dean
Herefordshire
Riverside Inn, Aymestrey
Hertfordshire
Lytton Arms, Knebworth
Kent
Bell Inn, Smarden
Black Bull, Cliffe
Three Chimneys, Biddenden
Lancashire
Eagle & Child, Bispham Green
New Inn, Yealand Conyers
Leicestershire
Old Barn Inn, Glooston
Norfolk
Fishermans Arms,
    Winterton-on-Sea

Lord Nelson, Burnham Thorpe
Red Lion, Stiffkey
Three Horseshoes, Warham
  All Saints
Northamptonshire
Queens Head, Sutton Bassett
Northumberland
Dipton Mill, Hexham
Manor House Inn, Carterway
  Heads
Olde Ship Hotel, Seahouses
Queens Head Inn,
  Great Whittington
North Yorkshire
Malt Shovel, Brearton
Plough Inn, Saxton
Three Tuns Inn, Osmotherley
Wombwell Arms, Wass
Nottinghamshire
Martins Arms, Colston Bassett
Oxfordshire
Falkland Arms, Great Tew
Tite Inn, Chadlington
Rutland
Noel Arms, Whitwell
Shropshire
Crown, Munslow
Hundred House Hotel, Norton
Red Lion, Llanfair Waterdine
Three Tuns, Bishop's Castle
Somerset
Horse & Groom, East Woodlands
Notley Arms, Monksilver
Suffolk
Angel, Lavenham
Cornwallis Arms, Brome
Crown, Westleton
De La Pole Arms, Wingfield
Froize Inn, Chillesford
Surrey
Plough Inn, Coldharbour
Warwickshire
Fox & Hounds, Great Wolford
West Sussex
Black Horse, Nuthurst
Cricketers, Duncton
Elsted Inn, Elsted Marsh
George and Dragon, Burpham

Halfway Bridge Inn,
  Halfway Bridge
Hare and Hounds, Stoughton
King's Arms, Fernhurst
Lickfold Inn, Lickfold
Three Horseshoes, Elsted
West Yorkshire
Old Bridge Inn, Ripponden
Wiltshire
Dove Inn, Corton
George & Dragon, Rowde
Horse and Groom, Charlton
King John Inn, Tollard Royal
Lamb at Hindon, Hindon
Owl, Little Cheverell
Worcestershire
The Talbot, Knightwick

SCOTLAND
Borders
Traquair Arms, Innerleithen
East Lothian
Waterside, Haddington
Fife
Ship Inn, Limekilns
Perthshire & Kinross
Tormaukin Hotel, Glendevon
Stirling
Clachan Inn, Drymen
Lade Inn, Kilmahog

WALES
Gwynedd
Grapes Hotel, Maentwrog
Harp Inn, Llandwrog
Monmouthshire
Boat Inn, Penallt
Clytha Arms, Clytha
Red Hart, Llanvapley
Pembrokeshire
Carew Inn, Carew
Tafarn Newydd, Rosebush
Powys
Nantyffin Cider Mill Inn,
  Crickhowell
Vale of Glamorgan
Blue Anchor Inn, East Aberthaw

Pubs serving better-than-average wine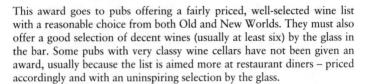

This award goes to pubs offering a fairly priced, well-selected wine list with a reasonable choice from both Old and New Worlds. They must also offer a good selection of decent wines (usually at least six) by the glass in the bar. Some pubs with very classy wine cellars have not been given an award, usually because the list is aimed more at restaurant diners – priced accordingly and with an uninspiring selection by the glass.

ENGLAND
Bedfordshire
Knife & Cleaver, Houghton
   Conquest
Berkshire
Bird in Hand, Knowl Hill
Inn on the Green, Cookham Dean
Royal Oak, Yattendon
Water Rat, Marsh Benham
Buckinghamshire
Angel Inn, Long Crendon
Annie Bailey's, Cuddington
Chequers Inn, Wooburn Common
Cambridgeshire
Anchor Inn, Sutton Gault
Chequers, Fowlmere
King William IV, Fenstanton
Pheasant Inn, Keyston
Queen's Head, Kirtling
Three Horseshoes, Madingley
Cheshire
Cholmondeley Arms,
   Cholmondeley
Grosvenor Arms, Aldford
Co Durham
Morritt Arms, Greta Bridge
Rose and Crown, Romaldkirk
Cornwall
Maltsters Arms, Chapel Amble
Pandora Inn, Mylor Bridge
Trengilly Wartha, Constantine
Cumbria
Pheasant Inn, Casterton
Punch Bowl Inn, Crosthwaite
Snooty Fox, Kirkby Lonsdale
Wheatsheaf, Beetham
Devon
Arundell Arms, Lifton
Castle Inn, Lydford
Cott Inn, Dartington
Drewe Arms, Broadhembury
Jack in the Green, Rockbeare

Kings Arms Inn, Stockland
Masons Arms, Branscombe
Masons Arms Inn, Knowstone
New Inn, Coleford
Nobody Inn, Doddiscombsleigh
Old Rydon Inn, Kingsteignton
Union Inn, Dolton
Dorset
Three Horseshoes, Powerstock
East Sussex
Griffin Inn, Fletching
Jolly Sportsman, East
   Chiltington
Ypres Castle, Rye
Essex
Bell Inn, Horndon on the Hill
Cricketers, Clavering
White Hart, Great Yeldham
White Horse, Ridgewell
Gloucestershire
New Inn, Coln St Aldwyns
Greater Manchester
White Hart, Lydgate
Hampshire
Fox Inn, Tangley
Globe on the Lake, Alresford
Peat Spade Inn, Longstock
Red Lion Inn, Boldre
Rose & Thistle, Rockbourne
Herefordshire
Roebuck, Brimfield
Ye Olde Salutation Inn, Weobley
Kent
Bell Inn, Smarden
Lancashire
Inn at Whitewell, Whitewell
New Inn, Yealand Conyers
Spread Eagle, Sawley
Leicestershire
Peacock Inn, Redmile
Lincolnshire
Black Horse Inn, Grimsthorpe

Norfolk
Rose & Crown, Snettisham
White Horse Hotel, Blakeney
Northamptonshire
Falcon Inn, Fotheringhay
Queens Head, Sutton Bassett
Northumberland
Manor House Inn, Carterway
    Heads
North Yorkshire
Abbey Inn, Byland Abbey
Angel Inn, Hetton
Black Bull Inn, Moulton
Blue Lion, East Witton
Buck Inn, Buckden
Crab & Lobster, Asenby
Foresters Arms,
    Carlton-in-Coverdale
Fox and Hounds, Carthorpe
Fox and Hounds, Sinnington
General Tarleton, Ferrensby
Nag's Head, Pickhill
Rose & Crown Inn,
    Sutton-on-the-Forest
Star Inn, Harome
Tempest Arms, Elslack
Three Hares, Bilborough
White Swan, Pickering
Wombwell Arms, Wass
Yorke Arms, Ramsgill
Oxfordshire
Bird in Hand, Hailey
Boar's Head, Ardington
The Goose, Britwell Salome
Lamb Inn, Buckland
Lamb Inn, Burford
Plough Inn, Clifton Hampden
Sir Charles Napier, Chinnor
Tite Inn, Chadlington
Shropshire
Hundred House Hotel, Norton
Somerset
Bell Inn, Buckland Dinham
Crown Hotel, Exford
George, Norton St Philip
Haselbury Inn, Haselbury
    Plucknett
Kings Arms, Montacute
Suffolk
Angel, Lavenham
Cornwallis Arms, Brome
Crown Inn, Snape

Surrey
Old Schoolhouse, Ockley
West Sussex
Crabtree, Lower Beeding
Horse Guards Inn, Tillington
King's Arms, Fernhurst
West Yorkshire
Kaye Arms, Grange Moor
Old Bridge Inn, Ripponden
Ring O'Bells, Thornton
Three Acres Inn, Roydhouse
Wiltshire
Dove Inn, Corton
George & Dragon, Rowde
Lamb at Hindon, Hindon
Royal Oak, Wootton Rivers
Seven Stars, Woodborough
Three Crowns, Brinkworth
Woodbridge Inn, North Newnton
Worcestershire
Kings Arms, Ombersley
The Talbot, Knightwick

SCOTLAND
Borders
Burts Hotel, Melrose
Dumfries & Galloway
Creebridge House Hotel,
    Minnigaff
Riverside Inn, Canonbie
Fife
Old Rectory, Dysart
Highland
Kylesku Hotel, Kylesku
Perthshire & Kinross
Tormaukin Hotel, Glendevon

WALES
Gwynedd
Penhelig Arms, Aberdovey
Monmouthshire
Clytha Arms, Clytha
Pembrokeshire
Tafarn Newydd, Rosebush
The Wolfe, Wolf's Castle
Powys
Bear Hotel, Crickhowell
Griffin Inn, Llyswen
Wrexham
West Arms, Llanarmon Dyffryn
    Ceiriog

New entries

The following pubs did not appear as main entries in the last edition of the *Guide*, although some may have been in the Out and About section, or may have appeared as main entries in previous editions.

ENGLAND
Berkshire
Harrow Inn, West Ilsley
Buckinghamshire
Russell Arms, Butlers Cross
Stag & Huntsman Inn,
    Hambleden
Cheshire
Bhurtpore Inn, Aston
Bull Inn, Shocklach
Dysart Arms, Bunbury
Grosvenor Arms, Aldford
Cornwall
Rashleigh, Polkerris
Cumbria
Black Bull, Coniston
Wheatsheaf, Beetham
Derbyshire
Cheshire Cheese Inn, Hope
Devonshire Arms, Beeley
Red Lion, Hognaston
Devon
Dartmoor Inn, Lydford
Duke of York, Iddesleigh
Hoops Inn, Horn's Cross
Maltster's Arms, Tuckenhay
White Hart, Dartington
Dorset
Acorn Inn, Evershot
Bottle Inn, Marshwood
East Riding of Yorkshire
Wellington, Lund
East Sussex
Horse and Groom, Rushlake
Jolly Sportsman, East
    Chiltington
Gloucestershire
Bathurst Arms, North Cerney
Churchill Arms, Paxford
Wild Duck Inn, Ewen
Hampshire
Augustus John, Fordingbridge

Dukes Head, Greatbridge
East End Arms, East End
Globe on the Lake, Alresford
Hawkley Inn, Hawkley
Red Lion Inn, Boldre
Yew Tree, Highclere
Isle of Wight
King's Head, Yarmouth
Kent
Dove, Dargate
King William IV, Littlebourne
Lancashire
Eagle & Child, Bispham Green
Spread Eagle, Sawley
Leicestershire
Bakers Arms, Thorpe Langton
Bell Inn, East Langton
Lincolnshire
Black Horse Inn, Grimsthorpe
Norfolk
Darby's, Swanton Morley
Lifeboat Inn, Thornham
Lord Nelson, Burnham Thorpe
Northamptonshire
George & Dragon, Chacombe
Shuckburgh Arms, Stoke Doyle
Northumberland
Saddle Hotel, Alnmouth
Tankerville Arms, Eglingham
North Yorkshire
Crown, Great Ouseburn
Fox and Hounds, Sinnington
Jefferson Arms, Thorganby
Yorke Arms, Ramsgill
Nottinghamshire
French Horn, Upton
Oxfordshire
Bull Inn, Charlbury
Falkland Arms, Great Tew
Feathers Hotel, Woodstock
The Goose, Britwell Salome
Red Lion Inn, Chalgrove

Rutland
Finch's Arms, Hambleton
The Sun, Cottesmore
Shropshire
Three Tuns, Bishop's Castle
Somerset
Full Moon, Rudge
Haselbury Inn, Haselbury
   Plucknett
South Gloucestershire
Anchor Inn, Oldbury-on-Severn
Dog Inn, Old Sodbury
Staffordshire
Red Lion Inn, Longdon Green
Suffolk
Cornwallis Arms, Brome
De La Pole Arms, Wingfield
Froize Inn, Chillesford
Trowel & Hammer Inn, Cotton
Surrey
Old Schoolhouse, Ockley
Warwickshire
Boot Inn, Lapworth
Chequers Inn, Ettington
Howard Arms, Ilmington
West Sussex
Black Horse, Nuthurst
The Fox Goes Free, Charlton
King's Arms, Fernhurst

Lickfold Inn, Lickfold
Wiltshire
Dove Inn, Corton
Grosvenor Arms, Hindon
King John Inn, Tollard Royal
Owl, Little Cheverell
Seven Stars, Woodborough
Worcestershire
Walter de Cantelupe, Kempsey

SCOTLAND
Highland
Plockton Inn, Plockton
Midlothian
The Howgate, Howgate

WALES
Conwy
Groes Hotel, Tyn-y-Groes
Kinmel Arms, St George
Pembrokeshire
Sloop Inn, Porthgain
The Wolfe, Wolf's Castle
Powys
Coach & Horses, Llangynidr
Farmers Arms, Cwmdu
Lion Hotel, Llandinam
Swansea
Fountain Inn, Pontarddulais

About the editor

Peter Haydon is a writer and journalist with a special interest in public houses, beer and English history. He is the author of *The English Pub: A History* (Hale) and *Known Treasures and Hidden Gems* (CAMRA Books), as well as former editor of *The Grist* (the journal of the International Brewers' Guild) and a member of the British Guild of Beer Writers. In 1997 he became General Secretary of the Society of Independent Brewers.

Introduction

What institution sums up the history and character of the British people better than a country pub? What other institution spans the millennium so comprehensively? In this guide you will find pubs that have their origins in the tenth century, while others date from every age since and have often done duty as court houses, smithies, chapels and farmhouses. Some started life as humble cottages, while others are built on manorial proportions. These hostelries have supplied board, and often lodging, to people from every walk of life, from gentry to drovers, from artisans to smugglers and, of course, to travellers of every description.

The best of our pubs are gems of our national heritage. Some are rough diamonds, it is true. But all fulfil a common purpose, which is to serve their communities, and many are a focal point – perhaps *the* focal point – of the village or market town in which they stand.

This fourth, and completely new, edition of *The Which? Guide to Country Pubs* features, as its predecessors have done, only pubs that have those exceptional qualities that make them worth a special visit – a detour from your route, a destination to make for when you feel like a small celebration, or maybe want to cheer someone up, or a base to start from or return to when you are exploring the countryside. If the pub features in these pages, you know in advance that your journey will not end in disappointment.

What we look for are pubs that offer a decent pint of beer, a reasonable selection of wines by the glass, a well thought-out menu featuring dishes made from high-quality, fresh produce, plus, of course, value for money and a congenial atmosphere. If a pub can offer something extra, such as locally caught fish or a particularly interesting line in vegetarian dishes, well-kept beers supplied by local producers, a pretty garden to sit in, or facilities for children, we will tell you about them. We will also tell you about the pub's policy on music, smoking and dogs, whether it is accessible to wheelchairs, whether it offers accommodation and whether it has a car park.

Sadly, we have found it more difficult, this time, to find such pubs. The reasons are several.

The country pub under threat

Three regrettable trends have emerged in the course of our research for this new guide. First, far too many pubs are being sold off as private dwellings, largely because they generally fetch more as homes than they do as going concerns. Second, an increasing number of establishments have ceased to be pubs in the accepted sense of the word, having been turned into full-scale restaurants where no attempt has been made to maintain a drinking area or any kind of pub atmosphere. A third reason for the decline is that many pubs have gone downhill after being bought up by brewing and catering chains, most of them bent on introducing standardised wine lists, identikit easy-to-cook or bought-in menus, a 'rationalised' ale list and, all too often, indifferent management and service.

Significantly, the vast majority of pubs in the main body of this edition are freehouses. While we acknowledge that plenty of awful freehouses exist, we are confident that those in this guide represent the cream of the licensed trade.

The numbers of freehouses, however, are sadly in decline. In 1998 the Office of Fair Trading looked at the effects of the emergence of the new pub chains, and in particular how it serves the interests of the large companies to reduce the number of freehouses in order to increase their own beer sales. Backed by City finance, these big companies are able to price potential individual buyers out of the market, or, more and more often, to make sitting freehouse owners 'an offer too good to turn down', as one departing landlord described it.

The OFT decided in its wisdom that while there were only a small number of dominant brewery firms, a significant number of large, non-brewing pub operators with countervailing market influence represented competition and were therefore a good thing.

The OFT also declined to establish a standard definition of the word 'freehouse' – there is none – so that genuine freehouses could try to derive some protection from the term, which has, for many people, positive connotations and which is frequently used by pubs that are in no true sense 'free' at all. Against this background the fall in the number of freehouses looks set to continue.

Corporatism and the country pub
The last edition of this guide identified some then-current worries and trends. How have things turned out?

The buying-up of pubs goes on, and 'dumbing-down' refurbishment, where character is destroyed in the name of corporate branding or – worse – of convenience, seems to be alive and well. Themed premises continue to spread through town and country alike, almost always to the detriment of what they replace.

A reader recommended an Oxfordshire pub to us in early 1998. Later in the year he wrote again saying, 'Don't bother . . . the building has been tarted up in the best tradition (false beams, old wood etc.), the elaborately described food is all bought-in –

[and it's] chips with everything. Why go on? . . . So sad, the other owners tried so hard.'

The last edition of the *Guide* also mentioned the welcome emergence of owners who believe the highest standards in food and drink are not incompatible with a pub atmosphere – and who were opening up more establishments founded on the same principles. This trend continues and we are pleased to be featuring a number of such pubs in this edition. They include the Three Horseshoes at Madingley, the Pheasant Inn at Keyston, the White Hart at Great Yeldham and the Falcon Inn at Fotheringhay, all owned by the Huntsbridge Group, whose MD, John Hoskins, summed up the group's philosophy thus: 'We stand or fall by the food and booze we deliver to the guest, not by virtue of any group marketing or group economics.'

Others, too, have set out to preserve the identity of the traditional pub while often giving the chefs their head: for example, Denis Watkins and John Topham at the Angel Inn at Hetton and General Tarleton at Ferrensby; Anne Voss-Bark and Philip Burgess at the Arundell Arms at Lifton and Dartmoor Inn at Lydford; and Leo Brooke-Little and Sonya Kidney at the Churchill Arms at Paxford and the Hare & Hounds at Foss Cross. These entrepreneurs, in contrast to some big companies that pay less attention to quality and authenticity than to profits, are driving standards up, and are a valuable restraint against those who would take things the other way.

Food developments

Pub food, for all sorts of reasons but fundamentally, perhaps, because of the drink/driving laws, has become even more important to the licensed trade. Without it, many pubs would struggle. A good number, unfortunately, have failed to realise that where the kitchen is small and the number of staff very limited, simple meals are the best solution. The pub with a short, attractive menu is still a rarity, and too many landlords bend over backwards to produce – say – a list of 20 main courses relying heavily on a catering trade supplier rather than a choice of half a dozen well-executed home-made dishes.

Potentially good news for consumers is the proposal by local Trading Standards authorities to introduce official definitions for words such as 'fresh', 'traditional' and 'home-made'. These terms have suffered from widespread misuse by some pubs which offer up 'fresh' fish straight from the freezer, 'traditional' steak and kidney pie from a caterers' pack, and 'home-made' soup rehydrated from a supermarket's packet. Whether the proposals result in firm, enforceable guidelines remains to be seen.

Some foreign cuisines work well in a pub context, which explains the continuing love affair between the pub and Thai cuisine. We could not help notice the sudden upsurge of Cajun and Creole dishes on menus: only time will tell if these prove more than a passing fashion. Despite fads and a tendency in many pubs towards upmarket, restaurant-style food, there will always be a place, we suspect, for the old standards – a well-made steak and kidney pie, or traditional roast beef served with Yorkshire pudding and two veg.

The news for vegetarians is good, with far more choice, and, as pubs embrace more Mediterranean and Eastern cooking styles, more creativity on menus. The heightened awareness in all areas of catering of the importance of obtaining foodstuffs from reliable suppliers, and the trend toward using local, often organic ingredients, has had benefits for meat eaters and non-meat eaters alike, and the commitment of a chef to locally sourced, and organic, produce is likely to be signalled on menus.

All this is indicative not only of a more adventurous and informed eating public, but also of a more questioning one. There are benefits, too, for a wider range of producers, including small local brewers, cheese manufacturers, makers of English country wines, local bee-keepers and others, all of whose products are increasingly seen on pub menus. The effect of patronage by a successful country pub can have an enormous effect on these businesses. Good food pubs are ideal showcases for regional produce, helping to create enviable 'word-of-mouth' reputations for producers.

Other trends
Since the last *Guide*, smoking in pubs and the possible tightening of drink/drive regulations have continued to be the subject of fierce debate. The pub trade has come under pressure to clean up the air quality in its establishments or have it cleaned up for them. To some extent pubs are doing just that: a large majority of the pubs in this edition have either a no-smoking area or an entire no-smoking room. If stricter drink/driving rules do become reality, food operations will be even more vital to a country pub's survival than they are now.

It also seems likely that the licensing laws will be further relaxed, and that later evening opening times will be with us before too long. This may signal the end of that ancient country tradition, the 'lock-in', and that equally ancient game of cat-and-mouse with the local constabulary, but it will allow licensees greater control over how they run their businesses, end the bizarre anomaly that exists between England and Wales on the one hand, and much of the rest of the world on the other, and extend consumer choice.

Real ale sales

Overall, real ale sales are thought to be falling by around 15 per cent per annum. Small brewers argue that they could sell all the beer they could make if more pubs were free to buy it, though some larger brewers prefer to invest in the new 'nitro-keg', or 'smooth-flow', beers. The jury is still out on this one.

Ironically there is more choice for the consumer than ever before. The number of small breweries continues to rise, but only a handful of names appear regularly in this guide. Britain's small brewers find it ever harder to get their beers in front of the public. Many landlords seem to be taking the beers which give them the best profit margins. We would like to see much more being done to support local brewers, even by the pubs in this guide.

What is undisputed is the issue of ale quality. Everyone is agreed that too much bad or indifferent ale is being sold to beer drinkers. Cask Marque is an initiative introduced in 1998 by the independent brewers Morland, Adnams, Greene King and Marston's. The 'Marque' – advertised by means of a plaque – is awarded after an inspection (paid for by the establishment) to pubs that serve properly looked-after ales. By early 1999, 21 brewers were supporting the initiative and 400 plaques had been awarded, though take-up had so far been low among freehouses in rural areas. Pubs have to 'volunteer' to be tested, and the award is made to the licensee and not the pub. Time will tell whether it makes a difference, but let us hope that increased consumer confidence in the quality of ale will help stem the drift away to other beer styles.

For a list of pubs serving exceptional draught beers, see pages 10–11.

Hopeful signs on the wine list

Wine in pubs is at last becoming a viable option, having for years been a Cinderella drink on which as little time, knowledge and money as possible were expended. Now, propelled by higher expectations and greater wine knowledge on the part of their customers, landlords have started to rectify the problem and pub wine is going from strength to strength. Wine lists are offering more quality and choice than ever before, as a result of which we have had to upgrade our criteria of what constitutes a 'good wine pub' (see list of award winners on pages 12–13). In this edition, to receive a wine award not only must a pub have a fairly priced, well-selected wine list with a reasonable choice from both Old and New Worlds, but it must also offer a fair selection of decent wines (usually at least six) by the glass.

The North wins again

Our analysis of the regions in terms of our awards for Top-Rated Pubs (see centre colour section for lists) caused much interest in the last *Guide*. In this edition North Yorkshire continues to be the culinary centre of British pub cooking, having won no fewer than six of the twenty-two double rosettes awarded, which is two more than in the last edition. It also has another six single-rosette winners, and thus comes in with around ten per cent of 'top pub' awards overall. In the South, by contrast, the biggest winners, Devon and Oxfordshire, have been awarded a total of six rosettes each. The South did far better, however, in terms of new main entries: topping the league is Hampshire with seven, followed by Devon, Oxfordshire and Wiltshire, with five each.

What is remarkable, however, is that Bedfordshire, Cheshire, Hertfordshire, Norfolk, Northamptonshire, Somerset, Staffordshire and Warwickshire have not managed a single rosette between them. There must be opportunities for bright entrepreneurs to fill these large gaps on the map with some first-class pub cuisine.

On that hopeful note, we would like to thank all of you who have contributed to this edition. Your reports, letters, emails, faxes and even hand-delivered messages have been immensely helpful in the research and preparation of the *Guide*. Please keep us informed about what you see, eat or drink – good or bad – in our country pubs, and in that way help us to keep you informed about these national treasures as they embark on their next thousand years.

E·N·G·L·A·N·D

Valiant Trooper

Trooper Road, Aldbury HP23 5RW TEL: (01442) 851203
off A41, 1½m W of Tring

The Valiant Trooper sits in this 'photogenically overloaded' Chiltern village which takes its name from the Saxon term for 'old-fashioned place': an old Roman road is supposed to have passed the spot where the pub now stands. The pub dates back to at least 1752 when it was known as the Royal Oak, becoming the Trooper alehouse in 1803 after the Duke of Wellington allegedly addressed soldiers at the inn. Records show it had become the Valiant Trooper by 1878. Once owned by Ind Coope, it has been a freehouse since 1980, when Dot O'Gorman (who retired in 1996) and her son Tim took it over. The O'Gorman formula is simple pub food prepared with good raw materials and served up in generous portions. The printed bar menu is an easy list of jacket potatoes, ploughman's, salads and sandwiches, and 'hot meals' such as cottage pie and mixed grill. More sophisticated meals are on the blackboard, which always features half a dozen starters and desserts, and a dozen main dishes. Typical specials might be carrot, honey and ginger soup, or smoked mackerel pâté wrapped in smoked salmon, followed by whole roast partridge forestière, or rump steak au poivre. A separate restaurant offers two- or three-course set meals. Puddings are along the lines of apple pie and rhubarb crumble. The pub serves Bass, John Smith's and Fuller's London Pride at all times, and a guest ale is likely to come from a national or large regional brewer. Ten wines are available by the glass. SAMPLE DISHES: melon with winter fruit compote £3; game pie cooked in port £6.50; fresh fruit salad £2.50.

Open *11.30 to 11, Sun 12 to 10.30, closed 25 Dec exc. 2 hrs at L; bar food and restaurant 12 to 2, 6.30 to 9.15 (2.30 Sun L and bank hols); restaurant closed Mon L*
Details *Children welcome in family room Car park Wheelchair access (also WC) Garden and patio No-smoking bar from 11.30 to 3.30 No music No dogs in restaurant Amex, Delta, Diners, MasterCard, Switch, Visa*

▲ *Bell*

Shipston Road, Alderminster CV37 8NY TEL: (01789) 450414
on A3400, 4m S of Stratford-upon-Avon

Just a few miles south of Stratford-upon-Avon, this unassuming seventeenth-century coaching-inn is an ideal stopping-off point for visitors to Shakespeare's birthplace. Further attractions come in the form of special events, such as French evenings and jazz nights. Keith and Vanessa Brewer have styled the Bell as a 'bistro and bar' and there is an upmarket feel about the place though the atmosphere remains informal and relaxed. Step to the left on entering and you are offered a menu and asked if you would like a table; step to the right and you are welcome just to have a drink in the small bar area, a neat, well-furnished room with polished flagstones, original timbers, farmhouse-style tables and an inglenook. There is also a conservatory dining-room at the rear, which makes the most of the lovely view of the Stour Valley. The printed menu opens with sweet-cured herrings, shellfish platter, sticky chicken wings and Parma ham, melon and artichoke salad, most of which are available as either a starter or a main. If you do want a further dish, try Moroccan chicken breast, curried lamb with fennel, or posh bangers and savoury mash. Samples from the pudding board include coffee and marshmallow mousse and cream, or baked vanilla cheesecake with marinated raspberries and strawberries. Beers are supplied by Greene King, and a wine list offers easy house quaffers, better bottles and a selection of personally chosen clarets and a list of vintages exclusively from Ch. Pindefleurs (a *grand cru* St Emilion), with which the pub has connections. SAMPLE DISHES: cucumber and mint soup £3.25; mini rack of English lamb £9.25; caramel ice-cream £4.

Open *12 to 3, 7 to 11, Sun 12 to 2.30, 7 to 10.30; bar food and restaurant 12 to 2, 7 to 9.30, Sun 12 to 1.45, 7 to 9*
Details *Children welcome　Car park　Wheelchair access (also WC)　Garden No smoking in restaurant　Live music　Dogs welcome in bar only　Delta, MasterCard, Switch, Visa　Accommodation: 6 rooms, B&B £25 to £55*

ALDERTON　　Gloucestershire　　　　　　　　　　map 5

Gardeners Arms

Beckford Road, Alderton GL20 8NL　TEL: (01242) 620257
off A438, 7m E of Tewkesbury

This half-timbered sixteenth-century thatched pub is set in the heart of a tiny village, and is spruced up with colourful hanging baskets in summer. The interior has a roomy seating area with sofas for drinkers, tables elsewhere for eating and attractive prints of horses adorning the walls. Ploughman's, pâtés and sandwiches are available at lunch-time, plus grilled king prawns and blackboard specials. The evening menu offers filled avocado pear or hot spicy Indonesian smoked mackerel as starters, followed by noisettes of lamb with herbs and garlic, grilled whole lemon sole or poached fillet of salmon in a wine, cream and dill sauce. Puddings are on the lines of baked lemon or pear and chocolate tart, plus home-made ice-cream. Beers come from Theakston, Wadworth and John Smith's, and a local beer called Stanney is also available. A short list of wines is chalked on a blackboard, and four are served by the glass. Hidcote Manor Gardens and the silk mill at Beckford are nearby. SAMPLE DISHES: grilled sardines £4.75; whole baby chicken in a cream and sherry sauce £8; sorbet meringue £3.

Open *11 to 2.30, 6.30 to 11, Sun 12 to 3, 7 to 10.30; bar food and restaurant all week 12 to 2, Tue to Sat D 7 to 9 (soup/sandwiches only Mon L)*
Details *Children welcome in eating areas   Car park   Wheelchair access (also WC)   Garden and patio   Live music   Dogs welcome in back bar only   Delta, MasterCard, Switch, Visa*

A L D F O R D   Cheshire   map 7

Grosvenor Arms 🍇   NEW ENTRY

Chester Road, Aldford CH3 6HJ   TEL: (01244) 620228
just off B5130, 5m S of Chester

This large, red-brick building is hard by one of the entrances to the Duke of Westminster's residence at Eaton Hall. Surprisingly, given its size, it was built as a pub for the estate. A profusion of flowers on the front gives it a French 'fleurie' look, and entering is a bit like stepping into a country house, with the first room resembling a library. In the main bar there is a supply of newspapers, magazines and games. The menu is the same on the blackboards as on the printed list and ranges from filled baguettes and ploughman's to an eclectic, cosmopolitan list of well-prepared dishes. Start with prawns marinated in Chinese spices and chillies on an oriental salad with toasted sesame seed dressing, or conchiglie pasta with cherry tomato and pesto cream sauce. Mussels cooked in white wine have been described as 'first class'. Similarly praised as a main course is half a roast crispy duck with hoisin sauce and pancakes – well up to Chinese restaurant standard. Also on offer are Thai chicken curry and Cajun spiced salmon burger and, for the more traditionally minded, Cumberland sausage on mustard and leek mash with onion gravy, or venison steak with a red wine and herb marinade. Puddings are of the crème brûlée variety, here served with fruits of the forest, or a hot waffle with honeycomb ice-cream and mixed berry sauce. The pub serves a good selection of well-cared-for beers: Flowers IPA, Jennings and Batemans, and a short but interesting wine list makes all bottles available by the glass. The pub is convenient for thirteenth-century Holt Castle. SAMPLE DISHES: roast duck thigh in blackberry sauce £4.25; salmon and haddock fish-cakes £6.50; raspberry and kiwi pavlova £3.75.

Open *11 to 11, Sun 12 to 10.30; bar food 12 to 10*
Details *Children welcome   Car park   Wheelchair access (also WC)   Garden Background music   Dogs in 1 bar only   Amex, Delta, MasterCard, Switch, Visa*

ALDWORTH   Berkshire   map 2

Bell Inn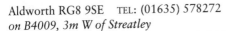

Aldworth RG8 9SE   TEL: (01635) 578272
on B4009, 3m W of Streatley

A delightfully unspoilt village pub with fourteenth-century origins has been in the same family for over 200 years. Ian Macaulay has been there since 1974. The Grade I listed building was formerly a manor hall. It stands opposite the village well in an attractive downland village close to the Ridgeway; making it an ideal spot for ramblers. Inside, it is 'typically simple, rustic as timeless pubs should be'. The cosy and characterful beamed bar with efficient woodburner, panelled walls and sturdy benches has a glass-panelled hatch, through which beers and food are served. You are advised to arrive early for the best seats, or squeeze into one of the candlelit snugs if you do not want to join the overspill in the hallway. The well-kept beers are, ambience apart, the pub's main attraction and are very reasonably priced. Arkells 3B and Kingsdown are favourites, West Berkshire Old Tyler may be on as well as some guests, and – something that may delight many – there are no draught lagers. Food is somewhat subsidiary to the main activities of drinking and talking, but good, hearty filled rolls are available. They arrive hot and crusty with a variety of generous fillings: Brie, Cheddar, salt beef, crab, or home-cooked ham, for example. In winter there is home-made soup with bread and cheese. Sweet-lovers can indulge with almond tart, sticky toffee pudding or various ice-creams. Three wines are available by the glass, at around £1.60. As one experienced inspector concluded: 'a timeless gem – long may it remain so.' SAMPLE DISHES: Stilton roll £1.30; smoked salmon roll £1.80; Tia Maria ice-cream £1.70.

Open *Tue to Sun (and bank hol Mon) 11 to 3, 6 to 11, Sun 12 to 3, 7 to 10.30; closed 25 Dec; bar food 11 to 2.50, 6 to 10.50, Sun 12 to 2.50, 7 to 10.20;*
Details *Children welcome in family room   Car park   Garden   No music Dogs welcome on a lead   No cards*

ALNMOUTH   **Northumberland**   **map 10**

▲ *Saddle Hotel*   **NEW ENTRY**

24-25 Northumberland Street, Alnmouth NE66 2RA
TEL: (01665) 830476
*from A1, take Alnwick turn-off, then Alnmouth exit at
mini-roundabout*

The Saddle Hotel is one of a string of Victorian-built pubs along
Alnmouth's main street, in which the houses face away from the
windswept beach. The main bar is divided into small bays with
simple, old-fashioned furniture. A lengthy printed menu offers
considerable choice with additional listings for senior citizens, children and vegetarians; there are also blackboard specials, plus a
separate à la carte menu for the restaurant. Among the usual range
of prawn cocktail, pâté and potato wedges you will find Craster
kipper, and smoked mackerel with horseradish, both served with
brown bread and butter. Hot platters include beef Elizabeth –
strips of beef in a mushroom, French mustard, red wine and cream
sauce, served with rice or chips – and local Northumberland
sausages, which you can have in a large Yorkshire pudding as an
alternative to the roast of the day. 'Hawaiian toast' is a grilled
combination of thick-cut bread topped with honey roast ham, a
pineapple ring and Cheddar cheese. Finally you might opt for a pie
of the day, or perhaps a chicken pancake which is advertised as
'only for the very hungry'. The pudding list is similarly extensive,
with old favourites like knickerbocker glory and banana split
tucked in among the dairy gateaux, pavlovas and steamed suet
puddings. The beer selection is short and simple – Ruddles Best
and Theakston Best. The 20-bottle wine list offers three house
wines by the glass. SAMPLE DISHES: egg and prawn cocktail £3;
chicken curry £5.25; profiteroles £2.50.

Open *11 to 3, 6 to 11, Sun 12 to 3, 6 to 9 (8.30 winter); closed 25 Dec; bar
food 12 to 2, 6 to 9 (no food Mon L Nov to Feb)*
Details *Children welcome in some areas   Wheelchair access (also WC)   No
smoking in restaurant   Background and live music   Dogs welcome
MasterCard, Switch, Visa   Accommodation: 7 rooms, B&B £25 to £30*

ALRESFORD   Hampshire   map 2

Globe on the Lake 🍇   ▢ NEW ENTRY ▢

The Soke SO24 9DB   *TEL:* (01962) 732294
on lower end of Broad Street on B3046 Basingstoke road

The Globe is an excellent summer lunch venue, enjoying a delightful
position at the bottom of the wide main street on the banks of a
reed-fringed pond, complete with swans and dabbling ducks. Inside
there is a carpeted main bar with roaring log fires at either end – for
those days when even the ducks do not feel like dabbling – one in a
splendid inglenook with a settle in front. A separate restaurant, with
French windows into the gardens and a raised terrace offering views
across the pond, is used as an occasional venue for jazz dinners in
summer. Landlady Linda O'Callaghan has smartened and upgraded
this old pub since her arrival in 1993, and it is gradually realising its
potential. Food is interesting and varied, all freshly prepared on the
premises, and appeals to a wide range of clientele; the emphasis is
very much on choice, presentation, attention to detail and the use
where possible of local produce. The bar menu is on an ever changing blackboard list of around some 20 items along the lines of
chicken liver parfait, or smooth and creamy Stilton and walnut paté
(something of a house speciality), to start, followed by salmon and
cod fish-cakes, game casserole, or a crispy-skinned, tender, duck leg
confit. All can be rounded off with a selection of home-made ices
with a plum compote, or perhaps smooth banana cheesecake served
with deep-fried bananas and excellent caramel sauce. Lighter snacks
such as meatloaf or cheese, tomato and onion flan as well as sandwiches are available too. Real ales are John Smith's, Courage Best,
Wadworth 6X and Marston's Pedigree, with the addition of
Cheriton Pots ale in the summer. Wines on a 48-strong list come
from Test Valley Wines and take a brisk trot round the world; a
generous 15 are offered by the glass. SAMPLE DISHES: tartlet of wild
mushrooms and Gruyère cheese £4; roast saddle of lamb with apricot and rosemary and a redcurrant jus £12.75; bread-and-butter
pudding £3.25.

Open *11 to 3 (2.30 winter), 6 to 11, Sun 12 to 3, 7 to 10.30; bar food 12 to
2, 6.30 (7 Sun) to 9.30*
Details *No children   Wheelchair access   Garden and patio   No smoking in 1
room   No music   No dogs in dining-room   Amex, Delta, MasterCard,
Switch, Visa*

---

*After the main section of the Guide is the special 'Out and About'
section listing additional pubs that are well worth a visit. Reports on
these entries are most welcome.*

AMBLESIDE   Cumbria   map 8

▲ *Drunken Duck Inn* 🍺

Barngates LA22 0NG   TEL: (015394) 36347
off B5286, between Ambleside and Hawkshead,
3m S of Ambleside

VIEWS

Enviably sandwiched between two of the Lake District's most popular touring and walking bases (Ambleside and Hawkshead), with
distant views of Windermere as a bonus, this classic Cumbrian pub is
understandably well patronised. So much so that getting served can
take a while at busy times. Fortunately, both the surrounding views
and the interior provide ample entertainment for the hungry hordes
anticipating a good feed: it is probably true to say that most people
eat here as well as drink. The Drunken Duck's narrow bar, quaint
and beamed, is crammed with fox masks, harness and rural bygones,
and there's always a cheerful blaze to sit by in winter. Near the fireplace, an apocryphal legend relates how the pub's name arose. When
space runs out, diners retreat outside to the picnic benches, or into
adjacent rooms furnished with simple wooden tables. Blackboards
announce varied and imaginative bar food, incorporating plenty of
Lakeland produce such as Cumberland sausage or black pudding as
well as child-oriented dishes. In the evenings the menu expands with
more elaborate and rather more expensive fare (sauté duck livers
perhaps, or sea bass with roast fennel). A separate, more formal
dining room at the rear serves pre-booked meals. Drinkers are by no
means neglected; the Drunken Duck brews its own real ale (Cracker
or Chesters Strong & Ugly) besides proffering Yates and Jennings
bitters or Theakston Old Peculier. Several decent wines are sold by
the glass, and there is a good range of malts. SAMPLE DISHES: chargrilled vegetables with minted yoghurt £3.25; beer-battered cod on
pommes pont neuf £6.50; Westmorland dream cake and double
cream £3.25 at lunch, slightly more at dinner.

Open *11.30 to 3, 6 to 11, Sun 12 to 3, 6 to 10.30; closed 25 Dec; bar food
and restaurant 12 to 2.30, 6 to 9*
Details *Children welcome   Car park   Wheelchair access (also WC)   Garden
No smoking in all eating areas   No music   Dogs welcome in bar area only
Amex, Delta, MasterCard, Switch, Visa   Accommodation: 9 rooms, B&B £45
to £90*

APPLEBY   Cumbria   **map 10**

▲ *Royal Oak Inn*

Bongate CA16 6UN   TEL: (01768) 351463
just off A66 at S edge of Appleby, 12m SE of Penrith

Shortly before the *Guide* went to press, new owners took over this substantial inn, but early signs indicate that they intend to maintain its status as a 'classic all-rounder'. Appleby is surrounded by wonderful countryside – the Lake District, the Pennines, the Yorkshire Dales, the Scottish borders – and this former coaching-inn with a long history (dating back to 1100 in parts) lies on the main road in the oldest part of town. Regulars like the cosy oak-panelled taproom, with its open log fire, stone walls and smoky-black beams, while the timber-walled lounge is comfortable in a chintzy way, still informal. Meals can also be taken in the two restaurants at the back (one of them non-smoking), which are popular with families at Sunday lunch-time. This is a pub which clearly aims to please everyone: at its simplest the bar menu offers baked potatoes, pâté and toast, cod and chips. More unusually you find tortilla wraps, toasted bagels, and open sandwiches made with ciabatta. Full meals might start with a Stilton, celery and walnut tart with sweet onion jam, little brown shrimps 'potted to Mrs Beaton's receipt', or roasted stove-top tomatoes. Vegetarians will continue to be pleased by three-bean crumble, leek and cheese sausages, or oyster mushrooms and roast hazelnut strudel, while others can waver between Cheddar chicken, smoked haddock and bacon fish-cakes, or Mr Ewbank's sirloin steak. Puddings are seasonally adjusted. Guest beers join John Smith, Tetley and Black Sheep, while cider-drinkers will be happy to find a Stowford Press presence. Seventy worldwide wines and 50 malt whiskies are further testimony to the inn's wide-ranging appeal. SAMPLE DISHES: roast local goats' cheese £5; Mrs Ewbank's Bongate lamb pudding with sweet leeks £7; vanilla pot with raspberries £3.

Open *11 to 11, Sun 12 to 10.30; bar food and restaurant 12 to 2, 6.30 to 9.30*
Details *Children welcome   Patio   No smoking in 1 dining-room   No music No dogs in public rooms   Amex, Delta, Diners, MasterCard, Switch, Visa Accommodation: 9 rooms, B&B £30 to £86*

Globe Inn

Appley TA21 0HJ   TEL: (01823) 672327
from M5 take Wellington exit, then W on A38; after 3m turn right to
Greenham; after 1m right at T-junction, signposted Stawley; pub
further ½m on left

This simple country pub in the hamlet of Appley has been run by two
couples, the Burts and the Morrises, for more than a decade. A large
garden at the rear has facilities for children. The place has a welcoming atmosphere, with coal-burning fires in each of the three bars, and
large portions of food help to give the Globe an air of generosity. The
regular beer is Tawny from the Cotleigh brewery in Devon, and there
is always a guest ale, while a traditional cider is laid on during the
summer months. A large menu is augmented by daily specials – usually
three starters, three main courses and two puddings – along the lines
of mackerel with fresh lime and mixed pepper dressing, or beef
Stroganov. Home-made soups and pâtés feature, as do a full range of
steaks, and less traditional items such as Peking-style crispy duck.
There are burgers and chips for the kids, and options for non-meat
eaters such as savoury vegetable crumble. Traditional roast beef comes
in two sizes at Sunday lunch-times. House wines start at £7.25, with
four wines available by the glass. SAMPLE DISHES: gravad lax (can be
shared) £7.75; steak and kidney pie cooked with stout £6.25; lemon
tart with clotted cream £3.25.

Open *Tue to Sat and bank hol Mon 11 to 3, Mon to Sat 6.30 to 11, Sun 12
to 3, 7 to 10.30; bar food and restaurant 12 to 2 (3 Sun), 7 to 9.30*
Details *Children welcome in family room and restaurant   Car park*
Wheelchair access   Garden   No smoking in restaurant   Background music
Guide dogs only   MasterCard, Switch, Visa

Jolly Waggoner

Ardeley SG2 7AH   TEL: (01438) 861350
off B1037 at Cromer, 5m E of Stevenage

This rambling pub is set in a village that is little more than a hamlet. It
looks big from the outside but actually is not: inside there is just one
bar with a step-up annexe. Beams and open timbers are everywhere,
the walls are pink and panelled and there are lots of dried flowers,
paintings of the pub, and knick-knacks on shelves between the beams:
it is all very cosy and homely. The lunch menu contains one or two
neat variations on the theme of sensible pub grub: omelette Arnold

Bennett is stuffed with smoked haddock and served with a light
béchamel sauce; burgers are home-made and come topped with
peppercorn sauce or Cheddar and bacon. More filling dishes are also
on offer: sirloin of Scotch beef provençale, or calf's liver with
Roquefort and horseradish sauce. Snackers can opt for a variety of
open toastie sandwiches with salad, and to finish there is lemon posset.
A restaurant menu is available in the evening offering the likes of
poached smoked haddock with cheese and mushroom sauce, or herb
crusted rack of lamb with port sauce. This Greene King pub serves the
brewery's staples, IPA and Abbott Ale, and there are three wines by the
glass. SAMPLE DISHES: carved ham salad £5; salmon fillet £11; chocolate
truffle torte £3.50.

Open *Tue to Sat 12 to 2.30, 6.30 to 11, Sun 12 to 3, 7 to 10.30; bar food
and restaurant Tue to Sun L 12 to 2, Tue to Sat D 6.30 to 9*
Details *Children welcome in bar eating area   Car park   Wheelchair access
Garden and patio   No music   No dogs   Delta, MasterCard, Visa*

ARDINGTON   Oxfordshire   map 2

Boar's Head 🍇

Church Street, Ardington OX12 8QA   TEL: (01235) 833254
off A417, 2m E of Wantage

The interior of the Boar's Head looks little different from the way it
did before new licensee Mark Stott took over in summer 1997,
though the opening up of a further room, painted pale yellow, has
made the whole pub more airy. Tables are generously spaced and
laid with rush mats, tall tumblers and flower arrangements. Much
simpler, shorter menus are on offer these days. Dishes like smoked
trout fillet with mild horseradish, smooth game pâté, and cassoulet
can be ordered in either large ('More') or small ('Less') portions.
From the main menu one could select confit of guinea-fowl, or
mushroom tart with quails' eggs and hollandaise, followed by roast
pork fillet with balsamic vinegar and red onions, or monkfish tails
with a mild Meaux mustard sauce. Puddings are possibly the pub's
forte: excellent burnt lemon cream, or the unusual elderflower jelly
with red berries, for example. Morland, Adnams and Butts beers are
served alongside an extensive, regularly changing list of 40 wines –
well-annotated and full of intriguing choices. Nine wines are served
by the glass. SAMPLE DISHES: crispy pork Chinese style £4.50; breast
of pigeon with apricot timbale £11; apple, cinnamon and ginger
syllabub £3.50.

Open *12 to 3, 6.30 to 11; bar food and restaurant 12 to 2, 7 to 9.15*
Details *Children welcome   Car park   Wheelchair access   Patio   No smoking
in restaurant   Background and live music   Dogs in bar area only   Delta,
MasterCard, Switch, Visa*

ARKESDEN   Essex   map 3

Axe and Compasses

Arkesden CB11 4EX   TEL: (01799) 550272
off B1038, 1m N of Clavering

A small stream, punctuated by little footbridges, runs alongside the narrow road through this pretty village. The Axe is right at the centre of things: 'friendly, comfortable and easy on the eye, both inside and out'. Accordingly you see a low-slung brick and thatch pub, with hardly a space left for another tub or hanging basket. The bars lead off each other, the public one with bare boards, settles and traditional pub games, the others, rather dimly lit, done out with swirly carpets, horse brasses, knick-knacks and velour seating. The blackboard and printed bar menu between them give a decent choice of fresh food with Mediterranean hints, without straying too far from the usual pub staples. Starters might be home-made pâté or baked avocado with prawns and cheese, followed by fresh grilled skate or lemon sole, or a very good pancake stuffed with mushrooms in a rich, creamy sauce and accompanied by nicely done vegetables; meaty options might be lamb's liver and bacon, beef casserole with dumplings or a Sunday roast. Sweets such as tiramisù or hazelnut meringue and raspberries come on a trolley. A full restaurant menu is also available but you can eat the bar food wherever you like. The 'splendid service' has been commended. This is a Greene King pub with IPA and Abbot Ale on handpump; a few wines can be had by the glass. SAMPLE DISHES: grilled sardines £3.25; grilled haunch-steak of wild venison with a brandy and redcurrant sauce £11.75; chocolate roulade £3.

Open *11.30 to 2.30, 6 to 11, Sun 12 to 3, 7 to 10; closed 25 Dec; bar food and restaurant 12 to 2, 6.45 to 9.30 (no food Sun eve winter)*
Details *Children welcome in dining-room   Car park   Patio   No music   No dogs   Delta, MasterCard, Visa*

ARLINGTON   East Sussex   map 3

Old Oak 🍺

Arlington BN26 6SJ   TEL: (01323) 482072
off A22, 4m SW of Hailsham outside village of Arlington

Near Michelham Priory and opposite the Abbot's Wood Nature Reserve, this handsome rural white-painted brick freehouse, licensed since 1733, serves Harveys Best and Badger Best as well as a guest beer 'and a not half bad Merlot' by the glass. A basset hound seems to rule the roost and 'everyone from babies to grannies, gumboots to floral dresses' comes to enjoy the views of the South Downs, the summer beer garden and barbecue, the winter fire in the hearth and the ales and victuals the pub has to offer. The same food is available in the spacious bar or the slightly more formal restaurant, the lunch menu sticking to staples like ploughman's, salads, baked potatoes and a few dishes on the lines of lasagne, fried haddock and a curry of the day. Evening snacks feature standard starters like pâté and prawn cocktail, then grilled trout or pork fillet with pepper sauce, and plenty of steaks. Blackboard additions are changed weekly. One visitor's Sunday-lunch roast pork was a star turn, with not only moist lean meat and crisp crackling, but five vegetables and two types of potato. Service is welcoming and efficient. SAMPLE DISHES: macaroni cheese and spinach £5; home-cooked ham salad £5.50; steak and mushroom pie £6.75.

Open *11 to 3, 6 to 11, Sun 12 to 3, 7 to 10.30; bar food and restaurant all week L 12 to 2, Tue to Sat D 7 to 9.15*
Details *Children welcome in dining-room   Car park   Wheelchair access Garden   No-smoking area   Background music   No dogs in restaurant   Delta, MasterCard, Switch, Visa*

ARMATHWAITE   **Cumbria**   map 10

▲ *Dukes Head*

Front Street, Armathwaite CA4 9PB   TEL: (01697) 472226
off A6, between Carlisle and Penrith

'A pleasant pub run by pleasant people,' concluded one reporter. Two generations of the Lynch family run the operation, and when the same reporter phoned to check if they did bar meals he was told that it was 'service with a smile' and if you booked the dining-room it was 'service with an even bigger smile'. A small public bar is almost entirely taken up with a pool table, but if you enter via the porch you will find yourself in a pleasant lounge bar with comfy chairs and well-spaced tables around the walls. Beyond the lounge is the dining-room of the big smiles (where the same menu operates). Cooking is in the traditional pub-grub style – home-made soups, deep-fried Camembert, and battered mushrooms with a garlic dip, for example – though pasta shells in a mild curry mayonnaise with strips of chicken makes an unusual starter. They are very proud of their roast duckling, which they claim is probably the best in Cumbria, or you could settle for grilled fillet of local trout in almonds and pistachios. There are children's portions and a selection of simpler meals, such as three-egg omelette, salads, ploughman's and sandwiches; puddings include home-made meringue with raspberries, or fresh orange and pineapple with sorbet. A 20-bin wine list offers plenty of choice and is a nice balance between France, Spain and the New World, while for beer drinkers there is Boddingtons. SAMPLE DISHES: pork and venison pâté £3.75; poached plaice in cheese and prawn sauce £7.75; brandy-snap basket with poached pears £3.

Open *11 to 3, 6 to 11; closed 25 Dec; bar food 12 to 1.45, 6.30 to 8.45;*
Details *Children welcome in eating areas   Car park   Wheelchair access (also WC)   Garden   No smoking in restaurant   Background music   Dogs welcome Delta, Mastercard, Switch, Visa   Accommodation: 5 rooms, B&B £29 to £49*

A S E N B Y   **North Yorkshire**   **map 9**

▲ *Crab & Lobster* 😊😊 🍇

Dishforth Road, Asenby YO7 3QL   TEL: (01845) 577286
off A168, between A19 and A1

You will know you have found the Crab & Lobster, for its exterior and setting are unmistakable. Straw crabs crawl up the thatched roof, flagpoles with flags of different nations line the car park and surrounding the pub is a flagstoned patio with colourful plant pots. Even the beautiful, heavy doors carry a marine theme with a crab motif and a porthole. The building is covered with old tin advertising signs for things like Colman's Mustard and Capstan Full Strength, and the roof is covered with knick-knacks such as an old butter churn, a rocking horse and lobster pots. Inside, the mood is set with jazzy background music, and one quickly becomes aware that the place is stuffed full of bizarre items, including a dentist's chair and more lobster pots. The whole place is dimly lit – though the restaurant has more natural light – and is all very atmospheric, with candles in champagne bottles completing the picture.

The cooking succeeds in drawing out the superlatives from our reporters. Ravioli with lobster is 'excellent', grilled turbot is 'without fault', scallops in garlic and bread crumbs and Gruyère cheese are 'very good', and roast sea bass with fennel and herbs is 'perfect'. The kitchen excels in the key area of timing when busy. This is frequently the downfall of many otherwise good food pubs, and numbers of reporters have commented on the Crab's ability to deliver dishes at the table together and piping hot. Fish is very much the thing here, and the kitchen is familiar with most known ways of cooking it, and a few more besides. Non-fish-eaters are catered for by way of bison casserole with chorizo dumplings, or Cajun chicken with tortilla chips and guacamole, but it is for such dishes as a galette of sea trout with sauce bonne femme, or crab and king prawn croustade thermidor that a well-heeled clientele come. The pub runs a series of theme evenings, ranging from jazz suppers and curry clubs, to puddings dinners and a posh 'fish 'n' chips supper'. A short selection of real ales consists of Bass, Worthington and Black Sheep. The extensive wine list is divided into categories from dry to full-bodied, and is whimsically annotated with picture symbols; 14 are available by the glass. SAMPLE DISHES: six Irish rock oysters £7; halibut and blue lobster Thai curry £13.50; banana and blackberry strudel with Malteser ice-cream £4.50.

Open *11.30 to 3, 6.30 to 11, Sun 12 to 3, 7 to 10.30; closed eve 25 Dec; bar food Sun to Mon 12 to 2, 7 to 9.30, Sat 6.30 to 10; restaurant 12 to 2, 7 to 9* **Details** *Children welcome   Car park   Garden and patio   No smoking in restaurant   Background and live music   No dogs   Amex, Delta, MasterCard, Switch, Visa   Accommodation: 9 rooms, B&B £75 to £105*

ASHPRINGTON   Devon   map 1

▲ *Durant Arms*

Ashprington TQ9 7UP   TEL: (01803) 732240
off A381 Totnes to Kingsbridge road, 2m SE of Totnes

This homely pub stands in the middle of the village square and at night it is well lit and impossible to miss. It has been run since 1995 by Graham and Eileen Ellis, who seem to have an ability to inspire affection almost immediately. There is a dining-room to the right of the entrance and a lounge bar to the left. This is a smart, well looked-after establishment, the lounge having the air of a homely domestic front room, with a log-burning fire, ornaments on the mantelpiece and pretty pictures on the walls. The bar counter occupies a corner of the room, which contains well-spaced tables laid with pristine cloths and formal place settings. A blackboard menu on the wall lists the day's specials, which could include avocado with prawns, pan-fried plaice fillets, steamed halibut with prawns in a spinach and cream sauce, seafood lasagne, or casserole of venison in red wine. The lunch menu might lead off with leek and potato soup or melon with a raspberry sorbet. There are also one-course bar meals such as chicken curry and rice, or steak and kidney pie, and a further selection of main courses like sliced Barbary duck in a gooseberry sauce, or pan-fried skate wing with wine and capers. Cooking is simple and unpretentious, and very caring service by Eileen gives the impression of nothing being too much trouble. Puddings include fresh fruit salad, banana split, or rhubarb and apple crumble. Graham serves up Flowers Original and Wadworth 6X, and offers a respectable list of reasonably priced wines. The pub has a self-catering cottage in the grounds, as well as in-house accommodation. SAMPLE DISHES: whole prawns in garlic dip £4; fillet of beef Stroganov £8.75; lemon meringue pie £3.

Open *11.30 to 2.30, 6 (6.30 in winter) to 11, Sun 12 to 2.30, 7 to 10.30; bar food and restaurant 12 to 2, 7 to 9.15*
Details *Children welcome in dining-room   Wheelchair access (also WC) Garden and patio   No smoking in 1 dining-room   Background and live music Dogs welcome   Delta, MasterCard, Switch, Visa   Accommodation: 3 rooms, B&B £25 to £30*

▲ *Waterman's Arms* 🍺

Bow Bridge, Ashprington TQ9 7EG
TEL: (01803) 732214

This solid stone-built inn, next to a bridge recorded in the Domesday Book, was formerly a brewhouse, once a haunt of the hated press gangs, and finally a smithy before its conversion into a hotel. It is a bit too smoothly managed to be a classic country pub, according to some fastidious reporters, who none the less concede that it is a pleasant place to stay. Brass, copper, dried hops, boating pictures, plates, beams and lamps create a comfortable upmarket country inn look, albeit one that has been efficiently and pleasantly modernised. Cooking is 'hotel-style' and the menu offers a choice of starters and light meals as well as full-blown main courses and daily specials. Antipasta is a nice touch with chilli-marinated olives, salami, mozzarella and chargrilled vegetables served with bread sticks. Crab and prawn cocktail would make a light meal in itself, and main courses on the menu hail solidly from the steak-and-kidney-pie and chilli-con-carne school of cooking. More modern dishes are available on the specials list – breast of chicken with an olive tapénade for example, or roasted salmon with sun-dried tomato butter sauce. There are interesting flavour combinations to try in the shape of a whole Brixham plaice with bananas and a light mustard sauce, or half a roasted duck rubbed with five spices. Puddings might include pear frangipane tart, carrot cake with clotted cream, or mango cheesecake. In addition to the Bass, Palmers, Exmoor and Flowers ales, Pig Squeal and Luscombe ciders are also on offer, and the two-dozen-strong wine list looks to France and Australia for its inspiration. SAMPLE DISHES: deep-fried calamari £8; loin of venison in a rosemary jus £15; baked rice pudding with maple syrup and jam £4.

Open *summer 11 to 11, Sun 12 to 10.30, winter 11 to 3, 6 to 11, Sun 12 to 3, 6 to 10.30; bar food and restaurant 12 to 2.30, 6.30 to 10*
Details *Children welcome in bar eating area   Car park   Garden and patio Background and live music   Dogs welcome   Amex, Delta, MasterCard, Switch, Visa   Accommodation: 15 rooms, B&B £40 to £64*

Recommendations for good country pubs will be very welcome.

▲ King's Arms Hotel

Askrigg DL8 3HQ   TEL: (01969) 650258
off A684 Sedburgh to Bedale road, ½m N of Bainbridge

The King's Arms is a major attraction on the Herriot Trail, best
known to fans as the Drover's in the TV series *All Creatures Great
and Small*. In the heart of Wensleydale country, the hotel in the
village of Askrigg (meaning 'ash trees in the nook') was built in 1760
for John Pratt to house his famous racing stable. In 1810 it became a
well-known coaching-inn on the Richmond to Lancaster turnpike.
Inside, there are three charming bars: a simply furnished back bar, a
high-ceilinged main bar, which betrays its origins as the tack room –
saddle hooks can still be seen – and a cosy, panelled front room with
beams and open fire. The emphasis of the food is on local game in
season and traditional Yorkshire dishes. In this vein you might start
with pigeon en croûte with Madeira, followed by singed panhaggerty
(pan-fried ham and spring onion potato cake). As well as traditional
dishes like steak and ale pie, or venison duet, you might also find
chicken hoisin, fajitas, or lamb with pesto. Sirloin steak comes in
Wensleydale sauce. Puddings are of the sticky toffee and bread-and-
butter variety. The separate 'Silks Room' offers the same menu as do
the bars in more formal surroundings and the Clubroom has a full
restaurant menu, featuring several dishes re-created from the inn's
Georgian heyday. Dent Bitter travels some 15 miles east across the
Yorkshire Dales to join Theakston XB and John Smith's from the
west. The wine list runs to some 30 well-chosen, mid-priced bottles,
plus three dessert wines by the glass and a short connoisseur's list, as
well as wines of the week and the month. SAMPLE DISHES: exotic
fruits with yoghurt and poppy seed dressing £3.75; pork cutlet on
sage and onion stuffing with prune and brandy sauce £8.25; hot
chocolate pudding £3.25.

Open *11 to 3 (5 Sat), 6.30 to 11, Sun 12 to 3, 7 to 10.30; bar food and
restaurant 12 to 2, 6.30 (7 Sun) to 9*
Details *Children welcome in eating areas   Car park   Wheelchair access (also
WC)   Patio   No smoking in restaurants   Jukebox   No dogs in restaurants
Amex, Delta, MasterCard, Switch, Visa   Accommodation: 11 rooms, B&B
£39.50 to £124*

ASTON Cheshire map 7

Bhurtpore Inn NEW ENTRY

Wrenbury Road, Aston CW5 8DQ
TEL: (01270) 780917
off A530, 5m S of Nantwich

Simon George bought the pub in 1991, and in freeing it from 90 years of the tie he restored it to his family, as he is the great-great-great-grandson of Joyce George, who took on the running of the Bhurtpore in 1849. The pub takes its name from the Siege of Bhurtpore, an Indian military campaign conducted in 1825 by local landowner Lord Combermere, a dandified but able British commander. The campaign was notable for witnessing the debut of Ghurka soldiers under the Union flag. Perhaps it is with an understanding of soldiers' thirst that Simon George offers such an impressive range of real ales. Hanby's Drawwell Bitter from Shropshire is the permanent presence on the bar counter, normally accompanied by nine ales chosen exclusively from independent small brewers. In addition there is usually one guest cider or perry, plus a massive selection of bottled British, German, Czech and Belgian beers. This unassuming pub, scattered with various relevant artefacts, serves interesting home-cooked food and above-average curries. If you are in an Indian mood, start with spicy lamb samosa with a cool yoghurt and mint dip and then select from a range of curries and baltis displayed on the specials board. Those with milder mouths could start with crispy coated vegetables with a blue cheese or mayonnaise dip and then lamb chops with a port and rosemary sauce. The wine list certainly plays second fiddle to the beer list – and even third fiddle to the extensive single malt whisky list – but manages none the less to contain some bottles that will not disappoint the 'I don't like beer' brigade. SAMPLE DISHES: soup of the day £1.75; braised steak with red wine and onions £6.50; lemon brûlée £3.

Open *12 to 2.30, 6.30 to 11, Sun 12 to 3, 7 to 10.30; closed 25 Dec and 31 Dec; bar food and restaurant 12 to 2 (2.30 weekends), 7 to 9.30*
Details *No children   Car park   Wheelchair access (also WC)   Garden and patio   No smoking in dining-room and part of lounge bar   Background and live music   Dogs welcome in games room only   No cards*

▲ *Tally Ho Inn* ✿

Aswarby NG34 8SA   TEL: (01529) 455205
on A15 Peterborough to Lincoln road, 5m S of Sleaford

Committed new owners, who took over early in 1998, have kept the
hunting theme going at this 'quintessential English pub, the kind it
would be hard not to like', that looms up on the A15 at the edge of
the village. A pub for over 100 years and a farmhouse for a couple of
hundred before that, it now attracts locals and others for bar snacks
taken on settles and Windsor chairs under beamed ceilings and with
the smell of wood smoke on the air. Staff are welcoming and courteous, bringing generous and 'super value' helpings of Lincolnshire
sausages, minty lamb steaks, huge salmon and spinach fish-cakes, or
blackboard specials such as lamb kidneys in cream sauce, or chicken
breast with ham and mushrooms. Praise comes easily for the 'crisp,
floury' chips and the excellent vegetables, though few will manage to
finish their greens if they have an eye on the puddings, which might
include 'soft, gorgeous' iced lemon curd cake, or mascarpone chocolate cheesecake. Prices are a little higher in the restaurant. On the
drinks front are 'superbly kept' Bateman's beers, plus Bass, Rudgate
and Tom Wood; also Scrumpy Jack, and a quick turnover of various
wines by the glass. SAMPLE DISHES: vegetable loaf with herby tomato
sauce £7; lamb and cider casserole £6.75; lemon soufflé with raspberries and almond biscuits £2.50.

Open *12 to 3, 6 to 11, Sun 12 to 3, 7 to 10.30; closed 26 Dec; bar food 12
to 2.30, 6.30 to 10; restaurant Sun 12 to 3, Mon to Sat 7.15 to 11*
Details *Children welcome   Car park   Wheelchair access (also WC)   Garden
and patio   Background music   Dogs welcome   Delta, MasterCard, Switch,
Visa   Accommodation: 6 rooms, B&B £33 to £48*

▲ *Red Hart Inn*

Awre GL14 1EW   TEL: (01594) 510220
off A48 Newnham to Chepstow road, 2m S of Newnham

This whitewashed fifteenth-century inn, close to the Forest of Dean,
lies on the flatlands of the Severn estuary. For summer eating, there
is bench seating in the pleasant garden, which has apple trees and an
old cider press. The interior of the L-shaped building has a central
bar and exposed dark oak beams decorated with dried hops and
brassware, all making for a relaxed country atmosphere; the separate

dining area has pine tables. An 'excellent value' printed bar menu lists 'robust and straightforward' food such as salads, sandwiches, baguettes, ploughman's and filled jacket potatoes, plus more substantial offerings such as scampi, cold poached salmon and a variety of steaks. A large blackboard contains the day's specials, which might include deep-fried mushrooms, chicken liver pâté, butterfly chicken or Thai-spiced crab-cakes, among many other choices. A more expensive *carte* offers dishes like marinated king prawns or smoked meat platter to start, followed by rack of lamb with a shallot and rosemary sauce, scallop and scampi thermidor, or medallions of pork with apricots in an apple and cream sauce. Desserts could be chocolate torte, apricot crème brûlée, or profiteroles. Real ales come from Bass, Fuller's or the local Freeminer brewery in Sling, bolstered by two guest beers and local cider. A 20-bottle wine list offers two house wines by the glass. SAMPLE DISHES: deep-fried whitebait £3.75; lamb in black-bean sauce £6; sticky toffee pecan cheesecake £3.25.

Open *Mon to Fri 12 to 3, 6.30 to 11, Sat 12 to 3, 6 to 11, Sun 12 to 3, 6.30 to 10.30; bar food and restaurant 12 to 2, 7 to 9*
Details *Children welcome in bar eating area   Car park   Garden   No smoking in restaurant   Background music   Guide dogs only   Amex, Delta, MasterCard, Switch, Visa   Accommodation: 2 rooms, B&B £55*

AXFORD   Wiltshire   map 2

▲ *Red Lion*

Axford SN8 2HA   TEL: (01672) 520271
*off A4, 3m E of Marlborough, between Mildenhall
and Ramsbury*

FISH

The sleepy village of Axford lies just a few minutes drive outside historic Marlborough, near the leafy banks of the Kennet & Avon Canal. This seventeenth-century brick-and-flint pub makes a good excuse to break a journey, or a base for exploring the Savernake Forest and the Kennet valley, which can be seen from its front garden. While the structure of this traditional hostelry (beams, open fireplaces, settle seating etc.) remains reassuringly intact, recent tidings speak of an even more ambitious approach to the food side of the business. Now marketed as a 'fully air-conditioned, non-smoking, fresh fish, seafood & game restaurant', the Red Lion has a wide-ranging but down-to-earth menu incorporating local produce such as wild game, cheeses and herbs. Fish remains an important part of the repertoire, delivered daily from the South Coast, and perhaps served up as deep-fried whitebait, or grilled monkfish with mixed herbs. Imaginative blackboard specials (potted Stilton and chestnut terrine, perhaps, or a crown of lamb with date and ginger stuffing) are chalked up weekly. For all those 'squires, farmers and ploughmen' who regularly stroll by, there are plenty of familiar bar snacks like steak and kidney pie, toasted sandwiches and rib-sticking platters of beef, Wiltshire ham and cheese. Trolley puds are described as 'good but sweet'. Six wines are served by the glass, while draught Wadworth and Hook Norton brews cater for real ale enthusiasts. If you are driving, you can expect a decent cup of tea or coffee. SAMPLE DISHES: spinach and mushroom lasagne £5; crevette platter £11.50; roast Gressingham duck £12.50.

Open *11 to 3, 6.30 to 11, Sun 12 to 3, 7 to 10.30; bar food and restaurant 12 to 2.15, 7 to 9 (10 Sat)*
Details *Children welcome   Car park   Wheelchair access   Garden   No smoking in restaurant   Background music   No dogs   Delta, MasterCard, Switch, Visa   Accommodation: 4 rooms, B&B £35 to £50*

AYMESTREY   Herefordshire   map 5

▲ *Riverside Inn*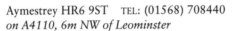

Aymestrey HR6 9ST   TEL: (01568) 708440
on A4110, 6m NW of Leominster

LOCAL PRODUCE

This Herefordshire pub is set on the River Lugg beneath superbly wooded hillsides, not far from Croft Castle, Croft Ambrey iron-age fort and the Capability Brown-landscaped Berrington Hall. The lines of the very long inn, half-timbered in the sixteenth century, are incongruously neat for its age. Inside is a maze of rooms, which descend to a lower-level dining-room with glass walls on two sides. Beers come from the inn's brewery and include Woodhampton, Kingfisher and Rooster. There has been a change of regime in the kitchen since the last *Guide*, though menus remain ambitious. Kick off with a mouclade of mussels in a tarragon sauce, or perhaps a sardine and anchovy escabèche with olive and lemon vinaigrette. Follow with fillet of Herefordshire beef coated with a red grape and mustard sauce, or fillet of Welsh venison on a noodle pancake with a roast shallot sauce. Ice-creams are home-made. The menu makes quality claims to reassure diners that all meat is local and humanely farmed. Bin ends on the wine list probably represent the best buys; five wines are served by the glass. SAMPLE DISHES: risotto with a sun-dried tomato and Cheddar wafer £5; suprême of brill with a salmon mousse and citrus cream sauce £11; apricot and Amaretto ice-cream £3.25.

Open *12 to 3, 6.30 (7 in winter) to 11, Sun 12 to 3, 7 to 10.30; closed 25 Dec; bar food and restaurant 12 to 2.30 (2 Sun), 7 to 9.30*
Details *Children over 7 welcome in dining-room   Car park   Garden Wheelchair access to dining-room only   Garden   No smoking in 1 dining-room   No music   No dogs in eating areas   Delta, MasterCard, Switch, Visa Accommodation: 6 rooms, B&B £30 to £60*

BAINBRIDGE   North Yorkshire   map 8

▲ *Rose & Crown Hotel*

Bainbridge DL8 3EE   TEL: (01969) 650225
on A684, between Hawes and Leyburn, 4m E of Hawes

The Forest Horn, blown nightly between late September and
Shrovetide to guide travellers through the treacheries of darkness
and mist, hangs in the hotel's hall. For this is a venerable place, 500
years an inn, and in a prime position on the village green. The
lounge bar with its antique settles, flagged floors, panelling, beams
and inglenook fireplace is the hub of the inn, while pub games are
played in the locals' bar. There is also a snug, and a more formal
restaurant which operates in the evenings and at Sunday lunch-times.
The bar menu, bolstered by a few blackboard items, is quite short
but likely to appeal to all comers by offering local produce turned
into simple home-made dishes – some traditional, some up to the
minute, with interesting sauces and dressings. Home-made terrine
comes with chutney, while more salady starters include Dales cottage
cheese with a fruit and nut salad. Main courses might be Bainbridge
rarebit with cheese, kidney and mushrooms, seared tuna with a herb
potato cake and stir-fried vegetables with oriental rice. Half a dozen
lunchtime-only sandwiches present an ideal selection: hot bacon with
home-made relish, chicken and mayonnaise with apricot chutney,
and of course Wensleydale cheese and tomato with pickle. Puddings
are the top pub favourites of sticky toffee pudding, banoffi pie and
fruit crumble. Beer is the drink to go for here: friendly bar staff
hand-pull pints of Webster's Yorkshire Bitter and John Smith's.
House wines are available by the glass. SAMPLE DISHES: smoked trout
with prawn and mango mayonnaise £4.25; chicken breast in garlic
butter £8; crème brûlée £3.75.

Open *11 to 11, Sun 12 to 10.30; closed 25 Dec, 1 Jan; bar food 12 to 2
(2.30 Sun), 6.30 to 9.30; restaurant Sun L 12 to 2.30, all week D 7 to 9.30*
Details *Children welcome   Car park   Wheelchair access   Garden
Background music; jukebox   No dogs in lounge or snug bars while food is
being served   Delta, MasterCard, Visa   Accommodation: 11 rooms, B&B £25
to £66*

NEW ENTRY *indicates that pub was not a main entry in the
previous edition (though it may have featured in the 'Out and
About' section.)*

BALLINGER COMMON   Buckinghamshire   map 3

Pheasant

Ballinger Common HP16 9LF   TEL: (01494) 837236
off A413 at Great Missenden, 3m W of Chesham

'Ballinger,' says the Pheasant's brochure, 'is a haven of tranquillity and charm,' and the white-pebbledash, flower-festooned nineteenth-century inn is very much at the heart of it, facing the village green and cricket pitch. The pub's owners are 'friendly, chatty' and concerned that people will have a good time and come again. The sign outside describes the pub as an 'eating house', and this is clearly its primary function. A long menu is supplemented by a specials board, which changes weekly. 'Beginnings and light meals' might include avocado baked with prawns and the Ballinger Burger, which contains a home-made 'pure' beef patty. Mixed seafood bake, and savoury vegetarian pancake are typical main courses, while the specials board might offer such alternatives as fresh fish, braised rabbit, or shank of lamb. Seasonal fruit pies are a regular feature. Beer drinkers can choose from a small but changing selection, with bottled Leffe Blonde an alternative aperitif. Stowford Press cider is also available. The wine list is competently chosen and presented, though wines by the glass are a little pricey. SAMPLE DISHES: leek and ham 'hotpot' au gratin £6.50; lemon chicken £11; hazelnut meringue £3.75.

Open *all week 12 to 3, Tue to Sat 6.30 to 11; bar food 12 to 2.15, 6.45 to 9*
Details *Children over 7 welcome in conservatory   Car park   Wheelchair access (also WC)   Patio   No smoking in conservatory   Background music No dogs   Amex, Delta, MasterCard, Switch, Visa*

BANTHAM   Devon   map 1

▲ *Sloop Inn*

Bantham TQ7 3AJ   TEL: (01548) 560489
off A379, 4m W of Kingsbridge

This sixteenth-century former smugglers' inn, once owned by a notorious local wrecker, is a bizarre construction consisting of an improbably tall and narrow building abutting one of more usual proportions. Located in a sprawling seaside village of a few well-spaced dwellings, it has views of the sea, Burgh Island and the River Avon, and with its adjacent accommodation is a great place for a surfing holiday. Cooking here sets out to deliver simple, quintessential pub grub: pasties, basket meals, ploughman's, salads and sandwiches form the vast bulk of the menu. Starters consist of all our old favourites – garlic mushrooms, home-made pâté and prawn cocktail – while mains are things like deep-fried scampi, steak, and grilled smoked gammon, though there are more ambitious specials which may include deep-fried squat lobster with lemon and tarragon mayonnaise, followed by grilled skate wing, or pork tenderloin in cider and apricot sauce. A range of Salcombe Dairy ice-creams is available to finish, along with lemon crunch, apple pie, or spotted dick. Service is prompt and attentive. The pub serves Bass, Usher's Best and locally brewed Blackawton, as well as Churchwards cider. A selection of 55 wines from around the world includes around ten by the glass. SAMPLE DISHES: barbecue spare ribs £4.50; chargrilled salmon with pesto and lemon oil £10; raspberry pavlova £3.

Open *11 to 2.30, 6 to 11, Sun 12 to 2.30, 7 to 10.30; closed eve 25 and 26 Dec; bar food and restaurant 12 to 2, 7 to 10 (no food 25 and 26 Dec)* **Details** *Children welcome in dining-room and family room   Car park Wheelchair access   Patio   No cigars or pipes   Background music   Dogs welcome   Delta, Switch   Accommodation: 7 rooms, B&B £29 to £62*

BARNARD GATE   Oxfordshire   map 2

Boot Inn

Barnard Gate OX8 6XE   TEL: (01865) 881231
off A40, between Witney and Oxford

Enjoying a relatively peaceful and convenient position just off the A40, the attractive and very civilised Boot Inn is a typical Cotswold stone building with a good front terrace. It is also a popular stop noted for its interesting bar food and fascinating collection of boots and shoes. The collection is made up of those donated by celebrities, such as Tim Henman, Geoff Hurst and the Bee Gees: you are asked to nominate a celebrity, and once 12 nominations have been made, the manager will write to the person concerned, asking him or her for a footwear donation. The spacious quarry-tiled bar with huge stone fireplace and log fire, mixture of solid tables topped with fresh flowers and candles, interspersed with boots and shoes, combine to create a warm and welcoming atmosphere. The emphasis here is on food, which is served brasserie-style. A new manager and chef have been installed as the *Guide* went to press and although popular dishes such as grilled prawns with garlic mayonnaise will remain, the new chef has yet to stamp his style. This freehouse, run by George Dailey since 1989, serves Hook Norton ales and Fuller's London Pride on handpump and offers about 30 wines, including four by the glass. SAMPLE DISHES: crostini with grilled goats' cheese served with a mango salsa £4.75; steak and kidney pudding with Colman's English mustard and bubble and squeak (limited numbers made daily – phone to reserve) £11; sticky toffee pudding £3.50.

Open *11 to 11, Sun 12 to 3, 7 to 10.30; bar food and restaurant 12 to 3, 7 to 10*
Details *Children welcome in bar eating area　Car park　Wheelchair access Patio　No-smoking areas　Background music　Dogs welcome　MasterCard, Visa*

BARNSTON　Merseyside　　　　　　　map 7

Fox & Hounds

Barnston Road, Barnston L61 1BW　TEL: (0151) 648 7685
off A551, 1¼m N of Heswall

This large, handsome 1930s pub, with extensive patio area, is as comprehensively oak-beam free as it is chips, burgers and pizza free. Good dining is the order of the day as licensee/chef Helen Leech is keen to stress. The lunchtime-only blackboard menu changes daily according to availability of produce and how Helen feels. Prices are very reasonable. Lamb hotpot with pickled red cabbage, and pork au poivre are both under £5. Nevertheless the pub seems to attract a fairly affluent Merseyside clientele, judging by the vehicles drawn up in the car park. Webster's Yorkshire Bitter, Courage Directors, Ruddles County, and Theakston Best and XB form the core of the beer range, which is augmented by guests, and there is also a list of 50 whiskies. Three wines are served by the glass. SAMPLE DISHES: minted lamb-burgers with yoghurt, mint and cucumber relish £4.25; baked suprême of salmon with honey and mustard glaze £6.75; toffee apple pie £2.25.

Open *11 to 11, Sun 12 to 10.30; bar food L only 12 to 2*
Details *Children welcome in family room　Car park　Wheelchair access Garden and patio　No music　Dogs welcome　No cards*

BEELEY   Derbyshire   map 9

Devonshire Arms   NEW ENTRY

Beeley DE4 2NR   TEL: (01629) 733259
off B6102, *5m N of Matlock*

A welcome new addition to the *Guide*, this civilised and fairly
upmarket retreat for visitors to the Chatsworth Estate and nearby
Haddon Hall is set in an attractive village. It is equally popular with
country-house visitors, and walkers exploring the beautiful and classic Peak District landscape. Built in 1726 as a row of cottages, it was
converted into an inn in 1741, and the name and dates of each and
every subsequent landlord are displayed on the menu. The comfortable and neatly furnished interior comprises three characterful,
beamed rooms: a small rear 'tap' room, where walkers with muddy
boots are directed; a civilised main bar with roaring open fire; and a
rear flag-floored dining-room. Food is served all day, and the style is
interesting home-cooked food, ranging from decent soups to sea
bass, all at value-for-money prices. 'To get things started', as the
menu puts it, there is a good choice of dishes from salmon
brochettes, salad of smoked venison, or Stilton-stuffed pears with
poppy-seed dressing. Main courses might be 'Pieces of Eight' – white
fish in breadcrumbs with lemon – Welsh rarebit, steak Balmoral, or a
Barnsley chop. Friday nights are fish nights, and pasta-style vegetarian dishes abound. The beer list might fool you into thinking you are
in the Dales, not the Peak District, for the Theakston and Black
Sheep breweries have exclusive run of the bar. A short wine list
offers reasonably priced generic wines. SAMPLE DISHES: seafood hors
d'oeuvre £5.50; venison in red wine sauce £9; treacle sponge £2.50.

Open *11 to 11, Sun 12 to 10.30; bar food and restaurant 12 to 9.30
(Victorian breakfast served on Sun from 10 to 12)*
Details *Children welcome   Car park   Wheelchair access   Patio   No-
smoking areas   No music   Guide dogs only   MasterCard, Visa, Switch*

BEER   Devon   map 2

▲ *Anchor*

Beer EX12 3ET   TEL: (01297) 20386
off A3052, between Seaton and Sidmouth

This white-painted building, standing on a hillside overlooking the
harbour and beach, looks more like a converted Victorian town
house than a pub. The interior is very much geared to eating, with a
small bar area in one corner and a large restaurant section with café-

like décor. A printed menu lists a selection of basket-type meals, but the blackboard offers much more adventurous dishes with a strong emphasis on fish. Try deep-fried squid dusted with paprika and rosemary and served with tartare sauce, or a tartlet of Stilton, prawns and chives on a bed of marinated vegetables. Main dishes may include steamed fillet of sea bass with king prawns and saffron sauce, or grilled fillets of John Dory and fresh salmon with prawns and lemon butter. Daily-changing home-made puddings come with clotted cream. Ales from the local Otter brewery are served, as well as regularly changing guests, while the wine list is uncomplicated and reasonably priced. The pub was taken over by the Old English Pub Company shortly before the *Guide* went to press, which means that the comments above may date rapidly. SAMPLE DISHES: moules marinière £4.50; roast breast of duck with orange and ginger sauce £11.50; blackcurrant roulade £3.25.

Open *summer 11 to 11, winter Mon to Fri 11 to 2.30, 5.30 to 11, Sat and Sun 11 to 11; closed eve 25 Dec; bar food and restaurant 12 to 2, 7 to 9.30* **Details** *Children welcome in bar eating area   Wheelchair access   Garden   No smoking in restaurant   Background music in restaurant   Dogs welcome in public bar only   Delta, MasterCard, Switch, Visa   Accommodation: 8 rooms, B&B £40 to £65*

BEETHAM   **Cumbria**   map 8

▲ *Wheatsheaf* ❦   NEW ENTRY

Beetham LA7 7AL   TEL: (015395) 62123
just off A6, 5m N of Carnforth

This fine, timbered sixteenth-century inn on the River Bela is convenient for Morecambe Bay and the Lake District. New owners have totally refurbished the Wheatsheaf, and all accommodation is now *en suite*. The small snug is for drinkers, but all the other areas have tables laid with place mats, cutlery and paper napkins. The beamed public bar has a tiled floor, brasses hanging above the bar, and a dartboard, while a separate carpeted first-floor restaurant (where booking is essential at weekends) has polished dark wood tables. This is very much a dining pub, with the same quite upmarket, but moderately priced menu served throughout. Normal pub staples are noticeable by their absence. Instead, you will find starters ranging from soup of the day (perhaps swede and tarragon) to a skewer of king prawns or pan-fried chicken livers with polenta, followed by main courses of marinated loin of venison, seared tuna steak or, for vegetarians, a spicy lentil samosa with satay sauce. Puddings cater for traditionalists – bread-and-butter pudding, for example – or choose pecan pie, or iced banana parfait. Sunday meals are set-price only, with traditional roasts. Beers come from Tetley or Jennings and might include the latter's Cumberland Ale or Sneck Lifter. An excellent 30-bottle wine list has a worldwide selection from good producers, with six available by the glass. SAMPLE DISHES: warm confit of duck £4.25; grilled salmon steak £9; dark coffee mousse £3.50.

Open *11 to 3, 6 to 11, Sun 12 to 3, 7 to 10.30; bar food and restaurant 12 to 2, 6 (7 Sun) to 9*
Details *Children welcome in bar eating area before 8.30pm Car park No smoking in restaurant Background music Dogs welcome in some areas Delta, MasterCard, Visa, Switch Accommodation: 6 rooms, B&B £55 to £70*

BENTWORTH Hampshire   map 2

Sun 🍺

Sun Hill, Bentworth GU34 5JT   TEL: (01420) 562338
off A339 Alton to Basingstoke, 3m W of Alton

A change of licensee in early 1997 seems not to have upset any applecarts at this friendly freehouse in deep-green countryside on the edge of a Hampshire village. Originally two cottages, dating from the seventeenth century, its white-painted walls billow with flowers during the summertime, providing customers who bag the lane-side picnic tables with colourful surroundings. Inside, log fires blaze in winter, and the three cosy, interconnected bar and dining spaces are cheerfully decorated with gleaming brass and pewter. It is very much a local, but increasingly popular with business people at lunch-time – hence the extra elbow room offered by a side extension, sympathetically matching the older style of brick-and-timber floors and low-beamed ceilings. Blackboard menus ring the changes on an assortment of hot dishes such as Cumberland sausage or beef in ale, bolstered with plenty of staple sandwiches, ploughman's lunches and filled jacket potatoes. Most of it springs no surprises, but there are a few more unusual suggestions, and enough choice to please nearly everyone, including vegetarians. Real ale fans should be more than pleased, with no fewer than eight handpumps dispensing enticing local brews like Bunces Pigswill or Ringwood Old Thumper. Other beers on offer may include Cheriton Pots Ale, Hogs Back TEA, Brakspear Bitter and Badger Best. Wine drinkers get a choice of Gales country wines, and three house wines by the glass. There is a decent selection of malts as well. SAMPLE DISHES: onion and cider soup £2.25; lamb and butter-bean casserole £6.50; chocolate shortbread with white chocolate sauce £2.50

Open *12 to 3, 6 to 11, Sun 12 to 10; closed eves 25 and 26 Dec; bar food 12 to 2, 7 to 9.30*
Details *Children welcome in family room Car park Wheelchair access Garden and patio No music Dogs welcome MasterCard, Switch, Visa*

BERWICK   East Sussex   map 3

Cricketers' Arms

Berwick Village BN26 6SP   TEL: (01323) 870469
just off A27 Lewes to Polegate road

A very pretty village pub, nesting in a quiet cul-de-sac, the Cricketers' Arms was formed from the conversion of two flint-faced cottages. The dead-end road leads only to the church, which houses wall paintings by Vanessa Bell and Duncan Grant. Attractive gardens at the front and rear of the pub have picnic tables for summer eating. Inside, the three separate rooms all have creaky floors, old wooden tables and chairs, heavy red curtains, cricketing prints on the walls and log fires in winter. The menu's 'light dishes' could tempt you with soup, deep-fried Camembert or garlic mushrooms. 'Local favourites' might be jacket potatoes with a variety of fillings, ploughman's, a vegetarian dish of the day, sausages or home-cooked honey ham. Daily specials have included local cod in batter, prawn platter, prime sirloin steak, and gammon steak with egg or pineapple. The desserts range from fruit crumble, steamed ginger and lemon pudding to deluxe ice-creams. Harvey's Best, Pale and Old Ales are drawn direct from casks, and 'wines of the month' are advertised along with a selection of English country wines. Altogether ten wines are available by the glass. SAMPLE DISHES: breaded Japanese prawns £4.50; garlic and herb chicken quarter £5.50; banoffi pie £2.75.

Open *Mon to Sat 11 to 3, 6 to 11 (all day Sat in summer), Sun 11 to 10.30 (12 to 10.30 in winter); closed 25 Dec; bar food 12 to 2.15, 6.30 to 9 (all day Sat in summer), Sun 12 to 9*
Details *Children welcome in eating area   Car park   Wheelchair access (also WC)   Garden   No music   Well-behaved dogs welcome   No cards*

BIDDENDEN   Kent   map 3

Three Chimneys 🍺

Biddenden TN27 7HA   TEL: (01580) 291472
on A262, 2m W of Biddenden

Look at the inn sign and you will discover that the pub does not have three chimneys; its name comes from a corruption of *trois chemins* (French for three roads) and refers to a nearby three-way crossroads, which during the Napoleonic wars marked the boundary beyond which French prisoners could not freely roam without being deemed to have absconded. The pub is pure Kentish picture-postcard, leaving you in no doubt that you are in the Garden of England. Opposite is that quintessentially Kentish sight, an oast house, and it may come as no surprise that hop bines decorate the bar. The menu here is always short; four choices at each course, chosen from a large repertoire and changing frequently to maintain interest, with vegetarian options available upon request. Particular favourites among customers, according to the landlord, are Danish blue and cauliflower soup, seafood kebab, duck and chestnut mousse, and more substantial pork and veal terrine, followed perhaps by hot cheese flan, artichoke chicken, or turkey fricassee; to finish there may be pear frangipane, date and walnut pudding, or prune and apple meringue. Biddenden is known for its cider, but real ales include Adnams Best, Brakspear Bitter, Harveys Best, and Morland Old Speckled Hen, all served from cask. The wine list offers a choice of bottles from each of the several regions and countries it visits. SAMPLE DISHES: potted Stilton in port and walnuts £3.50; pork loin in ginger beer sauce £6.50; upside-down marmalade pudding £3.

Open *11 to 2.30, 6 to 11, Sun 12 to 2.30, 7 to 10.30; closed 25 and 26 Dec; bar food 12 to 2, 7 to 10*
Details *Children welcome in dining-room   Car park   Wheelchair access Garden   No music   Dogs welcome on a lead   Delta, MasterCard, Switch, Visa*

BILBROUGH   North Yorkshire   map 9

Three Hares 🍇

Main Street, Bilbrough YO2 3PH   TEL: (01937) 832128
off A64, between Tadcaster and York

This ex-coaching inn in the pretty village of Bilbrough, a tranquil retreat from touristy York, is a good example of what has been happening to quite a few old Yorkshire pubs: namely a move away from basic, uninspired pub food towards a decent selection of imaginative, freshly prepared dishes. The Three Hares has a rather old feel, with willow-patterned plates on the walls, a beamed ceiling and traditional wooden tables and chairs. A one-page menu offers about ten starters, ten main courses, half a dozen puddings and some cheeses, and the food shows a number of modern touches. Starters, for example, might take in goats'-cheese soufflé or Thai salmon salad, followed by lamb and sun-dried tomato sausage, perhaps, or goujons of sole with a lemon poppy seed mayonnaise, or stir-fried chicken and king prawns with ginger, spring onions and chilli sauce with egg noodles. In addition, a blackboard displays a small number of specials of the day. Reporters have enjoyed chunky chicken-liver paté that arrives with warm olive bread, seared scallops in a light creamy sauce, and medallions of lamb in a red wine sauce. Likewise, praise has come in for desserts of tarte Tatin, and bread-and-butter pudding served with excellent custard. Black Sheep Bitter and Timothy Taylor Landlord are on tap, plus guest beers. Wines, displayed on blackboards, comprise mainly New World bottles, with eight available by the glass. SAMPLE DISHES: deep-fried vegetables in crispy yeast batter with a sweet-and-sour sauce £4; roast top side of venison, confit of butter beans and pancetta with roasted shallots £13; steamed banana sponge with caramel sauce £3.25.

Open *Tue to Sun 12 to 2.30 (3 in summer), 7 to 11, Sun 12 to 3; closed 25 Dec; bar food and restaurant 12 to 2.15, 7 to 9.30*
Details *Children welcome in eating areas   Car park   Garden   No smoking in restaurant   Background music   No dogs   MasterCard, Visa, Switch*

BIRCHOVER   Derbyshire   **map 5**

Druid Inn

VEGETARIAN

Main Street, Birchover DE4 2BL   TEL: (01629) 650302
from A6 near Haddon Hall take B5056, Birchover signposted on left after 2m

---

This ivy-covered eighteenth-century inn gets its name from the supposed druidical connection with Row Tor rocking stones, which loom from an outcrop above. It is situated in the heart of the Peak District's excellent walking country, and not far from many of the area's tourist attractions. Summer drinks can be taken on the front terrace overlooking fields, and the rambling interior has a small bar area, but the emphasis is on eating, in either the garden room or the two-storey dining extension. Food spans the globe and the extensive menu might offer Thai fish-cakes, Somerset pork casserole, or five-spice duck with noodles. Garlic mushrooms or various patés with toast and salad are lighter offerings, and vegetarians are well catered for with casseroles, rissoles, curries or half an aubergine filled with rice, mushrooms and peppers in a peanut and garlic sauce. For dessert lovers there is Bakewell pudding, or perhaps sherry trifle or steamed chocolate pudding. Draught beers are Morland Speckled Hen, Monksfield Cask and Marston's Pedigree. Three house wines are available by the glass. SAMPLE DISHES: deep-fried Buxton blue cheese with apricot dip £4.75; traditional steak and kidney pudding £8; apple and marzipan torte £2.75.

Open *12 to 3 (2 winter), 7 to 11 (10 or 10.30 winter); bar food 12 to 2 (2.30 Sun), 7 to 9.30 (9 winter)*
Details *Children welcome in dining-room before 8pm   Car park   Wheelchair access   Patio   No smoking in 2 rooms   Background music   Guide dogs welcome   Amex, Diners, MasterCard, Switch, Visa*

BIRCH VALE Derbyshire map 8

▲ *Waltzing Weasel*

New Mills Road, Birch Vale SK22 1BT TEL: (01663) 743402
on A6015, ½m W of Hayfield

The Weasel is a restaurant-style pub serving high-quality food, which
benefits greatly from good sourcing of raw materials. It is a low,
stone building with good views of Kinder Scout from its picture
windows and an easily accessible terrace with pretty and mature
gardens. The U-shaped main room has plenty of intimate corners
and oak settles around an open fire. The landlord serves behind the
bar, greeting arriving customers pleasantly. Many reporters have
come away satisfied and on a good day the pub can clearly do what
it does very well, with plenty of cheerful and helpful staff on hand.
The lunch menu may start with gravadlax, egg mayonnaise or chilled
melon, followed by home-baked ham, Peak pie, lamb and walnut
pie, or an 'excellent' seafood tart. In the evening, a separate but similar menu operates in the restaurant, while the bar menu may offer
hot buttered shrimps on toast, mussels in wine or hare pâté to start,
followed by Barnsley chop, or chicken and asparagus pie. Only
Burton Bitter and Marston's Pedigree are on handpump. The pub is
ideally suited for visiting a wide variety of attractions from Haddon
Hall to Alton Towers as well as the peaks themselves. SAMPLE DISHES:
crayfish tails £6; beef in whisky £9.50; raspberry crumble £3.

Open *12 to 3, 5.30 to 11 (10.30 Sun); bar food and restaurant 12 to 2, 7 to 9*
Details *Children welcome in bar eating area   Car park   Wheelchair access*
(also WC)   Garden   Background music   Dogs welcome   Amex, Delta,
MasterCard, Switch, Visa   Accommodation: 8 rooms, B&B £38 to £95

BISHOP'S CASTLE Shropshire map 5

▲ *Three Tuns* 🍺 NEW ENTRY

Salop Street, Bishop's Castle SY9 5BW TEL: (01588) 638797
on B4385, just off A488, 8m NW of Craven Arms

This late sixteenth-century timber-framed pub is in a quiet road off
the main street of this attractive village, which lies in the prettiest
part of Shropshire, close to the Welsh border. It has its own Grade
II-listed classic Victorian four-storey tower brewery providing Three
Tuns bitter, Sexton, Offa's and, at Christmas, Old Scrooge; wines
come from Tanners and four are offered by the glass. The pub interior retains many original features, including heavy oak beams, a
Jacobean staircase and a large open fireplace; the spacious lounge

bar has wooden tables, stools, and cushioned wall benches and pews. New owners have taken over since the last edition who now provide accommodation, and a reporter has described the pub's atmosphere as 'relaxed and a pleasure to eat and drink in'. Menus are chalked on blackboards and offer light choices such as sandwiches, soup, terrine or deep-fried goats' cheese. More substantial dishes could be beef in Three Tuns ale, chicken pie, or ratatouille with mozzarella and salad. Daily-changing fish dishes are listed on the specials board. Puddings might include chocolate brûlée, apricot and brandy bread-and-butter pudding, or lemon tart. SAMPLE DISHES: potato and fennel soup £2.50; chilli con carne with wild rice £5.50; French apple flan £3.

Open *Mon to Thur 12 to 3.30, 5 to 11, Fri to Sun 12 to 11 (10.30 Sun); closed 25 Dec; bar food and restaurant 12 to 2.30, 7 to 9.30*
Details *Children welcome   Car park   Wheelchair access   Garden and patio No smoking in lounge bar   Live music   Dogs welcome in bar only MasterCard, Switch, Visa   Accommodation: 4 rooms, B&B £75*

BISPHAM GREEN   Lancashire   map 8

Eagle & Child ✿ 🍺 NEW ENTRY

Malt Kiln Lane, Bispham Green L40 3SG
TEL: (01257) 462297
J27 from M6, take A5209 over Parbold Hill, right on B5246, fourth left signposted Bispham Green; pub ½m on right

PIGS

A holly tree and hanging baskets add some colour to this white-fronted pub in the middle of this designated conservation area. At the rear is a lawned garden bordered with trees, with fields beyond, and there is also a bowling green and a brick sty, home to some very contented pigs that are fun to visit. Inside are two fair-sized rooms plus a no-smoking room, one up a few steps and laid up for eating, although you can eat in the bar area too. Fireplaces with coal fires, and loads of hop bines hanging from beams, add to an overall impression of soothing light browns. A sign near the bar advertises forthcoming theme nights; they have quite a busy schedule, which takes in summer barbecues and a curry club. The cooking is definitely a notch up from the norm, offering a mixture of the traditional and modern – from roast beef and Yorkshire pudding to warm salad of rabbit and chorizo. Continental vegetable soup has a 'wonderful dusky flavour', gnocchi comes with fresh basil, asparagus and cheese topping, and seafood rendezvous is served in a mild cream curry sauce. Alternatively you could head for the 'standard menu' (which changes every six months) and go for steak and real-ale pie, or pan-fried pork fillet with apricot and sultana couscous.

Home-made puddings include Romanov fruit bavarois, or blueberry brûlée. Beers are well looked after and carefully poured 'like conjuring a snake out of a basket'; among them are Thwaites, Theakston and changing guests from local regional and microbrewers – Liverpool brewery is a regular choice. There is also an extensive range of malt whiskies. SAMPLE DISHES: goujons of fresh cod fillet and tartare sauce £3.25; medallions of beef fillet au poivre £11; apricot syllabub £3.

Open *12 to 3, 5.30 to 11, Sun 12 to 10.30; bar food 12 to 2, 5.30 to 9, Sun 12 to 8.30*
Details *Children welcome in dining-room   Car park   Wheelchair access (also WC)   Garden and patio   No smoking in 1 room   Background and live music Dogs welcome   Delta, MasterCard, Switch, Visa*

BLACKBOYS   **East Sussex**   **map 3**

Blackboys Inn

Lewes Road, Blackboys TN22 5LG   TEL: (01825) 890283
on B2192, 3m E of Uckfield

'An almost perfect English country pub,' enthused one reporter about this ancient black weatherboarded inn set back off the road. With a duck pond at the front and a large rear garden with rustic tables, it is an ideal spot for summer eating. Inside, the two bars have low-beamed ceilings, fresh hanging hops, a fine collection of old keys, displays of stuffed birds and fish, and a piano in the public bar. Typical dishes from the bar menu are ploughman's, soup, salads, steak butty, scampi, and sausages or beefburgers. A separate dining-room serves a more extensive menu that is available throughout the pub, offering grilled mushrooms with goats' cheese, king prawns, Blackboys smokie and crab and Gruyère tartlet, followed by Cajun chicken, roast duck or scallop of seafood. Reporters have drooled over the desserts, describing 'chocolate nemesis' as 'decadent and delicious' and a bruléed apple flan with apple and calvados sorbet as 'perfect'. Harveys best and pale beers are supplemented by Armada and Tom Paine in the summer, Porter in the autumn and Old in the winter. The 25-bottle wine list offers about six by the glass. SAMPLE DISHES: pork and spinach terrine £3.50; poulet à la forestière £9.50; bread-and-butter pudding £3.50.

Open *11 to 3, 6 to 11, Sun 7 to 10.30; bar food and restaurant all week L 12 to 2.15, Mon to Sat D 6.30 to 9.30 (10 some weekends)*
Details *Children welcome in dining-room   Car park   Garden and patio   No smoking in dining-rooms   Jukebox   Dogs welcome in some bar areas   Amex, Delta, MasterCard, Switch, Visa*

BLACKBROOK   Surrey   map 3

Plough

Blackbrook RH5 4DS   TEL: (01306) 886603
off A24, 1½m SE of Dorking

Robin and Christine Squires, who run this pleasantly atmospheric
King & Barnes pub, have been licensees here since the early '80s.
Framed memorabilia adorn the walls, and old bottles, one of which
is labelled 'anti gas ointment', on shelves in several eating areas help
create the mood. Beers and wines as well as the food menu, which
rotates rather than changes, are all written up on blackboards. For
starters there might be smoked salmon pâté, or marinated chargrilled
vegetable parmigiano, and to follow you could choose perhaps red
snapper with bitter orange sauce, or coconut, lime and beef curry.
For those sweet of tooth, a good way to end would be Austrian
chocolate cake with raspberry coulis. Portions tend to be generous,
and for those who might prefer a lighter bite at lunch-time a snack
menu offers bagels, jacket potatoes and ploughman's. King & Barnes
beers are served, and the guest is likely to be one of their seasonal
brews. Half the wines on the 36-bottle list are served by the (large)
glass. SAMPLE DISHES: Stilton, onion and chestnut soup £2.75;
Toulouse sausages with olive oil and parsley mash £6.75; Italian
nougat ice-cream £3.25.

Open *11 to 2.30, 6 to 11, Sun 12 to 3, 6 to 10.30; bar food all week L 12 to
2, Tue to Sun D 7 to 9*
Details *No children   Car park   Garden and patio   No-smoking area   No
music   Dogs welcome   No cards*

BLAKENEY   Norfolk   map 6

▲ *White Horse Hotel* ❦

4 High Street, Blakeney NR25 7AL   TEL: (01263) 740574
on A149, 5m W of Holt

This exceptionally well-run and well-maintained seventeenth-century
coaching-inn occupies a great location just up from the quay in the
tiny, narrow High Street, which the long L-shaped bar overlooks on
two levels. The civilised interior is softly lit and decorated in cream
colours and dark wood, and the accommodation is attractive.
Watercolours by local artists, depicting local themes and views of the
sea and salt marshes, are for sale. A separate bistro-style eating area
has pine tables and a separate à la carte restaurant. In the bar, a
blackboard lists an excellent selection of wines by the glass: wine is

taken seriously here and supplies come from Adnams. The beer also hails from Adnams, with Boddingtons and Bass on handpump as well. The printed bar menu offers reasonably priced dishes, such as home-made pâté, deep-fried herring roe (both served on toast), and 'hearty, satisfying' cockle chowder, while a specials board might turn out casseroled pork on tagliatelle, or fresh local mussels. Home-made puddings are served with cream, ice-cream or custard. Service is charming and the pub has a welcoming feel. Boat trips leave from the quay to the National Trust Blakeney Point Reserve where there is a seal colony. SAMPLE DISHES: deep-fried whitebait £3.75; fisherman's pie £5; treacle tart £2.50.

Open *11 to 3, 5.30 (6 winter) to 11 (10.30 Sun); bar food 12 to 2.30 (2 winter), 6 to 9.30 (9 winter); restaurant Tue to Sat D only 7 to 9*
Details *Children welcome in family room   Car park   Wheelchair access Garden and patio   No-smoking area   No music   No dogs   Amex, Diners, MasterCard, Switch, Visa   Accommodation: 10 rooms, B&B £25 to £80*

BLEDINGTON   Gloucestershire   map 5

▲ *Kings Head* 🍺

The Green, Bledington OX7 6HD   TEL: (01608) 658365
on B4450, 4m SE of Stow-on-the-Wold

Be prepared to share a table at Sunday lunch times at the Kings Head – it is that popular – but friendly and efficient staff manage to cope with the crowds that arrive at this creeper-clad fifteenth-century Cotswold-stone pub. Annette and Michael Royce have created a welcoming air and provide good-value food of 'excellent' quality. In the evenings, an extensive à la carte is supplemented with an 'extras' list. The main menu might offer pan-fried pork fillet with mustard seeds, or a range of chargrilled steaks. Local black pudding is very popular, the proprietors tell us, served with apple, bacon and honey, or on a crumpet with figs and marmalade; local game sausages are another speciality, served on mash with onion gravy. Temptations on the extras menu might include three-cheese terrine with port relish, or tomato and feta parcels with asparagus sauce, plus fish dishes such as chargrilled swordfish steak marinated in vodka, and a range of 'pasta bowl' options. At lunch-time, the menu is listed on blackboards and is equally wide but features mostly simpler dishes at lower prices, plus a children's selection; a good-value fixed-price menu is also available at either lunch or dinner. The extensive and eclectic wine list offers vintages priced to suit all pockets, and 15 wines are available by the glass. The pub also has a reputation for good real ales. Hook Norton and Wadworth 6X are permanent features, but there is also a regularly changing guest.

Stowford Press cider is also on offer, as well as a selection of over 50 malts, many quite obscure. In summer the rare game of Aunt Sally is played on the patio at the rear. SAMPLE DISHES: mushroom and basil Stroganov in a choux bun £3.75; half a honey-roast duck with parsnip purée £11; crème brûlée £2.50.

Open *11 to 2.30, 5.30 (6 in winter) to 11, Sun 11 to 2.30, 5.30 to 10.30; closed 24 and 25 Dec; bar food and restaurant 12 to 2, 7 to 10*
Details *Children welcome in restaurant   Car park   Wheelchair access Garden and patio   No-smoking area in restaurant   Background music   No dogs   Delta, MasterCard, Switch, Visa   Accommodation: 14 rooms, B&B £45 to £90*

B L E D L O W   **Buckinghamshire**   map 3

Lions of Bledlow

Church End, Bledlow HP27 9PE   TEL: (01844) 343345
off B4009, 2m SW of Princes Risborough; take West Lane, not Bledlow Ridge turning

Situated at the end of this Chiltern village, the Lions is popular with both locals and walkers using one of the countless tracks and footpaths in surrounding fields and woods. Fortuitously, one such path leads right up to the pub door. Step inside and you will find an unspoilt, characterful interior, with warming winter fire and al fresco facilities in summer. It is an unadorned simple series of low beamed rooms, with plenty of entry space. Walkers' pubs always seem to do baguettes – presumably because of the portable shape. The Lion offers a fair selection of fillings, which can also be ordered as a salad. There is a children's menu, and side orders inevitably include onion rings and chips. Turn the menu over for more substantial fare: deep-fried Brie and cranberry sauce to start, or Japanese-style prawns served with Cajun dips. Chicken tikka masala, the nation's favourite dish, appears alongside chicken burrito and gammon steak. Puddings are a mix of bought-in and home-made and are listed on blackboards. Courage Best, Marston's Pedigree, Wadworth 6X, Brakspear Bitter and guests from local breweries, such as Vale or Chiltern, are on handpump. The wine list is short but modern, with eight wines by the glass. SAMPLE DISHES: smoked salmon with prawns in marie rose sauce £4; lasagne £5.50; rhubarb crumble £2.95.

Open *11.30 to 3 (4 Sat), 6 to 11, Sun 12 to 4, 7 to 10.30; bar food and restaurant 12 to 2.30, 7 to 9.30*
Details *Children welcome in eating areas   Car park   Wheelchair access Garden and patio   No music   No dogs in dining-room   Amex, Delta, Diners, MasterCard, Switch, Visa*

BLYFORD   **Suffolk**   map 6

▲ *Queen's Head Inn*

Southwold Road, Blyford IP19 9JY   TEL: (01502) 478404
on B1123, 3m E of Halesworth

Its location – on the road to Southwold – should be enough of a
clue that this is an Adnams pub. At least, it is a pub during the
week. On Saturday nights it is much more of a restaurant and has a
different, more expensive menu. The building is a neat, two-storey
fifteenth-century inn painted a pinkish cream – much paler than
the usual oxblood colour so popular in East Anglia – and sits
beneath a neat thatch, which replaced one that burnt off a few
years ago. A subterranean passage runs from the cellar to the
church opposite, which is worth a visit for its medieval 'doom'
painting. Inside the large, oak-beamed bar there are plenty of intimate nooks and crannies, and a separate no-smoking room. Order
from a lunch selection that might include jumbo pork sausages,
chips and peas, or Lowestoft cod in a light beer batter. Children's
dishes are available. Sunday lunch offers roast pork, lamb and beef,
while the all-important Saturday evening menu steps up a rung to
offer venison with fruit and mushrooms braised in burgundy sauce,
or 24-hour marinated Greek-style spiced lamb. Beers are from the
Adnams range and the wine list runs to two dozen bottles. SAMPLE
DISHES: shell-on prawns in garlic butter £4.25; crab and prawn
salad £6.25; sticky toffee meringue £2.75.

Open *10.30 (11 winter) to 3.30, 6.30 to 11, Sun 12 to 3, 7 to 10.30; bar
food and restaurant 11.45 to 1.40, 7 to 9*
Details *Children welcome in dining-room and family room   Car park
Wheelchair access (also WC)   Garden   No smoking in restaurant   No music
Guide dogs only   No cards   Accommodation: 2 rooms, B&B £60*

BOLDRE   **Hampshire**   map 2

Red Lion Inn 🍇 NEW ENTRY

Boldre SO41 8NE   TEL: (01590) 673177
off A337, 2m N of Lymington

Dating from around 1650 and standing on the site of an alehouse
mentioned in the Domesday Book, this attractive pub can be found
in the village centre, opposite the green. An old cart outside is strewn
with flowers, and hanging baskets and troughs are a riot of colour in
summer. Inside, it is a series of interconnecting, beamed rooms
adorned with an amazing collection of old bottles, chamber pots,

various farm implements, man traps and hunting prints. Combined with open fires and comfortable furnishings, they make the Red Lion one of the better New Forest pubs. The menu offers a mix of starters/light snacks plus a short selection of simple, filling main courses and one or two pasta and vegetarian options. Salmon terrine, parcels of Brie cheese and Cajun chicken wings are among the more exciting of the light bites and mains are very much in the mould of saddle of lamb, or liver and bacon. Halfway between light and filling, you could settle for a seafood pasta, or a vegetable casserole. Puddings might include amaretti roulade, or steamed chocolate sponge. This Eldridge Pope pub serves Royal Oak, plus Webster's Green Label and Bass; the wine list of some 40 bottles offers nearly all of them by the glass. SAMPLE DISHES: New Forest game terrine £5; venison sausages and mash £7.25; apple pie £3.25.

Open *11 to 11, Sun 12 to 10.30; closed 24 Dec eve, 25 Dec; bar food and restaurant 11.30 to 2.30, 6.30 to 9.30*
Details *No children under 14   Car park   Wheelchair access (also WC) Garden and patio   No-smoking in 1 dining-room   No music   No dogs Amex, Delta, MasterCard, Switch, Visa*

BOLTER END   **Buckinghamshire**   map 3

Peacock

Bolter End, Lane End HP14 3LU   TEL: (01494) 881417
on B482 Marlow to Stokenchurch road

A distinctly Mediterranean influence seems to run through the cooking at this cheery, snug, low-ceilinged, roadside pub in the Chilterns, judging from the quantity of fresh fish, and the names of the menu dishes and the daily specials. How about stincotto (gammon hock simmered with herbs), albondigas (meatballs with pasta), Mediterranean lamb casserole, grilled salmon fillet with roasted vegetables, and side dishes of lamon beans or saffron rice? But tastes that prefer not to venture over the English Channel will be satisfied by home-made steak and kidney pie, grilled Lincolnshire pork sausages, or half a roast shoulder of lamb, and vegetarians by cheesy mushroom pancakes or vegetable lasagne. Save room for a Peacock Pud: a daily-changing crumble, orange and brandy crêpes, a quality ice-cream or sorbet, treacle and walnut tart or Devon clotted cream fudge cake. Alternatively, finish with cheeses, which may include Blue Vinney. Ale drinkers can choose from Brakspear Bitter, Adnams Bitter and one guest, while the wine choice includes six whites and four reds by the glass or bottle. SAMPLE DISHES: grilled marinated butterfly chicken breast £8; sweet-and-sour tiger prawns in filo £7.50; pannacotta £3.

Open *11.45 to 2.30, 6 to 11, Sun 12 to 3; bar food 12 to 2, 7 to 9.45*
Details *No children   Car park   Wheelchair access   Garden   No smoking in 1 bar area   No music   Dogs welcome   Amex, Delta, Diners, MasterCard, Switch, Visa*

BOOTHSDALE   Cheshire   map 7

Boot Inn

Boothsdale, Willington CW6 0NH   TEL: (01829) 751375
coming from Chester on A54 turn right to Oscroft Willington, then left at T-junction, then second right up Boothsdale to pub; from Knutsford on A556 turn left to Kelsall Willington, then second left up Quarry Lane, then left at end, then first left up Boothsdale to pub

Occupying an entire row of cottages in this pretty Cheshire village on the edge of the region known as 'Little Switzerland', the Boot is not exactly easy to find, but in the words of one, 'the effort is very worthwhile'. It was a beerhouse in 1848, and had its first licensee in 1872; if you are there, you can enquire why the pub is known locally as 'the cat'. Within, the ambience is peaceful and 'laid back': a wood-burning stove sits in the brick-fronted main bar, old political cartoons are on the walls, and there is a penny farthing cycle made from old Victorian coppers. Another room is furnished with old church pews, and opening out from the bar is a restaurant; the same menus are available throughout. Blackboard specials might take in fish chowder, or baked Brie rolled in nuts, followed by Indonesian lamb with couscous, or salmon with a lemon herb crust, while printed menus serve up devilled kidneys, or anchovy bake with egg and cheese, and main courses of Cumberland sausage, a horseshoe of gammon, or 'excellent' steak and kidney pie cooked in ale and with 'beautifully done' puff pastry. For the not-so-hungry there are salad platters, and vegetarians receive special treatment in the form of mushroom Stroganov, or pepper satay. Home-made puddings might run to crème brûlée, lemon syllabub or Bakewell tart. Real ales served are Flowers, Bass, Cains and Greenalls, plus a guest. The 20-bottle wine list is very reasonably priced and includes three house wines by the bottle or glass. SAMPLE DISHES: Norwegian shell-on prawns £3.50; sliced fillet of beef with mushrooms from £11; apple and damson crumble £3.50.

Open *Mon to Fri 11 to 3, 6 to 11, Sat 11 to 11, Sun 12 to 10.30; bar food and restaurant Mon to Fri 11 to 2.30, 6 to 9.30 (bar snacks available all day), Sat 11 to 11, Sun 12 to 10.30*
Details *Children welcome   Car park   Garden and patio   No music   No dogs Amex, Delta, MasterCard, Switch, Visa*

BORASTON   Shropshire   map 5

▲ *Peacock* ✿

Worcester Road, Boraston WR15 8LL   TEL: (01584) 810506
off A456, 1¼m E of Tenbury Wells

Its fourteenth-century origins are very much in evidence at this large, white-painted roadside inn that still has a very out of the way feel. Inside is a collection of little rooms, linked with open doorways and partition beams. Wood-panelled walls in the bar give a 'stately' feel, while the 'bistro' dining area is open to the rafters, conferring a lighter ambience. The pub's strength is undoubtedly its food. Chef Mark Flello uses good quality raw materials – particularly local game and fish – and has some interesting ideas; presentation is straightforward and uncluttered, and timing is generally spot-on. The menu is listed on a blackboard: start with corn tortillas with chilli and tomato salsa, perhaps, or terrine of wild rabbit with summer berries. Vegetarian options might include a mille-feuille of wild mushroom risotto with cherry tomatoes and basil sauce, while main courses come in the shape of feuilleté, noisettes, confits or parcels. There may be roast duck breast with kumquats, roast cod with roast fennel, grilled mackerel with sharp gooseberry sauce, and chicken breast with an Agen prune and honey sauce. Puddings are generally the heavy sort: sticky toffee, pavlova, or 'Peacock chocolate fetish'. At lunch-time the emphasis is on a shorter and simpler selection that may include beef baguettes, or home-made faggots with mash. Beers on tap are Tetley Bitter, Ind Coope Burton Ale and Bass. The wine list has been chosen personally by the proprietor, and has a good selection of half-bottles; wines are graded for sweetness (whites) and fullness (reds). SAMPLE DISHES: scallops and monkfish in curry and coriander sauce £7; whole baked sea bass with rosemary and garlic £16; cappuccino chocolate mousse £4.

Open *11.30 to 3, 6 to 11, Sun 12 to 3.30, 7 to 10.30; bar food and restaurant 12 to 2.15, 7 to 9.30*
Details *Children welcome in 1 room   Car park   Wheelchair access   Garden and patio   No-smoking area   Background music   No dogs   Delta, MasterCard, Switch, Visa   Accommodation: 3 rooms, B&B £40 to £65*

If you disagree with any assessment made in the Guide, write to tell us why – The Which? Guide to Country Pubs, FREEPOST, 2 Marylebone Road, London NW1 1YN.

BOROUGHBRIDGE   North Yorkshire   map 8

▲ *Black Bull*

6 St James Square, Boroughbridge YO5 9AR   TEL: (01423) 322413

This squat, two-storey pub, with white frontage and bowed, lace-curtained windows, lists its attractions in gothic lettering under the windows, while at first-floor level hanging-baskets of forget-me-nots, geraniums and lobelia give the appearance of a tea-room as much as a pub. This is clearly Boroughbridge's main eaterie. A welcoming lounge bar with roaring log fire in a huge fireplace is popular with local drinkers and, on a busy night, a stream of diners enjoying a pre-prandial drink and choosing from the menu before going through to the dining-room at the rear. The bar snacks menu is noted for its eclectic selection. Yes, Yorkshire pud filled with lamb casserole and home-made pork and sage sausages with gravy make their appearance, but so do Thai-spiced chicken and noodle broth, or chicken marinated in Indian spices with onion and pepper relish and minted cucumber yoghurt. There is the usual range of steaks, but also a more unusual range of stir-fries. The à la carte menu offered in the dining-room lists many of the same dishes, some at the same prices, and again there are nods towards the current fascination with Thai cooking, but choice is wider and some dishes are more expensive. Puddings are solidly traditional: warm chocolate pecan tart, or syrup sponge and custard. Beers are Black Sheep and John Smith's, plus a guest, which may well be from a Yorkshire microbrewery. The wine list is a jolly trot around the globe. The pub offers theme evenings, perhaps a jazz night or a 'Taste of Thailand' evening. Boroughbridge is convenient for visitors to Roman Aldburgh, Newby Hall or Ripon. SAMPLE DISHES: crab and salmon fish-cakes with dill and lemon butter sauce £4; stir-fried Thai-spiced beef and vegetables with fragrant rice £6.75; tarte Tatin £3.25.

Open *11 to 11, Sun 12 to 10.30; closed 25 Dec eve, no food 1 Jan; bar food 12 to 9; restaurant 12 to 2, 7 to 9.30 (9 Sun and Mon)*
Details *Children welcome in eating areas   Wheelchair access   No music   No dogs   Delta, MasterCard, Switch, Visa   Accommodation: 4 rooms, B&B £37 to £48*

BRAMDEAN   Hampshire   map 2

Fox Inn

Bramdean SO24 0LP   TEL: (01962) 771363
on A272 Winchester to Petersfield road, 3m SE of New Alresford

An oak carving of the Prince of Wales feathers stands proudly affixed to the outside wall of this white-painted pub because George IV, when still heir to the throne, deigned to enter the premises for refreshment – and was pleased. The pub also had a prime viewing position when soldiers on both sides of the Civil War marched past to do battle at Cheriton in 1644. The pub is neatly kept and comfortable with cushioned benches, warm-coloured brick walls, a roaring log fire, low ceilings and a large three-sided bar. Its regulars know that they are advised to book – otherwise the choice may be restricted to cold food, particularly at Sunday lunch-time – for this is a food pub, with the emphasis on fresh fish. The blackboard advertises that day's offerings: maybe simple avocado and prawns, or plaice stuffed with prawns and crab, or scallops with Parma ham, or halibut, red snapper and locally smoked trout. Non-fishy dishes might turn out to be 'excellent mushroom soup, creamy and thick with mushrooms', braised beef in red wine, or roast rack of lamb; vegetables are served plain. Evening main courses are more expensive than at lunch, and prices are generally on the high side but worth it. Dinner-party sweets might include chocolate St Emilion or lemon tart. This is a Marston's pub, with Pedigree on handpump, while the wine list offers three dozen bins, with four wines available by the glass. Older customers support the place admirably, liking the proper service as much as the food. SAMPLE DISHES: smoked salmon with dill sauce £5.50; pan-fried calf's liver with bacon and onions £9; forgotten lemon heaven £3.

Open *11 to 3, 6.30 (6 in summer) to 11, Sun 12 to 3, 7 to 10.30; bar food 12 to 2, 7 to 9 (no food Sun D Jan and Feb)*
Details *No children   Car park   Wheelchair access (also WC)   Garden and patio   No-smoking area   Background music   Small dogs welcome by arrangement   Amex, Delta, MasterCard, Visa, Switch*

BRANSCOMBE   Devon   map 2

▲ *Masons Arms* 🍺 🥂

Branscombe EX12 3DJ   TEL: (01297) 680300
off A3052, 5m E of Sidmouth

A new owner took over in April 1998, and so this pub might be one to watch, and best watched at different times of the year to enjoy the changing hues of the ivy creeper which surrounds the front door. Some lovely walks can be had during the day – a pebbly beach is only a half-mile away in one direction, and there is a pretty valley with steep, narrow lanes in the other. Outside the pub are two thatched 'parasols', and the split-level interior has polished stone floors, traditional and well-maintained décor, plus an inglenook fireplace. The printed menu changes daily, and the cooking, as one reporter noted, is 'faithful to St Delia and Gary Rhodes'. Having progressed beyond Delia's boiled egg, the chef is capable of turning out an excellent scrambled egg, which our inspector thought was beyond the ability of many. At lunch-time there is a full selection of sandwiches, ploughman's and a children's menu. Otherwise the style is fairly modern-British.

From the bar menu you might choose a classic Caesar salad, or chargrilled vegetables in a balsamic dressing with shaved Parmesan. Continue the modern theme with linguine with flat mushrooms and garlic, or a grilled fillet of salmon with salsa verde and seared vegetables. Home-made puddings are above average: white chocolate crème brûlée sounds like a confident rendition of this popular favourite. The pub always serves draught Bass, as well as Otter Bitter and Masons Ale, which is brewed for the pub by the Otter Brewery. The 30-bottle wine list is divided into European and New World bins, and around a dozen are available by the glass. SAMPLE DISHES: butterfly king prawns with Thai jam £5.50; rump steak with slow-roasted tomatoes, field mushrooms and garlic butter £10; bread-and-butter pudding £2.50.

Open *summer 11.30 to 11, Sun 12 to 10.30, winter Mon to Fri 11.30 to 3, 6 to 11, Sat 11.30 to 11, Sun 12 to 10.30; bar food 12 to 2.15, 7 to 9.30; restaurant D only 7 to 9*
Details *Children welcome   Car park   Wheelchair access (also WC)   Patio No-smoking area   Live music   No dogs in restaurant   Delta, MasterCard, Switch   Accommodation: 26 rooms, B&B £22 to £120*

If you visit any pubs that you think should appear in the Guide, write to tell us – The Which? Guide to Country Pubs, FREEPOST, 2 Marylebone Road, London NW1 1YN.

BRASSINGTON   Derbyshire   map 5

Ye Olde Gate Inn

Well Street, Brassington DE4 4HJ   TEL: (01629) 540448
just off B3035 Ashbourne to Wirksworth road, 4m W of Wirksworth

Dating back to 1616, Ye Olde Gate Inn is set in a pretty Derbyshire
village which sprawls up a hillside and which has many smartly
maintained, neat stone cottages. The pub itself is a long, low, stone
building in one of the streets near the church. There are three main
rooms, one to the left of the entrance set with long tables and
candles. The main room by the bar has an impressive Victorian
black-leaded range with an open fire, and the dining-room is non-
smoking. Food is a draw here, and locals and those from further
afield come for the Orkney crab pâté or French onion soup,
followed by a king prawn or spicy lamb Balti or something more
traditional like cottage pie, all made by landlord Paul Burlinson. For
pudding treat yourself to a hot lemon sponge with hot lemon sauce.
At lunch-time baguettes and ploughman's are also on offer, and in
summer come for the barbecues, where Cajun steaks might feature.
This is a Marston's pub, serving Pedigree and Head Brewer's Choice.
Three house wines from the basic list are served by the glass. SAMPLE
DISHES: venison pâté £4; lamb chump hotpot £6; New York cheesecake £3.25.

Open *Tue to Thur 12 to 2.30 (3 Fri and Sat), Tue to Thur (and Mon in
winter) 6 to 11, Sun 12 to 3, 7 to 10.30; bar food Tue to Sun 12 to 2, 7 to 9*
Details *No children   Car park   Wheelchair access (also WC)   Garden   No
smoking in dining-room   No music   Dogs welcome   No cards*

BREARTON   North Yorkshire   map 9

Malt Shovel 🍺

Brearton HG3 3BX   TEL: (01423) 862929
off A61 and B6165, 2m E of Ripley

'Homely and down to earth' sums up the Malt Shovel, which
modestly sets out to provide quality food and drink in a casual
atmosphere. However, the relaxed 'family run' feel of the place
should not fool visitors into thinking there is no commitment to
standards. The daily-changing blackboard menu offers seven each of
meat, fish and vegetarian dishes, plus the same number of desserts.
All ingredients are fresh ('nothing is frozen except the ice-cream,'
they tell us), and haggis is naturally served with tatties and neeps.
'Cajun' may be a popular adjective on countless pub menus, but here

it is fish rather than the usual chicken which gets the spicy treatment, while venison sausage with braised red cabbage marks another break from the ordinary. A 25-strong wine list features a wide range of good-value house wines, and there are never fewer than five real ales on offer. Theakston beers (out of the wood from the nearby Masham brewery, rather than the ersatz version from Newcastle) sit on the bar next to their neighbour, Black Sheep; Daleside Nightjar from Harrogate is another regular and the selection is augmented with two frequently changing guests from local microbreweries. SAMPLE DISHES: wild mushroom Stroganov £6; steak and ale pie £5.50; char-grilled banana with ice-cream and toffee sauce £2.50.

Open *Tue to Sat 12 to 2.30, 6.45 to 11, Sun 12 to 2.30, 6.45 to 10.30; closed 2 weeks Jan; bar food Tue to Sun 12 to 2, Tue to Sat 7 to 9*
Details *Children welcome   Car park   Wheelchair access (also WC)   Garden and patio   No music   Dogs welcome   No cards*

BRIMFIELD   Herefordshire   map 5

▲ *Roebuck* ♀ ❦

Brimfield SY8 4NE   TEL: (01584) 711230
just off A49 Leominster to Ludlow road, 4m W of Tenbury Wells

LOCAL PRODUCE

Carole Evans, who did much to give the Roebuck its reputation for good food, has moved, but has left her chef, Jonathan Waters, in the pub's kitchens. He, along with new owner and fellow chef David Williams-Lloyd, continues to provide classy fare. The pub itself has three bar areas with old-fashioned décor, lots of beams, and dark wood panelling. Despite its reputation for good food, it is still very much a village local, and visitors can take in a trip to the village's charming half-timbered church, which is not far from the inn. The dining-room (no longer called 'Poppies') is more modern in style, with pale bamboo chairs, parquet floors and pastel-coloured prints. The kitchen has stuck with the pub's remit to make good local produce the focus of its cooking. Menus are short and change seasonally, while the specials update daily to exploit what is freshly available. Everything is made in the kitchen, from the bread served with your soup, to the petits fours that arrive with your coffee.

The regular menu might tempt you to try smoked salmon with pickled cucumber and dill dressing, or crab filo parcels with a spicy tomato sauce, while the specials list, which has something of a bias towards fish, gears up more than a notch or two to offer starters such as cold gâteau of fresh crab, crayfish, avocado and tomato, or fillets of lemon sole stuffed with lobster mousse in a fennel and citrus sauce. These might be followed by roast monkfish with a fresh crayfish sauce or, for the less fishily inclined, roast saddle of new grouse with a rowan and wild bramble sauce. Fish pie is a bit of a house trademark. Although the pub is a freehouse, it serves only Tetley Bitter and Morland Old Speckled Hen. It pays rather more attention to its wine list, which has been revamped and is quite fashionable in both content and execution, offering odd-bins and bin-ends as well as six by the glass. Local farmhouse ciders and perry as well as brandies and malt whiskies are also available. SAMPLE DISHES: whole, boned and stuffed quail with a sherry and grape sauce £5.25; red sea bream with provençale vegetables and crispy leeks £12; rhubarb and ginger crumble with custard £3.50.

Open *11.30 to 3, 6.30 to 11, Sun 12 to 3, 7 to 10.30; closed eve 25 Dec; bar food and restaurant 12 to 2.30, 7 to 9.30*
Details *Children welcome in bar-eating area Car park Wheelchair access Garden and patio No smoking in dining-room No music No dogs in dining areas Delta, MasterCard, Switch, Visa Accommodation: 3 rooms, B&B £45 to £60*

BRINKWORTH   Wiltshire   map 2

Three Crowns 🍴 🍇

Brinkworth SN15 5AF   TEL: (01666) 510366
on B4042 Malmesbury to Wootton Bassett road

'A consistently good standard of a wide range of food' was one reporter's reason for recommending the Three Crowns. The area has been described as 'rural and rambling' and the same description could apply to the pub itself, a 'conglomerate' of different building parts. A large bar bustling full of unmatching, random tables and chairs and artefacts of varying ages leads to a conservatory dining-room which, though newish, maintains the same feel. Service is plentiful, friendly and prompt; 'the aim,' said one, 'is obviously not to slow the meal down with starters (there are none on the menu) but to encourage people with tempting desserts.' The large range changes daily according to market availability, the house style favours creamy, alcoholic sauces, and portions are very large.

Steaks are permanent – match your favourite cut to your favourite sauce, be it au poivre, Stilton and prawns, Diane, Café de Paris, or Borras (sliced shiitake and button mushrooms in a creamy red wine sauce). More creamy red wine sauce, as well as pear and rosemary jelly, come with rack of lamb, and for the adventurous there are dishes featuring the 'new' meats – crocodile, kangaroo and ostrich – which likewise get the creamy-sauce treatment. A lengthy pudding list tends to rich favourites like sticky toffee pudding, banoffi pie, or chocolate and Grand Marnier mousse. The 70-plus wine list contains some superior wines, and 14 are available by the glass. There are, unfortunately, few kangaroo or ostrich equivalents among the beers, which consist of Wadworth 6X, Bass, Boddingtons, Castle Eden and Archers. SAMPLE DISHES: half a smoked chicken in sherry and cream sauce £13.50; sauté marinated crocodile with onions and pink peppercorns in whisky and cream sauce £16.50; banana pancakes with home-made vanilla ice-cream £5.

Open *10 to 3, 6 to 11; closed 25 Dec; bar food 12 to 2, 6 to 9.30*
Details *Children welcome in dining-room   Car park   Garden and patio   No smoking in conservatory   Background music   Dogs welcome in bar only Amex, Delta, Diners, MasterCard, Switch, Visa*

BRITWELL SALOME   Oxfordshire   map 2

The Goose 😋😋 🍇   NEW ENTRY

Britwell Salome OX9 5LG   TEL: (01491) 612304
on B4009, 1¼m SW of Watlington

One would expect the food at the Goose to be first rate, and it is – after all, until taking over in January 1998, Chris Barber was personal chef to Prince Charles and before that spent two years as a commis chef in Buckingham Palace. Service is informal, and the staff exude relaxed confidence. Chris Barber, anxious to reassure locals that this was not to be another pub reinvented as a restaurant, knocked on all the doors in the village to explain what he was doing. The result is that the bar is as likely to be as crowded as the dining-rooms. A small, modern bar area, with terracotta-coloured walls and watercolour pictures, opens on to two dark-green painted dining-rooms, with dark wood tables, wheel-back chairs and candles.

Menus are short, with three choices for each course; evenings are strictly set price (two or three courses, for £20). The style is modern, minimalist, with the focus on fresh, good-quality ingredients fairly simply presented. A lunch menu might begin with a gratin of scallops, or porcini and field mushrooms on toast, followed by roast partridge and bubble and squeak, grilled swordfish with ratatouille and tomato butter, or loin of veal with chanterelle jus. Finish with chicory crème brûlée, pear and almond tart with cinnamon ice-cream, or a selection of cheeses. (Sandwiches are also available at lunch-time). In the evening expect a crab-cake in a bisque, or a delightfully simple penne with wild mushrooms, and follow with roast sirloin of Orkney beef with roast vegetables, or grilled tuna with ratatouille and lentils. Thirteen years of royal service is probably not the best schooling for learning about beer, and only one real ale is served. However, if you are going to serve just one, you can do much worse than Brakspear's. The short, well-chosen wine list has ten good, reasonably priced wines by the glass. SAMPLE DISHES: wild mushroom soup £4; pork chop with grainy mustard sauce £13; apple crumble with crème Anglaise £5.

Open *Tue to Sat 12 to 3, 6 to 11, Sun 12 to 4, 7 to 10.30; bar food and restaurant Tue to Sat 12 to 2, 6.30 to 10, Sun L only 12 to 3*
Details *Children welcome in dining-room   Car park   Wheelchair access   Garden   No smoking in dining-room   Background music   Dogs welcome   Delta, MasterCard, Visa, Switch*

BROADHEMBURY   Devon   map 2

Drewe Arms 🏵️🏵️ 🍺 🍇

Broadhembury EX14 0NF   TEL: (01404) 841267
off A373, between Cullompton and Honiton

Never complacent, the Drewe Arms continues to produce food of a consistently high standard (the word 'excellent' features in a slew of reports). Although just a few minutes drive from the M5, this hamlet of thatched cottages is remarkably quiet and traffic-free. The unspoilt nature of this seven-centuries-old pub seems to strike many visitors, as does the fish for which it is famous. It has been run by Kerstin and Nigel Burge for over a decade, and Kerstin's Scandinavian origins will occasionally show through in the cooking – marinated herring with aquavit, for example, is something of a speciality, or there might be gravlax with dill and mustard sauce. Among other fishy starters that might tempt you are scallops hollandaise, mussels in garlic and wine, and crab thermidor. They could be followed perhaps with sea bass stewed with pesto, John Dory with wild mushrooms, half a lobster with new potatoes, or – for meat eaters – 'the bookmaker's' (8oz fillet steak) open sandwich. Standard-sounding desserts such as bread pudding and crème brûlée are well above average, and pear tarte Tatin has been described as 'gorgeous'. A blackboard menu system operates, with all dishes available everywhere, and diners able to mix and match from different boards. The beers are locally supplied by the Otter brewery, only five miles away, and the wine list, which includes a healthy selection of half-bottles, concentrates on the popular accompaniments to fish, such as Chardonnay and Sauvignon; nine wines are available by the glass. Service is cheerful and very accommodating. SAMPLE DISHES: red mullet in herb butter £5; sea bream with chilli and orange butter £9.50; chocolate marquise £4.

Open *11 to 3, 6 to 11, Sun 12 to 3, 7 to 10.30; closed 31 Dec and 1 Jan; bar food and restaurant Mon to Sat 12 to 2, 7 to 9.30, Sun 12 to 2*
Details *Children welcome in eating areas   Car park   Wheelchair access (also WC)   Garden   No music   Dogs welcome by arrangement   No cards*

BROME Suffolk map 6

▲ *Cornwallis Arms* 🍺 🍇 NEW ENTRY

Brome IP23 8AJ TEL: (01379) 870326
at junction of A140 and B1077, midway between Norwich and Ipswich

Built in the sixteenth century as a dower-house to Brome Hall on the Cornwallis estate (visitors are often startled by the prospect of the impressive hall that looms before them at the end of a 200-yard driveway), the Cornwallis Arms is now a country-house hotel with a 'hugely atmospheric' pub-style bar attached to it. Enter through an old door into a flagged passageway, walk right over a deep well, which is thickly glassed over and greenly lit, into a large, well-proportioned room with beams and timbers, Windsor chairs, a mix of wood tables, a large log-burning stove, and classical music softly playing in the background. The Cornwallis is one of the outlets of St Peter's Brewery, and the core business here is beer. The pub serves the full range of St Peter's unique draught brews, plus ten of their bottled ales, wheat and fruit beers. Wines too are a cut above the average, with a good selection from around the world. The list has a useful smattering of half-bottles, and eight wines are available by the glass. Once you have sorted out what you want to drink, order your food either at the bar or at your table from a short printed menu or from the blackboards. You will find some conventional items – chicken liver pâté, fillet of haddock in ale batter with mushy peas and chips – alongside the more flamboyant – Gruyère and peppery rocket sandwich, casserole of beef and pickled walnuts (why aren't pickled walnuts on more pub menus?). Or go for guinea-fowl with wild mushrooms and red wine sauce, or turkey and bramble pie. Marmalade bread and butter pudding, or maybe down-to-earth plum crumble, will round things off neatly. Service is on the ball, even when the place is heaving. SAMPLE DISHES: wild mushroom and herb risotto £4; pan-fried John Dory with a red onion and tomato dressing £10; mulled berry pudding £3.25.

Open *11 to 11; bar food and restaurant 12 to 2.30, 6.30 to 10*
Details *Children welcome Car park Wheelchair access (also WC) Garden and patio Background music Guide dogs only Amex, Delta, Diners, MasterCard, Switch, Visa Accommodation: 16 rooms, £68 to £105*

Many pubs have separate restaurants with very different menus. These have not been inspected. A recommendation for the pub/bar food does not necessarily imply that the restaurant is also recommended.

BUCKDEN   **North Yorkshire**   map 8

▲ *Buck Inn* ❦

Buckden BD23 5JA   TEL: (01756) 760228
on B6160, between Kettleworth and West Burton

The imposing presence of Buckden Pike (2,300ft) rising up behind
the pub brings the walkers to this beautiful part of Wharfedale, and
to this popular Dales inn. It is an attractive, creeper-clad, Georgian
coaching-inn overlooking the village green in the heart of Upper
Wharfedale. Inside, the main bar, popular with locals, features a flagstone floor; there is an adjoining dining area, comfortably
modernised with tapestry banquette seating and wheel-back chairs
around 'pub' tables. Locals and walkers alike will enjoy the interesting food from a menu which changes twice a day. Typically there
will be modern British fare like terrine of duck encased in pancetta
with honey dressing, or black pudding parfait with grain mustard
brioche. From there the menu may go on to offer escalope of salmon
with egg noodles and beurre blanc, medallions of pork fillet and
black pudding risotto, or braised lamb in filo pastry with a pearl
barley jus or even a Toulouse sausage with champ potatoes and
Madeira and onion sauce. The evening menu is likely to be similar
with one important exception – no chips. At the rear is a restaurant
with a separate menu which also changes daily. Real ales offered are
Best, XB, Old Peculier and Black Bull Bitter, all from Theakston, and
a personally chosen wine list is divided into European, New World
and fine wine selections with plenty of half- bottles on offer. SAMPLE
DISHES: Greek salad £4.50; seared tuna and salsa £8.25; toffee and
apple parfait £3.25.

Open *11 to 11, Sun 12 to 10.30; bar food and restaurant Mon to Sat 12 to 2,
6.30 to 9 (9.30 Fri and Sat), Sun 12 to 5, 6.30 to 9*
Details *Children welcome   Car park   Wheelchair access   Garden and patio
No smoking in restaurant   Background music   Dogs welcome   Delta,
MasterCard, Switch, Visa   Accommodation: 14 rooms, B&B £33 to £72*

BUCKLAND   Oxfordshire   map 2

▲ *Lamb Inn* ❀ ❦

Lamb Lane, Buckland SN7 8QN   TEL: (01367) 870484
off A420, midway between Faringdon and Kingston Bagpuize

Commanding views of the Thames Valley flood plain, this eighteenth-century, honey-coloured Cotswold stone pub has acquired
quite a reputation for its food and wine since it was acquired by Paul

and Peta Barnard in 1992. The bar is in a plain rectangular room with an open fire, beams garlanded with hops and a blackboard menu, while the dining-room extension is a far cry from rustic-country-pub style, with its blue and yellow colour scheme and sophisticated air. Service is friendly, but can reflect the pressure on tables at peak times.

The menu changes regularly as the seasons progress, and over the course of a year a large and eclectic range of dishes will have been served up: grilled gurnard with tomato, anchovy and garlic sauce is a typically unusual starter, as are grilled halloumi with roasted peppers, tomato and basil, and warm pike mousse. Main courses seem a little more familiar – cassoulet, or shepherd's pie – though roast widgeon in plum, cinnamon and apple sauce is a rarely spotted bird, and fillet of turbot poached in champagne on a bed of samphire sounds wonderfully indulgent. Puddings too are a mix of the familiar and the rare: bread-and-butter pudding is almost obligatory in a pub, but junket is rarely seen at all. The only beer served is Wadworth 6X, reflecting the fact that most diners are mainly interested in the exceptional wine list, which includes many bottles featured at the Barnards' regular wine tastings. They also keep themselves busy, when not in the kitchen, managing an outdoor catering service and making their own pickles, chutneys and vinegars, as well as looking after the pub's accommodation. SAMPLE DISHES: curried apple soup £3.25; roast local partridge with roast onions, red cabbage and Madeira sauce £14.25; warm poached dates £4.

Open *11 to 3, 5.30 to 11, Sun 12 to 3, 7 to 11; closed 24 to 26 Dec; bar food and restaurant 12 to 2 (2.30 Sun), 6.30 to 9.30*
Details *Children welcome in dining-room   Car park   Garden and patio   No smoking in restaurant   Background and live music   No dogs   Amex, Delta, MasterCard, Switch, Visa   Accommodation: 4 rooms, B&B £35 to £55*

BUCKLAND DINHAM   Somerset   map 2

Bell Inn 🍇

High Street, Buckland Dinham BA11 2QT   TEL: (01373) 462956
on A362 Frome to Radstock road, 1½m NW of Frome

The ivy-clad Bell Inn, set atop a steep hill, made a big impression on one pair of reporters, who concluded that landlord Paul Hartley-Nadhar and his wife Lynda have succeeded in creating a 'really English' traditional public house. 'We were attended to almost immediately on arrival,' they wrote, 'and made to feel very welcome. Paul obviously loves what he is doing and enjoys talking to his customers. His enthusiasm is contagious. Being encouraged by the landlord to hurl more logs on to the fire really made us feel at home.' The pub has a large walled garden with play area including a boules piste and barbecue and a two-acre paddock where special events and picnics are held. As the *Guide* went to press, a new menu was planned to replace the previous profusion of menus and aims to take in everything from traditional pub fare to 'superb gourmet excitement'. Typical of the cooking style is dim-sum with sweet-and-sour dip, 'deep-fried just right'. Follow this perhaps with a generous main-course of extra hot chef's curry, or 'delicious' vegetable lasagne accompanied by a salad with a dressing of raspberry and balsamic vinegars with pesto and garden herbs. Finish with forest fruits yoghurt ice-cream or 'piping hot' treacle tart. Beers are a large selection of the usual suspects – Morland Old Speckled Hen, Courage Best, Theakston XB, Marston's Pedigree and John Smith's. The interesting wine list covers the world and includes four house wines by the glass or bottle; an unusual feature is that any bottle on the list costing under £12 is also offered by the glass. A selection of ports, sherries, malts and vintage cognacs are offered to round off your meal. SAMPLE DISHES: scallop and bacon brochette £4.50; haunch of venison in burgundy and juniper gravy £10; toffee apple sponge pudding with vanilla sauce £3.75.

Open *11.45 to 3, 5.30 to 11, Sun 12 to 3, 7 to 10.30; bar food and restaurant 12 to 2.30, 6.45 (7 Sun) to 9.30*
Details *Children welcome   Car park   Wheelchair access (also WC)   Garden and patio   No-smoking area   Background and live music   Dogs welcome on a lead   Amex, Delta, Diners, MasterCard, Switch, Visa*

B U N B U R Y   Cheshire   map 7

Dysart Arms   NEW ENTRY

Bowes Gate Road, Bunbury CW6 9PH   TEL: (01829) 260183
off A51, 5m NW of Nantwich

The Dysart Arms is next to the church of St Boniface, which is visible from the garden and makes quite a spectacle at night when it is illuminated. If you're there at the right time, you may even be serenaded by bell ringers. One of eight untied pubs run by a family company, the pub has been cleverly extended from the original bar and the three anterooms to include two extra dining areas – one for non-smokers – and a large library-like room for bigger parties. In its short life it has already become popular with locals, local diners and not- so-local diners, and the food is of a high standard. Although prices are slightly above average, portions are generous and some people may find that two starters will easily qualify as a filling meal – especially if they have already sampled some of the dim-sum type nibbles and deep-fried courgettes (a pleasant change from peanuts and crisps). The same shortish menu is both printed and chalked on a board by the bar, offering starters of leek, Stilton and mushroom tartlet with garden chutney, or perhaps a small Yorkshire pudding with chipolata sausages and onion gravy. For main courses there may be roast salmon fillet, braised shoulder of lamb or mild chicken curry with naan. The selection of half a dozen puddings is strong on inter-esting-flavoured ice-creams, such as apple and cider, or honeycomb, as well as more substantial options like chocolate sponge with custard. Boddingtons, Fuller's London Pride and Timothy Taylor Landlord plus two guests, constitute the real ales, and from an 18-strong wine list 14 are available by the glass. SAMPLE DISHES: carrot and orange soup £3.25; steak and ale pie £10; sweet waffles with fresh strawberries £4.

Open *11.30 to 11, Sun 12 to 10.30; bar food 12 to 9.30*
Details *No children under 14 after 7pm   Car park   Wheelchair access (also WC)   Garden and patio   No smoking area in dining-room   Background music   Dogs welcome in 1 bar area   Amex, Delta, MasterCard, Switch, Visa*

BURFORD   Oxfordshire   map 5

▲ *Lamb Inn* ❦

Sheep Street, Burford OX18 4LR   TEL: (01993) 823155

If you are looking for the archetypal Cotswold pub, come to the Lamb, which is set in a well-heeled village not far from Oxford. Burford boasts a large number of pubs, but the Lamb is particularly popular with tourists, who are drawn to the inn's ambitious and lengthy menu and wine list and genteel upper-middle-class décor. Diners are almost spoilt for choice. The frequently changing bar menu, which is available only for lunch, might lead off with cream of celery, walnut and Roquefort soup, duck liver, or pistachio and armagnac parfait with redcurrant dressing. They helpfully warn you that some items, such as steak and mushroom pie, or lamb with roast aubergines, will take 25 minutes to prepare. The pudding selection keeps a neat balance between heavy – plum and almond tart – and light – lemon mousse. The pub's deep armchairs and sofas are very comfortable if not ideal for eating, and the demand for food some-times exceed the seating available. Dinner and Sunday lunch are served only in the separate restaurant. The more interesting Hook Norton Best Bitter supplements a standard selection of beers, includ-ing Wadworth 6X and Adnams Bitter. The restaurant has its own extensive wine list, chock full of well-known names, and the bar list includes 15 by the bottle or glass. SAMPLE DISHES: Cornish crab and anchovy fritters on a pink peppercorn cream £6.25; salad of smoked

duck and orange on a balsamic and coriander olive oil dressing
£6.75; peach jalousie £3.25.

Open *11 to 2.30, 6 to 11, Sun 12 to 3, 7 to 10.30; closed 25 and 26 Dec;
bar food Mon to Sat L only 12 to 2; restaurant Sun L 12.30 to 1.45, all week
D 7 to 9*
Details *Children welcome   Car park   Garden   No smoking in dining-room
No music   No dogs in dining-room   No cards   Accommodation: 15 rooms,
B&B £60 to £115*

BURNHAM THORPE   Norfolk   map 6

Lord Nelson 🍺   [NEW ENTRY]

Walsingham Road, Burnham Thorpe PE31 8HN
TEL: (01328) 738241
off B1155/B1355, 2m S of Burnham Market

Burnham Thorpe is the birthplace of Lord Nelson and from where
he went to sea aged 12 in 1770. The pub was then called the Plough
and it was here that he gave a farewell party for villagers when he
returned to sea in 1793. The pub was renamed in 1807, two years
after his death at Trafalgar, and Nelson memorabilia, which has
accumulated there over the years, has made it into something of a
shrine. Set in a very pretty village, the pub itself is a 'gem': little has
changed since the last century. Visitors enter over a worn brick floor
to find rooms kept cosy and snug in cold weather with wood-burning fires. There is no bar at all for dispensing drinks, so beers are
brought to your table straight from the cask – Greene King IPA,
Abbot and Mild and, needless to say, Woodforde's Nelson's
Revenge. They also do a rum-based drink containing a secret ingredient called Nelson's Blood. On the blackboard menu you might find
chicken and mushroom soup, spare ribs in barbecue sauce or local
smoked salmon with mixed leaves and red peppers, and main
courses of grilled whole trout with lemon butter sauce, English
breakfast (served at any time), steak and mushroom pie or grilled
loin of pork with rosemary and garlic. Follow that, if you can, with
pecan pie, apple crumble or Bailey's parfait. A short wine list is very
reasonably priced. SAMPLE DISHES: pan-fried garlic mushrooms £3;
deep-fried chicken Kiev £6.50: bread-and-butter pudding £3.

Open *11 to 3, 6 to 11, Sun 12 to 3, 7 to 10.30; closed eves 25 and 26 Dec;
bar food 12 to 2, 7 to 9*
Details *Children welcome in eating areas   Car park   Wheelchair access (also
WC)   Garden   No-smoking area   Live music   Dogs welcome on a lead   No
cards*

BURPHAM   West Sussex   map 3

George and Dragon 🍺

Burpham BN18 9RR   TEL: (01903) 883131
*2½m up single track, no-through road signposted Warningcamp off
A27, 1m E of Arundel*

'Everything was cooked to such a high standard that, although the
menu was plain, the taste of the food was not,' wrote one enthusiastic reporter of the George and Dragon. It stands on the corner of a
very small village – one church, one pub and fifteen houses, and a
signposted circular walk starting from the pub. Inside, there are old
beams, floral curtains and country pine furniture. Bar tables fill up
fast at lunch-time and any overspill tumbles into the more formal
dining area, normally used for evening meals, when a more restaurant-style menu operates. A printed menu offers the regular items,
while the blackboard is the place to select the more ambitious dishes,
such as guinea-fowl suprême with orange sauce. One visitor's cream
of onion soup was 'unexpectedly delicious' with a delicate creami-
ness. Toad in the hole may sound ordinary but is made with good
farmhouse sausages with a batter 'of just the right texture'. Brill may
be lightly cooked with lime slices, and the ploughman's may inspire
raptures for the creamy taste of the pâté in one version, or the well-
kept state of the Stilton in another. To finish, chocolate mousse
leaves you in no doubt as to its home-made status, being made with
good-quality chocolate. Beers include a good selection from local
breweries such as Arundel, Bunces and Harveys, plus Timothy
Taylor from further afield. A 40-strong wine list offers decent drinking, with four wines available by the glass. SAMPLE DISHES: egg and
prawns in marie rose sauce £3.50; 8oz fillet steak with mushroom
and tomato £12.25; plum crumble £3.50.

Open *11 to 2.30, 6 to 11, Sun 12 to 3, 7 to 10.30; closed 25 Dec; bar food
12 to 2, 7 to 9.45 (no Sun D Sept to April); restaurant Sun L 12 to 2, Mon to
Sat D 7 to 9*
Details *No children   Car park   Wheelchair access (also WC)   Patio
Background and live music   No dogs   Amex, Delta, Diners, MasterCard,
Switch, Visa*

BUTLERS CROSS   Buckinghamshire   map 3

Russell Arms   NEW ENTRY

FISH

Chalkshire, Butlers Cross HP17 0ST
TEL: (01296) 622618

The variety and sheer quality of the fish dishes make this small white-washed pub, situated at the centre of the village near the cross-roads, worth a visit. The bar area, accessed through a small nondescript hallway, is dominated by a large brick-built fireplace to the right and colourful map prints of South Africa on the walls. Small bar tables are arranged to the left, and the dining-rooms are through to the back. A large stencilled blackboard lists the bill of fare. Starters include coquilles St Jacques, oysters, and snails in garlic butter, calamares and lobster bisque. Fillet of cod, haddock, plaice or whatever else has been landed from Grimsby or bought from the London fish market comprises the main courses. The portion of halibut au gratin enjoyed by a reporter was huge and visibly fresh, and lemon sole comes grilled, served off the bone, and timed just right. All dishes are served with fried potatoes and a crisp salad platter. Homemade apple and blackberry pie, chocolate mousse and tiramisù might feature among the desserts on offer. Licensee 'Pepe' Rivero-Cobrera, has installed a new Spanish chef in the kitchen and, not surprisingly, the wine list is now heavily dominated by French and Spanish choices. The pub's real ales are Brakspear and ABC Bitter from Carlsberg-Tetley. SAMPLE DISHES: moules marinière £4.50; swordfish steak £9.50; crème brûlée £3.

Open *11 to 3, 6 to 11, Sun 7 to 11; bar food and restaurant Tue to Sat 12 to 2.45 (2 restaurant), 6 to 9, Sun 12 to 2.45*
Details *Children welcome   Car park   Wheelchair access (also WC)   Garden No music   No dogs   Amex, Diners, MasterCard, Switch, Visa*

BUTLEY   Suffolk   map 6

Oyster Inn

Butley IP12 3NZ   TEL: (01394) 450790
on B1084, 4m W of Orford

This centuries-old inn, just outside the village, is a popular watering-hole. The small garden with tables, chairs, rabbits and birds makes a good spot for summer drinking. The unspoilt interior features a real coal fire in winter, swathes of hops hanging from low beams, scrubbed pine tables and settles, and local watercolours on the walls. With no background music or jukebox, music is restricted to live folk performances on Sunday evenings. As an Adnams pub, the Oyster carries the full range of their real ales, plus 17 of their wines, with the house selection also available by the glass. The menu changes most days but typical bar snack fare might be pâté, soup, filled jacket potatoes or a ploughman's; while more substantial offerings might include Cumberland sausage, mussels, venison with pepper sauce, steak and kidney pie or seafood/lobster platters. Homemade puddings range from treacle roly-poly to fruit crumbles or pies. Children have their own menu, providing chicken teddies, turkey dinosaurs and pizzas. SAMPLE DISHES: chicken liver pâté £3.50; fish pie £6; French citron pie £2.50.

Open *Sun to Fri 11.30 to 3, 6 to 11, Sat 11.30 to 11; bar food all week L 12 to 2, Tue to Sat D 7 to 9;*
Details *Children welcome by arrangement   Car park   Wheelchair access Garden and patio   Live music Sun nights   Dogs welcome   MasterCard, Switch, Visa*

BUTTERTON   Staffordshire

map 5

▲ *Black Lion Inn*

Butterton ST13 7SP   TEL: (01538) 304232
just off B5053, 6m E of Leek

New owners Timothy Lowes and his Canadian wife Lynn have made a few changes since their arrival in 1997. Essentially, however, this homely old inn dating from 1782 still offers the traditional hospitality and warm welcome for which it has previously been praised. The location on the edge of the Manifold Valley, with views over the Peak District National Park, attracts many visitors, especially walkers and outdoor types. A stone building opposite the parish church, the Lion has cottagey window panes and exposed timbers which impart a cosy feel inside, enhanced by an old-fashioned black range, open fires and a blizzard of brass, china and pictures around its interlocking rooms. Traditional pub games and a separate pool room attract a loyal band of locals as well as tourists, and Saturday nights are lively affairs. A no-surprises printed menu offers soups, sandwiches and family favourites, supplemented by blackboard specials: casseroles, steaks, a few fish and chicken dishes, vegetarian options and hearty puddings – all at reasonable prices. The 'Lion's Pride' dining-room offers a separate à la carte menu, and is bookable for functions and large groups. Ales include Theakston Best, Marston's Pedigree, Charles Wells Bombardier, and Hartington Bitter and IPA from the nearby Whim brewery. Four wines are served by the glass among a selection of 18 inexpensive bottles (most under £10). SAMPLE DISHES:

vegetarian lasagne £5; rumpstiltonskin (rump steak with Stilton) £9; apple sultana sponge £2.50.

Open *12 to 3, 7 to 11, Sun 12 to 3, 7 to 10.30; bar food and restaurant 12 to 2, 7 to 9*
Details *Children welcome in bar eating area   Car park   Wheelchair access Garden   Background music   No dogs during meal times   MasterCard, Visa Accommodation: 3 rooms, B&B £35 to £80*

BYLAND ABBEY   North Yorkshire   map 9

Abbey Inn 🍇

Byland Abbey YO6 4BD   TEL: (01347) 868204
off A170, between Thirsk and Helmsley, 2m W of Ampleforth

Byland Abbey, built by Cistercian monks in the twelfth century, gained fame in 1322 as the scene of an attack by the Scots, led by Robert the Bruce, while Edward II was dining there, but fell into ruin after the Reformation. The Abbey Inn next door enjoys fine views of the ruins and you can read a more detailed account of the abbey's history on the back of the pub's wine list. Martin and Jane Nordli took over in mid-1997and have made their mark on this already unusual inn. Its four splendid main rooms are decorated in eclectic style, comfortable, relaxing and full of charm and character, especially when candlelit in the evening. Floors are strewn with rugs, there are open fires, Jacobean-style chairs, settles with scatter cushions, stuffed birds, dried flower arrangements and numerous *objets d'art*. In short, there is much to interest the eye. There is much to interest the tastebuds too. At lunch tuck into an Abbey platter (a salad of ham, cheese, beef and pâté), or lamb shank with port and rosemary sauce. In the evening you will find Caesar salad, slices of pastrami and salami on ciabatta drizzled with olive oil, or gammon Singapore. Individual puddings may include champagne jelly with a citrus fruit salad. The pub serves only Tetley Bitter and Black Sheep, but a medium-length wine list offers decent drinking with wines divided into grape varieties for easy reference with eight by the glass. SAMPLE DISHES: duck and orange pâté £4.50; pan-fried medallions of venison £11.50; soft chocolate cake with espresso sauce £3.25.

Open *Tue to Sat and bank hol Mons 11 to 3, all week 6.30 to 11; closed 25 Dec; bar food 12 to 2, 6.30 to 9*
Details *Children welcome   Car park   Garden   Background music   No dogs Delta, MasterCard, Switch, Visa*

🍇🍇 *indicates a pub serving food on a par with 'seriously good' restaurants, where the cooking achieves consistent quality.*

CALVER　Derbyshire　　map 8

▲ *Chequers Inn*

Froggatt Edge, Calver S30 1ZB　TEL: (01433) 630231
on B6054, off A623 6m N of Bakewell

Originally four stone-built cottages, this eighteenth-century Grade II
listed inn is situated on an old packhorse road just below the steep
cliffs of Froggatt Edge. The inn enjoys a scenic location close to
many Peak District attractions, with a pretty rear garden backing on
to woodland. The smart refurbished interior has rag-washed yellow
walls, bare floorboards, comfortable settles, a log fire and attractive
prints. There is a separate dining area, but the same menu is served
throughout the pub. Choose from hearty sandwiches, soup, prawn
cocktail, pâté or potato skins to start. If you fancy something more
substantial there is pasta, grilled sea bream, grilled steak or gammon,
chicken fajitas, cottage pie or seven-spice salmon fillet. The daily-
changing specials board offers casseroles in winter and a large selection of fresh fish. Puddings range from black cherry clafoutis to
whisky parfait or profiteroles. Beers come from Ward's of Sheffield
and might include Thorne Best Bitter; a good selection of malt
whiskies is also available, and the short wine list includes four by the
glass. SAMPLE DISHES: celeriac fritters £3.25; liver and bacon £6;
Bakewell pudding £4.50.

Open *summer 11 to 11, winter Mon to Fri 11 to 3, 5.30 to 11, Sat, Sun and
bank hols 11 to 11; closed eve 25 Dec (L bookings only) and 26 Dec; bar food
Mon to Fri 12 to 2, 6 to 9.30, Sat 12 to 10, Sun and bank hols 12 to 9.30*
Details *Children welcome in bar eating area　Car park　Garden　No-
smoking area　Background music　No dogs　Delta, MasterCard, Switch, Visa
Accommodation: 6 rooms, B&B £46 to £68*

CARLTON-IN-COVERDALE　North Yorkshire　map 8

▲ *Foresters Arms* 🏵 🍇

Carlton-in-Coverdale DL8 4BB　TEL: (01969) 640272
off A684, 5m SW of Leyburn

Coverdale is quiet, with little traffic, perhaps because the narrow
roads discourage motoring but also because it is one of the lesser
known of the Dales. However, more and more people are prepared
to make the effort to wend their way here, to search out the
Foresters for its classy, restaurant-quality food served in a pub environment. One couple wrote, 'We only wish that the Dales were not
so far from Somerset [or] we would be going back to the Foresters

many times.' The pub dates from the 1600s, and although the bars have recently been refurbished they retain their traditional character, with beams, an open fireplace and flagged floor. Customers can choose from three main menus, and any of the dishes can be eaten anywhere. Tables are laid after you have placed your food order at the bar, and service is friendly and welcoming.

For the just-peckish there is a light lunch menu offering such things as scrambled eggs with smoked salmon, grilled Yorkshire ham and eggs, or tomato and basil pasta with a Toulouse sausage. Those with heartier appetites have a good choice from the main menu: starters such as bruschetta with Parma ham and sun-dried tomato dressing, or baked crab and asparagus gâteau with a soufflé-like texture and a wonderful taste of fresh crab, followed by veal cutlet sautéd with sage and garlic, or calf's liver with leek mash and Madeira sauce. Or you might be tempted by a dish from the short but imaginative vegetarian menu, or decide to dive in to the whole page of fish dishes: from fish soup with rouille to roast monkfish tails with mussel ragoût. Still hungry? Go for home-made puddings (which may take a while to prepare): baked treacle tart with ginger ice-cream, perhaps, or mango soufflé. Alternatively, opt for a selection of nine cheeses – including Stinking Bishop, Cornish Yarg, and Darrus and Gubbeen from Ireland – served with a glass of Ramos Pinto Port. Ubiquitous local brews Black Sheep, John Smith's and Theakston are joined by interloper Ruddles. The wine list offers ten good-value house wines as well as eight half-bottles and a separate list of fine and rare wines. SAMPLE DISHES: spiced chicken livers with pepper risotto £5.75; roast sea bream with onion marmalade, red wine and tarragon £10; feuilleté of berries and Kirsch sabayon £5.50.

Open *Tue to Sun 12 to 3, 6.30 to 11 (7 to 10.30 Sun); closed 3 weeks Jan; bar food Tue to Sun 12 to 2, 7 to 9, restaurant Sun L 12 to 2, Tue to Sat D 7 to 9.30*
Details *Children welcome in bar eating area   Car park   Wheelchair access Garden   No-smoking area   Background music   Dogs welcome in bedrooms by arrangement   Delta, MasterCard, Visa, Switch   Accommodation: 3 rooms, B&B £35 to £60*

CARTERWAY HEADS   Northumberland   map 10

▲ *Manor House Inn* 😋 🍺 🍇

Carterway Heads, Shotley Bridge DH8 9LX
TEL: (01207) 255268
on A68, 3m W of Consett

New owners took over in mid-1997, bringing a new chef with them, but reports suggest they have not departed far from the previous regime's successful formula. The new proprietors are clearly acquisitive types. Their collection of porcelain jugs, which hang from the beams in the dining-room, already numbers more than 100 and the other collection, malt whiskies, includes an impressive 150. The pub fronts on to the main road, but at the back it offers views of unspoilt and beautiful countryside. Popular with families and a young crowd, this long building houses two bars and a dining-room, with the same menu throughout. One reporter reckoned the long blackboard list was 'quite modern and sophisticated for the wilds of Northumberland, with the merest nod to pub stalwarts'. At the same time the kitchen avoids getting carried away and being trendy for the sake of it. Starters, which can all be ordered as main courses, take in warm salad of smoky bacon and mange-tout, green-lipped mussels in a Thai curry sauce, or creamy tomato pasta. To follow, try stir-fried Szechuan wild mushrooms and vegetables in filo pastry, chicken breast stuffed with sun-dried tomatoes and spinach, or maybe baked salmon with dill and dry Vermouth sauce. Finish with a sweet such as sticky toffee pudding, which has been described as 'beyond reproach', or, for those with a more savoury palate, a plate of local cheeses with onion marmalade. Theakston best and Courage Directors are supplemented with guests from regional independents like Mordue and Durham, and a sensible wine list offers good choices at good prices, with five available by the glass. SAMPLE DISHES: mackerel terrine £3.75; pigeon and lamb casserole with black pudding £10; banoffi pie £3.

Open *summer Mon to Fri 11 to 3, 6 to 11, Sat, Sun and bank hols 11 to 11, winter 11 to 3, 6 to 11, Sun 12 to 3, 7 to 10.30; bar food and restaurant 12 to 2.30, 7 to 9.30*
Details *Children welcome in bar eating area   Car park   Garden   No smoking in restaurant   Background music   Well-behaved dogs welcome   Amex, MasterCard, Switch, Visa   Accommodation: 4 rooms, B&B £25 to £46*

CARTHORPE   **North Yorkshire**   **map 9**

Fox and Hounds 🍇

Carthorpe DL8 2LG   TEL: (01845) 567433
off A1, 4m SE of Bedale

This pristinely kept former smithy is tucked away in a sleepy Yorkshire village not far off the A1. Howard and Bernadette Fitzgerald run a house orientated to serving above-average food, and as such it is much more of a dining pub than a propping-up-the-bar pub. A traditionally furnished lounge has plush wall seating, dark-wood furniture, open fires, plates, plants and bits and bobs. If the place is busy, go through to the high-ceilinged dining area with its array of smith's tools. 'A' and 'B' fixed-price and à la carte menus alternate weekly, and are supplemented by blackboard specials featuring mainly whatever fish have been delivered that day. From the set menus, kick off perhaps with black pudding with caramelised apple and onion marmalade, or bubble and squeak with a fried egg (depending whether you're there during an 'A week' or a 'B week') and proceed to pork loin with apple sauce, or vegetable curry with rice. From the *carte*, you might choose duckling with orange sauce, or rack of lamb on a blackcurrant croûton with redcurrant gravy. Among fishy specials could be mussels in cheese sauce, followed by dressed Whitby crab or Dover sole. Trifles, sticky toffee puds or treacle tarts also swap each week, though there's no swapping when it comes to beers, which areTheakston bitter and John Smith's. The wine list impresses with its good selection, helpful annotations and generous helping of half-bottles; in addition, about a dozen wines are sold by the glass. SAMPLE DISHES: bacon and Stilton tartlet £4.25; halibut steak with lobster and prawn sauce £11; meringue nest with raspberry and blackcurrant ice-cream (included with set-menu, or £3.75 on its own).

Open *Tue to Sun 12 to 2.30, 7 to 11; closed first week Jan; bar food and restaurant 12 to 2, 7 to 9.30*
Details *Children welcome　Car park　Wheelchair access (also WC)　No smoking in restaurant　Background music　No dogs　Delta, MasterCard, Switch, Visa*

CARTMEL FELL　　Cumbria　　　　　　　　　　map 8

Masons Arms

Strawberry Bank, Cartmel Fell LA11 6NW
TEL: (015395) 68486
off A5074, turn left at sign for Bowland Bridge, 1m up hill

There are wonderful views from the terrace of this Lakeland pub, which is particularly popular with walkers. The garden has plenty of tables and chairs for summer eating, while the three rooms inside have low black beams, flagstoned floors, wooden pews and 'bags of character'. The pub is the home of the Strawberry Bank Brewery, which produces a variety of cask-conditioned ales with wonderful names such as Ned's Tipple and Black Beck; there are also beers from Marston, Bateman and Barnsley on tap, as well as an extensive selection of bottled beers from around the world. Non-beer lovers might pick one of the eight wines available by the large or small glass. Pub favourites such as soup, sandwiches, pâtés, steak pie and chilli con carne appear on the printed menus, while for the more adventurous daily blackboards will deliver stuffed vine leaves, wild mushroom strudel,

Mexican turkey chilli, Greek lamb pie, or spinach and Puy lentil mous-saka. To round things off are profiteroles with chocolate sauce, or perhaps Manhattan baked cheesecake. SAMPLE DISHES: prawn platter £4; coachman's casserole £8; apple and hazelnut crumble £3.

Open *Mon to Thur 11.30 to 3, 6 to 11, Fri to Sun (and all week from mid-July to early Sept) 11 to 11; closed 25 and 26 Dec; bar food 12 to 2, 6 to 8.45*
Details *Children welcome   Car park   Wheelchair access   Garden   No smoking in upstairs dining-room   Background music   No dogs during meal times   Amex, Delta, MasterCard, Switch, Visa*

CASTERTON   Cumbria   map 8

▲ *Pheasant Inn* 🍇

Casterton, nr Kirkby Lonsdale LA6 2RX   TEL: (015242) 71230
on A683, 1m N of junction with A65

A mile or so from pretty Kirkby Lonsdale is the village of Casterton, well suited for visiting the Lakes and Yorkshire dales as well as many local National Trust properties, the scenic Settle to Carlisle railway, and for fishing on the River Lune. The inn itself has a residential air, and the exposed beams, polished brass and open fires and settles make it look more 'genuine' than 'olde worlde'. The clientele consists of residents, plus golfers from the local club, and a sufficient number of campers from caravan sites ensure it 'does not get too stuffy with the tweeds and cords set', in the view of one visitor. The printed menu is almost dwarfed by the selection of specials: tangy tomato soup, or four-cheese ravioli, might tempt you towards spicy lamb curry, roast pork with apple sauce, spaghetti bolognaise, or rainbow trout with ham and smoked garlic. Chargrills are a bit of a speciality: prawns, tuna steaks, or venison steak perhaps. Eve's pudding, banoffi pie, fudge cake, and various crumbles feature on the pudding list. Theakston Best and a weekly-changing guest, and over 30 malt whiskies, account for the barley-based beverages, while the grape selection is a 30-plus list of wines of which a dozen or so are available by the glass and a further seven by the half-bottle. SAMPLE DISHES: marinated herring fillets £4; rack of lamb with minted gravy £9.50; gooseberry crumble £3.25.

Open *11 to 3, 6 to 11 (10.30 Sun); bar food 12 to 2, 6.30 to 9 (9.30 Fri and Sat); restaurant Tue to Sun Apr to Oct and Tue to Sat Nov to Mar D only 7 to 9*
Details *Children welcome   Car park   Wheelchair access (also WC)   Garden and patio   No smoking in 2 rooms   Background music   Dogs welcome   Delta, Diners, MasterCard, Switch, Visa (credit cards accepted for payments over £15)   Accommodation: 10 rooms, B&B £37.50 to £68*

CHACOMBE   **Northamptonshire**   map 5

▲ *George & Dragon* `NEW ENTRY`

1 Silver Street, Chacombe OX17 2JR   TEL: (01295) 711500
off A361, just N of M40 junction 11

A picture in summer when the attractive façade is festooned with flowers, this mellow sandstone pub dating from the seventeenth century is tucked close to this pretty village's church and is popular with businessmen from nearby Banbury. There is a welcoming atmosphere inside the three comfortable bars. One, with a TV and rustic tables, is very much the locals' bar. The other two display flag-stones, an inglenook fireplace, low beams and terracotta-painted walls. Ray Bennett and his wife have built up the dining side of the pub during their four years at the George & Dragon, and employ two chefs who competently handle the preparation of a varied range of unusual pasta dishes, exemplary fresh fish and carefully sauced meat dishes. Lunchtime additions include sandwiches and jacket potatoes. The main boards change every three weeks, with the fish board reflecting local availability. Accompany your meal with one of the usual suspects: Marston's Pedigree, Wadworth 6X, Theakston Best and XB or Morland Old Speckled Hen, or alternatively with one of a selection of fruit wines. SAMPLE DISHES: Brie and smoked bacon fritter £5; sauté strips of lamb with chilli and mint £8.25; brandy-snap basket with melon and pineapple in a vanilla creamed cheese £3.25.

Open *12 to 11 (10.30 Sun); bar food and restaurant 12 to 7, full menu 7 to 9.30*
Details *Children welcome in bar eating area   Car park   Wheelchair access (also WC)   Patio   No smoking in restaurant   Background music   Dogs welcome   Amex, Delta, Diners, MasterCard, Switch, Visa   Accommodation: 2 rooms, B&B £38.50 to £55*

CHADLINGTON   **Oxfordshire**   map 5

Tite Inn 🍺 🍇

Mill End, Chadlington OX7 3NY   TEL: (01608) 676475
off A361, 2½m S of Chipping Norton

Seated atop its own valley in the Cotswolds this weathered, ochre-coloured inn offers exceptional views. It takes its name from the stream which flows beneath it. Dating from around 1600, the premises have been an inn for 200 years; the bar and cellars are the oldest parts and a ghost of an unknown woman has reputedly been seen around them. The open-plan, bare stone interior is 'spruce, uncluttered and immaculate', and the informal 'Garden Room' restaurant is notable for the grapevine clinging to the ceiling (try to spot its colourful denizens). Beers and wines are the house's forte. Well-kept ales from local and regional brewers are on constant rotation – consult the blackboards for availability – and the wine list is short but well chosen, with the emphasis on interesting, good-value New World wines. Food is simple, unfussy and reasonably priced, focused very much on the use of good-quality basic ingredients. Meat is sourced from the village butcher – 'the best for miles around', according to a local. The lunch menu tends to contain dishes that require little last-minute cooking, such as seafood salad, or pâté ploughman's. Similarly, starters on the evening menu might include avocado with prawns, or charcuterie, though there may be main courses of chicken breast in cider and honey sauce, or lamb curry 'with all the trimmings'. Sunday lunch sees a traditional roast added to the menu. SAMPLE DISHES: bobotie and salad £7; boeuf bourguignon £8; posh bread-and-butter pudding £3.

Open *Tue to Sat 12 to 2.30, 6.30 to 11, Sun 12 to 3, 7 to 10.30; closed 25 and 26 Dec, bank hol eves; bar food and restaurant Tue to Sun 12 to 2 (2.30 Sun), 7 to 9 (limited bar food only Sun eve)*
Details *Children welcome   Car park   Wheelchair access (also WC)   Garden No smoking in restaurant   Background music   Dogs welcome   Delta, MasterCard, Switch, Visa*

CHALE   Isle of Wight   map 2

▲ *Wight Mouse Inn*

Chale PO38 2HA   TEL: (01983) 730431
on B3399, 5m W of Ventnor

WHISKY

A formidable array of 365 malts and other whiskies can be enjoyed in this seventeenth-century stone-and-slate coaching-inn that has a great sense of history. It sits alongside the Clarendon Hotel, overlooking Chale Bay and encourages visitors of all ages. Children are welcome in three of the bars (games rooms), in a garden replete with swings, slides, and climbing frames, and can pick food from their own Mouse World menu. The children's bill of fare lists all the usual chicken teddy bears and Marmite sandwiches but also parent-pleasers such as cauliflower cheese and jacket potatoes. The main bar, however, remains children-free and is popular with locals, farmers and holidaymakers. The décor is cosy, with open log fires, decorated bar stools, plates and pistols. Live music every night of the year provides entertainment. The oak beams come from a three-masted sailing ship, the Clarendon, which sank 160 or so years ago with its cargo of turtles, molasses and rum. If whisky is not your tipple, try one of the six real ales – Marston's Pedigree, Wadsworth 6X, Morland Old Speckled Hen, Gale's HSB, Boddingtons Bitter and Fuggle's Imperial – or one of the wines, which includes a bottle from the Isle of Wight. The menu is full of pub favourites, including fried fish, steaks, ploughman's lunches and curries. SAMPLE DISHES: crab cocktail £4; shellfish Mornay £8; knickerbocker glory £2.75.

Open *11 to 12, Sun 12 to 10.30; bar food 12 to 10*
Details *Children welcome   Car park   Wheelchair access (also WC)   Garden and patio   No-smoking area   Background and live music; jukebox   No dogs Delta, MasterCard, Switch, Visa   Accommodation: 15 rooms, B&B £25 to £70*

CHALGROVE   Oxfordshire   Map 2

Red Lion Inn   NEW ENTRY

115 High Street, Chalgrove OX44 7SS   TEL: (01865) 890625
on B480, 4 miles NW of Watlington

Although the earliest record of the Red Lion Inn as a pub is 1637, parts of the building date from the eleventh century. The pub is unusual in that it is actually owned by Chalgrove parish church, and in times past – much to the disapproval of church leaders – provided free carousing to dissolute church wardens. With its cream and red façade, the Lion sits behind a well-kept front garden, which belies its high-street location. A stream in a channel runs the length of the street, and you have to cross this to reach the pub. Inside, a log-burning fire is at one end of the 'bar and beams' main room, and a wood stove at the other: the atmosphere is warm and unpretentious. The cooking shows some imagination and engages with a few inter-national touches: very spicy tiger prawns in tempura are served with a salsa of tomato, ginger and pineapple, for example, and crispy duck comes with dressed leaves in a sweet marinade. Bar meals, writ-ten up on a blackboard, are slightly smaller and cheaper than their à la carte versions, and might take in chicken Madras curry, rabbit with calvados, or monkfish medallions. Puddings have been described as excellent value. Lemon pavlova comprises three meringue mounds on a pool of lemon syrup, topped with lemon cream, while summer berries with Greek yoghurt, crème fraîche, crushed meringue and caramel pieces impressed our reporter so much with its intricate layers of fruit that she drew a diagram. The church sanctions the sale of Brakspear Bitter, Fuller's London Pride and a guest ale as well as a 24-strong wine list, which offers some reasonably priced bottles as well as more pricey *grand crus*. SAMPLE DISHES: moules marinière, steamed in cream, shallots, parsley and white wine £4.75; pot roast pheasant with rosemary, bacon, calvados and pink peppercorn sauce £12; banana fritter, caramel ice-cream, whisky and apricot sauce £3.50.

Open *Mon to Fri 12 to 3, 5.30 to 11, Sat 12 to 3, 6 to 11, Sun 12 to 3, 7 to 10.30; closed 25 Dec; bar food and restaurant all week L 12 to 2, Mon to Sat D 7 to 9.30*
Details *Children welcome in eating areas   Wheelchair access (also WC) Garden and patio   No smoking in dining-room   Background music   Dogs welcome   Delta, Diners, MasterCard, Visa, Switch*

CHAPEL AMBLE   Cornwall   map 1

Maltsters Arms 🍺 🍇

Chapel Amble PL27 6EU   TEL: (01208) 812473
off A39, 2m N of Wadebridge

CHEESE

You would expect the owners of a pub called the Maltsters Arms to know a thing or two about beer, and they certainly do. Alastair and Marie Gray serve a respectable range of ales. In addition to Bass, Young's and Fuller's, the local brewery Sharp's supply Cornish Coaster and also brew Maltsters especially for the pub. The inn, centrally located within the village, is whitewashed and features a thatched porch. Inside, the layout is semi-open-plan with rooms flowing into one another. A number of different menus are advertised, but the focus is on the range of cheeses, many of them local, and fresh fish dishes. The owners' suggestion to have a glass of whisky or a port with your St Endellion, Cornish Pepper, Village Green, or Ticklemore goats' cheese seems like an eminently sensible idea. Fish specials might include pan-fried sardines in garlic butter or fillet of wild trout with a saffron, wine and cream sauce. Meat eaters might want to try thickly sliced chicken liver pâté and follow that with sirloin steak garni, while vegetarians would be pleased with broccoli and Stilton bake. Traditional sponges and tarts feature on the pudding selection. The wine list is heavily French, but with plenty of New World offerings. SAMPLE DISHES: cheesy garlic mushrooms £3.50; fillet of John Dory with aromatic Chinese-style dressing £10.50; orange and Grand Marnier bread-and-butter pudding £3.

Open *11 to 2.30, 6 to 11, Sun 12 to 2.30, 7 to 10.30; closed 25 Dec eve; bar food 12 to 1.45, 6.15 to 9.15 (9.30 summer); restaurant 12 to 2 (1.45 Sun), 6.30 to 10 (9.30 Sun)*
Details *Children welcome in family room   Car park   Wheelchair access (also WC)   Patio   No smoking in restaurant   Background music   Guide dogs only Delta, MasterCard, Switch, Visa*

CHARLBURY   Oxfordshire   map 5

▲ *Bull Inn*   NEW ENTRY

Sheep Street, Charlbury OX7 3RR   TEL: (01608) 810689
on B4026, 6 miles SE of Chipping Norton

This good-sized sixteenth-century Cotswold stone hostelry has been
much renovated and redecorated, but retains some original features
such as heavy beams and bare stone walls. Customers can eat either
in the long, narrow main bar, where menus are chalked on a board,
or in the more expensive restaurant, which has its own blackboards
(which can be read in the comfort of a tiny lounge area) featuring
the bar menu plus a lot more. Bar food takes in the likes of Spanish
omelette, hummus with hot pitta bread, moules marinière, and pork
and chicken-liver terrine. For pie-lovers there's a 'smoky fish'
version, pasta fans will find tortellini with a creamy white wine and
wild mushroom sauce, while carnivores might opt for 'very succulent' rack of English lamb. Portions are generous and the food is
based on fresh ingredients neatly presented with style but without
pretension. Everything except the ice-cream and bread is home-
made, though plans are afoot to make the ice-cream in-house too. At
lunch-time a selection of hot and cold French baguettes is also available. Although the Bull Inn is a freehouse, it sells only Greene King's
regular range, now augmented with the brewery's hoppier brew,
Triumph. A somewhat pricey but useful wine list offers six wines by
the glass. The inn is situated in a triangle formed by Chipping
Norton, Burford and Oxford, and Blenheim Palace is less than ten
miles away. SAMPLE DISHES: plate of oak-smoked salmon with bread
and butter £7.25; pan-fried lambs' liver, bacon and onions with
chive mash and gravy £7.50; bitter-chocolate terrine with pistachio
sauce £4.

Open *Tue to Sat 12 to 2.30, 7 to 11.30, Sun and bank hol Mon 12 to 3;
closed 25 Dec, eve 26 Dec, 1 Jan; bar food and restaurant Tue to Sun L 12 to
2 (1.30 restaurant), Tue to Sat D 7 to 9 (9.30 Fri and Sat)*
Details *No children under 5   Car park   Wheelchair access   Patio   No
smoking in restaurant   Background music   Guide dogs only   Delta,
MasterCard, Visa, Switch   Accommodation: 3 rooms, B&B £50 to £60*

CHARLTON   Wiltshire   map 2

▲ *Horse and Groom* 🍺

The Street, Charlton SN16 9DL   TEL: (01666) 823904
on B4040 Malmesbury to Cricklade road, 2m E of Malmesbury

This handsome sixteenth-century stone coaching-inn, not far from
Malmesbury and handy for the Badminton Horse Trials, has been
run by Nichola King and Philip Gilder since 1994. Inside are two
charming bars done out with block stone floors, exposed walls and
open log fire. There are hearty snacks of the filled rolls, ploughman's
and jacket potato variety on offer in the Charlton Bar, with more
substantial meals listed on a blackboard and à la carte menu in the
lounge bar and dining-room. Peppered mackerel and smoked trout
terrine or venison paupiettes with shallots and cassis sauce might be
offered on the blackboard, while à la carte choices include roasted
guinea-fowl, or whole sole Veronique. The wine list runs to 42 bins
including some half-bottles, but only house wines are offered by the
glass. Beers are supplied by local Wiltshire brewers such as Archers,
Wadworth or Mole's. SAMPLE DISHES: smoked haddock pot £4.25;
duck and bacon salad £11; lemon meringue £3.50.

Open *Mon to Fri 12 to 3, 7 to 11, Sat and Sun 12 to 11; bar food and
restaurant 12 to 2, 7 to 10 (9.30 Sun)*
Details *Children welcome   Car park   Wheelchair access (also WC)   Garden
Background music   Dogs welcome in bar   Delta, MasterCard, Switch, Visa
Accommodation: 3 rooms, B&B £60 to £75*

CHARLTON   West Sussex   map 3

▲ *The Fox Goes Free*   [NEW ENTRY]

Charlton PO18 0HU   TEL: (01243) 811461
off A286 Chichester to Midhurst road, 1m E of Singleton

Formerly known as the Charlton Fox, this 400-year-old flint building, situated in a small village, has had its name changed after being
taken over by Olly Ligertwood and his French girlfriend, Ando, who
are aiming to provide a menu of 'quality food based on French and
English ideas'. Early reports indicate that they are succeeding. Inside
there are two bar areas of differing sizes and two extra seating areas.
All are low-beamed and the smaller bar has a large inglenook which
creates a very intimate atmosphere, made more so by the warm
welcome. Typical dishes include 'nicely runny' baked Brie with
almonds, or Chinese chicken wings, followed by spicy Mexican
tacos, venison in red wine, or pigeon breast with apple and calvados.
There is also a separate menu of casseroles – for a minimum of four

people and ordered 24 hours in advance – perhaps of rabbit, mustard and cider, or liver and bacon. Puddings might take in apple strudel or banoffi pie. The new owners were previously in the *Guide* at the Five Bells in Buriton, which was noted for its real ale, a reputation they hope to maintain here. At the time of going to press, Ballards and Ringwood were available and will remain to be joined by rotating guest beers, with perhaps as many as six during the summer. Reasonably priced house wines are on a blackboard, with a further selection on a printed list. One to watch. SAMPLE DISHES: Roquefort and walnut salad £4.50; duck breast with green peppercorns and brandy £9.50; treacle tart £2.50.

Open *11 to 3, 6 to 11, Sun 12 to 3, 7 to 10.30; bar food and restaurant 11 to 2.30, 6 to 10.30*
Details *Children welcome in eating areas   Car park   Wheelchair access (also WC)   Garden and patio   No smoking in 1 dining-room   Background music; no music in 1 dining-room   Dogs welcome   Delta, MasterCard, Switch, Visa Accommodation: 3 rooms, B&B £30 to £45*

CHENIES   Buckinghamshire   map 3

Red Lion 🍺

Chenies WD3 6ED   TEL: (01923) 282722
off A404, between Chorleywood and Little Chalfont

This attractive whitewashed roadside pub lies in the Chess Valley, and is made pretty in summer by hanging baskets and window-boxes. Interesting old photos and a brass model of Stephenson's Rocket decorate the bar area, which has wooden tables, stools and chairs. Standard bar food offerings include filled baguettes and baps, jacket potatoes, soup and salads (available in starter and main-course sizes). More substantial dishes might be pork escalopes, lamb fillet stuffed with capers and mushrooms, roughy in a Pernod sauce, or the 'internationally acclaimed' Chenies lamb pie, while a modern streak is shown in such dishes as grilled Mediterranean tomatoes with mozzarella, olives, basil and ciabatta bread, or warm Cajun spiced chicken with pineapple. Desserts are a similar mix of old-fashioned favourites such as apple pie and rhubarb crumble and not-so-traditional home-made jaffa cake. Apart from Vale's Notley Ale, Wadworth 6X and Benskins, there is Lion Pride, especially brewed for the pub by the Rebellion Beer Company in Marlow. Three wines are available by the glass. SAMPLE DISHES: prawns with garlic mayonnaise £5; sausage, leek and Cheddar bake £5.50; honey and whisky cheesecake £3.

Open *11 to 3, 5.30 to 11, Sun 12 to 3, 6.30 to 10.30; closed 25 Dec; bar food 12 to 2, 7 to 10 (9.30 Sun)*
Details *No children   Car park   Wheelchair access (also WC)   No music Dogs welcome   Amex, Delta, Diners, MasterCard, Switch, Visa*

CHERITON   Hampshire   map 2

▲ *Flower Pots Inn*

Cheriton SO24 0QQ   TEL: (01962) 771318
on B3046, 4m S of New Alresford

Let your nose lead you to the Flower Pots Inn: sweet, hoppy aromas drift out of its own award-winning Cheriton Brewhouse, which is adjacent to the pub. 'If only more pubs were like this . . . a delight,' wrote one reporter. The style is simple, with quarry-tiled floors, a log fire and solid furniture. The small family room is well above average with paper and colouring pencils supplied to young visitors. Food is simple too: hearty baps come with ham or prawns; sandwiches are toasted or not according to preference, and main courses are likely to include a hotpot, chilli or curry. This is principally an ale house, so the wine list is limited. The Pots Ale, Best Bitter and Diggers Gold – well-respected in the microbrewing fraternity – have only to travel across the car park, so are in excellent condition, and they are served in the best possible way: under gravity, straight from the cask. SAMPLE DISHES: home-cooked ham sandwich £2.25; lamb and apricot hotpot £4.50; Coronation chicken jacket potato £4.

Open *12 to 2.30, 6 to 11, Sun 12 to 3, 7 to 10.3; bar food 12 to 2, 7 to 9*
Details *Children welcome   Car park   Wheelchair access   Garden   No music Dogs welcome on a lead   No cards   Accommodation: 5 rooms, B&B £30 to £50*

CHIDDINGLY   East Sussex   map 3

Six Bells

COMMUNITY PUB

Chiddingly BN8 6HF   TEL: (01825) 872227
off A22 Uckfield to Eastbourne road at Golden Cross service station

This old village pub is where a community pub should be – next to the church, church hall and village shop – and it is clearly very much the focus of the community and the cricket team. The pub itself has brick floors, low ceilings, beams, nooks and crannies with tables and chairs in them. Real fires burn in winter and the walls are covered with old enamel advertisements. On offer here is exceptionally good-value pub grub – no frills and no fuss. The menu is exactly as you would expect: garlic prawns, pâté and French bread, ploughman's, cheesy vegetable bake, lasagne and shepherd's pie. Almost all items are under £5, though vegetables are charged separately. Chocolate nut sundae is a cool way to end a meal, or try banana split. The pub is a freehouse, but with just Harvey's and Courage Directors on tap one reporter's observation that the beers could be a little more exciting is probably fair comment. An English wine from Barkham is on offer, as well as five by the glass. SAMPLE DISHES: French onion soup £1.25; steak and kidney pie £2.50; raspberry pavlova £2.50.

Open *11 to 3, 6 to 11 (12 Fri and Sat), Sun 12 to 10.30; bar food 11.30 to 2.30, 6 to 10.30*
Details *Children welcome in family room   Car park   Wheelchair access (also WC)   Garden and patio   Live music   Dogs welcome on a lead   No cards*

CHIDDINGSTONE   Kent   map 3

Castle Inn

Chiddingstone TN8 7AH   TEL: (01892) 870247
off B2027, 4m E of Edenbridge

The Inn publishes a delightful set of sepia postcards showing off the village in an Edwardian summer, the men in breeches and boaters and the little girls in unsullied white frocks. The latest motor drawn up on the cobbles by the venerable tile-hung side of the inn – even then it was an artist's paradise. The heavily beamed building has been an inn for 250 years, and for 300 years before that it was a private residence known as Waterslip House. These days it is part of the National Trust's considerable responsibilities in Kent, and has had one tenant, Nigel Lucas, for over 34 years. Records show that the village itself dates back to the early ninth century. A bar menu offers simple, appetising dishes such as egg mayonnaise, a plate of smoked salmon or today's pasta dish. Or perhaps opt for hot local pork sausages, or 'death by chilli con carne', which comes with the warning 'very hot – please believe us'. Children are happily accommodated unless the only thing they will eat is chips. Sweets are a range of ice-creams 'from around the world' or something like cheesecake or fudge cake. A less pubby fixed-price two- or three-course fireside menu (not Sunday lunch-time) opens the doors to the likes of roast rack of lamb or poached salmon with caper and parsley sauce. A request for an ordinary or liqueur coffee, tea or fruit tea, will be easily fulfilled. Larkin's Traditional and Young's Ordinary are the real ales on offer, but this is an excellent pub for wine, with more than 150 bottles lovingly assembled and logically catalogued, though without descriptions and just three by the glass. SAMPLE DISHES: crudités £3.50; beef and vegetable curry £5.50; Dutch apple slice £3.50.

Open *11 to 11, Sun 12 to 10.30; bar food 11 to 10.45, Sun 12 to 10.15; restaurant 12 to 2, 7.30 to 9.30*
Details *Children welcome   Car park   Wheelchair access   Garden and patio   No music   Dogs welcome   Amex, Delta, Diners, MasterCard, Switch, Visa*

CHILLESFORD   Suffolk   map 6

▲ *Froize Inn* 🍺 [NEW ENTRY]

The Street, Chillesford IP12 3PU
TEL: (01394) 450282
on B1084, 7m E of Woodbridge

FISH

Situated on the coastal path, this pub dating from about 1490 was
built on the site of a former friary – the name is thought to be a
corruption of the word friary and 'froise', a kind of takeaway
pancake. The history of the Froize is too long to detail here, but
eventful. Today the pub has *en suite* accommodation, a beer garden
and a camping/caravan site. A large building, it boasts a low, beamed
ceiling and plenty of dining tables. The fireplace is fitted with a solid
fuel stove, there is lots of exposed brickwork and plenty of pictures
and memorabilia with nautical and rustic associations, including a
collection of clay pipes. Menus provide good choice, with a definite
focus on fish, which also comes with an unusual twist: fresh sea
lettuce florentine with eggs and cream, gravad lax pinwheels rolled
and stuffed with spinach and cream cheese, or fillet of kingfish
grilled with banana and served with Kenyan-style coconut sauce,
perhaps. For meat eaters there might be stir-fried beef with Chinese
vegetables, or griddled chicken with tarragon and garlic in a lemon
sauce, and pudding lovers can try caramelised apple froize or home-
made ice-cream. The pub is to be praised for its dedication to local
real ales, with house brews from Mauldons and beers from Greene
King and Adnams as well as Woodforde's, St Peter's, Earl Soham,
Green Dragon, Scotts, Iceni, Nethergate, Tolly Cobbold and Mighty
Oak . They lay down strong winter ales for a year, and it would be a
delight to see more pubs doing so. The wine list offers a good choice
by the glass and half-bottle. SAMPLE DISHES: 6 oysters served raw with
a shallot, tarragon and red wine vinaigrette £7; whole steamed local
sea bass on a bed of lime noodles £15; toffee and pistachio ice-cream
£3.50.

Open *Tue to Fri 12 to 3, 6 (6.30 winter) to 11, Sat and Sun 12 to 11 (10.30
Sun); closed last week in Feb, first 2 weeks in Mar and last week in Sept; bar
food and restaurant Tue to Sun 12 to 2, 7 to 9*
Details *Children welcome in eating areas   Car park   Wheelchair access (also
WC)   Garden   No smoking in dining area   Live music   Dogs welcome   No
cards   Accommodation: 2 rooms, B&B £30 to £60*

---

*Assessments of wine in pubs is based largely on what is available in
the bar. Many pubs also have full restaurant wine lists.*

CHINNOR   Oxfordshire   map 2

Sir Charles Napier 👥 👥 🍇
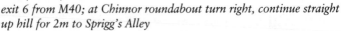

Sprigg's Alley, nr Chinnor OX9 4BX
TEL: (01494) 483011
*exit 6 from M40; at Chinnor roundabout turn right, continue straight
up hill for 2m to Sprigg's Alley*

This pub is renowned for three things: sculptures, dining and wine.
The sculptures are everywhere, inside and out, and while the pub
refers to its décor as 'eclectic', others have suggested the word
'eccentric', but it is none the less cheery for that. Helped along by
owner Julie Griffiths' friendly, relaxed manner, the atmosphere is
leisurely and informal, conducive to lingering over what readers
describe as 'innovative' and 'imaginative' food that is never pretentious or trendy for its own sake. The menu offers dishes that could
be conventional but receive a surprising tweak. Baked sardines, for
example, come with piccalilli, and pan-fried calf's liver is served
with a balsamic crème fraîche. Other dishes, such as crispy
Gressingham duck, are house specialities, while salsas and flavoured
oils are frequent treatments for seafood and meat. A special deal at
lunch or dinner is two courses including coffee for £15.50, which
might include cauliflower and Stilton soup, or Caesar salad to start,
and chargrilled Mexican chicken salad with guacamole, or salmon
fish-cake with sorrel sauce, to follow.

The wine list is enormous, with prices and choices to satisfy most
pockets and palates. For those who might be intimidated by its sheer
scope, the list helpfully starts with a short house selection. There is a
good choice of champagnes, half-bottles and dessert wines, and the
list concludes with a page of ports, brandies, Russian vodkas and
single malts. Four wines are available by the glass. Wadworth IPA
and 6X are served from the wood. SAMPLE DISHES: seared tuna with
lentil salsa £6.50; whole steamed Cornish crab with basil and chilli
oil £13.50; lime and ginger crème brûlée £5.50.

Open *Tue to Sat 12 to 3, 6.30 to 12, Sun 12 to 4; closed 26 and 27 Dec; bar
food and restaurant 12.30 to 2.15, 7 to 10, Sun 12.30 to 3.30*
Details *No children under 7 at D   Car park   Wheelchair access   Garden
No-smoking area   Background music   No dogs   Amex, Delta, MasterCard,
Switch, Visa*

---

*Prices quoted in an entry are based on information supplied by the
pub, rounded up to the nearest 25 pence. These prices may have
changed since publication and are meant only as a guide.*

CHOLMONDELEY   Cheshire   map 5

▲ *Cholmondeley Arms* 🍇

Cholmondeley SY14 8BT   TEL: (01829) 720300
on A49, 5½m N of Whitchurch

The Cholmondeley (pronounced Chumley) Arms, which stands almost opposite the gates of Cholmondeley Castle and Gardens, was the village school until 1982 and was converted into a pub in 1988. The old-fashioned school atmosphere can still be felt inside the inn, which features lofty pitched ceilings, school memorabilia (including old school desks), huge windows and enormous radiators in three rooms. It is furnished with tasteful pictures and prints, antique pine, old settles and pews, and across the former playground the old Schoolmaster's House provides accommodation. This is a popular dining pub, with a printed main menu offering grills, sandwiches, ploughman's and light lunches, supplemented by a varied and daily-changing list of blackboard specials. These might include starters of hot crab pâté, or goats'-cheese soufflé with devilled tomato sauce, followed by Kashmiri lamb curry, peppered rib-eye steak, or 'very enjoyable' salmon fish-cakes with hollandaise. A good light bite at midday would be the 'school lunch' (hot baguette containing a large spicy sausage with barbecue sauce), or perhaps devilled lambs' kidneys on toast with salad. Children under eight have their own chicken nuggets or fish finger or sausage and chips menu. Puddings, ices and sorbets are homemade: among them could be Bakewell tart, praline ice-cream or Grand Marnier pancake. Beers to wash it all down with include Marston's Bitter and Pedigree, Greene King Abbot Ale and Boddingtons as well as a guest. An extensive wine list contains representations from all the major producing countries, with seven wines available by the glass. SAMPLE DISHES: cold spinach roulade with a mushroom, cream and garlic filling £4.50; rabbit braised with wine, mustard and lemon thyme £8; hot baked syrup sponge with cream £4.

Open *11 to 3, 7 (6.30 Sat) to 11; closed 25 Dec; bar food 12 to 2.15, 7 (6.30 Sat) to 10*
Details *Children welcome   Car park   Wheelchair access (also WC)   Garden No music   Dogs welcome   MasterCard, Switch, Visa   Accommodation: 6 rooms, B&B £45 to £60*

CHURCHINFORD   Somerset   map 2

▲ *York Inn*

Honiton Road, Churchinford TA3 7RF   TEL: (01823) 601333
off B3170, 8m S of Taunton

'Well worth the detour for the range of interesting, home-cooked food, thoughtfully prepared by landlord Reg Ambrose,' wrote one enthusiastic reporter. On the outside, the white-painted pub is brightened with window boxes and hanging baskets, and potted trees stand either side of the front door. Inside, there is a good public bar area with darts, a pool table and simple furnishings, while the dining-room is complete with hop-strewn beams, rustic candle-topped tables and a warming wood-burning stove. Jugs and cups hang from the beams. The bar snacks menu and dining-room menu, both on blackboards, change frequently and there are daily specials of fish and game in season. From the bar snacks list you could choose sausages with onion gravy, mash and peas, or cod with chips and peas. For those wanting a full meal, the dining-room menu might open with smoked haddock and Welsh rarebit, or pan-fried mushrooms with grilled bacon, before moving on to glazed Gressingham duck breast with peppers and shallots, and 'tournedos' of pork with caramelised apple; finally, top it all off with cider cake with calvados sauce, or sticky toffee pudding. Choose your ale from either draught Bass or Otter Bitter. A short wine list is also short on information, but bottles are reasonably priced; four are available by the glass. SAMPLE DISHES: smoked chicken breast with Dijon vinai-grette £4.50; John Dory fillets with fried leeks and mushrooms £11.50; lemon and stem ginger roulade £3.25.

Open *Tue to Sun 12 to 3, all week 6 to 11 (10.30 Sun); bar food 12 to 1.45 (2 Sun), 7 to 9.30*
Details *Children welcome in bar eating area   Car park   Wheelchair access Patio   No smoking in dining-room   Background music; jukebox   Dogs welcome   Amex, Delta, MasterCard, Visa   Accommodation: 3 rooms, B&B £30 to £56*

CHURCH KNOWLE   Dorset   map 2

New Inn

Church Knowle BH20 5NQ   TEL: (01929) 480357
off A351, 4m S of Wareham

They work hard at their themed evenings here – everything from a casino party night and Halloween and St Valentine's evenings to a thigh-slapping Bavarian buffet party complete with oompah band.

The setting is congenial: white-painted brick walls, heavily beamed ceilings, a vast inglenook in each of the bars and lots of bric-à-brac define the pub, which is located in a gorgeous village within spitting distance of Corfe Castle and Lulworth Cove. But the main hallmark of this early sixteenth-century, thatch-and-Purbeck-stone hostelry is that all the food is home-made. Fresh fish – whatever has been brought in from Poole or Brixham – and English lamb come in all sorts of guises, such as fisherman's pie or lamb rogan josh. Good plain vegetables set off the dishes well, particularly those that lean towards traditional English recipes, like rabbit or pheasant casseroles, New Forest game pie or Dorset jugged lamb. Blue Vinney cheese soup is a long-standing favourite, and salads are enhanced by a 'terrific' dressing. Puddings such as apple strudel, lemon brûlée and spotted dick tempt. Beer drinkers can choose between Wadworth 6X, Flowers Original and Morland Old Speckled Hen; Georges Duboeuf fills the wine bill, and quite a thing is made of the malts, bourbons and coffees. The pub has a skittle alley and its own camp site. SAMPLE DISHES: mushrooms with garlic dip £3; haddock fillet in beer batter £9; treacle tart £3.50.

Open *10 (11 winter) to 3, 6 (7 winter) to 11; closed Mon Jan to Mar; bar food and restaurant 12 to 2.15, 6 (7 winter) to 9.15*
Details *Children welcome in bar eating area   Car park   Wheelchair access (also WC)   Garden and patio   No-smoking area   Background and live music   Guide dogs only   Delta, MasterCard, Switch, Visa*

CLAVERING Essex

map 3

▲ *Cricketers* 🍇

Clavering CB11 4QT   TEL: (01799) 550442
on B1038, off M11, between Saffron Walden and Bishop's Stortford

This 'beautiful little pub' on the edge of Clavering is only ten minutes from the M11 and half an hour from Stansted Airport. It is a long, white building whose former front garden is now a pretty terrace with benches and tables, while a side garden provides further outside seating. Inside, the highly polished wooden tables, brass knick-knacks and glasses at the bar positively gleam, the log fire glows and the place exudes a contented, well-cared-for charm. The place is surprisingly bright with a modern, open-plan layout broken up by dark wooden beams that were once part of dividing walls. (The main part of the long bar has a very low ceiling – six-footers beware!)

The cooking has been described as exhibiting 'a traditional Sunday roast style with a slight continental influence'. A reporter noticed that regular diners tended to head straight to the specials board, though the bar menu also has plenty to tempt, such as Arbroath smokies baked in a thermidor sauce under a flaked oat and herb breadcrumb crust; and the continental influence shows in a warm tossed salad of duck confit and artichokes with a sesame oil dressing. Main courses may include suprême of chicken, stuffed with mushroom duxelle, wrapped in puff pastry and sliced on to a wholegrain mushroom sauce, or roast pheasant with chestnut and fresh sage accompanied by Brussels sprouts, cranberries and gravy. Fish features in a big way: grilled whole lemon sole, half a lobster and prawn salad with palm hearts, and much more. Sweets, including sorbets and ice-creams, are home-made and include at least one hot pudding every day. A 'Pudding Club' is held Wednesday nights, with the focus on the sticky old-fashioned variety served with custard. Service is said to be 'wonderful'. On handpump at this freehouse are Flowers Original and IPA, Adnams, Wadworth 6X and Wethereds, and a 50-strong wine list features a range of prices and features a half-dozen or so by the glass. A more expensive restaurant is open evenings and for Sunday lunch. SAMPLE DISHES: blue cheese and broccoli tartlet £4; halibut steak on a crab bisque £10.25; apricot and blackcurrant cream tart £3.

Open *10.30 to 3, 6 to 11; closed 25 and 26 Dec; bar food 12 to 2, 7 to 10; restaurant Sun L 12 to 2, Mon to Sat D 7 to 10*
Details *Children welcome in bar eating area   Car park   Wheelchair access Garden   No-smoking area   Background music   No dogs   Amex, MasterCard, Switch, Visa   Accommodation: 6 rooms, B&B £60 to £80*

CLEY NEXT THE SEA   Norfolk   map 6

▲ *George & Dragon Hotel*

Cley next the Sea NR25 7RN
TEL: (01263) 740652
on A149 coast road, in centre of village

Watchers of marine bird life who enjoy a diet similar to that of their quarry will find this pub is made for them. Nine years in the building, this imposing Edwardian-style inn was completed in 1897 on the site of the original structure, and enjoys an enviable position in the village overlooking an unspoilt stretch of salt marsh, containing a wealth of exhilarating walks. Long popular as a base for naturalists, it is but a stone's throw from some of the most famous wildlife reserves on the north Norfolk coast. A homely main bar and adjoining dining area are adorned with simple furnishings, wildlife prints and various memorabilia relating to the Norfolk Naturalist Trust, which was founded in the pub by Dr Long in 1926 – the first such trust of its kind. Pride of place goes to the brass church lectern in the main bar on which rests the 'bird bible', a record of sightings of unusual birds, many of which have been spied from the pub's own hide.

Local produce, especially fish, features prominently on the menu. Cider-pickled herring and oak-smoked salmon come from the nearby smokehouse. Local crab will be stuffed into local mushrooms and then deep-fried. A fairly standard printed menu, strong on fish and salads, is topped up by a specials board that is certainly the better bet, and might offer you herring roes on toast, samphire in season, or seafood and melon salad with ginger and lime dressing. Main dishes might include jugged hare, or pan-fried slip soles or dabs. There is usually a curry on the board, as well as vegetarian options. Some rarely sighted specimens of the pudding family come in the shape of marmalade sponge with citrus sauce, or pear and cinnamon upside-down sponge. Beers fly in from Greene King at Bury St Edmunds, and the wine list has a number of migratory New World bottles under a 'for the more adventurous' heading. SAMPLE DISHES: country pâté £3; boned lemon sole fillet with crabmeat £7.50; strawberry and pear filo tart £2.50.

Open *11 to 3 (11.30 to 2.30 winter), 6 to 11 (7 to 10.30 winter), Sun 12 to 2, 7 to 10.30; closed 25 Dec eve; bar food 12 to 2, 7 to 8.45, Sun 12 to 1.45 (2 for cold food), 7 to 8.30*

Details *Children welcome in dining-room   Car park   Wheelchair access (also female WC)   Garden   No smoking in dining-room   Background music   Dogs welcome   No cards   Accommodation: 8 rooms, B&B £35 to £68*

CLIFFE   Kent   **map 3**

Black Bull 🍺

186 Church Street, Cliffe ME3 7QD
TEL: (01634) 220893
off B2000, 5m N of Rochester

FAR EASTERN

Cliffe is a small village with attractive weatherboarded properties, a fair number of pubs, and historical associations with Roman times and Dickens. It is set on marshy Hoo Peninsula, where bird-watchers and walkers will have plenty to keep them occupied. The Black Bull is a solid, black-and-white-painted red-brick building, with high ceilings and a central fireplace; downstairs is the Tapestries restaurant. Oriental food is what brings the customers to Michael and Sok Pek Berry's pub in this bleakish corner of Kent. He looks after front-of-house and the beer cellar, while she runs the kitchen, delivering a popular array of bar food along the lines of satay, spare ribs, king prawn sambal, chilli chicken, sweet-and-sour pork, nasi goreng, hokkein mee, and kofta curry (lamb meatballs in a spicy yoghurt sauce). There's even roti canai (Malaysian bread) to go with the curries if you would prefer that to rice. For the traditionally minded, there are ploughman's, salads, and scampi and chips. Finish off with jackfruit ice-cream or mango sorbet. Tapestries restaurant offers a number of set meals (for a minimum of two to four people), and a full *carte* with such things as crispy aromatic duck and 'three-taste salmon' with chilli sauce. Popular on Sunday in the restaurant is the 'Curry Tiffin' buffet: 20 or so hot and cold items for £10 a head (children half-price) for all you can eat. Oriental beers like Five Star State, Tsingtao, Tiger and Singha are available, and for those who prefer real ale there is plenty to choose from, including Morland Old Speckled Hen, Young's Special, Wadworth 6X, Marston's Pedigree, and Charles Wells Bombardier. The wine list features 27 bottles from round the world, including one from China, as well as saké. SAMPLE DISHES: spring rolls £4; boneless chicken cooked in a spicy sauce with stir-fried vegetables £6.25; Malaysian pancake with a coconut filling served with coconut ice-cream £3.

Open *12 to 2.30, 7 to 11; closed 25 Dec eve and 1 Jan; bar food and restaurant all week L 12 to 2, Tue to Sat D 7 to 10*
Details *Children welcome   Car park   Wheelchair access (also WC)   Patio No smoking in restaurant   Occasional live music; jukebox   Dogs welcome MasterCard, Visa*

CLIFTON HAMPDEN   Oxfordshire   map 2

▲ *Plough Inn* 🍇

Abingdon Road, Clifton Hampden OX14 3EG
TEL: (01865) 407811
S of A415 Clifton Hampden to Dorchester road

SETTING

This charming thatched and timber-framed sixteenth-century build-ing is only a short walk from the River Thames. There is an attrac-tive rear garden, a side patio and terrace for sunny days, while inside is a cosy main bar with deep-red painted walls and open fires at each end and two separate dining-rooms. This is definitely a food pub, but you are welcome to drop in for just a drink. Note also that the Plough is no-smoking throughout – and popular for it. Turkish proprietor Yuksel Bektas has stamped his own personality firmly on the place – expect to find him dressed in tail coat and exuding unstinting enthusiasm. Orders are taken by Yuksel and his wife at the bar. Blackboards list a short selection of sandwiches and specials – lamb kebab with rice and salad, perhaps, or smoked chicken stir-fry – while the printed menu offers a mixture of light, modern dishes and more traditional options. Some choices may be taken as either starters or main courses, such as crispy duck salad with a honey and grain mustard dressing, or tomato and mozzarella salad. Full main courses take in gâteau of roast provençale vegetables with tomato and basil sauce, or seafood pasta in a lemon, basil and mushroom sauce. As well as sticky toffee pudding and crème brulée, there may be more unusual desserts such as poached pear, iced chocolate parfait and Eton pudding – layers of summer fruits with meringue, crème anglaise, raspberry purée and vodka. A rather ordinary beer selection consists of just John Smith's, Courage Best and Directors, but an interesting wine list is moderately priced and, of course, the Turkish coffee is rather good. SAMPLE DISHES: trio of melons £5; chicken, leek and fennel pie £7; chocolate, prune and frangipane tart £3.50.

Open *11 to 11; bar food and restaurant 11 to 11*
Details *Children welcome   Car park   Wheelchair access (also WC)   Garden and patio   No smoking   No music   Guide dogs only   MasterCard, Switch, Visa   Accommodation: 12 rooms, B&B £55 to £75*

COLDHARBOUR   Surrey   map 3

▲ *Plough Inn* 🍺

Coldharbour RH5 6HD   TEL: (01306) 711793
4m S of Dorking, signposted Leith Hill and Coldharbour

Just below the top of Leith Hill, this whitewashed pub is reputed to be the highest in south-east England. It is situated in a narrow road, with a few tables and umbrellas outside, plus a magnificent new pub sign appropriately illustrating ploughing. Family run, this is a beer pub par excellence, with its own microbrewery offering Tally Whacker, a strong dark ale, and a fruity, full-flavoured bitter, 'Crooked Furrow' – the latter even converted a previously non-beer-drinking female reporter. Up to seven guest ales are also available, plus Biddenden farm cider and Gales country fruit wines; the full, 20-bottle wine list offers seven by the glass. The main bar has wooden tables for eating, while the separate red-carpeted dining area at a lower level has white cloths, and an enormous log fire in winter; a third area at the back has a pool table. In the pretty rear garden, with its pleasant countryside views, you will find a lily pond, and wooden benches and tables for summer eating. Inside, separate blackboards offer pub staples, main courses and puddings respectively. Ploughman's, filled baguettes and jacket potatoes are typical bar snacks. Starters might be prawn salad, or garlic mushrooms in a warm filo pastry basket, while main courses take in crispy duck breast with zesty orange sauce or toad-in-the-hole. Speciality fish dishes include chargrilled swordfish steak in Sicilian marinade and the pub's own version of fish pie, containing smoked haddock, tuna and cheese. For dessert try Sussex Duck Pond pudding (steamed lemon and apple) or real banoffi pie. SAMPLE DISHES: chicken-liver, smoked bacon and cognac pâté with wholemeal toast £3.50; pan-fried chicken breast with garlic and herbs £7.50; pavlova with whipped double cream and red fruits £3.

Open *11.30 to 3, 6 to 11, Sat and Sun 11.30 to 11; closed eves 25 and 26 Dec; bar food and restaurant 12 to 2.30, 7.30 to 9.30*
Details *Children welcome   Garden and patio   No smoking in restaurant Occasional background music   Dogs welcome on a lead   Delta, MasterCard, Visa, Switch   Accommodation: 1 room, B&B £55*

COLEFORD   Devon   map 1

▲ *New Inn* ❦

Coleford EX17 5BZ   TEL: (01363) 84242
off A377 Exeter to Barnstaple road, 4m W of Crediton

Local produce is just one of the star features at this white-painted rendered cob and thatched freehouse whose walls have seen more than 700 years of history. Other stars are the ales and the wines. Five beers are on handpump – 'regulars' such as Otter Ale, Badger Bitter and Wadworth 6X (although these may change from time to time), plus a more frequently changing guest beer – and wines are finely chosen by Christopher Piper Wines of Ottery St Mary, nicely vari-ous, fairly priced and helpfully described. One imagines that Captain the pub's parrot is pretty aware of his star quality too. The food is freshly prepared from local ingredients: the cheeses for the plough-man's are all from Devon, so are the clotted cream and the ice-cream, the eggs are free range, and the locally produced sausages are free from additives. Best of all is the fish, which comes straight off the boats at Brixham and is then conjured up into a creamy fish pie or a fillet of brill with a cream, lemon and butter sauce or a seafood platter. Roasted vegetables on couscous with a yoghurt and corian-der dressing, and wild mushroom, croûton and cashew-nut salad with garlic potato cake, will undoubtedly have a wide appeal too. Apple pie and treacle tart are crowned with clotted cream, and this is a pub that can rustle up a decent steamed pudding. Beams, a log fire, brass and copper, chintz, old plates and tankards provide the setting for all this indulgence, or you can sit at benches by the stream. SAMPLE DISHES: Dartmouth smoked trout with apple and mint jelly £5; lamb in sweet cinnamon sauce £7; ginger steamed pudding £4.

Open *12 to 2.30, 6 to 11, Sun 12 to 2.30, 7 to 10.30; closed 25 and 26 Dec; bar food and restaurant 12 to 2, 7 to 10*
Details *Children welcome   Car park   Wheelchair access (also WC)   Garden No smoking in restaurant   Background music   No dogs in restaurant   No cards   Accommodation: 5 rooms, B&B £46 to £85*

COLESHILL   Buckinghamshire   map 3

▲ *Red Lion*

Village Road, Coleshill HP7 0LN   TEL: (01494) 727020
off A355 Amersham to Beaconsfield road

No tarting up or 'theming' has been visited on this timber-framed
'time warp village pub', where the things that matter are conversation about village events, darts (men's league on Monday, women's
on Tuesday), quizzes and crib. Sixty years' worth of pub team photos
adorn walls left to yellow, and a fire burns in the brick fireplace in
winter. Tables are few and you may end up with one under the dartboard; outside you can sit under parasols gazing at the village pond.
The 'simple, homely and good-value' menu likewise lacks any
pretension. If you do not fancy a jacket potato, salad, sandwich or
toasted sandwich, the place to look is the blackboard. The menu
really does change daily: egg mayonnaise, leek and cauliflower soup,
lamb's liver and bacon, cold poached salmon and salad – you get the
drift. Seasonality plays a part, so do not expect braised pheasant in
summer or strawberry flan in winter. Greene King IPA and Tetley
are the two resident beers, joined in rotation by London Pride,
Rebellion Smugglers and Morrell's Varsity. Wines are very simple,
and they go in for whisky in quite a way here. SAMPLE DISHES: leek
and cauliflower soup £2.25; baked ham with parsley sauce £7.25;
plum crumble cake £2.50.

Open *Mon to Fri 11 to 3, 5.30 to 11, Sat 11 to 11, Sun 12 to 4, 7 to 10.30;
bar food 12 to 2.15, 7 to 9*
Details *Children welcome   Car park   Wheelchair access   Garden   No music
Dogs welcome on a lead   No cards   Accommodation: 2 rooms, B&B £25 to
£35*

COLNE BRIDGE   West Yorkshire   map 8

Royal and Ancient

19 Dalton Bank Road, Colne Bridge HD5 0RE
TEL: (01484) 425461
on B6118, 2m SE of M62 junction 25

Under its jumbled multi-pitched slate roof, the pub resembles an
overgrown gate house. It takes its name from the famous golf course,
and a golfing theme pervades the bar, while the restaurant goes
under the name of Mr Skeffington, inspired by the 1944 movie star-
ring Claude Raines and Bette Davis – clearly a favourite of chef
Kenny Robertson. Mr Skeffington is done out in movie memorabilia,

while the bar is full of warm colours from dark beams and bare stone walls. The informal bar menu features freshly baked baguettes with a range of fillings and is supplemented by a blackboard of daily specials, perhaps venison and duck casserole or mushroom Stroganov. The à la carte menu on offer in the restaurant and all day in the 'bistro' area of the bar is shortish, with competently made dishes such as roulade of salmon and plaice on a bed of peppered spinach, or apricot and candied-fruit stuffed pork loin. The pub has no accommodation, but nevertheless offers extensive breakfasts. The beer selection is less exciting than in previous years, with standards like Tetley Bitter, Marston's Pedigree and Timothy Taylor Landlord. The licensees write that the wine list centres on the New World, with all wines available by the glass, although we were not able to have a look at the wine list before going to press. SAMPLE DISHES: pork and chicken terrine with seared capsicums and smoked bacon £4.75; pan-fried duck breast with sweet cherry and wine sauce £11.75; chocolate and banana trifle £3.

Open *11 to 11, Sun 12 to 10.30; bar food 11 to 11, Sun 12 to 10.30, restaurant Mon to Sat eve only 6 to 9 (9.30 Sat), Sun 12 to 4*
Details *No children   Car park   Wheelchair access   Garden and patio   No smoking in restaurant   Background music   No dogs in restaurant   Delta, MasterCard, Switch, Visa*

COLN ST ALDWYNS   **Gloucestershire**   map 2

▲ *New Inn* 🍺 🍇

Coln St Aldwyns GL7 5AN   TEL: (01285) 750651
off B4425, Cirencester to Burford road, 2m SW of Bibury

Coln St Aldwyns is an old stone-cottage village in commuter land, and the inn is made of the same carefully kept stone as every other building in the village, although you would be hard pushed to notice since it is engulfed in ivy. The exterior is immaculate, with trimmed borders, hanging baskets, and flowers in pots and tubs. The New Inn is, in fact, very old and dates from the Elizabethan era. Inside, hops are strung along one edge of the ceiling, and the seating is a combination of old wooden chairs, old benches and a church pew. The pub is very popular with well-heeled country clientele, who seem to appreciate the mix of the traditional and fashionable in dishes such as Welsh rarebit with mixed leaves and basil pesto, chicken-liver and mushroom pâté served with toasted brioche, or grilled leg of lamb steak with tabbouleh. For one reporter, grilled lambs' liver and bacon with creamed potatoes, white wine and thyme jus would 'take some beating', and fish-lovers have fair choice: perhaps salmon fish-cakes with mixed leaves and chive velouté, or more straightforward fish and chips. A separate menu is available for vegetarians. Sweets might take in sticky toffee pudding with butterscotch sauce, or when in season summer pudding with clotted cream. A good selection of ales include Hook Norton, Wadworth 6X, Butcombe and Wychwood Shires, while a short, one-page wine list is on offer, taken from a fuller list, which can be viewed and ordered from if requested. Eight wines are served by the glass. SAMPLE DISHES: gravad lax with honey and mustard dressing £5.25; smoked haddock risotto with prawns, curry and garden herbs £9.25; fresh poached peach with red berry sorbet £4.25.

Open *summer 11 to 11, Sun 12 to 10.30, winter 11 to 2.30, 5.30 to 11, Sun 12 to 10.30; closed 1 Jan; bar food and restaurant 12 to 2 (2.30 Sun), 7 to 9 (9.30 Fri and Sat)*
Details *Children welcome in bar eating area   Car park   Wheelchair access (also WC)   Patio   No smoking in restaurant   Dogs welcome on a lead in bar only   Amex, Delta, MasterCard, Visa, Switch   Accommodation: 14 rooms, B&B £65 to £110*

COLSTON BASSETT   Nottinghamshire   map 5

Martins Arms ✿ 🍺

School Lane, Colston Bassett NG12 3FD   TEL: (01949) 81361
off A46 Leicester to Newark road, 4m S of Bingham

This splendid Jacobean pub, dating from 1690, was formerly the squire's dwelling. It is now a Grade II listed building, set in a peaceful conservation area in the Vale of Belvoir. Customers can play croquet in the sizeable garden or sit under parasols at outdoor tables. The charming interior has a country-house feel with tasteful window drapes, scatter cushions on a large sofa and settles, two warming winter log fires and hunting prints on the walls. There is also an equally attractive and well-decorated restaurant furnished with antiques and sporting its own lounge area.

The printed bar menu offers speciality sandwiches, warm salads and upmarket ploughman's as well as an adventurous selection of main dishes, which may turn out to be simpler on the plate than in their description. A reporter's 'firm, well-made' ham hock and oyster mushroom terrine was complemented by a 'delicious' home-made pear chutney and toasted brioche, while warm salad of bacon and poached eggs with vinaigrette dressing has been described as 'delicious and simple'. Dishes are constructed with care and attention, as shown in sliced loin of venison on puréed celeriac and red wine and raspberry sauce, or rabbit cooked with salsify and fruit Madeira sauce. The menu is not cheap, but dishes certainly are original. Desserts might include glazed lemon rice-pudding with orange and almond biscuits, or pear and almond tart with clotted cream. Ale lovers are tantalised with a wide selection that takes in Marston's Best and Pedigree, Bass, Greene King Abbot Ale, Morland Old Speckled Hen, Black Sheep Bitter, Batemans XXXB, Timothy Taylor Landlord, Fuller's London Pride and Vaux Waggledance. In addition to a selection of brandies and malts, Lay and Wheeler supply a wine list that offers a fair range of choice and prices, and eight half-bottles. SAMPLE DISHES: smoked salmon, rocket salad and ratatouille chutney £7; braised shoulder of lamb, lemon and thyme on pomme purée £12; dark chocolate tart with fruit purée £4.50.

Open *12 to 3, 6 to 11, Sun 7 to 10.30; bar food 12 to 2, 6 to 10; restaurant 12 to 1.45, 7 to 9*
Details *No children under 14 in bar; children welcome in family room and dining-room   Car park   Wheelchair access (also WC)   Garden   No dogs MasterCard, Switch, Visa*

COMBE HAY   Bath & N.E. Somerset   map 2

▲ *Wheatsheaf*

Combe Hay BA2 7EG   TEL: (01225) 833504
off A367, 3m S of Bath

VIEWS

The enjoyment of wholesome English food while taking in stunning views of English woods and fields is what brings in the summer crowds to this rather out-of-the-way location, high above a fold in the landscape. The bar has been described as a bit 'dark', although the restaurant area is quite cheerful; another option, weather permitting, is outdoor eating. A large range of dishes is chalked up on the blackboard and reporters have been pleasantly surprised by dishes that were much better than their descriptions suggested. Bar meals are of the ploughman's and lasagne variety, while the à la carte menu offers sound English fare such as breast of pheasant stuffed with cranberry, apricot and rosemary in calvados sauce, and fruit crumble and custard. Courage Best, Morland Old Speckled Hen and Butcombe Bitter are served in excellent condition, and there is an extensive range of malt whiskies. Around six wines are available by the glass. SAMPLE DISHES: smoked chicken and ham terrine £5.25; sauté guinea-fowl and ginger sausages and pork and leek sausages with grain mustard £7.50; apple pie £3.

Open *11 to 2.30, 6 to 10.30 (11 Sat), Sun 12 to 2.30, 7 to 10.30; bar food and restaurant 12 to 2, 6.30 to 9.30*
Details *Children welcome (not in B&B accommodation)   Car park   Garden and patio   No music   Dogs welcome on a lead   Delta, MasterCard, Switch, Visa   Accommodation: 3 rooms, B&B £45 to £75*

COMPTON   **Surrey**   **map 3**

▲ *Harrow Inn*

The Street, Compton GU3 1EG   TEL: (01483) 810379
on B3000, signposted Compton, off A3

This red-brick, tile-hung pub in the centre of the village is a popular
venue for a mixed bunch of regulars and travellers stopping off the A3
for a bite to eat. A series of small rooms are done out in traditional
style – bright patterned carpet, cream walls, dark woodwork and low
ceilings – and every part is used for eating. There is a bar snacks menu,
offering plenty of sandwiches and filled baked potatoes, as well as
deep-fried whitebait, or ham, egg and chips, plus an à la carte featuring fish – brill, salmon and cod roulade with creamy watercress sauce,
for example – steaks, and vegetarian options, supplemented by blackboard specials. Sunday lunch sees a roast or two added. Exotic fruit
pavlova and chocolate and Amaretto mousse stand out on the
puddings menu. The drinks list is short and reliable: Harveys Sussex
Best, and Greene King IPA and Abbot Ale are the draught beers; house
wines are mostly Spanish. SAMPLE DISHES: salmon and dill fish-cakes
£5.75; lamb steak with blueberry and rosemary jus £11.75; fresh
lemon tart with lemon sorbet and cream £3.75.

Open *11 to 11, Sun 12 to 4; bar food 12 to 2.30, 6 to 10; restaurant Mon to
Sat 6 to 10*
Details *Children welcome   Car park   Wheelchair access (also WC)   Garden
No music   No dogs in restaurant   Amex, Delta, MasterCard, Switch, Visa
Accommodation: 5 rooms, room only £37.50 to £42.50*

COMPTON MARTIN   Bath & N.E. Somerset   **map 2**

Ring O'Bells

Main Street, Compton Martin BS40 6JE   TEL: (01761) 221284
on A368, between Weston-super-Mare and Bath

Easy to spot in the village centre, this rambling whitewashed pub
handily placed halfway between Bath and the Somerset coast enjoys
rear views of the Mendip Hills. It has spacious facilities, including a
large garden with swings and climbing frames. For guests with
minors in tow, the Ring O'Bells provides plenty of child-oriented
games and amusements in a large family room, though this is some
way from the cosier stone-flagged bar at the front where food is
served. Menus are geared towards family favourites, featuring
starters such as garlic mushrooms or grills and pasta dishes for main
courses, and plenty of sandwiches, omelettes and salads on the side,

mostly accompanied by chips. Daily specials incorporate local produce (Chew Valley trout, perhaps, or Mendip lamb) and occasional exotica like wild boar steaks. Children are predictably thought of too – a Kiddie's Choice menu paddles through the shallows of chicken nuggets, beefburgers and beans on toast, with a chocolate bar bribe for the ones who clear their plates, and crayons on request. Older patrons may prefer to concentrate on Butcombe Bitter, or some of the other real ales stocked – Adnams, London Pride, Otter Ale, for example. Half a dozen wines by the glass appear on a short, simple list. SAMPLE DISHES: deep-fried Brie £3.25; Butcombe beef £5; lemon cream pie £2.25.

Open *11.30 to 3, 6.30 to 11, Sun 12 to 3, 7 to 10.30; bar food and restaurant 11.30 to 2, 6.30 to 9.30 (10 Fri and Sat), Sun 12 to 2, 7 to 9.30* **Details** *Children welcome in family room   Car park   Wheelchair access (also WC)   Garden   No smoking in family room   No music   Dogs welcome on a lead in bar only   Amex, Delta, MasterCard, Switch, Visa*

CONISTON   Cumbria

map 8

▲ *Black Bull* 🍺   NEW ENTRY

Yewdale Road, Coniston LA21 8DU
TEL: (015394) 41335/41668
off A593, 6m SW of Ambleside

BREW PUB

The Bradleys have run the Black Bull at the foot of the 'Old Man' mountain (the Old Man's toe is in the resident's lounge) since 1977 and son Ian, who runs the pub's award-winning micro-brewery, is looking to step into his dad's shoes. The L-shaped bar dates back to the time of the Spanish Armada, and the beams in the bars are from wrecked Spanish galleons. Numerous prints of Sir Donald Campbell, who made Coniston Water famous through his attempts at water speed records, hang on the walls; the area at the back of the pub is furnished in a more rustic style. A separate restaurant serves traditional French cuisine – moules marinière or entrecôte chasseur – but locals and walkers prefer the ambience in the bar, and the simple bar menu, which offers the usual staples plus fisherman's platter, half a roast chicken or duck, and locally smoked trout. The Black Bull's most recent claim to fame is its beers. Coniston Brewery was purpose-built at the rear of the pub, and Ian brews deceptively simple beers which are long on flavour and aroma. The first brew, Bluebird Bitter, was made on a Friday the 13th in 1995, but despite this inauspicious date won the Champion Beer of Britain award at the 1998 Great British Beer Festival. Other beers made in the brewery are a darker Old Man and a mid-range beer, Opium, named after Thomas De Quincey – the opium eater – who, like Ruskin, Turner

and Coleridge, all stayed at the inn. SAMPLE DISHES: egg mayonnaise
£3; Cumberland sausage platter £6; Lakeland ice-cream £2.50.

Open *11 to 11, Sun 12 to 10.30; closed 25 Dec; bar food 12 to 9 (9.30
weekends); restaurant all week summer D only 6 to 9 (9.30 weekends),
weekends only in winter; booking essential*
Details *Children welcome in bar eating area   Car park   Wheelchair access
(also WC)   Garden and patio   No-smoking area   No music   No dogs in
restaurant   Delta, MasterCard, Switch, Visa   Accommodation: 15 rooms,
B&B £33 to £40*

C O N S T A N T I N E   Cornwall   map 1

▲ *Trengilly Wartha* 🍺 🍇

Nancenoy, Constantine TR11 5RP   TEL: (01326) 340332
off A394 Falmouth to Helston road, signposted Constantine

As far as pubs are concerned, 'hard to find' is usually a euphemism
for 'good', and so it is with the Trengilly Wartha. One reporter had
been there before and still had to concentrate hard to find it. It may
be best to ask one of the friendly locals for help. The name means
'place above the trees', which is an apt description of this largish pub
halfway up the side of a wooded valley. Inside, décor and atmosphere are that of a typical Cornish local, while the restaurant has a
more upmarket feel. There are separate bar and restaurant menus,
and the style of cooking for both is fun and inventive. Bar dishes
display a distinctly modern, light touch – goats' cheese is a hardy
perennial on countless starters menus but goats'-cheese strudel makes
it all seem very new, and lobster is not usually served in ravioli with
fish mousse in a ginger broth. You can start with a frittura of mixed
fresh fish, or gambas con gabardina (king prawns in saffron beer
batter). Some oriental influences surface in, for example, marinated
beef fillet with stir-fried vegetables and Basmati rice. Fish dishes are
subject to availability but may include cod on boulangère potatoes,

or lemon sole with fries and garnish. Greengages are not found in every kitchen and with almonds make a tasty tart, while crème brûlée gets an upbeat twist with saffron and lime. Service is friendly and professional. Real ales are served directly from the cask. The one regular beer, Sharp's Cornish Coaster, may be joined by guests from local breweries. The pub also operates as a vintner's. Nigel Logan's wine list starts with a brief blurb explaining what the company has been up to for the last year. Their vintners list is impeccable and includes many half-bottles and 15 to 20 by the glass. SAMPLE DISHES: sugared cashew-nuts £1.50; gai pad mamuang (Thai chicken in tomato sauce) £6.25; mango, apricot and raspberry sorbet terrine £3.

Open *11 to 3, 6.30 to 11, Sun 7 to 10.30; bar food 12 to 2.15 (2 Sun), 6 to 9.30, restaurant all week, D only 7.30 to 9.30; no food 25 Dec*
Details *Children welcome   Car park   Garden   No smoking in conservatory No music   Dogs welcome   Amex, Delta, Diners, MasterCard, Switch, Visa Accommodation: 8 rooms, B&B £39 to £80*

COOKHAM DEAN   Berkshire   **map 3**

▲ *Inn on the Green* ❦
The Old Cricket Common, Cookham Dean SL6 9NZ
TEL: (01628) 482638
off A404, S of M40 junction 4

Tucked away in woody heights within a wide turn in the Thames, this mock-Tudor pub is set back from a large village green. It is characterful enough from the outside, but even more so within where the interior offers varied dining in a number of settings. Refurbishment of the kitchen in spring 1999 may result in some changes, but currently the bar menu – available only at lunch-time for reasons of space, though light meals such as starters can be served in the bar in the evenings – offers a good, albeit pricey, modern English repertoire. Starters feature such dishes as potato and goats' cheese gratin, Thai crab parcels, or terrine of wild boar, while main courses might take in steamed lobster, charged at market price, or pot roast quail. Vegetarians could settle for Roquefort and apple strudel, and dessert lovers might indulge themselves with home-made honey and whisky ice-cream in a biscuit cup before tucking into the cheeseboard. Brakspear and Fuller's London Pride comprise the regular ales, and guests are likely to be on the lines of Bishop's Tipple, or perhaps Red October from Rebellion Brewery. There are about 20 malts on offer plus a range of unusual digestifs, as well as a wine list which is strong on claret, with house wines from South Africa and 12 wines by the glass. SAMPLE DISHES: smoked salmon blinis £8; rack of lamb £17; white chocolate cheesecake £4.50.

Open *12 to 3, 5.30 to 11, Sun 7 to 10.30; closed 25 Dec and 1 Jan eves; bar food Mon to Sat L only 12 to 2.30; restaurant 12 to 2.30, 7.30 to 10*
Details *Children welcome in bar eating area   Car park   Wheelchair access Garden and patio   No music   Dogs in bar only   Amex, Delta, MasterCard, Switch, Visa   Accommodation: 8 rooms, B&B £50 to £95*

Jolly Farmer

Church Road, Cookham Dean SL6 9PD   TEL: (01628) 482905
off A404, S of M40 junction 4

One reporter described the Jolly Farmer as a 'thriving village local', and it should be as it is owned by the village, which put together a consortium to buy it in the late '80s. The eighteenth-century brick pub enjoys a traditional position opposite the parish church in this sprawling village high on a wooded hill above the Thames Valley. The small, simply furnished bars with their homely décor have a chatty, often very busy atmosphere and open fires. Menus are chalked on a board, where at lunch-time you might find potato skins and dips, steak and kidney pie, or ham, eggs and chips, while in the evening more substantial offerings are added, along the lines of half a roast duck with orange and ginger sauce, fillet steak, or pan-fried swordfish with crispy seaweed and lemon butter. Puddings tend towards the traditional – treacle tart perhaps. Courage Best is the village's chosen regular ale, and two guests may come from major regionals, with perhaps the odd better-established independent such as Rebellion or Titanic thrown in for good measure. Three wines are available by the glass. SAMPLE DISHES: pan-fried sardines in herbs and garlic £4; chicken and mushroom Stroganov £7; banoffi pie £3.

Open *11.30 to 3, 5.30 (6 Sat) to 11, Sun 11.30 to 3, 7 to 10.30; bar food and restaurant 12 to 2, 7.30 to 9*
Details *Children welcome in dining-room   Car park   Wheelchair access Garden and patio   No smoking in dining-room until after main courses   No music   Well-behaved dogs welcome   Delta, MasterCard, Switch, Visa*

CORSCOMBE   Dorset   map 2

▲ *Fox Inn*

Corscombe DT2 0NS   TEL: (01935) 891330
off A356, 6m SE of Crewkerne

You could describe the Fox as a picture-postcard pub, not least because it does appear on picture postcards, which bear the legend 'no chips or microwaves'. Reached by winding country lanes, this very pretty thatched pub was built as a cottage in the 1600s on the old droving route to Yeovil, and was later a cider house. Out front, climbing roses hug the walls and at the rear picnic tables permit drinkers to while away the hours contemplating the idly flowing stream. Inside, it is equally charming, with bare stone floors, a huge inglenook, beams, blue and white gingham tablecloths, stuffed birds and a fox, and hunting prints. At the back is a vine and plant festooned conservatory with a long table and benches, ideal for parties.

Chef Will Longman came here from another fish pub, the Three Horseshoes, Powerstock (see entry) and brought his passion for seafood with him, producing dishes such as roast cod steak with anchovies, garlic and olive oil, or pan-fried scallops with parsley, garlic and more olive oil. The daily-changing blackboard menu might kick off with fish soup or wild mushroom risotto with Parmesan. Whole roasted red mullet with a piquant vinaigrette was described by a reporter as full of flavour, very simple and successful. Game comes from local shoots and the New Orleans smothered rabbit impressed one seasoned reporter who thought the Creole-style sauce 'lifted the tender meat to a higher plane'. Puddings include a range of old favourites – sticky toffee and bread-and-butter, for example. Exmoor Ale, Fuller's London Pride and Shepherd Neame Spitfire make a satisfying choice of beers, and there are also home-made elderflower cordial, sloe gin and damson vodka on offer. The wine list offers a respectable selection, including a number of half-bottles and eight fine wines. SAMPLE DISHES: grilled local goats'-cheese salad £4.50; fish pie with cod, brill and prawns £7.75; crème caramel £3.25.

Open *Mon to Fri 12 to 2.30, 7 to 11, Sat 12 to 4, 7 to 11, Sun 12 to 4, 7 to 10.30; bar food and restaurant 12 to 2, 7 to 9 (9.30 Fri and Sat)*
Details *Well-behaved children welcome   Car park   Wheelchair access Garden and patio   No-smoking in 1 dining-room   No music   No dogs Delta, MasterCard, Switch, Visa   Accommodation: 3 rooms, B&B £45 to £75*

The Guide is totally independent, accepts no free hospitality and carries no advertising.

CORTON   Wiltshire   map 2

▲ *Dove Inn* 🍺 🍇   NEW ENTRY

Corton BA12 0SZ   TEL: (01985) 850109
off A36, 5m from Warminster

This brick and stone pub, dating from about 1850, is tucked away at the western end of a tranquil village near the River Wylye. It was known as the New Inn until 1969 when it was renamed the Dove after the dovecote on the front wall. A new extension was built in 1998-99, but the new owners have been careful to use authentic materials. The homely interior is simply furnished with attractive prints and has a welcoming atmosphere. Under its new stewardship the Dove is gaining a reputation as a good food pub. The cooking gives a modern treatment to traditional dishes. Avocado Patricia, for example, is hot avocado and prawns in a creamy mushroom sauce, and coarse country terrine comes with a spicy chilli and green-tomato chutney dressing. Other fashionable starters might be king prawns wrapped in filo pastry with a sweet chilli dip, or stir-fried baby scallops with ginger, spring onions and coriander. For a main course you might try red onion and pork sausages on a bed of bubble and squeak with a light cider gravy, or go East for Thai chicken curry with basmati rice and poppadums, or continental with smoked chicken, tomato and tarragon tagliatelle carbonara. Chocolate amaretti provides an up-to-date touch among the home-made treacle tart and cheesecake variety of desserts. The pub runs a 'visitors guest beer book', which in one two-month period managed to clock up 15 entries; ales on tap have included Buchanan's Best from Federation, and Black Magic Stout, Best and Yeoman 1767 from Oakhill. A 'fruit-driven' wine list contains lots of well-known names and offers seven by the glass. SAMPLE DISHES: deep-fried whitebait with a lemon mayonnaise £4; individual game casserole with cranberries, chestnuts, orange and a puff pastry lid £7.25; apple and pear crumble £3.50.

Open *Mon to Fri 12 to 3.30 (3 in winter), 6 to 11, Sat 12 to 4, 6 to 11, Sun 12 to 4, 7 to 10.30, closed eve 25 Dec; bar food and restaurant 12.15 to 2.30, 7 to 9.30 (9 Sun)*
Details *Children welcome   Car park   Wheelchair access (also WC)   Garden No smoking in dining-room   Background and live music   Well-behaved dogs welcome on a lead   MasterCard, Switch, Visa   Accommodation: 4 rooms, B&B £40 to £48*

The details under the text are taken from questionnaires that have been filled in by the pubs that feature in the book.

COTHERSTONE   Co Durham   map 10

▲ *Fox and Hounds*

Cotherstone DL12 9PF   TEL: (01833) 650241
on B6277, 3m NW of Barnard Castle

This 200-year-old whitewashed coaching-inn, which overlooks the village green, is convenient for Raby Castle, Barnard Castle, Rokeby Park and walking in Upper Teesdale. The heavily beamed interior is simply furnished, with welcoming log fires in both the bar and restaurant in winter. Cushioned banquettes, wooden furniture, and prints, local photographs and plates on the walls make for a comfortable ambience. Three *en suite* bedrooms have the use of their own first-floor lounge. Bar meals could be the 'Fox & Hounds brunch' (bacon, egg, sausage, black pudding, tomato and mushroom), soup, pâté or mussels, followed by gammon steak, salads or steak and kidney pie. More expensive dishes could be whole grilled Dover sole, roast half duckling or rack of Teesdale lamb, while a separate Italian menu offers minestrone, pasta and pizzas. As the *Guide* went to press, there were plans to open a separate Italian restaurant. Sunday lunch is a traditional roast. Desserts range from fruit salad to sponge puddings or knickerbocker glory. Beers come from the Black Sheep Brewery, and a list of 18 wines offers three by the glass; malt whiskies are also available. SAMPLE DISHES: bacon salad with garlic croûtons £5; chicken balti madras £7; banana split £3.

Open *11 to 3, 6 to 11; closed 25 Dec; bar food and restaurant 12 to 3, 6 to 9.30*
Details *Children welcome   Car park   Wheelchair access (also WC)   Patio No smoking in restaurant   Background music   No dogs in bedrooms   Amex, Delta, Diners, MasterCard, Visa, Switch   Accommodation: 3 rooms, B&B £38 to £60*

COTTERED   Hertfordshire   map 3

Bull

Cottered SG9 9QP   TEL: (01763) 281243
on A507, between Buntingford and Baldock

Above-average pub food, but with restaurant presentation, is served up at this Greene King pub, set in this pretty north Hertfordshire village. Inside are two bars and a tiny dining-room. Diners spill over into the lounge bar, while the public bar is the locals' drinking area. Staff are exceptionally helpful and friendly even when busy. The cooking is definitely pubby though food is presented restaurant-style on big white plates. Light snacks at lunch take in jacket potato or home-made soup. You can also choose from a range of main-course salads – Greek, stir-fried chicken or smoked salmon – or plough-man's. Hot dishes come from the chargrill, maybe a rack of smoked pork ribs, fillet or sirloin of beef, or garlic and herb chicken fillet. Alternatively try the local sausages or a pasta dish. In the evening the menu will be augmented by starters like smoked bacon and mush-room salad, or prawn salad, and the chargrill will turn out an extra roasted rack of lamb. Additionally, the specials board, which will be brought over to your table for perusal, might offer fried squid, feta salad or steak, Stilton and Guinness pie. Puddings are also listed on the specials board. Beers are, as you would expect, Greene King IPA and Abbott Ale, and a 20-strong wine list covers the basics and offers a range of prices to suit most pockets. SAMPLE DISHES: fried Brie £3.50; gammon steak and pineapple £7.50; bread-and-brandy pudding £3.

Open *12 to 2.30, 6.30 to 11, Sun 12 to 2.30, 7 to 10.30; bar food and restaurant 12 to 2, 6.45 to 9*
Details *No children under 7   Car park   Garden   Background music   No dogs   Delta, MasterCard, Visa*

COTTESMORE   Rutland   map 6

The Sun ♥ [NEW ENTRY]

Cottesmore LE15 7DH   TEL: (01572) 812321
on B668 between Oakham and Stretton (A1), 4m NE of Oakham

'A really good find and yet another serious dining pub in this upmar-ket part of the country,' concluded one enthusiastic reporter. This thatched, whitewashed, seventeenth-century pub, set back from the main street, is run by Sylvia and Frank Garbez, formerly of the Blue Ball, Braunston, and the Peacock Inn, Redmile (see entry). Inside, pastel-yellow rag-washed walls, flagged and wooden floors strewn with rugs, plus beams, open fires and woodburners throughout the comfortable and rambling series of rooms, combine to produce a civilised dining atmosphere. Food is Mediterranean-type dishes served in a brasserie style at reasonable prices, and it gets top marks for presentation. For lighter appetites there are sandwiches and 'quick meals', such as spicy salmon fish-cakes, or tagliatelle with wild mushrooms, palm hearts and spinach. Full meals could start with grilled scallops and sea bass with artichoke and 'sun-blushed' toma-toes, or warm Stilton soufflé on walnut salad, followed by half a roast pheasant flambéd with calvados and apples, or fillet steak topped with foie gras on fondant cabbage and Madeira jus. Finish with lime-infused crème brûlée with plum compote, or warm

Normandy apple pancake. This Everards pub offers Tiger supplemented by Adnams Best and Morland Old Speckled Hen, and nine wines are available by the glass. SAMPLE DISHES: crab ravioli with tomato, lemon and herb dressing £5; paupiette of saddle of rabbit with savoy cabbage, sweet pepper and basil £9.50; crème caramel £1.75.

Open *11 to 2.30, 6 to 11; bar food and restaurant 12 to 2, 6.30 to 10 (exc Sun eve)*
Details *Children welcome   Car park   Wheelchair access   Garden and patio No-smoking in 1 room   Background music   Delta, MasterCard, Switch, Visa*

COTTON   Suffolk   Map 6

Trowel & Hammer Inn   `NEW ENTRY`

Mill Road, Cotton IP14 4QL   TEL: (01449) 781234
6 miles N of Stowmarket, just off the B1113

Chicken-liver pâté and roast lamb will keep the more conservative of the regulars happy at this long, low, white-painted freehouse on the edge of the village, but the true nature of the menu is better summed up as traditional with a modern twist. Choosing may be hard: smoked duck breast with beetroot salsa or fish soup with rouille and croûtons to start? What about lamb fillet with Parmesan and a rich red gravy, kidneys and black pudding with a Dijon mustard sauce, or salmon in filo pastry with a lemon, lime and coriander sauce? Vegetables are carefully handled, including decent dauphinoise potatoes. A baker's dozen of blackboard puds tempts traditionalists and modernists alike with everything from apple and honey crumble to pancakes with red fruits and mascarpone cheese. The same menu applies throughout the pub but is served more formally in the comfortable yellow-washed, candlelit restaurant than in the dark-panelled traditional bar. You can also eat in the attractive garden. Guest beers such as Nethergate and Mauldons join the East Anglian regulars of Adnams Bitter and Greene King IPA and Abbot Ale, and there are some reasonable wines. And if vodka is your tipple, here is the place to come. SAMPLE DISHES: herring roes on toast £3.25; Cumberland sausage with bubble and squeak and onion gravy £6; coconut ice-cream with bananas £3.25.

Open *Mon to Fri 11.30 to 3, 6 to 11, Sat and Sun 12 to 11 (10.30 Sun); bar food 11.30 to 2, 6 to 10, Sun 12 to 2, 6 to 9.30*
Details *Children welcome in bar eating area   Car park   Wheelchair access (also WC)   Garden   Background and live music   Dogs welcome   Delta, MasterCard, Visa, Switch*

COXWOLD   North Yorkshire   **map 9**

▲ *Fauconberg Arms*

Main Street, Coxwold YO6 4AD   TEL: (01347) 868214

This old inn in an ancient village is well suited for visiting nearby historical sites. Coxwold is mentioned in the Domesday Book as Cucvalt and the inn itself was built some 500 years after the famous audit. It takes its name from the Fauconberg family, who were granted the village and estate by Henry VIII. A later Lord Fauconberg went on to marry Oliver Cromwell's daughter. As befits such stately patronage, the pub is of stately proportions. An extensive portalled frontage gives way to a fine old interior with a lounge bar with rugs on the stone floors, antique furniture and a splendid stone fireplace. At the rear is a public bar with TV and darts. The menu suggests confident cooking with some inventiveness going on behind the scenes, to offset the more traditional dishes. If the home-made soup does not appeal, try mousse of salmon and oak-smoked sea trout with dill mayonnaise and toast, or chicken liver and ham terrine. Again, if beefsteak and Guinness pie seems pedestrian, then asparagus and cashew-nut filo pastry plaits with port, red onion and honey glaze certainly will not. There is an afternoon tea menu with home-made scones and a high tea menu offering food like gammon steak with egg and pineapple. Puddings are available at all times – Grand Marnier white chocolate mousse appears regularly. Beers are John Smiths, Tetley and Theakston Black Bull, while the list of 20 wines covers the world and includes eight by the glass. Nearby places to visit include Thirsk races, Newburgh Priory, Shandy Hall (home of Lawrence Sterne), Byland and Rievaulx Abbeys, Ampleforth College and Abbey, and Castle Howard. SAMPLE DISHES: trio of puff pastry parcels filled with Red Leicester and chive pâté with red onion marmalade £3.50; chicken Barbados £6.50; butterscotch pudding £3.25.

Open *11 to 2.30, 6.30 to 11, Sun 12 to 2.30, 7 to 10.30; bar food and restaurant 12 to 1.45, 7 to 8.45 (no food Mon eve in winter)*
Details *Children welcome   Car park   Patio   Background music   No dogs MasterCard, Visa   Accommodation: 4 rooms, B&B £30 to £55*

CRANMORE   Somerset   map 2

Strode Arms

Cranmore BA4 4QJ   TEL: (01749) 880450
just S of A361, 4m E of Shepton Mallet

Unmistakably an old stone farmhouse inside and out, with chunky
doorways, exposed beams and squat windows, and simple farmhouse
furniture in keeping, this long, low pub opposite the village pond
goes in for fresh, simple food, good ales and friendly, prompt
service. Straightforward choices from the printed menu served in the
bar and the slightly more formal restaurant are boosted by blackboard specials and accompanied by vegetables or salad, a choice of
potatoes and even bubble and squeak sometimes. Much is made on
the premises, including that day's soup, shepherd's pie, faggots, meat
pies, and haddock and cod fish-cakes. Generous smoked trout and
chicken marinade on very fresh lettuce, and succulent wild boar
steak with apples made up one visitor's successful supper. If you are
a rice-pudding fan, this is the place to come; or home in on the apricot frangipane or apple strudel. Sunday lunch is a traditional roast
meal. Most people will look to the beers rather than the wines for
lubrication: Hook Norton, Flowers IPA, or that month's guest beer –
or Wilkins cider. SAMPLE DISHES: Swiss toast (Swiss cheese creamed
with white wine and grilled with Parma ham and mushrooms) £4.50;
cod and scallop pie £8.50; raspberry meringue and ice-cream £3.25.

Open *11.30 (12 Sun) to 2.30, 6.30 to 11; closed eve Sun Oct to end Mar; bar
food and restaurant 12 to 2, 7 to 9.30*
Details *Children welcome in dining-room   Car park   Wheelchair access (also
WC)   Garden and patio   No music   No dogs in restaurant   MasterCard, Visa*

CRAZIES HILL   Berkshire   map 3

Horns

Crazies Hill, nr Wargrave RG10 8LY   TEL: (01189) 401416
off A4 at Kiln Green, 3m N of Twyford

This attractive, whitewashed brick and timber cottage, nestling in a
small rural hamlet, was a hunting lodge in Tudor days, and a barn
was added some two hundred years ago. Sympathetic refurbishment
by owners Brakspear brewery earlier this decade has ensured that the
authentic character of the pub remains unspoilt. The relaxed atmosphere, without machines or music, is created throughout the three
small interconnecting bars, by the open fires, beams and sporting
prints, and the barn with its impressive vaulted ceiling, tiled floor

and farmhouse kitchen tables. Beers are Brakspear Bitter and Special with XXX Mild and Old Ale available seasonally. A snack menu, available only at lunch-time, offers baguettes, chilli, and Cumberland sausage with mash. Or be more adventurous and head for the blackboards, where you might find baked sea bass with a caper and saffron cream sauce, or roast partridge with peppercorn sauce. Alternatively, peruse the printed à la carte menu to find perhaps starters of warm bacon, avocado and goats'-cheese salad, or breaded butterfly prawns with garlic mayonnaise, followed by chicken breast with shallots, cherry tomatoes and wild mushroom sauce, or pancakes with oyster mushrooms in a creamy sage sauce. A 30-bin wine list includes several good vintages and a number of half-bottles; six house wines are available by the glass. The pub holds 'special evenings' such as curry nights every six weeks. SAMPLE DISHES: smoked salmon salad £5.95; rack of lamb with redcurrant and mint £11; caramelised lemon tart £3.75.

Open *11.30 to 2.30, 6 to 11, Sun 12 to 3, 7 to 10.30; closed 25 and 26 Dec, eve 1 Jan; bar food and restaurant all week L 12 to 1.45, Mon to Sat D 7 to 9.15*
Details *Children welcome L only   Car park   Wheelchair access (also WC) Garden   No music   Dogs by arrangement   Delta, MasterCard, Switch, Visa*

CROSLAND HILL   West Yorkshire   map 8

Sands House

Blackmoorfoot Road, Crosland Hill HD4 7AE
TEL: (01484) 654478
off A62, 2m SW of Huddersfield town centre

Huddersfield is a surprising place where satanic mills surrender abruptly to breathtaking vistas of open moorland. This pleasant building of local sandstone stands on the cusp, so to speak, of the urban zone, with views from the car park over the moors. The pub itself is just as eye-catching, displaying a magpie collection of old street furniture (telephone boxes, traffic lights etc.) in a children's play area outside, and an astonishing array of clocks inside. Décor is cosy and simple, with wooden tables and Windsor chairs in the three interconnected bar areas. One room functions as a drinkers' bar; the brasserie-style atmosphere in the adjoining dining-rooms is lively and bustling, and you may find groups and parties celebrating here. Daily menus are chalked on blackboards, often featuring hearty soups and sandwiches as well as vegetarian dishes and inventive creations with oriental touches (Bombay potatoes with peanut raita, or aubergine stuffed with Turkish tabbouleh, for example). Portions are generous, but if you've room, finish off with diet-busting sticky concoctions like chocolate squidgy cake or bread-and-butter pudding. Drinkers can enjoy an above-average range of well-priced, helpfully annotated wines as well as Theakston, Boddingtons and Courage real ales. Several house wines are available in half-litre carafes or by the glass. SAMPLE DISHES: chilli meatballs with tomato and garlic sauce £3.75; beef pepperpot with mash £6; raspberry and kiwi fruit roulade £2.75.

Open *11.30 to 11, Sun 12 to 10.30; bar food and restaurant 11.30 to 9.30*
Details *Children welcome in eating areas   Car park   Garden and patio*
Background music   No dogs   MasterCard, Switch, Visa

CROSTHWAITE   Cumbria   map 8

▲ *Punch Bowl Inn* ✸ ❦

Crosthwaite LA8 8HR   TEL: (015395) 68237
off A5074, 3m S of Windermere

This seventeenth-century inn is situated in the Lyth Valley, famous for its damsons, which are often found on the menu, and although Stephen Doherty has gone to take over the kitchen at his other pub, the Spread Eagle in Sawley (see entry), the Punch Bowl remains well above par. It is not really a place to drop in to for a quick pint, but most reporters agree that it is still a pub. Here, the food's the thing, with some imaginative touches in evidence. Pork terrine with pickle and home-made chutney comes wrapped in a sliver of bacon, while Jumbo prawns are presented in a circle on top of a nest of spinach and beneath a julienne of crispy threads of carrot, courgette and celery. On a plainer note, you will find that cod Florentine is a generous fillet with crisp skin in a well-balanced cheese sauce, and fillet steak comes pink under a crispy exterior. For afters, chocolate nemesis is a rich combination of chocolate, cream, milk and eggs baked in the oven and served with cinnamon ice-cream, while apple feuilleté comprises caramelised apples baked in filo pastry with almond and calvados cream, served with a vanilla sauce. Unlike many foodie pubs, the Punch Bowl does not neglect its beers, offering Theakston Best plus two guest ales; the wine list is a shortish selection of well-chosen vintages, covering a range of prices and including several half-bottles and dessert wine selections; nine wines available by the glass are listed on a blackboard. Service is cheerful and knowledgeable. SAMPLE DISHES: gravadlax with blinis £5; chicken schnitzel £7.25; Roux brothers' lemon tart £3.50.

Open *11 to 11, Sun 12 to 10.30; closed 25 Dec, eve 26 Dec, eve 1 Jan; bar food and restaurant 12 to 2, 6 to 9*
Details *Children welcome   Car park   Wheelchair access   Patio   No smoking in restaurant   No music   Dogs welcome in bar only   Delta, MasterCard, Switch, Visa   Accommodation: 3 rooms, B&B £35 to £50*

CUDDINGTON   **Buckinghamshire**   map 2

Annie Bailey's ❦

Upper Church Street, Cuddington HP18 0AP
off A418, 4½m W of Aylesbury   TEL: (01844) 291215

Cuddington is a picturesque village for urban strollers to enjoy and
offers public footpath walks for more serious walkers. The pub was
originally called the Red Lion until renamed in honour of Annie
Bailey – born in the village in 1794, she married a local licensed vict-
ualler and went on to have five children, the descendants of whom
still return to visit the pub. Inside, the décor is tasteful and stylish,
with a fairly small bar and bar area – as this is an eating-house, space
is devoted to tables, and there is a separate restaurant at the rear.
Since the last edition of the *Guide*, the beer served has improved and
now consists of Brakspear's, and Wychert from the Vale Brewery at
Haddenham. The pub describes itself as 'an English country pub
serving new-wave British cuisine', a style that shows up in starters of
toasted ciabatta with stir-fried chicken livers and mushrooms, or the
house salad of roasted red peppers, truffle oil, croûtons and flaked
Parmesan, and main-course dishes of suprême of chicken with Stilton
and pancetta. Fish lovers will not be disappointed to find halibut
steak in a filo pastry parcel with basil and tomato, or monkfish with
smoked bacon in a red wine sauce. No fewer than 14 wines are available by the glass from a list which covers many regions and countries, but focuses on Burgundy and Bordeaux. SAMPLE DISHES:
Scottish black pudding on baked red cabbage £4.50; fresh tagliatelle
with aubergine pesto £10; chocolate truffle cake £4.75.

Open *Sun and Tue to Fri L 12 to 3, Tue to Sat eve 6 to 11; bar food and
restaurant 12 to 2.30, 6.30 to 10*
Details *Children welcome   Car park   Wheelchair access   Garden and patio
Background music   No dogs   Amex, Delta, Diners, MasterCard, Switch, Visa*

CUMNOR   Oxfordshire   map 2

Vine Inn ✿

11 Abingdon Road, Cumnor OX2 9QN   TEL: (01865) 862567
off A420, 4m W of Oxford

This is a real pub that sells exceptional food. It is a large whitewashed building dating back to 1743 with the eponymous vine trailing across its front. Cumnor village itself is a quiet outpost of Oxford
with charming thatched cottages and two well-maintained pubs, the
most central of which is the Vine. Cooking here is a fusion of the

traditional and new wave, so if you order calf's liver it will come with lime sauce, and pasta could be crab linguine with poppy seeds. Gazpacho is one of a number of starters that can also be enjoyed as a main course, while other starters might take in pan-fried chicken livers with prunes, bacon and nutmeg, or hot or cold potato and leek soup. Tempting main courses could be duck and ginger stir-fry or salmon tapénade. Seating is arranged in a warren of open-plan rooms, including the main bar area with its glass-fronted real fire, and a more modern dining area to the rear. People eat where they wish, though if you choose one of the two comfortable settees, you may have to move one or both of the pub's resident dogs to get a seat. A large beer garden at the rear features a wooden climbing frame for children, and a tidy games area is also provided inside. Wadworth 6X and Adnams seem to be the hardy perennials, with other beers making guest appearances. A short wine list includes a selction of half-bottles and five by the glass. SAMPLE DISHES: crab soup with red chilli £3.50; Cajun chicken platter £6; chocolate marquise £3.75.

Open *11 to 2.30, 6 to 11, Sun 12 to 3, 7 to 10.30; closed 25 and eve 26 Dec; bar food and restaurant 12.30 to 2.15, 6.30 (7 Sun) to 9.15*
Details *Children welcome in eating areas   Car park   Wheelchair access (also WC)   Garden and patio   No smoking in conservatory   Background and live music   Dogs welcome on a lead   Delta, MasterCard, Switch, Visa*

DANEHILL   East Sussex   map 3

Coach & Horses

School Lane, Danehill RH17 7JF   TEL: (01825) 740369
on A275, 8m S of East Grinstead, 1m down School Lane, signposted Chelwood

---

Danehill is set high on the rolling slopes of the Ashdown Forest and, as fans of A.A. Milne may know, is not far from Upper Hartfield, where the famous Pooh Sticks Bridge can be found, and Five Hundred Acre Wood (known in *Winnie the Pooh* as Hundred Acre Wood). This pleasing old pub is a simple, low-slung construction of local stone, standing at a junction of major and minor roads. The gardens are an added bonus in summer, with an excellent play area for children. The food is wholeheartedly praised as honest and fair-priced, promising no more than it achieves. Snacks include a good range of sandwiches and light meals like scampi or chilli-con-carne. More elaborate dishes are served at lunch-time and in the evenings – lime and sorrel fish platter, or home-made fisherman's pie – with a traditional roast for Sunday lunch. Drinks include those to be found on a short but respectable wine list with nothing over £15 and three house wines available by the glass. The house bitter is Harveys

Sussex Best, accompanied by a couple of weekly changing guest ales such as Woodforde's Wherry or Wolf Best, and Thatcher's cider in summer. SAMPLE DISHES: prawns in filo pastry £4.25; pork roulade with polenta £8; treacle tart £3.

Open *Mon to Fri 11 to 2.30, 6 to 11, Sat 11 to 3, 6 to 11, Sun 12 to 3, 7 to 10.30; closed 25 and 26 Dec; bar food all week L 12 to 2, Mon to Sat D 7 to 9*
Details *Children welcome in bar eating area   Car park   Wheelchair access   Garden   No smoking in bar eating area   No music   No dogs in bar eating area   Delta, MasterCard, Switch, Visa*

DARGATE   Kent

map 3

Dove ♣   NEW ENTRY

Plum Pudding Lane, Dargate ME13 9HB   TEL: (01227) 751360
signposted off A299, 4m SW of Whitstable

'My idea of a country pub,' wrote one visitor to this pretty, cottagey pub, in the bucolic sounding Plum Pudding Lane in the sleepy hamlet of Dargate. 'There is a smell of wood smoke as you approach and in the summer the lane must be a riot of flowers.' Inside the pub there is a series of rooms, which are open-plan but still feel separate. You will find bare floorboards, scrubbed wood tables, plain chairs, candles stuck in wine bottles, a roaring log fire, hop garlands, photos of the pub in old days, plus china doves around the fireplace – it is simple and charming. One look at the blackboard tells you that this is no standard pub menu. Note there are no steak and kidney puds, chips or filled jacket potatoes – instead the lunchtime snack menu offers the likes of croque monsieur, minute steak, or baked goats' cheese crottin wrapped in bacon with salad and a 'delicious, lively, unusual' fresh tomato chutney. Ingredients are very local – mallards, pheasant and partridge are shot down the road, while fresh fish (perhaps lemon sole, plaice or cod) comes from Hythe. They may be used in such dishes as confit of duck salad with French beans and grain mustard, sardines grilled with olive oil and garlic, or smoked haddock fish-cakes in a light curry sauce. Roast chump of lamb is served with ratatouille, breast of chicken with sweet red pepper and chorizo, or there could be daube of beef provençale, and lobster with samphire in season.

This is first-class cooking offering good technique and with freshness of ingredients paramount. A reporter's tomato and basil soup was packed with flavour, and lemon tart to finish was reckoned to be up to the standard of a top London chef – delicate, creamy texture, very lemony with a light pastry crust. Alternatively, finish with coffee parfait or a selection of British and Irish cheeses. Somehow the right balance between drinking and food has been kept. It has all the look and feel of a rural pub, and the food, despite the imagination at play has a certain rustic appeal. It is a Shepherd Neame pub with Master Brew on handpump. The wine list runs to around 25 bottles with eight on offer by the very reasonably priced glass. SAMPLE DISHES: pan-fried crevettes with garden herbs £4.50; whole crown of mallard with glazed root vegetables £13; passion-fruit and orange crème brûlée £3.75.

Open *11 to 3, 6 to 11.30, Sun 12 to 3, 7 to 10.30; closed 25 Dec; bar food Tue to Sun L 12 to 2, Tue to Sat D 7 to 9*
Details *Children welcome Car park Garden Background music Dogs welcome Delta, MasterCard, Switch, Visa*

DARTINGTON   Devon

map 1

▲ *Cott Inn* 🍇

HISTORY

Dartington TQ9 6HE   TEL: (01803) 863777
S of A385, 2m NW of Totnes

The legend on the front of the building states that the Cott Inn has been licensed since 1320. Its name comes from its first licensee, Johannes Cott, a wealthy Dutch burgher who spotted the gap in the market for an inn to service the needs of packhorse drivers and travellers. It is a truly archetypal English pub, with its long, low, white-painted exterior and a thatched roof that is believed to be one of the longest in Britain. It does not stretch very far backwards, but extends sideways in a series of stepped, interconnecting rooms (it was originally a row of cottages) with an open log fire burning at either end of the bar. There are heavy, blackened beams in abundance, uneven walls, and seating is a mix of old settles and wooden chairs. A hot and cold buffet is served at lunch, which is reckoned to be good, but it is in the evenings when things really happen. Much is made of fish and seafood, delivered daily from Brixham and Plymouth. There may be paupiettes of plaice with asparagus cream and tarragon sauce, or scallops wrapped in bacon with white wine, cream and garlic. A simple starter may be a plate of antipasto, or melon with mango and strawberries, or go for a hot rainbow trout with creamed leek and a Dijon mustard and dill dressing. Non-fishy main courses might take in steak and kidney pie, navarin of lamb with redcurrants and shallots, or a curry. For pudding there could be raspberry and sherry trifle. Real ales from Bass, Butcombe and Otter are served, and the short wine list contains some very good selections, with ten wines available by the glass. The Cott Inn was taken over by the Old English Pub Company shortly before the *Guide* went to press, which means that the comments above may date rapidly; we would welcome news of any changes. SAMPLE DISHES: scallops in saffron batter and tartare sauce £4.75; fillet of salmon with shrimp and cucumber sauce £10; lemon and mango posset £3.50.

Open *11 to 2.30, 5.30 to 11, Sun 12 to 3, 7 to 10.30; closed 25 Dec; bar food and restaurant 12 to 2.15, 6.30 to 9.30*
Details *Children welcome in dining-room   Car park   Garden and patio No-smoking area in bar; no smoking in dining-room   Live music   Dogs welcome   Amex, Delta, MasterCard, Switch, Visa   Accommodation: 6 rooms, B&B £45 to £65*

▲ *White Hart* ❀ [NEW ENTRY]

ORGANIC

Dartington Hall, Dartington TQ9 6EL
TEL: (01803) 866051
from A384 follow signs for Dartington and then to Dartington Hall

---

The White Hart is tucked away in a corner of the fourteenth-century medieval courtyard of Dartington Hall, originally built for John Holand, half-brother of Richard II. It is now part of a 1,000-acre estate with conference facilities, a cinema, three dairy farms and an organic market garden, and features a programme of literary and artistic events throughout the year. Make time to explore the 28 acres of landscaped gardens or stroll along their section of the River Dart. To find the bar once you have arrived at the Hall, look for tell-tale clues like the beer barrels that stand outside. Using the original stonework with the addition of a light oak dado, very simply designed oak tables and chairs and a York stone floor, the owners have crafted an interior that successfully and stylishly combines elements of the traditional and contemporary. It is a small L-shaped room with an open log fire against one wall and a small bar against another, and overlooks the Great Lawn.

Organic produce is used whenever possible – the estate is in the process of switching to organic farming – and local produce features strongly. The lunchtime menu is a laminated card supplemented by a short blackboard selection of delicious-sounding baguettes and doorstep sandwiches, with fillings such as Riverside pork and apple sausages with fried onions and mustard. The evening blackboard menu lists the likes of pan-fried pigeon breasts with mustard dressing, local game casserole, or red snapper in a white wine sauce. Finish with organic raspberries with cream or local cheese with biscuits. Accompany your meal with Butcombe Bitter, Blackawton Bitter, or Dartmoor IPA. SAMPLE DISHES: home-cured gravad lax £4.25; organic Cornish lamb steak £9; Italian walnut tart £2.75.

Open *summer 11 to 11, Sun 11 to 10.30, winter11 to 3, 5.30 to 11, Sun 11 to 3, 5.30 to 10.30; bar food 12 to 2.30, 6 to 9*
Details *Children welcome in restaurant   Car park   Wheelchair access (also WC)   Garden and patio   Background music   No dogs   Delta, MasterCard, Switch, Visa   Accommodation: 48 rooms, B&B £31.50 to £105*

DOBCROSS   **Greater Manchester**   **map 8**

Navigation Inn

Wool Road, Dobcross OL3 5NS   TEL: (01457) 872418
on A670, 4m NE of Oldham

If brass bands are your scene, the Navigation Inn is an ideal retreat in traditional North Country heartland. This unassuming roadside pub offers an amiable welcome to a mixed clientele of locals, families and visitors to the popular showcase village of Uppermill, which is nearby. Built in solid local stone, it is traditionally kitted out with copper-topped tables. Tankards line the bar and collections of miniature buses and photographs of brass bands (a passion of the landlord) catch the eye on walls and windowsills – the musicians' stirring tones are to be heard over the sound system at lunchtimes. Menus are highly traditional and inexpensive, featuring items like cod, chips and mushy peas or steak and kidney pie, though Yorkshire pudding strays daringly across the great Pennine divide from time to time, and the chef's specials range more widely. Beers are from Camerons, Banks's and Marston's; wine selections are very limited. SAMPLE DISHES: prawn cocktail £2.50; chicken suprême with leek and Stilton sauce £6; apple pie £1.75.

Open *Mon to Fri 11.30 to 3, 5 to 11, Sat and Sun 11.30 to 11; bar food and restaurant all week L 12 to 2 (2.30 Sun), Mon to Fri D 5 to 8 (7.30 Mon and Tue), Sat 6 to 9, Sun 6 to 8.30*
Details *Children welcome   Car park   Wheelchair access (also WC)   Patio Background music   Guide dogs only   No cards*

DODDISCOMBSLEIGH   **Devon**   **map 1**

▲ *Nobody Inn*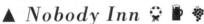

Doddiscombsleigh EX6 7PS   TEL: (01647) 252394
3m W of A38, Haldon Racecourse exit

'Choice' would seem to be the best word to describe the Nobody Inn: 40 different cheeses, 230 whiskies and 800 wines are on offer at this hard-to-find, certainly very rural pub. The interior has a wonderfully atmospheric mix of darkness and shadow, with an oxblood ceiling and low lighting. The cooking places great emphasis on local produce and, accordingly, both the bar and restaurant menus change frequently. Regulars on the bar menu include Nobody Soup, 'made from loads of ingredients', and pork sausage, mash and mustard and onion gravy. Cheeses on offer vary owing to seasonal availability, or 'because the animals have gone on holiday';

Devonshire cheeses take centre stage (and that includes blue cheese made from milk from Devon's own Romanian buffalos) but from time to time may share with 'imported selected "foreign" cheeses from Dorset, Somerset and even Cornwall'.

Bar meal specials show more than a little imagination: local ostrich liver is ground into pâté; Blue Vinney cheese is turned into soup; mutton is cooked in a turmeric, cinnamon and prune sauce; and chicken is served in orange marmalade. Desserts might include apple and lovage strudel or treacle tart. The separate restaurant menu might start you off with terrine of white fish and smoked salmon with a vermouth sauce, before proceeding to sirloin of beef in a red wine, shallot and mushroom sauce. The pub serves an eclectic range of real ales: Bass, Pilgrim's Pudding, and Teign Valley Tipple, as well as their own Nobody's Best from Branscombe Vale brewery. The extent of the round-the-world 800-bin wine list is explained by the fact that the pub is also a wine merchant; around 25 wines are available by the glass. SAMPLE DISHES: six local cheeses £4.25; chicken in an orange and tarragon sauce £6.25; syrup sponge pudding £3.

Open *12 to 2.30, 6 to 11, Sun 12 to 3, 7 to 10.30; closed 25 Dec and 26 Dec eve; bar food and restaurant 12 to 2, 7 to 10*
Details *No children   Car park   Garden   No smoking in restaurant   No music   Guide dogs only   Delta, MasterCard, Switch, Visa   Accommodation: 7 rooms, B&B £22 to £64*

DOLTON   Devon   map 1

▲ *Union Inn* 🍺 🍇

Fore Street, Dolton EX19 8QH   TEL: (01805) 804633
on B3217, 7m S of Great Torrington

It has been said that you do not pass through Dolton unless it is your destination, so out of the way is this peaceful village on a fold of hills above the River Torridge. However, the village is now part of the Tarka Trail and business is brisk at the centrally located Union Inn. The pub was originally built as a Devon Longhouse before being converted into a hotel in the early nineteenth century. Within, the two low, beamed bars are small and filled with settles, benches, a log fire, country-style prints and horse brasses. Not surprisingly, Ian and Irene Fisher concentrate on cooking fish, without neglecting carnivores. A lunchtime bar menu offers baguettes and ploughman's, while burgers and local ham with egg and chips can also be ordered on quiet evenings. The full dining menu features the Fishers' well-regarded Japanese-style prawns, a range of steaks and above-average vegetarian dishes such as mushroom Stroganov. You'd be advised to scour the specials board: this might feature dishes such as whole local plaice grilled with butter, wine and herbs, or – in season – game dishes like venison steak with port and juniper sauce, or woodpigeon braised with Madeira, onions and sultanas. Pudding selections are short but inventive – try hot summer fruits cooked in vodka and served with home-made meringue. This is another pub that does what freehouses are best placed to do: serve quality ales from individualistic local breweries. Here they sell Sharp's Doom Bar, Hicks Special Draught, John Davy Bitter and many other beers from small West Country brewers. Most of the wines on the short but interesting list are supplied by Christopher Piper wine merchants. There are four half-bottles, and six wines are served by the glass, including the house Australians. SAMPLE DISHES: sardines grilled with olive oil and sea salt £3.50; fish mixed grill with salmon, mackerel and squid £8; chocolate truffle torte £3.

Open *Thur to Tue 12 to 2.30, 6 to 11; closed first 2 weeks in Feb; bar food and restaurant Thur to Tue 12 to 2, 7 to 9.30*
Details *Children welcome in dining-room   Car park   Wheelchair access Garden   No smoking in restaurant   No music   No dogs in restaurant   Delta, MasterCard, Switch, Visa   Accommodation: 3 rooms, B&B £22.50 to £45*

DOWNHAM   Lancashire   map 8

Assheton Arms

Downham BB7 4BJ   TEL: (01200) 441227
off A59, 3m NE of Clitheroe

This delightful stone-built pub, in a classic estate village, is named after the family who bought the settlement in the mid-sixteenth century. A traditional atmosphere pervades the bar and eating areas, which boast low ceilings, solid oak tables, settles, window seats and a central stone fireplace. The printed menu offers pub staples of soup, pâté, ploughman's and sandwiches. More substantial dishes such as chicken Kiev, steaks, chilli con carne or home-made pies are also available. A specials board offers fish dishes such as oysters from Loch Fyne, moules marinière, monkfish, or even half an English lobster. Children under 12 have their own menu of burgers, fish and chips or chicken nuggets. Puddings are of the spotted dick or jam roly-poly variety, and there is also a choice of ice-creams; or try cheese and biscuits, followed by decent coffee from the coffee machine. Beers come from Boddingtons or Castle Eden; a reasonably priced 30-bottle wine list offers seven by the glass. SAMPLE DISHES: Stilton pâté £3.50; casserole of venison, bacon and cranberries £8; syrup sponge £2.50.

Open *12 to 3, 7 to 11; bar food 12 to 2 (2.30 Sun), 7 to 10*
Details *Children welcome   Car park   Wheelchair access (also WC)   Patio No-smoking area   Background music   Dogs welcome   Amex, Delta, MasterCard, Switch, Visa*

DUNCTON   West Sussex   map 3

Cricketers

Duncton GU28 0LB   TEL: (01798) 342473
on A285, 3m S of Petworth

Prior to 1860 this pub was known as the Swan, becoming the
Cricketers in that year, when it was purchased by John Wisden of
the eponymous *Almanac*. A two-storey, white-painted farmhouse
with a moss-covered roof, the pub lies before one of the most
dramatic ascents of the scarp slope of the South Downs. At the rear,
a garden over which much care has been taken creates a sense of
harmony. On entering, you will find a clearly defined layout: a long,
low space and, opposite the front door, a hatch with fixed blackboards on either side. The bar is set to the left so food ordering does
not disturb the serious business of drinking, and a fine inglenook
with a log fire commands the end of the room. The pub boasts an
impressive range of real ales, including Archers, Friary Meux, and
Burton Ale, with about three guests. Cooking is in a simple English
tradition, well executed and with fine ingredients. Start with grilled
sardines or a mille-feuille of mushrooms, then sample either steak
and kidney pie or Sussex Downs partridge, but note that different
menus operate at lunch and dinner. A wine list of about thirty bins
offers five by the glass. Bignor Roman Villa is nearby. SAMPLE DISHES:
vegetable terrine with tomato and basil coulis £4; pigeon breast in
rich red wine sauce £8; apple pie £3.50.

Open *11 to 2.30, 6 to 11, Sun 12 to 3.30; bar food and restaurant 12 to 2
(exc Mon), 7 to 9*
Details *Children welcome in dining area   Car park   Wheelchair access (also
WC)   Garden   No music   No dogs   Delta, MasterCard, Switch, Visa*

DUNSFOLD   Surrey   map 3

Sun Inn

The Common, Dunsfold GU8 4LE   TEL: (01483) 200242
off B2130, 4m SW of Cranleigh

Despite the weekend and holiday crowds that converge at this distin-
guished-looking Georgian pub, high standards and good value are
maintained. Lunch in the garden on a quiet day, watching horses
being exercised on the common, could be a tranquil experience.
Inside, sit at small polished tables in a traditional setting of low-
beamed ceilings, horse brasses, pictures and blackboards of what is
on offer. Simple starters such as deep-fried Brie, or mozzarella salad,

lead on to steaks, grilled plaice and the mainstay of sausages in various ways – perhaps venison sausages in a rich and intense gravy – and traditional roasts. Tuna steak with chargrilled vegetables, and home-made steak and kidney pie might be other possibilities, and do not forget the printed menu listing sandwiches and ploughman's. Vegetables come in separate dishes: roast parsnips have won a particular thumbs up. Sweets are also home-made, such as hazelnut and raspberry roulade and banoffi pie. Ales are Marston's Pedigree, Friary Meux Bitter, King & Barnes Sussex, plus an occasional guest, alongside a decent range of wines including English and New World representatives. SAMPLE DISHES: home-made cream of tomato soup £3.50; venison sausages £7; treacle tart £3.25.

Open *11 to 3, 6 to 11, Sun 12 to 4, 7 to 10.30; bar food Mon to Sat 12 to 2.15, 7 to 10, Sun 12 to 2.30, 7 to 9.30*
Details *Children welcome in dining-room   Wheelchair access (also WC) Garden and patio   Occasional live music   Well-behaved dogs welcome in bar; no dogs in dining-room   Amex, Delta, MasterCard, Switch, Visa*

DUNWICH   **Suffolk**   map 6

▲ *Ship Inn*

St James Street, Dunwich IP17 3DT
TEL: (01728) 648219
off B1125, 4m SW of Southwold

SEASIDE

So much of Dunwich has fallen into the sea that local fishermen claim they sometimes hear Church bells tolling beneath the waves. The Ship is one of the few buildings left in the village, which was once a major medieval port. At one time the haunt of smugglers, the pub retains a nautical flavour. The beach is close at hand and the front of the Ship overlooks the marshes – Minsmere Nature Reserve is nearby and Dunwich Heath and Forest are there to be explored. This pretty pub has a friendly, cheerful atmosphere. There is a small bar with a log fire, plus a conservatory where you can eat and a restaurant which is so popular that you may need to book several days in advance. The short lunchtime menu is very pubby – fish and chips, pork and beans, ploughman's, and a salad platter are what you are likely to find. In the evening a more comprehensive menu operates, perhaps opening with marinated sardines in a lime and dill dressing, avocado with prawns and a beetroot dressing, or an unusual Stilton and port cheesecake. Fresh fish of the day depends upon the local catch, though deep-fried plaice and cod are always on the menu. There may also be fish pie, half a roast chicken on asparagus sauce or lamb chops with redcurrant gravy. Puddings may include 'spicy and delicious' passion-cake, stuffed full of peel and nuts. Portions are not over-large but are good value, and children's and vegetarian options are available. Adnams beers from nearby Southwold are on tap and Adnams also supply the 23-strong, French-dominated wine list. SAMPLE DISHES: crispy Camembert parcels with Suffolk jelly £4.75; steak and stout vol au vent £8.25; Bakewell tart £2.75.

Open *11 to 3, 6 to 11, Sun 12 to 3, 6.30 to 11; closed eve 25 Dec; bar food 12 to 2, 7 to 9.15*
Details *Children welcome exc in bar   Car park   Wheelchair access   Garden and patio   No smoking in dining-room   No music   Dogs welcome MasterCard, Switch, Visa   Accommodation: 3 rooms, B&B £37 to £58*

EASINGTON   **Buckinghamshire**   map 2

Mole & Chicken

Easington HP18 9EY   TEL: (01844) 208387
off B4011, 1m N of Long Crendon on Chilton road

If you are looking for a pub offering adventurous bar food in a relaxed but stylish atmosphere, come to the Mole & Chicken. This nineteenth-century former village stores was built to supply the workers' estate and was licensed only to sell ale and cider until 1918, when it was known as the Rising Sun. In 1922 it was taken over by a Mr Chick and a Mr Heather (known to all as Moley), hence its modern name. Today it offers truly magnificent views from this tiny hamlet across the Oxfordshire and Buckinghamshire countryside, especially from the splendid summer garden. Well-heeled diners travel from miles to enjoy not only the food and views, but also the tastefully decorated interior with its oak and pine tables, rag-washed terracotta walls with sten-cilling, two log fires, candlelight (even at lunch-time) and flagged floors. If you are planning to eat, it may be worth booking, especially on a Sunday. From the restaurant-style menu, you could start with honey-marinated chicken breast satay with spicy dip, or a seafood flan in hollandaise sauce. Follow with one of the large selection of house salads, juniper-marinated duck breast perhaps, or, if more peckish, a half-shoulder of English lamb, or pan-fried calf's liver flambéd with brandy and orange juice. Beers to enjoy include Mansfield Bitter, Adnams, Morland Old Speckled Hen, and Notley Ale from the Vale Brewery. A short handwritten wine list is well priced and strong on France and South Africa. SAMPLE DISHES: large field mushrooms with ratatouille and a trio of cheeses £6; turkey escalopes with a julienne of vegetables £9; chocolate chestnut tart £4.25.

Open *12 to 3, 6 to 12, Sun 12 to 11; closed 25 Dec; bar food 12 to 2, 6.30 to 10, Sun 12 to 9*
Details *Children welcome   Car park   Wheelchair access (also WC)   Garden and patio   Background music   No dogs   Delta, MasterCard, Switch, Visa*

EAST CHILTINGTON   East Sussex   map 3

Jolly Sportsman ✿ 🍺 🍇   NEW ENTRY

Chapel Lane, East Chiltington BN7 3BA   TEL: (01273) 890400
off Novington Lane between B2116 and Plumpton Green

Set in a Sussex garden, the pub looks north with sweeping views across the Weald towards Godfrey Broster's – the brewing vicar's – Rectory Brewery. Not surprisingly, the pub sells the brewery's beers direct from the cask. The building itself is a rambling mixture of the old and the new, and recent landlords have spent some time creating a soft warm interior that is both modern and rustic. A combination of wooden furniture and floors and brick paving and walls have produced an ambience that is comfortable and unpretentious. Added to that is the quality of the food here, produced by a kitchen that has the advantage of owner Bruce Wass's experience as a successful restaurateur in Tunbridge Wells. The style focuses on using fine raw materials, original ideas and good timing.

Seafood mousseline with sauce béarnaise has a light and eggy texture and good fishy taste, while main-course duck confit with plums and ginger is a large duck leg with meat falling off the bone and oozing with flavour. Try Alsatian-style 'perfectly judged and unsurpassable-good' choucroute, and then, perhaps, choose stuffed pig's trotter with rich mash and Puy lentils. Apricot, walnut and ginger toffee pudding puts other toffee puddings in the shade, and home-made fig ice-cream with prune and plum compote comes with a very buttery toffee sauce, and 'a lot of it'. The bar menu includes items in smaller portions and at lower prices than the restaurant menu, which offers fixed-price dining in the evening. Apart from beers from the 'brewing vicar', the pub also serves Harveys and King & Barnes ales, and a praiseworthy range of bottled beers. The extensive wine list is mainly French with the odd New World bottle, nine half-bottles and six by the glass. SAMPLE DISHES: smoked haddock and chive puff £5.25; sea bass, sweet pepper and honey sauce £11; tiramisù £5.

Open *Tue to Sat (and bank hol Mon) 12 to 3, 6.30 to 11, Sun 12 to 4; closed 25 Dec; bar food and restaurant Tue to Sun L 12.30 to 3, Tue to Sat D 7 to 10*
Details *Children welcome   Car park   Wheelchair access (also WC)   Garden   No music   Dogs welcome   Delta, MasterCard, Switch, Visa*

✿ ✿ *indicates a pub serving food on a par with 'seriously good' restaurants, where the cooking achieves consistent quality.*

🍺 *indicates a pub serving exceptional draught beers.*

EAST DEAN   East Sussex   map 3

Tiger Inn

The Green, East Dean BN20 0DA   TEL: (01323) 423209
off A269 Seaford to Eastbourne road, 4m W of Eastbourne

The beast on the sign above the door is less of a raging tiger than an indulged pussycat, satisfied by a good meal and a pint of the free-house's well-kept ales. Visitors have the choice of five beers: Harveys Best, Adnams Best, Flowers Original, Morland Old Speckled Hen and Timothy Taylor Landlord. Alternatively, they could plump for one of the six wines available by the glass. Many of the meals incorporate local produce, such as locally cured gravad lax with a mustard and dill sauce, smoked haddock, ginger and spring onion fish-cakes, sausage ploughman's, or a whole lobster. Apart from the good bill of fare, the pub wins on atmosphere. Its bars are beamed with low ceilings, and the furnishings and furniture traditional, with plenty of pewter, china and antique settles. Families can retreat to a non-smoking upstairs room, play pub games, or sit outside at one of the many trestle tables by the war memorial on the village green. From there they can enjoy the window boxes, flowering climbers and the beautifully kept 'fabric' of the white-painted, tiled inn, which is a favourite with Morris dancers. SAMPLE DISHES: grilled goats' cheese on field mushrooms with pesto salad £5; Harveys steak and ale pie £6.25; Captain Morgan's bread-and-butter pudding £3.

Open *summer 11 to 11, winter Mon to Fri 6 to 11, Sat 11 to 11, Sun 12 to 10.30; closed eves 25 and 26 Dec; bar food 12 to 2, 6.30 to 9 (9.30 Fri and Sat)*
Details *No children   Car park   Patio   No-smoking room   No music   Well-behaved dogs welcome on a lead   No cards*

EAST END   Hampshire   map 2

East End Arms ❀   NEW ENTRY

East End SO41 5SY   TEL: (01590) 626223
off B3054, 2m E of Lymington; follow signs for Isle of Wight ferry and continue 2m

This traditional pub tucked away down quiet lanes at the edge of the New Forest is a popular destination for walkers, and has received several positive reports since it was bought by the owners of the George Hotel in Yarmouth. But this is by no means a clone of the upmarket George: although the lounge has been comfortably refurbished, the bar with its open fire remains simple and rustic. Apart from Ringwood Best and Fortyniner, both served directly from cask behind the bar, there is usually a guest beer and a real cider. In addition, the pub stocks an impressive selection of bottled beers from a variety of British brewers large and small. The wine list has been described as being a little top-heavy pricewise, but is respectably short (though lacking in New World offerings).

The menu is also short with plenty of interesting brasserie-style dishes, and cooking, timing and presentation have all been praised. Dill-marinated salmon with crème fraîche is a pretty permanent starter, though you might get an inventive baked egg curry, or ham and Gruyère ciabatta croque-monsieur as a hearty lunchtime snack. Local produce and country dishes appear everywhere on the menu. Slow-roast lamb shank with parsnips has come in for special praise; monkfish tail is supremely fresh; and partridge breasts 'came very pink as requested, utterly tender, with chestnuts in bacon, and a venison liver jus giving a classic rounding of forest flavours'. Menus change monthly and puddings are likely to be chocolate and hazelnut roll, or apple and blackberry pie, depending upon the season. SAMPLE DISHES: spiced lamb sausage with sweet pepper sauce £4; sweet tenderloin of pork with forest mushrooms, Madeira and marrow liquor £9; banana ice-cream £3.75.

Open *11.30 to 3, 6 to 11, Sun 12 to 3, 7 to 10.30; bar food (not Mon) 12 to 2, 7 to 9 (10 Fri and Sat)*
Details *Children welcome   Car park   Wheelchair access (also WC)   Garden   Background music   Dogs in public bar only   No cards*

EAST HADDON   Northamptonshire   map 5

▲ *Red Lion Hotel*

Main Street, East Haddon NN6 8BU   TEL: (01604) 770223
off A248, 8m NW of Northampton

It would be difficult not to find something of interest on the daily-changing bar menu of this thatched, stone pub a few miles north-west of Northampton, close to Althorp House and Guilsborough Grange Wildlife Park. Even if you are only after a sandwich or a plough-man's, at least take a look at the other options, especially if you are a vegetarian. The choices might include hot spiced baked aubergines, goats'-cheese toasties, or Parmesan-crusted almond and sweet potato cakes with tomato and basil sauce. Those in search of 'meat and two veg' need not be alarmed, as pheasant casserole, lamb's liver and onions, and steak and mushroom pie in a rich Guinness sauce all making regular appearances. Fish and chips devotees can relax too, as can fans of old-fashioned puddings with the likes of mincemeat tart, syrup sponge or sherry trifle there to tempt you. Sunday lunch is a traditional three-course roast affair. The bar itself is green-painted and wood-panelled with traditional plates, brass and open fires. Charles Wells own the premises, so the choice of ales is Bombardier, Eagle and Broadside, but there is also Morland Old Speckled Hen. Some reasonable finds crop up in the wine list, with offerings from both the Old and New World. SAMPLE DISHES: carrot and coriander soup £3; lemon-crusted deep-fried Brie and halloumi with Cumberland sauce £8; Bakewell tart £3.50.

Open *11 to 2.30, 6 to 11, Sun 12 to 2.30, 7 to 10.30; closed 25 and 26 Dec; bar food and restaurant 12.15 to 2, 7 to 9.30 (exc Sun D)*
Details *Children welcome in bar eating area   Car park   Wheelchair access (also WC)   Garden and patio   No smoking in dining-room   Background music   No dogs   Amex, Delta, Diners, MasterCard, Switch, Visa*
Accommodation: 5 rooms, B&B £60 to £75

EAST LANGTON   Leicestershire   map 5

▲ *Bell Inn*   [NEW ENTRY]

CHIPS

Main Street, East Langton LE16 7TW
TEL: (01858) 545278
just off B6047, 4m N of Market Harborough

Set back from the village within a pleasant front-walled garden, this creeper-clad listed pub dates from the sixteenth century. Landlord Alistair Chapman ran a nearby pub in Church Langton for 14 years before buying and refurbishing the Bell Inn three years ago, and has turned it into a thriving, popular and friendly pub with well-kept ales and its own style of cooking. The interior is warm and welcoming, with a long, stripped stone bar, sturdy pine tables, and log fire fronted by a pair of sofas; its beams are head-crackingly low. The emphasis is on home-cooked food, with all the chips hand-cut (how many pubs can say that these days?). The same food is served in the bar and the no-smoking green dining-room. Specials change monthly and might include locally shot pigeon breast with apple and gooseberry sauce, chicken roulade, or chicken tikka masala. These supplement the extensive lunchtime and evening menus, which overlap in parts. So at either sitting you could have deep-fried Oxford blue cheese, Brixworth pâté, or a steak sandwich. Common main courses include chicken and prawn satay, steak and kidney pie or broccoli-stuffed chicken. At the time of inspection, the pub was serving Greene King IPA, Abbot Ale and Jennings Cumberland Ale on hand-pump, and Ridleys Rumpus from cask. A half-dozen or so wines are available by the glass. SAMPLE DISHES: seafood au gratin £4.25; game and port casserole £10; lemon and sultana cheesecake £3.

Open *11.30 to 2.30, 7 (6.30 Fri and Sat) to 11; closed 25 Dec; bar food and restaurant 12 to 2.15, 7 to 10*
Details *Children welcome   Car park   Wheelchair access   Garden   No smoking in dining area   No music   Dogs welcome   Delta, Diners, MasterCard, Switch, Visa   Accommodation: 2 rooms, B&B £37.50 to £55*

EAST WITTON   **North Yorkshire**   map 8

▲ *Blue Lion* 🍷🍷 🌼

East Witton DL8 4SN   TEL: (01969) 624273
on A6108 Masham to Leyburn road, 2m SE of Middleham

The rather austere exterior of this late-eighteenth-century coaching-inn hides an interior of considerable opulence and a lavishness that definitely extends into the kitchen. Real fires and dark wood settles and tables give a warm glow to the place, creating an ideal ambience for the enjoyment of chef John Dalby's cooking. The use of local ingredients and imaginative menus have helped establish the Blue Lion's reputation as one of the best eating places in the Dales. There is a separate restaurant with its own menu, open most evenings for dinner, but the bar menu is of equally high standard, with dishes such as cherry tomato and tapénade tart, peppered duck breast with port and blackberry sauce, or spiced monkfish with oriental sauce on fresh tagliatelle. Service has been described as 'exemplary, very pleasant, polite and obliging'. The wine list, which runs to 128 bins, is primarily French but the New World is not neglected. Prices are very reasonable, but for those who wish to spend more there are several *grand cru* clarets, as well as selections of pudding wines and vintage ports. For beer drinkers there are Black Sheep and Theakston ales. The pub's accommodation makes it a popular base for visitors to the region, especially shooting parties and racing types with business in nearby Middleham, the 'Newmarket of the North'. SAMPLE DISHES: onion and blue Wensleydale tart with tomato chutney £4; trio of fish with fricassee of leeks and oyster mushrooms £11.50; pear tarte Tatin with honey ice-cream £3.75.

Open *all week 11 to 11; bar food 12 to 2.15, 7 to 9.30; restaurant Sun L 12 to 2.15, Tue to Sat D 7 to 9.30; no food 25 Dec*
Details *Children welcome in dining-room   Car park   Wheelchair access (also WC)   Garden and patio   No music   No dogs in restaurant   MasterCard, Switch, Visa   Accommodation: 12 rooms, B&B £47.50 to £85*

The details under the text are taken from questionnaires that have been filled in by the pubs that feature in the book.

EAST WOODLANDS   Somerset   map 2

Horse & Groom 🍺

East Woodlands BA11 5LY   TEL: (01373) 462802
off A361, 2m S of Frome

The Horse & Groom is located at the end of a rural road in a tiny farm hamlet not far from the Marquis of Bath's estate. Whether the Marquis drops in for a pint or two is uncertain, though he has every reason to – he owns the pub. The area offers good country walks in and around the local Mendip-stone villages and such places of interest as Stourhead and Nunny Castle. This means there is plenty of passing trade to keep the pub busy and lively. Inside are two bars, the public bar and a lounge with an inglenook which makes the place cosy when lit. There is also a garden room/restaurant in the rear conservatory. The bar menu runs from filled baguettes and ploughman's through to more exciting fare like smoked haddock risotto, or pork escalope with a Tewkesbury mustard and mushroom sauce. Beers are well-kept; Wadworth 6X and Butcombe Bitter are always on and guests tend to be of the likes of Bateman's XB and Greene King IPA. The wine list offers around 15 bottles, of which seven available by the glass are advertised on a blackboard. SAMPLE DISHES: smoked pheasant £4.25; fresh salmon fillet with pink grapefruit and peppercorn sauce £8; Bramley apple tart £3.25.

Open *11.30 to 2.30, 6.30 to 11, Sun 12 to 3, 7 to 10.30; bar food and restaurant Tue to Sun L 12 to 1.45, Tue to Sat D 6.30 to 9*
Details *Children welcome in bar eating area   Car park   Wheelchair access Garden   No smoking in dining-room   No music   No dogs   Delta, MasterCard, Visa*

EGLINGHAM   Northumberland   map 10

Tankerville Arms   `NEW ENTRY`

Eglingham NE66 2TX   TEL: (01665) 578444
on B6346, 6m N of Alnwick

A well-heeled dining pub, the Tankerville Arms is owned by the same family as the Cook and Barker down at Newton-on-the-Moor (see entry). It is set by itself in the village's main street of Northumbrian stone cottages. The three rooms – main bar, snug and restaurant – are attractively furnished in pine and warm pink fabrics. Although a printed bar menu exists, in the evening you can also choose from the restaurant menu. Even if you did not stray from the bar menu proper, you could dine handsomely and very reasonably on dishes with unusual twists. How about oak-smoked duck with a roast shallot and orange pesto, or melon gateau with prawns, lime and coconut? Even the straightforward-sounding deep-fried cod comes in a coriander batter. Vegetarians may be pleased by spinach and oyster mushroom rösti, or deep-fried pepper gnocchi, and salads and sandwiches also look good. Add the blackboard and evening menu and you may find sauté monkfish with cumin-roasted carrots, lemon sole with capers, and 'beautifully tender' guinea-fowl with a creamy green peppercorn sauce. Soft meringue with a bitter orange sorbet and summer fruits, or blackcurrant jelly with passion-fruit, offers no less interesting a prospect. The friendly licensee provides three regularly changing real ales, such as Ruddles, Directors, John Smith's, Jennings and Theakston Best Bitter. French and Australian wines are likewise good value. SAMPLE DISHES: baked courgette soup £2; lambs' kidneys with bacon and black pudding £6; lime parfait with strawberries £3.

Open *11 (12 winter) to 3, 6 to 11, Sun 12 to 3, 6 (7 winter) to 10.30; bar food 12 to 2, 6 to 9*
Details *Children welcome   Car park   Wheelchair access (also WC)   Garden Smoking in bar area only   Background music   Amex, Delta, MasterCard, Switch, Visa*

E G L O S H A Y L E   **Cornwall**   map 1

Earl of St Vincent

Egloshayle PL27 6HT   TEL: (01208) 814807
on A389, just E of Wadebridge

This whitewashed pub, bedecked with glorious hanging baskets in summer, may be hard to find but with the commendation 'still the best for food and ale' it is certainly worth tracking down. Named after one of Nelson's admirals, it originally functioned as a boarding-house for masons building the local church. Inside, open fires, heavy beams and wood panelling create a relaxing atmosphere completed by landlord Edward Connolly's collection of antique timepieces, which occupy every wall space and surface and imbue the pub with a continual but soothing ticking. All are in perfect working order, so produce a regular 'cacophony of chimes, bongs and cuckoos'. If you have some time on your hands, you could count the calories rather than the seconds with a melon boat, soup of the day, or avocado pear with prawns, and then choose from a selection of salads, fish dishes, grills, or the chef's specials – which might comprise beef Stroganov, roast duckling, or mushroom and broccoli au gratin. Sunday lunch features a roast. Indulgent puddings strictly *not* for the figure conscious include death by chocolate, and sticky toffee and hazlenut meringue. The pub's 'reasonable' food prices have won praise. This St Austell tenancy serves Tinners and HSD, and the wine list offers mostly French choices with some German whites and a smattering of New World bottles. SAMPLE DISHES: pâté and toast £2.50; steak au poivre £12; treacle tart £2.

Open *11 to 3, 6.30 to 11, Sun 12 to 3, 7 to 10.30; bar food 12 to 2, 7 to 9, Sun 12 to 2*
Details *Children welcome in bar eating area   Wheelchair access (also WC) Garden and patio   No-smoking area   Background music   No dogs   Delta, MasterCard, Switch, Visa*

ELSLACK   North Yorkshire   map 8

▲ *Tempest Arms* 🍇

Elslack BD23 3AY   TEL: (01282) 842450
off A56/A59, 4m W of Skipton

Although this stone-built pub is on the main road, it is surrounded by countryside on the edge of the Yorkshire Dales National Park, and foliage and bushes mask the noise of the cars. The interior, with its oak beams, wooden floors and real log fires, is comfortable and unspoilt. In the entrance is an original butter churn, while jam pans, mock oil lamps and bedpan warmers add character in the bar area. The dining-room is candlelit and has soft music in the evening, and a small garden and patio with chairs and tables makes for summer eating. The same menu is served throughout and starts with typical pub snacks of sandwiches, soup, pâté, garlic prawns or smoked chicken Caesar, plus more substantial dishes such as smoked fish platters, scampi, pie of the day, chicken Dijon, steak or a smorgasbord platter (roast meats, fish, cheese and salads, with a bowl of home-made soup and crusty bread). Puddings might be sticky toffee or bread-and-butter, and a wide variety of coffees makes an excellent finish to a meal. Jennings cask ales such as Cumberland Ale and Sneck Lifter are on offer, plus an extensive wine list, with 25 by the glass kept in good condition by the Verre de Vin system. SAMPLE DISHES: Mushroom and Stilton casserole £3.50; lamb Jennings £7.25; jam roly poly £4.

Open *11 to 11, Sun 12 to 10.30; bar food and restaurant Mon to Fri 12 to 2, 6 to 10, Sat and Sun 12 to 9*
Details *Children welcome in eating areas   Car park   Wheelchair access Garden   Background music   No dogs   Amex, Delta, MasterCard, Visa, Switch Accommodation: 10 rooms, B&B £49.50 to £57.50*

ELSTEAD　　Surrey　　　　　　　　　　　　　　　map 3

Woolpack

The Green, Elstead GU8 6HD　TEL: (01252) 703106
on B3001 Milford to Farnham road, 4m W of Godalming

A much-modernised pub, the Woolpack is divided into two bars. Both have log-burning fires, but the more atmospheric has low ceilings and beams, while the other, more modern bar, has high ceilings and a lighter, brighter feel to it. Wool trade memorabilia – looms, shuttles, scales and other bric-à-brac – dotted around the walls, along with Victorian black and white engravings and country prints. Beer is served from chilled casks behind the bar. Greene King Abbott Ale and Fuller's London Pride are on offer, and seven wines are available by the glass. If you are feeling hungry, look to the blackboard for an interesting selection of specials. You could kick off with deep-fried Camembert in port and cranberry sauce, or an avocado and seafood salad. Move on to an unusual ostrich steak in pesto, mustard and honey sauce, pork steak in apricots, schnapps and thyme sauce, or a casserole. Puddings, home-made and fresh every day, are a bit of a speciality here and include lots of pavlovas and mousses. SAMPLE DISHES: turkey strips in almond and mustard breadcrumbs with an orange and port sauce £5; lamb steak in creamy rosemary and onion sauce £9; banoffi pie £3.25.

Open *11 to 2.30, 6 to 11, Sun 12 to 2, 7 to 10.30; closed eve 25 Dec and 26 Dec; bar food and restaurant 12 to 2, 7 to 9.45, Sun 12 to 2, 7.15 to 9*
Details *Children welcome in dining-room　Car park　Wheelchair access Garden　No music　Dogs welcome on a lead　Delta, MasterCard, Switch, Visa*

ELSTED　　West Sussex　　　　　　　　　　　map 3

Three Horseshoes 🍺

Elsted GU29 0JY　TEL: (01730) 825746
off A272, 3m W of Midhurst

'Has it all really,' wrote one of our more experienced reporters: you may concur if on your wish-list are unspoilt rustic charm, tip-top real ales drawn from the cask, hearty home-made food from a reasonably short and daily-changing menu, and a splendid summer garden with glorious views of the South Downs. Built as a drovers' alehouse in the sixteenth century, this pretty inn in a peaceful, unspoilt village is, in many ways, the quintessential country pub. Outside, you encounter a lovely cottage with an extensive rear garden complete with roaming chickens. Inside, low ceiling beams, latch doors and a vast inglenook surrounded by a motley mix of antique settles, oak benches and sturdy tables (candlelit in the evenings) contribute to an old world atmosphere. The menu may offer leek and potato soup, rabbit and prune casserole, baked Brie with cranberry sauce, asparagus and prawns au gratin, braised lamb with apples and apricots, or apple and date pie; all good English fare. This is a popular pub with walkers, the highlight of whose calendar is the annual Ballard's Brewery charity walk, which takes in several local pubs selling Ballard's ale such as the Elsted Inn (see entry below), and takes place on the first Sunday in December. Apart from Ballard's beers, the pub serves Cheriton Pots ales, Ringwood Fortyniner and Hop Back Summer Lightning in the warmer months. As befits an alehouse, the wine list is short and offers two white and one red house wine by the glass. SAMPLE DISHES: avocado with Stilton and mushroom sauce topped with bacon £6; steak, kidney and Murphys pie £9; treacle tart £4.

Open *11 to 2.30, 6 to 11, Sun 12 to 3, 7 to 10.30 (closed Sun eve winter); bar food 12 to 2, 6.30 (7 Sun) to 9.30 (sometimes 9 in winter)*
Details *Children welcome   Car park   Wheelchair access   Garden   No music Dogs welcome in bar areas   MasterCard, Switch, Visa*

ELSTED MARSH   West Sussex   map 3

▲ *Elsted Inn* ▮

Elsted Marsh GU29 0JT   TEL: (01730) 813662   LOCAL PRODUCE
off A272, 3m W of Midhurst and 1m N of Elsted

'We are still a simple and unpretentious village pub, with all the fun and nonsense of the local. We will certainly never be called a restaurant pub!' So Tweazle Jones and her partner, Barry Horton, describe the Elsted Inn. The pub was built to serve the railway in the steam age as the station was once next door, and though this has now gone, the railway age lives on in pictures on the walls of this unmodernised pub. There are two simple bars with a lot of original wood in evidence, original shutters, wooden floors and three open log fires. A small dining-room – candlelit at night – with patchwork curtains, boasts an old oak dresser, and a collection of old polished tables and chairs rescued locally and restored. Tweazle describes her cooking as 'good English with the odd fascinating foreign dish thrown in'. Local produce, especially game, features strongly in such dishes as braised venison, quail in garlic, Sussex cassoulet, Gascony duck confit, and traditional Spanish paella. Sausages are made locally, and chunky sandwiches are prepared from hand-made bread from the National Trust bakery at Slindon. Vegetarians are well cared for with roulade, bakes or roast vegetables with couscous, and children can have half-portions mixed and matched to order. In addition, Wednesday evenings (book please) are theme nights, usually with a curry, but often with a paella or smorgasbord, or whatever has been suggested. The pub is notable for being the original home of Ballard's brewery and still sells their beers today alongside Arundel, Fuller's, Cheriton and other guest ales from independent brewers. Wines are supplied by the pub's neighbour, Midhurst Wine Shippers, and Charles Hennings of Pulborough. SAMPLE DISHES: creamy onion soup £3; beef in beer pie £8; fresh rhubarb crumble £4.

Open *11.30 to 3, 5.30 (6 Sat) to 11, Sun 12 to 3, 7 to 10.30; closed 25 Dec eve and no food L; bar food 12 to 2, 7 to 9.30 (10 Fri and Sat)*
Details *Children welcome in dining-room   Car park   Garden and patio Occasional live music   Dogs welcome   Delta, MasterCard, Visa, Switch Accommodation: 4 rooms, B&B £35 to £50*

ELTERWATER   **Cumbria**   **map 8**

▲ *Britannia Inn*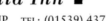

Elterwater LA22 9HP   TEL: (01539) 437210
off A593, 3m W of Ambleside

A mecca for walkers, the pretty stone hamlet of Elterwater stands at the head of Cumbria's magnificent Langdale Valley. During the tourist season (which lasts practically all year in Lakeland), this simple whitewashed inn is all but overwhelmed, and in fine weather visitors spill out on to the village green where white chairs and tables offer ringside views of the local Morris men's bells and hankies from time to time. Inside, the Britannia is unpretentious, though a discerning eye may spot a fine antique or two, and an impressive array of naval bric-à-brac amid the wheelbacks and plain wooden tables. Blazing fires cheer up the cosy bar on chilly days, and diners may be forced to migrate into adjacent rooms for hearty traditional pub fare like steak and mushroom or Cumberland pie, filling crusty rolls and baked potatoes. More elaborate special meals – poached halibut with red and yellow pepper sauce, say, or breast of chicken waterzooï – are served, but residents take precedence in the dining-room during the evenings. Children's meals are available too, with boredom-beating activity sheets and crayons served up alongside. Real ale fans can choose from Jennings Bitter, Dent Aviator or Coniston Bluebird, plus a couple of guest beers on draught. Country wines (damson, strawberry, etc.) accompany an undemanding but respectable selection of about 30 conventional bottles, mostly under a tenner. SAMPLE DISHES: Cumberland pâté with Cumberland sauce £2.50; Hungarian bean goulash £6; lemon brûleé £2.75.

Open *11 to 11, Sun 12 to 10.30; closed 25 Dec and eve 26 Dec; bar food 12 to 2, 6.30 to 9.30 (light snacks served 2 to 5.30)*
Details *No children after 9pm   Patio   No smoking in dining-room   No music   No dogs in dining-room   Amex, Delta, Diners, MasterCard, Switch, Visa   Accommodation: 13 rooms, B&B £24 to £68*

ETTINGTON   Warwickshire   map 5

Chequers Inn   NEW ENTRY

91 Banbury Road, Ettington CV37 7SR
TEL: (01789) 740387
off A422, 6m SE of Stratford-upon-Avon

PASTA

This white-painted village inn with a neat, comfortable interior has been sympathetically refurbished by new owner Paul Russell, a businessman who bought the pub as a hobby. Not only does he have the wherewithal to refurbish it but he can also afford a Raymond Blanc-trained chef, so this counts as a serious dining pub. An eye to detail includes the employment of courteous Italian front-of-house staff who are unencumbered by the British belief that service is not a profession. The very promising food is imaginatively cooked, modern-style. Although the restaurant menu is served in the bar, the same is not true vice versa, and the bar menu blurs distinctions between starters and main courses. A blackboard lists light snacks such as tomato and basil bruschetta and Greek salad. Cream of pumpkin soup lacks the blandness often associated with that vegetable and has some bite to it. Pasta wears the laurels here: try pesto pasta topped with grilled salmon and fresh parsley, or (from the restaurant menu) fettucine with chargrilled chicken and avocado with Neapolitan sauce, and pasta calamari with coriander and ginger pesto – both can be served as a starter or a main. Other main courses can be chosen from seasonally changing fish, grill and vegetarian sections or a 'from the oven' category, which contains dishes such as sweet chilli duck with Thai noodles. Brûlées typically flavoured with Baileys or brandy dominate the sweet selection – all home-made. The pub always serves Hook Norton Bitter plus one other guest, usually from one of the regional brewers, and a judiciously chosen global wine list runs to some 45 bins and includes bottles like Cloudy Bay Sauvignon Blanc or Chardonnay at fair prices. SAMPLE DISHES: Caesar salad £5.50; steak baguettes £6.25; peach crumble £4.

Open *Tue to Sat 12 to 2.30, 6.30 to 10.30, Sun 12 to 2.30; bar food and restaurant Tue to Sun L 12 to 2.30, Tue to Sat D 6.30 to 10.30*
Details *Children welcome   Car park   Wheelchair access (also WC)   Garden and patio   No smoking in restaurant   Background music   Guide dogs only Delta, MasterCard, Switch, Visa*

EVERSHOT   Dorset   map 2

▲ *Acorn Inn*   NEW ENTRY

Fore Street, Evershot DT2 0JW   TEL: (01935) 83228
*2m off A37 Yeovil to Dorchester road; 4m off A356
Crewkerne to Dorchester road*

Fans of Thomas Hardy may recognise Evershot and the Acorn from
Tess of the d'Urbervilles, though he called them Evershed and the
Sow and Acorn. The village is situated on a steep hill; halfway up is
this thatched sixteenth-century coaching-inn which has recently been
taken over by Martyn and Susie Lee, who also run the Fox at
Corscombe (see entry). It is a rambling building, with two stone-
walled bars, a skittle alley and a wood-panelled restaurant, and as the
Guide went to press the cellar was due to be converted to provide
extra seating and a venue for live jazz. The influence of the Fox is
felt in the menu: try starting with cockle chowder, potted shrimps,
or mussels in celery, cider and chervil. The fishy theme continues in
the form of baked local sea bass with caramelised shallots and red
wine sauce, or dressed Portland crab on a bed of continental leaves.
Meateaters can tuck into venison sausages with a traditional red
cabbage and mustard sauce accompaniment, or carved duck breast
on champ potatoes with a strawberry jus. Puddings are solidly traditional – treacle tart or spotted dick, for example – and come with
clotted cream or custard. As at the Fox, Exmoor Ale and Fuller's
London Pride are served on draught along with a guest ale – Otter
Bright, perhaps. The wine list, also identical to that at the Fox,
comes from Christopher Piper wines, and four wines are served by
the glass. SAMPLE DISHES: pan-fried chicken livers on juniper and
orange rösti £4.25; pan-fried Hooke trout with caper butter sauce
£9; sunken ginger pudding £3.25.

Open *12 to 11, Sun 12 to 10.30; bar food 12 to 2, 7 to 9 (9.30 Fri and Sat)*
Details *Children welcome   Car park   Wheelchair access   Patio   No smoking
in restaurant   Jukebox   No dogs   Amex, Delta, MasterCard, Switch, Visa
Accommodation: 9 rooms, B&B £45 to £120*

EWEN   Gloucestershire   map 2

▲ *Wild Duck Inn*   [NEW ENTRY]

Drakes Island, Ewen GL7 6BY   TEL: (01285) 770310
off A429 Cirencester to Malmesbury road, 3m SW of Cirencester

A gem of a Cotswold pub, the Wild Duck is a comely fifteenth-century inn, built and roofed in typical golden Cotswold stone. It is long, low, and barn-like with a central clock tower. At the front an open garden with one or two seats offers views of trees and woods. Inside is warm and welcoming with flagstone floors, wooden beams festooned with hops, coral walls, open fireplaces, a variety of clean, scrubbed tables all with candles, and farmhouse chairs and settles. The walls are adorned with a number of stuffed animals and a variety of country paintings and portraits. Numerous niches and alcoves on two levels allow parties of various sizes to socialise in relative privacy. There is a large, rather cluttered bar at the far end where locals congregate. Food is cooked to order and this can cause delays when the pub is busy, which it frequently is. The bill of fare might take in starters of giant garlic prawns with honey and cumin dressing, or avocado and goats'-cheese salad, followed by half-roast duckling with a chive and cream cheese sauce, or perhaps Cajun chicken burger with coleslaw, salad and chips. Vegetarians have a fair choice, fish dishes change daily, and portions tend to be generous. Real ales on offer include Theakston Old Peculier, Courage Directors, Smiles and Fuller's London Pride. Champagnes head the wine list which, reflecting current trends, slightly favours the reds. SAMPLE DISHES: chicken liver pâté with home-made piccalilli £5; gnocchi in a Stilton and sun-dried tomato cream £7.25; passion-fruit cheesecake £3.50.

Open *11 to 11, Sun 12 to 10.30; bar food and restaurant 12 to 2, 6.45 to 10*
Details *Children welcome in eating areas   Car park   Garden   Background music   Dogs welcome   Amex, Delta, MasterCard, Switch, Visa*
Accommodation: 12 rooms, B&B £44 to £90

EXFORD   Somerset   map 1

▲ *Crown Hotel* 🍇

Exford TA24 7PP   TEL: (01643) 831554
on B3224, 9m SW of Minehead

This immaculately maintained village pub, with its many gables, has a smart upmarket interior. The décor has tones of a hunting lodge and has found favour with the huntin', shootin' and fishin' crowd. There is a welcoming fire as you enter a small ante-room with a number of small tables. This in turn leads into the main bar area, an L-shaped room with a bar along one side. The polished wood of the tables, banquettes and even the beams has a deep sheen. The hunting motif is everywhere, with candleholders of deer antlers on the tables, and well-secured guns and an array of hunting trophies on the walls. An extensive and interesting blackboard menu tries to tempt you with such starters as grilled goats' cheese with pine-nut salad, or baked eggs with black pudding and bacon. Main courses may include fillet of Devon beef with Stilton sauce and gaufrette potatoes, Scottish salmon with cumin seeds and spinach, or hake and vegetable samosa with shellfish sauce. The desserts on offer might be hazelnut créme brûlée, caramel cream cheesecake, or chocolate terrine with chocolate sauce. In addition to Lanes Farmhouse cider the pub serves Wadworth 6X and Exmoor Ale and Brakspear Bitter. The wine list is predominantly French and an impressive 16 house wines are available by the glass. Many different types of cognac, Armagnac and calvados are available as well as a range of English country wines, including dandelion, birch and parsnip. SAMPLE DISHES: melon cocktail with Sauternes wine and tomato sorbet £4; grilled tuna steak on tomato fondue £9.50; red fruit cream cheesecake £3.50.

Open *11 to 3, 6 to 11; bar food 12 to 2, 6.30 to 9.30; restaurant Sun L 12 to 2, all week D 7 to 9.30*
Details *Children welcome in bar eating area   Car park   Wheelchair access Garden   No music   Dogs welcome   Amex, Delta, MasterCard, Switch, Visa Accommodation: 17 rooms, B&B £39 to £110*

EXLADE STREET   Oxfordshire   map 2

▲ *Highwayman*

Exlade Street RG8 0UA   TEL: (01491) 682020
off A4074, between Reading and Wallingford, 4m NE of Pangbourne

This civilised freehouse overlooks open fields on the edge of the Chilterns. It is a sizeable, rambling building dating from 1625, with tall chimneys and low-slung rooflines. The owners are experienced innkeepers, and the dining areas hum with trade at lunch-times in this popular and populous part of the Thames Valley. The original building has been sympathetically expanded to incorporate a modern conservatory dining-room, which leads out to a rear courtyard and terraced garden. The bar is cosy, with oak beams and barrel stools, while the two candlelit dining areas are pleasingly set out with bench seating and plenty of pictures and china. Food ranges from garlic mushrooms and home-made soups through an appetising, if fairly expensive, choice of meat and fish dishes – perhaps a smoked salmon and crab parcel or half a roast duck with cherry sauce. Innovative specials change fortnightly, and puddings are rich and filling. Hearty sandwiches and snacks are also available. There is a good range of real ales, fetched from the cellar, such as Hall & Woodhouse Tanglefoot, London Pride, Bishop's Tipple and Hook Norton Old Hooky. Besides five house wines, even bubbly is available by the glass. SAMPLE DISHES: scallops in bacon £7; chilli prawns £14; chocolate marquise £5.

Open *11 to 11, Sun 12 to 10.30; bar food and restaurant 12 to 2.30, 6 to 10.30, Sun 12 to 4, 7 to 10.30*
Details *No children   Car park   Garden and patio   No smoking in conservatory   Background music   Dogs in bar only   No cards*
Accommodation: 5 rooms, B&B £50 to £60

EYAM   Derbyshire

map 8

▲ *Miners Arms*

Water Lane, Eyam S32 5RG
TEL: (01433) 630853
off B6521, 5m N of Bakewell

HAUNTED

In the heart of the Peak District lies the picturesque and historic village of Eyam. As the pub's name suggests, the village was once a lead-mining centre, but what captures most visitors' attention is the poignant story of the Plague, brought here from London in 1665 in a bale of cloth, and the villagers' brave decision to quarantine themselves rather than flee to safety and spread the infection further. The harrowing death toll is recounted in Eyam's museum, and Eyam Hall, built soon after the epidemic, is also worth a visit. The Miners Arms, a pre-plague row of cottages dating from 1630, is perhaps, not surprisingly, haunted, the most famous spectres being Sarah and Emily, who perished in a fire. However, prospective customers need not be apprehensive; the interior is thoroughly cheerful and unspooky, with hefty rafters and cosy alcoves. Brass, china and old photographs decorate interior walls, and in summer the roadside façade is bright with hanging baskets. At lunch-times, home-cooked bar food comprises snacks, and blackboard specials such as crispy roast duck or poached salmon in white wine sauce. In the evenings a more elaborate and expensive menu is available in the restaurant – perhaps hot stuffed tomatoes with ham and mushroom or crayfish cocktail, followed by medallions of veal with a Madeira and shallot sauce or pot roast guinea-fowl. Desserts are all home-made. Tetley and Stones bitters are on draught, and the wine list is short and sweet, with six choices by the glass and several half-bottles. SAMPLE DISHES: Parma ham and feta cheese £3.85; braised lamb cutlets £6.25; Bakewell pudding £2.25

Open *Tue to Sun L 12 to 3, Mon to Sat eve 7 to 11; closed first 2 weeks in Jan; bar food Tue to Sat L 12 to 2; restaurant Sun L 12 to 1.30, Tue to Sat D 7 to 9*
Details *Children welcome   Car park   Wheelchair access (also WC)   Garden No music   No dogs in eating area   Delta, MasterCard, Visa, Switch Accommodation: 7 rooms, B&B £30 to £55*

E Y N S F O R D   Kent   map 3

Malt Shovel

Station Road, Eynsford DA4 0ER   TEL: (01322) 862164   **FISH**
on A225, 2m SE of Swanley

The Malt Shovel is a typical mock-Tudor pub of the 1930s, with an interior to match, and Roy and Linda Swallow offer a friendly welcome. Fish and seafood is the speciality of the house, as the tank of live lobsters and oysters shows: a blackboard lists specials, but devilled whitebait, grilled sardines and moules marinière are all available often enough to feature on the printed menu. Main courses are uncomplicated, the preferred cooking style being simple grilling, whether of trout, sole (Dover or lemon), plaice, sea bass or monkfish. Burgers, ploughman's, and venison pie may be fish-free, but jacket potatoes and sandwiches get the prawn and crab treatment. There are also vegetarian options and sweets come from the trolley. The house stocks Fuller's London Pride, Wadworth 6X, Flowers Original, Brakspear Bitter and Harveys Armada, and seven wines are offered by the glass. SAMPLE DISHES: fresh oysters from the tank £1.45 (each); grilled lemon sole £7.50; crème brûlée £2.75.

Open *11 to 3.30, 7 (6 Sat) to 11, Sun 12 to 4, 7 to 10.30; closed 25 and 26 Dec; bar food and restaurant 12 to 2.30 (3 Sun), 7 to 9.30*
Details *Children welcome in eating areas   Car park   Wheelchair access Patio   No smoking in dining-room   Background music   No dogs   Amex, Delta, MasterCard, Switch, Visa*

F A R N H A M   Dorset   map 2

▲ *Museum Hotel*

Farnham DT11 8DE   TEL: (01725) 516261
off A354, 9m NE of Blandford Forum

Dating in part back to Cromwellian times, this sturdy pub was once the museum for the local estate. The Coopers bar boasts an inglenook fireplace, green-cushioned seats and an original bread oven, while locals favour the Woodlands bar, also with a fireplace, for its selection of pub games such as darts. Additional dining space is provided by a brick-built conservatory, and a sheltered terrace and garden, with swings, are popular in summer: bedrooms are in a converted former stables. Pub staples such as sandwiches, soups, ploughman's, salads and steak and kidney pie are permanently on the menu, but daily specials evoke more of a fanfare. These might be baked stuffed mushrooms or potato and aubergine tart to start, followed by fish pie, lasagne or spiced lamb and apricots. More expensive dishes in the evening could be fritto misto (a selection of deep-fried fish), guinea-fowl with green peppercorn sauce or pork Normande. For dessert opt for, say, baked banana with cinnamon cream. Wadworth 6X and Hook Norton, plus a guest beer, are always available; the 22-strong wine list offers six by the glass. SAMPLE DISHES: butterfly prawns with sweet-and-sour sauce £5; home-made game pie £7.25; bread-and-butter pudding £3.25.

Open *11 to 3, 6 to 11, Sun 7 to 10.30; closed 25 Dec; bar food and restaurant 12 to 2, 7 to 9.30*
Details *Children welcome in dining-room Car park Wheelchair access Garden and patio Background and occasional live music; jukebox No dogs Delta, MasterCard, Switch, Visa Accommodation: 4 rooms, B&B £45 to £65*

FAVERSHAM   Kent   map 3

Albion

Front Brents, Faversham ME13 7DH   TEL: (01795) 591411
on Faversham Creek, near town centre

What is one to do if one is French and owns a pub in the middle of Kent by the name of Albion? Stay ever so French, is the answer. Thus the menu at this waterside pub, set in the middle of a row of pretty cottages, excels at things like fish soup with rouille and garlic croûtons, hazelnut and Roquefort terrine, creamy-winey fish dishes and well-made crêpes, all cooked to order. If you can forgo a wonderfully tart steamed date and apple pudding or black cherry yoghurt ice-cream, just sink your teeth into 'smelly French cheese'. Other temptations have more of an English feel, such as beef, mushroom and ale pie with crisp pastry, lunchtime filled rolls (albeit called baguettes) and knickerbocker glory. The choice is large for a pub of this size, just one long, light room with the bar in the middle, painted pale green in keeping with the watery setting by the weeping willows along the towpath, and decorated with nets, dried flowers and nautical prints. If you sit at the picnic benches you can enjoy the peaceful setting opposite a nineteenth-century warehouse complex. When it comes to drinks, celebrate the English half of the business with Master Brew, Bishop's Finger or Spitfire from the Shepherd Neame brewery just down the road, or stay French with one of the five good-value house wines. SAMPLE DISHES: deep-fried sesame-breaded Brie with port and fruit compote £4.25; slow-cooked braised knuckle of lamb with garlic, tomato, rosemary and flageolet beans £10.25; apricot streusel with Greek yoghurt £3.75.

Open *Mon to Thu 11 to 3, 6.30 to 11, Fri and Sat 11 to 3, 6 to 11, Sun 12 to 3, 7 to 10.30; bar food 12 to 2, 6.45 to 10, Sun 12 to 2, 7 to 9*
Details *Children welcome in bar eating area   Car park   Wheelchair access (also WC)   Garden and patio   Background music   No dogs   Delta, MasterCard, Switch, Visa*

FAWLEY   **Buckinghamshire**   map 2

▲ *Walnut Tree* ✿

Fawley RG9 6JE   TEL: (01491) 638360
off A4155 Henley to Marlow road, 4m N of Henley

This tree is planted deep in the countryside at the end of a single-track road that seems to go on forever, but it is 'well worth the tortuous journey'. A raised patio along the entire frontage is dotted with tables, and to the rear is a garden. Stepping inside there is a stylish bar to the right with Don Quixote prints and to the left is the main bar, with a small log fire and 'bar style' rectangular tables set up for eating. Further to the left are two conservatory dining-rooms (non-smoking), with cane furniture in one and more traditional furnishing in the other. People come primarily to eat, although there is ample space for drinkers. The menu is not the cheapest but the cooking is well executed and offers good, unfussy, traditional English food. Start with smoked Scottish salmon and quails' eggs served with a salad garnish and brown bread and butter, or a more unusual salt and pepper calamari with chilli. Otherwise there may be grilled goats' cheese, or sauté chicken livers. From the main courses, chicken with Stilton and walnuts sounds like good English fare, as does roasted rack of lamb with a rich rosemary jus. Specials of the day might include grilled lemon sole, medallions of venison, or seared slices of salmon fillet, and for vegetarians there is home-made ravioli or an oriental vegetable stir-fry. Ice-creams and sorbets come in flavours such as stem ginger and Acacia honey, pistachio, and passion-fruit, and you can have these with your sticky toffee pudding, spiced apple torte, or treacle tart. This Brakspear pub serves their Ordinary and Special bitters as well as their seasonal ales. The wine list runs to around 50 bins and offers two or three respectable selections from each region or country, including Mexico and Chile. Five house wines are available by the glass. SAMPLE DISHES:

chef's terrine of the day £4.25; whole roast guinea-fowl £10.75; chocolate truffle torte £3.25.

Open *all week 12 to 3, Mon to Sat 6 to 11; bar food and restaurant 12 to 2, 7 to 9.30*
Details *Children welcome in dining-room   Car park   Wheelchair access Garden and patio   No smoking in conservatory   Occasional background music   No dogs in conservatory or dining-room   Delta, MasterCard, Switch, Visa   Accommodation: 2 rooms, B&B £35 to £55*

FELSHAM   Suffolk   map 6

Six Bells

Church Road, Felsham IP30 0PJ   TEL: (01449) 736268
off A14, 7m SE of Bury St Edmunds

Being hard to find, the Six Bells is very much a locals' pub: it is something of a 'local community centre' in the middle of the village, but one where lucky travellers will, if they stop, find a friendly welcome. Simply furnished with tables that have seen better days, a darts board and a bar-billiards table, there is plenty of space for eating. Food is listed on blackboards which will require you to walk around the pub to read them all, and since you will be on your feet, you go and order your food from the bar, which is then cooked to order. Starters might be soup, or perhaps garlic mushrooms. Steak and ale pie, and lasagne are typical mains, and the salads contain a bit of everything. Puddings are all home-made – the banoffi short-cake is reckoned to be a prime example of the species. The pub belongs to Greene King, so IPA, Abbot Ale and the infrequently seen XX Dark Mild are served straight from the cask. Bottled Strong Suffolk, St Edmund's Ale and Barley Wine are also available. Five wines change regularly, and three are available by the glass. As one correspondent wrote, 'This is what a real pub should be, and I would return, provided I could find my way again through those wretched country lanes.' SAMPLE DISHES: feta cheese salad £3.50; salmon steak salad and new potatoes £6.75; apple, plum and blackberry crumble £3.25.

Open *Wed to Sat 12 to 2 (also Tue and bank hol Mon in summer), Mon to Sat 6 to 11, Sun 12 to 3, 7 to 10.30; bar food and restaurant Tue to Sat L 12 to 1.45, Mon to Sat D 6.30 to 9.30*
Details *Children welcome   Car park   Wheelchair access   Garden   No smoking in restaurant   Background music   Well-behaved dogs welcome   No cards*

King William IV 🍇

High Street, Fenstanton PE18 9JF   TEL: (01480) 462467
off A604, 5m SE of Huntingdon

Close to the clock tower in the centre of the village is a row of cream-painted cottages that together make up the King William. The knocked-through interior has retained a number of fireplaces and standing beams to create a lively locals' bar and a separate dining area, which incorporates the plant-filled, no-smoking 'Garden Room'. The lunchtime bar menu offers a large range of sandwiches, including baguettes and 'double-deckers', and simple things such as jacket potatoes, or venison sausages with creamed potatoes. The main menu gears up a notch to take in deep-fried cheese-stuffed mushrooms, seared scallops, or steak and kidney pudding, but the specials board is where the kitchen shows off its strengths, with six weekly-changing fish options – maybe suprême of halibut with white wine and dill – appearing alongside the likes of honey-glazed ham hock with creamy calvados, cider and apple sauce. Vegetarian options are always available: perhaps spinach and ricotta roulade with salad. There are also some interesting puddings – iced whisky and raspberry soufflé, for example. This Greene King pub offers IPA and Abbott Ale as well as Morland Old Speckled Hen, Wadworth 6X, Marston's Pedigree and a monthly guest. House wines are available in litre or half-litre carafes, as well as by the glass, and seven come from the New World. Landscaper Capability Brown is buried in the nearby churchyard. SAMPLE DISHES: three-cheese gnocchi in white wine, cream and herb sauce £4; rosettes of pork with confit of peppers and wild berry and mint dressing £10; brandy-snap basket with mango sorbet £3.

Open *11 to 3.30, 6 to 11, Sun 12 to 10.30; closed 1 Jan; bar food and restaurant 11.30 to 2.15, 7 to 10, Sun 12 to 3.30*
Details *Children welcome   Car park   Wheelchair access   Patio   No-smoking area in restaurant   Background and live music   Dogs welcome on a lead Amex, Delta, MasterCard, Switch, Visa*

FERNHURST   West Sussex   map 3

King's Arms ✪ 🍺 ❀   [NEW ENTRY]

Midhurst Road, Fernhurst GU27 3HA
TEL: (01428) 652005
on A256, 1m S of Fernhurst on sharp bend

This attractive Sussex stone pub stands on a corner of the main
Midhurst road on the Surrey–West Sussex border. An unusual tiled
porch runs the length of the front, from which hanging baskets are
suspended, while at the rear is a garden with a willow tree, white
lilacs and views over surrounding fields. Within the grounds a wisteria-clad Sussex barn is used for functions such as music evenings, wine
tasting and barbecues. Inside, the décor is as one would expect of a
seventeenth-century pub: beams, oak tables, settles and a big fireplace. There is one large L-shaped bar with tables around the edge
and a separate dining area. The pub was taken over in October 1996
by Michael and Annabel Hirst; he was previously head chef and she
manager of restaurants in London, and their experience shows.

The contemporary menu, presented on a blackboard which is
carried from table to table, changes fortnightly and is based firmly on
seasonal ingredients. Wild mushrooms on brioche offers a good
selection of assorted fungi, with a well-balanced dressing of balsamic
vinegar, garlic and herbs; and smoked duck breast salad is a generous
portion served on a pancake with a good designer leaf salad. Scallops
are lightly cooked, plentiful and with good flavour, and arrive on a
rösti and a pyramid of leeks; while tender and juicy rack of lamb is
cooked pink and served with spinach on a bed of bubble and squeak.
All dishes are home-made, including puddings, ice-creams and
sorbets. Depending upon the season, you may find plum and blackberry crumble, raspberry mousse, or warm cider and raisin cake with
toffee cream and caramelised apples on the lengthy pudding menu.
King's Arms Ale is brewed specially for the pub by the Brewery on
Sea. Otter Bright and Gales HSB are also available, plus two regularly changing ales from independent breweries. A user-friendly wine
list offers plenty of reasonably priced good-value drinking from
around the world, and includes 13 half-bottles and six by the glass.
SAMPLE DISHES: smoked salmon and scrambled egg £6.50; fillet of red
snapper with oven baked provençale vegetables and Parmesan £9.75;
citrus mousse with lemon biscuits £3.75.

Open *Mon to Fri 11.30 to 3, 3.30 to 11, Sat 11.30 to 3, 6.30 to 11, Sun 12
to 3; closed 25 Dec, bank hol Mon eve; bar food and restaurant 12 to 2.30, 7
to 9.30*
Details *Children welcome in eating areas   Car park   Wheelchair access (also
WC)   Garden   No-smoking area   Live music   Dogs welcome   Delta,
MasterCard, Switch, Visa*

▲ *General Tarleton* ❦ ❧

Harrogate Road, Ferrensby HG5 0QB   TEL: (01423) 340284
off A6065, 3m N of Knaresborough

If you ever drop into a Marquis of Granby it is a fair bet you are
drinking in a pub set up by one of that 'going at it bald-headed'
gentleman's former sergeants. Similarly, the General Tarleton was
set up by a former comrade in arms of Sir Banastre Tarleton,
former MP for Liverpool and soldier under Wellington. No
mention of the pub is complete without reference to the Angel at
Hetton (see entry), which has a widespread reputation and was the
first venture of the General's owners, Denis Watkins and John
Topham. In 1998 the General had a quarter of a million pound
makeover, including the creation of a covered courtyard, which
with a few kicks and scuffs should weather into a more atmospheric setting.

Cooking has been described as 'British at heart with a toe dipped
firmly in the Mediterranean.' Arrive early or late in the brasserie to
stand the best chance of getting a table, and if you want to eat in the
restaurant book in advance. If you can get a brasserie table you
might like to try the AWT, an Angel import which consists of an
open sandwich with salmon, cream cheese, smoked bacon, and
home-made chutney, or – another Angel speciality – 'little money
bags', which is seafood baked in filo pastry. Baked tomato tart drizzled with pesto is an example of that toe in the Med, as is the deli
platter of chicken liver and foie gras parfait, Cheddar, Somerset Brie,
pastrami, salami, roast ham and goose rillettes, served with bread,
fruit and pickles. From the toe move up to the heart with fish and
chips, rib-eye steak, or slow-cooked shoulder of English lamb.
'Hetton Mess' is a pun as well as a pudding, comprising meringue,
sweetened farmhouse yoghurt and raspberry coulis, and summer
pudding is about as English as you can get. The General issues Black
Sheep Bitter, Tetley Bitter and Timothy Taylor Landlord to the other
ranks, while wine drinkers can choose from an exceptional list with
plenty of half-bottles and 18 by the glass. SAMPLE DISHES: rustic fish
soup £4: chargrilled spring lamb leg steak £11; brandy-snap basket
£3.75.

Open *12 to 3 (2.30 in winter), 6 to 11, Sun 12 to 3, 6.30 to 10.30; closed 25
Dec; bar food 12 to 2, 6 to 10, Sun 12 to 2, 6.30 to 9; restaurant Sun L 12 to
2, Mon to Sat D 6 to 10*
Details *Children welcome   Car park   Wheelchair access (also WC)   Garden
No smoking in dining-room and 1 bar area   No music   Guide dogs only
Amex, Delta, MasterCard, Switch, Visa   Accommodation: 14 rooms, B&B
£68 to £85*

FIR TREE   Co Durham   map 10

▲ Duke of York

Fir Tree DL15 8DG   TEL: (01388) 762848
on A68, 4m S of Tow Law

A pub since 1760, this important staging-post between Edinburgh and York has been in the Suggett family for four generations. The last major changes took place in 1966 when the old practice of fetching beer direct from the cask was abandoned and a proper bar counter was installed by the famous craftsman 'Mouseman' Thompson. Black Sheep Bitter is the only cask-conditioned ale on offer and the daily-changing blackboard menus are similarly brief. Fresh seasonal produce is very much the house emphasis, with steaks from local farms available in a variety of sauces. The other house speciality is 'sauces of inspiration' which are prepared individually according to each order. A typical selection of specials might include dim-sum or smooth chicken liver pâté to start; hot roast beef in a bun or gammon steak as bar meals; a 'sauce' dish of lamb in hot pepper; and strawberry Amaretto, or Dime Bar pie for dessert. The wine list is supplied by Yorkshire Fine Wines and offers four choices by the glass. SAMPLE DISHES: prawn cocktail £4; chicken princess £9.50; orange and Cointreau ice-cream £3.

Open *11 to 3 (2.30 winter), 4.30 to 10.30; bar food and restaurant 12 to 2, 6.30 to 9*
Details *Children welcome   Car park   Wheelchair access (also WC)   Garden No music   No dogs   Delta, Diners, MasterCard, Switch, Visa Accommodation: 4 rooms, B&B £52 to £69*

FLETCHING   East Sussex   map 3

▲ Griffin Inn 🌼 🍺 🌾

VIEWS

Fletching TN22 3SS   TEL: (01825) 722890
off A272, between Maresfield and Newick, 3m NW of Uckfield

The pub's own blurb points out that 'the Griffin Inn has been at Fletching for over 400 years'; which might prompt one to ask, where was it before that? This unspoilt Sussex village is where Simon de Montfort is believed to have camped on the eve of the battle of Lewes in 1264. The Norman church spire can be seen for miles around and Sheffield Park Gardens, the Bluebell Railway, Glyndebourne, Firle Place, Kipling's house Bateman's and Bodiam Castle are all nearby. The success of this sixteenth-century inn is largely a result of the efforts of the Pullan family, who have run the pub for 20 years. There is obvious intelligence at work in the kitchen and on a good day reporters are quick to praise more or less everything.

The menu changes twice daily and is chalked up in the cosy, beamed bar. If you are looking for something unusual, try soused mackerel fillets with pickled vegetables on red mustard leaves, or crab and prawn fritters with a coriander dip on Mizuno leaves, while goats' cheese is made into a light mousse and served with Melba toast. Main courses might include a late summer salad of broad beans, Jersey Royals, cherry tomatoes and soft boiled eggs. Traditional bouillabaisse, and penne with wild mushrooms, roasted red onions, basil pesto and Parmesan, show a Mediterranean influence, while 'moules, frites and mayo' will be popular with Belgians. From closer to home come chargrilled Scottish rib-eye steak with chips, or chargrilled local sausage with flavoured mash and mustard sauce. To finish, elderflower and juniper sorbet sounds delightfully delicate. Dark chocolate and coffee mousse, on the other hand, sounds delightfully indelicate. There is also a selection of hot ciabatta sandwiches. The pub serves Harveys Best Bitter, Tanglefoot, Ballard's Best and a varying guest. The wine list runs to over 100 bottles, with separate pages for dessert wines and digestifs, and there is even a separate list devoted to some 15 wines by the glass. SAMPLE DISHES: Sussex asparagus with basil and Parmesan shavings £5; confit of duck on rocket leaves with a shallot and red onion sauce £7.50; strawberry ganache £4.

Open *12 to 3, 6 to 11, Sun 12 to 3, 6 to 10.30; closed 25 Dec; bar food and restaurant 12 to 2.30, 7 to 9.30 (9.45 Fri and Sat; restaurant closed Sun D in winter)*
Details *Children welcome   Car park   Wheelchair access (also WC)   Garden and patio   Live music; jukebox   No dogs in restaurant   Amex, Delta, MasterCard, Switch, Visa   Accommodation: 8 rooms, B&B £40 to £95*

FORD   **Buckinghamshire**   map 3

Dinton Hermit
Water Lane, Ford HP17 8XH   TEL: (01296) 748379
off A418, 4m SW of Aylesbury

The pub takes its name from one John Bigg, who died in 1696 and whose portrait hangs in the bar. He was clerk to Simon Mayne, one of the signatories to Charles I's death warrant. Mayne ended his days in the Tower of London, while Bigg ended his as a recluse. The food has been described as unpretentious but skilful home-cooking, and portions are sufficiently generous to render dessert an ambition too far for some. The pub is shut on Mondays, which is when Jane Tompkins and her daughter buy ingredients for the next week. The lunch menu favours simple dishes, such as a half-pint of prawns, plus a few hot main courses like steak and mushroom pie. The evening menu is more ambitious, perhaps offering chicken florentine, or duck in orange and ginger sauce. Beers offered are ABC, Wadworth 6X and Adnams, and four wines are available by the glass. SAMPLE DISHES: egg mayonnaise £3.25; veal escalope with ham, cheese and asparagus £11.75; home-made fruit pie £3.25.

Open *Wed to Sat 11 to 2.30, Tue to Sat 6 to 11, Sun 12 to 2, 7 to 10.30; bar food Wed to Sat 12 to 2, 7 to 9*
Details *Car park   Wheelchair access (also WC)   Garden   No music   Guide dogs only   No cards*

F O R D H A M   Cambridgeshire   **map 6**

White Pheasant

Market Street, Fordham CB7 5LQ   TEL: (01638) 720414
on A142, 5m N of Newmarket

Tasteful simplicity defines the interior of this seventeenth-century, white-painted inn, situated in a Fenland village close to Ely, with rugs on otherwise bare floorboards, a motley mix of old tables and chairs, prints and paintings on walls, attractive tartan curtains and candles on tables, creating a relaxing and cosy ambience. A printed à la carte menu is supported by a weekly-changing specials board, both available throughout the pub. It serves a local lunchtime business trade and offers dishes like lamb's liver with onion gravy as a midday top up. Otherwise, specials could include roast chicken breast filled with ricotta cheese and tomato relish, Scottish rainbow trout with peach and apricot sauce, or grilled plaice with garlic butter. Puddings present some individual choices: hot chocolate and mint pudding with ice-cream, or a light, moussey strawberry and Cointreau flummery. This freehouse offers Theakston Best and Courage Directors, plus guest ales – perhaps supplied by the City of Cambridge Brewery. The wine list offers between around two dozen wines with reasonably priced house wines and three available by the glass. SAMPLE DISHES: spicy sausage and red onion warm salad £4; Barnsley lamb chop with bramble and mint sauce £10.75; apple and rhubarb crumble £3.25.

Open *12 to 3, 6 to 11, Sun 12 to 3, 7 to 10.30; closed 25 and 26 Dec, eve 1 Jan; bar food 12 to 2.30, 6 (7 Sun) to 10*
Details *Children welcome   Car park   Wheelchair access   Garden Background music   No dogs   Delta, MasterCard, Switch, Visa*

FORDINGBRIDGE   Hampshire   **map 2**

▲ *Augustus John*   NEW ENTRY

116 Station Road, Fordingbridge SP6 1DG   TEL: (01425) 652098

In the days when this pub was known as the Railway Hotel, it was a regular haunt of the famous hard-drinking artist it is now named after. He was for many years a resident of Fordingbridge, and the pub's sign is based on one of his self-portraits. Inside, it is decorated with copies of his pictures and has been smartly refurbished to give it a warm and welcoming atmosphere. An area with plush bench seating is provided for drinkers, but these days it is principally a dining pub, and a popular one – booking is advisable as space is limited. Regularly changing blackboard menus might offer 'most enjoyable' tomato and fennel soup, or 'very tasty' grilled king prawns in garlic to start. Lunchtime specials could include steak and Guinness casserole, Thai-style pork or chicken curry, and regular main courses are solidly traditional: steak au poivre with port and Stilton, calf's liver and bacon, monkfish tails in bacon, or sea bass in fennel and Pernod. If you have room, finish with a home-made pudding like chocolate and rum torte. There is a short wine list, while Hardy Country Bitter and Draught Bass are provided to satisfy the ale lover. SAMPLE DISHES: scallops with herb and garlic butter £4.25; whole Poole plaice £7; treacle, brandy and pecan pie £2.75.

Open *11am to midnight (11.30 Sun); bar food and restaurant 12 to 2.15, 6.30 to 9.30*
Details *Children welcome in dining-room   Car park   Wheelchair access Garden and patio   No-smoking area   Background music   Dogs welcome in bar only   Delta, MasterCard, Switch, Visa   Accommodation: 4 rooms, B&B £35 to £50*

FORDWICH   Kent   **map 3**

Fordwich Arms

King Street, Fordwich CT2 0DB
TEL: (01227) 710444   HAUNTED
off A28, 3m NE of Canterbury

Fordwich and Manningtree (Essex) are at daggers drawn as to which is England's smallest town. The arguments rage, though at least Fordwich has a pub fully worthy of an appearance in these pages, and one that has the honour of being opposite the tiny sixteenth-century town hall. But this brick mock-Tudor pub with gardens leading down to the Stour has no chips on its shoulder about size – and no chips on the menu either. Everything is cooked fresh and prepared to order, from the numerous sandwiches, 'double-filled' cottage rolls, salads, jacket potatoes and ploughman's, to the '90s numbers of Thai crab-cakes, pork fillet in filo pastry, or confit of duck with onion marmalade. Blackboard main courses all come with four fresh vegetables and potatoes. You could stay cool with iced lemon brûlée or pear and almond tart, or instead cock a snook at modernity and go for one of the blackboard 'hot puds' with custard. The separate non-smoking restaurant comes to life with regular 'Gourmet Evenings', considerably influenced by that country just over the Channel. There is also a folk club evening on the first and third Sunday each month. Local Theobalds cider may be of interest, or try the pub's own-label French house wines (including seven by the glass), or stick to Boddingtons, Flowers or Shepherd Neame Master Brew. And do not look too hard at that black-coated guest sweeping down the corridor – it is probably just the ghost of Captain Short putting in an appearance. SAMPLE DISHES: grilled goats' cheese £4; Tuscan lamb £6.75; baked chocolate cheesecake £3.

Open *11 to 11, Sun 12 to 3, 7 to 10.30; bar food and restaurant all week L 12 to 2, Mon to Sat D 6.30 to 10*
Details *Children welcome in dining-room   Car park   Wheelchair access (also WC)   Garden and patio   No smoking in dining-room   Background music No dogs in dining-room   Delta, MasterCard, Switch, Visa*

FOSS CROSS   Gloucestershire   map 5

Hare & Hounds 🏵 🏵

Foss Cross GL54 4NW   TEL: (01285) 720288
on A429, between Cirencester and Northleach

Now under the direction of Leo Brooke-Little and Sonya Kidney of the Churchill Arms, Paxford (see entry), the Hare & Hounds has lost a little of its 'simple pubbiness' but not so much that it jars: the old red pub carpet has been replaced by natural-looking matting ('goes well with the bare stone walls,' thought one visitor), and some colourful modern prints now hang alongside the odd farming implement and stuffed bird. Bigger changes have arrived, however, in terms of what appears on the menu, and the skill with which the dishes are produced. As with all the best kitchens, the focus at the Hare & Hounds is on first-class raw materials skilfully rendered, rather than on reliance on pretentious or fussy preparation. Consequently, a starter such as seared scallops with saffron dressing on a 'bonfire of leaves' shows 'brilliant main components and timing', and a main course of duck breast with ginger and lime sauce is a bird of 'superior provenance' that for one reporter even 'smelled wonderful'.

The daily blackboard might also deliver celery and apple soup, or salad of avocado, bacon and spiced tomato to start, and main courses of faggots with split pea purée and onion gravy, grey mullet with lemon butter sauce, or pork chop with curried aubergine. Excellent home-made ice-creams feature in a number of desserts – poached pear with caramelised walnuts and 'intense' coffee ice-cream, for example, or mango ice-cream served with elderflower jelly in a brandy-snap basket – or you could go down a more traditional pub route for sticky toffee pudding. Arkell's beers are what's on tap, and a short wine list, with six by the glass, contains some good offerings. SAMPLE DISHES: flaked salmon with beetroot, sour cream and spring onions £4.50; grilled cod with red pepper sauce and coriander pesto £7.50; iced raspberry and passion-fruit crème with raspberries £3.50.

Open *11 to 3, 6 to 11, Sun 12 to 3, 7 to 11; bar food 12 to 2, 7 to 9*
Details *Children welcome in bar eating area   Car park   Wheelchair access Garden and patio   Live music   No dogs   MasterCard, Switch, Visa*

FOTHERINGHAY   Northamptonshire   map 6

Falcon Inn 🍇

Fotheringhay PE8 5HZ   TEL: (01832) 226254
off A605, 4m NE of Oundle

There are some pub companies whose mere acquisition of a pub is virtually sufficient to get it dropped from this guide. Huntsbridge Ltd, however, is that rare operator whose takeover of a pub is almost bound to ensure its inclusion. Like its sister pubs, the Pheasant at Keyston, Three Horseshoes at Madingley and White Hart at Great Yeldham (see entries), the Falcon is true to Huntsbridge's winning formula: eat what you like, where you like, and wash it down with well-kept beers and superb-value wines. Part of the success of that formula is the right property in the right village and the Falcon is no exception, nesting as it does on the main street of this unspoilt village, facing the church. The toilets are still outside, although this does not seem to deter customers, and inside are a tiny self-contained snug, a bar at the front, then a dining-room with a conservatory extension at the back. The modern-style dining-room has not abandoned the air of a pub.

On the food front, bold flavours figure in dishes such as penne pasta with raddichio, bacon, Parmesan and balsamic vinegar, or perhaps bruschetta with goats' cheese, roast peppers, plum tomatoes, garlic and olives. The menu changes every six to eight weeks to match seasonal availabilities. In May you can choose pasta with spring vegetables, herbs, chilli oil and more Parmesan; in November, look for saddle of venison with horseradish, mashed potato, honey-roast carrots and celeriac with a juniper sauce. Likewise, summer pudding will give way as the season changes to apple and blackberry crumble tart with crème Anglaise. A selection of dessert wines appears below the sweet choices on the menu. The beer list is longer than usual for Huntsbridge: besides the ubiquitous Adnams there are Greene King IPA and a guest ale. The wine list, selected seasonally by Master of Wine John Hoskins, contains expertly chosen vintages; 14 are available in half-bottles and 10 by the glass, and all are served in over-sized glasses the better to bring out their aromas. SAMPLE DISHES: fresh asparagus with Parmesan and lemon £4; chargrilled chicken in beer sauce £8; chocolate and orange crème brûlée £4.75.

Open *Tue to Sat L 11.30 to 3, Mon to Sat D 6 to 11, Sun 12 to 3, 7 to 10.30; bar food and restaurant 12 to 2.15, 6.15 to 9.15*
Details *Children welcome   Car park   Wheelchair access (also WC)   Garden and patio   No smoking in restaurant   No music   Dogs welcome in bar only   Amex, Diners, MasterCard, Switch, Visa*

F O W L M E R E   **Cambridgeshire**   **map 6**

Chequers 🍇

High Street, Fowlmere SG8 7SR   TEL: (01763) 208369
off B1368, between A10 and A505, 5m NE of Royston

A bone, a child's shoe and an iron oar in the huge inglenook fireplace were probably placed as talismans to ward off evil spirits by William Thrift, the owner of the inn in the seventeenth century; he is also thought to be responsible for installing the priest hole above the bar. Latterly the pub was popular with World War II Spitfire pilots. There is more history to ponder in the two beamed bars, comfortable with tapestry print banquettes and restrained in atmosphere, but you may be too busy deciding what to eat and drink. The menu (available in both the bar and the conservatory restaurant) roams worldwide, but in among all the complicated descriptions can be found good-looking cold beef with sauté new potatoes, ploughman's with mature Lancashire or Stilton, grilled Dover sole and some excellent Parma ham with 'plump, ripe, jammy' figs and fresh herbs. Freshness and good buying are keynotes. Sweets sound interesting, such as baked banana with cardamom syrup and vanilla ice-cream. The 50-strong wine list has an excellent New World selection, plus eight half-bottles and ten by the glass. Adnams is joined by various guest beers, including Farmer's Glory and Old Baily, but then again you might be lured by the 30-odd malt whiskies or indeed by freshly squeezed orange juice. SAMPLE DISHES: confit of Barbary duck leg with ginger, anise and chilli sauce £6; pheasant breast with wild mushroom sauce and bubble and squeak £9; Irish farmhouse cheeses £4.

Open *12 to 2.30, 6 to 11, Sun 12 to 2.30, 7 to 10.30; closed 25 Dec; bar food and restaurant 12 to 2, 7 to 10, Sun 12 to 2.30, 7 to 9.30*
Details *Children welcome   Car park   Wheelchair access   Garden and patio No smoking in restaurant   No music   No dogs   Amex, Delta, Diners, MasterCard, Switch, Visa*

FOWNHOPE   Herefordshire   map 5

▲ *Green Man Inn*

Fownhope HR1 4PE   TEL: (01432) 860243
on B4424, 6m SE of Hereford

When first recorded in 1485, the pub was known as the Naked Boy, for reasons which are now lost to us. Like many ancient inns in this part of the world, it was witness to the Civil War, when the Roundhead Colonel Birch rested his mounted troops here between the siege of Goodrich Castle and the occupation of Hereford. It then became a coaching-inn, but also saw service as a court. The iron bars to which prisoners were chained, the cell and the judge's chamber with its special lock are still visible. A former landlord was the famous boxer Tom Spring. Just half a mile from the River Wye, the tall, half-timbered inn is well situated for a number of first-class salmon reaches, but despite physical appearances is not at all pretentious. It is very much the village local and is popular with families. Chicken wings with BBQ dip or egg mayonnaise are typical bar meal starters. Chicken Kiev, breaded scampi and chilli con carne are indicative of the remainder of the dishes. Kids can have burgers or fishfingers, and vegetarians might try vegetable lasagne or home-made quiche. A restaurant menu offers some of the same dishes, but provides greater choice, and a long list of puddings includes profiteroles and banoffi toffee pie. Service is fast and friendly even when hard-pressed. This freehouse serves beer from Hook Norton as well as Marston's Pedigree and Courage Directors, while the wine list offers value for money with a selection of Three Choirs English wines and three by the glass. SAMPLE DISHES: deep-fried Brie wedges and cranberry sauce £2.50; duck à l'orange £13; Alabama chocolate fudge cake £3.

Open *11 to 11, Sun 12 to 10.30; bar food 12 to 2, 6 to 10; restaurant Sun L 12 to 2, Mon to Sat D 7 to 9*
Details *Children welcome   Car park   Wheelchair access   Garden   No-smoking area   Background music   No dogs in restaurant   Amex, Delta, Diners, MasterCard, Switch, Visa   Accommodation: 19 rooms, B&B £34.50 to £56*

FRILSHAM   Berkshire   map 2

Pot Kiln 🍺

HOME BREW

Frilsham RG16 0XX   TEL: (01635) 201366
*off B4009; in Yattendon take road opposite church, left
at next T-junction, go over M4 motorway bridge and straight
on – do not turn right to Frilsham*

This unspoilt brick-built, seventeenth-century rural pub lies down a narrow country lane in peaceful countryside, which makes it particularly popular with walkers: a pleasant garden has picnic benches and tables. The name of the pub results from it once having been the site of old brick kilns. Three simply furnished rooms have cushioned wall benches, wooden floors and open fires; there is sometimes folk music on Sunday evenings. Blackboards offer daily specials, while a small range of starters might take in tomato, bean and sage soup, ploughman's, pâtés, quiche or a daily pasta dish. More substantial offerings could be chicken with tarragon cream sauce, salmon and broccoli fish-cakes or steak and kidney pudding. Ice-creams and sorbets are the only desserts. No food is available on Tuesdays, and on Sunday only hot filled rolls are served. Excellent real ales come from Arkells and Morland, and from the West Berkshire Brewery, which operates from the rear of the pub, providing Black Kiln Bitter and Dr Hexter's Healer. House red and white wines are available by the glass, bottle or litre. SAMPLE DISHES: ham roll £1.50; macaroni cheese £4.50; orange sorbet £2.50.

Open *Mon and Wed to Sat 12 to 2.30, Mon to Sat 6.30 to 11, Sun 12 to 3, 7 to 10.30; bar food Mon and Wed to Sat 12 to 1.45, 7 to 9.30, Sun (hot filled rolls only) 12 to 2*
Details *Children welcome in family room   Car park   Wheelchair access Garden   No smoking in family room; no-smoking area in bar   Occasional live music   No dogs in saloon bar or family room   No cards*

GEDNEY DYKE   Lincolnshire   map 6

Chequers �»

Main Street, Gedney Dyke PE12 0AJ   TEL: (01406) 362666
just off B1359, from Gedney roundabout on A17, 3m E of Holbeach

Food is certainly the focus at the Chequers: an inspector thought that a competent hand in the kitchen was displaying some flair in menu choice, with well-chosen ingredients and unfussy but attractive presentation, without shortcuts. In short, this is pub food at something like its best. The exterior is whitewashed and has red doors and window frames matching the profusion of fiery colours droop-

ing from hanging baskets, which gives it a jaunty air. Inside there is a
modern extension to the dining area, leading to a patio eating area,
and at the rear towards the bar is a small open fire beneath a blackboard menu which bears the legend 'Welcome to the Chequers at
Gedney Dyke'. The dishes listed on the board illuminate rather than
extend the printed menu, but clearly there are some favourites – the
catch of the day is an important feature and vegetarians are catered
for at each course.

As to the food itself: try, perhaps, foie gras parfait on a bed of
marinated apple, Bradan Orach (apparently Gaelic for 'golden
salmon'), or in-season shellfish (Cromer crab, langoustines or scallops). For a modest main course go for Cajun spiced chicken
suprême on warm salad, or, if you are feeling more gastronomic, try
breast of Gressingham duck stuffed with prunes and pine-nuts and
glazed with a Marsala sauce. Follow this with sticky toffee pudding
in butterscotch sauce and wash it all down with a pint of either
Adnams Bass, Morland Old Speckled Hen or Elgood's Pageant. If
you prefer wine, the 60-strong list is provided by Adnams and
includes around 18 half- bottles with seven house wines offered by
the glass. SAMPLE DISHES: tian of fresh crab with sauce gazpacho
£5.50; breast of guinea-fowl with caramelised shallots and balsamic
dressing £9; chocolate ganache with coffee sauce £3.50.

Open *12 to 3, 7 to 11 (10.30 Sun); closed Sun eve in Jan and Feb, 25 and 26
Dec; bar food 12 to 2, 7 to 9 (no food eve 24 Dec and all day 26 Dec)*
Details *Children welcome   Car park   Garden and patio   No smoking in
garden room   Background music   No dogs   Amex, Delta, Diners,
MasterCard, Switch, Visa*

GIBRALTAR   Buckinghamshire   map 3

Bottle and Glass

Gibraltar HP17 8TY   TEL: (01296) 748488
on A418, between Thame and Aylesbury

This charming, well-maintained and pretty sixteenth-century
thatched inn is set back from the A418 north of Thame. It is a real
picture in summer with its overflowing hanging baskets and tubs a
riot of colour among the patio tables, offering delightful al fresco
eating at front and rear. Inside, there is a spotless interior with a
rambling series of beamed rooms around a central bar with cosy
alcoves, low ceilings, quarry-tiled floors, open fires and Windsor
chairs. It is a popular dining destination not least because of the
warm welcome offered by June Southwood, who has built a superior
operation, serving well-presented fish dishes on large white plates
with plenty of care to detail. The menu changes daily according to

what fish is delivered that morning. Choices could range from seared tuna loin with cracked pepper and roast fennel sauce to grilled Dover sole, or whole lobster thermidor. Meat dishes might include chilli beef with peppers, ginger, garlic and chilli sauce, or a rack of lamb with Anna potatoes and a sage and rosemary jus. Home-made sweets include summer pudding, or lemon posset. The pub serves the Morrells range of beers: Oxford, Varsity and Mild. Four wines are available by the glass. SAMPLE DISHES: spicy crab cocktail £6; baked sea bass with lemon and chive sauce £16; chocolate bread-and-butter pudding £4.50.

Open *10 to 3, 6 to 11, Sun 10 to 3; closed 25 and 26 Dec; bar food and restaurant 12 to 2, 7 to 9.30*
Details *Children welcome   Car park   Patio   Background music   Dogs welcome in some areas of bar   Amex, Delta, Diners, MasterCard, Switch, Visa*

GLOOSTON   Leicestershire   map 5

▲ *Old Barn Inn* 🍺

Andrews Lane, Glooston LE16 7ST   TEL: (01858) 545215
off A6, 6m N of Market Harborough

This secluded whitewashed sixteenth-century freehouse is in the heart of hunting country close to Rutland Water. The large cellar bar has stripped pine tables and a log fire in winter. Although the pub is open only at weekend lunch-times and in the evening all week except Sunday, blackboard menus provide plenty of choice and some innovative offerings. These might range from home-made soups, a variety of home-made pastas (with deep-fried chicken and bacon, perhaps, or salmon and spinach) and vegetarian dishes (stuffed red pepper, maybe, or parsnip and pear sauté), to more substantial, often seasonal offerings such as Moroccan chicken, or fillet of pork with apple and elderflower honey. To end things nicely is a good range of home-made ice-creams and puddings. More ambitious set-price and à la carte meals are served in the comfortable beamed dining-room, and could offer roast partridge, or medallions of beef in a Guinness and port sauce. Beer drinkers will be happy to note the wide range available – from Jennings, Bateman, Hook Norton, Adnams, Shepherd Neame and others. Nine wines are served by the glass, and the main list changes with the seasons to complement the menu. SAMPLE DISHES: seafood soup £3.25; paupiettes of lemon sole and smoked salmon £11.50; chocolate pecan tart £3.50.

Open *Mon to Fri eve only 7 to 11, Sat 12 to 2.30, 7 to 11, Sun 12 to 1.45; bar food and restaurant Sat and Sun L 12 to 1.30, Mon to Sat D 7 to 9.30*
Details *Children welcome in eating areas   Car park   Patio   No smoking in restaurant and bedrooms   No music   Dogs welcome on a lead in bar, and in bedrooms   Amex, Delta, MasterCard, Switch, Visa   Accommodation: 3 rooms, B&B £37.50 to £49.50*

GOOSNARGH   Lancashire   map 8

Bushell's Arms

Church Lane, Goosnargh PR3 2BH   TEL: (01772) 865235
off B5269, 3m W of Longridge

Goosnargh is a dormitory village between Preston and Longridge, handy for the M6 and the good walking country of the Forest of Bowland. The Bushell's Arms stands on the rural side of the village, where parking is rarely a problem. The bar space is open plan but divided into more intimate spaces by a series of alcoves furnished with red plush banquettes and small tables. The tables are significant because the food is possibly the most important side of the business. Licensee David Best is a keen food and wine writer. By any standards the menu is remarkably wide-ranging, galloping around the globe from Middle Eastern falafel, or Burmese spring rolls to Moroccan chicken, or an authentically South American version of chilli con carne. Puddings return closer to home with reassuring nursery favourites such as ginger sponge or rhubarb and strawberry crumble. Even more local are the award-winning Lancashire cheese, and Westmorland tart. The wine list shows exceptional flair; over 50 enticingly described bins are listed, all carefully dated (three by the glass). Hand-pumped ales include Timothy Taylor Best Bitter, Flowers IPA and Boddingtons. If you are driving, the range of Douwe Egberts coffees verges on designer chic. Despite the gastronomic ambitions of the Bushell's Arms, its prices remain consistently reasonable. SAMPLE DISHES: Stilton and chestnut paté £2; salmon puff pastry parcel £6.50; wild blackberry pie £2.

Open *12 to 3, 6 to 11, Sun 12 to 'until quiet', 7 to 10.30; closed 25 Dec, some Mons; bar food 12 to 2, 7 to 9.15*
Details *Children welcome in bar eating area   Car park   Wheelchair access (also WC)   Garden and patio   No-smoking areas   No music   Guide dogs only   No cards*

GOSFIELD   Essex   map 3

Green Man

The Street, Gosfield CO9 1TP   TEL: (01787) 472746
on A1017, 4m NE of Braintree

'We know of no better pub/restaurant for a traditional style of
Sunday lunch,' commented a reporter. This Greene King tenancy is a
popular dining pub, with a friendly, cheerful atmosphere where
customers can tuck into a wide selection of well-cooked food chosen
from daily-changing menus chalked on blackboards. Try, for a first
course, salmon smoked in nearby Hedingham, or flavoursome home-
made brandy and chicken liver pâté. Roast beef is mandatory, beautifully cooked and tender, or rebel and go for pheasant casseroled in
red wine. Blackcurrant pie with a scoop of vanilla ice-cream is likewise a must. The well-kept beers are Greene King IPA and Abbot ale,
while a reasonably sized wine list contains some bottles starting at
£6, and around five are usually offered by the glass. SAMPLE DISHES:
fan of melon with fruit and sorbet £4; home-made steak and kidney
pudding £7; lemon syllabub £3.

Open *12 to 3, 6.30 to 11, Sun 7 to 10.30; bar food 12 to 2, 6.30 to 9, Sun L
only 12 to 2*
Details *Children welcome   Car park   Wheelchair access   Garden   Jukebox
No dogs in eating areas   Amex, Delta, MasterCard, Switch, Visa*

GRANGE MOOR   West Yorkshire   map 8

Kaye Arms ❧

29 Wakefield Road, Grange Moor WF4 4BG   TEL: (01924) 848385
off A642 and B6118, 4m S of Dewsbury

This fairly large roadside pub stands on its own a considerable way
away from any houses. Its remote location has affected drinking
trade, and the pub, which has served food for many years, now does
so on an increasingly significant basis. The spacious interior boasts a
fair-sized bar; although it is still very much a pub layout, the many
tables now wear tablecloths. Staff take no bookings except for parties
of six and over, and get good trade from visitors to the nearby
Yorkshire Mining Museum. The short printed menu is strong on
house specialities, all pleasing and well presented. Mature Cheddar
cheese soufflé is popular with regulars, and grilled scallops in garlic
butter and Gruyère cheese are 'exactly as described'. In addition
there will be daily recommendations; goats' cheese in filo pastry, say,
or French black pudding on a fresh spinach tart. Mains of the day

might include roast fillet of salmon with lemon butter sauce, or roast marinated venison with pear and rosemary sauce. A range of side orders is available for an extra charge. A reporter tells us that the separately listed puddings, which consist of an inviting hot and cold selection, have improved over the past few years. Try, perhaps, chocolate pudding with cream or ice-cream, or sticky toffee pudding with butterscotch sauce and fresh cream. Theakston Bitter is the only real ale available, but some 14 wines are available by the glass: seven white, five red, one rosé and one sparkling. SAMPLE DISHES: Cumbrian ham with sweet-and-sour fruit £4.50; poached salmon, strawberry and cucumber salad £9; pavlova with banana and cassis sauce £3.25.

Open *Tue to Sun 11.30 to 3, 7 to 11, Sat 6.15 to 11; closed 25 and 26 Dec; bar food Tue to Sun 12 to 1.45, 7 to 9.45*
Details *No children   Car park   Wheelchair access (also WC)   No-smoking area   Background music   No dogs   Delta, MasterCard, Switch, Visa*

GRASMERE   Cumbria   map 10

▲ *Travellers Rest*

Grasmere LA22 9RR   TEL: (01539) 435604
just off A591 Keswick road, ½m N of Grasmere

Set in magnificent scenery, this sixteenth-century coaching-inn is a typical long, low, whitewashed Lakeland pub that nestles into the hills behind it. It caters for the occasional effete motorist, cyclists and walkers on the coast-to-coast route, who will be glad of the open log fire that hits full frontally upon entering on a cold day. The interior is a simple arrangement of three interconnected rooms with a bar in the middle, all done out in rough-cast whitewashed walls, beams and low ceilings; one of the rooms is a games room. Despite the carpets, those with rucksacks and heavy boots are made to feel welcome. Jennings beers are on offer – there's Sneck Lifter, Cumberland Ale and Bitter – with Marston's Pedigree as a bonus. The menu is very similar to that on offer at a sister establishment, the King's Head at St John in the Vale at the other end of Thirlmere, which, curiously, looks almost identical. Food is good value for money and local produce features strongly. Blackboards display the daily specials, the catch of the day and wines of the week. Apart from a selection of open and closed sandwiches, there might be starters like garlic mushrooms, moules marinière, or deep-fried squid. Reasonably priced main courses include chicken tikka masala, steak and kidney pie, beef burger, or chicken Kiev. For puddings, you could choose between chocolate pecan pie, or pear and ginger pudding with custard. There is a children's menu and the pub is very child-friendly. The Wordsworth Museum is nearby. SAMPLE DISHES: deep-fried squid £3; roast half-duck £7.25; blackberry and apple pancake £3.

Open *12 to 11, Sun 12 to 10.30; bar food and restaurant 12 to 3, 6 to 9.30 (May to Oct 12 to 9.30)*
Details *Children welcome   Car park   Wheelchair access   Garden   No smoking in dining-room   Background and live music; jukebox   No dogs in dining areas   Delta, MasterCard, Switch, Visa   Accommodation: 8 rooms, B&B £16 to £58*

GREATBRIDGE   Hampshire   map 2

Dukes Head   NEW ENTRY

Greatbridge Road, Greatbridge SO51 0HB   TEL: (01794) 514450
on A3057 Romsey-Stockbridge road, 1m N of Romsey

Positive feedback has increased during the past year on this pleasant, cream-painted riverside inn dating from 1583. An Eldridge Pope pub, though you would not know it from the individualistic décor, it stands on a sharp bend, catching passing motorists' attention with a colourful display of hanging basketry in summer. The rambling interior, with an inglenook fireplace in the main bar, boasts themed rooms including one dedicated to fishing, and a rear garden of rustic tables and benches secludes customers from traffic noise. Food is a high point: one reader's Saturday night meal was described as 'tremendous', with the unexpected bonus of a magician between courses! Extensive, seasonal menus show wide-ranging influences – Creole, Mediterranean, even Russian dishes rub shoulders with home-grown items like Hampshire venison. A house speciality is gumbo, a stew-like soup of seafood, chicken or vegetables ladled from a tureen, served with rice and garlic bread. Local bitters from Eldridge Pope and Hampshire Brewery include Hardy Country, Pride of Romsey (praised as 'spot on') and King Alfred's. Nearly 30 competently selected and reasonably priced wines are on offer, including many by the glass as well as fine ports and champagnes. Service is rated 'friendly and efficient'. SAMPLE DISHES: game terrine £4.50; mustard-glazed ham hock £9; bread-and-butter pudding £3.25.

Open *11 to 11; bar food 11 to 3, 6 to 10*
Details *Children welcome in some areas   Car park   Garden   No-smoking room   Background music   No dogs   Amex, Delta, Diners, MasterCard, Switch, Visa*

Hampden Arms

Great Hampden HP16 9RQ   TEL: (01494) 488255
*off A4010 or A413, midway between Princes Risborough and
Great Missenden*

The Hampden is most certainly an eating house: portions are large,
and so are the menus. The pub is brick, timber-framed and plaster-
panelled with a large, attractive garden to the back and side. In the
small L-shaped interior is a corner bar; wooden beams and horse
brasses abound and every table is laid up, leaving little space, even at
the bar, for social drinking without eating. Yet the atmosphere is
homely and cosy enough to remind people that this is indeed a pub.
Chequers, the Prime Minister's country residence, is not far away,
and the area is popular with walkers and cyclists. The lobby blackboard even offers a 'walkers' special' – a large plate of chips with
cheese and onion on top. A long, printed menu is doubled in length
by the choices on the blackboard list: home-made onion soup, or
cheese salad, followed by lasagne, steak Diane, or chicken Maryland.
A vegetarian menu offers five choices – from baked Stilton avocado
to Californian fried vegetables – and a light brunch menu presents
some high-tea-style dishes such as buck rarebit or Spanish omelette.
Puddings accommodate all our old friends, from crème brûlée to
apple crumble, as well as banana pancake, and you may opt to end
things nicely with one of the ten liqueur coffees on offer. Hampden
Bitter and Tetley are the beers on offer. About a dozen bottles
feature on the wine list; house wines are £9.95 and three wines are
available by the glass. SAMPLE DISHES: Coquilles St Jacques £7;
chicken and bacon pie £7.25; profiteroles £3.50.

Open *12 to 2.30, 6.30 to 11, Sun 12 to 3, 6.30 to 10.30; closed some Sun in
winter; bar food 12 to 2, 6.30 to 9.30 (9 Sun)*
Details *Children welcome in family room   Car park   Garden   No music
Dogs welcome at licensee's discretion   Amex, Delta, MasterCard, Switch, Visa*

GREAT OUSEBURN   North Yorkshire   map 9

Crown NEW ENTRY

Main Street, Great Ouseburn YO26 9RF   TEL: (01423) 330430
off B6265, 4m S of Boroughbridge

Great Ouseburn lies conveniently close to the Great North Road,
north-west of York. As the name suggests, the River Ouse flows close
by. The Crown is a warm, welcoming pub with ancient beams and
huge log fires in the main bar. Both landlord and staff engender a
friendly atmosphere and many customers are local regulars who
know each other. An outside courtyard provides additional drinking
space on summer evenings. Food is served in a separate dining-room,
agreeably decked with Wedgwood china and portraits of local
worthies. Regular printed menus are given variety with blackboard
specials, perhaps including queen scallops or fresh mussels, followed
by seafood kebabs or a venison casserole. Vegetarian options might
run to a wild mushroom, spinach and mixed pepper tart or vegetables and Brie en croûte. Many dishes are elaborately sauced and
puddings are all home-made. At weekends, large baguettes make
hearty lunchtime snacks. Real ales include John Smith's, Black
Sheep, Theakston and Timothy Taylor Landlord. There's a fair selection of bottled beers and New World wines (six by the glass). Note
that the pub is open only in the evening on weekdays, but all day at
weekends. SAMPLE DISHES: spicy Thai fish-cakes with mint raita dip
£5; chargrilled pork medallions with cream, brandy, mushroom and
tarragon sauce £10.50; 14oz sirloin steak £13

Open *Mon to Fri 5 to 11, Sat and Sun 11 to 11; bar food and restaurant Mon
to Fri 6 to 10, Sat 12 to 3.30, 6 to 10, Sun 12 to 9.30*
Details *Well-behaved children welcome   Car park   Wheelchair access
Garden and patio   Background music   Guide dogs only   Delta, Diners,
MasterCard, Switch, Visa*

GREAT TEW   Oxfordshire   map 5

▲ *Falkland Arms* 🍺 NEW ENTRY

Great Tew OX7 4DB   TEL: (01608) 683653
off B4022, 5m E of Chipping Norton

Dr Johnson and Samuel Pepys would not be out of place in this
sixteenth-century, creeper-clad pub. Made of local golden stone, it
nestles in a row of thatched cottages, opposite the village school. The
atmosphere inside is 'classic country pub', with worn flagstones,
rough stone walls, a splendid inglenook fireplace, rustic settles and

heavy oak-beamed ceiling adorned with large mugs. The rear garden, complete with dovecot, is shady and peaceful. The ever changing (though limited) menu boasts hearty, traditional, home-made food, and the kitchen prides itself on its use of fresh ingredients. At lunchtime, baguettes, jacket potatoes and a few hot dishes are on offer, while in the evening you can choose from soup or pâté, pork in cider, chilli, steak and ale pie, or lamb and rosemary casserole. Our inspector noted the absence of chips. A superb range of eight to ten ales are on offer, including Farmers Glory, Hall & Woodhouse Tanglefoot, Hook Norton Best and Adnams Broadside. The wine list includes 16 English country wines available by the bottle or glass, and four house wines by the glass. Westons Old Rosie Scrumpy is available for cider drinkers. SAMPLE DISHES: mushrooms cooked in double cream with port and Stilton £4; blade of lamb roasted with honey £10; apple and cinnamon pie £3.

Open *11.30 to 2.30, 6 to 11, Sun 12 to 3, 7 to 10.30 (all day Sat and Sun in summer); bar food L only 12 to 2; restaurant Mon to Sat D only 7 to 8 (booking advised)*
Details *Children welcome in eating areas at L only   Garden and patio   No smoking in restaurant   Live music on Sun eves   No dogs in restaurant or bedrooms   MasterCard, Visa, Switch   Accommodation: 6 rooms, B&B £40 to £65*

GREAT WHITTINGTON   Northumberland   map 10

Queens Head Inn 😋 😋 🍺

Great Whittington NE19 2HP   TEL: (01434) 672267
off A68, 4m N of Corbridge at Stagshaw roundabout, then 1½m to village

Arrive late on a Monday night, without booking, if you like. It is not a problem; nothing, it seems, is an inconvenience at this first-rate pub. Definitely in the hard-to-find category, possibly because those who know of it are reluctant to divulge its whereabouts, it is nevertheless worth a detour off the A68 to sample cooking that could hold its own in the West End of London. The date 1701 is carved into the stone lintel over the main doorway of this handsome pub, and as you enter you will find a small bar area to the left, with a coal fire burning beneath a broad mural of a hunting scene painted across the width of the chimney-piece. Sit here awhile and consult the printed menu, or choose from the extensive blackboard. To the right of the bar is a raised seating area and beyond that, behind a row of pew seating, is the dining area, which becomes progressively more formal the further from the bar you go. Country prints adorn the bare stone walls and there is a Welsh dresser at the back of the dining-room.

Service is knowledgeable and chatty, and timing is just about right for the degree of preparation and presentation involved.

Your food, when it arrives, will look terrific; there is clearly considerable skill in this kitchen, and a reliance on good-quality raw materials. Cream of chicken and leek soup is thick and smooth; avocado and prawns with a lime and chive vinaigrette is tangy and well-balanced. Lamb cutlets arrive beautifully presented; and roast peppers with oyster mushroom salad contains wonderfully flavoursome mushrooms. Finally, if you or one of your number does not select the iced nougatine on a fruit coulis for you all to have a taste, then you are fools unto yourselves. Well-kept beers come from Yorkshire independents Hambleton Ales and Black Sheep. About 30 wines from all over the world feature on the wine list; three are available by the glass. SAMPLE DISHES: salad of smoked bacon, tomato fillets and croûtons with fresh pesto dressing £4.50; breast of duck with a compote of herbs £12; duo of chocolate mousse on a café Anglaise £3.50.

Open *Mon 6 to 11, Tue to Sat 12 to 2.30, 6 to 11, Sun 12 to 3, 7 to 10.30; bar food and restaurant 12 to 2 (exc Mon), 6.30 to 9*
Details *Children welcome in eating areas   Car park   Wheelchair access (also WC)   Garden   No smoking in restaurant   Background music   No dogs Delta, MasterCard, Switch, Visa*

GREAT WOLFORD   **Warwickshire**   map 5

▲ *Fox & Hounds* 🍺

Great Wolford CV36 5NQ   TEL: (01608) 674220
off A44, 3m NE of Moreton-in-Marsh

The hamlet of Great Wolford is just east of the Warwickshire–Gloucestershire border and is convenient for the antique shops of Moreton-in-Marsh and the Rollright stone circle. Licensed since 1540, the pub has a venerable feel about it, with low ceilings, hanging mugs, jugs and hop garlands, and a rough, open stone fireplace. Whereas the printed menu lists the usual range of pub fare – ploughman's, jacket potatoes, a curry and steaks – blackboard specials head into more ambitious territory. Salmon and crab fish-cake with a saffron and leek sauce could be a starter, followed by roasted lamb noisettes with a herb crust served with risotto. Seven beers are on offer, mostly from the larger regionals, including Jennings, Adnams, Hook Norton and Black Sheep, and there is a wide selection of malt whiskies. Five wines are available by the glass from the fairly basic 28-strong list. SAMPLE DISHES: smoked goose breast on potato salad £5; délice of Scottish salmon on scented couscous £10; icky sticky pudding served with ice-cream quenelles £3.50.

Open *Tue to Sun L 12 to 3, Tue to Sat eve 7 to 11; bar food 12 to 2, 7 to 9.15*
Details *Children welcome in dining-room   Car park   Wheelchair access (also WC)   Garden   No music   Dogs welcome   No cards   Accommodation: 5 rooms, room only £35*

GREAT YELDHAM   Essex   map 6

White Hart 🏵🏵 🍇

Poole Street, Great Yeldham CO9 4HJ   TEL: (01787) 237250
on A604 between Haverhill and Halstead, 6m NW of Halstead

This half-timbered classic Tudor pub, built in 1505, has been owned by the Huntsbridge group (see also Three Horseshoes, Madingley, Pheasant Inn, Keyston and Falcon Inn, Fotheringhay) and run by chef-proprietor Roger Jones since he moved here from the Pheasant in 1995. Despite the 'heaviness' of the beams, it has been sympathet-ically refurbished to make the most of the structural features inside and out, and the atmosphere is informal, with customers welcome to eat in the bar or more formal 'restaurant' as they choose. The cook-ing style is decidedly modern, and both menus are available in all parts of the house: a 'snack' list – offering the likes of pasta, plough-man's, sausages and mash – and a lengthy à la carte. The latter might open with pan-fried fillet of trout with warm new potato and caper salad and salsa verde, perhaps followed by fillet of lamb with rata-touille, stuffed aubergine and another salsa, this time of rocket and mint. The wide range of home-made breads are frequently praised by reporters, and the sweets list also features its own selection of dessert wines and port – chargrilled nectarines with honey and crème fraîche may be accompanied with a glass of 1990 Ch. Loubens or a 1993 Tokay Aszu, for example. Reports suggest that standards of food and service can be a little variable, but when on form are excellent.

The main list of 'around 100 of the most interesting wines we can lay our hands on' offers good choice without pretension and at a range of prices; nearly all of the 16 house wines are available by the glass. The beer selection is a large offering of regional ales including Adnams, Fuller's London Pride, Bateman, XB, Charles Wells Bombardier, Shepherd Neame Spitfire and Marston's Pedigree. SAMPLE DISHES: Thai-style mussel soup with lemon grass, spring onion and noodles £4; seared fillets of John Dory with stuffed pepper and borlotti bean salad £11; raspberry crème brûlée £3.25.

Open *11 to 3, 6 to 11, Sun 12 to 2, 7 to 10.30; closed eve 25 and 26 Dec, and 1 Jan; bar food and restaurant 11 to 3, 6 to 11, Sun 12 to 2, 7 to 10.30*
Details *Children welcome   Car park   Garden and patio   No smoking in restaurant   No music   No dogs   Amex, Delta, Diners, MasterCard, Switch, Visa*

GRETA BRIDGE   Co Durham   map 10

▲ *Morritt Arms* ❦

Greta Bridge DL12 9SE   TEL: (01833) 627232
off A66, 6m W of Bowes

This substantial creeper-covered seventeenth-century coaching-inn, just by the River Greta, is only three miles from Barnard Castle. A pleasant garden is available for summer drinking. The public rooms have polished wood block floors strewn with rugs, comfortable armchairs and sofas, log fires, and tasteful paintings and prints on the walls. The Dickens bar has huge murals depicting characters from the novelist's books – he stayed here in 1839. The hotel is open all day with a lounge menu offering morning coffee or afternoon tea, including cream teas, and more substantial sandwiches available all day. The bar menu also goes in for sandwiches, such as hot ciabatta with pesto, tomato and mozzarella; rare roast beef; prawn and salmon decker; or Italian charcuterie. Otherwise start with soup, ploughman's or marinated mushrooms, going on to braised lamb shank, steak and kidney pie or salmon fish-cakes; vegetarians are offered vegetable Wellington with four-cheese sauce. Puddings might be profiteroles, sticky toffee or bread-and-butter. Set-price meals are available in the Copperfield restaurant and could start with a fan of avocado followed by roast guinea-fowl, finishing with strawberry and raspberry cheesecake. Beers are from Tetley, Theakston, Landlord from Timothy Taylor or Conciliation from the nearby Butterknowle Brewery at Bishop Auckland. An extensive wine list of some 200 bottles, predominantly New World, is available with around a dozen by the glass. SAMPLE DISHES: home-made chicken liver pâté £3; spicy sausages with Parmesan mash £6; chocolate and orange torte £4.25.

Open *11 to 11, Sun 11 to 10.30; bar food and restaurant 12 to 2.30, 6 (7 restaurant) to 9.30*
Details *Children welcome   Car park   Wheelchair access (also WC)   Garden No smoking in eating areas   Background and live music; jukebox   No dogs in restaurant   Amex, Delta, Diners, MasterCard, Switch, Visa   Accommodation: 23 rooms, B&B £60 to £86*

The Guide is totally independent, accepts no free hospitality and carries no advertising.

GRIMSTHORPE   Lincolnshire   map 6

▲ *Black Horse Inn* 🍇 | NEW ENTRY |

Grimsthorpe PE10 0LY   TEL: (01778) 591247
On A151, between A1 and A15, 4m NW of Bourne

Built in 1717 as a coaching-inn, and nestling in the shadows of
Grimsthorpe Castle – used in TV adaptations of *Middlemarch* and
Moll Flanders – the Black Horse Inn is a very worthy new entry in
the *Guide*. It was taken over in late 1996 by Brian and Elaine Rey,
who are obviously aiming high. Separate bar menus operate at lunch-
time and evening and there is also a restaurant with its own menus.
Bar lunches might start with pan-fried halloumi cheese with lime and
caper vinaigrette, hot buttered Arbroath smokie, or Piedmont pepper
stuffed with tomato, garlic, mozzarella and anchovies. Main courses
are meatier options such as kidneys sautéd in Madeira sauce, roast
Scotch beef with Yorkshire pudding and onion gravy, or
Gressingham duck breast in a red wine sauce. If you prefer fish,
there might be poached salmon steak with dill sauce. Finish with
'excellent' toffee-apple pie with home-made vanilla ice-cream, or
lemon tart with orange sauce. The pub serves Bateman's XXXB as
well as two house beers, and a massive wine list, complete with
index, offers pudding wines, ports and liqueurs, half-bottles, nine
house wines by the glass, bin-end specials and a faultless selection of
drinking at all prices. SAMPLE DISHES: field mushrooms filled with
Stilton £4; rare-breed pork chop with red wine gravy £6.50; warm
toffee-apple pie £3.25.

Open *11.30 to 2.30, 6 (6.30 in winter) to 11, Sun 12 to 3, 7 to 10.30; bar
food and restaurant 12 to 2, 7 to 9.30*
Details *No children under 14   Car park   Wheelchair access (also WC)
Garden and patio   No smoking in restaurant   Background music   Guide dogs
only   Amex, Delta, MasterCard, Switch, Visa   Accommodation: 6 rooms,
B&B £55 to £90*

GUNWALLOE   Cornwall   map 1

▲ *Halzephron Inn*

Gunwalloe TR12 7QB   TEL: (01326) 240406
*from A3083 1½m S of Helston take small lane
towards Church Cove*

This old smugglers' inn sits on the cliff top from where a tunnel
leads down to the beach, where goods from wrecked ships were
carried ashore. The name means 'hell's headland' in Cornish, and on

windy days it can be a very dramatic setting. The pub has come a long way since the mid-1990s as a small outlet offering snacks: the bar has been extended and an effort has been made to increase the number of tables for diners, including a family room with a stack of toys for small hands. The same menu is available in all three dining areas, and there is a wide selection of specials. Starters might include home-made chicken liver pâté, smoked salmon and avocado mousse, or pan-fried scallops, followed by roast noisettes of lamb with root vegetables and rosemary jus, or perhaps beef stew with mustard dumplings in a rich stock. Or you could choose local fishmonger Mr Kearsley's crab salad platter, or local butcher Mr Retallack's chargrilled steak. There is almond and apricot meringue or chocolate rum mousse to finish things off nicely. Beers come from the local brewery, Sharp's; one reporter particularly enjoyed the Doom Bar. St Austell Dartmoor Best is also on offer, as are a selection of whiskies to warm you up after a brisk walk along the cliff top. The mainly European wine list is reasonably priced but offers only three by the glass. SAMPLE DISHES: fillet of smoked trout with horseradish sauce £4.25; devilled lambs' kidneys £8.50; Yarde Farm dairy ice-creams with home-made butterscotch sauce £3.

Open *11 to 2.30, 6 to 11, Sun 12 to 2.30, 6 to 10.30; closed 25 Dec; bar food and restaurant 12 to 2, 7 to 9.30 (9 Sun)*
Details *Children welcome in family room   Car park   Wheelchair access Garden   No smoking in restaurant   No music   No dogs   Amex, Delta, MasterCard, Switch, Visa   Accommodation: 2 rooms, B&B £35 to £64*

HAILEY   Oxfordshire

map 5

▲ *Bird in Hand* ☙

Whiteoak Green, Hailey OX8 5XP   TEL: (01993) 868321
off B4022 Charlbury to Witney road; turn right ½m after Hailey village

Described by a reporter as 'one of England's best-kept secrets', the Bird in Hand is a much extended Cotswold stone seventeenth-century inn, now more a small hotel. Situated in the rolling country-side of West Oxfordshire, it is an ideal base for visiting Oxford, Blenheim Palace or Bicester village. Staff are described as 'welcoming and friendly'. Light snacks of sandwiches or ploughman's are available, plus traditional items like fish and chips with mushy peas, steak and kidney pudding or sugar-glazed ham with egg and chips. More challenging items on the menu include warm salad of seared tuna or shredded crispy duck and bacon, followed by main courses of pan-fried chicken livers, chargrilled pork fillet or various steaks; vegetarians are offered summer tomato and mozzarella tart or a pasta dish. The daily-changing blackboards focus on fish, perhaps red mullet roasted with peppers and garlic, or cod with mussel sauce. Finish with chocolate and brandy torte, strawberry cheesecake, or a selection of British cheeses. There is a separate restaurant furnished in red and green where a choice of roasts is served for Sunday lunch. Beers are Marston's Pedigree, Boddingtons and Wadworth 6X, while 12 wines are offered by the glass from £2.50. SAMPLE DISHES: grilled goats' cheese £4.50; stuffed breast of chicken £9; blackcurrant and cassis bavarois £3.75.

Open *11 to 11, Sun 12 to 3, 7 to 10.30; closed 25 and 26 Dec; bar food and restaurant 12 to 2, 7 to 9.30*
Details *Children welcome in bar eating area   Car park   Wheelchair access (also WC)   Garden   No smoking in restaurant   Background music   No dogs in restaurant   Delta, MasterCard, Switch, Visa   Accommodation: 16 rooms, B&B £55 to £75*

HALFWAY BRIDGE   West Sussex   map 3

Halfway Bridge Inn 🍺
Halfway Bridge GU28 9BP   TEL: (01798) 861281
on A272, midway between Midhurst and Petworth, just S of Lodsworth

The Inn is a hotchpotch of buildings of varying ages. Visitors approach through an archway covered in jasmine and roses, then a garden dotted with extremely weathered tables and half-barrel tubs of pansies and lobelia threatening to burst the cooper's hoops. Inside are low ceilings, polished wooden tables, the standard indolent pub dog, and paintings and bric-à-brac in a succession of small rooms clustered around the bar area. The laid-back ambience is created in no small part by sincere and friendly antipodean staff. A short menu has plenty of interesting choices, such as spinach and rocket Caesar salad, or a warm salad of chicken livers and balsamic dressing for starters, and seared red mullet with spicy stir-fried egg noodles, or walnut and mushroom strudel with crème fraîche and chives for main courses. To finish try the 'chocolate thingy' – a slab of frozen chocolate confection including nuts and dried fruit – a 'wickedly good dessert'. Good beers are in abundance: Cheriton Pots Ale, Gale's HSB and Fuller's London Pride as well as guests from Harveys, Brewery on Sea, Hampshire Brewery and Hop Back. Orval and Chimay Trappist beers are available by the bottle. A 25-strong wine list includes offerings from Chile and Lebanon. SAMPLE DISHES: moules marinière £5; confit of duck with red wine sauce £10.75; walnut treacle tart £3.

Open *11 to 3, 6 to 11, Sun 12 to 3, 7 to 10.30; closed 25 Dec, and Sun eve when clocks go back; bar food and restaurant 12 to 2 (2.30 Sat and Sun), 7 to 10*
Details *Car park   Wheelchair access   Garden and patio   No-smoking area in restaurant   Live music   Dogs welcome on a lead   Delta, MasterCard, Switch, Visa*

HALLATON   Leicestershire   map 5

Bewicke Arms

1 Eastgate, Hallaton LE16 8UB   TEL: (01858) 555217
off A47, 7m NE of Market Harborough

An unspoilt pub in an unspoilt village surrounded by rolling countryside, this 400-year-old thatched inn stands opposite the green, with its
unusually shaped stone cross. There is also a rural museum where you
can find out about the village's traditional Hare Pie Scrambling and
Bottle Kicking, which take place each Easter Monday. Long-serving
and popular landlord Neil Spiers has made unchanging consistency the
pub's strength. He serves Ruddles Best Bitter and County, Marston's
Pedigree and a fortnightly-changing guest beer, and produces a single
printed lunch and evening menu with simple fish and steak dishes.
There are also more adventurous blackboard specials, such as chicken
puttanesca, or Eastern casserole of lamb with naan bread. The modest
wine list provides a dozen bottles and three by the glass. The pub also
operates a tea-room and gift shop in a converted former coach house.
SAMPLE DISHES: warm goats'-cheese salad £4.75; creamy seafood
pancakes £7; treacle sponge and custard £3.

Open *12 to 2.30, 7 to 11; bar food and restaurant 12 to 2, 7 to 9.45*
Details *Children welcome   Car park   Garden and patio   Background music
No dogs   Delta, MasterCard, Switch, Visa*

HAMBLEDEN   Buckinghamshire   map 3

▲ *Stag & Huntsman Inn* NEW ENTRY

Hambleden RG9 6RP   TEL: (01491) 571227
off A4155 Henley to Marlow road, 1m from Mill End

Film-makers favour the quaint Chiltern village of Hambleden for its
idyllic setting. The pub, in every respect a tourist destination in itself,
is no exception. The very cosy public bar is full of crooked nooks,
and splashes of green – chairs, picture frames, tablecloths – punctu-
ate the red dining-room. Henley is in the catchment area and the pub
is very popular during the Regatta, but despite its upmarket location
has not lost the common touch. Curry and quiz nights are just some
of the entertainments provided, and locals clearly feel very at home
here. Food comes courtesy of a printed menu, short but offering
plenty of variety, and a blackboard for daily specials; you can eat
what you like, where you like. Home-made soup with a bread roll is
good traditional pub fare, but artichoke and feta cheese salad illus-
trates willingness to keep up with popular tastes. Crab-cakes and

aïoli are reported to be 'excellent', garlicky and rich. Portions are generous: liver and bacon with spring onion mash and gravy was 'copious', while stew of the day comes innovatively served in a giant Yorkshire pudding. Ploughman's and children's meals are available, and the puddings list is remarkably short, with tiramisù probably the most adventurous selection. Since this is Henley, it seems only sensible that the pub serves Brakspear Ordinary and Special, but it also stocks Wadworth 6X and Old Luxters Barn Ale. A short laminated wine list runs to 20 wines, offering – except for certain areas of France – one red and one white per region. SAMPLE DISHES: Spanish omelette and salad £4.50; chilli bowl with a bread roll £5.25; blackberry and apple crumble £3.

Open *11 to 2.30, 6 to 11, Sun 12 to 3, 7 to 10.30; closed bank hol Mon eves; bar food 12 to 2, 7 to 9.30 (9 Sun)*
Details *Children welcome in bar eating area   Car park   Garden   Background music   Dogs welcome on a lead in public bar only   Delta, MasterCard, Switch, Visa   Accommodation: 3 rooms, B&B £58 to £68*

HAMBLETON   Rutland   map 6

▲ *Finch's Arms*   NEW ENTRY

Oakham Road, Upper Hambleton LE15 8TL   TEL: (01572) 756575
off A606 E of Oakham

Located in a sleepy village on the peninsula in Rutland Water, this unassuming stone pub is a stone's throw from Hambleton Hall. Owned by the proprietors of the Peacock Inn at Redmile (see entry), it has been refurbished in keeping with the style of that establishment, and offers a modern menu of upmarket, Mediterranean-influenced dishes. Diners get stunning views of the reservoir in a pleasant setting of yellow-washed walls, wooden floors and cane furnishings. Should you not want a full meal, light snacks served in the bar include smoked haddock chowder and lasagne of oyster mushroom and Parmesan. Examples of the kind of 'Peacockesque' fare on offer would be, in the starters department, warm Roquefort tart with crispy Parma ham and red onion jus, or mussel, celery, cream and vermouth stew; mains might include blackened Cajun chicken breast, savoury couscous and tomato oil salsa, or confit of duck leg with Caesar salad and ginger vinaigrette. There are several pasta dishes on the menu, which is supplemented by daily specials such as cream of leek and mushroom soup, and pan-fried duck breast. Desserts are along the lines of cappuccino crème brûlée and apple and pear tarte Tatin with calvados sauce. Service sometimes comes under pressure – the price of growing popularity. The pub offers quaffers Marston's Pedigree, Adnams and Timothy Taylor Landlord, while sippers get a

40-bin list, including six by the glass. SAMPLE DISHES: Moroccan spiced crab-cakes, mint and watercress pesto £4.50; hay-roasted pork loin with pistachio and dried apricot stuffing £9.50; rum chocolate and pine-nut tart £4.

Open *summer 11 to 11, Sun 12 to 10.30, winter 10.30 to 3, 5 to 10.30; bar food and restaurant 12 to 2.30, 6.30 to 9.30 (no food Sun eve in winter)*
Details *Children welcome Car park Wheelchair access Garden No smoking in restaurant Background music No dogs Delta, Diners, MasterCard, Switch, Visa Accommodation: 9 rooms, B&B £65 to £85*

HAMSTEAD MARSHALL   Berkshire   map 2

▲ *White Hart*

Kintbury Road, Hamstead Marshall RG20 0HW
TEL: (01488) 658201
off A4, 4½m W of Newbury

This smart, very English-looking sixteenth-century inn with a neat walled garden and six *en suite* bedrooms in a converted barn has been run by Nicola and Dorothy Aromando since 1982. Their imaginative and popular Italian food uses herbs from the garden and beef from Elm Farm, whose organic fields surround the pub on all sides. Indeed, a two-mile 'appetiser' walk round the farm could start and end at the White Hart. Inside, the L-shaped bar is informal with beams, a central open brick fireplace with log fire, red plush seats, a mix of sturdy tables and attractive prints. The same menu operates in both the bar and the restaurant, and the food and 'excellent' espresso coffee are brought by smartly attired waitresses. Printed menus list the starters, such as Parma ham with melon, and Napoli salami with olives, as well as frittata (Italian-style omelette) and pasta dishes – lasagne, quadroni or spaghetti al olio. From the specials boards you could choose fritelle (organic meatballs stuffed with mozzarella), or salmi di cervo, a venison and Guinness pie. Tiramisù is a well-praised dessert. Wadworth 6X is on offer along with Hardy Country or Ringwood Best and, not unnaturally, the wine list is rather pro-Italian, with an organic Soave to go with your organic food. SAMPLE DISHES: insalata of mozzarella with tomato, olive oil and basil dressing £4.50; agnello (lamb cutlets with a wine and balsamic vinegar sauce) £12.50; warm apple pie and mango ice-cream £4.50.

Open *Mon to Sat 12 to 2.30, 6 to 11; closed 25 and 26 Dec, 2 weeks summer; bar food and restaurant 12.15 to 2, 6.30 to 9.45*
Details *Children welcome in eating areas Car park Wheelchair access Garden No smoking area in restaurant Background music No dogs MasterCard, Visa Accommodation: 6 rooms, B&B £50 to £75*

HAROME   North Yorkshire   map 9

Star Inn ✿ ✿ ❧

Harome YO6 5JE   TEL: (01439) 770397
off A170, 3m SE of Helmsley

The Star, by all accounts, is definitely heading up – something you should not do on entering the pub, for the thatched roof comes down to head height. Inside this 600-year-old building you are likely to be met by licensee Jacquie Pern, whose husband Andrew is chef. When they took it over in 1996 it was largely unchanged from the days when J.B. Priestley used to nurse a pint at the bar. Today it is, in the words of one correspondent, a 'Star reborn'. It is very much an eating pub, where the Perns, as Andrew says, 'try to produce good wholesome northern food with a bit of flair'. The menu changes every fortnight to follow the gradual movement of the seasons, while the specials blackboard is updated daily. The lunch menu offers some unusual variations on pub grub, like venison burger with melted Wensleydale cheese, or Loch Fyne oak-smoked salmon sandwiches, and the lunchtime pudding menu differs from the evening's. Andrew's cooking favours classic, often creamy sauces, with highly inventive twists: there may be saffron fried squid on a lake of gazpacho, or roast monkfish wrapped in air-dried ham with a langoustine cream sauce, for example. Beers are very much the local standards, with the addition of ales from Hambleton in summer; the wine list is comprehensive with prices to suit all and is divided into recommended wines for particular types of food. The Star can be quite busy and it is not unknown to have to share your table. SAMPLE DISHES: roast black pudding with pan-fried pigeon breast and Waldorf dressing £5; breast of guinea-fowl with celeriac mash £10; brûlée of blood oranges with fresh blueberries and shortbread £4.

Open *Tue to Sat 11.30 to 3, 6.30 to 11, Sun 12 to 10,30; closed 3 weeks Jan; bar food and restaurant Tue to Sat 11.45 to 2, 6.45 to 9.30, Sun 12 to 6* **Details** *Children welcome Car park Wheelchair access Garden and patio No smoking in restaurant Background music No dogs MasterCard, Switch, Visa*

HASELBURY PLUCKNETT   Somerset   map 2

Haselbury Inn 🍇   NEW ENTRY

Haselbury Plucknett TA18 7RJ   TEL: (01460) 72488
off A30, 2m from Crewkerne

Over 20 years in the business have helped new licensees Pat and Jan Howard promote the Haselbury from an Out and About to a main entry in the *Guide*. Originally part of the local sail- and rope-making industry, the pub is now comfortably appointed with open fires, three-piece suites, exposed beams and brickwork, and a formal restaurant area at the rear. Food is cooked to order and seasonal and fresh ingredients are used wherever possible. Daily specials boards always include six fish dishes – perhaps chargrilled tuna with Caesar salad, or haddock and prawn bake. There is also plenty to choose from on the printed menu: start with mushroom tartlet, tagliatelle with garlic and herbs, or prawn and pineapple cocktail. An entire page is dedicated to various steaks and grills, such as Haselbury Hog, a thick-cut pork chop stuffed with Stilton and grilled. A curry of the month made with hand-mixed spices and home-made ghee is also available. Where puddings are bought in they admit it, but there is an alternative selection of sweets made by the pub's own patisserie chef Joanna. She will daily prepare such delights as orange mint and honey dessert, or meringue pear Belle Hélène. A good selection of beers is available: Thomas Hardy Country, Wadworth 6X, Otter Best and St Austell Dartmoor Best. The wine list is impressive, well laid out, with good descriptions and plenty of superior but well-priced house wines and ten specially selected half-bottles. A dozen or so wines are available by the glass. SAMPLE DISHES: mussels au gratin £4; Thai pork Marsala £8; chilled zabaglione £3.25.

Open *Tue to Sat 11.45 to 3, 6.45 to 11, Sun 12 to 3, 7 to 10.30; bar food and restaurant Tue to Sun 12 to 2, 6.45 (7 Sun) to 9.30*
Details *Children welcome   Car park   Wheelchair access (also WC)   Garden and patio   No smoking in restaurant   Background music   No dogs   Amex, Delta, MasterCard, Switch, Visa*

HASSOP   Derbyshire   map 9

Eyre Arms

Hassop DE45 1NS   TEL: (01629) 640390
on B6001, 2m N of Bakewell

This substantial, creeper-clad roadside pub would be a useful stop for anyone exploring the southern part of the Peak District, which claims Bakewell, Chatsworth, Haddon Hall, Eyam (the 'plague village'), and various nature trails all within a five-mile radius. Staff are friendly and the lounge bar is welcoming, with its coal fire burning in a large stone hearth, beamed ceilings, longcase clock, cushioned settles and blown-up photos of local scenes. The printed menu presents straightforward choices of both starters and main courses, some with an Indian twist, such as onion bhajia and lamb balti. Venison makes an appearance in steak and pie forms, and vegetarians could opt for aubergine and mushroom lasagne or bulgar wheat and walnut casserole. Or then again the blackboard might persuade you in favour of sea bass steak, duck with mango sauce, or a Sunday roast. Most main dishes are accompanied by salad and coleslaw or fresh vegetables and potatoes. Here they stick to the draught beers their customers know and like: Black Sheep Special, John Smith's, Marston's Pedigree. SAMPLE DISHES: pear and parsnip soup £2.50; rabbit pie £9; chicken with lime and coriander £7.50.

Open *11.30 to 3, 6.30 (7 winter) to 11; bar food 12 to 2, 6.30 (7 winter) to 9*
Details *Children welcome in bar eating area   Car park   Wheelchair access (also WC)   Garden   No smoking area   Background music   No dogs   No cards*

HAWKLEY   Hampshire   map 2

Hawkley Inn 🍺 NEW ENTRY

Pococks Lane, Hawkley GU33 6NE   TEL: (01730) 827205
off A3, 2½m N of Petersfield

Tucked away well off the beaten track amid rolling, unspoilt Hampshire countryside, this friendly, rustic and unpretentious village local has become a favourite watering-hole among walkers hiking the Hangers Way. 'Rustic' is also an appropriate description of the relaxing, small, opened-up bar, with its rather individual simple décor and furnishings. 'Bohemian' is a word that has also been used. The pub has regular live music, and attracts an eclectic range of people, not least to its annual Beer Festival. This is both a good food pub and a good ale pub, offering quite ambitious fare such as pheasant and cep terrine, Tunisian fish tart, smoked salmon pâté, followed by grilled duck breast with green peppercorn sauce, cassoulet, or confit of duck breast, as well as a range of sandwiches. Puddings are likely to include treacle tart, or crème brûlée. There is an ever-changing beer list, with six handpumps serving ales from such independents as Ballard's, Cheriton, Beckett's, RCH and Itchen Valley, and home-made cider is on sale in the summer. A short list of seven wines is also available. SAMPLE DISHES: fish soup £4.25; cassoulet £10.50; apple and red fruit crumble £3.25.

Open *12 to 2.30 (3 Sat), 6 to 11, Sun 12 to 3, 6 to 10.30; bar food all week L 12 to 2 (2.30 Sat and Sun), Mon to Sat D 7 to 9.30*
Details *Children welcome before 8pm   Garden and patio   Background and live music   Dogs welcome on a lead   MasterCard, Visa*

HAWKSHEAD   Cumbria   map 8

▲ *Queen's Head Hotel*

Main Street, Hawkshead LA22 0NS
TEL: (015394) 36271
on B5285, 4m S of Ambleside

VEGETARIAN

They are past masters at handling a weight of visitors to this black and white all-day pub in the centre of a village made traffic-free thanks to William Wordsworth and Beatrix Potter. Mercifully, the hotel has remained homely, and although you may be urged to share tables when the going gets busy, you are unlikely to feel unloved by any inefficiencies of service. The beamed and panelled bar is surprisingly large, adorned with brass, china and toby jugs, and cosy, with a log fire in winter. Tables are set up outside in summer, and there is a separate lacy-clothed restaurant. The bar menu embraces pub favourites, plus plenty of adventurous specials; lunchtime and evening menus differ slightly. Choosing will be difficult: how about goats'-cheese crostini, terrine of pork and bacon with apples and prunes, or crab fritters to start with? Main courses are equally well presented, whether smoked haddock in a creamy sauce with mashed potato, boneless roast quail with grapes, mushrooms and bacon, or Moroccan chicken. At lunch-time you can also plump for an interestingly filled baguette or baked potato. Vegetarians will have a field day of delightful dilemmas. Chocolate and banana pudding and sticky toffee pudding are typical sweets. Wines are reasonably priced, and you get the choice of Hartleys XB from the barrel or hand-pumped Robinson's Frederics. SAMPLE DISHES: smoked haddock with Welsh rarebit £4.50; Caribbean sweet potato casserole £7; pheasant in creamy celery and onion sauce £10.

Open *11 to 11, Sun 12 to 10.30; bar food and restaurant 12 to 2.30, 6.15 to 9.30*
Details *Children welcome in family room   Wheelchair access (also WC) Patio   No smoking in restaurant   Background music   No dogs   Delta, MasterCard, Visa, Switch   Accommodation: 13 rooms, B&B £30 to £45*

Quarry House Inn

Bingley Road, Lees Moor, Haworth BD21 5QE
TEL: (01535) 642239
off A629, 2m E of Haworth

Hats off to the Smith family for banning the word 'Brontë' from both
their printed bar menus and the descriptions of the blackboard
specials. For this remote stone freehouse, with great views of the
Worth Valley and its steam railway, is only two miles from touristy
Haworth (although it is within Keighley's boundary). It is thought to
have been a quarry manager's residence at one time; now its bar is
plain and unpretentious with round tables, plush seating and pleasant
waitress service. Sunday lunch is a traditional roast; otherwise the bar
menu consists of all the favourites you might hope to find: pâté and
toast, home-made soup, fried fish, roast chicken, grills, steaks,
omelettes, jacket potatoes, salads and sandwiches. Children are
offered the usual kids' fare but can also choose small helpings from
the rest of the menu. The blackboard specials are what they should be
– a little more elaborate – but call on the same fresh fish and fine local
meat. Depending on the season, you might find grilled sardines, hake
on tomato salsa, chicken stuffed with asparagus mousse, or pork
tenderloin with Bramley purée and bacon pieces. Vegetarians have
some nice dilemmas too. A separate restaurant caters for fancier occasions. Traditionally kept ales are Tetley's, Timothy Taylor Landlord
and Golden Best, plus an occasional guest beer, and many of the 40-
odd wines from around the world are to be had by the glass. SAMPLE
DISHES: celery and apple soup £2; pan-fried monkfish with bacon and
mushrooms £9; lemon meringue pie £2.50.

Open *12 to 3, 7 to 12; closed 25 and 26 Dec, 1 Jan; bar food and restaurant
12 to 2, 7 to 10.30*
Details *Children welcome   Car park   Wheelchair access (also WC)   Garden
Background music   Dogs welcome   MasterCard, Visa*

Rose and Crown

Hawridge Common HP5 2UQ   TEL: (01494) 758386
off A416 N of Chesham, take road towards Cholesbury

A rather ordinary frontage is enlivened with flowers, but more of the
pub's real character is displayed at the rear, where a very attractive
garden, ending in a spread of mature trees, has a raised patio with

benches and a children's play area tucked discreetly out of sight. The pub dates from the seventeenth century, and the renovated interior's exposed bricks and beams make the most of the original features. Partly because it is in good walking country in the Chilterns, the clientele tend to be a healthy mix of regulars and passers-by. The menu is more static than its blackboard presence might suggest – there is usually only one daily special – and offers traditional pub fare alongside some more eclectic items: steak and ale pie, and rack of lamb, for example, as well as spinach and feta cheese goujons with sun-dried tomatoes, and roast duck served on bean sprouts. Lighter (and less expensive) meals and snacks such as chilli con carne and omelettes are not available when the dining-area is fully booked – often at weekends. Service is speedy and friendly. Beers are Wadworth 6X, Ruddles Best and a guest, while 20 or so wines feature on the fairly basic list; six wines are served by the glass. The pub also hosts barbecues and regular themed evenings – 'curry night', 'Italian night', etc. – for which booking is necessary. SAMPLE DISHES: gravad lax £5.50; beef Wellington £14; jam roly-poly £4.

Open *all week 12 to 3, 5 to 11 (all day Sat and Sun in summer); bar food and restaurant Tue to Sun 12 to 2, 7 to 10*
Details *Children welcome in restaurant   Car park   Garden and patio   No smoking in restaurant   Background music   No dogs in restaurant   Amex, Delta, Diners, MasterCard, Switch, Visa*

HAYDON BRIDGE   Northumberland   map 10

General Havelock Inn

Ratcliffe Road, Haydon Bridge NE47 6ER   TEL: (01434) 684376
on A69, 8m W of Hexham, 100yds from junction with B6319

Do not drive too fast or you will miss this terraced pub with its dark green frontage, which backs on to the South Tyne River. Tetley Bitter is the only beer served in the front bar, which leads through to an open space with a bench seat, decorative furniture and old advertising signs. Beyond is the dining-room, where formally laid-out tables are flanked by pink banquettes and spindleback chairs. Bare stone walls are enlivened with prints, just enough military memorabilia to justify the pub's name, and elaborately ruched curtains. The menu is handwritten; different menus operate at lunch-times and in the evenings, and food can be eaten either in the bar or in the restaurant. Lunch fare might start with Stilton and mushroom bake, followed by roast loin of pork with apple. In the evening you might commence with fresh mussels in dry cider and move on to roast duck in Cumberland sauce, or perhaps fresh North Sea haddock in a soy sauce – all finished off with one of a selection of home-made puddings. A 30-strong wine list concentrates on France with a sprin-kling of New World bottles and three by the glass. SAMPLE DISHES: Galia melon £2; roast sirloin with horseradish £6; Danish chocolate bar £3.

Open *Wed to Sun 12 to 2.30, 7 to 11; closed first 2 weeks in Jan, first 2 weeks in Sept; bar food and restaurant Wed to Sun 12 to 1.30, 7.30 to 8.45 (exc Sun eve)*
Details *Children welcome   Wheelchair access (also WC)   Garden   No music No cards*

HAYFIELD   Derbyshire   map 8

▲ *Sportsman*

Kinder Road, Hayfield SK22 2LE   TEL: (01663) 741565
on A624 Glossop to Chapel-en-le-Frith road

Set in beautiful countryside at the foot of Kinder Scout, this white stone-built pub stands on a narrow road leading up to the bleaker moors and is particularly popular with walkers. The white-walled, beamed interior has two main rooms, plus a bar area and a pool room; there is a garden at the rear for summer eating and seven *en suite* bedrooms are available. Red carpeting, wooden tables, Windsor chairs and settles, fresh flowers and a log fire in winter create a comfortable ambience, while the rifles on the wall emphasise the pub's connections. Service has been described as 'friendly and effi-cient from relaxed staff'. Blackboards display daily dishes and Sunday lunch is a traditional roast. Typical pub offerings might be filled baguettes, soup, pâté, sandwiches, or ploughman's, while main courses run to Thai-style pork fillet, Caucasian lamb or grilled Scottish plaice. From the dessert menu, try caramelised rice pudding or green apple ice-cream. Hand-pulled Thwaites and Daniels beers are on offer, plus Georges Duboeuf red and white house wines – also available by the glass. SAMPLE DISHES: mushrooms with hot garlic butter £3; 'boozy' beef pie £7; blackberry and apple pie £3.25.

Open *12 to 3 (exc Mon), 7 to 11 (10.30 Sun); bar food 12 to 2 (exc Mon), 7 to 9 (exc Sun); closed Mon L*
Details *Children welcome   Car park   Garden   Background music   No dogs in bedrooms   Delta, MasterCard, Visa   Accommodation: 6 rooms, B&B £35 to £45*

Use the maps at the centre of the Guide to plan your trip.

If a pub has a special point of interest, this is indicated by a 'flashed' word or phrase at the top right of the entry.

HAYTOR VALE   Devon   map 1

▲ *Rock Inn*

Haytor Vale TQ13 9XP   TEL: (01364) 661305
turn off A38 at Bovey Tracey on to A382; after 2 miles join B3387 to
Haytor, then left at phone box

The setting amid Haytor's distinctive granite outcrops attracts many
visitors to this peaceful moorland hamlet on the edge of Dartmoor.
Inside the inn, which takes its name from the surroundings, familiar
furnishings and open fires are the style, with fresh flowers and
candles adding warmth. Hotel residents have a separate restaurant
and menu, but there is plenty of choice in the large bar area, where
blackboard suggestions supplement a lengthy printed menu of light
and full meals. Sandwiches and sausages are served at lunch-time
only; otherwise you can pick from bread and cheese platters with
salad and chutney (for walkers), ham, beef and cheese platters (for
quarrymen), sirloin steak with Stilton (for coachmen) and other
hearty staples for such typical patrons. Rock Inn favourites could be
Innkeeper's chicken (with Stilton and bacon in a leek sauce), or
Squire's English lamb (in a minty rosemary and red wine sauce). Real
ales on offer include Bass, St Austell Dartmoor Best, and Hardy
Royal Oak, and half a dozen wines are available by the glass. SAMPLE
DISHES: caramelised red onion tart with red pepper dressing £5.75;
Dartmoor rabbit in mustard sauce £7; Rock Inn chocolate pot with
clotted cream £3.75.

Open *summer 11 to 3, 6 to 11, Sun 12 to 3, 7 to 10.30, winter 11 to 2.30, 7*
to 10.30; closed 25 Dec; bar food and restaurant 12 to 2.15, 7 to 9.45
(restaurant open to residents only)
Details *Children welcome in dining-room   Car park   Wheelchair access*
Garden and patio   No-smoking rooms   No music   No dogs   Amex, Delta,
MasterCard, Switch, Visa   Accommodation: 9 rooms, B&B £48 to £91

HECKINGTON   Lincolnshire   map 6

▲ *Nags Head*

34 High Street, Heckington NG34 9QZ   TEL: (01529) 460218
off A17, 5m E of Sleaford

'A good local village pub for both the drinker and those wanting
simple, good-value food' is one summing up of this tall brick inn on
the main road by the village green. The licensees who took over in
the summer of 1998 do not appear to be new brooms sweeping clean
but for the time being are carrying on much as before, offering

generous helpings of freshly cooked food. Stilton pops up in several guises; with pears on toast as a starter, in a Stilton and Guinness pâté, or with ham in a fine quiche: 'full of flavour with light, crumbly pastry – perfect pub food.' Homity pie, made from potatoes, cheese, onions and herbs, has long been popular here, and vegetarians are not going to have to scour the printed menu or the blackboard specials for other interesting choices. Sunday roasts are popular, and sweets of the apple pie or treacle tart variety. You may have to wait in the cosy bar for even simple dishes but the staff are friendly. Ward's Best is the main ale on offer along with Samson Bitter and one guest beer such as Magnificent Mouse or Adnams Broadside. SAMPLE DISHES: garlic mushrooms £3.25; roast chicken £5.50; syrup tart £2.50.

Open *11 to 3, 5 to 11, Sun 12 to 3, 5 to 10.30; bar food and restaurant 12 to 2, 7 to 10*
Details *Children welcome in dining-room   Car park   Wheelchair access (also WC)   Garden and patio   No-smoking area   Background music and jukebox No dogs   Delta, Diners, MasterCard, Switch, Visa   Accommodation: 3 rooms, B&B £17.50 to £35*

H E T T O N   **North Yorkshire**   **map 8**

Angel Inn 🏆🏆 🍇

Hetton BD23 6LT   TEL: (01756) 730263
off B6265, 5m N of Skipton

Without doubt, the Angel remains one of the country's top eating pubs. Just outside Skipton, this 400-year old ivy-clad farmhouse building with colourful window boxes, miniature conifers and a small walled courtyard at the front is traditionally decorated, and the presence of staff in aprons and waistcoats lends a nineteenth-century feel. The hard-to-book dining-rooms are relatively formal, with good linen and polished glasses, but it is equally possible to eat in the bar (if you can get a seat). Many satisfied customers report to the *Guide* and it would seem that no one leaves without becoming a fan of Denis Watkins's Inn. A signature dish of 'little money bags' – a treasure of seafood baked in filo pastry – is now also available at his second establishment, the General Tarleton, (see entry Ferrensby), as is the AWT, or open smoked salmon sandwich.

There are plenty of exciting dishes to choose from: crispy tomato tart with deep-fried basil, pesto and Parmesan shavings, or Angel seafood hors d'oeuvre, which is recommended as a starter for two people or a main course for one. Naturally, there is parfait of chicken liver foie gras, but at the Angel it is served with grape chutney and a toasted brioche. Confit of duck comes with a cassoulet of haricot beans, Toulouse sausage and smoked bacon. Be prepared to wait, as everything is cooked to order, and the kitchen can get very busy; if there is a delay, proficient and committed staff will do their best to help. Finish off your meal with a sticky toffee pudding with hot butterscotch sauce or lemon tart with strawberries and clotted cream accompanied, perhaps, by a Tokai or Muscat wine. This is not a beer drinkers pub, but Tetley's Bitter, Black Sheep and Timothy Taylor Landlord are on offer, plus a range of malt whiskies, Armagnacs and their own label Cognac. An extensive wine list of over 300 bottles, many chosen in France and shipped direct, offers unsurpassable drinking; over 30 half-bottles and 26 by the glass make for a magnificent choice. SAMPLE DISHES: Caesar salad £4; risotto of fresh basil, spinach and home-dried cherry tomatoes £6; chocolate tart with malted chocolate ice-cream £4.50.

Open *12 to 3, 6 to 11 (10.30 Sun and winter); bar food 12 to 2, 6 to 10 (9.30 Sun); restaurant Mon to Sat 12 to 2, 6 to 10, Sun 12 to 2*
Details *Children welcome   Car park   Wheelchair access (also WC)   Patio No-smoking area in restaurant and bar   No music   No dogs   Amex, MasterCard, Switch, Visa*

HEXHAM   Northumberland   map 10

Dipton Mill 🍺

WALKS

Dipton Mill Road, Hexham, NE46 1YA
TEL: (01434) 606577
S of Hexham towards Blanchland and Hexham racecourse

This simple but charming country pub, with a single bar, is known locally for its real ale and good-value home-cooked food. Set in a dip in the road by the river, it was once a watermill, and now looks like a country cottage. Surrounded by wooded countryside, it is situated in ideal walking country. Hadrian's wall, Chesters and Housesteads Roman forts, and Hexham's ancient abbey, all of which are nearby, are well worth a visit. Inside the pub itself the tables are set around the walls, allowing visitors, mostly locals, to enjoy the open log fire and the warm and friendly atmosphere. The cooking is simple. You could start with soup and then, depending on how hungry you are, try the ploughman's, which comes with a variety of cheeses: the Doddington, Cuddy's Cave and Berwick Edge, all from the local Doddington Dairy. If you are a bit more peckish tuck into steak and kidney pie, chicken breast in cherry sauce, mince and dumplings, or a bacon chop in cider sauce. If you still have room try some more cheese or perhaps a syrup sponge and custard. The beers are supplied by the local Hexhamshire Brewery, which sells Shire Bitter, Devil's Water and Whapweasel. Four house wines are available by the glass. SAMPLE DISHES: cheese and broccoli flan £4.50; lamb steak in a wine and mustard sauce £5.50; bread-and-butter pudding £1.75.

Open *12 to 2.30, 6 to 11, Sun 12 to 4.30, 7 to 10.30; closed 25 Dec; bar food 12 to 2.30, 6.30 (7.30 Sun) to 8.30*
Details *Children welcome   Wheelchair access (also WC)   Garden and patio No music   Dogs welcome in back room and garden   No cards*

HIGHCLERE   Hampshire   map 2

▲ *Yew Tree*   NEW ENTRY

Andover Road, Highclere RG20 9SE   TEL: (01635) 253360
on A343, ½m S of Highclere

Built three hundred and fifty years ago, the attractive brick Yew Tree stands just south of the village and is well placed for visitors looking round Highclere Castle. This busy dining pub with cottagey bedrooms retains much of its traditional character: the bar sports plenty of old beams and floor tiles, two log fires, old scrubbed pine tables and a couple of deep sofas, while several interconnecting rooms comprise the more formal dining area. You can also eat outside on the front terrace and in the garden. The same menu operates throughout the inn, with a blackboard announcing the identity of today's soup or whatever unusual starters might be on. Cheese balls with home-made Bramley apple chutney sounds an absolute must for a novel starter, and pan-fried venison haunch steak with a juniper and rowanberry jelly sauce is every bit as mouthwatering. Hats off to that rare pudding – baked Bramley apple stuffed with dates and served with hot custard – as well as to Welsh rarebit and herring roes on toast served as savouries. The range of drinks runs from Wadworth 6X and King Alfred from the Hampshire Brewery, through various local ciders, ten wines by the glass from a worldwide list, a selection of schnapps, and summertime home-made lemonade. SAMPLE DISHES: Thai fish-cakes £5.50; slow-braised beef in local beer £12.75; chocolate truffle cake £4.

Open *11 to 3, Sun 5.30 to 11, 7 to 11; bar food 12 to 2.30, 6.30 to 10, Sun 12.30 to 2.30, 7 to 9.30*
Details *Children welcome in eating areas   Car park   Wheelchair access (also WC)   Garden and patio   No-smoking area in restaurant   Background music Dogs in tiled part of bar only   Amex, Delta, Diners, MasterCard, Switch, Visa Accommodation: 6 rooms, B&B £45 to £60*

If you disagree with any assessment made in the Guide, write to tell us why – The Which? Guide to Country Pubs, FREEPOST, 2 Marylebone Road, London NW1 4DF.

HIGHER BURWARDSLEY   Cheshire   map 7

▲ *Pheasant Inn*

Higher Burwardsley CH3 9PF   TEL: (01829) 770434
off A41 6m SE of Chester, signposted Tattenhall and Burwardsley

Stunning views of rolling Cheshire countryside are a plus at this
seventeenth-century half-timbered inn. The building is set on a
central courtyard along with a clutter of outhouses, which are home
to workshops where you can see hand-carved candles being made. In
the bar is a log fire, which is open on both sides and is claimed to be
the largest in Cheshire. The décor has a nautical influence owing to
proprietor David Greenhaugh's former occupation as a pilot on the
Manchester Ship Canal. These days his passion is Highland cattle – a
prize-winning herd grazes in a field nearby. The printed bar menu is
backed up with a blackboard selection of daily specials. There may
be watercress and potato soup, or Welsh mussels, followed by Malay
chicken curry, fresh Cornish hake, or home-produced rump steak,
and to finish choose from a selection of home-made desserts of the
spotted dick and bread-and-butter pudding variety. A separate set-
price menu operates in the restaurant, perhaps offering parcels of
Scottish smoked salmon filled with prawns, followed by minted
spring lamb leg steak. The pub serves draught Bass and Weetwood
Ale, and in the Highland Room more than 40 malts are available.
The wine list is strongly New World and one house red and three
house whites are available by the glass. Accommodation makes the
pub a useful base from which to visit Chester, and ramblers will find
it placed midway along the Frodsham to Whitchurch 'Sandstone
Walk', with Beeston, Peckforton and Cholmondeley castles all
nearby. SAMPLE DISHES: Greek salad £3.50; game casserole £6; lemon
and lime cheesecake £3.

Open *12 to 3, 6 to 11, Sun 12 to 3, 7 to 10.30 (summer Sat 12 to 11, Sun 12
to 10.30); bar food and restaurant 12 to 2.15, 7 to 9.15*
Details *Children welcome in family room and dining-room   Car park
Garden and patio   No smoking in some rooms   Background music   Dogs
welcome in some rooms   Amex, Delta, Diners, MasterCard, Switch, Visa
Accommodation: 10 rooms, B&B £45 to £80*

HILDERSHAM   Cambridgeshire   map 6

Pear Tree

Hildersham CB1 6BU   TEL: (01223) 891680
off A604, 8m SE of Cambridge

There is only one pub in the pretty village of Hildersham and there is only one bar in the pub, around which village gossip will go as surely as upholstered wooden settles go around its walls. The bar has plenty of space for eating without intimidating drinkers and vice versa. Vegetarian cooking is a speciality of the house, though not to the detriment of meat dishes. Thus on the bar meals' printed list Lincolnshire sausages sits next to vegetable nuggets, and home-made liver pâté rubs shoulders with a note saying that only vegetarian cheeses are used in ploughman's and sauces. More enterprising items can be found on the daily specials board: chicken suprême with a white wine and tarragon sauce, for example, or butterfish fillet with a mango sauce, as well as the usual steaks and grills. Vegetarian specials, too, come into their own here – perhaps leek roulade with a cream cheese filling, or spicy blackeye beans with rice and salad. Greene King IPA and Abbott Ale are served in excellent condition and are supplemented by a guest ale. Ten wines feature on the list, with house and New World wines sold by the glass. SAMPLE DISHES: crispy crab pancakes with sweet and sour dip £3.50; liver grill £6; lemon layer pudding £2.25.

Open *11.45 to 2, 6.30 (6 Sat) to 11, Sun 11.45 to 2, 7 to 10.30; bar food 12 to 2, 6.30 to 9.30, Sun 12 to 2, 7 to 9*
Details *Children welcome in bar eating area   Car park   Garden   No music Dogs welcome   Delta, MasterCard, Switch, Visa*

HILL TOP   Leicestershire   map 5

Nags Head Inn

Hill Top DE74 2PR   TEL: (01332) 850652
4m from M1, junction 24; on B6540, at S end of Castle Donington

Although it looks quite ordinary from the outside, the inventive, modern-style cuisine ensures that this plain, whitewashed building must rank as one of the top food pubs in the 800-strong Marston's estate. Inside, chances are that the neat, traditionally furnished bar area with open fires and well-decorated dining-rooms either side will be a hive of activity; located close to the Castle Donington motor-racing circuit and East Midlands Airport, the Nags Head is popular with businessmen, locals and airport staff who appreciate the quirky and challenging food. Blackboards offer a range of upmarket sandwiches, baguettes and ciabattas with generous fillings, as well as more substantial fare like lamb fillet with saffron and tomato mash, beef fillet with peppercorn sauce, pan-fried black pudding with bacon and onion, and blackened haddock with fennel and orange. The regular menu provides similarly exciting combinations: pan-fried pigeon breast with green beans and bacon, and grilled cod with pease pudding and bacon, for example. Finish with a chocolate whisky trifle or the equally unusual treacle oat tart, and wash it all down with a pint of Marston's Pedigree or Banks's Bitter. The reasonably priced wine list largely ignores France, with the exception of the medium-bodied reds, and six house wines are offered by the glass. SAMPLE DISHES: crab quenelles with tartare dressing £4; sliced fillet of beef with Cajun spice and tzatziki dressing £15.50; bread-and-butter pudding £3.50.

Open *11.30 to 2.30, 5.30 to 11, Sun 12 to 3, 7 to 10.30; bar food 12 to 2, 5.30 to 9; restaurant 12 to 2, 5.30 (7 Sun) to 9.30*
Details *No children   Car park   Wheelchair access (also WC)   Garden   No smoking in restaurant   No music   Dogs welcome in bar area only   Amex, Delta, Diners, MasterCard, Switch, Visa*

HINDON   Wiltshire   map 2

▲ *Grosvenor Arms* 🏆🏆   NEW ENTRY

High Street, Hindon SP3 6DJ   TEL: (01747) 820696
1m from A350 between Warminster and Shaftesbury

The Grosvenor Arms is a fine example of a pub that manages to serve restaurant-quality food without falling into the trap of becoming a restaurant. At the time of going to press, an exterior facelift for the inn was on the cards, but the inside has already been done up 'stylishly, consistently, sparingly and very much in keeping with the character and Georgian age of the building'. Ambitious new owners took over in early 1998 and have installed a highly rated chef. The same menus are available in both bar and dining-room. A snacks list offers familiar pubby items like warm salad of goats' cheese, and grilled Cumberland sausages with 'killer' mash and onion gravy, but also more unusual things such as spring roll of local rabbit. The main menu is divided into 'adequate' (starter) and 'ample' (main) size dishes, some available in both. The range takes in pan-fried wood pigeon on mushroom and leek risotto, or warm tian of chargrilled vegetables layered with mozzarella and aged balsamic vinegar with a tomato compote. One reporter was surprised at seared snapper on creamed leeks and cherry tomatoes, admitting she had no idea that snapper could be so interesting, while roast saddle of locally farmed rabbit with mushroom stuffing, wrapped in Parma ham and served with mustard sauce was 'alive with flavour'. Puddings are individual creations such as whole poached pear topped with a nutty caramel sauce and cinnamon ice-cream. Wadworth 6X, Bass and Tisbury form a short beer selection, while the wine list makes enjoyable reading as well as drinking, with six house wines by the glass. SAMPLE DISHES: salad of seared Cornish scallops £6.75; wild game casserole with winter root vegetables in real ale on sage bubble and squeak £13; warm baked blueberry muffin on vanilla custard £4.

Open *11 to 3, 6 to 11, Sun 11 to 3, 7 to 10.30; bar food and restaurant 12 to 2, 6.30 to 9.30, Sat D only 6.30 to 7.30*
Details *Children welcome   Car park   Patio   No smoking in dining-room No music   Dogs welcome in bar only   Delta, MasterCard, Switch, Visa Accommodation: 7 rooms, B&B £45 to £75*

▲ *Lamb at Hindon* 🍺 🍇

High Street, Hindon SP3 6DP   TEL: (01747) 820573
on B3089, 16m W of Salisbury

Stop at the Lamb, on the main crossroads of this village of stone-built houses, and you will catch echoes – perhaps the sound of hooves – from the days when coaches plied the London–West Country road. Beams set in an oxblood ceiling, a mighty log-burning inglenook and gently ticking clocks that might well be counting the seconds to the arrival of the next mailcoach define the atmosphere, and a vast painting of Salisbury Plain hangs in the dining-room. Cooking has been described as homely, and an extensive bar menu, chalked up on blackboards, should contain sufficient choice to appeal to everyone. Bar dishes are very much in the 'one-plate meal' style and offer everything from grilled whole plaice, Greek salad, sausage platter, chicken breast and garlic, to seafood and pasta, venison and mushroom casserole, or seared Cornish scallops with smoked bacon. Puddings are likely to be of the sticky toffee or bread-and-butter school. In the evening a separate dinner menu is available in the restaurant. Beer lovers will find Wadworth 6X on offer as well as less ubiquitous beers from independent brewers such as Ashvine, Butcombe, Slaters, Otter and Tisbury. A wine list of over 100 bins offers plenty of good New World drinking and lots of well-priced vintages, 14 of which are available by the glass. SAMPLE DISHES: deep-fried squid £4; glazed lamb chops with hawthorn jelly £7; nutty treacle tart £3.

Use the maps at the centre of the Guide to plan your trip.

Open *11 to 11, Sun 12 to 10.30; bar food and restaurant 12 to 2, 7 to 10*
Details *Children welcome   Car park   Wheelchair access (also WC)   Garden*
No smoking in restaurant   No music   No dogs in restaurant   Amex, Delta,
MasterCard, Switch, Visa   Accommodation: 14 rooms, B&B £43 to £75

HOGNASTON   Derbyshire   map 5

▲ *Red Lion* ۞   NEW ENTRY

Main Street, Hognaston DE6 1PR   TEL: (01335) 370396
off A5035 between Ashbourne and Winksworth

This unpretentious white-painted inn nestles in the sleepy village of
Hognaston, close to Carsington Water, the UK's newest reservoir.
Behind the unassuming façade is a delightful country pub with some of
the best pub food for miles around. The friendly and very welcoming
L-shaped bar has three open fires, a beamed ceiling, quarry tiled floors
dotted with colourful rugs, an interesting mix of old tables, chairs and
pews and a carved stone fireplace. It is not cluttered, having just a few
pictures and the odd piece of china, and there is a rear room with a
large table ideal for families or a private party. In the evenings it takes
on more of a restaurant atmosphere, especially at weekends when it is
generally full of diners, but early and late the bar is lively with local
drinkers and it manages to balance both successfully.

This worthy new entry produces imaginative and competently
cooked contemporary dishes in a restaurant style served in an informal
yet civilised pub atmosphere. Stilton, celery, pear and walnuts on a bed
of leaves is a generous and enjoyable starter, or perhaps choose warm
vol-au-vent filled with ricotta cheese and caramelised red onions with
cherry tomatoes and a raspberry vinaigrette, or Italian salad. The
main-course selection is full of tempting offerings, such as tagine of
Moroccan lamb, Thai chicken curry, or slices of glazed Barbary duck
breast with plum sauce and Chinese pancake, and ostentatious diners
might go for a duo of poached salmon and cod set on a pool of creamy
lobster sauce topped with caviar. Desserts are home-made with some
traditional and some more imaginative offerings: apple, gooseberry,
honey and muesli crumble, for example. This freehouse takes the full
range of Marston's beers, plus Morland Old Speckled Hen, and the
wine list consists of 20 varietal types which change regularly. SAMPLE
DISHES: garlic mushrooms with melted cheese £3.50; boeuf en croûte
£13; lemon cheesecake with toffee and pecan sauce £3.25.

Open *Tue to Sat 12 to 3, Mon to Sat 6 to 11, Sun 12 to 3, 7 to 10.30; bar
food Tue to Sun L 12 to 2 (2.30 weekends), Mon to Sat D 6.30 to 9*
Details *Children welcome in conservatory before 8pm   Car park   Wheelchair
access (also WC)   Patio   Background and live music   No dogs in the evening
Delta, MasterCard, Switch, Visa   Accommodation: 3 rooms, B&B £40 to £65*

HOLNE   Devon   map 1

▲ *Church House Inn* ▮

Holne TQ13 7SJ   TEL: (01364) 631208
off A38 and A3357, just S of Ashburton

Charles 'Water Babies' Kingsley was born at the vicarage while his
father was the village curate. A stained-glass window in the church is
dedicated to him and by way of secular commemoration a room in
the pub has been named after the author. You enter the inn (dating
from around 1329 but 'looking more like half-timbered Victorian')
through a wide pillared porch complete with benches; within, the
décor is very simple, drawing attention to the heavy oak partition
that divides the two bars. Here they take pride in serving local
produce, and actually suggest that some starters can act as a light
meal in themselves, such as home-made soup or pâté with locally
baked bread, and spinach and ricotta tortellini. Local lamb and beef,
home-cooked gammon in lunchtime-only sandwiches or ploughman's, chicken and leek pie, venison casserole, omelettes – this is
accomplished homely fare. The Dartmoor rabbit pie chosen by one
visitor was thick and meaty with a puff pastry top. The choice of
simply cooked fish depends on what has been landed but you might
strike lucky with John Dory, mullet or bream. Vegetable dishes may
include cauliflower cheese. Salcombe Dairy ice-cream or clotted
cream accompany the puddings, such as fruit crumble or treacle tart.
Sunday lunch and more formal evening meals are served in the
Maison de l'Eglise restaurant. The beers, including Dartmoor Best
Bitter, Butcombe and Wilmot's are also proudly local, as are the
ciders: Luscombe cask-conditioned and Tom Grey's farm cider. The
welcome is warm, and the local countryside stunning, with
Dartmoor and the Dart Valley on the doorstep. SAMPLE DISHES:
Greek salad £4; venison casserole £9; bread-and-butter pudding £3.

Open *11.30 to 3, 6.30 to 11, Sun 12 to 3, 7 to 10.30; bar food and
restaurant 12 (12.15 Sun) to 2.30, 7 to 9.30 (Sun 7.15 to 9); restaurant Tue
to Sat 7 to 9.30, Sun 12.15 to 2.30*
Details *Children welcome in eating areas   Wheelchair access   Patio   No
smoking in restaurant   No music   No dogs in restaurant   MasterCard, Visa
Accommodation: 6 rooms, B&B £22.50 to £55*

♔ *indicates a pub offering above-average bar food that shows
ambition and good ideas, or simple pub fare prepared particularly
well.*

♔ ♔ *indicates a pub serving food on a par with 'seriously good'
restaurants, where the cooking achieves consistent quality.*

HOPE   Derbyshire   map 8

▲ *Cheshire Cheese Inn*   NEW ENTRY

Edale Road, Hope Valley S33 6ZF   TEL: (01433) 620381
on A625 between Chapel-en-le-Frith and Hathersage

There is another pub of the same name in nearby Castleton which
sometimes causes confusion. This inviting mellow stone sixteenth-
century inn lies at the heart of the Peak District National park. Its
name comes from being on the old salt-carrying route from Cheshire
across the Pennines to Yorkshire, when payment for lodgings was
actually made in cheese – the original cheese hooks can still be seen in
the lower room. A small and cottagey interior comprises three snug,
oak-boarded rooms on different levels, with a cosy atmosphere of
open fires, horsebrasses and old local photographs. Food is home-
cooked and wholesome, with good snacks and specials and plenty of
vegetables. Well-priced starters might include deep-fried potato skins
or moules marinière. Main courses could be a Cheshire cheese mixed
grill, or fillet of fresh salmon, and specials might be black pudding in
mustard and cream or jugged hare. Puddings contain some unusual
choices, such as apple and caramel granny pie or ginger pudding with
ginger and lemon sauce. The pub serves Ward's Best Bitter, plus two
guest beers, and a 20-strong wine list offers three by the glass.
Castleton Caverns are nearby. SAMPLE DISHES: jalapeño peppers
£4.25; mallard breast £18; rum and raisin sponge £3.

Open *summer Mon to Fri 12 to 3, 6 to 11, Sat 11 to 11, Sun 12 to 10.30;
winter Tue to Fri 12 to 3, 6.30 to 11, Sat 11 to 11, Sun 12 to 4; bar food 12
to 2.30, 6.30 to 8.30*
Details *Children welcome   Car park   Wheelchair access   Patio   No smoking
in dining area   Background music   Dogs welcome   Delta, MasterCard,
Switch, Visa   Accommodation: 2 rooms, B&B £50 to £60*

HOPTON WAFERS   Shropshire   map 5

▲ *Crown Inn*

Hopton Wafers DY14 0NB   TEL: (01299) 270372
on A4117, 2m W of Cleobury Mortimer

At right angles to the main road, this large, creeper-clad inn is
fronted by a patio with flower-filled window boxes. A garden slopes
down towards a meandering stream. Inside, it is 'very English, very
traditional, very upper-middle class'. Ceiling beams are garnished
with dried hops and there are real fires in the bar and in the restaurant's inglenook. The bar is known as the Rent Room, as this was
where rents were collected from tenants by stewards of the local

estate. 'Very hands-on' owners Alan and Elizabeth Matthews took over in 1997, and have introduced no fewer than four printed menus: two for the bar, and two for the more expensive restaurant. Of the bar menus, 'Rent Room Standards' are an unchanging list of sandwiches, grills and salads, while the more ambitious daily-changing 'Rent Room Crown Cuisine' list might offer grilled stuffed quail with wild mushroom sauce, followed by roast monkfish wrapped in bacon with garlic and red wine jus. Cream and cheese play a part in a number of dishes, such as feta cheese wrapped in prosciutto, and breast of chicken stuffed with banana on a curry cream. Vegetables, both cooked and in salads, get the thumbs up for quality from a reporter. Service is 'genuinely friendly'. Draught ales include rarely seen Marston's Bitter as well as Pedigree, and Adnams Bitter along with two house ales. The wine list is a good balance between Old and New Worlds; most bottles are in the £11 to £20 range, and six wines are available by the glass. SAMPLE DISHES: Galia melon on raspberry coulis with cottage cheese £4; pork fillet medallions with Marsala and mushroom sauce £9.50; Normandy apple tart and cream £3.50.

Open *11 to 3, 6 to 11 (10.30 Sun); bar food and restaurant 12 to 2.30, 6 to 9.30 (restaurant closed Mon; no bar food 25 Dec L)*
Details *Children welcome in eating areas   Car park   Wheelchair access Garden and patio   No smoking in restaurant   Background music   Guide dogs only   Delta, MasterCard, Switch, Visa   Accommodation: 8 rooms, B&B £35 to £75*

HORNDON ON THE HILL   Essex   map 3

▲ *Bell Inn* ✿ ▮ ❧

High Road, Horndon on the Hill SS17 8LD   TEL: (01375) 642463
off M25 at junction 30/31, signposted Thurrock, Lakeside; take A13, then B1007 to Horndon

The Bell has been in Christine Vereker's family for 60 of its 500 years. She and husband John have run it together since 1970 and have endeavoured to make it into a 'destination' pub. Staff training plays a big part in reaching that goal, and it clearly pays off. Chef Sean Kelly, who runs a kitchen of nine, and general manager Joanne Uttridge both joined the Bell from college. Joanne is one of the few women to hold the advanced sommelier certificate from the Court of Master Sommeliers and this is reflected in the wine list. Many staff hold wine certificates.

The cooking at this long, vaulted roofed pub, with fine views down to Basildon, is modern Anglo-French. The menu changes daily, is available throughout the pub and is commendably short. Readers have praised aubergine and goats'-cheese gâteau, peppered venison and blue-cheese salad, and pigeon breast with haggis, potato rösti and thyme. For dessert try steamed orange pudding in a light citrus sauce, or poached peaches in saffron and star anise jelly. Service scores consistently highly with reporters. There is a permanent range of popular ales on tap: Greene King IPA, Morland Old Speckled Hen, Fuller's London Pride, and Bass, plus two regularly changing guests (around 140 a year). The wine list reflects the skill of the staff, and a strong selection of French bins from well-known shippers is supported by plenty of New World offerings, all at prices to suit most pockets. Six wines by the glass start at £1.70. SAMPLE DISHES: tuna carpaccio with cucumber and sesame dressing £5.25; roast rack of lamb, colcannon and braised Puy lentils £12; trio of hot English puddings £3.50.

Open *11 to 2.30, 6 to 11, Sun 12 to 3, 7 to 10.30; no bar food 25 and 26 Dec 1998 and closed millennium holiday week; bar food and restaurant 12 to 1.45, 6.45 to 9.45*
Details *Children welcome in eating areas   Car park   Wheelchair access Courtyard   No smoking in restaurant   No music   Dogs welcome on a lead in bar   Amex, Delta, MasterCard, Switch, Visa   Accommodation: 15 rooms, room only £45 to £85*

HORNINGSEA   Cambridgeshire   **map 6**

Plough and Fleece

High Street, Horningsea CB5 9JG   TEL: (01223) 860795
off A45, 4m NE of Cambridge

A simple, rustic appearance, with stone floors, wooden settles and a real fire indicate some antiquity and, indeed, the Grade II listed, Dutch-style building is over 300 years old. A popular refuge from Cambridge, it is frequented by students and business-people alike, drawn by its comfortable, relaxed atmosphere and traditional cooking. Unusually, the lunch menu is more extensive than the evening menu, which is a slimmed-down version of the former, suggesting that lunch is the busier period. The cooking is hearty pub fare with some nice touches, such as devilled crab on buttered toast, or oysters and bacon on toast. Main courses are of the hotpot and fish pie variety, with beef Wellington for those who wish to splash out. The wine list offers generic choices, rather than wines of specific provenance, at very reasonable prices. Beers are Greene King IPA and Abbot Ale.

SAMPLE DISHES: hot garlic cockles £3.75; shepherd's pie £4.50; plum pudding £3.

Open *Mon to Sat 11.30 to 2.30, Tue to Sat 7 to 11, Sun 12 to 2, 7 to 10.30; closed eve 25 and 26 Dec; bar food and restaurant all week 12 to 2 (1.30 Sun), Tue to Sat 7 to 9.30*
Details *Children welcome in dining-room; no babies or toddlers   Car park   Wheelchair access   Garden and patio   No smoking in restaurant   No music   Dogs welcome in public bar only   Amex, Delta, MasterCard, Switch, Visa*

HORN'S CROSS   Devon   map 1

▲ *Hoops Inn*   [NEW ENTRY]

Horn's Cross EX39 5DL   TEL: (01237) 451222
on A39 just W of Horn's Cross, 5m SW of Bideford

Although of undoubted antiquity and a certain amount of local fame, this thirteenth-century smugglers inn, a long, low building with Wheaton-reed thatch and thick cob walls, was stumbling along in the doldrums until a few years ago when Gay and Don Marriot took it over and began to turn it around. Now their efforts are starting to pay dividends. It is clean and smart, with rustic, bare floorboards and the place retains an historic atmosphere. There are two menus, each chalked up on boards at either end of the bar. One is a 'regular' menu of pub grub staples with one or two more interesting additions: pan-fried herring roes on toast, chicken livers and pancetta, half-shoulder of lamb with cinnamon and mint, or venison steak. The other is the 'marine menu' and is a selection of Devonshire fish and shellfish. This ranges from simple fish and chips, or shark steak with salad, to monkfish with green pepper sauce, or turbot with orange and saffron sauce. The separate restaurant has its own menu. A fine selection of real ales is served, notably Dorothy Goodbody from Wye Valley and Norman's Conquest from the Cottage brewery, and the pub has occasional beer festivals. Close to 40 bottles feature on the wine list, with a couple of dozen or so available by the glass. Famous customers at the Hoops have included Sir Richard Grenville, Raleigh, Drake and Hawkins, and it is not far from Hartland quay, where tobacco and potatoes were first imported.
SAMPLE DISHES: mushrooms filled with bacon and Brie £3.50; crackly pork £10; banoffi pie £2.75.

Open *8am to 11pm, Sun 8am to 10.30pm; closed 25 Dec; bar food and restaurant Mon to Fri 12 to 3, 6 to 9.30, Sat and Sun 12 to 9.30*
Details *Children welcome; no children under 10 in restaurant   Car park   Wheelchair access   Garden   No smoking in restaurant and 1 bar   Background music   Guide dogs only   Delta, MasterCard, Switch, Visa   Accommodation: 12 rooms, B&B £40 to £122*

HORRINGER   Suffolk   map 6

Beehive

Horringer IP29 5SJ   TEL: (01284) 735260
on A143, 3m SW of Bury St Edmunds

A *'strong'* stone's throw from Ickworth Rotunda (National Trust),
the Beehive is an attractive, flint pub with creepers up the walls and
a small front garden, plus a further garden around the back with a
seating area. The dark interior, with plenty of corners, feels homely;
there is one small bar which serves well-kept beers from Greene King
and at which you give your food order, taken from blackboard
slates. The menu changes on a rotation system, with eight choices at
each course, including light snacks. The food here is well executed
and frequently simple. Thus goats' cheese will appear on a salad, and
chicken liver pâté will also include sun-dried tomatoes. Snacky meals
are equally modern and may take in vegetarian options such as
grilled beef tomato with minted couscous and salad, or baked
aubergine with ratatouille, while bouillabaisse, or cold poached
chicken with samphire, salad and coriander dressing, might crop up
as a main course. Puddings might be banana and crème fraîche
cheesecake with toffee sauce or fresh ginger crème brûlée. A 20-bin
wine list of well-priced and well-described bottles offers four wines
by the glass, which change regularly. SAMPLE DISHES: trout and crab
pressed terrine with a lime and lemon mayonnaise £5.25; roast
lemon sole with herbs, sea salt and olive oil £10; cold peaches and
cream soufflé £3.75.

Open *11.30 to 2.30, 7 to 11, Sun 12 to 2.30, 7 to 10.30; closed 25 and 26
Dec; bar food 12 to 2, 7 to 9.30*
Details *Children welcome   Car park   Wheelchair access   Garden and patio
No music   Guide dogs only   Delta, MasterCard, Switch, Visa*

HORSEBRIDGE   Hampshire   map 2

▲ *John of Gaunt*

Horsebridge SO20 6PU   TEL: (01794) 388394
1m off A3057, 8m W of Winchester

This warm and welcoming village freehouse has plenty of space but
not many tables at which to eat (so book or get there early). What is
on offer is wholesome, home-made and down-to-earth pub food.
Soups, roasts, grills, casseroles and pies form the backbone of the
printed menus and blackboard specials, with plenty of fish too – not
surprising for somewhere so close to the River Test – including

smoked eel and local trout. Anyone wanting something less substantial than steak and kidney pudding, wild duck with good vegetables or half a shoulder of roast lamb could go instead for a jumbo roll, ploughman's or a burger with salad and chips. Ringwood Best and Fortyniner, Inch's Stonehouse and Palmer's IPA are the draught ales available. If beer is not your preferred tipple, there are French wines, including a few good clarets, and 28 single malt whiskies. The Atkinses now offer twin-bedded B&B accommodation in a separate bungalow, which could be useful for visitors making the recommended evening assault on the rose garden at Mottisfont Abbey Garden a few miles away. SAMPLE DISHES: Stilton and onion soup £2; Lynda's fish pie £5.75; rhubarb crumble £2.

Open *11 to 2.30 (3 Fri and Sat), 6 to 11, Sun 12 to 3, 7 to 10.30; closed last week Jan and first week Feb; bar food 12 to 2, 7 to 9.30*
Details *Children welcome in bar eating area   Car park   Garden   Background music   No dogs in eating area   No cards   Accommodation: 2 rooms, B&B £23 to £45*

HOUGHTON CONQUEST   **Bedfordshire**   map 6

▲ *Knife & Cleaver* ❦

The Grove, Houghton Conquest MK45 3LA
TEL: (01234) 740387
between A6 and B530, 5m S of Bedford

FISH

You would never guess by looking that the Knife & Cleaver was once an abattoir and butcher's – hence the name – since it resembles a comfortable private house in the stockbroker belt; the tasteful atmosphere is further enhanced by a patio garden at the rear with trees and a pergola clad in climbing flowers. Most customers choose to eat in the light, conservatory-style restaurant, but there is bar fare to be enjoyed before the open fire, such as cream of paprika and truffle soup, or asparagus and smoked chicken with thyme and garlic tortellini. A fish specials menu, the pub's forte, backs up the bar menu. Fishy starters may include Loch Fyne oysters, smoked halibut on toasted brioche with sauté wild mushrooms, or crab minestrone with sesame seed croûtons. Next you could try panaché of red mullet, pithiviers of red snapper with Parma ham and ricotta in a langoustine and grape sauce – or really push the boat out with a whole lobster served to your liking. Carnivores may prefer deep-fried belly of pork marinated in orange, smoked garlic and chilli, or beef shin with black olives and tarragon sauce. For pudding why not plump for fresh pineapple poached in summer fruits, or warm apple and amaretti meringue sponge with butterscotch sauce? The pub offers a restrained but superior selection of Bateman's Best and

Adnams, as well as Stowford Press cider and a large selection of malts. The 80-strong international wine list starts with 'value' wines before moving on to prices aimed at the discerning connoisseur, and provides around 26 by the glass using the Verre du Vin preservation system. SAMPLE DISHES: melon with sorbet £4; sauté baby squid with chorizo, chickpeas and roast garlic £13.50; raspberry sorbet with white chocolate sauce £3.25.

Open *11 to 3, 6.30 to 11, Sun 11 to 3; bar food 12 to 2, 7 to 9.30, Sun 12 to 2; restaurant Sun to Fri L 12 to 2, Mon to Sat D 7 to 9.30; closed eve bank hols and 26 to 30 Dec*
Details *Children welcome in eating areas   Car park   Wheelchair access Garden and patio   No smoking in restaurant   Background music   No dogs Amex, Delta, Diners, MasterCard, Switch, Visa   Accommodation: 9 rooms, B&B £49 to £74*

HUBBERHOLME   **North Yorkshire**   **map 8**

▲ *George Inn*

Hubberholme BD23 5JE   TEL: (01756) 760223
off B6160 at Buckden, 20m N of Skipton

This splendid character inn is located at the head of Wharfedale in the tiny hamlet of Hubberholme, opposite the bridge over the River Wharfe and the ancient church, famous for 'Mouseman' Thompson's carvings and where J.B. Priestley's ashes are scattered. Bridge, church and pub together form a tiny conservation area. The local clientele is augmented by numerous walkers and cyclists, attracted by the beauty of the Dales, and the pub fare reflects their desire to receive sustenance rather than to sample epicurean delights. Warming carrot and coriander soup and filling pepper steak fortify hardy outdoor types who frequent the region in all weathers. Beers come from Theakston, Younger and Black Sheep, and three of the 40-strong wine list are available by the glass. SAMPLE DISHES: home-made chicken liver pâté £3.25; pan-fried breast of duck with raspberry saupiquet £7.25; moussaka £7.

Open *11.30 to 3, 6.30 to 11.30, Sun 12 to 3, 6.30 to 10.30; closed 2 weeks Jan; bar food 12 to 2, 6.30 to 8.45*
Details *Children welcome in bar eating area   Car park   Wheelchair access Garden and patio   No music   Dogs welcome   Delta, MasterCard, Switch, Visa   Accommodation: 7 rooms, B&B £20 to £59*

🍺 *indicates a pub serving exceptional draught beers.*

🍇 *indicates a pub serving better-than-average wine.*

ICKLINGHAM   Suffolk   map 6

Red Lion

The Street, Icklingham IP28 6PS   TEL: (01638) 717802
on A1101, 7m NW of Bury St Edmunds

Pubs and churches are often very near each other, the rigours of worship triggering a tremendous thirst, and so it is with the Red Lion and both All Saints opposite (thirteenth-century, thatched, largely unspoilt) and St James's (along the road, housing an ancient iron scroll work chest). The pub, too, is thatched, sixteenth-century but this time with antiques, plenty of exposed beams, rugs on the floorboards and a log fire. Simple and appetising bar food items are supplemented by daily specials, with the emphasis on fish and notable not least for the absence of chips. Fancier cooking can be experienced in the restaurant. The mixed hors d'oeuvre is a platter of prawns and three smoked fish: trout, mackerel and salmon, or you could plump for soup or home-made pâté. Straightforward treatment of good ingredients is the hallmark of main courses too: one summer visitor commended her excellent salmon that really tasted of salmon. The choice you get depends on what has been delivered that day, perhaps Torbay sole or skate wings with nut brown butter. Meaty options include lamb's liver and bacon with onion gravy or gammon steak with sweet-and-sour sauce. Main courses (other than salads) come with three vegetables and new potatoes. Puddings are big on chocolate, so expect hot nut chocolate pudding or chocolate Baileys cheesecake. Greene King Abbot Ale and IPA are the ales, and interesting alternatives are 15 or so English country wines and elderflower pressé. SAMPLE DISHES: Tiger Bay prawns in garlic butter £5.25; whole grilled plaice £10.25; rich chocolate pot £3.50.

Open *all week 12 to 3, 6 to 11; closed 25 Dec, eve 26 Dec, eve 1 Jan; bar food and restaurant 12 to 2.30, 6 to 10, Sun 12 to 2.30, 7 to 9.30*
Details *Children welcome   Car park   Wheelchair access (also WC)   Garden Background music   No dogs   Delta, MasterCard, Visa, Switch, Visa*

IDDESLEIGH   Devon   map 1

▲ *Duke of York* 🍺 [NEW ENTRY]

Iddesleigh EX19 8BG   TEL: (01837) 810253
on B3217, 3m NE of Hatherleigh

This long, low, thatched, white-painted pub on a hill in the middle of this remote village has an atmospheric bar, simple with scrubbed oak tables and cosy with a log fire. The menu is written on cards pinned to the wall, and 'wholesome', 'generous', 'freshly prepared' and 'well-presented' are adjectives earned by the food. A thick home-made soup, for instance, or port and Stilton pâté, followed by salmon fish-cakes, steak and kidney pudding, vegetable korma, or lasagne, are typical choices, and a fair bit of fish is in evidence. A selection of ten puddings makes for a difficult choice: should it be brown sugar meringues with raspberries in whipped cream, Caribbean rum bananas, or chocolate tart? Smiles Golden might be a summary of the cheerful hospitality as well as being one of the real ales on offer. Other beers available include Cotleigh Tawny, Adnams Broadside, Sharp's Doom Bar, Barum Original and Wye Valley Dorothy Goodbody's. There is also a choice of proper ciders – Thatcher's Farmers Tipple scrumpy and Stowford Press, and 30 or so varied wines include English Down St Mary. Three cheers too for freshly squeezed orange and grapefruit juice. SAMPLE DISHES: celery and watercress soup £2.75; turkey and mushroom pie £6; coffee, walnut and butterscotch sponge pudding £3.

Open *11 to 11, Sun 12 to 10.30; bar food 11 to 10, restaurant 6 to 10*
Details *Children welcome in eating areas   Wheelchair access   Garden and patio   Live music   Dogs welcome   Delta, MasterCard, Switch, Visa Accommodation: 8 rooms, B&B £25 to £50*

IGHTHAM   Kent   map 3

Harrow Inn ♥

Common Road, Ightham TN15 9EB   TEL: (01732) 885912
just off A25 Sevenoaks to Borough Green road

This creeper-clad seventeenth-century inn, close to the A25 but enjoying a rural setting, attracts swarms of devotees. Inside, two small bars are divided by a log fire. The cramped front bar squeezes in a few tables, adorned with fresh flowers and candles. Books line the window shelves, and pictures of racing cars and an ancient dash-board suspended over the bar create an ambience which is somewhat ruffled by obtrusive pop music. The adjoining bar has a pool table and more seating, and the popular restaurant at the back offers an à la carte menu. At the helm are Claire Butler and her partner John Elton. Claire's menu changes daily and is short enough to ensure that attention is paid to each dish. The bar menu encourages one-course eating, offering fare along the lines of grilled goats' cheese on toasted ciabatta with a sweet red pepper dressing, the chef's own coarse country pâté, or traditional moules marinière. The bumper-sounding 'Kent Korker' is a dish of locally produced sausages with mash and onion gravy, while vegetarians can take refuge in a warm leek tart with new potatoes and a mixed-leaf salad. Puddings are in the banoffi pie, creme brûlée and bread-and-butter tradition. Clare and John's current supply arrangement with Greene King has recently expired and although some Greene King beers will still be available, they are looking forward to the chance to exercise greater freedom in their purchasing of beers and wine, particularly from local suppliers. SAMPLE DISHES: cream of leek soup £4; tagliatelle Alfredo £6; summer pudding £3.50.

Open *12 to 3, 7 to 11; bar food 12 to 2.30, 7 to 9.30; restaurant Sun L 12 to 2, Tue to Sat D 7 to 9.30*
Details *Children welcome in dining-room   Car park   Garden   Background music   MasterCard, Switch, Visa*

ILMINGTON   Warwickshire   map 5

▲ *Howard Arms*   NEW ENTRY

Lower Green, Ilmington CV36 4LN   TEL: (01608) 682226
off A3400, 4m NW of Shipston on Stour

As it is a couple of miles from National Trust owned Hidcote Manor Gardens as well as Kiftsgate Court Gardens, it is hardly surprising that the Howard Arms does not do too badly in the flower stakes itself. Situated on the edge of the village, the pub faces a tiny green which is almost entirely shaded by a chestnut tree. The building is a deep honey-coloured Cotswold stone affair extending across three linked houses dating back some 300 years. At the front every available space is occupied with window boxes and hanging baskets 'flowering away madly'. At the rear is a raised central flowerbed surrounded by a lawned seating area and flower borders. The traditional menu is more interesting than at many places, but not pretentious or over-ambitious. The dishes are all described on blackboards hung over the hearth and there are plenty to choose from, with quality above par for pub food. Tossed salad with smoky bacon, potato and house vinaigrette has been described as a 'good idea with decent vinaigrette'. Lamb chops in minted gravy are prepared with above-average ingredients and vegetables are well timed. A non-savoury and trendy starter would be Ogen melon with passion-fruit sorbet, and roast Brie and smoky bacon with sun-dried tomato vinaigrette sounds a superior rendition of an otherwise stalwart dish. Main courses might take in a solidly traditional dish such as steak and kidney pie, or perhaps escalope of veal, or braised pheasant with red wine. Draught beers are an unusual mix – Wychwood Special, Everard's Tiger and Marston's Pedigree. The 30-bottle wine list offers four by the glass, including a house wine of the month. SAMPLE DISHES: crispy calamari with dips £4.50; lamb and rosemary pie £6.75; apple Bakewell £3.75.

Open *11 to 2.30, 6 to 11, Sun 12 to 3, 7 to 10.30; bar food and restaurant 12 to 2.30, 7 to 10.30 (exc Sun in winter)*
Details *Children welcome in eating areas   Car park   Wheelchair access Garden   No smoking in restaurant   Background music   No dogs   Amex, Delta, MasterCard, Switch, Visa   Accommodation: 2 rooms, B&B £35 to £55*

INGBIRCHWORTH   South Yorkshire   map 9

▲ *Fountain Inn*

Wellthorne Road, Ingbirchworth S36 7GJ   TEL: (01226) 763125
just off A629 Huddersfield to Sheffield road, 6m W of Barnsley

Regular theme nights are the thing at the Fountain Inn. They change every couple of months, but Monday night might be Steak Night, when beef and traditional British dishes dominate the menu, and Tuesday could be Wine and Fish Night. This very traditional pub is much larger than first impressions suggest, being a collection of interconnecting, white-walled rooms. The pub has a very cheery atmosphere. Customers are attracted by a menu that scores highly on value and offers an extensive choice of puddings. Dishes are traditional with occasional flashes of colour, such as Bombay potato and spinach parcels. There is chicken tikka masala as well as chicken suprême. The shortish wine list is influenced by regular customers' preferences, but the menu points out that they are happy to consider suggestions. About eight wines are available by the glass, while the beers served are Mansfield Riding Bitter and Old Baily. Accommodation has recently been added; ten *en suite* rooms in all. SAMPLE DISHES: game sausage £4; steak, Guinness and Stilton casserole £7; brandy-snap basket £3.

Open *11.30 to 2.30, 5 to 11, Sun 12 to 10.30; bar food Mon to Sat 12 to 2, 5 to 9.30, Sun 12 to 9.30*
Details *Children welcome   Car park   Wheelchair access (also WC)   Garden and patio   No-smoking area   Background music   Guide dogs only   Access, Delta, Switch, Visa   Accommodation: 10 rooms, B&B £40 to £70*

ITTERINGHAM   Norfolk   map 6

Walpole Arms

The Common, Itteringham NR11 7AR   TEL: (01263) 587258
off B1354, 4m NW of Aylsham

On the edge of the village, the Walpole Arms may look like a straggling collection of farm buildings from the road – indeed the pub was at one time a barn and stables – but inside the atmosphere is convivial and welcoming. Fairly recent renovations have endowed the red-brick barn with upright and slanted beams which divide this large room into more intimate areas. There is a restaurant too, though it is the bar that has the edge on character; in winter it is cheered by an open fire. Licensee Paul Simmons generates community spirit with a pub newsletter outlining regular events such as a seafood night, or visits by a local theatre group or craft fair. The pub has its own smokehouse, from which salmon and Norfolk smoked sausages are available to take away. The menu changes daily and, as all dishes are individually prepared, diners are asked to be patient if things get busy, which it can. It is best to book if you wish to eat. Dishes can be adventurous – Thai fish-cakes with stir-fried oriental vegetables and noodles, or loin of pork with Gruyère and basil on a Mediterranean compote, for example – although one reporter noted the most popular choice on a Saturday night seemed to be giant platters of steak or scampi with onion rings and chips. About six home-made puddings are offered, as well as Swiss ice-creams and sorbets. Beers are a draw, with Adnams and Woodforde's predominating, though M&B Mild is a rare and welcome stranger in these parts. The long wine list covers the world and includes four half-bottles and seven by the glass. SAMPLE DISHES: smoked mackerel pâté £3.25; Cajun stir-fry with noodles £8; raspberry fool with home-made shortbread £3.

Open *12 to 3, 6 to 11 (10.30 Sun); closed 25 Dec eve; bar food and restaurant 12 to 2, 7 to 9 (not Mon and Sun eves in winter)*
Details *Children welcome in eating areas   Car park   Wheelchair access (also WC)   Garden   No smoking in restaurant   Background and live music   No dogs during food-serving times   Delta, MasterCard, Switch, Visa (5% surcharge on credit cards, 50p on debit cards)*

IXWORTH   Suffolk   map 6

Pykkerell

High Street, Ixworth IP31 2HH   TEL: (01359) 230398
off A143 Bury St Edmunds to Diss road

This brick-built fifteenth-century coaching-inn on the main street (named after the old English word for a small pike) has an imposing colonnaded portico, and a Grade II listed barn at the rear. The rambling interior has lots of atmosphere created by old panelling, beams, wooden floorboards with rugs, shelves of books, and brass candlesticks, while a separate restaurant has tables with crisp white cloths. At lunch-time expect the usual staples of ploughman's, sandwiches, sausages, ham and eggs or salads, fish-cakes, Suffolk back bacon chop or lasagne. In the evening a more expensive à la carte menu operates, featuring fish from Lowestoft and local game. Starters might be smoked fish platter, salmon carpaccio, or terrine of venison, and main courses could include oven-roasted duck breast, steak au poivre, or Barnsley lamb crown chops. On the daily-changing fish board are choices ranging from whitebait to moules marinière or deep-fried monkfish. Puddings could be profiteroles, sticky treacle tart or dark chocolate ganache. Greene King IPA and Abbot Ale are supplemented by seasonal guest beers, such as Marston's Pedigree, while a 27-bottle wine list offers three house wines by the glass or bottle. SAMPLE DISHES: deep-fried Camembert £4.50; steak and ale pie £7; lemon meringue pie £3.50.

Open *12 to 3, 6 to 11, Sun 12 to 3, 7 to 10.30; bar food and restaurant 12 to 2.30, 6 (7 Sun) to 10*
Details *Children welcome   Car park   Wheelchair access   Patio   Background music   Dogs welcome   Delta, MasterCard, Switch, Visa*

KEMPSEY   **Worcestershire**   **map 5**

Walter de Cantelupe ✿   NEW ENTRY

Main Road, Kempsey WR5 3NA   TEL: (01905) 820572
on A38, 4m S of Worcester

This tiny pub is named after the thirteenth-century Bishop of Worcester, who helped Simon de Montfort and his 5,000 troops cross the River Severn – a futile gesture, as de Montfort was captured by Prince Edward and his troops massacred, while the bishop was excommunicated. In a more peaceful context, at the pub nowadays flowers in hanging baskets and window boxes decorate the outside and, within, one area has comforting red walls, a gold ceiling and curtains, and a welcoming log fire. A larger non-smoking room has gold walls with green fleur-de-lys stencils, and a large Walter de Cantelupe Golf Society honours board high up on the wall. The pub is individually run, with home cooking by the landlord. Start with a rustic ploughman's lunch – half a loaf with a hefty wedge of cheese and apple chutney – or thick, earthy mushroom soup, sandwiches, hot baguettes or maybe Cumberland sausage with onion gravy. In winter, fisherman's pie, at least three types of fish and steak and mushroom pie are likely to feature, and summer may deliver local asparagus to start, followed by a choice of fresh fish, such as turbot or bass. More elaborate dishes in the evening might be game pie, roasted lamb fillet, roast breast of Barbary duck or sauté chicken. Desserts range from traditional sticky toffee pudding and locally made ice-creams to more unusual Tia Maria and dark chocolate pancake. Ales from Timothy Taylor and Marston's are joined by St George's Pride from a local brewery; otherwise try local Norberry's perry, Stowford Press cider or Tiltridge wine. A wine list of about two dozen bottles also offers eight by the glass. SAMPLE DISHES: hot garlic tiger prawns £4.25; Barnsley chop £6; bread-and-butter pudding £2.50.

Open *11 to 2.30, 6 to 11, Sun 12 to 3, 7 to 10.30; bar food 12 to 2 (2.30 summer, 3 Sun in summer), 6.30 to 9 (10 Fri and Sat)*
Details *Children welcome in bar eating area before 8.15pm   Car park Wheelchair access (also WC)   Patio   No-smoking area   No music   Dogs welcome   Amex, Delta, MasterCard, Switch, Visa*

KEYSTON   Cambridgeshire   map 6

Pheasant Inn ♥ ❦

Keyston PE18 0RE   TEL: (01832) 710241
on B663, 1m S of junction with A604

As part of the Huntsbridge Group (also see entries for The Three Horseshoes, Madingley, the White Hart, Great Yeldham, and the Falcon Inn, Fotheringhay), visitors may well expect high standards at the Pheasant, and they will not be disappointed. Chef/patron Martin Lee runs an eating establishment that attracts great praise but has not forgotten that it is, above all, a pub. The long-fronted, thatched building contains a traditionally furnished lounge and more formal dining areas, but you can eat anywhere. As one enthusiast wrote, 'This is a clever operation, designed to appeal to all comers, all ages and all pockets. You could as easily bring your 80-year old granny as your eyebrow-pierced, magenta-haired 18-year-old daughter.' The menu is imaginative, but not over-ambitious; although it borrows from other cuisines, it does so with real understanding of them. It is long enough to excite, but short enough to guarantee time in the kitchen for first-rate preparation.

Pan-fried scallops have attracted frequent endorsement, whether with balsamic vinegar, coriander and stir-fried vegetables, or with courgette chutney, thyme and orange. Simple dishes like tomato and basil soup with Selvapiana olive oil have also received the thumbs up, and best end of lamb cutlets come pink and full of flavour, while pigeon breasts in wild mushroom risotto alternate crispy slices of meat with tender ones. Portions are generous, and that goes for the puddings, too, which might include vanilla soufflé with grappa and raspberry sauce, for example. Alternatively, opt for the cheese selection with walnut bread, oatmeal biscuits and salad. Young staff are friendly and accommodating. Real ales consist of Adnams Best as a permanent fixture and two changing guests. The exceptional wine list covers many regions, vintages and prices, with 14 wines available by the glass, including Laurent Perrier champagne. SAMPLE DISHES:

pumpkin soup with kirsch and Gruyère £4; fillets of brill with aubergine purée £10; roast pear with spice sauce and cinnamon ice-cream £4.50.

Open *12 to 2, 6.30 (6 Sat) to 10, Sun 12 to 2, 7 to 9.30; closed eve 25 Dec, 31 Dec L; bar food 12 to 2, 6.30 (6 Sat) to 10, Sun 12 to 2, 7 to 9.30*
Details *Children welcome   Car park   Wheelchair access   Patio   No-smoking area   Live music   Dogs in bar only   Amex, Delta, Diners, MasterCard, Switch, Visa*

KINGSTEIGNTON   Devon   map 1

Old Rydon Inn ❦

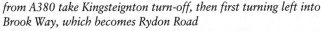

HISTORY

Rydon Road, Kingsteignton TQ12 3QG
TEL: (01626) 354626
from A380 take Kingsteignton turn-off, then first turning left into Brook Way, which becomes Rydon Road

This Grade II listed farmhouse with a sheltered walled garden dates from the time of Henry II, the Devon name 'Rydon' coming from the Old English 'ryge dun', which means hill of rye. The restaurant, which has its own bar, is the oldest part of the building, where you find thick, rough-painted walls, small rooms, lots of nooks and crannies, and the original early-sixteenth-century elm screens. Although under the same roof as the restaurant, the pub part is in the former stable, with an old cider apple loft upstairs to which families with children are despatched. Bar meals range from baguettes, jacket potatoes and salads, with toasted English muffins an unusual departure from the norm. Blackboard fare might include smoked haddock, lemon and herb fish-cake (fish and seafood are delivered from Brixham), followed by guinea-fowl Stroganov or nasi goreng, an Indonesian-style spicy chicken dish, which makes frequent appearances. Puddings are also a little special, such as rice-pudding with apricots, and apple and custard pancake with caramel sauce. A separate restaurant menu is strong on Italian cooking. The well-priced wine list offers some interesting choices and some fine vintages, and five wines are available by the glass. Wadworth 6X and Bass are the usual beers on tap, plus one guest. SAMPLE DISHES: parsnip and apple soup £2.50; Brixham fish pie £7; lemon layer pudding £3.

Open *11 to 2.30, 6 to 11, Sun 12 to 3, 7 to 10.30; closed 25 Dec bar food 12 to 2, 7 to 9; restaurant 7 to 9.30 (exc Sun)*
Details *Children welcome in bar eating area   Car park   Garden and patio Background music   No dogs   Amex, Delta, Diners, MasterCard, Switch, Visa*

KINGSTON NEAR LEWES   East Sussex   map 3

Juggs

The Street, Kingston near Lewes BN7 3NT   TEL: (01273) 472523
off A27, 2m SW of Lewes

The tiny village of Kingston has a flint church near one end where it runs into a steep slope of the South Downs; a few houses and cottages, among them the Juggs, line the street as it leads up from the village green. The pub, originally a low-ceilinged, tile-hung and white-painted brick cottage, has been much extended over the years, but it has all been done with a careful eye to scale and materials. Sound ales are served from Harveys of Lewes and King & Barnes. The pub does a brisk trade in good-value home cooking and serves generous portions. A small number of specials are added daily to the printed menu, which offers prawn pot, taramasalata, or curry spiced vegetable soup for starters. Sausage fans might try the 'banger tray', featuring three locally produced sausages served with chips. Potato skins are a main course and come with a blue cheese dip; and both smoked salmon and spinach kedgeree, and Brie and leek quiche have been favourably reported on. Apple strudel and chocolate brownies make slightly out of the ordinary puddings. The short wine list features bins from Australia and New Zealand as well as from Lebanon and England, with plenty of bottles under £10. SAMPLE DISHES: mackerel pâté £3.50; spaghetti bolognese £5.25; butterscotch toffee ice-cream £3.

Open *summer 11 to 11 (Sun 10.30), winter 11 to 3, 6 to 11 (10.30 Sun);
closed 25 Dec eve, 26 Dec, 31 Dec eve, 1 Jan; bar food and restaurant 12 to 2,
6 to 9.30 (3 Sun)*
Details *Children welcome in family room   Car park   Wheelchair access
Garden and patio   No smoking in restaurant   No music   Dogs welcome on a
lead   Delta, MasterCard, Switch, Visa*

KINTBURY   Berkshire   map 2

▲ *Dundas Arms* ✿ ▮

53 Station Road, Kintbury RG17 9UT
TEL: (01488) 658263
1m S of A4, between Newbury and Hungerford

CANAL

Located on the banks of the Kennet and Avon canal at the point where it joins the River Kennet, the Dundas Arms is a popular place for a bit of al fresco eating and so atmospheric waterside tables are soon bagged. If the weather does not oblige, diners can retire to the restaurant, decorated with wine racks displaying the extensiveness of the cellar, or to an adjoining modern room with white ash chairs.

Locals hang out in the public bar, which has a rustic feel with wood panelling, heavy furniture and views of the canal.

The cooking here, in the view of an inspector, is 'very competent', with an emphasis on the use of quality ingredients. Daily specials appear on a chalk board and might include celeriac soup, flat mushrooms on Italian bread, duck liver pâté, home-made potted shrimps, home-cured gravlax and the like. The restaurant menu is also available in the bar, and offers a larger selection with some modern and eclectic touches such as lemon grass and cep sauce. Ham hock terrine is a 'masterly' construction of well-prepared ingredients; gratin of crab is 'overflowing with sizzling juice'; and roast partridge arrives ultra-tender with real bread sauce. Landlord David Dalzell-Piper embodies the hands-on approach, both working in the kitchen and serving tables. He serves beers from Morland on a regular basis, together with guests such as Ringwood, Butts and Bass. SAMPLE DISHES: crab au gratin £4.50; white bean and vegetable casserole with grilled chorizo sausage £5; sticky toffee pudding £4.

Open *11 to 2.30, 6 to 11, Sun 12 to 2.30, 7 to 10.30; bar food and restaurant Mon to Sat 12 to 2, 7 to 9 (exc Mon eve)*
Details *Children welcome Car park Garden and patio No music No dogs Amex, Delta, MasterCard, Switch, Visa Accommodation: 5 rooms, B&B £60 to £70*

KIRDFORD   West Sussex   map 3

▲ *Half Moon Inn*

Kirdford RH14 0LT   TEL: (01403) 820223
off A272, 2m W of Wisborough Green

FISH

The Moran family have had links with London's Billingsgate fish market for over 125 years, and their opening of a seafood shop in nearby Loxwood confirms their reputation for fresh shellfish and seafood. Meanwhile the Half Moon continues to reel in the crowds. This pretty, tile-hung Whitbread lease with a charming cottage garden dates back to the seventeenth century – the era of the inglenook. As you would expect from a fish pub of this reputation, the blackboards are the place to look. The bar menu could include moules marinière, filo prawns, crab cakes or buffalo shrimp, while the 'catch of the day' could be anything from simply grilled lemon sole to more adventurous dishes with unusual fish like swordfish, scabbard and barracuda. Hungry types can try the Half Moon Platter, a large plate of fish and shellfish. Meat-eaters are not neglected: they can tuck into a steak and kidney pie or chicken Kiev. Puddings are of the crème brûlée and crumble variety. To wash it all down there is a good selection of ales: King & Barnes Sussex Ale, Fuller's London Pride and Wadworth 6X, as well as guests from local independents like Arundel and Ballard's. Three wines are available by the glass. SAMPLE DISHES: potted shrimps £5; grilled plaice £8.50; chocolate marquise £3.50.

Open *11 to 3 (2.30 winter), 7 to 11 (10.30 Sun); closed eve 25 Dec and some Sun eves in winter; bar food and restaurant all week L 12 to 2.15, Mon to Thur D 7 to 9.15*
Details *No children in dining-room after 8.30   Car park   Wheelchair access Garden   No-smoking area   Background music   Amex, Delta, MasterCard, Switch, Visa   Accommodation: 3 rooms, B&B £30 to £60*

KIRKBY LONSDALE   Cumbria   map 8

▲ *Snooty Fox* 🏆 🍇

Main Street, Kirkby Lonsdale LA6 2AH   TEL: (01524) 271308

This whitewashed, listed Jacobean inn stands right on the main street of this touristy town. The interior consists of a series of small, open-plan, carpeted rooms, with a central bar, large wooden tables, pews and armchairs, and log fires in winter. A hunting theme prevails, with stuffed birds and animals, hunting horns, plus fencing masks and foils. Appropriately, a large stuffed fox stands in a glass case in the entrance hall. Tables to the side and back are set for eating, though you can eat anywhere. Printed menus feature starters along the lines of home-made soup, goats' cheese and scallions baked en croûte, or Snooty Fox terrine, while main courses take in roast barbary duck, collops of marinated venison, or grilled whole sea bass. Typical pub offerings are also available, such as jacket potatoes, filled baguettes or salads. Chalked on a board are perhaps four or so daily specials, such as lemon and honey-glazed chicken, haddock and prawn bake, or rabbit casserole with dumplings. Sticky toffee pudding has been described as 'very rich, with a lovely flavour and an interesting texture, surrounded by lots of sticky sauce'. Other desserts might be crème brûlée, home-made ice-creams and sorbets. Timothy Taylor Landlord, Hartleys XB and Theakston Best beers are on offer, plus eight wines by the glass all around the £2 mark. The main list rises to a staggering £250 for a 1953 *premier cru* Ch. Haut Brion, but otherwise prices are reasonable for a selection of bottles from around the world. SAMPLE DISHES: three-cheese soufflé £4; pan-fried suprême of chicken £9.75; steamed chocolate pudding £3.25.

Open *11 to 11, Sun 12 to 10.30; closed 25 Dec and 1 Jan; bar food 12 to 2.30, 6.30 to 10*
Details *Children welcome in dining-room   Car park   Wheelchair access (also WC)   Garden   No-smoking area in dining-room   Jukebox   Dogs welcome on a lead; no dogs in restaurant   Amex, MasterCard, Switch, Visa Accommodation: 9 rooms, B&B £30 to £58*

KIRTLING   Cambridgeshire   map 6

Queen's Head 🍇

Kirtling CB8 9PA   TEL: (01638) 731737
off B1063, 5m SE of Newmarket

If you find Kirtling you will find the Queen's Head. The pub started life in 1558 as an Elizabethan dwelling, and within its series of rooms on different levels, some with floorboards, some flagged, and warmed by two log fires, you can sit at stripped wood tables on wooden chairs as well as comfy chesterfields. The place clearly appeals to the horsey set from nearby Newmarket, who make up a good proportion of the clientele. Light lunches and puddings appear on separate blackboards, but the bulk of the menu is chalked up on ingenious blackboard strips, enabling dishes to be added or removed as appropriate. Gary and Dianne Kingshott also operate the Beehive in Horringer (see entry) and similar standards apply at the Queen's Head. The Beehive is noted for its soups and those here are every bit as good – 'one of the best I've had for a long time,' commented one of our inspectors. Other starters might include terrine of chicken breast, asparagus and bacon with melba toast, or warm cheese, tomato and black olive tart. Well-prepared main courses are the likes of collops of pork with a sherry, grain mustard and cream sauce, baked fillet of salmon with fennel and Pernod sauce, or a rich beef and potato goulash with sour cream. Light snacks are available in the form of local sausages in a rich onion gravy, a steak sandwich, or whole grilled sardines with basil and tomato sauce, while a baked raspberry and blackberry cream pot, caramelised oranges, or baked date and rum cheesecake might turn up as the home-made puddings. This being Suffolk, beers likely to be served are Greene King IPA and Adnams Bitter, while a 40-strong wine list, wide-ranging in both style and price, offers half a dozen wines by the glass. SAMPLE DISHES: spinach soup with bread £3.50; mignons of beef fillet in a Stilton sauce £13; crêpes with hot chocolate sauce and ice-cream £3.75.

Open *11.30 to 2.30, 7 to 11, Sun 12 to 2.30; closed 25 and 26 Dec, first week Jan; bar food 12 to 2, 7 to 9.30 (exc Sun D)*
Details *Children welcome   Car park   Wheelchair access   Garden and patio No music   No dogs   Amex, Delta, MasterCard, Switch, Visa*

Red Lion

The Street, Kirtling CB8 9PD   TEL: (01638) 730162

At the other end of this long village from the Queen's Head (see previous entry) sits the Red Lion. This timber-framed, tile-roofed building is a freehouse, though the beer selection – Greene King IPA, Adnams Broadside and Morland Old Speckled Hen – could perhaps be a little more adventurous. The wine list, however, is a good selection from the Adnams range, including a sprinkling of half-bottles, four wines by the glass and prices to suit most pockets. The food continues to please reporters, one of whom thought the lunchtime bar meals 'looked and tasted like evening restaurant meals', and reckoned his Cajun pork chop 'excellent'. Some offbeat items feature on the menu: fried avocado in tempura batter, for example, or grilled horse mushrooms filled with spinach and Brie; otherwise there might be smoked duck breast on a salad of endive and orange, medallions of beef fillet wrapped in bacon and cooked in a red wine sauce, or even chilli con carne. Summer pudding was described by one visitor as 'the best I have ever eaten'. Good-value three-course Sunday lunches offer a choice of three roasts, a fish and vegetarian dish. SAMPLE DISHES: smoked salmon and prawns £7; griddled chicken suprême with caramelised pepper sauce £12; fruits-of-the-forest pavlova £3.50.

Open *Tue to Sat 12 to 2.30, 7 to 11, Sun 12 to 10.30; bar food and restaurant Tue to Sat 12 to 2, 7 to 10, Sun 12 to 2.30, 7 to 9*
Details *Children welcome in eating areas   Car park   Wheelchair access Garden   Background music   Dogs welcome   Amex, MasterCard, Switch, Visa*

KNAPP   Somerset   map 2

▲ Rising Sun

Knapp, North Curry TA3 6BG   TEL: (01823) 490436
off A358 Taunton to Langport road at Thornfalcon garage, signed North Curry

This fifteenth-century longhouse – only a pub for 40 years – is in a tiny hamlet reached down high-hedged, narrow lanes. The small front sun-trap terrace has a few tables, pretty roses and shrubs and wonderful views. Inside is a wealth of beams, with a bar area and two separate restaurant areas (one used as a family room at lunchtime on weekdays). Horse-brasses and plates decorate the walls, and a huge log stove is lit in winter. The bar menu takes in soup, ploughman's, pâtés, a variety of double open sandwiches, Welsh rarebit, ham and eggs, and scampi. The separate restaurant menu majors on fish, with dishes such as grilled skate wing, whole Dover sole, or medallions of monkfish. Vegetarians are offered a nut roast or seasonal vegetable pancakes. Sunday lunch includes a roast, such as prime rib of English beef with Yorkshire pudding. Chef's specials could be a whole crab, half a lobster, or grilled gurnard fillet. Desserts range from treacle tart to raspberry pavlova, or Devonshire farm ice-creams. Beers on hand-pump are Bass, Boddingtons and Exmoor ale, and the local village cider is available in summer. A list of some 20 wines covers Europe and the New World, with three available by the glass. SAMPLE DISHES: soup of the day £3; half-pint of prawns £4.50; frozen mocha cream £3.75.

Open *11.30 to 2.30, 6.30 to 11, Sun 12 to 3, 7 to 10.30; bar food and restaurant all week L 12 to 2, Sun to Thu D 7 to 9.30*
Details *Children welcome in dining-room   Car park   Wheelchair access (also WC)   Patio   No smoking in 1 dining-room   Occasional music   Dogs welcome in bar only   Delta, MasterCard, Switch, Visa   Accommodation: 3 rooms, B&B £25 to £36*

KNEBWORTH   Hertfordshire   map 3

Lytton Arms 🍺

Park Lane, Old Knebworth SG3 6QB
TEL: (01438) 812312

BOTTLED BEER

'A great pub', commented our inspector, who liked the changing range of beers and the attractive setting. Designed by Sir Edward Lutyens – a brother-in-law of Lord Lytton, whose family still own the neighbouring Knebworth Estate – in about 1877, the pub is now a freehouse. Beer is very much the thing here: Bass, London Pride and Woodforde's Wherry are permanents along with Theakston Best and Adnams Broadside, and there are an astonishing six extra guest ale pumps which have served a truly impressive 2,600 cask-conditioned beers over the past decade. As if this were not enough, a vast range of bottled Belgian beers is on offer, including Orval, Rochefort and Rodenbach. Not to be outdone by Knebworth, the pub organises its own festivals – beer rather than rock – which take place in summer and autumn when the garden is a riot of colour thanks to the countless hanging baskets. Giant chess is a novel outdoor attraction when the weather allows. The menu at this hop-garlanded, child-friendly pub is divided between a fairly fixed menu and changing daily specials. 'Pub staples' is perhaps the best description of what is on offer, with the speciality sausages being particularly well worth a try, or go for home-made lasagne, battered haddock or chilli con carne, with spotted dick to finish. If you must drink wine in this beer paradise, you will find the list good value for money. SAMPLE DISHES: king prawns £4; minted lamb steak £7; chocolate pudding with chocolate sauce £2.50.

Open *Mon to Wed (also Thur in winter) 11 to 3, 5 to 11, Thur (summer), Fri to Sun 11 to 11 (10.30 Sun); bar food 12 to 2 (2.30 Sun), 6.30 to 9.30*
Details *Children welcome in bar eating area   Car park   Wheelchair access (also WC)   Garden   No smoking in dining area or conservatory   Background music   No dogs   Amex, Delta, Diners, MasterCard, Switch, Visa*

KNIGHTWICK   Worcestershire   map 5

▲ *The Talbot* ♀ ▮ ❀

Knightwick WR6 5PH   TEL: (01886) 821235
*on B4197; turn off A44 just S of River Teme crossing,
between Worcester and Bromyard*

Way off the beaten track, this 500-year-old pub is very much a family affair. Phillip Clift runs the Teme Valley Brewery, located at the rear (ask and they will show you around) and also has the distinction of being the owner of one of the largest hop farms in England. He also grows his own barley so can claim to be one of the very few wholly self-sufficient brewers. Sisters Wiz and Anne run the hotel where his creations are served: This, That and T'other are beers much admired by those keen to demonstrate that hop varieties can be as individual as grapes. In September, they brew hop varietal beers with green hops plucked from the bine that day.

In terms of food, too, the emphasis is on freshly sourced ingredients (often given an inventive twist), including locally gathered fungi, traditionally reared meat and poultry, game from the pub's own 'farm', and fresh fish. Menus are chalked on a large board, and are changed daily; the price at lunch for a three-course meal is around £11 (£9 for two courses), and at dinner £17 (£15 for two). There might be crab and lobster blinis, falafel, or warm beetroot salad to start, followed by pan-fried scallops in nori seaweed, polenta with courgettes and Parmesan, or pot roasted mutton with caper sauce. Desserts take in plum compote or banana cake. Also available at lunch-times is a bar menu offering imaginative snacks such as lamb- or cheese-stuffed filo parcels, and herring roe and mushroom tart, as well as ploughman's and rolls. The excellent wine list travels the world, offering bottles from good producers and over a dozen by the glass. SAMPLE DISHES: pork, orange and cognac pâté; wild boar loin; plum compote: all three courses £12 lunch, £17 dinner.

Open *11 to 11; closed 25 Dec eve; bar food and restaurant 12 to 2, 6.30 to 9 (9.30 weekends)*
Details *Children welcome in eating areas   Car park   Wheelchair access (also WC)   Garden   Occasional live music   Dogs by arrangement   Delta, MasterCard, Switch, Visa   Accommodation: 10 rooms, B&B £30 to £67.50*

KNOWL HILL   Berkshire   map 3

▲ *Bird in Hand* 🍇

Bath Road, Knowl Hill RG10 9UP   TEL: (01628) 826622
on A4, 3m NE of Twyford

The Bird in Hand is a historic hostelry for all the best reasons. First, it has been a family business for over 35 years. Second, parts of the building date back to the fourteenth century and though other parts look fairly modern, there is enough authenticity in the accommodation and conference facilities to avoid the total character assassination that has befallen so many of our former pubs and hotels. Third, legend has it that George III threw a horseshoe while riding in Windsor Great Park and enjoyed hospitality here as his mount was reshod. In gratitude he granted the inn a licence to sell beer and wine day and night. Whether this was before or after he went mad remains unclear. The interior has a relaxing wood-panelled main bar with leather armchairs and a canopied open fireplace, plus some cosy alcoves. This fairly upmarket establishment offers a quite traditional menu: Welsh rarebit, shell-on prawns, braised shank of lamb and the like, and, quaintly, non-English dishes like nasi goreng and prawn jambalaya are labelled 'Continental'. An imaginative cold buffet of meat, fish and salads is also available at lunch-time. The separate restaurant menu offers dishes such as crispy duck pancakes or pan-fried queen scallops, followed by roasted loin of monkfish, or Chinese-style marinated magret of duck. The pub serves Brakspear's seasonal beers, as well as London Pride, but it is the wine list that warrants serious consideration, with a dozen choices available by the glass from a 60-bottle list, all kept by the Verre du Vin method. SAMPLE DISHES: bruschetta of wild mushrooms £4.25; stir-fried beef with noodles £7.50; steamed orange and pineapple pudding £3.75.

Open *11 to 3, 5.45 to 11, Sun 12 to 3, 7 to 10.30; bar food 12 to 2.30, 6 to 10; restaurant 12 to 2, 7 to 9.30*
Details *Children welcome in bar eating area   Car park   Wheelchair access (also WC)   Garden and patio   No music   Dogs welcome   Amex, Delta, Diners, MasterCard, Switch, Visa   Accommodation: 15 rooms, B&B £50 to £100*

▲ *Masons Arms Inn* 🍺 🍇

Knowstone EX36 4RY   TEL: (01398) 341231
1½m N of A361, midway between South Molton and Tiverton

This white-painted medieval building was freshly thatched in autumn 1998, though perhaps the pub's new top knot needs to weather in a bit to lose its Bavarian farmhouse look. Passing through two ancient doors, you enter the small stone-floored bar which is equipped with a short counter, a large inglenook with a log fire and a collection of ancient bottles on the mantelpiece above. Converted oil lamps and candles illuminate the scene. Wooden stools surround the few tables in the bar and there is a pretty separate dining-room. But do not be misled by the rustic surroundings: a short yet varied menu on a blackboard in the bar holds out promises of the good-quality home cooking you might expect from a small rural pub – dishes such as smoked mackerel and cider pâté, cheese and leek pie or game pie with rabbit and pheasant; and curry lovers will find chicken tikka masala or vegetable korma. A notable selection of local West Country cheeses includes Vulscombe goats' cheese, Tower Farm Cheddar, Curworthy, Nancarrow, Sharpham Rustic and Yarg, and desserts take in banana in rum, little chocolate pot, gooseberry crumble and crêpes suzette. Inspiration is not merely local – you might arrive on a theme evening such as a New Orleans night offering Creole and Cajun food. The pub serves Dorset Best from Hall & Woodhouse and Tawny Bitter from Cotleigh plus the occasional guest. The majority of wines come from Christopher Piper, with eight to ten available by the glass. The pub is in a conservation area and National Trust properties like Arlington Court and Knightshayes are nearby, as are the Royal Horticultural Society Gardens at Roseover. SAMPLE DISHES: game terrine £3; Devon cassoulet £6; chocolate and nougat ice-cream £2.25.

Open *11 to 3, 6 (7 winter) to 11, Sun 12 to 3, 6 (7 winter) to 10.30; closed eves 25 and 26 Dec; bar food and restaurant 12 to 2, 7 to 9, Sun 12.30 to 2, 8.30 to 9 (no food L 25 Dec)*
Details *Children welcome in dining-room   Car park   Garden and patio   No smoking in dining-room   Live music   Well-behaved dogs welcome   No cards Accommodation: 5 rooms, B&B £21 to £55*

Report forms are at the back of the book; write a letter if you prefer, or email your pub report to guidereports@which.co.uk.

The Guide is totally independent, accepts no free hospitality and carries no advertising.

LANERCOST   Cumbria   map 10

▲ *Abbey Bridge* 🍺

Lanercost CA8 2HG   TEL: (016977) 2224
off A69, 3m NE of Brampton; follow signs to Lanercost Priory

Lanercost Abbey is within walking distance and Hadrian's Wall not
far away from this inn on the banks of the River Irthing, beside a
seventeenth-century bridge, from which you might just glimpse a
kingfisher or an otter. An old blacksmith's forge has been converted
into a small bar and eating area, the bar with high chairs and some
small pews, its rough stone walls decorated with horseshoes and
collars, and the dining area in the balcony up spiral stairs. The pub is
notable not only for the fact that you have to ring the doorbell to
gain entry, but also for its changing real ales. Yates will quite likely
be on but landlord Philip Sayers changes the other beers on the three
handpumps as soon as the cask is emptied. The result is that he
serves 400 different beers a year. The menu looks fun. For starters,
Texas toothpicks are strips of jalapeño and onion, Cajun-coated and
deep-fried, while mushroom balti caters for the popular British
palate. More traditional dishes are offered up as main courses – roast
duckling with Cumberland sauce or coq au vin – although seafood
paella and Thai vegetable schnitzel also pop up. For pudding indulge
yourself with Chantilly profiteroles with toffee sauce, or baked
Alaska. Three house wines are available by the glass. SAMPLE DISHES:
chicken yakatori £4.25; beef and ale pie £10; chocolate rumpot £3.

Open *12 to 2.30, 7 to 11; bar food 12 to 2, 7 to 9 (10.30 Sun)*
Details *Children welcome   Car park   Wheelchair access   Garden   No
smoking in dining area   Live music   Dogs welcome   Amex, Delta,
MasterCard, Switch, Visa   Accommodation: 7 rooms, B&B £25 to £50*

LANGTON GREEN   Kent   map 3

Hare

Langton Road, Langton Green TN3 0JA   TEL: (01892) 862419
on A264, 2½m W of Tunbridge Wells

This airy Victorian roadside pub has French windows opening on to
a patio and the village green beyond. Rugs cover bare boards in the
front area; plenty of tables and benches are available for eating, and
ornamental plates, Victorian memorabilia and a collection of chamber pots make for an eclectic décor. The constantly changing blackboard menu offers soup, roasted chicken wings, pasta, deep-fried
spicy Thai crab, and cod patties as starters. Main courses might be

ostrich steak on a bed of leeks in a red wine sauce, seared salmon fillet, roast shoulder of lamb with a herb crust or half a roast duck. Puddings are of the banoffi pie, bread-and-butter or lemon cheesecake variety, backed up by ice-creams and sorbets. Greene King Rayments and Abbot ales are supplemented by a selection of 50 malt whiskies and a 30-bottle wine list (mainly lacking producers' names), with around a dozen by the glass, including three house wines under £2. SAMPLE DISHES: spinach roulade £5; salmon and haddock fishcakes £6.25; chocolate pecan pie with fruit coulis £4.

Open *11 to 11, Sun 12 to 10.30; closed eve 25 Dec; bar food 12 to 9.30 (9 Sun)*
Details *Children welcome in dining-room   Car park   Wheelchair access Patio   Background music   Dogs welcome in bar area only   Amex, Delta, MasterCard, Switch, Visa*

LANGTON HERRING   Dorset   map 2

Elm Tree

Shop Lane, Langton Herring DT3 4HU   TEL: (01305) 871257
off B3157, 5m NW of Weymouth

This old whitewashed inn in a delightful village is particularly popular with walkers, because of its location close to the Dorset coastal path. A profusion of hanging baskets and flower tubs make it a colourful place; the comfortable interior has three beamed rooms, with flagstones, inglenook fireplaces, old-fashioned settles and cushioned window seats. A wealth of copper and brass artefacts and Toby jugs add to the ambience. The Elm Tree is noted for its daily home-cooked specials, which supplement the printed menu. Staples of home-made soup, sandwiches, jacket potatoes, ploughman's, and pâtés are followed by more substantial dishes such as chilli con carne, lamb Madras with pilau rice, Langton beefsteak and ale pie or grilled sirloin steak. At lunch-time, the Elm Tree brunch menu is available, consisting of garlic breads, toasted sandwiches, and burger baps. Traditional bar meals – all served with chips and salad – are ham and eggs, deep-fried cod, jumbo sausages, or grilled gammon steak. Ice-creams feature in many desserts – from banana split to knickerbocker glory – or there might be treacle tart on the specials board. Children under 12 are offered burgers, sausages, scampi pieces, fish fingers or veggie nuggets, all with chips. Greenalls and Boddingtons beers are supplemented by a good choice of wines from around the world, including 12 by the glass. SAMPLE DISHES: artichoke hearts and mushrooms £5; baked crab Mornay £8; butterscotch banana fritters £3.75.

Open *11 to 3, 6 to 11, Sun 12 to 3, 7 to 10.30; bar food 12 to 2, 7 to 9*
Details *Children welcome in bar eating area   Car park   Wheelchair access (also WC)   Garden   Background music   No dogs   No cards*

LANLIVERY   Cornwall   map 1

 Crown

Lanlivery PL30 5BT   TEL: (01208) 872707
off A390, 2m W of Lostwithiel

This very simple pub is tucked away down a narrow country road in the shadow of the church from which bellringers may serenade your meal. The rough stone slate-roofed building dates from the twelfth century and from both its external appearance and interior layout was clearly once a row of cottages. Enter by the public bar with its massive slate stone floor and built-in wall settles and turn right into the middle bar with a worn burgundy velour sofa, dark cushioned settles and a ceiling that consists of the upper storey's floorboards supported by beams. This is a place with atmosphere – not to mention lots of creaking when someone walks upstairs. Behind the pub is a lovely sheltered garden which you cross to reach the bedrooms in a comfortable outbuilding. Simple grub on offer could be Cornish pasty with chips, ploughman's, huntsman's (honey-roast gammon), plus poached or grilled fish according to the day's catch. Home-made curries are a bit of a speciality and vegetarian options include ratatouille en croûte and Stilton-stuffed mushrooms on a gooseberry sauce. For pudding you can indulge yourself with pavlova, nutty treacle tart or a chocolate fudge gâteau. Apart from Bass, real ales are supplied by local brewer Sharp's, and a very short wine list offers half a dozen choices by the glass. SAMPLE DISHES: soup of the day £2.60; deep-fried plaice fillets £5; apple pie and cream £2.75.

Open *11 to 3, 6 to 11, Sun 12 to 3, 6.30 to 10.30; bar food and restaurant 12 to 2, 7 to 9.15*
Details *Children welcome in dining-room   Car park   Wheelchair access (also WC)   Garden   No-smoking area   Live music   No dogs in restaurant MasterCard, Switch, Visa   Accommodation: 2 rooms, B&B £25 to £40*

LAPWORTH   Warwickshire   map 5

Boot Inn   NEW ENTRY

Old Warwick Road, Lapworth B94 6JU   TEL: (01564) 782464
on B4439 Old Warwick road

This smart red-brick pub enjoys a pleasant location beside the Grand Union Canal, with an attractive side terrace for al fresco drinking and access to the canal. The interior has been tastefully refurbished, with both the lively, small bars sporting an interesting mix of sturdy, rustic tables, bench seating, quarry-tiled floors with rugs, fresh flowers everywhere and interesting prints and paintings throughout. The upstairs restaurant has a very relaxing atmosphere. This is very much a dining pub – the food is generally Mediterranean in style – although sandwiches and filled baguettes are available in the bar. A reporter particularly praised a starter of feta and chickpea salad, followed by duck with pineapple, papaya and spring onion salsa. Other starters might be Thai salmon gravad lax with lime crème fraîche; mussels in cider, leeks and cream; or penne pasta with courgettes, pine-nuts and buffalo mozzarella. Main courses could be salmon fish-cakes, baked free-range chicken, roast Moroccan rump of lamb, or chargrilled calf's liver. A specials board lists the day's fresh fish dishes based on the daily catch. End things nicely with steamed chocolate, date and walnut pudding, or lemon and vanilla tart. On tap are Boddingtons, Flowers Original, Wadworth 6X and Morland Old Speckled Hen, while a 30-bottle wine list offers South African house wines by the glass. SAMPLE DISHES: fried squid with tabbouleh and crème fraîche £5; Japanese-style rump of pork with soy broth £9; lime and Tequila cheesecake £3.50.

Open *summer 11 to 11, winter 11 to 3, 5.30 to 11; bar food and restaurant 12 to 2.30, 6.30 to 9.30*
Details *No children   Car park   Wheelchair access (also WC)   Garden Background music   Dogs welcome   Amex, Delta, MasterCard, Switch, Visa*

LAVENHAM   **Suffolk**   map 6

▲ *Angel* 🏆 🍺 🍇

Market Place, Lavenham CO10 9QZ   TEL: (01787) 247388
on A1141, 6m NE of Sudbury

Standing on the exceptionally pretty old market place, just across from the Guildhall, is the Angel, the oldest part of which was licensed as an inn in 1420, and is heavily beamed and dominated by a enormous fireplace. In the front are bay windows and the 'piano table' (because of its shape), the most coveted spot in the pub. It has built up a regular clientele – one enthusiastic diner sent in six reports in eight months – who describe it as 'a friendly eating pub'. The menu is deceptively simple-sounding and for the most part eschews modern treatments. Game terrine with Cumberland sausage, or warm salad of scallops and bacon, are traditional treatments of traditional ingredients. The lunch menu offers lighter main courses, such as Suffolk cheese and ham pie, or fresh salmon salad with new potatoes. Lamb in paprika and cream may be available lunch or evening, and a speciality is vegetable tarts, such as tomato and sweet potato, or tomato and mozarella. Sticky toffee pudding is as modern as the puddings get. Only beers from Suffolk are served, but this is no bad thing given the choice this encompasses: perhaps Adnams Bitter, Mauldons Suffolk Punch and Nethergate Bitter. House wines are sold on a part-bottle basis, so you only pay for what you drink, and a friendly enough list includes a bottle of Shawsgate from nearby Framlingham; there is also a regularly changing menu of malt whiskies. SAMPLE DISHES: carrot and coriander soup £2.75; chicken breast with orange and ginger £8.25; coffee cheesecake £3.25.

Open *11 to 11, Sun 12 to 10.30; closed 25 and 26 Dec; bar food 12 to 2.15, 6.45 to 9.15*
Details *Children welcome   Car park   Wheelchair access (also WC)   Garden and patio   No-smoking area   Background and live music   Dogs welcome in bar   Amex, Delta, MasterCard, Switch, Visa   Accommodation: 8 rooms, B&B £43 to £69 (£115 for two on Sat inc dinner)*

LEVINGTON   Suffolk   map 6

Ship

Church Lane, Levington IP10 0LQ   TEL: (01473) 659573
off A45 to Felixstowe, 6m SE of Ipswich

William and Shirley Waite have run this (now Pubmaster) tenancy since 1991, and judging by the number of businessmen and Londoners eating here at the time of inspection, they have built up quite a reputation for good-value pub food. The exterior is immaculate, with wooden tables set in a row and hanging baskets providing a blaze of colour against the pristine whitewashed walls and tidy thatch. Inside, cushioned, modern settles are ranged throughout several interconnecting rooms and practically all the wall space is covered with pictures and plates, many ship-related. Real log fires add a cosy glow. A short menu changes daily, ensuring both quality and variety, and is very much in the one-course-meal mode. So choose between Suffolk ham salad, steak and kidney pie, mussels in white wine and garlic butter, kippers even, or a half-lobster salad. Puddings might be cranberry and almond pie, or lemon meringue pie. The pub serves Greene King IPA and Abbot Ale, Flowers IPA, Tetley Bitter and Tolly Cobbold's St George Bitter, and there is a 20-strong wine list offering four by the glass. Levington has a marina and the terrace overlooks the nautical goings-on of the Orwell estuary. SAMPLE DISHES: vegetable soup £3.25; braised knuckle of lamb £6.50; banana cream pie £3.

Open *11.30 to 3, 6 to 11, Sun 12 to 3, 7 to 10.30; bar food and restaurant Sun to Tue 12 to 1.50, Wed to Sat 12 to 1.50, 7 to 8.50*
Details *No children   Car park   Garden and patio   No-smoking area   No music   No dogs   Delta, MasterCard, Switch, Visa*

LICKFOLD　　West Sussex　　　　　　　map 3

Lickfold Inn ☻ 🍺 [NEW ENTRY]

Lickfold GU28 9EY　TEL: (01798) 861285
off A272 Midhurst to Petworth road, signposted Lodsworth, 4m NE of Midhurst

The Lickfold Inn was closed for a year for refurbishment after it was bought by a consortium of 'whizzkids and pop stars', and the result is a trendy, food-orientated pub popular with weekending Londoners. In summer the patio area is 'almost OTT' with luxuriant hanging baskets and flowers 'spilling out from almost every aperture', and romantic fairy lights. It is here that they do barbecues. Inside, the pub has more than its fair share of old beams, flagged floors, big open fires and agricultural implements. The cooking is fashionable and not cheap, but it scores highly. Sweet potato and goats'-cheese fritter, squid and king prawns with chilli sauce, and a well-dressed salad of 'interesting designer leaves' all scored 'ten out of ten' for one reporter. Sweet potato makes a second appearance on the pub menu in the shape of a galette served with roasted rump of lamb, while other main courses might take in Thai chicken curry, or chargrilled tuna with stir-fried mushrooms and ginger. For pudding there could be 'sensational-looking' rum baba, or very untraditional and 'very sweet' treacle tart with cream and bananas. For the merely peckish, a separate blackboard lists sandwiches with interesting fillings and home-made bread. A good range of half a dozen beers comes from a refreshing mix of microbreweries – Ballard's, Cheriton, Brewery on Sea – and family regionals, such as Shepherd Neame, Fuller's and Gale's. Local scrumpy and some quality foreign bottled beers round off the longer drinks. The wine list is pricey but well chosen. Divided into New and Old World sections, it has interesting choices in each, with plenty of half-bottles, dessert wines, ports and brandies. There is also a restaurant on the first floor. SAMPLE DISHES: smoked goose breast and artichoke salad £6.25; wild boar and apple sausages with mustard mash £8.50; grilled peaches with mascarpone £4.25.

Open *11 to 11, Sun 12 to 10.30; bar food 12 to 2.30, 7 to 9.30; restaurant Tue to Sat D only 7 to 9.30*
Details *Children welcome　Car park　Wheelchair access (also WC)　Garden Background and live music　Dogs welcome　Amex, Delta, MasterCard, Switch, Visa*

Assessments of wine in pubs is based largely on what is available in the bar. Many pubs also have full restaurant wine lists.

LIDGATE   Suffolk   map 6

Star Inn ✿
Lidgate CB8 9PP   TEL: (01638) 500275
on B1036, 6m E of Newmarket

Here is one they rave about, with reporters denoting it a 'cracking pub' with 'great atmosphere'. Lidgate is just a few hundred yards over the Suffolk border from Essex, and the pretty, pink-washed Star is made up of two obviously conjoined Elizabethan cottages, with a pretty garden front and back. Because of the make-up of the pub, there are two separate dark-beamed bars, both traditionally furnished with heavy oak and pine tables, candles in iron holders, a log fire and prints of racehorses (Newmarket is nearby) – as well as a smaller, quite plain dining-room. Enticing cooking smells greet you on entering, and Catalan posters and plates above the bar give some hint as to the provenance of the food. The landlady is Catalan, and Mediterranean fish soups, Spanish omelette, paella, wild boar in port, roast lamb in garlic and red wine, monkfish meunière, and tomato and goats'-cheese salad are her stock-in-trade. Otherwise there are more traditional offerings, such as lasagne, sirloin steak and chips. Paella comes in the pan and includes chicken, mussels, langoustines, shrimps, chorizo, peas and peppers in sticky Arborio rice. The pub is owned by Greene King and serves IPA and Abbot. Not surprisingly, Rioja rather than Rhône dominates the wine list, which offers five by the glass. SAMPLE DISHES: prawns in garlic £4.50; Spanish meatballs with squid £10.50; tiramasù £3.50.

Open *11 to 3, 5 to 11; bar food and restaurant 12 to 2, 7 to 10, Sun 12 to 2.30*
Details *Children welcome   Car park   Garden   Smoking not encouraged in restaurant   Background music   No dogs at weekends   Amex, Delta, Diners, MasterCard, Switch, Visa*

LIFTON   Devon   map 1

▲ Arundell Arms ✿ ❦
Lifton PL16 0AA   TEL: (01566) 784666
just off A30, 4m E of Launceston

Anne Voss-Bark, the owner/manager of this sixteenth-century creeper-clad country hotel, with its 20 miles of fishing rights on the River Tamar, knows her clientele. Whereas other pub newsletters chart the fortunes of the darts team, that of the Arundell Arms records the season's best catches, the prospects for snipe shooting and how to enrol on a fly fishing course. Having ridden, shot and waded, the Arundell's customers are naturally more keen to eat than they are to drink. In the restaurant, customers will be looked after by chef Philip Burgess and might choose spiced fillet of red mullet or shallot soup to begin, and roasted English partridge or a saffron risotto with leeks and asparagus to follow. The hotel's Arundell Bar, with its small log fire, polished oak tables and framed fishing flies on the walls, offers cheaper substantial one-course meals such as Spanish omelette, or fritters of sea fish deep-fried in a light saffron batter with a tossed leaf salad and a green mayonnaise, as well as light snacks such as toasted fillet steak sandwich or croque-monsieur. Ask at the bar for the day's choice of desserts or opt for the Cheddar or Stilton with oatcakes and Bath Olivers. Courage Best Bitter and occasional guest beers are on offer, plus an excellent, well-chosen wine list offering around 30 half-bottles and six by the glass. There is even an English representative from Bovey Tracey. Note that the Arundell Bar is through the main entrance and that there is another bar in the hotel called the Courthouse, which is leased to tenants. Anne Voss-Bark and Philip Burgess have combined their experience and skills to rejuvenate the nearby Dartmoor Inn at Lydford (see entry). SAMPLE DISHES: salad of avocado, late summer tomatoes and French beans £4.50; lightly seared smoked haddock £8; roasted hazelnut and almond meringue £3.75.

Open *11 to 11; closed eves of 24, 25 and 26 Dec; bar food 12 to 2.30, 6.30 to 9.30; restaurant 12.30 to 2, 7.30 to 9.30*
Details *Children welcome   Car park   Wheelchair access   No-smoking area in bar; no smoking in restaurant   Background music   No dogs in restaurant Amex, Diners, MasterCard, Visa, Switch   Accommodation: 28 rooms, B&B £44 to £110*

LINTON   West Yorkshire   map 8

Windmill Inn

Main Street, Linton LS22 4HT   TEL: (01937) 582209
off A58, 1m S of Wetherby

This compact stone pub in a pretty village was the mill owner's house until some 300 years ago. It is every inch the proper country pub, complete with beams, old benches and horse brasses, as well as a ghost, a secret passage to the church, and a pear tree grown from a pip brought back from the Napoleonic wars (so they say). The enthusiastic family team offer the same fairly long menu in bar, dining-room or conservatory; put on a good-value 'early bird' evening meal of two or three courses (£6 to £8) providing you are out by 8; encourage reduced portions of Sunday lunch for those with smaller appetites; and tempt children with interesting choices, including one of the grown-up favourites of wild boar sausages with mash and gravy. Interesting sandwiches and baguettes are available only at lunch-time, or choose leek and potato soup, Yorkshire pudding with leek gravy, or one of a dozen blackboard starters. For main courses, sea bream fried with capers and almonds sounds appealing, and there are plenty of meaty dishes, including boozy beef pie. The sweets come with cream, custard or good ice-cream. John Smith's and Theakston are joined by three guest beers each week, perhaps Fat Controller from Rudgate, plus Scrumpy Jack and eight wines by the glass. SAMPLE DISHES: smoked bacon and Brie baguette £5.25; haddock in beer batter £6.25; caramel pavlova £3.

Open *Mon to Fri 11.30 to 3, 5 to 11.30, Sat and Sun 11 to 11; closed 25 Dec L; bar food and restaurant all week L 12 to 2, Tue to Sat D 6 to 9 (9.30 Fri and Sat); early bird menu Tue to Fri 5.30 to 7*
Details *Children welcome   Car park   Garden and patio   No-smoking area Background music   Dogs welcome by arrangement   Delta, MasterCard, Switch, Visa*

LITTLEBOURNE   Kent   map 3

▲ *King William IV*   NEW ENTRY

4 High Street, Littlebourne CT3 1ST   TEL: (01227) 721244
on A257, 6m E of Canterbury

'For the type of pub, they pitch the menu just right,' observed one contented visitor to this sturdy white-painted brick freehouse in a pretty village. Locals obviously think the same, attracted by the cosy atmosphere and pleasant chatty service, the hoppy decorations, the golfing and cricketing paraphernalia and the flexibility of the menu. Although at lunch-time there is a set two-course meal as well as bar snacks, and an à la carte lunch and dinner, you can actually eat whatever you like. Settle in front of the log fire or in the restaurant part, with its prints of the eponymous monarch and 'real red flock wallpaper', ready for well-flavoured food that does not aim to be too ambitious. This could be Stilton and celery soup with herby croûtons, or a warm croissant filled with bacon, mushrooms and Brie, and a good salad alongside. Rabbit braised in red wine with parsley dumplings, and pheasant with game chips and bread sauce could well be examples of the pub's commitment to local produce, but you are just as likely to enjoy simple egg and chips or fried cod. Bass and Shepherd Neame Master Brew are firm fixtures, with a guest beer added occasionally. An extensive wine list covers the world, at reasonable prices, although lacking vintages; house wines are offered by glass and bottle. SAMPLE DISHES: leek and potato soup £2.50; grilled salmon fillet with prawn and scallop risotto £8.25; poached pears in sloe gin £3.25.

Open *11 to 11, Sun 12 to 10.30; bar food and restaurant 12 to 2.15, 7 to 9.15*
Details *No children   Car park   Wheelchair access   Patio   Background music No dogs   Amex, Delta, MasterCard, Switch, Visa   Accommodation: 7 rooms, B&B £25 to £40*

LITTLE CHEVERELL　　　Wiltshire　　　　　map 2

Owl 🍺 NEW ENTRY

Low Road, Little Cheverell SN10 4JS
TEL: (01380) 812263
¼m off A360 Salisbury road at West Lavington

SETTING

'A real find,' wrote our inspector, and as rare as an owl too. It is that odd bird, the perfectly decent but unexceptional pub which has revamped itself into something special without a change of ownership. As ever, simplest is best; the deal is honest home-made food, unpretentiously served in a pretty setting, with good ales. The pub is set well off the main road and its beer garden descends in terraces to the river – very secluded and quiet on a hot day. Inside, the walls are covered with ancient farming implements and there are fresh flowers on every table. The menu is meaty pub fare in generous helpings, and not unadvisedly does the menu warn: 'Skinny they are before they eat, but when they leave they're fat and replete!' Look to the specials board for the unusual stuff like whole knuckle of lamb, or a 'ludicrously large' pheasant in gooseberry and white wine sauce. The friendly landlord, Mike Hardham, who can talk the knuckles off a lamb, runs his own small real ale wholesale business and consequently West Country independents feature strongly on the beer list. Wines are basic, with house red or white offered by the glass. Though the pub is hard to find, it is well worth a visit. SAMPLE DISHES: greenlip mussels in garlic butter £4.25; Wiltshire ham, egg and chips £5; lemon meringue pie £2.

Open *Tue to Sat 12 to 2.30, 7 to 11, Sun 12 to 3, 7 to 10.30; closed Sun eve in winter; bar food 12 to 2, 7 to 9.30*
Details *Children welcome   Car park   Wheelchair access (also WC)   Garden and patio   No-smoking dining area   Occasional live music   Dogs welcome No cards*

Use the maps at the centre of the Guide to plan your trip.

LITTLE COMPTON Warwickshire map 5

▲ Red Lion

Little Compton GL56 0RT TEL: (01608) 674397
off A44, 4m NW of Chipping Norton

Two secluded, pretty gardens set off this Cotswold stone building not far from the Warwickshire–Gloucestershire border. Exposed stone is a feature inside the house too, and fresh floral table arrangements rather than pub bric-à-brac help to create the atmosphere. This is a friendly locals' house. There is a public bar, where drinkers will be cheered by BB and SBA beers from the Donnington Brewery, and where there might be a game of darts or dominoes in progress, and a lounge bar and a restaurant where the diners congregate. A good local supplier of meat is a strong plus here: joints are cut from the rump or fillet and you are charged by weight, which allows real trenchermen to go for a 32oz steak, or more. Cooking is not hugely ambitious, but provides all-round good value: on the printed menu are soups, steaks and lasagna, and on the frequently changing blackboards might be sardines grilled with lemon and garlic, pork and herb sausages with mash, and roast Barbary duck with apricot and Grand Marnier. Wines provide an interesting, good-value mix with a strong presence in France and the New World; house wines come by the glass, half-litre and litre. SAMPLE DISHES: deep-fried whitebait £3.50; 8oz rump steak au poivre £11; whisky trifle £2.75.

Open *12 to 3, 6 to 11, Sun 12 to 3, 7 to 10.30; closed 25 and 26 Dec eve; bar food and restaurant 12 to 2 (2.30 Sun), 7 to 10.30 (9.30 Sat)*
Details *Children welcome in eating areas Car park Wheelchair access (also WC) Garden No smoking in restaurant Background and live music; jukebox in public bar No dogs Delta, MasterCard, Switch, Visa Accommodation: 3 rooms, B&B £25 to £38*

LLANFAIR WATERDINE Shropshire map 5

▲ Red Lion 🍺

Llanfair Waterdine LD7 1TU TEL: (01547) 528214
*4m NW of Knighton, off B4355 Knighton to Newtown
road, over Teme bridge at Lloyney*

Throw a stone from the doorway of this half-timbered sixteenth-century drovers' inn and it will probably land in Wales. The border, the Teme River, runs past the back of Chris and Judy Stevenson's old-fashioned alehouse, which is well off the beaten track. Indeed, apart from the tiny B-road the busiest local thoroughfare is the

Offa's Dyke path. The pub's interior is homely, with a great fireplace containing an iron stove, heat from which can be enjoyed from the comfort of deep armchairs. Spicy dishes such as piri-piri chicken and rice, and beef Beijing, appear on the bar menu alongside more conservative alternatives like steak Madeira, and salmon fish-cakes, while weekly-changing specials might include organic wild boar steak with Cumberland sauce. The well-kept beers come from Tetley and the Wye Valley Brewery in Hereford. Service is relaxed and convivial. SAMPLE DISHES: crispy prawn balls, salad and hot chilli dip £3; chicken Tuscany style £8.25; seasonal steamed puddings £3.

Open *Wed to Mon L 12 to 2, all week D 7 to 11 (10.30 Sun); bar food and restaurant Wed to Mon (Wed to Sun in winter) L 12 to 2, all week D 7 to 9* **Details** *No children   Car park   Garden and patio   No smoking in restaurant Background music   Guide dogs only   Accommodation: 2 rooms, B&B £30 to £50*

LLANYMYNECH   Shropshire   map 5

Bradford Arms ♥

Llanymynech SY22 6EJ   TEL: (01691) 830582
on A483, 6m S of Oswestry

Llanymynech straddles the A483, which marks the boundary between England and Wales. Though the village is unprepossessing, the pub's cocoon-like interior is spruce and smartly snug. This is above all a dining-pub, with the emphasis on fine raw materials – everything except the ice-cream is made on the premises, including excellent bread baked fresh every day. Timing is spot on and many dishes are built on good stock- and booze-based sauces. Despite its length, the menu is surprisingly cliché-free. Prawn cocktail comes as a 'rémoulade' with capers, gherkins, dill and mayonnaise, and some very original starters include grilled eggs 'old Bruge style' with tarragon, prawns, Dijon mustard and cream, and brochette Jurasienne (deep-fried breaded Gruyère cheese wrapped in thin slices of smoked ham). There is a selection of main-course salads, while hot mains embrace individual dishes like lamb 'Tkemaly' – served with plums, dill, garlic, wine and soured cream – or suprême of chicken in fennel, Pernod and cream sauce. Sweet-lovers have a wide selection to choose from: white chocolate bavarois, rum and walnut gâteau, or maybe crème caramel. Or head for the cheese board, where you can choose three from an international selection of 15 that might include home-grown Yorkshire Blue, French Vignotte and Italian Taleggio. Only in the beer department is the selection modest, with Shepherd Neame Spitfire and Greene King Abbot Ale on draught. The wine list trots around the world and includes several old and rare bottles over £100; four wines are available by the glass. SAMPLE DISHES: large king prawn tails £6; grilled fillet steak au poivre vert £8.75; gooseberry and honey cream pudding £2.75.

Open *Tue to Sun 12 to 3, 7 to 11; closed 25 and 26 Dec, first 3 weeks in Jan; bar food and restaurant Tue to Sun 12 to 2, 7 to 10 (9 Sun)*
Details *Children welcome in dining-room   Car park   Wheelchair access (also WC)   Patio   No-smoking area   Background music   Guide dogs only   Delta, MasterCard, Switch, Visa*

LODERS   Dorset   map 2

▲ *Loders Arms*

Loders DT6 3SA   TEL: (01308) 422431
off A3066, 2m NE of Bridport

This is a homely village local, situated in a delightful stone-and-thatch village tucked away in a narrow valley deep in the Dorset hills, close to Bridport. To the rear is a skittles alley and garden with picnic tables and views of the wooded hills. Within, open fires blaze and the small bar is well patronised by local drinkers. It would be stretching things to describe the interior as smart, but it is warm and welcoming and positively bustles in the evenings. Dining is so popular that booking is advisable; the draw is the intriguing range of home-cooked dishes offered by hard-working tenants Helen and Roger Flint. All the menus are up on blackboards, which change frequently, though some core dishes are virtually always available. These include first courses of Brie in filo, devilled kidneys, and chicken liver parfait, and main courses of baked sea bass with salsa verde, rump steak, venison steak, and rack of lamb. Occasional starters might be baked polenta, garlic mushrooms and mozzarella, or fresh anchovies with basil and tomato salad. Visiting main dishes have included chicken breast pieces with tarragon, sun-dried tomatoes and pasta, and rabbit in cider. Puddings are refreshingly different: sticky pudding is of the apricot or date variety rather than toffee, and cheesecake might be walnut and praline. The pub is a Palmers tenancy, so serves that brewer's 200, IPA and Bridport Bitter. A selection of wines from all over the world offers six by the glass. SAMPLE DISHES: crostini, sun-dried tomatoes, tapénade and mozzarella £4.25; smoked haddock fish-cakes £7; steamed lemon and ginger pudding £3.

Open *Mon to Fri 11.30 to 2.30, 6 to 11, Sat 11 to 3, 6 to 11, Sun 12 to 10.30; bar food and restaurant 12.30 to 2, 7.15 to 9*
Details *Children welcome   Car park   Wheelchair access   Garden and patio Smoking discouraged in dining area   Background music   Dogs welcome MasterCard, Visa   Accommodation: 2 rooms, B&B £25 to £45*

▲ *Angel Inn* 🏵 🍇

Bicester Road, Long Crendon HP18 9EE
TEL: (01844) 208268
on B4011, 2m NW of Thame

Steve and Angie Good took over the Angel in spring 1997 but have continued with the former owners' emphasis on fish dishes, which are chalked up daily on a board. Chargrilled squid and sausage, or crab and Gruyère tartlet with ginger and lime sauce, are typically imaginative starters. Well-presented main courses might include whole lobster, or fillet of cod on olive mash. Non-fish dishes are on the printed à la carte menu, which takes in chargrilled medallion of highland venison in port and juniper sauce with a haggis fritter, or vegetarian options such as deep-fried tomato and aubergine stuffed with goats' cheese. The pub itself is of some antiquity – customers can contemplate a section of original 400-year-old exposed wattle and daub protected behind glass. The atmosphere is homely: there are armchairs in the bar area, and the conservatory dining area is arranged with well-spaced, candlelit tables and low-level lighting, which gives a pleasant, intimate feel. The extensive wine list, which runs to over 100 bins, is divided according to the 'weight' of the wine, oaked or unoaked, sweet or dry, and includes a section of 'reserve' wines, most of which are over £30; a reasonable number are available in half-bottles and by the glass, and further, less-expensive wines are chalked on a board behind the bar. Beers include Hook Norton Old Hooky, Shepherd Neame Spitfire and Ridleys Rumpus, and there is a selection of malt whiskies. SAMPLE DISHES: pan-seared Spanish sardines with chilli butter £4.25; pan-fried fillet of snapper on vegetable stir-fry £14.50; hot roast pineapple with cinnamon ice-cream £4.50.

Open *Mon to Sat 11 to 11, Sun 12 to 2.30; bar food and restaurant 12 to 2.30, 7 to 9.30, Sun 12 to 3*
Details *Children welcome　Car park　Patio　No-smoking area　Background music　Guide dogs only　Delta, MasterCard, Switch, Visa　Accommodation: 3 rooms, B&B £55 to £65*

LONGDON GREEN   Staffordshire   map 5

Red Lion Inn   ⬛NEW ENTRY⬛

Longdon Green WS15 4QF   TEL: (01543) 490250
just off A51 Lichfield to Rugeley Road, 2m N of Lichfield

This upgraded pub on the village green now serves as a popular
restaurant, though it has not lost its former appeal as an unpretentious country local in Victorian red brick. The present incumbents
are relative newcomers from the dynamic world of computing. With
plenty of energy to spare, they have already made a promising
impact on the Staffordshire dining scene, offering a recognisable but
upbeat range of traditional dishes like smoked barbary duck, or roast
pheasant with juniper and port sauce varied with occasional forays
into Italian or other ethnic theme cooking. Good-value fixed-price
supper menus offer three courses. Surroundings are tidily simple,
with wheelback chairs and open fires, and service is personal and
attentive. Beers have a Midland bias, with Bass and Worthington on
tap, while wines stray further afield with plenty of New World bins
among well-chosen European classics, including guest wines by
British producers based in France. Three are served by the glass.
SAMPLE DISHES: foccacia with peppers £4.50; rack of lamb with black
cherry sauce £12; lemon cheesecake £3.50.

Open *all week L 11 to 3, Mon to Sat eve 6.30 to 11; bar food 12.30 to 2, 7
to 9 (10 Fri and Sat), Sun 12.30 to 2.30*
Details *Children welcome   Car park   Wheelchair access (also WC)   Garden
and patio   Background music   Delta, MasterCard, Switch, Visa*

LONGSTOCK   Hampshire   map 2

▲ *Peat Spade Inn* 🍺 🍇

Longstock SO20 6DR   TEL: (01264) 810612
off A3057, 1m N of Stockbridge

Sarah Hinman and Bernard Startup run a tight ship at the Peat
Spade, prompting *Guide* readers to write in to compliment the quality of the cooking offered – 'what a find,' one enthusiastic diner
exclaimed. This pleasant red brick, slate-roofed pub sits solid and
comfortable-looking in the centre of a well-heeled village. The
immediate impression on entering is of a well-maintained interior
exuding comfort and cleanliness. Shelves of knick-knacks include
collections of Toby jugs and an assortment of ancient pipes, and
there are prints and watercolours (some for sale) and open log fires.
It would be a joy to see more pubs adopt the Peat Spade's policy on

real ale; a short selection of fine ales from local brewers, in this case King Alfred's from the Hampshire Brewery and True Glory and Fortyniner from Ringwood. Food is served in a stylish and thoughtful way, from a short menu that demonstrates commitment to good raw materials. You might like to kick off with Orkney herring fillets in sour cream, or perhaps a walnut and mushroom terrine. Meaty mains include Aberdeen Angus sirloin steak or Ayrshire lamb cutlets with claret and rosemary. Fish lovers can choose between escalope of salmon or red bream fillets with mussel and shrimp sauce. Among the selection of 'light lunches' could be smoked haddock and horseradish bake, and warm salad of smoked chicken and chorizo. Puddings include one or two out-of-the-ordinary dishes like walnut and raisin fudge tart, or chocolate and Tia Maria torte. Six house wines and one pudding wine are available by the glass from a short, well-chosen list. SAMPLE DISHES: pumpkin and fresh coriander soup £3.50; medallions of pork tenderloin with flageolet beans £10; fresh lemon tart £3.75.

Open *Tue to Sat 11.30 to 3 (2.30 winter), 6 to 11 (10.30 winter), Sun 12 to 3; closed 25 and 26 Dec, 2nd week in May, 2nd week in Oct; bar food 12 to 2, 7 to 9.30 (9 Tue and Wed)*
Details *Children welcome   Car park   Wheelchair access (also WC)   Garden No-smoking area   Background music   Dogs on a lead welcome   No cards Accommodation: 2 rooms, B&B £53 to £59*

LONGWORTH   Oxfordshire   map 2

Blue Boar Inn

Tucks Lane, Longworth OX13 5ET   TEL: (01865) 820494
off A420 at Kingston Bagpuize, 7m W of Abingdon

'A real delight' was one reporter's summary of this pretty thatched and creeper-covered village pub. Inside, it has a buzzing atmosphere, enhanced by terracotta walls, jolly curtains, hop-strewn beams and genuinely old tables. There is space for drinkers, but most people come here to eat. Many of the dishes are interestingly and often richly sauced: Thai chicken curry on the hot side and authentically fragrant with lemon grass and coconut, or baked skate wings with a Cajun butter sauce. Home-made Blue Boar burger with Brie or Stilton, steaks with various sauces, and gammon, egg, tomato and chips are 'old favourites', while starters include basil and tomato soup, pigeon terrine and cheesy garlic bread. Sandwiches are a lunchtime option, and there is a handful of pubby puddings. Beers are Morrells Bitter and Varsity, while wines are good-value, wide-ranging and highly quaffable, with six by the glass. SAMPLE DISHES:

smoked salmon and scrambled egg £5; monkfish with roasted vegetables and a herbed crust £10.50; bread-and-butter pudding £3.

Open *Mon to Fri 12 to 3, 6 to 11, Sat 12 to 11, Sun 12 to 10.30; closed 25 Dec; bar food Mon to Sat 12 to 2.30, 7 to 10, Sun 12 to 3, 7 to 9*
Details *Children welcome in bar eating area Car park Wheelchair access (also WC) Garden Background and live music No dogs Amex, Delta, MasterCard, Switch, Visa*

LOSTWITHIEL   Cornwall   map 1

▲ *Royal Oak* 🍺

Duke Street, Lostwithiel PL22 0AG   TEL: (01208) 872552
off A390, 5m SE of Bodmin

The Royal Oak, like much of the village of Lostwithiel, dates back to the thirteenth century and was originally the gatehouse to the Castle Estate. It is rumoured that a tunnel once connected the pub cellars with Restormel Castle one and a half miles away. The pub is located on a steep hill and a rather plain exterior hides a much richer interior, with beams and exposed stone walls, warm red colours and settle seating. Over the bar is a blackboard showing the beers on offer: Bass, Marston's Pedigree, Fuller's London Pride, Sharp's and two changing guests from local independent brewers, as well as an impressive range of over 40 bottled beers from around the globe. The 50-plus-bottle wine list is half-French, half the rest of the world, with seven wines available by the glass. Cooking is the province of landlady Eileen Hine, who can be seen rustling up the dishes of the day. Canny eaters will opt for the specials board though the fixed menu will offer such starters as smoked fish platter, and avocado and orange salad, as well as the usual pâtés, soups and prawn cocktails. There is a large selection of steaks, including filet mignon, as well as veal Cordon Bleu, and roast Barbary duckling. Fish dishes are encouragingly simple; grilled trout, pan-fried scallops, and salmon steak in dill and cucumber sauce; sweets are good pubby puds and, this being Cornwall, come with clotted cream. SAMPLE DISHES: stuffed mushrooms £3.25; crab salad £5.75; cherry pie £2.

Open *11 to 11 (10.30 Sun); bar food and restaurant 12 to 2, 6.30 to 9.30*
Details *Children welcome in eating areas Car park Wheelchair access Garden Jukebox No dogs in restaurant Amex, Delta, Diners, MasterCard, Switch, Visa Accommodation: 6 rooms, B&B £34 to £55*

If a pub has a special point of interest, this is indicated by a 'flashed' word or phrase at the top right of the entry.

LOWER BEEDING West Sussex map 3

Crabtree 🏆🏆 🍇

Brighton Road, Lower Beeding RH13 6PT   TEL: (01403) 891257
on A281, 4m S of Horsham

The Crabtree is a large, sturdy, roadside building with more of a restaurant than a pub feel to it, but staff are charming and efficient. There are several bars and even the tables available for bar lunches are laid up with crisp white linen cloths. Otherwise, it is plainly decorated with a few quirky artefacts, some wine-orientated sayings painted on the wall, and some (decent) graffiti by customers. The blackboards tend to replicate the printed menus, and the lunchtime one- or two-course specials are very good value. Start with marinated herrings and a green salad with red onion in sour cream, or beef carpaccio with capers and rosemary on caramelised onions. Move down the short menu to choose between fish-cakes and a leek compote, together with baby spinach and grilled tomatoes, or grilled lamb chops with rosemary on Savoy cabbage and sauté mushrooms and red wine sauce. Baked apple, this one stuffed with sultanas and hazelnut in marsala, is yet another of those dishes one wishes one saw on more pub menus. Being a tied house, the Crabtree serves King & Barnes Sussex and Festive as well as their seasonal ales. A lengthy selection of house wines kicks off a list which covers a variety of styles at generally fair prices. SAMPLE DISHES: chilled gazpacho with balsamic vinegar and garden herbs £4; grilled salmon on fresh spinach with a chive hollandaise £10.25; apricot sorbet £3.50.

Open *11 to 3, 6 to 11, Sun 12 to 3, 7 to 10.30; closed 25 Dec; bar food and restaurant all week L 12.30 to 2, Mon to Thur D 6 to 10*
Details *Children welcome in eating areas   Car park   Wheelchair access Garden and patio   No-smoking area   No music   No dogs   Amex, Delta, Diners, MasterCard, Switch, Visa*

LOWER CHICKSGROVE Wiltshire map 2

▲ Compasses Inn

Lower Chicksgrove SP3 6NB   TEL: (01722) 714318
1m NW of A30 between Swallowcliffe and Fovant

This charming thatched and timbered allegedly fourteenth-century pub in a peaceful spot is hidden away down narrow lanes in unspoilt Wiltshire countryside, with just a few cottages for company. Picnic benches deck the front lawn and, in summer, the old cobbled path leading to the pantiled entrance porch. The unspoilt appearance of the main bar is reinforced by a partly flagstoned floor, low heavy beams, an assortment of traditional furniture in secluded alcoves, and a wood-burning stove sitting beneath an inglenook adorned with an assortment of farming implements. A small rear dining-room is a more recent extension, and in the evenings candlelit tables create an intimate and cosy atmosphere. The blackboard menu changes regularly and is short enough to support the management's request to be patient, as dishes are all cooked to order. Dudley and Eileen Cobb, who took over the pub in late 1997, inherited the existing chef, and the style of the cuisine has not notably altered. A number of starters – moules marinière (a house speciality), tiger prawns in garlic butter or coquilles St Jacques – are available as main courses. Fishy mains include Brixham sea bass grilled in tomato butter, or seafood tagliatelle, while meat eaters could tuck into fillet steak Dijonnaise; duck breast with orange, cream and Grand Marnier sauce; or boned quail with leeks, onions, grapes and port. If you do not feel up to the challenge, sandwiches and light bites are also available. Desserts are prepared by the chef and displayed on the blackboard. The pub serves Wadworth 6X, Bass and a brew from Tisbury Brewery, and a mid-priced wine list has some reasonable choices. SAMPLE DISHES: escargot à la Chablaisienne £4.75; ribeye steak in garlic £11; raspberry rhapsody £3.

Open *11 to 3, 6.30 to 11, Sun 12 to 3, 7 to 10.30; bar food and restaurant Tue to Sat 12 to 2, 7 to 9, Sun L only 12 to 2*
Details *Children welcome   Car park   Garden   No music   Dogs welcome Delta, MasterCard, Switch, Visa   Accommodation: 5 rooms, B&B £35 to £45*

LOWER ODDINGTON   Gloucestershire   map 5

Fox Inn 🌣

Lower Oddington GL56 0UR   TEL: (01451) 870555
off A436, E of Stow-in-the-Wold

Fronting on to the main street of straggly Lower Oddington, this pub of mellow Cotswold stone is largely obscured by a massive creeper that covers the whole building from kerb to eaves. The Fox is surrounded by some of Gloucestershire's most beautiful countryside, not far from the National Trust property Chastleton House. Its spacious interior is equally attractive, with most of the clutter being the human beings who flock here. Visitors spread throughout a number of small, interconnected rooms set around the central kitchen, and the atmosphere is 'busy, buzzy and trendy'. The menu changes only gradually and some dishes seem rock-solidly permanent: baked stuffed mushrooms with garlic mayonnaise, or a good-value 'quad' of four Cotswold sausages, for example. From there you can move on to upmarket pub-grub-style food. Rack of lamb with onion sauce, and warm chicken, bacon and avocado salad, say, or Thai chicken curry with basmati rice. Desserts include old favourites like bread-and-butter pudding and sticky toffee pudding. Vicky Elliot and Lilli Birch serve customers Hook Norton Best Bitter, Hampshire Brewery's Pride of Romsey and Marston's Pedigree, and a fairly static wine list offers average house wines as well as a decent world selection, including wines from Chile and Argentina. SAMPLE DISHES: courgette and basil soup £3; Gloucestershire pie £8; raspberry and lemon baked pudding £3.25.

Open *12 to 3, 6.30 to 11, Sun 12 to 3, 7 to 10.30; bar food 12 to 2, 7 to 10 (9.30 Sun)*
Details *Children welcome   Car park   Wheelchair access   Garden Background music   No dogs   MasterCard, Visa*

LUND   **East Riding of Yorkshire**   **map 9**

Wellington | NEW ENTRY |

19 The Green, Lund YO25 9TE   TEL: (01377) 217294
on B1284 between Beverley and Driffield

'A great old village pub, recently refurbished,' wrote one enthusiastic reporter. There's a taproom bar, with dartboard and pool table, and a very comfortable and friendly main bar, with a large log-burning fireplace, where lunchtime bar meals are served; in the evenings you have to use the separate restaurant. Similarities exist between the menus but main-course prices are higher in the evenings. Food comes well served and prepared with fresh ingredients, good sauces and good vegetables. Kick off with smoked haddock fish-cakes with a mild curried apple sauce, or a blue Wensleydale and port pâté with granary toast; also at lunch try beef bourguignonne with horseradish mash, or goats'-cheese, tarragon and pine-nut flan with roasted pepper sauce, or prawn Madras with saffron rice. Follow with chocolate sponge, chocolate sauce and vanilla ice-cream, or poached pear with warm fudge sauce. The pub serves some of the big Yorkshire names – Black Sheep, Timothy Taylor Landlord and John Smith's – with Bateman Dark Mild travelling up the A1 specially. A wine list runs to 80 bins and carries an impressive selection of 20 half-bottles and pudding wines. SAMPLE DISHES: chestnut and orange soup £3; pheasant casserole £7.25; jam sponge and custard £2.50.

Open *12 to 3, 7 to 11 (10.30 Sun); bar food Tue to Sun L 12 to 2; restaurant Tue to Sat D 7 to 10*
Details *Children welcome in bar eating area at L   Car park   Wheelchair access (also WC)   Patio   No-smoking area   Background music   Dogs welcome on flagged floors   Delta, MasterCard, Switch, Visa*

LUSTLEIGH   Devon   map 1

Cleave

Lustleigh TQ13 9TJ   TEL: (01647) 277223
off A382, 4m SE of Moretonhampstead

The pretty, sheltered garden outside this fifteenth-century white-washed inn makes a splash of colour in summer. Lustleigh Cleave, the source of the pub's name, is a noted beauty spot and the village is reputed to date from the days of Alfred the Great. Inside the pub you will find two low-beamed bars, one with a vast inglenook complete with bread oven, the other with a piano and pool table. At the back is a family room, well equipped with games, books and crayons. Quick and efficient service reflects the pub's popularity, and a simple printed menu operates throughout the bars and dining-room; blackboard specials, such as spaghetti bolognese and cottage pie, are also available. A reporter thought cooking 'careful and sound', with a nod in the direction of local ingredients. There are plenty of sandwiches, plough-man's and salad options. Main meals such as cheese and onion flan, home-cooked ham, roast chicken or fillet of plaice in breadcrumbs are all served with chips and salad. Vegetarians can tuck into a nut roast in spicy tomato sauce and meat eaters can get their teeth into roast beef and Yorkshire pudding. The children's menu features scaled-down versions of main dishes, and puddings are along the lines of apple pie, rich chocolate fudge cake and warm treacle tart. Beers include Bass, Flowers Original and Hardy's Royal Oak. SAMPLE DISHES: mushrooms in garlic butter £4.50; wholetail breaded scampi £7; Dutch apple crumble £2.50.

Open *summer all week 11 to 11, winter Mon to Fri 11 to 3, 6 to 11, Sat and Sun 11 to 11; bar food 12 to 2, 6.30 to 9 (no D Mon in winter)*
Details *Children welcome in family room   Car park   Wheelchair access Garden and patio   No smoking in family room   No music   Dogs welcome Delta, MasterCard, Switch, Visa*

LUXBOROUGH   Somerset   map 1

▲ Royal Oak of Luxborough

Luxborough TA23 0SH   TEL: (01984) 640319
off A396, 4m S of Dunster

This stone-built pub, in a long straggling village in Exmoor National Park, was once a group of cottages and dates back to the fourteenth century. A small garden holds a few tables, while the interior consists of two bars with flagstone floors, low beams and brasses, and a sepa-rate dining-room which contains hunting prints, wooden tables and cane-seated chairs. A snack menu offers soup, pâté, ploughman's, filled jacket potatoes, sandwiches, salads or Royal Oak prawns for starters, with main dishes of fillet or rump steak, half a roast chicken or breaded plaice with chips. In the evening the kitchen moves up a notch or two to deliver venison casserole, breast of duck with cran-berry sauce, or perhaps pork fillet with apricots in brandy cream sauce. A specials board offers the day's catch from Brixham, and children get to choose from sausages, scampi or fishfingers with chips and beans. The range of home-made desserts includes choco-late mud pudding, spotted dick and bread-and-butter pudding, all served with clotted cream or custard. Flowers, Cotleigh and Exmoor ales are supplemented by Somerset ciders, malt whiskies and a reasonably priced wine list from fine producers (but with only two by the glass). SAMPLE DISHES: port and Stilton pâté £4.25; steak and ale pie £6; lemon and lime cheesecake £3.

Open *11 to 3, 6 to 11, Sun 12 to 2.30, 6 to 10.30; bar food and restaurant 12 to 2, 7 to 9.30*
Details *Children welcome in dining-room   Car park   Wheelchair access (also WC)   Garden and patio   No smoking in bedrooms   Live music   Dogs welcome   No cards   Accommodation: 11 rooms, B&B £30 to £65*

LYDDINGTON   Rutland   map 5

Old White Hart

51 Main Street, Lyddington LE15 9LR   TEL: (01572) 821703
off A6003, 2m S of Uppingham

This honey-coloured stone pub dates back to the seventeenth century and stands by the green in this attractive, out-of-the-way village, high above the Welland Valley. There is a pretty walled garden whose flowers can be enjoyed by players of pétanque waiting their turn on one of the 12 pistes the pub maintains. Inside is a cosy bar with heavy beams, dried flower arrangements, traditional furnishings and a splendid log fire. The pub's emphasis on food shows in the three distinct dining areas, and there is a separate tiled-floor room with a wood-burning stove popular with the local dominoes aficionados. Polly Dane has taken over since the last edition of the *Guide* and under her guidance the pub turns out a broad menu of modernish cooking. For a starter you might try duck confit, smoked applewood cheese tartlet, or sauté of scallops and prawns, local roast pheasant, pork escalope, or monkfish and salmon filo parcel. A short beer list offers Greene King IPA and Abbot as well as Timothy Taylor Landlord, and six wines are available by the glass. SAMPLE DISHES: venison and pork terrine £4.25; breast of Lonsdale duck £11.25; lime cheesecake with blackberry coulis £3.25.

Open *12 to 3, 6.30 to 11; bar food 12 to 2, 6.30 to 9.30, Sun L only 12 to 2*
Details *Children welcome   Car park   Wheelchair access (also WC)   Garden
No-smoking area   Background music   No dogs   Delta, MasterCard, Switch,
Visa*

LYDFORD   Devon   map 1

▲ *Castle Inn* 🍺 🌸

Lydford EX20 4BH   TEL: (01822) 820241
off A386, 7m N of Tavistock

This Tudor pub, standing next to the castle – a ghostly ruin of a
square keep on a mound now inhabited exclusively by pigeons – is
wisteria-clad and atmospheric. The focal point of this popular and
busy local in the village centre is the narrow, cosy public bar. A large
inglenook fireplace is situated opposite the bar, and a delightful no-
smoking snug is secreted away down a narrow corridor and screened
from it by two curved, high-backed settles (ideal for couples). The
wonderful lounge, with its ample, deep settees and warm old-fashioned appeal, is crammed with all sorts of pictures, plates and
polished brass ornaments. A daily-changing blackboard menu above
the fireplace supplements the lengthy printed bar menu and à la carte
eating in the Foresters restaurant. The bar menu changes constantly,
so you may or may not find such fare as lamb curry with basmati
rice, pickles and poppadom; leek, cream cheese and sweetcorn
roulade; Dartmouth smoked mackerel with horseradish, wild mushrooms and pine-nuts; tagliatelle with mascarpone sauce; or an
unusual-sounding dolcelatte, cranberry and chestnut layered pie.
Sauté potatoes are a popular accompaniment to most dishes, all of
which are served in a caring fashion by staff for whom 'nothing is
too much effort'. In addition to local Luscombe cider, the pub serves
London Pride, Butcombe Bitter and up to three guests from regional
microbreweries. There are separate lists for wines by the glass and
dessert wines, while the lengthy main list boasts some superior
choices, a good New World selection and a handful from Devon.
Sixteen wines are offered by the glass. SAMPLE DISHES: curried banana
soup £2.75; Devon turkey, ham and mushroom pie £6.25; treacle
tart £3.25.

Open *11.30 to 3, 6 to 11, Sun 12 to 3, 6 (7 winter) to 10.30; closed eve 25
Dec bar food 12 to 2.30, 6.30 to 9.30, Sun 6.30 (7 winter) to 9; restaurant 7
to 9.30 (9 Sun)*
Details *Children welcome in dining-room   Car park   Garden and patio   No-
smoking area   No music   No dogs in restaurant or lounge   Amex, Delta,
Diners, MasterCard, Switch, Visa   Accommodation: 9 rooms, B&B £34.50
to £85*

Dartmoor Inn   NEW ENTRY

Lydford EX20 4AU   TEL: (01822) 820221
on A386 Tavistock to Okehampton Road

The kitchen was first to be refurbished at this pub now owned by
Anne Voss-Bark and Philip Burgess of the Arundell Arms at Lifton
(see entry), and since opening for meals in July 1998 the Dartmoor
Inn has rapidly built up a reputation for high-quality, traditional
food at reasonable prices. There is plenty to do in the area if outdoor
activities are your cup of tea: the moor rises up behind the pub and
High Down is popular with walkers; picnickers swim in deep
sections of the River Lyd in summer; and Brat Tor attracts hang-glid-
ers. If you prefer just to admire the scenery, the National Trust-
owned gorge is a spectacular sight. Despite the rather untempting
exterior, a warm welcome awaits inside. The atmosphere is New
England, with tongue-and-groove wood panelling painted sea green,
muted lighting, bunches of dried flowers and plenty of real log fires.
There is limited bar space as most of the room is designated table
seating for diners, who can enjoy the cosy and intimate surroundings
of several small rooms.

   From the fairly short daily-changing menu you might find
'intensely flavoured and creamy' roasted tomato soup with nutmeg
cream, or a pint of deliciously creamy mussels, heavily flavoured with
saffron and 'lightly cooked to perfection'. If you arrive on a Sunday,
you might enjoy tender roast sirloin of beef with horseradish cream
served with excellent Yorkshire pudding. Otherwise there might be
linguine with Parmesan, toasted hazelnuts and cream sauce; fillet of
guinea-fowl with charcoal-grilled polenta and pesto; or coq au vin
with noodles and croûtons. The dessert menu contains a selection of
organic ice-creams and local cheeses, as well as lemon meringue pie,
hot chocolate pudding with chocolate sauce, and treacle tart, all
served with clotted cream. The wine list is reasonably priced and the
wines change quarterly – four are available by the glass. Draught Bass
is the house beer but there are always another three real ales in
summer and perhaps two in winter. SAMPLE DISHES: smoked salmon
with avocado and herb relish £4; farmhouse sausages with mashed
potato and onion gravy £5; baked ricotta cheesecake £3.

Open *Tue to Sat 11 to 3 (2.30 winter), 6 (6.30 winter) to 11, Sun 12 to 3,
6.30 to 10.30; closed Mon, 2 weeks in Feb; bar food and restaurant 12 to
2.30 (3 Sun), 6 to 10 (10.30 Fri and Sat in summer)*
Details *Children welcome in bar eating-area   Car park   No smoking in
restaurant   Background music   Dogs welcome   Delta, MasterCard, Switch,
Visa*

🌽 *indicates a pub serving better-than-average wine.*

LYDGATE   **Greater Manchester**   **map 8**

▲ *White Hart* 🍴🍴 🍇

51 Stockport Road, Lydgate OL4 4JJ   TEL: (01457) 872566
on A6050, 3m E of Oldham

Perched high on a hillside with impressive views down over Oldham and Manchester, the White Hart has commanded its heights since 1788. When Charles Brierley and John Rudden took it over in 1994, however, it had become rather run down and they have laboured hard to create a food pub of considerable local reputation. The large building combines a bar and brasserie on the ground floor and a restaurant on the first, though as the food operation has expanded the bar area has been reduced. Everything is spacious and pristine.

On the brasserie menu is a good choice of often inventive dishes: terrine of rabbit, hare and confit of duck with a jus dressing, perhaps, or crab risotto cake with a sweetcorn relish, followed by roast fillet of beef with grilled peppered goats' cheese, or pan-fried salmon fillet with smoked haddock brandade, topped with a poached egg. For those in a hurry, there are some 'quick dishes' – omelette with glazed wild mushrooms, crème fraîche and chives, or cream soup of the day – and desserts might run to pear tarte Tatin with liquorice ice-cream, or something traditional like sticky toffee pudding – or even, for the unsweet of tooth, a selection of British cheeses. The upstairs restaurant offers a three-course fixed-price menu with a small number of regularly changing choices, which are sufficiently eclectic to satisfy most palates. On tap are beers from Lees and Boddingtons as well as Flowers IPA. A short version of the lengthy main wine list is available in the bar and brasserie, and includes nine wines by the glass. SAMPLE DISHES: chicken and sweet-bread sausage with an apple and mustard dressing £4.50; pan-fried pepper calf's liver with smoked bacon and spinach, topped with crème fraîche £12.50; strawberry crème brûlée £4.50.

Open *12 to 11, Sun 12 to 10.30; bar food 12 to 2.30, 6 to 9.30; restaurant Sun L 12 to 2.30, Tue to Sat D 7 to 9.30*
Details *Children welcome   Car park   Wheelchair access (also WC)   Garden No smoking in restaurant   Background music   Guide dogs only   Amex, Delta, MasterCard, Switch, Visa   Accommodation: 6 rooms, B&B £55 to £85*

MADINGLEY　　Cambridgeshire　　　　　　map 6

Three Horseshoes 🍷🍷 🍇

High Street, Madingley CB3 8AB　TEL: (01954) 210221
off A1303, 2m W of Cambridge, close to M11 junction 13

The Three Horseshoes is a pretty thatched pub situated on the village high street. It is another member of the highly successful Huntsbridge group (see also entries for Pheasant Inn, Keyston, White Hart, Great Yeldham and the Falcon Inn, Fotheringhay), and operates the same 'eat what you like where you like' system, offering a bar or a pleasant conservatory restaurant extension overlooking the garden. A mixed tapas starter includes radishes with butter, gazpacho, chorizo, almonds and manchego cheese with raisins and honey, while chargrilled scallops come with more chorizo, plus black pudding, onions, cream, parsley and garlic. Several dishes can be ordered as starters or main courses. Chargrilling seems to be the preferred cooking method, perhaps applied to leg of lamb, which comes with new potatoes, salsa verde, green and yellow beans and red onions in balsamic vinegar, or marinated beef fillet, accompanied by herb polenta, vine tomatoes, lemon braised fennel, tarragon mustard and olive oil and chilli dressing. Puddings also show up the kitchen's skill. A simple sticky toffee pudding was described as the best one reporter ever had, and grilled oranges with rosewater and crème fraîche is a definite 'try me' dish. The pub serves the group's preferred brew Adnams, plus a guest which changes at the end of each firkin. Master of Wine John Hoskins chooses the wines for the group and the list offers a fine selection at good value for money, with around a dozen available by the glass. SAMPLE DISHES: peppered veal with a salad of baby vegetables and truffle mayonniase £6; roast halibut with beetroot, horseradish and parsley and tumeric oil £13; fruit salad of blueberries, nectarines and mango with star anise and chilli syrup £4.50.

Open *11.30 to 2.30, 6 to 11, Sun 12 to 2.30, 7 to 10.30; bar food and restaurant 12 to 2, 6.30 to 9.30, Sun 12 to 2, 7 to 9*
Details *Children welcome　Car park　Wheelchair access　Garden　No smoking in restaurant　No music　Guide dogs only　Amex, Delta, Diners, MasterCard, Switch, Visa*

The Guide is totally independent, accepts no free hospitality and carries no advertising.

MAIDENSGROVE   Oxfordshire   map 2

Five Horseshoes

Maidensgrove RG9 6EX   TEL: (01491) 641282
off B480 and B481, 5m NW of Henley-on-Thames

This seventeenth-century vine-covered pub, not far from Henley-on-
Thames and Stonor House, steals the edge on some pretty keen local
competition. The success of the Five Horseshoes is due mainly to
Graham and Mary Cromack, who have, over the years, become
experienced caterers well able to cope with the volume of diners
who descend upon them. However, the splendid view of the
Chiltern Hills, which can be enjoyed from the bistro-style conservatory restaurant as well as the garden, is also a great attraction, and in
summer the barbecue in the garden is popular. Inside is a series of
rambling, low-ceilinged bars with carpeted or quarry tiled floors. A
mix of old furnishings, a wood-burning stove and collections of old
tools, photographs, prints and bank notes from around the world
add character. The menu is varied, delivering usual pub dishes like
soup or grilled goats' cheese, but also a more imaginitive carpaccio
of tuna, or Brie and mushroom fondue. Consult the specials board to
see if anything takes your fancy; otherwise try Scotch salmon fillet as
a main course, or wild boar sausages, or perhaps chargrilled calf's
liver. Beers come from the nearby Brakspear Brewery, with some
independent brewers' beers as guests. A printed wine list offers some
quality French bottles and some cheaper New World drinking.
SAMPLE DISHES: warm salad of bacon and Stilton £6; pancake of
seafood £11.25; double-baked chocolate mousse cake on mango
coulis £3.50.

Open   *11.30 to 2.30, 6 to 11, Sun 12 to 3, 7 to 10.30; bar food and
restaurant all week L 12 to 2, Mon to Sat D 7 to 10*
Details   *Children welcome in dining-room and club room   Car park
Wheelchair access   Garden and patio   No cigar smoking in restaurant
Background music   Dogs welcome   Delta, MasterCard, Switch, Visa*

MARKET OVERTON   Rutland   map 6

▲ *Black Bull*

2 Teigh Road, Market Overton LE15 7PW   TEL: (01572) 767677
off B668 Oakham to Stretton road, 2m N of Cottesmore

Eaters and drinkers alike will be happy at this thatched village pub,
which stays warm, welcoming and convivial even on the dreariest
rainy evening. Staff bustle cheerfully through a series of intercon-

nected bars kitted out in traditional olde-worlde-meets-*Country Life* décor amid dark beams and thick walls. The food is a major feature of the Black Bull's attractions. Listed on a huge blackboard, it features filling but imaginative fare. Even in the heart of the shires, it seems, fresh fish is in plentiful supply, and there is plenty for meat eaters too. Kick off with garlicky pan-fried sardines, or tiger prawns with a sweet chilli sauce, continue with a Rutland chicken (stuffed with cheese in a mushroom sauce), or maybe try rack of lamb, and finish with one of the many home-made, constantly changing desserts. Theakston, Wadsworth 6X and Hook Norton are on handpump, and wines include four by the glass. SAMPLE DISHES: mushrooms in wine, cream and garlic £3.50; red bream Cajun style £9; lasagne verdi £7.

Open *11.30 to 2.30, 6 to 11, Sun 11.30 to 2.30, 7 to 10.30; bar food and restaurant 12 to 2, 6.45 to 9.45, Sun 12 to 2, 7 to 9.30*
Details *Children welcome Patio Background music Dogs welcome Delta, MasterCard, Visa, Switch Accommodation: 2 rooms, B&B £30 to £45*

MARSDEN   West Yorkshire   map 8

▲ *Olive Branch* ✿

Manchester Road, Marsden HD7 6LU   TEL: (01484) 844487
on A62, 7m SW of Huddersfield

The converted pub stands on the old cross-Pennine road in a particularly inhospitable part of the moors but offers a warm welcome on a cold evening. Inside, it has a bistro atmosphere with scrubbed pine tables, a fire burning on cold nights in a black leaded grate, and a collection of Gerald Scarfe cartoons on the walls. The first-time visitor will need to know that there is no menu, but names of dishes are written on cards dotted around the room, so choosing your meal can be a bit like a treasure hunt. Food is prepared in full view in the open kitchen and shows some highly experimental touches. Hot avocado comes glazed with Stilton, celeriac is served with a seafood jus, and seared diver-caught scallops are accompanied by a confit of tomato and white truffle oil. Main courses take in pan-fried sirloin in a red wine and black grape sauce, or a hot chilli sauce, or even a creamy roasted sweet pepper sauce. Chicken may be shallow fried and served with brioche, tomato fondue and basil oil, in a light curry and banana sauce, braised in amaretto with toasted almonds or flambéd in sherry with pine kernels and sultanas. Puddings are more run-of-the-mill, with crème brûlée and sticky toffee pudding the order of the day, but there is still room for aniseed parfait with blackberry coulis. Unfortunately the pub serves no real ales, but the wine list spans the globe; four wines are available by the glass. SAMPLE DISHES:

hot spicy mushrooms with chorizo and toasted nuts £5; grilled haddock dusted in tabasco and cracked pepper £10.50; banana and toffee cheesecake £4.50.

Open *Wed to Fri 12 to 2, Mon to Sat 6.30 to 11, Sun 12 to 10.30; closed first 2 weeks Jan, second week June; bar food 12 to 1.45, 6.30 to 9.30 (8.45 Sun and Mon)*
Details *Children welcome in bar eating area   Car park   Wheelchair access   Garden   Background music   No dogs   Delta, MasterCard, Switch, Visa   Accommodation: 3 rooms, B&B £55*

MARSH BENHAM   Berkshire   map 2

Water Rat 🍇

Marsh Benham RG20 8LY   TEL: (01635) 582017

Now managed by Carole Evans, whose impressive past performance at the Roebuck in Brimfield (see entry) can be nothing but a good omen, this attractive, thatched inn will certainly be one to watch. As the *Guide* went to press, an interim menu was in operation, and there were plans afoot to incorporate the present restaurant into the bar area, build a new bar, add a conservatory restaurant, and revamp and refurbish everything totally. Even B&B accommodation is planned. If that interim menu signals something of what is to come, expect dishes such as crab pot with 'toasted fingers', game casserole, and orange burnt cream. Note the pub will be closed in early 1999 while refurbishment takes place. Prior to closure, Wadworth 6X and Courage Best were the ales offered, but this too may change. An interesting mid-range wine list has already been put together, with six by the glass. SAMPLE DISHES: carrot and orange soup £3; haddock tart served with creamed leeks £5.50; autumn fruit pavlova with cream £4.

Open *11.30 to 3, 6 to 11, Sun 12 to 3, 7 to 10.30; bar food and restaurant 12 to 2, 7 to 9*
Details *Children welcome in bar eating area   Car park   Garden   Background music   Dogs welcome   Delta, MasterCard, Switch, Visa*

MARSH GIBBON Buckinghamshire map 5

Greyhound Inn

Marsh Gibbon OX6 0HA   TEL: (01869) 277365
off A41 Bicester to Aylesbury road, 4m E of Bicester

An idiosyncratic menu and above-average beer are what mark out the Greyhound as somewhere worth a visit. On the outskirts of this village of rough stone buildings, the pub is typical of its companions, complete with a sagging roof as testament to its antiquity. Families may be happy to hear that the small garden contains a mini football field and climbing frames. Inside, there are two small, secluded and uncluttered dining areas, and the whole place is neither trendy nor pushy. Run by a couple who hail from Bangkok, the menu – with the exception of the salad garnishes – is entirely Thai, so do not expect sandwiches or ploughman's. Even the eight-ounce steak is called 'Weeping Tiger' and comes cut into thin slices accompanied by a neatly made hot sauce. For starters, try a spicy Thai salad and then sample a roast duck curry, or the intriguingly named 'never sober beef', fried with garlic, chillies, bamboo shoots and French beans. Puddings are a combination of exotic fruits and ice-creams or cakes, and the Greene King Abbot Ale and IPA, and Fuller's London Price are well kept. Wines are more basic, with three whites and one red offered by the glass. SAMPLE DISHES: satay £4.50; never sober chicken £6.75; coconut ice-cream £2.25.

Open *12 to 3, 6 to 11 (12 to 2 only on 25 Dec); bar food and restaurant 12.15 to 2.15, 6.30 to 9.30*
Details *Children welcome in bar eating area   Car park   Wheelchair access Garden   No smoking in restaurant   Background music   No dogs   Amex, Delta, MasterCard, Switch, Visa*

MARSHSIDE Kent map 3

Gate Inn

Marshside CT3 4EB   TEL: (01227) 860498
between A28 and A299, 3m SE of Herne Bay

Located in a rural setting in a tiny village, the Gate has been described as a 'smashing' pub. A stream runs through the lovely garden with its picnic tables and shady trees. Inside, the two simple rooms have a rustic feel, enhanced by cricketing photos, old benches, tables and settles. The menu divides lists under slightly whimsical headings such as 'pasta and pesto', 'ploughpersons', 'torpedoes' (filled french bread) etc. Light meals might be a bowl of garlic mushrooms with bread, gammon and pineapple, or grilled steak. A selection of vegetable hotpots come topped with grilled sausage chunks, black pudding or various other choices, and a vast array of sandwiches are made with chunky wholemeal bread. 'Gateburgers' come with cheese, egg or pineapple. For a more substantial dish, try the Gate Inn grill of steak, sausage, bacon, black pudding, mushrooms and chips. Desserts are mainly home-made ice-creams. Shepherd Neame Master Brew and Spitfire, plus seasonal beers, are drawn direct from casks behind the bar. Eight wines by the glass are also available, as are country wines. SAMPLE DISHES: vegetable flan £4.75; pasta with coronation chicken £5; banana split £2.

Open *11 to 2.30 (3 Sat), 6 to 11, Sun 12 to 3, 7 to 10.30; bar food 11.45 to 2, 6 (7 Sun) to 9*
Details *Well-behaved children welcome in bar eating area   Car park Wheelchair access (also WC)   Garden   No-smoking area   No music   Dogs welcome   No cards*

MARSHWOOD   Dorset   Map 2

Bottle Inn 🍺 [NEW ENTRY]

Marshwood DT6 5QJ   TEL: (01297) 678254
On the B3165 between Crewkerne and Lyme Regis, 4m SW of Broadwindsor

---

The approach road to Marshwood from Lyme Regis forms the Dorset/Devon boundary, and roadside notices by this village inn announce you have just reached (or just passed) the 'First Real Pub in Dorset', so there is no mistake where allegiances lie. Other signs promise the finest cask ales, a beer garden, a skittle alley and vegetarian specialities. It is a classic old thatched building (the date 1585 is inscribed above the doorway). After dark, lightbulbs deck its outline, a cheery beacon on the narrow, unlit bends round Marshwood. The Bottle is a genuine, unspoilt local, with friendly service from its resident host and hostess. It has plain wooden furnishings and minimal amounts of bric-à-brac. On chilly nights, inglenook fire-irons take on more than decorative roles to chivvy a decent blaze. The layout is simple, with two small rooms extending either side of the serving counter.

Steer right if you are hungry: daily menus are chalked up on boards, one for carnivores – perhaps Thai pork curry or game pie – and the other offering an interesting range of vegetarian dishes, such as homity pie or stuffed aubergines with fresh spicy tomato coulis. The landlady cooks and serves; expect a wait long enough to indicate that meals are freshly prepared. Organic produce is used wherever possible, from lamb and pork to ice-cream and frozen yoghurt, and is clearly marked as such on the menu. Drinkers have difficult decisions to make between cask beers, an exceptional range of organic bottled beers and ciders, or several wines by the glass. If quizzed, the landlord may suggest his well-kept and highly recommendable Otter, a local Honiton brew. Otherwise, Morland Old Speckled Hen and Wadworth 6X are joined by guests such as Fuller's London Pride and Oakhill. SAMPLE DISHES: moules marinière £4; pumpkin and coconut curry, rice, poppadum and chutneys £8; Dorset apple cake with calvados sauce and vanilla ice-cream £3.

Open *12 to 3, 5.30 (6.30 Sat in winter, Sun) to 11 (10.30 Sun); bar food Tue to Sun L 12 to 2, all week D 6.30 to 9 (exc Mon D winter)*
Details *Children welcome   Car park   Wheelchair access   Garden Background and live music   No dogs from Fri eve to Sun L   MasterCard, Switch, Visa*

MELLOR   Lancashire   map 8

▲ *Millstone*

Church Lane, Mellor BB2 7JR   TEL: (01254) 813333
off A677, 3m NW of Blackburn

This substantial grey-stone building, originally a coaching-inn, is set high above the Ribble Valley and provides a good base from which to explore the Forest of Bowland. It is more of a hotel than a pub, but has a large, comfortable public bar, an open-plan panelled room, with a fireplace, well-spaced tables and comfortable high-backed chairs. A short bar menu offers a range of bistro-style dishes such as soup of the day (maybe carrot and coriander) with fresh bread; rustic winter salad of warm sauté chicken livers, lardons and mushrooms; Miller's cheese sausage with rocket and tomato chutney; local black pudding on sage and onion mash with haricot beans and bay sauce; Loch Fyne Queen scallops baked in the shell with garlic and Gruyère; or Italian steak sandwich on ciabatta bread with mozzarella, tomato and red onions and a side helping of fries. Daily specials are listed on a blackboard, and there is a separate restaurant with its own 'fine dining' menu. This Shire Inns pub serves beers from Daniel Thwaites and a list of about 30 wines, with a selection by the glass listed on a board. SAMPLE DISHES: Millstone prawn cocktail £4.50; casserole of beef in stout £7; chocolate fudge brownie £3.50.

Open *11 to 11, Sun and bank hols 11 to 10.30; bar food 12 to 2, 6.30 to 9.30*
Details *No children   Car park   Wheelchair access (also WC)   No smoking in dining-room   No music   Amex, Delta, Diners, MasterCard, Switch, Visa Accommodation: 24 rooms, B&B £36 to £84*

MELLS   Somerset   map 2

▲ *Talbot*

High Street, Mells BA11 3PN   TEL: (01373) 812254
3m W of Frome

The Talbot is a charming fifteenth-century coaching-inn, set on the
edge of the Mendips. The village was once owned by the Abbey of
Glastonbury until the Dissolution, when parts were sold to the
Horner family (the nursery rhyme Little Jack Horner is mistakenly
thought to have originated at the Talbot). The Earl of Oxford and
Asquith, a Horner descendent and the pub's freeholder, has his
manor-house next door. Inside, the front bar is very much the local
watering-hole, while the rear is set out for eating. Fish specials are
chalked up on boards daily. Otherwise choose from the printed
menu and give your order to the smiling, young staff. Fresh shellfish
soup comes with toasted cheese muffins, and warm salad of pigeon
breast is dressed in a walnut oil vinaigrette. Mix and match your cut
of steak to your choice of sauce, or choose from a meaty menu of
lamb cutlets, saddle of roe deer, fillet of pork, or breast of duck.
There is also an above-average selection of vegetarian dishes. Beers
are very well kept; Bass and Butcombe offer a pleasant balance
between big and small breweries. A respectable wine list includes five
house wines available by the glass. SAMPLE DISHES: mousse of Cornish
crab and Pernod £4.50; barbecue ribs, salad and fries £10; home-
made cheesecake £3.25.

Open *12 to 2.30, 6 to 11, Sun 12 to 3, 7 to 10.30; closed eve 25 Dec; bar
food and restaurant 12 to 2, 7 to 9.30*
Details *Children welcome in dining-room   Car park   Wheelchair access (also
WC)   Garden and patio   Background music   Dogs welcome in bar only
Delta, Diners, MasterCard, Switch, Visa   Accommodation: 7 rooms B&B £30
to £65*

MELMERBY   Cumbria   map 10

Shepherds Inn

Melmerby CA10 1HF   TEL: (01768) 881217
on A686 Penrith to Alston road, 8m NE of Penrith

Nestled in the foothills of the Pennines, the pub has expanded out of
its original premises to engulf the row of terraced cottages attached.
It overlooks the village green and is surrounded by fields and fell
land. Breadth of choice in the chosen house specialities – beer,
cheese and whisky – is the main attraction. Jennings is the permanent

brew while ales from Black Sheep, Hesket Newmarket, Morland or Wychwood may be among the visitors. There is a small selection of bottled European beers, including one or two classics like the Trappist-brewed Orval, and sometimes a German wheat beer: ideal on a hot day. No fewer than seventeen cheeses are on offer, and if you do not specify which cheeses you desire in your 'Ultimate' ploughman's you put yourself at the whim of the kitchen. They might decide upon a nutty Cotherstone, a sharp Lancashire, a buttery Swaledale, an oak-smoked Westmorland, or a mature two-year old Cheddar. There is always a roast on offer, and popular house dishes include Cumberland sausage hotpot, or – what else? – Shepherd's pie. The sweets selection includes one or two unusual choices: zuccotta, for example, or blackcurrant and hazelnut roulade. Over 50 malt whiskies are on offer, and the wine list, like the food menu, is very good value. SAMPLE DISHES: dill marinated herring £3.75; 'Ultimate ploughman's' £5.25; rhubarb and strawberry compote £2.

Open 11 to 3, 6 to 11, Sun 12 to 3, 7 to 10.30; closed 25 Dec; bar food 11 to 2.30, 6 to 9.45, Sun 12 to 2.30, 7 to 9.45
Details Children welcome   Car park   Wheelchair access   Garden   No-smoking area   Live music; jukebox   Dogs welcome in 1 bar   Amex, Delta, Diners, MasterCard, Switch, Visa

MICKLEHAM   Surrey   map 3

King William IV

Byttom Hill, Mickleham RH5 6EL   TEL: (01372) 372590
off A24, between Leatherhead and Dorking, 2m S of Leatherhead

The King William IV was once an alehouse for staff on Lord Beaverbrook's estate, and parts of the building date from the late eighteenth century. This is a real walkers' pub – if you come by car leave it in the public car park down the hill and be prepared to climb lots of steep steps up to the pub. There are good views from the pretty rear garden with its white wrought-iron tables and chairs. A small public bar is reached through the lower entrance, while the larger bar and eating area are at the top. Stools outnumber chairs and there is a log fire in winter. Although the same menu is served throughout, it is reduced at Sunday lunch-times and on bank holidays, and only the starters are available at evening sessions. Among the normal pub staples are excellent sandwiches, a variety of jacket potatoes and ploughman's, plus pasta dishes, steak and kidney or seafood pies. These are supplemented by blackboard specials such as Torbay sole, calf's liver with smoked bacon, or roast duckling with orange sauce. Vegetarians are offered four choices: tostados (crispy corn pancakes with spicy beans), perhaps, or Brie and leeks in filo pastry. Puddings range from charlotte russe to apple strudel, or hot chocolate fudge cake. Draught beers from Adnams, Badger and Hogs Back Brewery are augmented by a monthly guest beer. The short wine list offers only a red and white house wine by the glass. SAMPLE DISHES: pâté maison £3.25; pan-fried trout with ginger and lime £7.75; fruit crumble £3.25.

Open *11 to 3, 6 to 11, Sun 12 to 3, 7 to 10.30; closed 25 Dec and 1 Jan; bar food all week L 12 to 2, Tue to Sun D 7 to 9.30*
Details *No children under 12   Garden and patio   Background and live music No dogs   MasterCard, Switch, Visa*

MIDFORD   Bath & N.E. Somerset   map 2

Hope & Anchor Inn
Midford BA2 8QX   TEL: (01225) 832296
on B3110, 3m S of Bath

Most people driving this road will either completely miss this unassuming stone pub or fail to give it a second glance as they carefully negotiate the steep hill and bends. So take care, but note it is worth stopping at the Hope & Anchor not least for its interesting food. Inside the comfortably furnished main bar there is a mix of flag and board floors, cushioned wall benches, an open fire in a stone fireplace and a homely and welcoming atmosphere, enhanced by light jazz music. The pub attracts a mixed clientele, from walkers to couples out enjoying Sunday lunch. The same menu is available throughout the pub and cooking is both above-average and imaginative. Roast aubergine, courgette and sweet pepper tart is a typical starter, as is smoked salmon, cream cheese and dill wrapped in smoked salmon with cucumber relish. Main courses might include pan-fried breast of barbary duck with rhubarb and apples, or fillet of pork wrapped in bacon with apples and calvados, or a chicken and shellfish paella. Or try one of the specials: scallops on a bed of wilted bok choi with chilli and saffron sauce, or maybe roast partridge with blueberries and shallots. Puddings keep things interesting with creations like chocolate, fig and hazelnut torte, or home-made peach ice-cream with a raspberry coulis. Butcombe Bitter, Bass and Bellringer from the Abbey Brewery make an alliterative beer list and a 25 strong wine list offers half a dozen by the glass. The pub is handy for walks along the River Frome, or to Westwood Manor and the American Museum at Claverton. SAMPLE DISHES: smoked salmon with toasted blinis £4.50; fillet of beef with wild mushrooms and green peppercorn sauce £14; tarte Tatin with calvados and crème anglais £2.75.

Open *11.30 to 2.30, 6.30 to 11, Sun 12 to 3, 7 to 10.30; bar food and restaurant 12 to 2, 6.30 (7 Sun) to 9.30*
Details *Children welcome in bar eating area   Car park   Wheelchair access Garden and patio   No smoking in restaurant   Background music   No dogs Delta, MasterCard, Switch, Visa*

MILTON ABBAS   Dorset   map 2

▲ *Hambro Arms*

Milton Abbas DT11 0BP   TEL: (01258) 880233
off A354, 6m SW of Blandford Forum

Two hundred years ago Lord Milton had the ancient village of Milton Abbas pulled down as it was too close to Milton Abbey. This late eighteenth-century village – built at a respectable distance – is the result. A long, low, white thatched building, the inn fits in well with its orderly surroundings. This Greenalls pub specialises in solid pub food and is mainly geared up for eating. The beamed front bar has well-spaced dining tables, a log fire and a blackboard menu to supplement the printed one. A formal restaurant follows on from that, with a bar-cum-games room at the rear. Some imaginative daily specials like venison steak in port and wild mushroom sauce, breast of chicken filled with ham and mozzarella, and partridge and pheasant in season, are available. Otherwise you will meet typical pub fare along the lines of soup of the day, country pâté, gammon, jumbo sausage and scampi, plus sandwiches and ploughman's. Puddings are slightly unusual – Amaretto slice or chocolate bavarois, for example. The pub serves Bass and Boddingtons, and the wine list is compiled by the operators. Oh, and Milton Abbey is nearby. SAMPLE DISHES: smoked Scotch salmon £5; beef and Guinness pie £8.50; raspberry cheesecake £4.

Open *Sun to Thur 11 (12 Sun) to 3, 7 to 10.30, Fri and Sat 11 to 11; bar food 12 to 2, 7 to 9.30 (9 winter), Sun 12 to 2, 7 to 8.30*
Details *No children   Car park   Patio   No music   No dogs   MasterCard, Switch, Visa   Accommodation: 2 rooms, B&B £35 to £55*

Sussex Ox

Milton Street BN26 5RL   TEL: (01323) 870840
off A27, 1m NE of Alfriston

'Less a typical English pub, more a decent-value family country restaurant with fine, friendly service' sums up this large, white weatherboarded pub with great views over the South Downs. Eclecticism rules: nostalgia for Sussex past in some accomplished photographs (majoring on oxen, of course) competes with a new gladiator-style adventure playground. Ramblers and serious hikers, perhaps en route to or from the Long Man of Wilmington, feel as at home as families, perhaps because no children are allowed in the main bar, though they are in the family room and dining room. The menu too will appeal to most tastes, with decent ploughman's, jacket potatoes and grilled whole plaice at one end of the scale, to duck cassoulet and Mexican bean dip at the other. Sussex Ox slabs are open sandwiches. Blackboard specials might include garlic mushrooms with coriander and nuts or crispy bacon and smoked sausage salad. Sweets are family favourites of the death by chocolate ilk. Everything is cooked to order and the same menu can be had in the separate Harness Room restaurant. On the drinks front, Scrumpy Jack is the cider, and Greene King Abbot and Harveys the beers; 14 wines come by the glass, including local English ones. SAMPLE DISHES: continental meat platter £3; garlic and herb chicken £7.25; summer pudding £3.

Open *11 to 3, 5.30 to 11 (6 to 10.30 winter), Sun 12 to 3, 5.30 to 10.30; closed 25 Dec; bar food and restaurant 12 to 2, 6 to 9, Sun 12 to 9*
Details *Children welcome in family room and dining-room   Car park Wheelchair access (also WC)   Garden and patio   No smoking in family room Background music   Dogs welcome on a lead   Switch, Visa*

Miners Arms

Mithian TR5 0QF   TEL: (01872) 552375
on B3285, 2m E of St Agnes

In one of Cornwall's oldest villages, this unassuming sixteenth-century pub was once a chapel, then the wages office for local miners. The three separate areas inside all have irregular beam and plank ceilings, one of which is highly decorated and has the date of 1577 clearly marked; two large wall paintings are of Elizabeth I and

'The Royalist'. Water for the pub used to come from a well in what is now the Cellar bar; there is also a passage behind a fireplace which used to lead to a tunnel to the manor-house and was probably used by monks in turbulent times in the past. Apart from the usual soups, pâtés, ploughman's and cheese and meat platters, more substantial dishes appear on the menu, such as lamb curry, chicken tikka masala, vegetable lasagne, or steak, kidney and oyster pie. Puddings range from treacle sponge to lemon brûlée or 'nuts about chocolate', plus local Callestick farmhouse ice-creams. Beers come from Wadworth, Bass or there might be Doom Bar from local Sharp's Brewery; a short wine list offers five by the glass. SAMPLE DISHES: carrot and coriander goujons £3; breaded scampi £6.50; saffron and honey bread-and-butter pudding £2.75.

Open *summer 12 to 3, 5.30 to 11, Sun 12 to 3, 6 to 10.30, winter 12 to 3, 6 to 11, Sun 12 to 3, 7 to 10.30; bar food 12 to 2.30, 6 (7 Sun in winter) to 9.30*

Details *Children welcome exc in bar   Car park   Garden and patio   No-smoking in 1 room   Background music   Well-behaved dogs welcome   Delta, MasterCard, Switch, Visa*

MONKSILVER   Somerset   map 2

Notley Arms 🍺

Monksilver TA4 4JB   TEL: (01984) 656217
on B3188, 5m S of Watchet

The Notley Arms is a well-run village pub with bags of charm and character, set next to a pretty stream running alongside, offering views of the delightful countryside. On entering the L-shaped bar one is immediately struck by the simple, yet comfortable and homely style of the place. There are shelves crowded with books on the plum-coloured walls, amid a motley collection of pictures and ornaments. The log fires effectively ward off wintry chills. Antiques, old pine settles, scatter cushions and scrubbed pine tables with vases of fresh flowers and candles attest to a well-loved and cared-for establishment which is deservedly popular. The black-board menu consists of a shortish but varied selection of tempting snacks and more substantial meals, including coarse country pâté, chicken and bacon pie, lamb and rosemary pudding, home-made pasta, and aubergine filled with couscous. Also available are sand-wichy items like the Richman's Pouch (wholemeal pitta filled with hot garlic beef), the Poorman's Pocket (as before but with cheese and salad), or the Beggarman's Bag, (with bacon, mushrooms and salad). Puddings are home-made and of the treacle tart variety, and service is unfailingly prompt and friendly. Apart from national brands Bass and Wadworth 6X, the pub also serves local independent brews Smiles Best and Exmoor Ale. In addition to the wine list, which offers about ten choices by the glass, there is also a selection of English country wines such as plum, rose petal and rhubarb. SAMPLE DISHES: wild mushroom strudel £5.75; cod fillet £7.50; lemon tart £2.75.

Open 11.30 to 2.30, 6.30 to 11, Sun 12 to 2.30, 7 to 11 (10.30 winter); closed 2 weeks end Jan/early Feb; bar food 12 to 2, 7 to 9.30 (9 Sun)
Details Children welcome in family room   Car park   Wheelchair access Garden   No smoking in family room   Background music   Dogs welcome MasterCard, Switch, Visa

---

MONTACUTE   Somerset   map 2

▲ Kings Arms 🍇

Bishopston, Montacute TA15 6UU   TEL: (01935) 822513
just off A3088, 4m NW of Yeovil

The inn was taken over by the Old English Pub Company during 1998, but the only noticeable change so far has been that the highly distinctive Fuller's London Pride beer that used to be available on draught has regrettably been ousted, although Bass is still served. We would welcome readers' comments on any other developments. The pub is sixteenth-century, covered with creepers, and built of hamstone like the rest of the unspoilt and picturesque village; it was once an alehouse owned by the nearby Abbey. National Trust woodland and the landscaped park of Montacute House, also Trust-owned, lie all around. The window seats of the pubby Pickwick bar, with its darkwood tables and chairs, and a log fire, are understandably popular. There is also a candlelit restaurant. One winter bar menu offered such starters as Somerset smokie (haddock), slices of smoked duck breast with pear chutney, and a fan of melon with fruit sorbet. To follow there might be more good English pub stuff: steak and kidney pie, grilled whole lemon sole or a grilled pork chop with an apple and sage sauce. Sweets are of the sticky toffee pudding variety, and the comprehensive wine list includes eight wines by the glass. SAMPLE DISHES: grilled sardines in tomato and basil sauce £5; braised meatballs with tomato sauce and blue cheese gratin £8.25; mint and cherry parfait £3.50.

Open 11 to 11, Sun 12 to 3, 7 to 10.30; bar food and restaurant Mon to Sat 12 to 2, 7 to 9
Details Children welcome in bar eating area   Car park   Wheelchair access Garden   No smoking in dining areas   Background music   No dogs   Amex, Delta, MasterCard, Switch, Visa   Accommodation: 30 rooms, B&B £49 to £105

▲ *Carrington Arms*

Moulsoe MK16 0HB   TEL: (01908) 218050
1m E of M1 junction 14 towards Cranfield

This large, Grade II-listed red-brick building makes 'a pleasant relief from the geometric sprawl of Milton Keynes'. Since Edwin and Trudy Cheeseman took over this former estate manager's residence in 1995, they have created a lively atmosphere and built a reputation for an unusual approach to food. Diners are instructed to 'find a table, set up a tab at the bar' and then head for the meat and fresh fish counter, perhaps stopping at the oyster bar on the way. The centre of the pub resembles a butcher's-cum-fishmonger's. Select a cut of meat or fillet of fish, all priced by weight, from the raw produce displayed – the wide range might include bourbon marinated steak, or duck breast in gin and chillies – then instruct the chef on how you prefer it prepared. Cooking is done on a large range in full view. There is also a small bar snacks menu, showing strong Thai influences in green chicken, or red beef and rice. Beers are Theakston Old Peculier, Charles Wells Bombardier, Adnams Bitter, Morland Old Speckled Hen and Boddingtons. The wine style-guide is as quirky as everything else and the list is suitably varied. SAMPLE DISHES: tom yum (Thai fish stew) £7; meat or fish course (by weight); Um Ali (Egyptian bread-and-butter pudding) £3.

Open *11 to 2.30, 6 to 11, Sun 12 to 3, 7 to 10.30; bar food Mon to Sat 12 to 2, 6.15 to 10, Sun 12 to 2.15, 7 to 9.30*
Details *Children welcome   Car park   Wheelchair access (also WC)   Garden and patio   Background music   No dogs   Amex, Delta, Diners, MasterCard, Switch, Visa   Accommodation: 8 rooms, B&B £44 to £57.50*

Black Bull Inn ❀ ❦

Moulton DL10 6QJ   TEL: (01325) 377289
1m SE of Scotch Corner

Audrey, Sarah and George Pagendam have built up quite a reputation since they first took over the Black Bull over 35 years ago. One of the pub's most distinctive features is the 1932 Brighton Belle Pullman carriage out at the back which houses the restaurant, but it should not be too hard to find as it is the only pub in this tiny village. As well as what is offered in the Pullman restaurant, there is an extensive bar menu (available at lunch-time only), which has a strong emphasis on fish. To start, you may have a choice of oysters, plain or grilled in garlic butter; or smoked salmon, again *au naturel*, or salmon in various other forms, including gravad lax. For hot snacks, there is seafood pancake thermidor; mussels and queen scallops with garlic, Cheddar and breadcrumbs; or seafood in wine with pancetta and curried sauce. Non-fish dishes might include Welsh rarebit and bacon, steak baguette, barbecued spare ribs or a spicy lamb kebab. To finish, there are above-average home-made puddings such as a grand-sounding coeur à la crème with fruit compote, or meringue with chocolate sauce. An excellent wine list offers quality drinking at reasonable prices, and eight selections listed on a blackboard are available by the glass. Theakston Best Bitter is the only ale on draught. SAMPLE DISHES: cured fish platter £6; feuilleté of smoked haddock, prawns, parsley and mash £5.75; hot orange liqueur parcels £3.50.

Open *Mon to Sat 12 to 2.30, 6 to 10.30 (11 Fri and Sat), Sun L only 12 to 2; closed 24 to 27 Dec; bar food Mon to Sat L only 12 to 2; restaurant Mon to Fri L 12 to 2, Mon to Sat D 6.45 to 10.15*
Details *No children   Car park   Wheelchair access   Patio   No music   No dogs   Amex, Delta, Diners, MasterCard, Switch, Visa*

MUNSLOW   Shropshire   **map 5**

Crown 🍺

Munslow SY7 9ET   TEL: (01584) 841205

This tall higgledy-piggledy building is set in attractive walking country and is rather older than it looks, hiding Tudor origins behind a Georgian façade. Inside, it is quickly apparent that this is a food pub, with most of the space given over to eating, although beer is also taken seriously – the pub's own brewery is visible from the bar. House beers are known as Boys Pale and Hundred in view of the fact that this Tudor house was already the local hundred house and court before becoming an inn in the late seventeenth century. Blackboard menus are divided into starters and main courses, snacks, filled baguettes, 'bar meals' (steaks, chicken in gravy, vegetable chilli, ratatouille) and a selection for children, and are supplemented by another board of daily specials. The latter may offer white anchovy salad, or tomato and horseradish soup, followed by chicken in Stilton and pecan sauce. Popular starters from the main board include tom yum (Thai hot and sour soup). Thai tiger prawns in lemon sauce keep up the oriental theme, though there could just as easily be pork with prosciutto and pimento sauce, lamb with rosemary and sherry, or salmon Normandy to demonstrate influences closer to home. A separate restaurant has its own 'international' menu. Wine is selected from a 35-strong list; three wines are available by the glass. SAMPLE DISHES: fish soup £4.50; chicken asparagus £9; syrup sponge £2.25.

Open *Mon to Fri 12 to 2.30, 7 to 11, Sat 12 to 3, 7 to 11, Sun 12 to 3, 7 to 10.30; bar food and restaurant 12 to 2, 7 to 9.30*
Details *Children welcome   Car park   Garden   Background music   Dogs welcome   Amex, Delta, MasterCard, Switch, Visa*

MYLOR BRIDGE   Cornwall   map 1

Pandora Inn 🍇

Restronguet Creek, Mylor Bridge TR11 5ST
TEL: (01326) 372678
off A39 from Truro, take B3292 signposted Penryn, then Mylor Bridge road, and follow steep road down to Restronguet

This thatched pub, 'full of history and Cornwall, but not themed', stands a few feet from the edge of the water at Mylor, which at high tide almost spills over on to the quay. The pub is clearly at risk from global warming. A huge anchor embedded in the quayside separates the car park from the outside seating area overlooking the estuary, and in summer you can also sit out on the pontoon and enjoy the waterside views. Inside, flagstone floors are used to coping with those arriving by boat or with wet feet. There are numerous seating areas, some with settles and one with a real fire, and the scrubbed pine tables and rough white-painted plaster walls feel quite in keeping with the pub's history. Part of the building, we are told, dates from the thirteenth century. Later on, it became known as the Passage House, being on the post road between Falmouth and Truro, and later still was renamed in memory of the *Pandora*, the naval ship sent to Tahiti to capture the mutineers of Captain Bligh's *Bounty*. The ship struck part of the Great Barrier Reef in 1791 and sank with the loss of many crew and mutineers. The captain survived to be court-martialled on his return to England, after which he retired to Cornwall and bought the inn.

The bar menu is aimed at one-course tourists and not surprisingly features plenty of fish, including Restronguet fish pie, baked mackerel, crab-cakes and moules marinière. One of the more substantial dinners is the seafood platter, with crab, prawns, cockles, smoked mackerel and fresh salmon; diners can also pick from an evening restaurant menu. Sandwiches, a children's menu and selection of salads – Cornish crab, perhaps, or home-cooked ham with apple chutney – are also on offer. A small choice of puddings may tempt, perhaps home-made treacle tart or ginger crunch sundae. This St Austell tenancy serves the brewery's beers. The 40-bottle wine list covers the world and extends to 20 by the glass. SAMPLE DISHES: half-pint of shell-on prawns with lemon mayonnaise £5; Jim's Mylor Bridge pasties with chips £3.25; lemon meringue pie £3.25.

Open *summer 11 to 11, Sun 12 to 10.30; winter Mon to Fri 12 to 2.30, 7 to 11, Sat 12 to 11, Sun 12 to 10.30; bar food 12 to 2, 7 to 9; restaurant D only 7 to 9.30*

Details *Children welcome in bar eating area Car park Wheelchair access (also WC) Garden No smoking in restaurant and part of bar No music No dogs in restaurant Amex, MasterCard, Switch, Visa*

NAYLAND **Suffolk** **map 6**

White Hart ☻

11 High Street, Nayland CO6 4JF
6m N of Colchester TEL: (01206) 263382

It is not clear which description best fits this large fifteenth-century coaching-inn. Reporters were not sure whether the White Hart is an inn-cum-pub, a hotel or a restaurant, but what is certain is that this is not a drinkers' pub. The well-to-do clientele are here to eat. The pub is divided into three rooms, with bare boards, scrubbed pine tables, and a roaring log fire in winter. Small flickering lights on each table give the place a Dickensian feel.

The same menu is served throughout, and although steak sandwiches, ploughman's, and omelettes with chips are served at lunchtime, most dishes are more upmarket, with set-price lunches and a *carte* in the evening. During the day, a printed menu lists five starters – perhaps soup or local game terrine – six main courses main courses, including whole Dover sole, braised lamb shank or confit of duck, and five or six puddings, ranging from iced passion-fruit soufflé to crème caramel. Dishes from the grill could be Scotch lobster, sirloin steak or lamb cutlets. Service is 'quiet, efficient and unobtrusive', and the cooking has been described as 'quality'. Beers come from Greene King or nearby Adnams, while the 32-bottle wine list, supplemented by a short list of fine wines, includes half a dozen by the glass. SAMPLE DISHES: deep-fried Brie with chutney £4.25; breast of woodpigeon with bacon and red wine sauce £9.50; bread-and-butter pudding £4.

Open *12 to 3, 6.30 to 11 (10.30 Sun); closed 26 Dec, 1 Jan; bar food 12 to 2 (2.30 Sun), 7 to 9 (9.30 Fri and Sat, 8.30 Sun)*
Details *Children welcome Car park Garden Background and live music No dogs Amex, Delta, Diners, MasterCard, Visa, Switch*

▲ *Marquis of Lorne*

Nettlecombe DT6 3SY   TEL: (01308) 485236
off A3066, 4m NE of Bridport

Parts of this flower-covered, stone-built pub date back to the sixteenth century. It is in a tiny hamlet up narrow lanes, overlooking the village of Powerstock, and nestles under Eggardon Hill, an ancient earth fort. Excellent *en suite* bedrooms are available, as is self-catering accommodation in a nearby thatched cottage. Outside there is a large children's play area, plus a separate beer garden for summer eating with pretty flower borders. The very friendly owners offer a warm welcome, good home-cooked food and well-kept ales from the local Palmers brewery; about 15 wines are also available, with eight by the glass. The main bar has panelled walls, an open fire and wall bench seating, while the separate dining area is carpeted. A wide range of food is chalked up on blackboards and changes daily, offering local fish, seasonal stews and game, and some more inventive dishes in the evening (particularly on Friday and Saturday). The usual pub staples of ploughman's, sandwiches and soup are always present; other light snacks might be Dorset pâté, garlic mushrooms or deep-fried prawns. Main courses range from roast poussin to faggots with onion gravy or honey-roast duck breast, and fish of the day could be pan-fried skate wing, moules, or grilled whole plaice. For pudding, there is sticky toffee or perhaps almond and apricot strudel. SAMPLE DISHES: avocado with curried chicken £4; roast partridge with orange and honey sauce £8.75; profiteroles £3.

Open *11 to 2.30, 6 (6.30 winter) to 11, Sun 12 to 3, 7 to 10.30; closed eve 25 Dec; bar food 11.30 to 2, 7 to 9.30 (no food 25 Dec)*
Details *Children welcome in bar eating area   Car park   Wheelchair access (also WC)   Garden   No-smoking area   Background music   Dogs in one bar only   Delta, MasterCard, Switch, Visa   Accommodation: 6 rooms, B&B £38 to £58*

George Inn

44 The Street, Newnham ME9 0LL   TEL: (01795) 890237
off A2, 5m SW of Faversham

This pretty, multi-chimneyed house has tiles on the first-floor walls, and window boxes and flower baskets adding colour to the light brickwork on the ground floor. At the rear is a large, attractive garden with tables. Inside, the fittings reveal the building's 1540 pedigree, though it was a private dwelling until 1718. Genuine beams are heavily garlanded with hops in true Kentish style, and prints of old pubs, cigarette cards and brewery paraphernalia contribute to the informal atmosphere. A bar snacks menu offers traditional pub fare, strong on home-made pies, plus a couple of balti dishes and a long selection of hot and cold sweets. A more formal dining area offers a similar menu, though starters and main courses are a little more adventurous – chargrilled tiger prawns in lemon juice, sweet chilli and noodles may tempt; otherwise there are traditional dishes such as steak, or fillet of salmon hollandaise. Beers are from Shepherd Neame, which owns the pub, and the wine list is short and competent, with ten available by the glass. SAMPLE DISHES: avocado and seafood medley £4; steak, kidney and mushroom pie £6; home-made banoffi pie £3.25.

Open *11 to 3, 6.30 to11, Sun 12 to 3, 7 to 10.30; bar food and restaurant 12 to 2.15, 7 to 9.30*

Details *Children welcome   Car park   Garden   Background and live music Dogs welcome   MasterCard, Switch, Visa*

NEWTON-ON-THE-MOOR   Northumberland map 10

▲ *Cook and Barker Inn* ❁

Newton-on-the-Moor NE65 9JY   TEL: (01665) 575234
¼m W of A1, in middle of village

Professionalism and attention to detail seem to be what visitors find most appealing about this isolated but comfortable old stone inn with views across rolling fields to the North Sea. This is definitely a 'dining pub', attracting clientele from far and wide. You can eat in the pine-furnished long bar with its open fires and local prints on the wood-panelled walls, or, in the evenings, in the separate stone-walled restaurant (items on the restaurant menu can also be ordered in the bar). Lunchtime offerings in the bar might include starters along the lines of beef and chicken salad, or seafood soup flavoured with Pernod, and main courses of mixed grill or fillet of sole au gratin. For lighter biters, there are salads and creative sandwiches. The dinner menu goes further afield to take in perhaps Thai salmon with spinach, and Cajun chicken with stir-fried vegetables. The restaurant's 90-strong wine list is also available in the bar, and includes a fairly priced selection from around the world, including about a dozen half-bottles and six wines by the glass. Beers on offer are Theakston Best and XB, Courage Directors and Stones Bitter. SAMPLE DISHES: pork and bacon terrine with pistachio nuts and garlic £3.50; braised lamb shank with roasted onions £7; cheese and biscuits £4.

Open *11 to 3, 6 to 11 (10.30 Sun); bar food 12 to 2, 6 to 8; restaurant D only 7 to 9*
Details *Children welcome in bar eating area   Car park   Wheelchair access Garden   No smoking in 1 room   No music   No dogs   Garden   Amex, Delta, MasterCard, Switch, Visa   Accommodation: 4 rooms, B&B £37.50 to £80*

NEWTON UNDER ROSEBERRY   Redcar   map 10

King's Head

Newton under Roseberry TS9 6QR   TEL: (01642) 722318
on A173, 3m SW of Guisborough

In a bit of a pub-food desert the red-brick and stone King's Head is situated on the Cleveland Way, with a dominating peak rising behind. It is set in the heart of Captain Cook country – as the heritage industry would like to designate the area – and brings in the walking fraternity. A short weekday fixed-price lunch menu changes some of its clothes daily, but is firmly set in the 1970s, offering starters like chilled grapefruit juice or avocado and prawns with marie rose sauce, or breadcrumbed plaice fillets, followed by rhubarb crumble and custard. More adventurous starters from the *carte* might be crunchy Camembert, garlic and cream mushroom pot or chicken and prawn stir-fry, with mains such as of rack of lamb, huntsman's chicken or fillet of codling. On Sundays the set-price menu is more extensive, but in a similar vein with help-yourself hors d'oeuvre, roast silverside of beef, or chicken suprême, followed by sweets from the trolley. More inventive is the Sunday 'alternative menu', which also offers interesting sandwiches (standard and toasted). With John Smith's Magnet as the only real ale, the modern world arrives only in the form of the wine list, which offers bottles from the New World, as well as from France. SAMPLE DISHES: crispy Danish mushrooms £4.75; pork cordon bleu £11; cinder toffee snap £4.

Open *11.30 to 3, 6.30 to 11; closed 25 and 26 Dec, 1 Jan; bar food 11.45 to 2.30 (3 Sun), 7.15 to 10.30*
Details *Children welcome in bar eating area   Car park   Wheelchair access (also WC)   Garden and patio   No-smoking area   Background music   Guide dogs only   Delta, MasterCard, Switch, Visa*

Prices quoted in an entry are based on information supplied by the pub, rounded up to the nearest 25 pence. These prices may have changed since publication and are meant only as a guide.

NORTH CERNEY   Gloucestershire   map 2

▲ *Bathurst Arms* `NEW ENTRY`

North Cerney GL7 7BZ   TEL: (01285) 831281

off A435, 4m N of Cirencester

RIVERSIDE

A rambling, pink-washed building on a country road, with gardens stretching to the banks of the River Churn, this is an ancient inn in an enviably romantic location. Church bells ring nearby, and Rosemary Verey's celebrated gardens at Barnsley House attract many visitors. The sprucely kept interior is described as 'traditional, but clean and uncluttered' with hunting prints and coaching scenes, fine carved stone fireplaces and wooden settles. Food is freshly prepared, an appetising choice of crowd-pleasers such as mixed grills or deep-fried scampi interspersed with more adventurous dishes incorporating sun-dried tomatoes or basmati rice. Barbecues are served in the gardens in summer, where mature trees shade trestle tables set on the lawns. Hook Norton, Arkell's and Wadworth ales are regular fixtures, while guest beers such as Bellringer or Timothy Taylor Landlord take a bow on a weekly basis. SAMPLE DISHES: warm salad of Cerney goats' cheese, smoked bacon and walnuts £4.50; home-made salmon fish-cakes with prawn and dill sauce £7; raspberry meringue roulade £3.

Open *11 to 3 (3.30 Sat), 6 to 11, Sun 12 to 3.30, 7 to 10.30 Sun; closed 25 Dec; bar food 12 to 2, 7 to 9.30*
Details *Children welcome in dining-room Car park Wheelchair access (also WC) Garden and patio No-smoking area Background and live music; jukebox No dogs in eating areas Delta, MasterCard, Switch, Visa Accommodation: 5 rooms, B&B £22.50 to £58*

NORTH NEWNTON   Wiltshire   map 2

▲ *Woodbridge Inn* 🍇

North Newnton SN9 6JZ   TEL: (01980) 630266

on A345, 3m S of Pewsey, on roundabout

MEXICAN

In the heart of the Vale of Pewsey, on the banks of the River Avon that runs down to Hampshire, stands this cream-painted, square-porched, sixteenth-century inn. Fly fishing is one of the activities organised by the pub; another is *pétanque* (boules). The food is a balanced mixture of traditional English and overseas. Mexico features strongly on the bar menu, which – besides pastas, plough-man's and burgers – takes in con queso (Mexican fondue), nachos, burritos and chimichangas. On the restaurant menu – which is also available in the bar – the repertoire gets even more international with stir-fried chicken and prawns in Thai green curry sauce, tournedos Rossini, and stincotto, as well as offering more near-to-home items such as roast lamb, and salmon with cracked peppercorn crust. For pudding lovers there's death by chocolate, or warm pecan pie. Children eating in the bar have their own menu. The beers come from Wadworth with, usually, a guest ale. The mostly French wine list makes a few overseas excursions, and offers around 20 wines by the glass – including a dozen by the 'friendly size' 350ml glass. SAMPLE DISHES: bang bang chicken salad £4.50; beef fajita with guacamole, soured cream, salsa and tortillas £11.25; black cherry surprise £3.25.

Open *11 to 3, 5.30 to 11, Sun 12 to 3, 7 to 10.30; closed 25 Dec; bar food and restaurant 11 to 2.30, 5.30 to 10.30, Sun 12 to 2.30, 7 to 10*
Details *Children welcome in eating areas   Car park   Wheelchair access (also WC)   Garden   No smoking in restaurant   Background music   Guide dogs only   Amex, Delta, Diners, MasterCard, Switch, Visa   Accommodation: 3 rooms, B&B £30 to £45*

NORTON   Shropshire   map 5

▲ *Hundred House Hotel* 🎗 🍺 🍇

Bridgnorth Road, Norton TF11 9EE
TEL: (01952) 730353
on A442, 6m S of Telford

There are now five members of the Phillips family running the Hundred House, and standards too seem to be constantly rising. The Phillipses have been in charge here since 1986 and their enthusiasm for what they do is clearly infectious. This tall, creeper-clad red-brick pub has extensive and beautifully maintained gardens at the rear, creating a charming setting. Inside, it is decked out with dried flowers, gourds and bouquets. There are open log fires, lots of exposed brickwork and warm hues of brown and red. Each member of the family has his or her own area of responsibility. Henry Phillips brews his own beer, Heritage Bitter, and makes his own damson gin, as well as selling Wood's Shropshire Lad and Everards Tiger. Sylvia looks after the gardens, which supply herbs to the kitchen, which is Stuart's domain. The brasserie menu offers a range of styles from traditional steak and kidney pie, local sausages with mash and onion gravy, or rich duck liver pâté, to modern dishes such as coriander-cured salmon with lime, peanuts and beansprouts, or a tower of aubergine fritters with goats' cheese, tomato and red wine provençale sauce. Side orders include home-made focaccia bread with garlic, onions and rosemary. Finish with crème brûlée or an individual apple tart. The restaurant menu shows a more formal style with some crossover of dishes from the brasserie menu. A well-chosen wine list offers around ten wines available by the half-bottle, bottle or glass, and a selection of superior bottles for aficionados. SAMPLE DISHES: Greek salad £4.50; pork chop marinated with lemon and sage, served with polenta and seasonal vegetables £8.50; apricot and almond flan £4.50.

Open *11 to 3.30, 6 to 11, Sun 11 to 3.30, 7 to 10.30; closed 25 Dec eve; bar food and restaurant 12 to 2.30. 6.15 to 9.45*
Details *Children welcome   Car park   Wheelchair access (also WC)   Garden No-smoking area   Background music   No dogs   Delta, MasterCard, Switch, Visa   Accommodation: 10 rooms, B&B £69 to £110*

NORTON ST PHILIP   Somerset   map 2

▲ *George*

High Street, Norton St Philip BA3 6LH
TEL: (01373) 834224
on A366 at junction with B3110, 7m S of Bath

This half-timbered Grade I listed building in the centre of the village dates from 1375, and can number Oliver Cromwell, Samuel Pepys and the Duke of Monmouth among the guests who have passed through its huge Gothic entrance. It has undergone a massive refurbishment, supervised by English Heritage, during which two flower murals from the time of Henry VIII were uncovered. The breathtaking interior has thick curtains and carpets, beamed ceilings, tapestries and enormous fireplaces, all in keeping with its age. One menu is served throughout, with the addition of interesting ploughman's and hefty sandwiches in the bar. Typical dishes might be soup, moules marinière, baked ratatouille, or crab and cod fish-cakes with lobster sauce. One reporter enjoyed an exemplary game and ale pie, with tender meat, which came topped with home-made shortcrust pastry that had absorbed the rich gamey juices. Staff have been described as 'extremely pleasant and welcoming'. Desserts could be spotted dick with custard, bread-and-butter pudding, apple and apricot crumble or 'death by chocolate'. Beers include Wadworth 6X, Henry's IPA and seasonal guest ales, such as Restoration (how appropriate). An excellent list of wines by the glass runs to some 32 from around the world. SAMPLE DISHES: soup of the day £4; beef and Guinness sausages with mash £8; ginger pudding with orange sauce £4.

Open *11 to 11, Sun 12 to 10.30; bar food 12 to 2, 6.30 to 9.30, Sun 12 to 2.30, 7 to 8.30*
Details *Children welcome in eating areas   Car park   Wheelchair access (also WC)   Garden   No smoking in 1 dining-room   Background music   Dogs welcome on a lead   Delta, MasterCard, Switch, Visa   Accommodation: 8 rooms, B&B £65 to £150*

Royal Oak

Church Street, Nunnington YO6 5US   TEL: (01439) 748271
B1257, 2m N of Hovingham

This stone-built pub is situated on a narrow village street just below
the parish church and up the hill from the three-arch bridge span-
ning the River Rye. Nunnington is a peaceful rural backwater
nestling on the scenic Howardian Hills, just a short drive from the
North Yorkshire Moors, Rievaulx Abbey and Castle Howard. In
summer, the pub is bustling with the visitors attracted to
Nunnington Hall, a seventeenth-century manor owned by the
National Trust and within walking distance of the Royal Oak. Inside,
the open-plan bar and separate dining area are neat and tidy, with
plenty of stone jugs, old keys and assorted farm implements adorning
the heavy beams and stone walls. The warming open fires and
comfortable mixture of furnishings – from old pews and settles to
scrubbed pine, farmhouse kitchen chairs and sturdy tables – give the
place a welcoming feel, and the comfortable dining atmosphere is
enhanced by light classical music.

'Home-cooked'-style dishes rub shoulders with pub favourites, and
you will find prawn cocktail, ploughman's, lasagne, roast chicken,
and steak pie. Fish lovers could try a fisherman's pot, salmon and
prawn tagliatelle or a seafood platter, and vegetarians will find something spicier than normal in sweet-and-sour vegetables. For pudding
try the Snow Queen, which is crushed meringue, cream and brandy
folded together and frozen before being served with the fruits of the
forest, or go for traditional treacle sponge and custard. Theakston
Bitter and Old Peculier plus Tetley Bitter are on draught, and the
wine list offers 13 bottles and four by the glass. SAMPLE DISHES:
smoked mackerel pâté £4; chicken breast in orange and tarragon
sauce £8; sticky toffee pudding £3.50.

Open *Tue to Sat 12 to 2, 6.30 to 11, Sun 12 to 2, 7 to 10.30; bar food Tue
to Sun 12 to 2, 6.30 (7 Sun) to 9*
Details *Children welcome in dining-room   Car park   Patio   Background
music   No dogs   Delta, MasterCard, Visa, Switch*

NUTHURST   **West Sussex**   **map 3**

Black Horse 🍺 NEW ENTRY

Nuthurst RH13 6LH   TEL: (01403) 891272
off A281, 3m S of Horsham

At the rear of the pub is a woodland garden complete with running stream crossed by a wooden bridge. Pooh sticks, anyone? There is lots of outdoor seating, both here and in front of the pub and underneath countless hanging baskets by the road. Inside there are three bar rooms and one restaurant area, with 'mind-your-head' beamed ceilings, flagged floors, dried flowers and hops and even rarely sighted corn dollies. The whole has a cosy natural atmosphere to it. This unspoilt, rural pub excels at above-average food at reasonable prices. Since assuming new ownership in May 1997, Karen Jones and Julian Clayton have turned their menu around, cutting the regular bar snacks and expanding the blackboard specials. The bar snacks are as bar snacky as they come: sandwiches, ploughman's, jacket potatoes and even that epitome of 1970s chic, the basket meal. The pub starts to score points with a main menu that sets out to provide what people seem to want, so chicken liver pâté, wedges of brie and goat's cheese are all there, but lettuce and nutmeg soup 'looked good and tasted better', mussels in white wine has mussels floating in a good cheesy soup, while special dishes might include Thai green chicken curry, or steak and kidney pie. Puddings might include favourites such as sherry trifle, or even rhubarb crumble. Friday night is Belgian night when a menu of spring chicken with beer and mustard, carbonnade flamande and, of course, moules & frites, is served as well; and in addition to a good range of regional beers offered from Bateman, Charles Wells, Adnams, Hall & Woodhouse and Shepherd Neame there are Trappist and Abbey style Belgian beers. All the wines on the short list are available by the glass, including some English country wines. SAMPLE DISHES: stuffed mushrooms £4.25; cannelloni £7; fresh strawberry brûlée £3.

Open *11 to 3, 6 to 11, Sun 11 to 4, 7 to 10.30; bar food and restaurant 12 to 2.30, 6 to 9.30*
Details *Children welcome   Car park   Wheelchair access   Garden and patio No smoking in snug bar and dining-room   Background and live music   Dogs welcome   Delta, MasterCard, Switch, Visa*

Licensing hours and bar food times are based on information supplied by each establishment and are correct at the time of going to press.

Assessments of wine in pubs is based largely on what is available in the bar. Many pubs also have full restaurant wine lists.

OAKWOODHILL   Surrey   map 3

Punch Bowl Inn

Oakwoodhill RH5 5PU   TEL: (01306) 627249
off A29 Dorking to Horsham road, 5m NW of Horsham

Under new ownership since January 1997, the Punch Bowl is making
efforts to put itself on the map. The half-tiled pub with whitewashed
ground floor and hanging baskets opens to an interior of light-wood
tables, bench wall seats and settles, an old stone floor and an enormous recessed log fire with brasses above. The aim is to serve
uncomplicated, nicely cooked and well-presented basic pub food – a
reporter summed it up as 'very much a soup, salad, ham and egg,
potato wedges, mixed grill, and steak type place'. It also serves an
all-day breakfast. A separate dining-room (offering the same menu)
has prints on the walls and hanging lanterns. A competent wine list is
on offer but the emphasis is more on the well-served ales from Hall
& Woodhouse. SAMPLE DISHES: chicken and smoked bacon stuffed
peppers £4; cod surprise marinated in citrus and cracked black
pepper £8; Punch Bowl hot raspberries £3.50.

Open *11 to 11, Sun 12 to 10.30; bar food Mon to Sat 12 to 2.30, 6 to 9 (10
Fri and Sat), Sun 12 to 9*
Details *Children welcome   Car park   Wheelchair access (also WC)   Garden
No smoking in restaurant   Background and live music; jukebox   Dogs
welcome   Amex, Delta, MasterCard, Switch, Visa*

OARE   Kent   map 3

Shipwrights Arms

Hollowshore, Oare ME13 7TU   **WATERSIDE**
TEL: (01795) 590088
*from A2 just W of Faversham take exit to Oare, then right towards
Davington, left into Ham Rd; follow signs across the marshes*

Water is inescapable at the Shipwrights. For a start, most customers
arrive along the creek and, having moored, step *down* to the pub,
which is protected from inundation by a dyke. Next to the pub is a
working boatyard, plus a house, and then nothing save marsh and
sheep. 'I loved this place for its simplicity, remoteness and genuine
friendliness,' said one, who noted that there is not even mains electricity. Built of homely brick and clad in weatherboard, the pub dates
from the seventeenth century, and inside you will find open areas
divided by original standing timbers and with fireplaces or pot-
bellied stoves, and a relaxed, no-frills but comfortable atmosphere.

Pub-grub-style food helps keep the place unspoilt: for the really hungry there is 'The Full House' breakfast (served until 1pm) with all the trimmings including black pudding and hashbrowns. Or go for soup of the day – perhaps with garlic bread with melted cheese – and then steak and kidney pud or maybe fish & chips, followed by spotted dick. Think 'warming' and you'll have the menu summed up. The landlord serves Shepherd Neame ales, as well as Goacher's Real Mild Ale and Pawley Farm cider. Four whites and four reds feature on the basic wine list, with three house wines available by the glass. SAMPLE DISHES: chips with melted Cheddar cheese £1.50; lamb and mint pudding £6; chocolate sponge £2.50.

Open *11 to 11, Sun 12 to 10.30; bar food 12 to 3, 7 to 9.30*
Details *Children welcome in family room and bar eating area   Car park Wheelchair access   Garden and patio   No smoking in family room Background and live music   Dogs welcome   No cards*

OCKLEY   Surrey   map 3

Old Schoolhouse ❧   NEW ENTRY

Stane Street, Ockley RH5 5TH   TEL: (01306) 627430
on A29 Bognor Regis road, 8m S of Dorking

A very restauranty pub is the Old Schoolhouse but, like many aspiring restaurant pubs, it is one that still has locals dropping in to prop up the bar and sup on King & Barnes ales – Sussex, Broadwood and Festive. The interior shows signs of the pub's age and has plenty of character; the central feature is an inglenook fireplace with a copper hood. Fish is a mainstay on the menus, both in 'Bryce's seafood restaurant' (which operates a fixed-price menu) and on the bar menu. The latter takes in pasta, open sandwiches, vegetarian dishes (roasted red pepper and aubergine tart, for example), fish-cakes, and deep-fried jumbo scampi in beer batter. In the restaurant, you might find ravioli of spinach and smoked haddock, or half a dozen Loch Fyne oysters to start, and Thai fish stew, or baked Selsey crab en croûte to follow. Otherwise, the daily specials board offers perhaps fillet steak or calf's liver for non-fish eaters, plus more fish options, such as whole Cornish lemon sole. The desserts list is the only fish-free zone. Crumble and cream come together in roasted rhubarb crème brûlée with apple crisps, while bread-and-butter pudding is flavoured with apricot and ginger and topped with date syrup. The wine list is, naturally, a little longer on the whites, and includes 15 by the glass. SAMPLE DISHES: Mediterranean chargrilled vegetables on bruschetta with Parmesan £4.25; fillet of smoked haddock on Cheddar mash with a poached egg £7.50; caramelised apple with a citrus cream £3.50.

Open *11 to 3, 6 to 11, Sun 12 to 3, 6 to 10.30; closed Sun eves Nov to Feb; bar food and restaurant 12 to 2, 6.30 (7 restaurant) to 9.30 (9 restaurant)*
Details *Children welcome   Car park   Wheelchair access (also WC)   Patio No smoking in restaurant   Background music   No dogs in restaurant   Delta, MasterCard, Switch, Visa*

ODELL   Bedfordshire   map 6

Bell

Horsefair Lane, Odell MK43 7AU   TEL: (01234) 720254
off A6, 8m NW of Bedford

This extended stone and thatch pub is on the River Ouse, with a garden stretching down to the water, which helps make it a popular summertime destination, especially for families. Inside are five simply furnished interconnecting rooms decorated in mellow colours and warmed in winter by three open fires, all helping to create a relaxing atmosphere. This Greene King-owned pub stocks the brewery's usual range of ales, including IPA, Abbot Ale, and Rayments Special Bitter, as well as seasonal guest brews. Wines, meanwhile, number just a dozen, with four available by the glass. Cooking is simple-modern rather than simple-pubby, with pancakes, flans, omelettes (including a 'five-filling' version) and pizzas featuring on the printed menu, which is augmented by a changing specials board offering somewhat more adventurous fare. There could be creamy fish, broccoli and mushroom pie; or pork, apple and cider casserole; or a summer cold dish of spinach, bacon and cream cheese roulade. Puddings, which are all home-made, include pecan pie, orange cheesecake and boozy chocolate mousse. SAMPLE DISHES: bacon flan with salad and chips £3.75; beef, bacon and red wine casserole £6.50; jam and sponge pudding £2.25.

Open *11 to 2.30, 6 to 11, Sun 12 to 2.30, 7 to 10.30; bar food all week L 12 to 2, Mon to Sat D 7 to 9.30*
Details *Children welcome in 1 bar eating area   Car park   Wheelchair access Garden and patio   Background music   No dogs   Delta, MasterCard, Switch, Visa*

OFFHAM   East Sussex   map 3

Blacksmith's Arms

London Road, Offham BN7 3QD   TEL: (01273) 472971
off A275, 2m N of Lewes

'An unexpected delight. . . we would never have visited it without recommendation – it was so easy to pass by,' was how our inspector summed up the Blacksmith's Arms. Unfortunately, many people do pass by, and at great speed. The pub is located on an accident black-spot, so great care is needed when visiting. A warning on the menu tells customers not to turn right when leaving the car park, and the original front door leading directly on to the road is permanently shut; customers use the safer side door instead. On offer here is first-rate food in a good, traditional pub atmosphere. Pork and chicken-liver pâté has an excellent, freshly made taste, and its accompanying gooseberry sauce complements it well. Crabmeat, smoked bacon and sweetcorn tartlet comes on a fresh tomato coulis, breast of chicken in sesame seeds with Creole sauce has chicken pieces that are crispy on the outside and moist within, and swordfish with pizzola sauce is beautifully presented – 'worthy of a competition entry'. Puddings are also winners, including chocolate, banana and almond pie with Amaretto crème Anglaise, or pancake filled with compote of rhubarb and apple served with gingerbread ice-cream. Beers are from Harveys, and the 36-bin wine list favours the Old World but has a smattering of bottles from the New; seven house wines are available by the glass. SAMPLE DISHES: grilled sardines in garlic butter £4.50; meatballs à la Blacksmith's Arms £7.25; pancake and banana mille-feuilles with butterscotch sauce £3.50.

Open *11.30 to 3, 6.30 to 11, Sun 12 to 3; bar food and restaurant all week L 12 to 2, Mon to Sat D 7 to 9.30*
Details *Children over 5 years welcome in eating areas   Car park   Wheelchair access (also WC)   No music   Dogs welcome in bar area only   Delta, MasterCard, Switch, Visa*

OLDBURY-ON-SEVERN   South Gloucestershire   map 2

Anchor Inn   NEW ENTRY

Church Road, Oldbury-on-Severn BS35 1QA   TEL: (01454) 413331
off B4061, 2m NW of Thornbury

This timeless mill house on the banks of the Severn, once used as a tie-up spot for barges, sits in a truly serene spot of the Gloucestershire countryside, and is adorned outside with flowers and old anchors. As one enthusiastic reporter advised, 'If you over-indulge, which is quite possible given the size of the portions, you can step across the road and walk it off through superb meadows to the main Severn estuary.' The split-level lounge bar has carpet-covered block floors and a beamed, coral-plastered ceiling, while the main bar is attractively furnished with polished tables, easy chairs, settles and window seats, country prints on plain walls and a stone fireplace.

There is one menu for everywhere; no blackboards, no starters, no ploughman's or rolls, just large portions of varied dishes carefully cooked and presented. The charcoal grill is used to cook marinated Barnsley chops and 'Snorkers' – locally reared pork and garlic sausages – while honeyed Welsh lamb consists of meltingly tender lamb pieces in rich gravy, and 'Oldbury flat 'at' is a large Yorkshire pudding containing beef and onion gravy. Madras beef and cashew-nut curry, or ratatouille niçoise show a more cosmopolitan side. Puddings are also large: the 'excellent' blackcurrant supreme consists of hot, juicy blackcurrants poured over blackcurrant sorbet and ice-cream. Beers are well-kept Theakston Best and Old Peculier, Bass, Butcombe Bitter and Worthington Best, as well as Black Sheep. Inch's cider and 75 malt whiskies are also on offer, as well as a range of Frobisher's natural fruit juices. The wine list includes 13 by the glass as well as local St Augustine's wines. SAMPLE DISHES: Worthington pork with cheddar cheese and mustard £6; mango trifle with mascarpone cheese and mango purée £3.25.

Open *weekdays 11.30 to 2.30, 6.30 to 11, Sat and Sun 11.30 to 11; closed 25 and 26 Dec; bar food and restaurant 11.30 to 2, 6.30 to 9.30, Sun 12 to 4, 7 to 9.30*
Details *Children welcome in dining-room   Car park   Wheelchair access (also WC)   Garden and patio   No smoking in restaurant   No music   Dogs welcome in bar   MasterCard, Visa*

OLD HEATHFIELD   East Sussex   map 3

Star ❀

Old Heathfield TN21 9AH   TEL: (01435) 863570
off B2203 or B2096, just S of Heathfield

'Like stepping into a picture postcard of an English pub,' wrote one enthusiastic visitor. The pub stands in the gorgeous grounds of All Saints Church, its original purpose being as a dormitory for the stonemasons who were rebuilding the church in the early fourteenth century. Sue and Mike Chappell, who also own the Horse and Groom at Rushlake Green (see entry), have clearly managed to create something special in the half-dozen years they have been here. 'Outstanding food, imaginative choice and welcoming staff – just how you want an English pub to be,' continued our reporter, noting candlelit tables, a fire roaring in the inglenook, pewter beer mugs hanging from the ceiling, a dog lying in front of the fire and lots of locals propping up the bar. There are books and cushions to ease the passage of time on rather rickety furniture. Scan the blackboard menus before choosing perhaps chicken liver pâté, then smoked salmon marinated in brandy and herbs, pan-fried, and served with a sweet-and-sour mayonnaise, or oven-roast duck breast flavoured with maple syrup and garlic, together with sauté potatoes, or even half a dozen anchovies with brown bread and butter. Be prepared to wait a while for your food to be cooked – not a hardship with such an atmosphere to absorb. Salcombe's famous ices feature prominently on the puddings menu, and the pub serves beers from Harveys and Greene King. A round-the-world wine list offers two by the glass. SAMPLE DISHES: warm smoked chicken salad £5; steak and kidney pie £6.50; bread pudding £3.25.

Open *11.30 to 3, 5.30 to 11, Sun 12 to 3, 7 to 10.30; bar food and restaurant 12 to 2.30, 7 to 9.30 (9 Sun)*
Details *Well-behaved children welcome   Car park   Wheelchair access Garden   Background music   Dogs welcome by arrangement   Delta, MasterCard, Switch, Visa*

OLD SODBURY   South Gloucestershire   map 2

▲ *Dog Inn*   NEW ENTRY

Old Sodbury BS37 6LZ   TEL: (01454) 312006
from M4 junction 18 take A46 Stroud road for 2m, left on A432

This very busy whitewashed roadside pub has a large lawned garden with plenty of seating, a children's play area and pets corner. The attractive bar/lounge/dining area interior has open stonework, dark beamed ceilings, wheelback chairs and settles, wrought-iron work and log fires in winter which all contribute to a warm, welcoming atmosphere described by a reporter as 'just what one expects of a country pub'. An exceptionally long menu states that 'as all meals are freshly prepared, please allow time for cooking'. Typical bar snacks are soup, sandwiches, pâté, sausages, prawn cocktail, whitebait and ploughman's, while more substantial offerings include scampi, moussaka, steak and kidney pie, chilli and curry. Steaks range from rump, via fillet, to chateaubriand (for two people). A separate fish board lists the catches of the day: perhaps giant prawns, lobster, salmon or cod. Vegetarians are well catered for, with dishes such as salads, pasta and nut roast. Children have their own menu, called 'Puppy Food!', covering burgers, fishfingers, chicken, ham, and cottage pie. A large selection of puddings might have rhubarb crumble, blackcurrant cheesecake, jam roly-poly or sticky toffee. Real ales come from Marston's, Wadworth and the local Wickwar BOB (Brand Oak Bitter). Stowford Press cider and nine malt whiskies are available, and six wines are offered by the glass. SAMPLE DISHES: mushrooms in garlic butter £2.75; scampi and chips £6.50; spotted dick and custard £2.25.

Open *11 to 11, Sun 12 to 3, 7 to 10.30; bar food 12 to 11, Sun 12 to 2.30, 7 to 9.30*
Details *Children welcome in bar eating area   Car park   Garden   No-smoking area   Jukebox   No dogs   Amex, MasterCard, Switch, Visa Accommodation: 6 rooms, B&B £18 to £38*

OMBERSLEY   **Worcestershire**   map 5

Kings Arms 🍇

Ombersley WR9 0EW   TEL: (01905) 620315 or 620142
off A449 Worcester to Kidderminster road, 4m W of Droitwich

The Kings Arms is a flower-festooned roadside house off the A449, with patios and pergolas, the sides of which are crammed with climbers. Inside is a warren of little rooms, many separated only by partition beams, decorated with horse brasses and hanging copper pans, and furnished with green plush seating. Carved coats of arms adorn the ceiling. The lunchtime menu offers fairly modern dishes, vegetables with salsa dip, chargrilled teriyaki wings, or chargrilled steak sandwich on toasted ciabatta. Sandwiches are on a board, and, again, ciabatta is popular. Fairly standard dishes get modern treatments. Game sausages get served on a chive mash, calf's liver arrives with red onion marmalade, while crispy cod is deep-fried in coriander batter is served with crème fraîche tartare. Daily specials may include crispy duck with orange and watercress salad, or lamb cutlets with crispy parsnip rösti. Fish specials have a board of their own, which might list oysters in Tabasco and cracked black pepper, baby mullet in Pernod sauce, skate wings with black butter, or scallops sautéd with chilli and lemon grass. Customers are invited to phone two days in advance to order what fish they would like. Puddings include banana and toffee pancakes with clotted cream, or cheeses poached in port and vanilla. On tap are Bass, Fuller's London Pride, Morland Old Speckled Hen, Banks's Bitter, Marston's Pedigree, plus guests, and up to 30 interesting wines are usually available from a full list of around 70. Ten wines, including a dessert wine and a champagne, are served by the glass. SAMPLE DISHES: marinated sardines on toast £4; wild mushroom ravioli with flaked Parmesan and baby spinach £7.25; English cheese with grapes and Bath Olivers £4.50

Open *11 to 2.30, 5.30 to 11, Sun 12 to 10.30; closed 25 Dec; bar food 12 to 2.15, 6 to 10, Sun 12 to 10*
Details *No children   Car park   Wheelchair access   Patio   No music   Guide dogs only   Amex, Delta, MasterCard, Switch, Visa*

OSMOTHERLEY   North Yorkshire   map 9

▲ *Three Tuns Inn*

Osmotherley DL6 3BN   TEL: (01609) 883301
1m off A19, 6m NE of Northallerton

The Three Tuns sits among a row of solid stone seventeenth-century cottages in the centre of Osmotherley, an attractive village on the edge of the North Yorkshire Moors. Convenient for walkers wishing to tackle the Hambleton Way, Lyke Wake Walk or the Cleveland Way, the pub offers a welcome respite. Benches in front (underneath colourful hanging baskets in summer) provide customers with the opportunity to sit and watch the world go by, while the small garden at the rear, with its rustic furniture, affords delightful views. Three connecting rooms are served by a central bar. The two front rooms are delightfully unspoilt with a good pubby atmosphere, padded bench-style seating, simple wooden tables, sporting prints and an open log fire. The third room is a more formal dining-room, but at weekends diners sit anywhere. The printed menu, which offers a range of food, from wholesome sandwiches and ploughman's to roast breast of barbary duck or home-cooked York ham, is supplemented by a blackboard of daily-changing specials – perhaps a parcel of fresh salmon, spinach, giant prawn tail and plaice with lobster sauce, or half a shoulder of lamb with Madeira sauce. Fish is likely to come from nearby Whitby, and the pub prides itself on its freshly cooked food. Puddings are a combination of old favourites plus one or two house specialities, perhaps a Tia Maria parfait, or a raspberry and whisky trifle. An above-average selection of beers is on offer, including Theakston Old Peculier, Best and XB, John Smith's Bitter and Old Legover from Daleside in Harrogate. A 30-plus wine list focuses most heavily on the burgundies but has some good Australian wines too. SAMPLE DISHES: cream of fresh watercress soup £3; braised oxtail in red wine £8; death by chocolate £3.25.

Open *11.45 to 3.30, 6.45 (7 Sun) to 10.30 (11 summer); bar food and restaurant all week L 12 to 2.30 (3 Sun), Mon to Sat D 7 to 9.30*
Details *Children welcome   Garden and patio   No music   Dogs welcome in snug only   MasterCard, Switch, Visa   Accommodation: 3 rooms, B&B £49.50 to £65*

▲ *Dog Inn*

Well Bank Lane, Over Peover WA16 8UP   TEL: (01625) 861421
*off A50 between Knutsford and Holmes Chapel; turn at Whipping
Stocks pub and continue for 1½m*

This eighteenth-century whitewashed brick and pebbledash pub is set
well back from the road, with wooden tables and benches on the
front patio and a garden behind. Inside, there is a lively bar area
popular with locals, and the red patterned carpets, 'bottle bottom'
windows, stone fireplaces and framed prints – some of which are for
sale – all help to create a cosy atmosphere. The menu is long, with a
choice of about 20 main courses and more than a dozen starters. The
range of sandwiches is extensive, or you might prefer a prawn,
poached salmon or roast turkey salad. Those who like ploughman's
can choose between Red Leicester, blue cheese and Cheddar. You
could start a more substantial meal with garlic mushrooms, black
pudding, smoked trout or duck and port pâté, and continue with a
roast or a pie, scampi, deep-fried cod or fresh spinach lasagne. Rack
of lamb has been described as featuring good-quality meat and comes
with an apricot gravy. Puddings are displayed in a cabinet and might
include bread-and-butter, sticky toffee or fruit pies. On tap are beers
from Tetley, Flowers, Boddingtons and local Weetwood Ales Old
Dog. Three dozen wines are graded as to sweetness (white) and fullness (red), and three house wines are available by the glass or bottle.
SAMPLE DISHES: deep-fried Brie with salad £4; steak and ale pie £8;
strawberry pavlova £3.50.

Open *11.30 to 3, 5.30 to 11, Sun 12 to 4, 7 to 10.30; bar food 12 to 2.30, 7
to 9.30*
Details *Children welcome   Car park   Wheelchair access (also WC)   Garden
and patio   No smoking in restaurant   Background music   Guide dogs only
Amex, Delta, MasterCard, Switch, Visa   Accommodation: 6 rooms, B&B £50
to £70*

Royal Oak

Over Stratton TA13 5LQ   TEL: (01460) 240906
*off A303, take Ilminster town centre turn away from South
Petherton, turn left after 300yds*

A good family pub with an attractive garden and its own play area in
which to deposit the children safely for a while. In the heart of this
pretty village, the pub is a conversion of three four-hundred-year-old

stone cottages. The interior has bags of charm and atmosphere with many original features on display. There are flag floors, open fires, hop bines and dried flowers and tasteful hand-painted vine murals, low lighting and candlelit tables. The printed menu lists some staple pub favourites, but extends to toasted goats' cheese and spinach pancakes to start, and medallions of monkfish or steaks from the char-grill as main courses. A specials board provides dishes that show what the chef can do: tagliatelle with fresh mussels, clams, tiger prawns and aïoli in sorrel sauce, or chicken chilli masala perhaps. Vegetarians and children are given special attention on the menu. This is a Hall & Woodhouse pub, serving Badger Best, Badger IPA and Tanglefoot. The wine list features a selection of fifty wines from around the globe and 3 by the glass. SAMPLE DISHES: mushrooms with Roquefort cheese and redcurrants £3.75; supreme of chicken £12; apple cheesecake £3.75.

Open *11 to 3, 6 to 11, Sun 12 to 3, 7 to 10.30; bar food and restaurant 12 to 2.30, 7 to 10*
Details *Children welcome   Car park   Wheelchair access (also WC)   Garden No smoking in restaurant   Background music   Dogs welcome   Delta, MasterCard, Switch, Visa*

PAXFORD   Gloucestershire   map 5

▲ *Churchill Arms* 🏵 🏵 NEW ENTRY

Paxford GL55 6XH   TEL: (01386) 594000
2m E of Chipping Campden

The only pub in the very Cotswold hamlet of Paxford, the Churchill Arms is situated diagonally opposite the church. It has a few trestle tables at the front and more at the rear, and a separate room where the game of Aunt Sally is played. Inside, it is open plan with very well-spaced furniture, which is just as well because it has tended to get very packed after Leo Brooke-Little and Sonya Kidney, who run the Marsh Goose restaurant in nearby Moreton-in-Marsh, took over in mid- 1997 (they have also recently taken over the Hare & Hounds in Foss Cross – see entry). The owners stress that they are running a pub which serves food and not a restaurant with beer; the presence of reasonably priced Hook Norton and Arkell's ales bears them out. The Churchill has a different identity from the Marsh Goose, but the cooking is just as good, as it should be with Sonya alternating between the two establishments: the ideas behind the dishes are fresh and bring out the essential nature of the ingredients they use. The menu is up on blackboards and the fare is colourful, straightforward and unadorned. Ease yourself into the food with courgette and dill soup, or hot cheese fritters with grain mustard sauce, or Evesham asparagus, shallots and herbs in olive oil with strips of smoked goose breast. Move on to fillets of lemon sole with aubergine ragoût and parsley cream sauce, or breast of chicken with Parmesan risotto, mushroom and Madeira cream sauce. Round the meal off with poached pear and rhubarb served with rhubarb ice-cream, or a sticky toffee pudding. This pub has produced a number of favourable reports in a fairly short time: one to watch. SAMPLE DISHES: smoked Scottish salmon with lemon £4.50; sauté lambs' kidneys with pilau rice in pancetta, port and green peppercorn sauce £8; raspberry praline terrine with melon and white chocolate sauce £3.

Open *11 to 3, 6 to 11, Sun 12 to 3, 7 to 10.30; bar food 12 to 2.30, 7 to 9*
Details *Children welcome   Car park   Wheelchair access   Garden and patio
Background music   Dogs welcome   Delta, MasterCard, Switch, Visa
Accommodation: 4 rooms, B&B £30 to £60*

PEMBRIDGE   Herefordshire   map 5

▲ *New Inn*

Market Square, Pembridge HR6 9DZ
TEL: (01544) 388427
on A44, between Kington and Leominster, 6m E of Kington

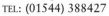
HISTORY

There is nothing new about the New Inn, which was built in 1311 and was for many years known as 'the inn without a name'. In its time it has seen service as a court and a jail, and it is believed that the treaty giving Edward IV the English crown was signed here after the battle of Mortimer's Cross in 1461. Traditionally furnished with flagstone floors and old settles, it is an important stop on the local history trail, which also takes in Offa's Dyke. Food is traditional too, and hearty as one would expect, with dishes like game pie and roast duckling conjuring up images of the 'groaning board' of days gone by. Sandwiches and ploughman's are staple alternatives to main dishes of Cumberland sausage with Yorkshire pudding on the printed menu, while specials such as lamb casserole with minted dumplings appear on the blackboard. Ruddles Best and County are the permanent beers, while rotating guest ales are selected from local independents, and there is an impressive range of 32 malts and blended whiskies, plus Weston's Organic Cider. Wine is the only area where the New World is allowed to intrude into this Old World environment, and a selection of English country wines also features. SAMPLE DISHES: Stilton and port pâté with toast £3.25; beef and horseradish stew with dumplings £5.50; lemon tart £2.75.

Open *11 to 3 (2.30 winter), 6 to 11, Sun 12 to 3, 7 to 10.30; bar food and
restaurant 12 to 2, 7 to 9.15*
Details *Children welcome in eating areas   Car park   Garden   No smoking in
lounge bar while food is served   Live music   No dogs   Accommodation: 6
rooms, B&B £18.50 to £37*

The top-rated pubs

England

Berkshire
Royal Oak, Yattendon

Cambridgeshire
Three Horseshoes, Madingley

Devon
Drewe Arms, Broadhembury

Essex
White Hart, Great Yeldham

Gloucestershire
Churchill Arms, Paxford
Hare & Hounds, Foss Cross

Greater Manchester
White Hart, Lydgate

Lancashire
Spread Eagle, Sawley

Northumberland
Queens Head Inn, Great Whittington

North Yorkshire
Angel Inn, Hetton
Blue Lion, East Witton
Crab & Lobster, Asenby
Plough Inn, Saxton
Star Inn, Harome
Yorke Arms, Ramsgill

Oxfordshire
Bell, Standlake
The Goose, Britwell Salome
Sir Charles Napier, Chinnor

Queens Head Inn

Star Inn

West Sussex
Crabtree, Lower Beeding

Wiltshire
George & Dragon, Rowde
Grosvenor Arms, Hindon

Red Lion Inn

WALES
Powys
Red Lion Inn, Llanfihangel
nant Melan

indicates a pub offering above-average bar food that shows ambition and good ideas, or simple pub fare prepared particularly well.

ENGLAND

Berkshire
Dundas Arms, Kintbury
Harrow Inn, West Ilsley

Buckinghamshire
Angel Inn, Long Crendon
Chequers Inn, Wooburn Common
Walnut Tree, Fawley

Springer Spaniel

Cambridgeshire
Anchor Inn, Sutton Gault
Pheasant Inn, Keyston

Co Durham
Rose and Crown, Romaldkirk

Cornwall
Springer Spaniel, Treburley

Cumbria
Bay Horse Hotel, Ulverston
Punch Bowl Inn, Crosthwaite
Queens Head, Troutbeck
Snooty Fox, Kirkby Lonsdale

Derbyshire
Red Lion, Hognaston

Red Lion

Nobody Inn

Devon
Anchor, Beer
Arundell Arms, Lifton
Jack in the Green,
Rockbeare
Nobody Inn,
Doddiscombsleigh
Peter Tavy Inn,
Peter Tavy
White Hart, Dartington

Fox Inn

Dorset
Fox Inn,
Corscombe
Three
Horseshoes,
Powerstock

East Sussex
Griffin Inn,
Fletching
Jolly
Sportsman,
East Chiltington
Star,
Old Heathfield

Essex
Bell Inn,
Horndon on the
Hill

Griffin Inn

Gloucestershire
Fox Inn, Lower
Oddington

Hampshire
East End Arms,
East End
Red House, Whitchurch

Herefordshire
Roebuck, Brimfield
Sun Inn, Winforton

Kent
Dove, Dargate
Harrow Inn, Ightham

Sun Inn

Lancashire
Eagle & Child,
Bispham Green

Leicestershire
Peacock Inn,
Redmile

Lincolnshire
Chequers,
Gedney Dyke
Tally Ho Inn, Aswarby

Northumberland
Cook and Barker Inn,
Newton-on-the-Moor
Manor House Inn,
Carterway Heads

North Yorkshire
Black Bull Inn,
Moulton
Foresters Arms,
Carlton-in-Coverdale
Fox and Hounds,
Sinnington
General Tarleton, Ferrensby
Sportsmans Arms,
Wath-in-Nidderdale
Wombwell Arms, Wass

Chequers

Nottinghamshire
Martins Arms,
Colston Bassett

Oxfordshire
Feathers Hotel,
Woodstock
Lamb Inn, Buckland
Vine Inn, Cumnor

Rutland
The Sun,
Cottesmore

Shropshire
Bradford Arms,
Llanymynech
Hundred House
Hotel, Norton
Peacock, Boraston

Hundred House Hotel

Suffolk
Angel, Lavenham
Angel Inn,
Stoke-by-Nayland
Crown Inn, Snape
Star Inn, Lidgate
White Hart, Nayland

West Sussex
Hamilton Arms,
Stedham
Horse Guards Inn,
Tillington
King's Arms, Fernhurst
Lickfold Inn, Lickfold

West Yorkshire
Olive Branch, Marsden
Three Acres Inn,
Roydhouse

Wiltshire
Three Crowns, Brinkworth

Worcestershire
The Talbot, Knightwick
Walter de Cantelupe,
Kempsey

Angel, Laveham

Lickfold Inn

SCOTLAND

Borders
Wheatsheaf, Swinton

Perthshire & Kinross
Tormaukin Hotel, Glendevon

WALES

Cardiff
Caesar's Arms,
Creigiau

Conwy
Kinmel Arms,
St George
Queen's Head,
Glanwydden

Penhelig Arms Hotel

Gwynedd
Penhelig Arms Hotel,
Aberdovey

Pembrokeshire
Tafarn Newydd, Rosebush

Powys
Bear Hotel, Crickhowell
Nantyffin Cider Mill Inn,
Crickhowell
Seland Newydd, Pwllgloyw

Bear Hotel

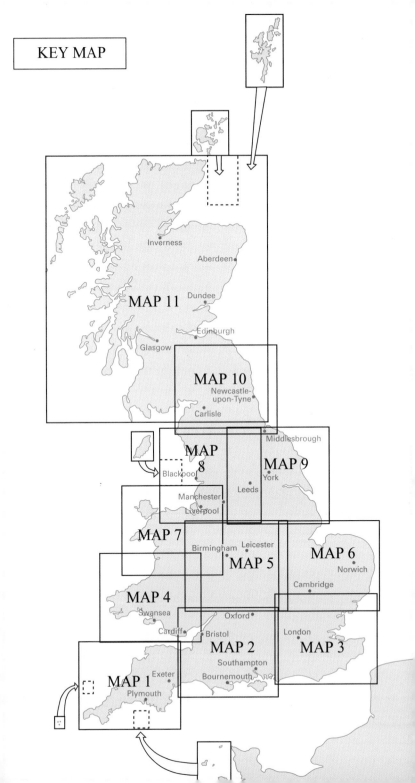

KEY MAP

MAP 11

Inverness

Aberdeen

Dundee

Edinburgh

Glasgow

MAP 10

Newcastle-
upon-Tyne

Carlisle

Middlesbrough

MAP
8

Blackpool

MAP 9

York

Leeds

Manchester

Liverpool

MAP 7

Birmingham

Leicester

MAP 5

MAP 6

Norwich

Cambridge

MAP 4

Swansea

Oxford

London

MAP 3

Cardiff

Bristol

MAP 2

Southampton

Bournemouth

MAP 1

Exeter

Plymouth

MAP 1

- ▐ Main entries
- ▐ Main entry with accommodation
- ▯ Out & About entries
- ▐ Main and Out & About entries
- ▐ Main entries with accommodation, and Out & Abouts

0	5	10 miles
0		15 kms

Isles of Scilly
28 miles WSW of Land's End

Bryher

St Martin's

▯ Tresco

St Mary's

St Agnes ▯

Lundy Island

B u d e
B a y

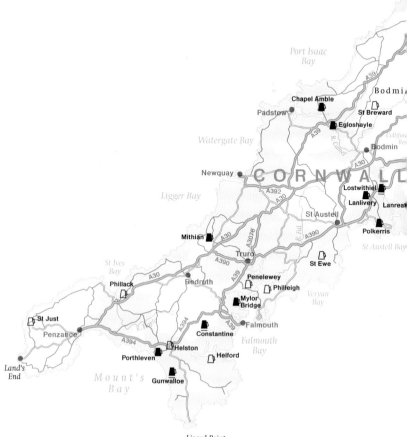

Port Isaac Bay

A39

B o d m i

Chapel Amble ▐

Padstow

St Breward ▯

Egloshayle ▐

Watergate Bay

A39

R. Camel

Colliford Res

Bodmin

Ligger Bay

Newquay

C O R N W A L L

A392

A30

Lostwithiel ▐

Lanlivery ▯

Lanrea

St Austell

R. Fal

A390

Polkerris ▐

Mithian ▐

A30

A3075

St Austell Bay

St Ives Bay

Truro

A390

St Ewe ▯

Phillack ▯

A30

Redruth

Penelewey

Philleigh ▯

Veryan Bay

Mylor ▐
Bridge

St Just ▯

Penzance

R. Hayle

A394

Constantine ▐

Falmouth

Falmouth Bay

Land's End

A394

Helston ▐

Helford ▯

Porthleven ▐

Mount's Bay

Gunwalloe ▐

Lizard Point

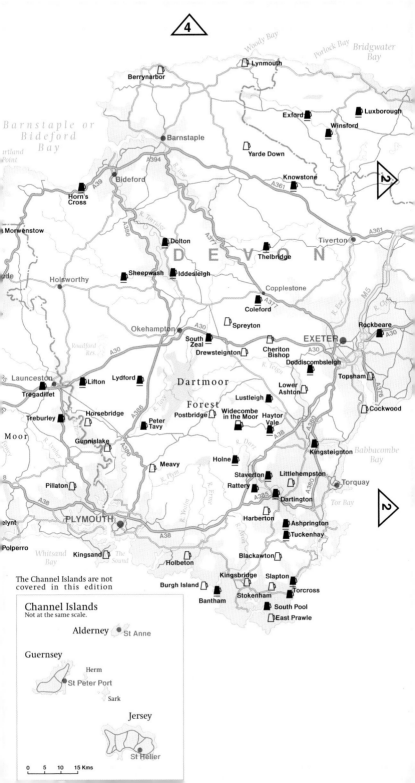

4

Woody Bay

Porlock Bay

Bridgwater Bay

Lynmouth

Berrynarbor

Exford

Luxborough

Winsford

Barnstaple or Bideford Bay

ortland Point

Barnstaple

Yarde Down

2

Bideford

A394

A39

R. Taw

Knowstone

A361

Horn's Cross

A386

R. Torridge

A377

Tiverton

A361

Morwenstow

Dolton

D E V O N

Thelbridge

M5

R. Exe

R. Clyst

Holsworthy

Sheepwash

Iddesleigh

Copplestone

de

A377

Coleford

Rockbeare

Spreyton

A30

EXETER

A30

Okehampton

A30

South Zeal

Cheriton Bishop

Drewsteignton

Doddiscombsleigh

Roadford Res.

A30

R. Teign

Topsham

A376

Dartmoor

Lower Ashton

Cockwood

Launceston

Lifton

Lydford

Lustleigh

Tregadillet

Forest

R. Tavy

Widecombe in the Moor

Haytor Vale

Treburley

Horsebridge

Postbridge

A38

A380

Kingsteignton

Babbacombe Bay

Peter Tavy

Moor

A386

Gunnislake

Meavy

Holne

R. Dart

Staverton

Littlehempston

Torquay

R. Lyd

R. Plym

Rattery

Dartington

A385

Tor Bay

2

Pillaton

A38

PLYMOUTH

Harberton

A380

elynt

R. Erme

R. Yealm

Ashprington

Tuckenhay

Polperro

Whitsand Bay

Kingsand

The Sound

Holbeton

Blackawton

Burgh Island

Kingsbridge

Slapton

Torcross

Bantham

Stokenham

South Pool

East Prawle

The Channel Islands are not
covered in this edition

Channel Islands
Not at the same scale.

Alderney ● St Anne

Guernsey

Herm

● St Peter Port

Sark

Jersey

● St Helier

0   5   10   15 Kms

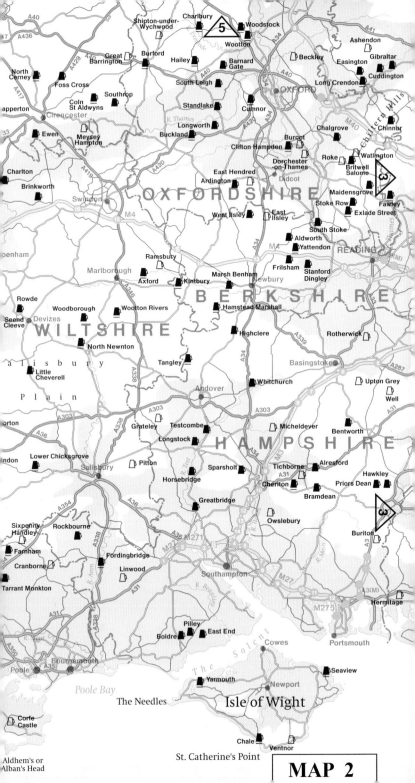

MAP 2

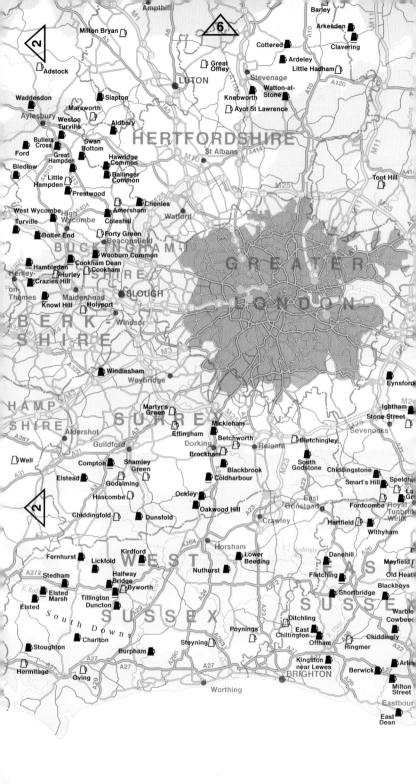

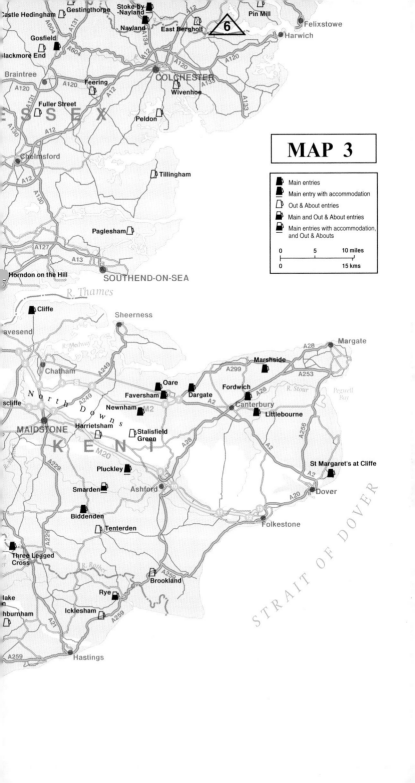

MAP 3

Main entries
Main entry with accommodation
Out & About entries
Main and Out & About entries
Main entries with accommodation, and Out & Abouts

| 0 | 5 | 10 miles |
| 0 | | 15 kms |

Castle Hedingham
Gestingthorpe
Stoke-by-Nayland
Nayland
East Bergholt
Pin Mill
Felixstowe
Harwich
Gosfield
Blackmore End
Braintree
Fuller Street
Feering
COLCHESTER
Wivenhoe
E S S E X
Peldon
Chelmsford
Tillingham
Paglesham
Horndon on the Hill
SOUTHEND-ON-SEA

R. Thames

Cliffe
Sheerness
Gravesend
R. Medway
Margate
Chatham
Marshside
Oare
Fordwich
R. Stour
Pegwell Bay
North Downs
Faversham
Dargate
Canterbury
Ascliffe
Newnham
Littlebourne
MAIDSTONE
Harrietsham
Stalisfield Green
K E N T
St Margaret's at Cliffe
Pluckley
Smarden
Ashford
Dover
Biddenden
Tenterden
Folkestone
Three Legged Cross
R. Rother
Brookland
Rye
Icklesham
STRAIT OF DOVER
Hastings

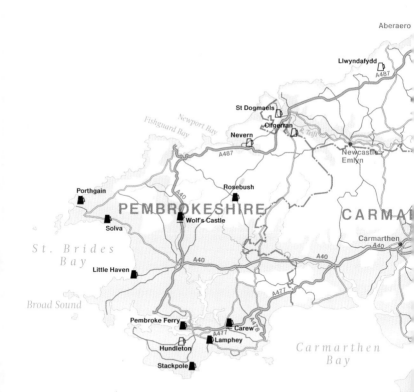

7

MAP 4

Main entries
Main entry with accommodation
Out & About entries
Main and Out & About entries
Main entries with accommodation, and Out & Abouts

0	5	10 miles
0		15 kms

CARDIGAN

BAY

Aberaero

Llwyndafydd
A487

St Dogmaels
Cilgerran
Nevern
R Teifi
Newcastle
Emlyn
A487

Fishguard Bay   Newport Bay

Rosebush

Porthgain

PEMBROKESHIRE   CARMA

Wolf's Castle

A40

Solva

Carmarthen
A40

St. Brides
Bay

Little Haven

A40   A40

Broad Sound

A477

Pembroke Ferry
Carew   A47
A477   Carmarthen
Lamphey   Bay
Hundleton

Stackpole

Reyno

BRISTOL

MAP 5

7

Bunbury
Higher Burwardsley
Marford
Gresford
Wrexham
Shocklach
Cholmondeley
Aston
Crewe
Barthomley
Shraleybrook
Newcastle-under-Lyme
Onecc
STOKE-ON-TRENT

WREXHAM

Oswestry

Llanyblodwel
Llanymynech
Nesscliffe
Bwlch-y-Cibau

STAFFORDSHIRE

Stafford

SHIRE

Shrewsbury

Welshpool

TELFORD

Montgomery

SHROPSHIRE

Much Wenlock
Norton
WOLVERHAMPTON

Wentnor
Cardington
Wenlock Edge
Brockton
Bridgnorth

Little Stretton
Bishop's Castle
Munslow
Wistanstow
Corfton

Llanfair Waterdine

Hopton Wafers
Kidderminster
Bewdley

POWYS

Boraston

Menithwood

Aymestrey
Brimfield
Ombersley

Shobdon
Old Radnor
Pembridge
Leominster
WORCESTER
Worcester
Inkberrow

Llanfihangel nant Melan

HEREFORD

Weobley

Knightwick

SHIRE

Whitney
Winforton
Dorstone
Lugwardine
Kempsey

Hay-on-Wye
Hereford

Bredon

Woolhope
Fownhope

Carey
Playley Green
Tewkesbury
Alderton

Sellack
Upton Bishop

Llanthony

GLOUCESTER

Ashleworth

Llanvihangel Crucorney
SHIRE
Cheltenham

Crickhowell
Gloucester

Llangattock
Llanvapley

Blaisdon

MONMOUTHSHIRE
Monmouth
Penallt
Sheepscombe
North Cerney

2

Clytha
Awre

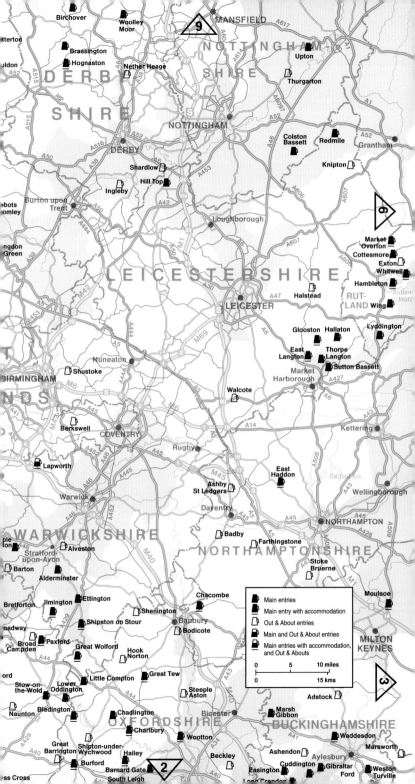

Map Legend

- Main entries
- Main entry with accommodation
- Out & About entries
- Main and Out & About entries
- Main entries with accommodation, and Out & Abouts

Scale:
0 — 5 — 10 miles
0 — 15 kms

Place names

DERBYSHIRE
- Birchover
- Woolley Moor
- Brassington
- Hognaston
- Nether Heage
- Shardlow
- Hill Top
- Ingleby
- Burton upon Trent

NOTTINGHAMSHIRE
- MANSFIELD
- Upton
- Thurgarton
- NOTTINGHAM
- DERBY
- Colston Bassett
- Redmile
- Grantham
- Knipton

LEICESTERSHIRE
- Loughborough
- Market Overton
- Cottesmore
- Exton
- Whitwell
- Hambleton
- LEICESTER
- Halstead
- RUTLAND
- Wing
- Glooston
- Hallaton
- Lyddington
- East Langton
- Thorpe Langton
- Sutton Bassett
- Market Harborough
- Walcote

WARWICKSHIRE
- BIRMINGHAM
- Shustoke
- Berkswell
- COVENTRY
- Lapworth
- Warwick
- Nuneaton
- Rugby
- Kettering
- Wellingborough
- East Haddon
- Ashby St Ledgers
- Daventry
- NORTHAMPTON
- Alveston
- Stratford-upon-Avon
- Barton
- Alderminster
- Ilmington
- Ettington
- Shenington
- Bretforton
- Shipston on Stour
- Paxford
- Great Wolford
- Hook Norton
- Broad Campden
- Little Compton
- Great Tew
- Stow-on-the-Wold
- Lower Oddington
- Steeple Aston
- Naunton
- Bledington
- Chadlington
- Charlbury
- Great Barrington
- Shipton-under-Wychwood
- Hailey
- Burford
- Barnard Gate
- South Leigh
- Wootton

NORTHAMPTONSHIRE
- Badby
- Farthingstone
- Stoke Bruerne
- Chacombe
- Banbury
- Bodicote
- Moulsoe

OXFORDSHIRE
- Adstock
- Marsh Gibbon
- Bicester
- Beckley
- Easington
- Long Crendon

BUCKINGHAMSHIRE
- Waddesdon
- Marsworth
- MILTON KEYNES
- Ashendon
- Cuddington
- Aylesbury
- Gibraltar
- Weston Turville

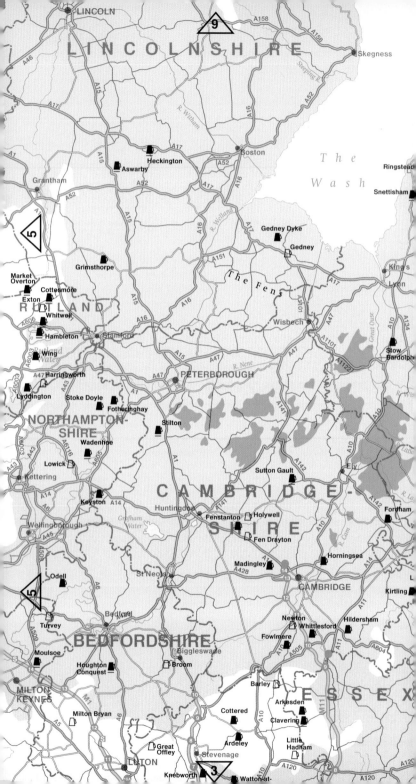

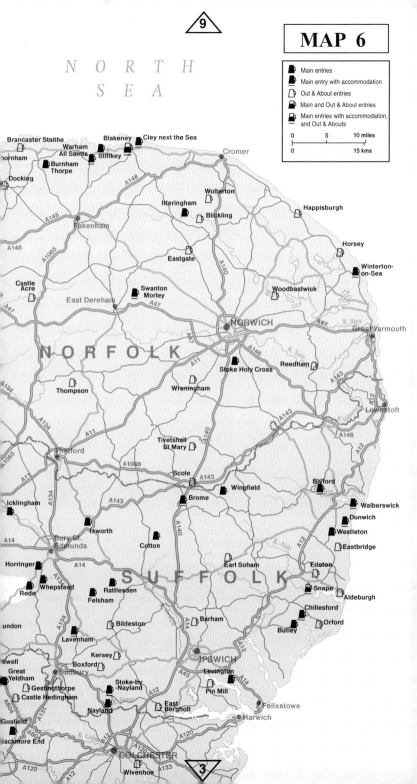

MAP 7

IRISH

SEA

Holyhead
Bay

Llyn Alaw

ISLE
OF
ANGLESEY

Red Wharf
Bay

Conwy
Bay

Holyhead

Red Wharf Bay

Glanwydden

Holy Island

Beaumaris

Tyn-y-Groes

Coly
Ba

A55

Bangor

Foel Fras
942

CONW

Menai Strait

A5

Carnedd
Dafydd
1044

Caernarfon

A487

A5

Glyder Fawr
999

Capel
Curig

A470

Betws-y-
Coed

Caernarfon

Bay

Llandwrog

Rhyd-Ddu

1085
Snowdon

872

Carnedd
Moel-Siabod

GWYNEDD

A487

Afon Glaslyn

Porthmadog

Maentwrog

Lleyn Peninsula

Pwllheli

Tremadog
Bay

A470

Aran Ben
884

Aran Fawr
905

A494

Bardsey Sound

Bontddu

Dolgellau

Bardsey Island

Barmouth

Cader Idris
893

A487

Cambrian Mountains

CARDIGAN

Macynlleth

Aberdovey

BAY

Afon Dy

A487

Aberystwyth

A44

CEREDIGION

4

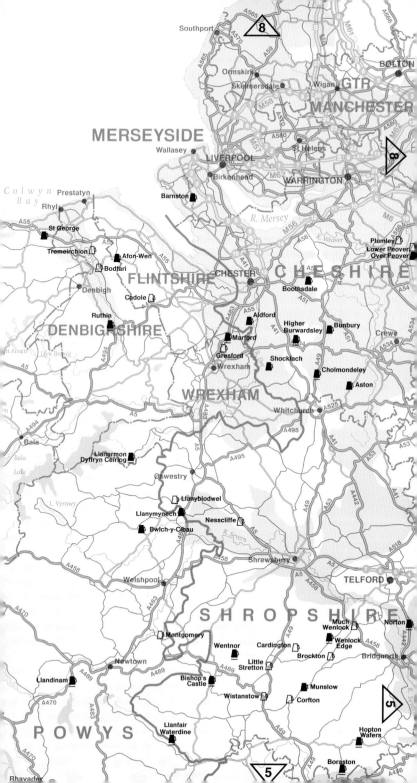

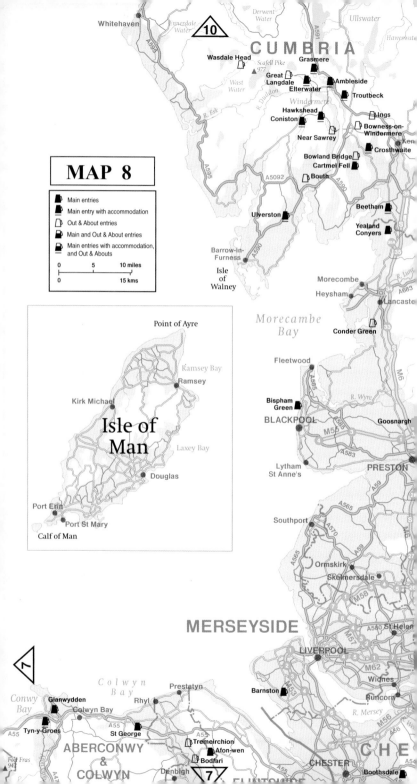

MAP 8

Main entries
Main entry with accommodation
Out & About entries
Main and Out & About entries
Main entries with accommodation, and Out & Abouts

0   5   10 miles
0   15 kms

CUMBRIA

Whitehaven
Wasdale Head
Scafell Pike 977
Great Langdale
Elterwater
Grasmere
Ambleside
Troutbeck
Hawkshead
Coniston
Ings
Bowness-on-Windermere
Near Sawrey
Ken
Crosthwaite
Bowland Bridge
Cartmel Fell
Bouth
Ulverston
Beetham
Yealand Conyers
Barrow-in-Furness
Isle of Walney

Morecombe
Heysham
Lancaster

Morecambe Bay
Conder Green

Fleetwood
Bispham Green
BLACKPOOL
Goosnargh
Lytham St Anne's
PRESTON

Point of Ayre
Ramsey Bay
Ramsey
Kirk Michael
Isle of Man
Laxey Bay
Douglas
Port Erin
Port St Mary
Calf of Man

Southport
Ormskirk
Skelmersdale

MERSEYSIDE

St Helen
LIVERPOOL
Widnes
Runcorn
R. Mersey

CHE

Prestatyn
Barnston
Colwyn Bay
Glanwydden
Colwyn Bay
Rhyl
Conwy Bay
Tyn-y-Groes
St George
Tremeirchion
Afon-wen
Bodfari
ABERCONWY & COLWYN
Denbigh

CHESTER
Boothsdale

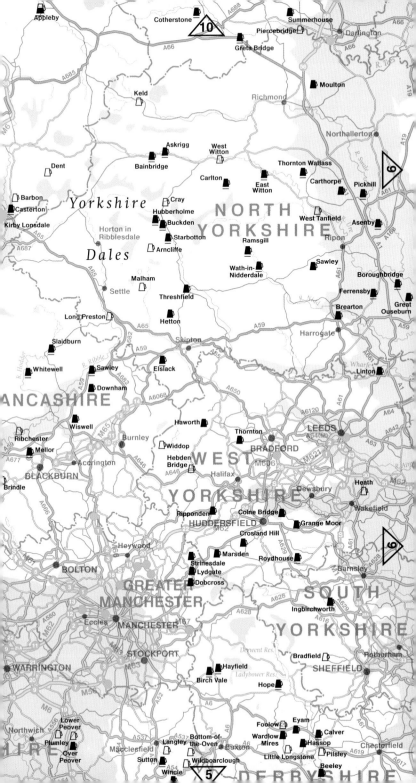

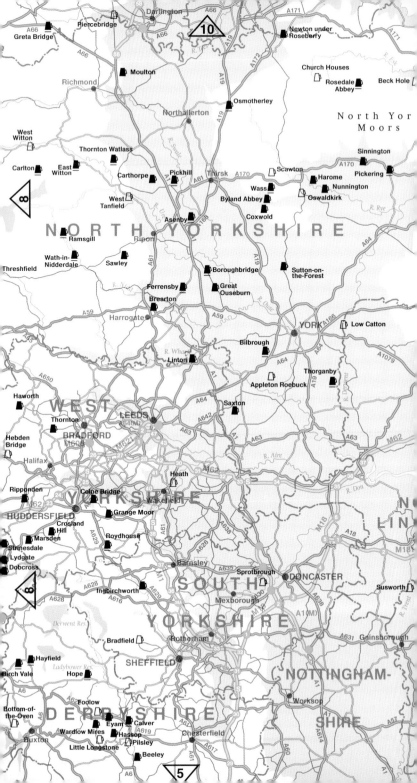

MAP 9

Main entries
Main entry with accommodation
Out & About entries
Main and Out & About entries
Main entries with accommodation, and Out & Abouts

| 0 | 5 | 10 miles |
| 0 | | 15 kms |

Whitby

Robin Hood's Bay

A171

Scarborough

A170

A64

A65

Flamborough Head

A166
Bridlington

Bridlington Bay

Yorkshire Wolds

66

Driffield

A165

A163
EAST RIDING

Lund

OF YORKSHIRE

South Dalton

A1035

A1079

A165

A63

KINGSTON
UPON HULL

KINGSTON
UPON HULL

R. Humber

Barton-upon-Humber

TH

NSHIRE

A160

Scunthorpe

Spurn Head

A18

M180

Grimsby

Cleethorpes

N.E.
LINCOLNSHIRE

A173

A15

Rothwell

A46

A16

A1103

A631

A15

Market
Rasen

Louth

Mablethorpe

The Wolds

A46

A16

A158

A57
LINCOLNSHIRE

A158

LINCOLN

A158

Skegness

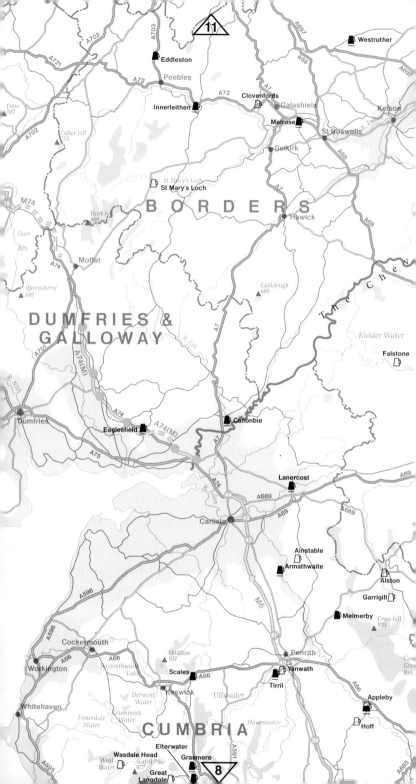

MAP 10

11

Berwick-upon-Tweed

Swinton

Coldstream
Wark

Holy Island

Farne Is.

The Cheviot
815

Seahouses

Low Newton
-by-the-Sea

Eglingham

Craster

R. Aln
Alnwick

Alnmouth

Newton-on-the-Moor

NORTHUMBERLAND

Morpeth

Matfen

Haydon
Bridge

Anick

Great Whittington

NEWCASTLE
UPON TYNE

Tynemouth

TYNE
&
WEAR

Hexham

R. Tyne

SUNDERLAND

Carterway
Heads

Stanley

Derwent Re

Consett

Chester-le-
Street

Pittington

Durham

DURHAM

Bishop
Auckland

Hartlepool

HARTLEPOOL

Fir Tree

Tees Bay

Redcar

Romaldkirk

STOCKTON-
ON-TEES

Summerhouse

MIDDLESBROUGH

Cotherstone

Piercebridge

Darlington

MIDDLES
BROUGH

REDCAR

Greta Bridge

Newton under
Roseberry

9

Main entries

Main entry with accommodation

Out & About entries

Main and Out & About entries

Main entries with accommodation,
and Out & Abouts

0   5   10 miles

0   15 kms

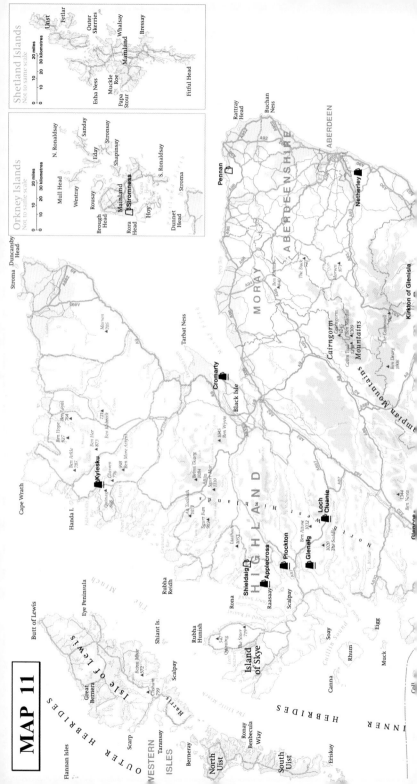

MAP 11

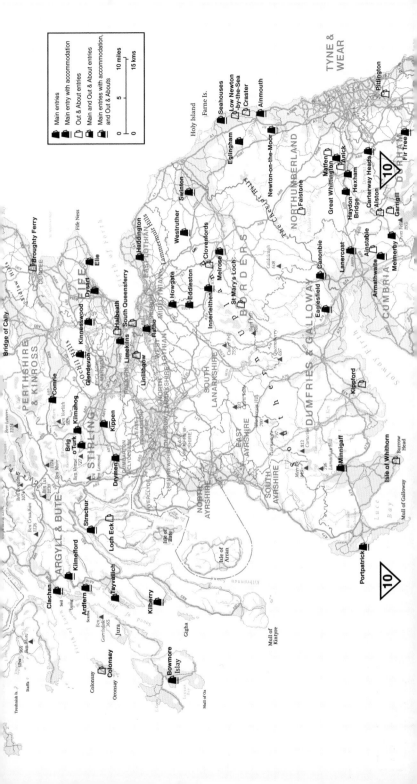

Something to look out for . . .

RIVERSIDE Here and there in the Guide, you will see small barley-ear symbols with words inside them, such as 'Home Brew', 'Haunted', 'Riverside' or simply 'Eccentric', indicating that the pub in question has something special, perhaps unique, about it.

Canal	Seaside
Views	Waterside
Walks	Wildlife
Setting	Riverside
Fishing	
Fish	Puddings
Spanish	Ploughman's
Vegetarian	Buffet
Oriental	Italian
Welsh	Cheese
Scottish	Thai
Fijian	Fish & Chips
Sausages	Old English
Far Eastern	Mexican
Belgian	Steaks
Indian	Pasta
Organic	French
English Regional	Local Produce
Home Brew	Cider
Whisky	Bottled Beer
History	Heritage
Haunted	Rare Breeds
Curios	Smugglers
Pigs	Activities
Community Pub	Eccentric
Clocks	Books
Shop	

PETER TAVY   Devon   map 1

▲ *Peter Tavy Inn* ❀ 🍺

Peter Tavy PL19 9NN   TEL: (01822) 810348
off A386, 3m NE of Tavistock

The Peter Tavy scored very highly with one of our harder to please
inspectors, so the new owners are clearly doing things right. This
deservedly popular pub is approached down a lane that is almost a
farm track by the time you get there and it can easily be mistaken for
a farmhouse but, in fact, was built to accommodate masons working
on the local church. It has a cosy interior with flagstone floors, a
small bar on the right as you enter and, to the left, a couple of rooms
divided by upright beams where a wall has, at some stage, been
removed. Tables are candlelit in the evening and the light from the
enclosed fire reflecting on horse brasses and brass ornaments gives
the place a pleasing atmosphere. Blackboard menus feature starters
and mains on one and puddings on another. Typical starters are
cream of tomato soup, baked avocado with prawns, or port and
Stilton pâté. Mains might be roast shoulder of lamb with minted
pear, venison steak with pepper sauce, fillet of pork with sage, apple
and cider sauce or grilled fillet of salmon with a prawn sauce; for
vegetarians there is lasagne, vegetable cottage pie and cashew nut
paella. Our inspector found the country pâté to be delicious – served
in a small ramekin and carefully seasoned, it arrived with a fresh
salad and good vinaigrette and was generous enough to count as a
snack all on its own. Baked cod with cheese and tomato was enormous, wonderfully fresh and the texture was yielding but not flaky –
'outstanding, quite faultless'. Treacle tart is correctly made with
black treacle, not golden syrup, which an inspector said was his first
sighting in 20 years. An outstanding selection of ales from Bass,
Badger, Cotleigh, Princetown, plus guests, rounds off the picture,
save for the wine list which offers one bottle per country per colour.
SAMPLE DISHES: spinach pancake with savoury mushrooms £3.75;
game casserole £6; toffee pear crumble £3.

Open *Mon to Thur 11.30 to 2.30, 6.30 (7 winter) to 11, Fri and Sat 11.30 to
3, 6 to 11, Sun 12 to 3, 6 (7 winter); bar food 12 to 2, 7 to 9*
Details *Children welcome in family room   Car park   Wheelchair access
Garden and patio   No smoking in family room   Background music   Dogs
welcome   Delta, MasterCard, Switch, Visa   Accommodation: 3 rooms, B&B
£20 to £45*

---

*All details are as accurate as possible at the time of going to press, but
pubs often change hands, and it is wise to check beforehand by
telephone anything that is particularly important to you.*

▲ *White Swan*

Market Place, Pickering YO18 7AA
TEL: (01751) 472288
turn off at roundabout at junction of A169 and A170

At the heart of this charming little market town stands the White Swan, a comfortable stone coaching-inn that has been enthusiastically run by the Buchanan family for the past 14 years. The homely and traditional front bar and adjacent lounge both overlook the main street. Locals congregate in the wood-panelled bar with its open fire, cushioned bench seating and tasteful prints. Both rooms are fairly small so space is at a premium for bar meals. A warm atmosphere prevails, aided by friendly, smartly attired staff who are willing to strike up a conversation and make you feel very welcome. There is an above-average printed menu and changing daily specials appear on the blackboard. Lunchtime bar dishes might be grilled lamb's liver with bacon, or steak and kidney pie. Vegetarian dishes are a speciality and several can be taken as either a starter or a main course. For some reason beetroot tends to be a stranger to British pub menus, but here that oversight is remedied with beetroot fritters served with caramelised onion, mustard cream and herb rice. Root vegetables come in an 'array' with balsamic vinegar, nut oil syrup and capsicum risotto, while tagliatelle is bound with coconut cream and fresh garden mint and served with apple crisps. At dinner you may wish to start off with assiette charcuterie with shaved Parmesan and truffle oil, or a salad of smoked goose breast with endive and citrus fruits, and proceed to pan-fried magret of duck with prunes, Armagnac and orange, or fricassee of rabbit with ham, mushrooms and saffron basmati rice. The pub serves Black Sheep Best Bitter and Special and Hambleton, while the vast 170-strong wine list reflects the Buchanans' interest in the wines of St Emilion, which number some 70 bottles. SAMPLE DISHES: chargrilled platter of vegetables with polenta £3.75; fresh Whitby crab-cakes with seared apple and pesto mayonnaise £5.50; chocolate marquise with coffee-bean sauce £3.

Open *Mon 12 to 11, Tue to Sat 11 to 3, 6 to 11, Sun 12 to 3, 7 to 10.30; bar food 12 to 2.30 (2 winter), 7 to 9.30 (9 winter); 24 to 26 Dec open for L only*
Details *Children welcome in bar eating area   Car park   Wheelchair access Patio   No smoking in restaurant   No music   Dogs welcome   Amex, Delta, MasterCard, Switch, Visa   Accommodation: 12 rooms, B&B £50 to £90*

Report forms are at the back of the book; write a letter if you prefer, or email your pub report to guidereports@which.co.uk.

PICKHILL   North Yorkshire   map 8

▲ *Nag's Head* 🍇

Pickhill YO7 4JG   TEL: (01845) 567391
off A1, 5m SE of Leeming

About a mile off the A1, with Fountains, Jervaulx and Rievaulx
abbeys all close at hand, this much-extended seventeenth-century inn
can be found right in the middle of the village. The pub has been run
since 1972 by the Boyntons, who ensure visitors receive a warm
welcome. While locals favour the tap bar with its collection of jugs
and ties, eating takes place in the more comfortable lounge with its
plush wall benches, and watercolours and oil paintings (for sale) on
the walls. Starters on the wide-ranging menu kick off with soup of the
day and go on to various items featuring mussels, scallops or prawns,
plus spring lamb kebabs, and assorted dim-sum. Among main courses
could be pork chops, pan-fried pigeon breast, or chicken vindaloo,
while puddings might be burnt Oxford cream or knickerbocker glory.
Beers on offer are Theakston Black Bull, Hambleton Bitter, and Black
Sheep Special, plus guest ales. Wine lovers are well served with eight
monthly-changing choices at £2 a glass or £10 a bottle, with the full,
reasonably priced list offering a good selection from around the
world. SAMPLE DISHES: prawns créole £4.75; steamed sea bass with
black bean sauce £12; truffle torte £3.25.

Open *11 to 11, Sun 12 to 10.30; closed 25 Dec; bar food and restaurant 12
to 2, 6 to 10*
Details *Children welcome   Car park   Wheelchair access (also WC)   Garden
and patio   No-smoking area   Background music   Dogs welcome in bedrooms
only   Delta, Diners, MasterCard, Switch, Visa   Accommodation: 15 rooms,
B&B £40 to £55*

PILLEY   Hampshire   map 2

Fleur de Lys

Pilley Street, Pilley SO41 5QB   TEL: (01590) 672158
off A337, 1m NW of Lymington

This charming thatched cottage-style pub has been an inn since 1096
and a list of all the landlords back to 1498 has pride of place at the
entrance. Not surprisingly, an inn of this antiquity is haunted, in this
case by two lively ghosts, one a mischievous but friendly grey-haired
lady. Original features abound: the inglenook was used for smoking
hams until comparatively recently and the tackle can still be seen.
Indeed, they still cook with a cauldron on the open fire in the

winter, serving ancient dishes like rabbit broth and dumplings, and lamb stew. In summer there are barbecues outside. Reporters tell us that service can be pressed when the pub gets particularly busy, which it can, as its character and its home-cooked food have made it very popular.

Order food at the bar either from the printed menu or the specials board. Starters are of the game pâté, hot Brie, pear-and-Stilton-bake variety, with one or two modern touches like filled potato skins or pesto pasta. Traditional-style main courses might be steamed pudding of the day with mash and mushy peas, venison sausages, or fish and chips, while the specials board might produce chicken satay with plum sauce, lamb cutlets marinated in oyster sauce, or pan-fried bream with garlic roast peppers. There's a fair choice for beer-drinkers: Morland Old Speckled Hen, Flowers Original, Marston's Pedigree and Wadworth 6X – as well as Ringwood Best from one of the UK's largest new-wave brewers, also located in the New Forest. The short wine list is reasonably priced, and nine wines are available by the glass. Fleur de Lys is handy for Beaulieu, Bucklers Hard and the New Forest. The nearby church is also worth a visit. SAMPLE DISHES: giant woodland mushrooms filled with garlic butter and Stilton £4.50; escalope of local salmon £9.25; fresh fruit pavlova £5.

Open *Mon to Fri 11.30 to 3, 6 to 11, Sat 11.30 to 4, 6 to 10.30, Sun 11.30 to 4; bar food and restaurant 12 to 2 (2.30 Sat and Sun), 6 (7 Sun) to 9.30* **Details** *Children welcome in eating areas   Car park   Wheelchair access (also WC)   Garden and patio   No-smoking areas   Background music   Dogs welcome   Delta, Diners, MasterCard, Switch, Visa*

PLAYLEY GREEN   Gloucestershire   map 5

Rose & Crown

Playley Green, Redmarley D'Abitot GL19 3NB
TEL: (01531) 650234
on A417, 5m SE of Ledbury

'Bright, uncontrived, very welcoming and with excellent service' is one summing up of this large, cream-washed stone pub by a main road in fine rolling Gloucestershire countryside. Flowers rather than knick-knackery are the penchant of landlady Kathy Bunnett, who lovingly tends the garden, tubs and hanging baskets. Flowers are the ales served, too, although the pub is no longer owned by that brewery, with Flowers Original and one guest beer – perhaps the 'chocolate-liquorice' Tapster's Blackdown Porter from Dorset – on tap, as well as Flowers IPA and Best Bitter available; Weston's Stowford Press is the draught cider. You can eat your meal in one of the two light and airy bar areas to either side of the front door, both with low ceilings, half-panelling and plaster above, or in the no-smoking restaurant area at the back (this is where to go for the Sunday roast). The printed menu points to filled rolls, omelettes, ploughman's and salads (which include home-made coleslaw); black-board specials major on meat, such as 'our ever-popular' lamb and apricot curry, honey-grilled gammon steak, and weekend steaks done in a variety of ways, and whatever fish has been brought in that day – maybe poached salmon fillet, grilled swordfish steak, plaice or halibut. The single vegetarian option might be cauliflower cheese. Customers do not allow puddings to change much either, so the odds of finding lemon and ginger tart, hot apricots in brandy with ice-cream, and chocolate rum crunch are high. SAMPLE DISHES: deep-fried Camembert with redcurrant jelly £4; beef and ale casserole £6.50; summer fruits cheesecake £2.75.

Open *11 to 2.30, 6 to 11, Sun 12 to 3, 7 to 10.30; closed 25 Dec bar food 11.30 to 2.15, 6.15 to 9.15, Sun 12 to 2.30, 6.15 to 9.15, restaurant open on request*
Details *Children welcome in bar eating area   Car park   Garden and patio No smoking in restaurant   Background music   No dogs in restaurant   Delta, MasterCard, Visa*

PLUCKLEY   Kent   map 3

▲ *Dering Arms*

Station Road, Pluckley TN27 0RR
TEL: (01233) 840371
off B2077, close to Pluckley railway station

FISH

The first thing you will notice about this striking, manorial-style building – at one time a hunting-lodge – are the arched, leaded windows. In the seventeenth century a member of the Dering family escaped through a window this shape when pursued by Roundheads, and it was decreed that all buildings built on the estate thereafter should have similar windows; many local houses still do. Inside, the pub is stylish, with a couple of hop-garlanded bars hung with farm-ing artefacts, guns and old prints. The landlord, Jim Buss, is a fish fan and travels to the coast two or three times a week to buy his raw materials; he also prides himself on the vegetables and fruit used in his cooking, some of which are supplied by his father's farm nearby. The specials board is the place to look if you are a fish lover. Start with crab Newburg or potted shrimps, and follow with red bream meunière, a whole crab salad or a simply grilled sole – Dover or lemon. Meat eaters might find rabbit in mustard and ale, or pheasant casseroled in red wine; both should still have room for fresh straw-berries or raspberries in season (or whatever fruit Jim's dad has to offer). The pub also specialises in seasonal game, and in the winter holds a series of black-tie, seven-course gourmet evenings offering food 'customers have often wanted to sample but never had the opportunity'. For example, frogs' legs provençale, estouffade of salmon with a red wine sauce, or snails with cream and hazelnuts. The pub serves ales from long-established microbrewery Goacher's and has a 100-strong wine list. SAMPLE DISHES: herring roes with crispy smoked bacon £4; skate with caper butter £9.75; fruit crumble with ice-cream £2.75.

Open *11 to 3, 6 to 11, Sun 12 to 3, 7 to 11; closed 26 to 28 Dec; bar food and restaurant 11.30 to 2, 7 to 9.30*
Details *Children welcome in eating area of Car park Wheelchair access Garden Occasional live music Dogs welcome Amex, Delta, MasterCard, Visa Accommodation: 3 rooms, B&B £30 to £80*

PLUSH   **Dorset**   **map 2**

Brace of Pheasants

Plush DT2 7RQ   TEL: (01300) 348357
off B3143, 2m N of Piddletrenthide

The long frontage of this very attractive sixteenth-century thatched inn is explained by the fact that it was formerly the village smithy and two adjoining cottages. At the rear is a garden with an aviary; ideal for children, who are not allowed into the characterful bar, with its low beams and massive inglenook. You may find yourself competing for the best position in front of the fire with Mollie and Bodger, the pub Labradors. A printed menu of dishes such as steak with port and Stilton, or game pie, is backed up by a specials board, and regular theme nights provide excellent value: Thursday is 'Curry Nosh' night, while 'Pasta Prego' evening is on Tuesday. A 'Wine and Dine' club meets around ten times a year to enjoy a didactic matching of food and drink, and bin ends from these events are available to take away or drink with your meal. Beers come from Smiles Brewery and Butcombe, and London Pride is also on tap. The regular wine list runs to a dozen choices, of which six are available by the glass. SAMPLE DISHES: crab savoury with sage and garlic topped with cheese and prawns £4; honey-roast chicken on a bed of stir-fried veg £11; summer pudding £4.

Open *12 to 2.30, 7 to 11, Sun 12 to 3, 7 to 10.30; bar food and restaurant 12 to 1.45, 7 to 9.30*
Details *Children welcome Car park Garden and patio No smoking in family room or restaurant No music Dogs welcome on a lead Delta, Mastercard, Switch, Visa*

POLKERRIS   Cornwall   map 1

Rashleigh 🍺   NEW ENTRY

SEASIDE

Polkerris PL24 2TL   TEL: (01726) 813991
off A3082, 2m W of Fowey

Strikingly situated on the edge of an isolated beach, the Rashleigh is frequented largely by people walking along the Cornish Coastal Path who stop off for sustenance during their efforts and by car drivers who know about it and who take a chance of getting into its tiny car park (the village nearby boasts a larger car park). Actually you could go there by boat too, since there is a restored jetty on the beach. The best place to enjoy the view of the beach, and across St Austell and Mevagissey bays, is the terrace, from where glimpses may also be had through small windows of the open, stonewalled, warm and cosy interior of the pub, which is on two levels. A good range of freshly made soups, sandwiches and hot meals is available from a menu headed 'snacks for hungry people'. Daily specials might include venison and bacon pie, seafood lasagne, or chicken curry Hawaii. The pub has a large range of interesting beers, from both nationals and independents, so as well as Bass and Burton Ale you could get Tanglefoot from the Badger Brewery, Old Hooky from Hook Norton, Sharp's Doom Bar, Otter Ale, Lancaster Bomber from Mitchell's, and Hicks Special from St Austell served from the wood. On offer, too, are 37 whiskies, a dozen brandies and a 48-strong wine list with plenty of selections from Australia, Chile, New Zealand and South Africa. SAMPLE DISHES: local mushrooms with pâté £3; chicken with broccoli in a pepper sauce £6.50; banoffi pie £3.

Open *summer 11 to 4.30, 5.30 to 11, Sun 12 to 3, 6.30 to 10.30, winter 11.30 to 2.45, 6.30 to 11, Sun 12 to 3, 6.30 to 10.30; bar food and restaurant 11.30 (12 Sun) to 2.15, 6.30 to 10*
Details *Children welcome in bar eating area   Car park   Wheelchair access Garden and patio   Smoking discouraged in restaurant   Background and live music   No dogs   Delta, MasterCard, Switch, Visa*

PORTHLEVEN   Cornwall   map 1

Ship Inn

Porthleven TR13 9JS   TEL: (01326) 572841
off B3304, 2m SW of Helston, on W side of harbour

Ten out of ten for atmosphere at this 'real local' built into the cliff at
the bottom of the steep harbour road: the rough stone walls are
festooned with nets, rugs lie on bare boards, candles flicker, and a
log fire crackles at each end of the bar. Fighting your way in from
the gales you could easily pretend to be a smuggler, intent on storing
some contraband in a hidey-hole. As if that weren't enough colour,
two ghosts are said to roam: one Mrs Ruberry and a French prisoner
of war; the chatty landlord will no doubt fill you in. Now, calm
down and choose your food. Here they refuse to offer chips but go
in for lots of sandwiches, toasties, ploughman's, crusties (half a leop-
ard loaf) and jacket potatoes, all with a variety of fillings, including
ham, prawn, Stilton and apple or walnut, and the pub's speciality,
crab. A blackboard runs to up to 14 daily specials, many of them
fishy. Everything is prepared to order. Bananas in rum with clotted
cream seems the right sort of pud to have in a smuggler's haunt, and
Sharp's Doom Bar Bitter or Courage Best the right sort of beer for a
pub near treacherous seas; others on offer are Morland Old Speckled
Hen and Greene King Abbot Ale. SAMPLE DISHES: smoked fish platter
ploughman's £7; crab salad £8; steak and kidney pie £7.

Open *11 to 11 (10.30 Sun), 11 to 3.30, 6.30 to 11, Sun winter 12 to 3, 7 to
10.30; bar food 12 to 2.15, 7 to 9 (9.30 summer)*
Details *Children welcome in family room   Garden   Background music   Dogs
welcome   No cards*

POWERSTOCK   Dorset   map 2

Three Horseshoes 🏵 🍇

Powerstock DT6 3TF   TEL: (01308) 485328
off A3066 at Gore Cross, 4m NE of Bridport

Mark and Susan Johnson took over this gabled stone pub in one of
the most striking landscapes in Hardy country in 1997. They have
maintained the former owners' reputation for fish and get their
supplies from catches landed at nearby West Bay and Lyme Regis.
The cooking has become slightly simpler than previously, with the
quality of the ingredients being allowed to do most of the work. The
dining-room and bar offer different menus and ambiences, the
former noted for its views, while the bar is 'tongue and groove' top,

bottom and ceiling, and is warmed by a roaring fire on cold days. Menus and wine lists are chalked on to blackboards which form an integral part of the décor. Fish starters might include grilled Cornish scallops, or gratin of Portland crab, which may tempt you to follow with grilled West Bay lemon sole, or a more piquant John Dory baked with sea salt and lime juice. Non-fish dishes may well feature local game in season, with pigeon breasts frequently appearing. Filled baguettes and ploughman's are also available at lunch-times. The wine list does not favour the whites and offers a healthy New World selection. Beers are well-kept pints of Palmer's Bridport and Best bitters. SAMPLE DISHES: seafood minestrone £5; cracked Lyme Bay crab salad £10.50; walnut and maple syrup flan £3.50.

Open *12 to 3, 6 (7 winter) to 11, Sun 12 to 3, 7 to 10.30; bar food and restaurant Mon to Fri 12 to 2, 7 to 9.30, Sat 12 to 2.30, 7 to 10, Sun 12 to 3, 7 to 9*

Details *Children welcome in bar eating area   Car park   Wheelchair access (also WC)   Garden and patio   No smoking in restaurant   No music   Dogs welcome in bar   Delta, MasterCard, Switch, Visa*

PRESTWOOD   **Buckinghamshire**   map 3

Polecat Inn

170 Wycombe Road, Prestwood HP16 0HJ   TEL: (01494) 862253
on A4128 Great Missenden to High Wycombe road, 2m W of Great Missenden

---

'The garden is very large,' wrote one reporter, 'the car park is very large, the inside is very large.' However, the Polecat Inn manages to maintain a 'cosy' feel because it is spread out over four separate rooms, decked out with stuffed birds and animals in glass cases. Landlord John Gamble and his staff manage to find time to talk to customers even when busy and are keen to stress that dishes are home prepared wherever possible. There is a standard menu which changes twice a year, while the more exotic dishes are chalked up on a daily specials board. A 'standard' starter might be pan-fried garlic mussels, while a specials starter could be twice-baked Stilton soufflé. Similarly, a 'standard' main course might be Cajun spare ribs, as opposed to a specials choice of stewed fillets of brill with potato gnocchi and tartare dressing. The well-priced wine list is arranged in a similar fashion, with a list and 'guest' wines on a board. There is a good vegetarian selection and the pies are made to order. The cooking has been described as light and demonstrating skill, a fact that is reflected in the inn's local popularity (bookings will be accepted only for parties of eight or more). Beers are Theakston Best and XB, Marston's Pedigree, Wadworth 6X and Morland Old Speckled Hen. There is also a selection of approximately

20 malt whiskies. SAMPLE DISHES: smoked duck salad with sage, apple and spring onion salsa £4.50; ragoût of beef and Mediterranean vegetables with pesto crust £8; meringues with caramel sauce £3.50.

Open *11.30 to 2.30, 6 to 11, Sun 12 to 3; bar food all week L 12 to 2, Mon to Sat 6.30 to 9*
Details *Children welcome in family room   Car park   Wheelchair access Garden   No smoking in 1 room   Background music   Dogs welcome   No cards*

PRIORS DEAN   Hampshire   map 2

White Horse Inn 🍺

SETTING

Priors Dean GU32 1DA   TEL: (01420) 588387
from Petersfield, take road signposted Steep and Froxfield for 5m, turn right at crossroads signposted East Tisted, then second right; from A32, 5m S of Alton, turn on to Steep and Froxfield road, left at crossroad, then second right

A Gale's pub, this rambling split-level seventeenth-century village local offers a truly impressive range of cask-conditioned ales. It enjoys a lofty position on downland surrounded by fields; First World War poet Edward Thomas wrote his first published work, 'Up in the Wind', in the area. The pub is known locally as the 'Pub with No Name' because it has no pub sign, and no one has seen fit to rectify this particular oversight. Two rustic parlours are unspoilt by modernity; some might say that they have a rather neglected air, but others would urge that this is all part of the charm. Each has an open fire fronted by old rocking chairs or sofas. The interior is candlelit in the evenings, and the ambience is enhanced by an array of antique furniture – settles, a grandfather clock, prints, farm implements and rugs. The clientele are a local crowd, plus those visitors who eventually manage to find the place. If you are intending to eat, arrive early, especially at weekends. There are lunch and evening blackboards: evening fare might include garlic mushrooms, kidneys in red wine, or Stilton-stuffed pear, and there is an emphasis on one-plate suppers. Ales served are Gale's HSB and Best, Ballard's, Fuller's London Pride, Ringwood Fortyniner, Bass, Wadworth 6X and Marston's Pedigree. The reasonably priced wine list includes about 20 country wines, and ten wines by the glass. SAMPLE DISHES: mussels in white wine £6; shoulder of lamb £8; ginger sponge £3.25.

Open *11 to 2.30, 6 to 11; closed eve 25 Dec; bar food 12 to 2, 7 to 9 (exc Sun eve)*
Details *Children welcome in dining-room   Car park   Wheelchair access (also WC)   Garden and patio   No smoking in dining-room   No music   No dogs in dining-room   Amex, Delta, Diners, MasterCard, Switch, Visa*

RAMSGILL   **North Yorkshire**   **map 8**

▲ *Yorke Arms* ♥♥ ❀   [NEW ENTRY]

Ramsgill HG3 5RL   TEL: (01423) 755243
take the Low Wath road from Pateley Bridge, then 4m to Ramsgill

There is no shortage of plaudits for the Yorke Arms, since Gerald
and Frances Atkins took over in 1997 (after stints in restaurants in
London and Scotland), with reporters approving both the quality of
the cooking and the professionalism of the operation. Once a shooting lodge, built in the eighteenth century, the pub has a grand,
manorial frontage, softened with crimson creepers. Once inside the
pub's thick walls, one finds Gerald Atkins behind his lounge bar,
where you can give him your food order and then settle into spindle-
backed chairs dotted around the room, or move into one of the
warren of small rooms.

Quiet restraint is Frances's forte, with food to be savoured, not
rushed, so you might linger over mushroom and tarragon soup, or
dawdle around a beetroot, feta and walnut salad, both dishes demonstrating an ability to be light and inventive as well as traditional.
Dally over tangy roast grouse with bilberries and whisky sauce, or
muse upon ricotta fritta with artichoke, spring onion and mozzarella.
A lot of thought and imagination goes into food preparation. Beef is
combined with pine-nuts and Stilton, ribbon vegetables and red
wine; or, in a more old-fashioned vein, Nidderdale lamb pie comes
with mash and greens. Seasoned menu watchers will know that
Yorkshire curd tart with rum custard is a bit out of the ordinary, and
that steamed syrup pudding is not – but you may well find both at
the Yorke Arms. Only one real ale is served, Black Sheep Special, but
the wine list is rather more comprehensive, changes quarterly and
does not bother with the 'just-give-me-a-glass-of-wine' approach, but
heads straight into a serious list of wines by the glass: there are six
including a champagne. SAMPLE DISHES: warm salad of black pudding,
poached eggs and apple £5.25; venison steak with celeriac, wild
mushrooms and port sauce £9; chocolate truffle cake £4.25.

Open *11 to 11, Sun 12 to 10.30; bar food and restaurant all week 12 to 1.45
(1 Sun in summer), 7 to 8.45 (exc Sun)*
Details *Children welcome in family room and bar eating area   Car park
Wheelchair access   Garden and patio   No smoking in restaurant   Background
music   No dogs   Amex, Delta, MasterCard, Switch, Visa   Accommodation:
13 rooms, B&B £55 to £120*

---

*After the main section of the Guide is the special 'Out and about'
section listing additional pubs that are well worth a visit. Reports on
these entries are most welcome.*

RATTERY   Devon   map 1

Church House Inn

Rattery TQ10 9LD   TEL: (01364) 642220
1m off A385, from A38 S of Ashburton, 4m W of Totnes

This ancient inn has achieved special status as a building of outstanding historical and architectural interest. It dates from 1028, when it
was built as a rest home for monks, and later it was used by the
builders of the Norman church next door. The surrounding village,
too, is charming, and full of classic Devon cottages. The pub itself,
though altered over the centuries, with its original small rooms now
amalgamated into one long bar, boasts quaint beams, exposed
stonework and plenty of taproom bric-à-brac. Historical photographs
of the village and its inhabitants deck the walls. An arched doorway
conceals a spiral staircase thought to date from 1030. Dartmoor
Best, Greene King Abbot Ale and Marston's Pedigree feature among
the handpumps, along with a long and global selection of wines, and
some decent malts. Food ranges from filled rolls and ploughman's
lunches to more unusual dishes chalked on blackboards: venison
casserole, deep-fried seafood parcels, turkey escalopes or lamb in
garlic and ginger with apricots. Puddings might be mixed fruit crumble, chocolate mousse or a fruit pie. SAMPLE DISHES: smoked trout
and prawn pâté £3.50; chicken jambalaya £7.50; strawberry and
kiwi meringue surprise £3.50.

Open *11 to 2.30, 6 (6.30 Jan and Feb) to 11, Sun 12 to 2.30, 7 to 10.30; bar
food and restaurant 12 to 2, 7 to 9 (8.30 in winter, 10.30 Fri and Sat)*
Details *Children welcome in eating areas   Car park   Wheelchair access (also
WC)   Patio   No music   Dogs welcome   No cards*

RATTLESDEN   Suffolk   map 6

Brewers Arms

Lower Road, Rattlesden IP30 0RJ   TEL: (01449) 736377
off A14, 5m W of Stowmarket

During the Second World War, the pub was a popular haunt of the
airmen of the USAF, who, like visitors today, probably found it a
fine spot to drive out to in summer. Naturally, the food has
improved since those days, especially under the stewardship of
foodie triumvirate Jeff and Nina Chamberlain and assistant chef
Paddy Allen, whose weekly-changing menus aim to feature dishes
from around the world. 'We do not do chips or have a children's
menu' (though children are welcome), writes Jeff Chamberlain, who

instead may deliver pork steak and apple, or Thai red prawn curry, plus desserts such as Greek yoghurt with honey and toasted flaked almonds. The wine list is less cosmopolitan, with only four non-French wines featuring on the 15-bottle list; three wines are available by the glass. Beers on offer are Greene King IPA and Abbot Ale, and Morland Old Speckled Hen. The pub itself is of interest. A glance at the interior shows it is clearly older than the exterior suggests, with genuine beams and original brickwork once more on display. SAMPLE DISHES: shish kebab with spicy yoghurt dressing £4.25; chicken breast with sour cream and paprika sauce £8.50; toffee and banana sponge £3.95.

Open *Tue to Sat 12 to 3, 6.30 to 11, Sun 12 to 3, 7 to 10.30; bar food and restaurant Tue to Sun L 12.30 to 2, Wed to Sat D 7 to 9.45*
Details *Children welcome in bar eating areas   Car park   Wheelchair access Garden   Background music   Dogs welcome   No smoking in restaurant Access, Amex, Switch, Visa*

R E D E   Suffolk   map 6

Plough

Rede IP29 4BE   TEL: (01284) 789208
off A143 Bury St Edmunds to Haverhill road

At the end of one of the small roads in the pretty village of Rede, noted for its traditional working farm with heavy horses, this attractive pub is in a beautiful setting, with pale pink walls and a thatched roof and garden in front. This is not a drinkers' pub, and both bar and restaurant are set out for eating. The bar is filled with small wooden tables with pink banquettes against the walls, and in the restaurant diners are seated at 'olde tea shoppe' chairs. Atmosphere is generated by the log fire and varnished black beams. This Greene King pub serves the usual range of bitter, plus their quarterly seasonal ales (dispensed under pressure, rather than by handpump or gravity). Wines are listed on a blackboard in the dining-room. There may be as many as 38 dishes on the menu, divided into four sections – vegetarian, fish, grills and meat. Cooking is very traditional but with an eye for what is fashionable, and there is a large range of daily-changing fresh fish dishes. Plaice, salmon, sole, monkfish Creole, seafood Mornay and crab au gratin might be there. Meat dishes could include Napoleon beef (as opposed to Wellington, presumably) in brandy and wild mushroom sauce, or honeyed pork with whole-grain mustard and honey sauce, or Tuscany lamb in a rich tomato, garlic and herb sauce. Grilled steaks are a house speciality. SAMPLE DISHES: smoked scallops with spinach and bacon £9;

braised pheasant in calvados and apple sauce £9; pecan and maple tart £3.

Open *11 to 3, 7 to 11, Sun 12 to 3, 7 to 10.30; bar food and restaurant 12 to 1.45, 7 to 9*
Details *Children welcome   Car park   Wheelchair access (also WC)   Garden Background music   No dogs   Amex, Delta, MasterCard, Switch, Visa*

REDMILE   Leicestershire   map 5

▲ *Peacock Inn* ❦ ❧
Main Street, Redmile NG13 0GA   TEL: (01949) 842554
off A52, 7m W of Grantham

The Crawfords have recently acquired the Finch's Arms in Hambleton (see entry), and fans of the Peacock may wish to see the formula of good, modern continental cooking in a traditional English inn environment replicated there. This splendid, tasteful inn is beautifully furbished and full of charm and character. Although it is a smart dining establishment, the bars have a civilised pubby atmosphere, and drinkers can quaff pints of excellent Timothy Taylor Landlord, or Tetley, as well as guests from Greene King, Adnams and Theakston. The same menu runs throughout the pub, so you can either eat in front of the fire in the bar or reserve a table in the spacious modern conservatory-style restaurant. Sandwiches are available in the bar at lunch-time only.

Cooking has a strong Mediterranean character, so duck liver and grape pâté will come on a toasted brioche with tossed salad leaves in walnut oil, or a tartlet of fresh salmon confit will be glazed with a warm caper and tomato sabayon. The French influence will carry through to a risotto of wild mushrooms and garlic roasted chestnuts, escalope of turkey breast, pan fried in nut butter with a fig and armagnac sauce, or a complex-sounding seared fillet of sea bass on olive oil mash scented with horseradish and celeriac with roast veal jus. After that indulge yourself with a romantic panache of dark and white chocolate mousse cake served with chocolate sauce, or a rarely seen crème caramel with a marinated orange salad. Relax and digest with a range of teas, coffees, liquor coffees and brandies after you have finished your wine picked from a heavily pro-French list, although with a smattering of New World representatives and around a dozen by the glass. SAMPLE DISHES: Thai-spiced fish-cakes £6; noisette of pork fillet wrapped in smoked bacon, with prune and red-wine sauce £13; iced apricot and tangerine parfait with blackcurrant coulis, served with almond shortbread biscuits £4.

Open *11 to 11; bar food and restaurant 12 to 2.30, 7 to 9.30 (9 Sun)*
Details *Children welcome   Car park   Wheelchair access (also WC)   Garden
and patio   No smoking in restaurant; no-smoking area in bar   Background
music   No dogs   Delta, MasterCard, Switch, Visa   Accommodation: 8 rooms,
B&B £65 to £90*

RIDGEWELL   Essex   map 6

White Horse 🍺 🍇

Mill Road, Ridgewell CO9 4SG   TEL: (01440) 785532
on A604, 10m N of Halstead

The landlord of this East Anglian village pub says he doesn't allow
dogs, and unknown children only 'if they are on a lead'! But this
unusual injunction (which may well please a substantial proportion
of clients) is probably a bark rather than a bite, for he is described as
'very obliging' and service as 'efficient and courteous'. The village
itself is notably pretty, with thatched cottages and a village green.
The pub stands on the main road skirting the village, and is decked
with flowers in summer. Since the local post office closed, it has
taken on the unusual sideline of selling stamps, in addition to
decently prepared food and a wide, constantly varying range of well-
kept ales from near and far – around 70 different guest beers during
the year. Bottled beers hail from the Nethergate Brewery (Old
Growler or Umbel Ale), and a serious wine list changes frequently,
with quality rather than price being uppermost; they are all offered
by the glass and bottle. Regular dishes include 'properly made'
chicken curry (with spices, rather than powder), lots of fresh fish on
Friday nights, and traditional Sunday roast beef with home-made
Yorkshire pudding. Sandwiches are made with locally baked bread.
SAMPLE DISHES: deep fried mushrooms stuffed with cream cheese
£3.75; steak and ale pie £5.50; apple crumble £2.

Open *11 to 3, 6 to 11, Sun 12 to 3, 7 to 11; closed 25 Dec; bar food 12 to
2.15, 7 to 9.45; restaurant Sun 12 to 2.15, Wed to Sat 7 to 9.45*
Details *Children welcome   Car park   Wheelchair access (also WC)   Garden
and patio   Background and live music   No dogs   Delta, Diners, MasterCard,
Switch, Visa*

Old Bridge Inn 🍺 ❦

Priest Lane, Ripponden HX6 4DF
TEL: (01422) 822595
off A58, 6m S of Halifax

Unusual food arrangements operate at this ancient early fourteenth-century pub – a help-yourself fixed-price buffet at lunch-time, and blackboards in the evenings and at weekends; while for a more formal meal you can take the shortest of strolls over the packhorse bridge to the restaurant. Top marks for setting: the long, low building by the church is painted white, the road and the bridge are cobbled, and the splashing of the river somehow lets you forget the nearby A58. Inside, a fragrant log fire burns in each of the three bar areas, which are comfortable with large, well-spaced tables, pleasing upholstery, metalwork lamps, copper kettles and porcelain. Blackboard choices might be the soup of the day or mushrooms parisienne to start, with a hotpot, meat pie, pasta bake or savoury pancake to follow. Meatballs with garlic bread or smoked haddock and spinach Mornay could be other choices, and if you fancy something afterwards with the words 'sticky' and/or 'toffee' in its title you will not be disappointed. Clark's, Black Sheep Best, and Timothy Taylor Golden Best and Landlord, are joined by a weekly guest; the pub also does a nice line in unusual bottled beers. The bar wine list only extends to some 15 bottles, but the restaurant's extensive 100-bottle list can be requested; 13 of the wines are available by the glass and are good partners for the food. SAMPLE DISHES: deep-fried Camembert £3.50; chicken, broccoli and Stilton pie £5; sticky oatmeal parkin with ginger sauce £2.50.

Open *Mon to Fri 12 to 3, 5.30 to 11, Sat 12 to 11, Sun 12 to 10.30; closed 25 Dec; bar food 12 to 2, 6 to 9.30; restaurant Tue to Sat 7 to 9*
Details *Children welcome in bar eating area   Car park   Wheelchair access Patio   No music   No dogs   MasterCard, Visa*

Jack in the Green ✿ 🍺 ❦

London Road, Rockbeare EX5 2EE   TEL: (01404) 822240
on A30, Exeter to Honiton road, 3m NE of Exeter

'Classy pub food with all the right modern touches' is how one reporter summed up the strength of this neat, well-maintained roadside pub. The menu changes monthly and offers a selection of fashionable dishes ranging from venison haunch steak with bubble and squeak, to grilled red mullet with pancetta, sage and garlic butter, or warm chicken and bacon salad with fried mushrooms and balsamic dressing, and always at least 12 versions of ploughman's. There are separate menus for Sunday lunch, as well as a bar snacks menu serving up old favourites like macaroni cheese, or braised faggots, or a lighter pitta bread with chicken strips, basil, tomato, cashew nuts, mayonnaise and chips. There is also a fixed-price restaurant menu. The wine list is extensive and informatively annotated. The 100 or so bins are reasonably priced, but include a smattering of more expensive selections, with 12 available by the glass. Cotleigh Tawny, Otter Ale and Teignworthy sit next to Bass and Hardys on the bar alongside other local brews. Like many in this part of the world, this pub boasts a skittles alley. SAMPLE DISHES: lamb and apricot pie £5.75; duck kebabs with tomato salsa and potato wedges £7.25; iced banana parfait £3.25.

Open *Mon to Thu 11 to 2.30, 6 to 11, Fri and Sat 11 to 3, 6 to 11, Sun 11 to 3, 7 to 10.30; closed 25 to 27 Dec; bar food and restaurant 12 to 2 (2.30 Fri to Sun), 6 to 9.30 (10 Fri and Sat)*
Details *Children welcome in eating areas and games room   Car park Wheelchair access (also WC)   Patio   No-smoking area   Background music No dogs   Delta, MasterCard, Switch, Visa*

ROCKBOURNE   Hampshire   map 2

Rose & Thistle 🍇

Rockbourne SP6 3NL   TEL: (01725) 518236
off B3078, 3m NW of Fordingbridge

The Rose & Thistle is an attractive sixteenth-century thatched pub, originally two cottages, set in rolling countryside, with a pleasant garden set out with bench tables and umbrellas for summer eating. Inside, there is a wealth of beams in the two interconnecting rooms, which both have log fires in winter. The bar area has barrel chairs and stools, while the comfortable dining-room has polished oak tables and low-backed settles, with old pictures and brasses adding character. Lunchtime menus range from soup of the day, scrambled eggs with smoked salmon, or Welsh rarebit, to main courses of lamb's liver and bacon or various steaks. Daily blackboard and fish specials add items such as game pies, seafood tagliatelle, monkfish, sea bass and John Dory. More sophisticated dishes in the evening might be wild boar terrine, or warm goats'-cheese salad, followed by Deben duck breast, or pork fillet in apricot and brandy sauce. Puddings vary from sticky toffee to lemon mousse with kiwi fruit. Draught beers on offer include Theakston XB, Marston's Pedigree and Morland Old Speckled Hen. Six wines are £2.50 for a 1.75cl glass or £9.50 a bottle, while the main list offers a good selection from around the world. SAMPLE DISHES: broccoli and cheese pancake £4.50; loin of pork with Dijon mustard sauce £9; rum truffle torte £2.75.

Open *11 to 3, 6 to 11, Sun 12 to 3, 7 to 10.30; bar food and restaurant 12 to 2.30, 7 to 9.30*
Details *Children welcome　Car park　Wheelchair access　Garden　No-smoking area　No music　No dogs in restaurant　Delta, MasterCard, Switch, Visa*

ROMALDKIRK　　Co Durham　　　　　　　　　　**map 10**

▲ *Rose and Crown* 🍴 🍇
Romaldkirk DL12 9EB　TEL: (01833) 650213
on B6277, 6m NW of Barnard Castle

'In lonely and beautiful Teesdale there sits this old village inn,' wrote one reporter, adding, 'we felt it to be welcoming, comfortable and efficient and offering good-value accommodation; it was a pleasant place to keep warm on a December night.' Built in 1733, the Rose and Crown still retains much of the feel of its days as a coaching-inn. Chef/licensee Christopher Davy's cooking at its best is excellent. His menu follows the seasons and uses local produce in dishes such as chargrilled sausages with black pudding, and 'Mr Cooke-Hurle's smoked chicken' with lardons and salad, or weekly-changing blackboard specials such as pan-fried breast of wood pigeon, though lighter Mediterranean touches also appear. Local Cotherstone cheese is a popular ingredient, used in dishes ranging from ploughman's to monkfish tails to gnocchi. The separate restaurant offers a good-value set-price dinner menu with a similar style. Beers offered are Theakston Best and Marston's Pedigree; an above-average selection of wines is available by the glass from a list which features both New and Old Worlds. SAMPLE DISHES: Greenland prawns with brandied tomato and fresh herb sauces £6; sauté chicken livers with smoked bacon, roasted walnuts and sherry £6; dark chocolate torte with two sauces £3.25.

Open *11.30 to 3, 5.30 to 11, Sun 12 to 3, 7 to 10.30; closed eve 25, 26 and 31 Dec; bar food 12 to 1.30, 6.30 to 9.30; restaurant Sun L 12 to 1.30, Mon to Sat D 7.30 to 9*
Details *Children welcome　Car park　Wheelchair access (also WC)　Patio No smoking in restaurant　No music　No dogs　MasterCard, Switch, Visa Accommodation: 12 rooms, B&B £62 to £90*

ROSEDALE ABBEY   North Yorkshire   map 9

▲ *White Horse Farm Hotel*

Rosedale Abbey YO18 8SE   TEL: (01751) 417239   **VIEWS**
on A170 turn right signposted Wrelton and Rosedale,
3m NW of Pickering

High up in Rosedale overlooking the moors, with spectacular views
from the front terrace, the White Horse is an old stone building
which has been a hotel for nearly 300 years. The bar is stone-walled
and beamed, with a collection of farming implements, stuffed birds,
horse harnesses and animal heads, while the separate restaurant
(open in the evening and for the Sunday roast lunch) is decorated in
blue and red. Yorkshire fare features strongly, a particular speciality
being a giant Yorkshire pudding filled with onion gravy and with or
without the chef's roast. Starters and 'lite bites' might be soup,
chicken liver and whisky pâté or White Horse Brie (breadcrumbed,
deep-fried and served with apricot conserve); sandwiches and salads
are also available. From the grill come steaks, chops or bangers and
mash, while other main courses could be salmon fillet, steak and
kidney pie or coq au vin. Under-13s have their own menu. The
restaurant offers three- and four-course set-price menus: perhaps
smoky mussels, followed by home-made soup, then duck confit and
ending with cheese or a sweet. Puddings are of the crumble and
crêpe variety. Beers come from Black Sheep, John Smith and
Theakston, plus there is a big choice of malt whiskies. The 30-bottle
wine list has six house wines by the litre, half-litre bottle and two
sizes of glass. SAMPLE DISHES: calamaris provençale £3.25; mixed grill
£10; bread-and-butter pudding £2.50.

Open *summer 11 to 11; winter 11.30 to 2.30, 6.30 to 11; Sun all year 12 to
2.30, 6.30 to 10.30; bar food 12 to 2 (3 Sun), 6.30 to 9 (10 summer);
restaurant Mon to Sat D 7 to 8.45, Sun L 12 to 2.30*
Details *Children welcome in family room   Car park   Garden and patio   No
smoking in restaurant   Background and live music   Dogs welcome   Amex,
Delta, Diners, MasterCard, Switch, Visa   Accommodation: 20 rooms, B&B
£35 to £87*

George & Dragon 🏵️🏵️ 🍺 🍇

High Street, Rowde SN10 2PN   TEL: (01380) 723053

A couple of miles from Devizes is the village of Rowde, and in the centre of the village on a bend of the road is the yellow pebble-dashed George & Dragon. The interior is deceptively small, with a bar area selling locally produced microbrewery beers now that Tim and Helen Withers have turned the pub into a freehouse. To the right of the bar is a small, cosy, bare-boarded restaurant, and while locals come and play cribbage before the fire, diners arrive for the spankingly fresh fish dishes that have given the pub its reputation.

Delivered daily, fish is well presented and delivered to table by efficient, well-informed, white-aproned staff. Reporters have endorsed main courses of skate with capers and black butter, steamed sea bass with ginger, stir-fried monkfish with bacon and crème fraîche, and fried squid with lemon and garlic. For non-fish-eaters there might be cheese soufflé, lamb curry, or a plate of local ham (or cheese) with salad, bread and pickles. Puddings are home-made and might feature pear poached in red wine with cinnamon, or ricotta al caffé. Good, bitter coffee is served with fudge cubes. In addition to the draught beers, there is Nadder Valley draught cider and an above-average selection of bottled beers from west country brewers as well as some German and Belgian favourites. The helpfully annotated wine list offers some classy – if expensive – drinking but also includes a helpful smattering of half-bottles and ten wines by the glass. There is a good selection of malts, cognacs, armagnacs and liqueurs. SAMPLE DISHES: 'fishy hors d'oeuvres' £5; red gurnard baked with cider and cheese £9; chocolate torte and coffee bean sauce £4.50.

Open *Tue to Sun 12 to 3, 7 to 11 (10.30 Sun); closed 25 Dec and 1 Jan; bar food and restaurant Tue to Sat 12 to 2, 7 to 10*
Details *Children welcome   Car park   Garden   No smoking in restaurant No music   Dogs welcome in bar only   Delta, MasterCard, Switch, Visa*

▲ *Three Acres Inn* 🏵️ 🍇

Roydhouse HD8 8LR   TEL: (01484) 602606
off B6116 (from A629), 1m E of Kirkburton

'A place one could feel comfortable going to on one's own', wrote one reporter, which may be just as well if you wish to avoid the waitresses 'cornering at high speed' at this busy former coaching-inn with stunning Pennine views. Cooking is fairly modern with plenty of pan frying and chargrilling, and there is an ice-laden seafood counter in the main bar area where brisk turnover ensures freshness. The latter offers a fruits de mer platter, costing as much as an entire meal, but it does contain lobster, crab claws, clams, crevettes, oysters, scallops, mussels and langoustine. At half the price you can have coquilles St Jacques, or fresh chargrilled Loch Fyne queenie scallops with Gruyère. Alternatively the busy kitchen will send out crispy Japanese chicken with wok fried greens, thread noodles and sweet chilli sauce as a starter, or Iranian Sevruga caviar on melba toast with crème fraîche – not something seen on many pub menus. The modern theme may be continued in the form of twice-cooked crispy belly pork with aubergines and bok choi on more thread noodles, or pepper crusted rump of beef with Roquefort butter and oyster mushrooms. For those not wanting a restaurant-sized bill, the large range of sandwiches may be more appropriate. Everything from chip butties or steak to locally smoked salmon is on offer. Brown-bread ice-cream is another modern touch, but crème brûlée and summer pudding are a bit more trad. The real ales consist of Timothy Taylor Landlord, Adnams Bitter, Morland Old Speckled Hen and Mansfield Bitter. There is a range of malts and cognacs, and the wine list, with around six by the glass (including the house champagne) is clearly aimed at those who can tell fine wine from plonk. SAMPLE DISHES: six Irish oysters £7; charcuterie with Mediterranean salad £8.25; chocolate tart and orange crème anglaise £4.25.

Open *12 to 3, 7 to 11 (11.30 Sat, 10.30 Sun); closed 25 Dec; bar food and restaurant 12 to 2, 6.45 to 9.45*
Details *Children welcome in eating areas   Car park   Wheelchair access Patio   Background music   No dogs   Amex, Delta, Diners, MasterCard, Switch, Visa   Accommodation: 19 rooms, B&B £40 to £65*

R U D G E   Somerset   map 2

▲ *Full Moon*   [NEW ENTRY]

Rudge BA11 2QF   TEL: (01373) 830936
off A36/A361, NE of Frome

This old cider house is worth a visit for its peaceful location, warm welcome and relaxed atmosphere, with fresh, simple food and good ales to boot. The front garden is the place to sit and watch the horses, walkers and cyclists go by. In both the main bar and the taproom you will find a happy mix of adults and children, most of whom will be tucking into a full menu; one visitor recommends reserving a table in the very pretty taproom with its fireplace and flagstoned floors. The menu contains many pub staples, such as baguettes and jacket potatoes, lasagne, pâté and steaks, as well as more exciting specials on the blackboard, perhaps venison, swordfish or a spicier dish. Fish is very popular, and daily-changing puddings might include chocolate mousse, honey and plum cheesecake and banoffi pie. Ales on offer are Bass, Butcombe and London Pride, with cider from Thatcher's, and the ten-strong wine list with five by the glass is put together by Stowells of Chelsea. SAMPLE DISHES: caramelised red onion tart £5; tenderloin of pork medallions in sweet sherry and Dijon mustard sauce £11; sticky toffee pudding with butterscotch sauce £3.25.

Open *12 to 3, 6 to 11, Sun 7 to 10.30; bar food 12 to 2.30, 6 to 9.30 (7 Sun)*
Details *Children welcome   Car park   Wheelchair access (also WC)   Garden No music   Dogs welcome on a lead   Amex, Delta, MasterCard, Switch, Visa Accommodation: 5 rooms, B&B £40 to £70*

RUSHLAKE GREEN   East Sussex   map 3

Horse and Groom   NEW ENTRY

Rushlake Green TN21 9QE   TEL: (01435) 830320
off B2096, 4m SE of Heathfield

Sue and Mike Chappell, who run the Star at Old Heathfield (see entry), took over here in August 1998, and if their other pub is anything to go by we can expect good things. The pub, slightly run down outside, is right on the green – you can understand why the village is called Rushlake Green, with more green than houses. Note, however, that the pub is slightly below the road and set back, and when cars are parked along the roadside they can easily obscure it. Inside, there are two little bars in a cosy, traditional style, with horse brasses, rural prints and black and white photographs of the village, and a log fire in one room. The menus are displayed on blackboards right at the entrance, which caused a logjam on the day we visited. If you get to the front you might catch sight of fish pie, steak and kidney pie, local pheasant, venison, Hastings cod and chips, mussels or salmon goujons, reflecting both the pub's rural location and its proximity to the sea. Our inspector enjoyed an 'excellent' smoked salmon fillet and thought the staff were charming and professional. Wines are taken seriously and the list appears well chosen, while Harveys Bitter, Greene King IPA and a guest from a major regional are on offer for the ale lover. SAMPLE DISHES: kedgeree £4.50; half a roast duckling with intense honey and ginger sauce £10.50; cappuccino jelly £4.

Open *11.30 to 3, 6 to 11, Sun 12 to 3, 7 to 10.30; bar food 11.30 to 2.30 (Sun from 12), 7 to 9.30*
Details *Children welcome   Car park   Wheelchair access   Garden and patio Background music   Dogs welcome   Delta, MasterCard, Switch, Visa*

R Y E   **East Sussex**   **map 3**

Ypres Castle

Gun Garden, Rye TN31 7HH   TEL: (01797) 223248
behind Ypres Tower Museum in centre of Rye

Many points go to make this seventeenth-century freehouse a place
of distinction. Take its situation, for instance, behind the Ypres
Tower, four centuries its senior, which now houses a museum of
local history, and from which there are even better views to Rye
Harbour than from the pub's sheltered terrace and garden. Or take
the half-dozen fine cask-conditioned ales, from dark to mild, including Charles Wells Bombardier, Adnams Broadside and local Pett
Progress from the Old Forge Brewer. Another unusual feature is the
32-bottle wine list which includes an excellent choice of 16 by the
glass. Add to this the fact that for part of the summer the pub serves
food all day, including late into the evening.

And then there is the food itself, much of it reliant on local
produce. Start with soup, say tomato, basil and orange, or with
several fishy starters, such as crab terrine or prawn brochettes. Main
courses are mostly based on meat or fish – Marsh lamb in a red wine
and rosemary gravy, pork loin escalopes with orange and mustard
sauce, and queen scallops marinière exemplify the style. Other fish,
including squid, sea bass, smoked cod and brill, show up periodi-
cally. Vegetarians should find something appetising among the pastas
and, like others, will appreciate that all main courses are served with
stir-fried vegetables and a choice of potatoes – jacket, roast, gratin,
chips. Traditional pub fare of filled baguettes, jacket potatoes and
ploughman's are all available. Puddings also cut a dash, such as treacle and walnut tart or black cherry cheesecake. Sunday lunch is a
carvery meal including a choice of roasts. SAMPLE DISHES: garlic
mushrooms £4; minty lamb and vegetable pie £7.75; apple and
blackberry pie £3.25.

Open *12 to 11 (10.30 Sun); closed eve 25 Dec; bar food 12 to 2.30, 7 to
10.30 (all day at certain times in summer)*
Details *Children welcome in family room   Garden   Background and live
music   Dogs welcome on a lead   Amex, Delta, MasterCard, Switch, Visa*

ST MARGARET'S AT CLIFFE　　Kent　　　map 3

▲ *Cliffe Tavern*

High Street, St Margaret's at Cliffe CT15 6AT
TEL: (01304) 852400
off A258 Dover to Deal road, 4m NE of Dover

The Cliffe Tavern is a sprawling, white, weatherboarded building which has been considerably extended from the original sixteenth-century house; it has previously been a shoemaker's shop, a corn merchant's, and an 'academy for young gentlemen', and became a hotel in 1887. Situated in the heart of this picturesque village on top of the cliffs just north of Dover, the inn is open all day and also offers morning coffee and cream teas. The interior consists of a main bar, smaller rear bar/eating area and dining-room, plus a walled garden. Old-fashioned posters and pictures decorate the walls. The bar menu offers traditional pub fare of soup, hot filled baguettes, curry of the day and so on, but the best bet is to look at the daily blackboard specials. Here you might find half a dozen fish options – plaice in prawn and caper sauce perhaps, or prawn and seaweed stir-fry – plus dishes such as pork and beef with stir-fried noodles. The 'Beef 'n' Reef' menu presents more fish, as well as grilled steaks of all types, with a couple of vegetarian options (vegetable samosa maybe, or cheese bake) thrown in for good measure. Desserts might be apple pie, sherry trifle or steamed puddings of various kinds. Three or four regularly changing real ales are available, plus three wines by the glass. The inn is a useful stop when using the Channel ports or visiting Dover Castle. SAMPLE DISHES: soup with crusty bread £2.50; moules marinière £4.75; coffee and hazelnut gâteau £3.50.

Open *11 to 11, Sun 12 to 10.30; bar food 12 to 2.30, 7 to 9.30; restaurant Thu to Sat D only 7 to 10*
Details *Children welcome in eating areas　Car park　Garden　Background and live music　No dogs in restaurant　Diners, MasterCard, Switch, Visa Accommodation: 12 rooms, B&B £40 to £55*

SAWLEY　　Lancashire　　　　　　　　　map 9

▲ *Spread Eagle* ✿ ✿ ❦ [NEW ENTRY]

Sawley BB7 4NH
TEL: (01200) 441202
off A59, 4m NE of Clitheroe

The Spread Eagle had a reputation in the '50s and '60s as a pioneer of good pub food under its former owner Geoffrey Truman, but lapsed into microwaved decline after his death. It was rescued in summer 1997, by Steven and Marjorie Doherty of the Punch Bowl, Crosthwaite (see entry), which they still operate. Steven is a chef of considerable ability, having earned a reputation as Albert Roux's 'enforcer' at Le Gavroche in London, but do not be fooled into thinking the Spread Eagle is yet another pub that has been transformed into a restaurant. It remains a pub, but one that serves modern British food of superior quality at prices that would make his old Gavroche colleagues weep. Going through the front door, you enter a comfortable lounge bar where you can have a drink while studying the menus – there are several – and once you have ordered you will be shown into the large, split-level dining-room, dominated by four large picture windows giving spectacular views of the Ribble Valley.

Menus are short and change according to time of day and day of the week. In the evening, prices on the specials menu vary depending on the time; so arrive early – and be sure to book. Meals do not come much more pubby – or fashionable, ironically enough – than sausages and mash, though baked aubergine and polenta is, perhaps, a dish that has travelled north with the Dohertys. There may also be gravad lax, or red onion tart, alongside chicken liver parfait and pea and ham soup. Grilled breast of duck comes in Chinese five spice, with wholewheat noodles and oyster mushrooms, and chicken breast comes in Thai green curry sauce with rice. If you want to avoid the spices then look out for chicken schnitzel, pan-fried with lemon parsley butter. Puddings are where good chefs get to have fun; poached meringue on vanilla custard with caramel and almonds is clearly something you are unlikely to find anywhere else, even if lemon crème brûlée is. Black Sheep Bitter makes a first-rate regular beer, and guests may come from major regionals or local independents such as Dent. An 'ungreedy' wine list includes bottles of individuality and quality and is rather better than at many restaurants. Fifteen wines are available by the half-bottle and several by the glass. SAMPLE DISHES: smoked salmon blini £5; baked salmon fillet in creamy wine and dill sauce £8; fudge brownie with ice-cream £3.25.

Open *11 to 11, Sun 11 to 10.30; closed 25 and 26 Dec, eve 1 Jan; bar food Sun to Fri 12 to 2, 6 to 9, Sat 6.30 to 9.15*
Details *Children welcome   Car park   Wheelchair access (also WC)   Garden No smoking in dining area   No music   No dogs   Amex, Delta, MasterCard, Switch, Visa   Accommodation: 10 rooms, £35 to £60*

Prices quoted in an entry are based on information supplied by the pub, rounded up to the nearest 25 pence. These prices may have changed since publication and are meant only as a guide.

SAWLEY   **North Yorkshire**   map 9

Sawley Arms

Sawley, nr Ripon HG4 3EQ   TEL: (01765) 620642
off B6265 Pateley Bridge to Ripon road, 5m SW of Ripon

June Hawes has been running the Sawley Arms since 1969, and as
long as she continues to do so, in the words of one, 'it will remain
constant, offering a short and satisfying menu of home-cooked
dishes, a warm welcome and a pub that is ablaze with colour in
summer.' Colourful it certainly is. The building resembles a private
house and on either side of the low stone porch are countless tubs
and urns, heavy with foliage and flowers. At the rear is a walled
garden which has won several awards. The interior is comprised of
four interconnecting rooms with armchairs and wall benches, creating a homely atmosphere. A short menu emphasises the home-made
nature of the food. Salmon mousse, and duck liver pâté in tangy
Cumberland sauce are typical starters. Halibut steak in prawn and
white wine sauce, and sauté breast of chicken in mushroom and herb
sauce are indicative too. Theakston ales and John Smith's are the
hardy perennial brews in this part of Yorkshire, and three wines are
served by the glass in addition to a selection of malt whiskies. The
pub is a short walk from Fountains Abbey. SAMPLE DISHES: cream of
pea, mint and lemon soup £2.75; home-made steak pie with butter-
crust pastry £8.50; crème caramel £3.25.

Open *11.30 to 3, 6.30 to 11, Sun 11.30 to 3; closed Mon eve in winter; bar
food and restaurant 11.30 to 2.15, 6.30 to 9*
Details *Car park   Wheelchair access (also WC)   Garden   No smoking in
restaurant   Background music   No dogs   Delta, MasterCard, Switch, Visa*

SAXTON   **North Yorkshire**   map 9

Plough Inn

Headwell Lane, Saxton LS24 9PB   TEL: (01937) 557242
off A162, between Tadcaster and Sherburn in Elmet

Located in the tiny village of Saxton, the Plough is nevertheless a
frequently very busy place – testimony to its far-reaching reputation
for quality restaurant-standard food delivered in a friendly pub
atmosphere. The small bar is simply decorated with wallpaper and
prints, while the dining-room is deep-red throughout, with drapes,
candles, polished tables and polished glass. The overall effect is one
of unelaborate confidence. Service is genuinely polite, attentive and
pleasant, and Nicky and Simon Treanor clearly inspire loyalty in

staff, who tend to stay. The same menu applies in both the lounge and the restaurant, but in the evening food is served only in the restaurant, as the bar is rather small.

The menu is very appealing, imaginative and varied, and you can either dine cheaply or push the boat out. Melted goats' cheese sits on half a red pepper, also stuffed with chopped pepper and all served warm with a delicious oily dressing. You could start with a chilled gazpacho with fresh basil and Parmesan, or maybe seafood parcel in lobster sauce or go East for Thai spiced spring rolls with a chilli dipping sauce. Follow with tender braised lamb shank, or 'perfectly cooked' fillet of salmon. Other options might include fillet of venison with bubble and squeak cake and juniper butter jus, or pan-fried calf's liver with olive mash, smoked bacon and Madeira sauce. The home-made and very traditional desserts might be crème brûlée, lemon tart or sticky toffee pudding with caramel sauce, while cheese and biscuits come with port. The pub has an extensive beer list, including microbrewed beers from Rooster's and Rudgate as well as some bigger Yorkshire brewers like Theakston and Timothy Taylor. The 60-bottle wine list has representatives from around the world, and includes six by the glass. SAMPLE DISHES: warm salad of mushrooms, bacon and prawns £5; breast of chicken stuffed with leeks, bacon, mushrooms and chestnuts, with a sherry vinegar sauce £10; dark chocolate tart £3.75.

Open *Tue to Sun 12 to 3, 6 to 11; closed first 2 weeks in Jan; bar food Tue to Sat L only 12 to 2; restaurant Tues to Sun 12 to 2, Tue to Sat D 6.30 to 10*
Details *Children welcome   Car park   Wheelchair access   Garden and patio No smoking in restaurant   Background music   No dogs   Delta, MasterCard, Switch, Visa*

SCALES   **Cumbria**   map 10

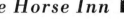

White Horse Inn
Scales CA12 4SY   TEL: (01768) 779241
just off A66, Keswick to Penrith road, 5m NE of Keswick

Once a farmhouse, with the dairy now the non-smoking area, this pub is just high enough off the main Keswick to Penrith road to escape the noise and bustle of passing traffic, and behind the pub lie footpaths up Blencathra fell. Although the interior is virtually open plan, low ceilings, with plenty of black beams and plenty of brass give a warm, cosy feeling. The inn is popular as a place to drop in for a reasonably priced snack and a pint of Jennings Best, Cumberland ale, or local Hesket Newmarket's Blencathra Ale; a 26-bottle wine list is also available, with house wines by the glass. Service has been described as 'friendly and efficient'. A full three-course meal (offered at midweek lunch-times in the winter) would be good value, but 'a main course and a beer would satisfy all but the hungriest walker off the fells'. The lunch menu is divided into starters, light bites and main courses. Soup and pâtés typify the first category; three-egg omelette or jacket potatoes the second; and Waberthwaite sausage with their own pickled cabbage, or home-made steak and ale pie the third. A blackboard menu lists the day's specials including, usually, about four fish dishes – salmon, halibut or shark, all from the West coast. For pudding perhaps choose fudge nut sundae or meringue basket from the large selection. SAMPLE DISHES: rolled oak-smoked salmon with stuffed prunes £4.50; lamb chops glazed with honey and coarse grain mustard sauce £7; home-made gingerbread with rum butter and whipped cream £2.75.

Open *11 to 11, Sun 12 to 10.30; sometimes closed between 4 and 6 in winter; bar food 12 to 3, 6 to 9.30*
Details *Children welcome   Car park   Wheelchair access (also WC)   Garden and patio   No smoking in 1 room   Background music   No dogs   Delta, Diners, MasterCard, Switch, Visa*

SEAHOUSES   Northumberland   map 10

▲ *Olde Ship Hotel* 🍺

9 Main Street, Seahouses NE68 7RD
TEL: (01665) 720200
on B1430, 3m SE of Bamburgh

SETTING

The Olde Ship sits above a tiny bustling harbour full of local fishing boats. From the pier you can take a boat trip to the bird and seal sanctuary on the Farne Islands or take a bracing coastal walk to the birthplace of Grace Darling at Bamburgh. The pub itself sits at right angles to the sea. The main bar is a gem; dark walls and floors set off a cornucopia of compasses, sextants, ships wheels and other nautical items. The food here is good value and mainly home-cooked, and the fish is caught locally. Choose from the blackboard or printed bar menu. Crab soup is creamy with a good fish flavour, baked herring and oatcakes sounds like a regional dish, and brown Windsor soup deserves to be tried for its rarity value. Bosun's fish stew contains onions, tomatoes and bacon with prawns, squid and cod, or you could settle for a spicy lamb stew with diced lamb, sieved tomatoes, peppers, onions, button mushrooms and Eastern spices, served with rice. Fortify yourself for a walk along the cliff tops with carbohy-drate-packed fudgy chocolate pudding or plum crumble. The pub serves an extensive range of real ales, with usually four on in winter, more in summer, possibly including Bass, Marston's Pedigree, Theakston, McEwans, Ruddles, John Smith's and Morland Old

Speckled Hen. A generic wine list contains a number of varieties, including wines of the month. SAMPLE DISHES: curried egg mayonnaise £3; casserole of liver and onions £6; coconut ice-cream £3.

Open *11 to 3, 6 to 11, Sun 12 to 3, 7 to 10.30; bar food 12 to 2, 7 to 8.15; no food 25 Dec*
Details *Children welcome in family room   Car park   Wheelchair access (also WC)   Garden   No-smoking area   Background music   Guide dogs only MasterCard, Switch, Visa   Accommodation: 16 rooms, B&B £37.50 to £75*

S E A V I E W   Isle of Wight   map 2

▲ *Seaview Hotel*

High Street, Seaview PO34 5EX   TEL: (01983) 612711
on B3340, 2m E of Ryde

No chance of misrepresentation under the Trades Descriptions Act here; a sea view is what you get at this pub/hotel with a distinctly nautical air, which is popular with both visitors to the island and local sailing types. Flags flying and bunting flapping gives the impression of awaiting the return of a naval hero. Should he walk into the 'Ward Room' bar he would feel immediately at home, for it is absolutely stuffed with nautical bric-à-brac, memorabilia and prints of ships. There is a tastefully decorated dining-room where the nautical theme persists in a toned-down fashion and a public bar at the rear where the younger clientele congregate. The pub serves Flowers IPA and Goddard's Special from the island's brewery. Cooking is naturally fishy, with specials varying according to the daily catch, but otherwise is fairly modern pub grub, with one or two individual touches in the shape of prawn, celeriac and Pernod cocktail or hot island crab ramekin. Lighter dishes are garlic mushrooms with pasta salad and pine kernels, or melted goats' cheese and walnut salad. More substantial dishes would include twice roasted knuckle of lamb with couscous and lime pickle. Puddings are a touch individual too – frozen peach yoghurt perhaps, or burnt vanilla custard cream. The lengthy wine list includes an Isle of Wight offering from Adgestone, as well as some superior clarets, and even a double magnum of 1987 Ch. Petrus, but only two wines by the glass. SAMPLE DISHES: cognac and liver parfait with green peppercorn chutney £4.50; grilled entrecote steak with Stilton sauce £10; poached meringue with banana toffee cream £4.

Open *11 to 2.30, 6 to 11, Sun 12 to 3, 7 to 10.30; closed 4 days over Christmas; bar food 12 to 2, 7 to 9.30; restaurant 12 to 1.45, 7.30 to 9.30 (not Sun exc bank hols)*
Details *Children welcome   Car park   Wheelchair access   Patio   No-smoking area   Background music   Dogs welcome   Amex, Delta, Diners, MasterCard, Switch, Visa   Accommodation: 16 rooms, B&B £60 to £115*

Lough Pool Inn

Sellack HR9 6LX   TEL: (01989) 730236
off A49, 3m NW of Ross-on-Wye

This charming black-and-white-framed seventeenth-century inn, where every straight line seems to be broken by dormer windows or crooked chimneys, is high on the list of 'hard to finds'. Two miles of tortuous lanes separate the pub from the main road. However, local opinion is that it is worth the detour. Formerly a wheelwright's workshop, the main bar has been opened up to make the most of the open fires and flagstone floor. Two dining areas lead off this room, but there is one menu available throughout. The 'bar meals' section offers jumbo sausage, gammon and pineapple, and ploughman's-type fare, while starters/light meals are of the order of deep-fried Brie, or soup of the day. Main courses might include chicken korma, and noisettes of lamb with minted dumplings, and there is a specials board which might feature wild boar casserole, or honey, mustard and sesame chicken. Interesting choices on the puddings menu take in cherries jubilee, or date and walnut pudding. House wines are from Le Sejour and beers are Wye Valley Hereford Supreme, John Smith's and Bass; local draught ciders such as Stowford Press and Scrumpy Supreme are also available. SAMPLE DISHES: marinated herring £3.50; Greek-style goat casserole £9.25; sticky toffee pavlova £3.75.

Open *11.30 to 2.30, 6.30 to 11, Sun 7 to 10.30; no food 25 Dec; bar food and restaurant 12 to 2, 7 to 9.30 (9 Sun)*
Details *Children welcome in dining-room   Car park   Wheelchair access Garden   No smoking in restaurant   Background music   Guide dogs only Delta, Diners, MasterCard, Switch, Visa*

▲ *Half Moon Inn*

Sheepwash EX21 5NE   TEL: (01409) 231376
off A3072, 4m W of Hatherleigh

Brothers Benjie and Charles Inniss have run the Half Moon in the centre of the old market town of Sheepwash since 1958 and have built a business of which Izaak Walton would have been mightily pleased. The pub has everything the fly fisherman could wish for: rights to ten miles of the middle and lower reaches of the River Torridge, a limited ghillie service, a rod room, drying facilities, and a

tackle and hire shop – and Charles will give tuition to novices. Drink
– Benjie's department – is the pub's other strong suit. The back bar
in the main lounge is crammed full of bottles of whisky, which
ideally should be drunk before the log fire burning in the huge
inglenook. Mainbrace Bitter is brewed especially for the house by
Jollyboat Brewery, and Courage Best and Marston's Pedigree are
also on draught. In addition there is a wine cellar that runs to over
200 bins and which is available for inspection. The bar lunch menu is
very simple: sandwiches (toasted or not), ploughman's, and home-
made pasties are about as sophisticated as it gets, but are reckoned to
be good. In the evening, a more formal dinner menu operates in the
separate dining-room. SAMPLE DISHES: ham salad £3.75; pasties with
salad or pickles £3; orange and brandy mousse £2.50.

Open *11 to 2.30, 6 to 11, Sun 12 to 2.30, 7 to 10.30; closed 25 Dec; bar
food L only 12 to 2; restaurant D only 8 to 8.30 (booking advisable)*
Details *Children welcome L, in games room only D   Car park   Wheelchair
access (also WC)   Patio   No music   Dogs welcome   MasterCard, Switch, Visa
Accommodation: 16 rooms, B&B £27.50 to £75*

SHIPSTON ON STOUR   Warwickshire   map 5

▲ *White Bear*

4 High Street, Shipston on Stour CV36 4AJ   TEL: (01608) 661558
just off A429 Ettington to Moreton-in-Marsh road

In a plum position in the middle of the Oxford/Stratford touring
circuit, this welcoming country town inn manages the trick of
appealing also to locals. Pass through its elegant Georgian frontage
for morning coffee with the papers, a light or full meal in the characterful beamed bars or bistro-style dining-room, or even a game of
Aunt Sally in the beer garden. You keep changing your mind as you
read down the good-value and wide-ranging menu: the 'combo' of
filo-wrapped king prawns, buffalo prawns and beer-battered
mozzarella sticks looks interesting. How about a bacon and Brie
warm salad (as a starter or a main course), sustaining cannelloni or
lasagne, or even a Dutch side order of chips, onions, ketchup and
mayonnaise? Settle on Wendy's steak and kidney pudding – or confit
of duck on mashed potato – but then you see the fresh fish blackboard offering chowder, garlicky pan-fried sardines, plaice with
lemon and parsley, or chargrilled tuna with a chilli and soy glaze. If
that weren't enough, there is a choice of a pudding or a savoury:
mushrooms on toast might also be a good children's dish unless they
prefer to pick from the Bear Cub menu. Good ales are Marston's
Pedigree, Mitchell & Butler's Brew XI and Bass, while the wine list
is a more than decent example of what all pubs could aspire to – not

too much, not too expensive, with interesting examples to suit all but the Liebfraumilch lover. Plenty of malt whiskies, too, savoured perhaps over live music on Sunday nights. SAMPLE DISHES: tomato and basil soup £2.25; Thai chicken curry £7.75; bread-and-butter pudding £3.25.

Open *11 to 11, Sun 12 to 10.30; closed 25 Dec; bar food and restaurant 12 to 2.30, 6.30 to 9.30 (10 Fri and Sat); residents only Sun eve*
Details *Children welcome   Car park   Wheelchair access (also WC)   Garden and patio   Live music on Sun eve   Dogs welcome   Amex, Delta, MasterCard, Switch, Visa   Accommodation: 10 rooms, B&B £22.50 to £50*

SHOBDON   Herefordshire   map 5

Bateman Arms

Shobdon HR6 9LX   TEL: (01568) 708374
on B4362, 6m W of Leominster

The Bateman Arms is a black-and-white pub right on the road, with a large bay window jutting out. At the rear, a patio garden has pretty rose bushes and tables for eating out, and extends into a secluded lawned area with more tables, sheltered by tall shrubs and trees. Although the pub changed hands at the end of 1997, no major changes appear to have taken place. The interior with its large open fireplace, settles, old photographs, books and glass ornaments retains an 'old-fashioned, traditional, personal' feel, although one reporter thought the modern background music somewhat at odds with that. A non-smoking dining-room is down a few steps. Very reasonably priced menus, with fish a speciality, are chalked on blackboards, and may offer soup, grilled goats' cheese or a hot mushroom tartlet as starters, and traditional steak and kidney pudding, chicken suprême in a light Madeira sauce, or pan-fried duck breast with a bramble and port sauce as main-course options. Fish of the day might be 'elegant' fish and chips, red snapper fillet with a spicy sauce, or grilled whole rainbow trout stuffed with leeks. Puddings are home-made and are of the sticky toffee and treacle tart variety. Bass and Wood supply the draft beers, and the short wine list includes three by the glass. Nearby properties of interest are Berrington Hall and Croft Castle (both National Trust). SAMPLE DISHES: deep-fried Brie £4.25; half-shoulder of lamb £10; Bailey's cheesecake £3.

Open *12 to 2.30, 7 to 11, Sun 12 to 3, 7 to 10.30; bar food and restaurant 12 to 2, 7 to 10*
Details *Children welcome   Car park   Wheelchair access   Garden   No smoking in restaurant   Background music   No dogs   Delta, MasterCard, Switch, Visa*

SHOCKLACH   Cheshire   map 7

Bull Inn   NEW ENTRY

Shocklach, nr Malpas SY14 7   TEL: (01829) 250239
off A534 Wrexham to Nantwich road, turn right after crossing river
Dee, then 3m to village

This fairly plain Victorian village pub, tucked away in unspoilt and
very rural countryside is approached down a myriad of lanes and is a
popular destination for diners enjoying a drive out for simple, home-
cooked dishes at value for money prices. Open plan and simply
furnished, it has a rear extension which gives the place a bit of a barn
like atmosphere broken only by tables, wall benches and the occasional print. The landlady has been described as friendly, jolly and
chatty. The daily typed menu is fairly extensive and traditional.
Home-made soups and pâtés will lead you into lamb and apricot
casserole, duck in orange and ginger, honey-roast ham and steak in
ale type main courses; fish dishes might be smoked fish pie, or local
trout with almonds and vegetarians are offered chilli pecuitos, pasta
dishes or a hazelnut and courgette loaf. A reporter's Basque chicken
had a rich tomato sauce with sausage, herbs and olives and came
with four vegetables. Finish with profiteroles, banoffi pie, hot chocolate fudge cake or sherry trifle. Only two real ales are served, Bass or
Burtonwood Bitter, and a standard wine list offers just four wines by
the glass. SAMPLE DISHES: spiced rollmop herring £3.25; medallions
of pork £8; apple pie and custard £2.

Open *12 to 3, 7 to 11; closed Mon L exc bank hols; bar food Tue to Sun 12
to 2 (open bank hol Mons), all week 7 to 10*
Details *Children welcome   Car park   Wheelchair access   Patio   Background
music   No dogs   No cards*

SHORTBRIDGE   East Sussex   map 3

Peacock Inn

Shortbridge, Piltdown TN22 3XA   TEL: (01825) 762463
just off A272 SW of Uckfield

Two mature yews stand sentinel at the top of the steps that lead up
to this pretty black and white, half-timbered brick pub on the
outskirts of this tiny Sussex village. One of the two bars is given over
mainly to dining, but both have log fires, horse brasses, parquet
flooring with large rugs, small windows and soft lamplight.
Competent dinner-party dishes, pleasantly served, characterise the
menus. For instance, you could pick the likes of deep-fried goats'

cheese with cranberry sauce, moules marinière, warm Brie and bacon salad, or, as a reporter remarked, a 'generous, fresh and well-flavoured' slice of salmon and haddock terrine, served with decent granary bread. Main courses also appeal to most tastes: perhaps seafood or chicken and asparagus pancake, grilled lamb cutlets with redcurrant and rosemary sauce, and Peacock chicken with a stuffing of cashews and garlic and a mozzarella topping. Alcoholic and creamy puddings feature largely, and an espresso machine can provide an indulgent finish. Sunday lunch is a traditional roast. Thirty well-chosen wines would suit most tastes and pockets, and the half-dozen beers on handpump include Morland Old Speckled Hen, Wadworth 6X and Harveys Best. SAMPLE DISHES: Sussex smokie £4; Shortbridge pie (chicken and leeks in Stilton) £6.75; caramelised oranges in Grand Marnier £3.25.

Open *11 to 3, 6 to 12; closed 25 and 26 Dec, eve 31 Dec; bar food 12 to 2.30, 6 to 10; restaurant all week, D only 7 to 10*
Details *Children welcome   Car park   Garden   Background music   Dogs welcome   Delta, MasterCard, Switch, Visa*

SINNINGTON   North Yorkshire   **map 9**

▲ *Fox and Hounds* ♀ ❦   NEW ENTRY

Main Street, Sinnington YO18 6SQ   TEL: (01751) 431577
off A170 between Helmsley and Pickering

Tardis-like, this tidy and bustling stone pub in the middle of an unspoilt North York Moors village holds much more than would seem possible from beyond the outside railings – a traditionally furnished bar with next-door pool room, a simple lounge bar with beams, panelling and an open fire, a candlelit restaurant and ten bedrooms. The same menu applies throughout the inn: many dishes have an attractive contemporary slant. Important things like interesting home-made breads and dressings, farmhouse cheeses and good vegetables are handled well. One successful starter was creamy duck and ginger pâté with a blueberry dressing; others that catch the eye are fresh seafood cocktail with a mild curry dressing, and smoked chicken sautéed with mushrooms and garlic on a bed of fusilli and chicory. 'Excellent' char-grilled gammon, steak pie with crisp shortcrust pastry and pan-fried salmon with fennel braised in orange juice, one of the weekly changing specials, were praised by autumn visitors, and the chef lets loose wild boar and kangaroo on to the menu from time to time. Puddings are also imaginative – how about chestnut and apple tart, or banana and caramel ice-cream cake? Requests for teas, coffees and hot chocolate are treated sympathetically. For beer you have the choice of Theakstons XB, Camerons Best and Bass, and the descriptive wine list offers six wines by the glass. Visitors have commended the 'crisp and attentive service'. SAMPLE DISHES: salmon gravlax with a mixed-leaf salad £5.25; lamb shank on bacon and spinach with mint gravy £8.75; caramelised citrus tart with champagne sorbet £3.25.

Open *12 to 2.30, 6 (6.30 winter) to 11.30 (11 Sun); bar food and restaurant 12 to 2, 6.30 (7 Mon to Thurs in winter) to 9 (8.30 Sun in winter); closed eve 25 Dec, eve 1 Jan*
Details *Children welcome in bar eating area   Car park   Wheelchair access (also WC)   Garden   No smoking in restaurant   Background music   Dogs welcome   Amex, MasterCard, Switch, Visa   Accommodation: 10 rooms, B&B £34 to £64*

SLAIDBURN   Lancashire   map 8

▲ *Hark to Bounty*
Slaidburn BB7 3EP   TEL: (01200) 446246
on B6478, 7m N of Clitheroe

This ancient stone-built coaching-inn is in the heart of Bowland forest. Its name is said to derive from an incident in 1875 when the hunt called at the pub – then called 'The Dog' – and were disturbed by the barking of the hounds. As the squire's dog Bounty was a particular culprit, the squire was heard to call 'hark' to quieten it, and thereafter the pub was rechristened. Inside, the long-carpeted lounge bar has plain wooden tables, ladderback chairs and a friendly atmosphere; there is also a remarkable courtroom, used by travelling justices from the fourteenth century until 1937, now a function room. The same menu is available throughout, offering light dishes such as soup of the day, pâté, wedges of Brie, or the Bounty special: prawn cocktail salad. More hearty traditional favourites might be pork chops topped with mustard, sirloin steak, fillet of cod, or steak and kidney pie. In addition, jacket potatoes, sandwiches, salad platters, and pasta and curry dishes of the day are always available. Children have the choice of burgers, fish fingers or sausages with chips and beans. Set-price three-course Sunday lunches at around £10 include a choice of nine main courses, two of which are roasts. Desserts range from jam roly poly to apple and blackberry pie or fruit crumble. Theakston and Courage beers feature, plus a short wine list with three by the glass. SAMPLE DISHES: grilled fresh sardines £3.50; mixed grill £9.50; sticky toffee pudding £2.50.

Open *10.30 to 11, Sun 12 to 10.30; bar food and restaurant Mon to Sat 12 to 2, 6.30 to 9 (9.30 Fri and Sat), Sun 12 to 2.30, 5.30 to 8*
Details *Children welcome   Car park   Wheelchair access   Garden Background music   No dogs when food is being served   Delta, MasterCard, Switch, Visa   Accommodation: 9 rooms, B&B £25 to £50*

Carpenters Arms

Slapton LU7 9DB   TEL: (01525) 220563

off A4146, 3m S of Leighton Buzzard

The attraction of this red-brick pub is much more cerebral than aesthetic, for across the courtyard from the pub (in a converted barn) is a second-hand bookshop of some 15,000 titles. This is an incitement to dwell which many will find impossible to resist, especially with Edgar's Golden and Notley Ale on offer from the local Vale Brewery to enable the alternation of sipping and page turning. If you can tear yourself away from the page for long enough to eat, there is a menu that contains a happy mix of pub staples – pâté, smoked salmon, ham and melon – as well as slightly unusual dishes – pastrami with roasted peppers and chillies, or a fish bisque. Ploughman's, sandwiches and filled baguettes are available at lunchtime on weekdays. Main courses might include a fillet of red snapper Cajun style or grilled lamb chops, and specials might range from beef stew and dumplings to chicken curry and rice. Saturday evening specials rise to whole grilled Dover sole, half a roast duckling with brandy and orange sauce or roast pork tenderloin with calvados. Puddings are solidly traditional as in spotted dick or profiteroles. SAMPLE DISHES: bacon with melted Brie on balsamic dressed leaves £4.75; steak and onion pie £8; chocolate mousse £3.25.

Open *12 to 3 (exc Sat), 7 to 11; bar food and restaurant Mon to Fri 12 to 2, all week 7.30 to 10*
Details *No children   Car park   Wheelchair access   Patio   No smoking while others are eating   No music   Dogs welcome   MasterCard, Visa*

▲ Tower Inn ▯

Church Road, Slapton TQ7 2PN   TEL: (01548) 580216
off A379, 5m SW of Dartmouth

If people forget that the pub is an institution as old as the church, older than the monarchy and older than parliament, they might be reminded of the fact in Slapton. The Tower Inn takes its name from the ancient ruins of a tower standing opposite, all that remains of a monastic college; the inn was established in 1374 to cater for the workmen building the college. The college is long gone, the pub endures; such are the priorities of the British. You would be wise to approach it on foot down a narrow lane, then step through the porch into a low-ceilinged, rustic bar with beams and pillars, scrubbed oak tables, church pew seating, log fires, wine-coloured walls, plum carpets and bare boards. Separate lunch and evening menus are offered up to a good mix of locals, tourists, all sorts. Lunchtime fare is good-value pubby food: sandwiches, baguettes, lasagne, gammon and chips. Several dishes also appear on the evening menu, which goes in for the likes of mussels, Dartmouth smoked mackerel or smoked salmon on salad, followed by rainbow trout and prawns, or tenderloin of pork in apricot and cider. One reporter's pea and ham soup was pleasantly thick, well seasoned and warming, and for an unusual dish you could try a 'pomarola', chicken with onions, tomatoes, garlic, basil, black pepper and red wine sauce on a bed of spaghetti, or minus the chicken. Sometimes they do themed menus, such as African, Thai, Italian or Oriental, and Sunday lunch is a roast. A children's menu is available in the evenings. An exciting range of beers comes in the form of Tanglefoot, Rebellion, Badger, Bishop's Tipple, Exmoor, Dartmoor and Broadmoor (just kidding), and a well put together wine list also represents good value for money. SAMPLE DISHES: crispy coated Camembert £3.50; steak and ale pie £5.50; treacle tart £3.

Open *12 to 3, 6 to 11, Sun 7 to 10.30; bar food 12 to 2.30, 6 to 9.30, Sun 7 to 10.30*
Details *Children welcome in eating areas   Car park   Wheelchair access Garden   Background and live music   Well-behaved dogs welcome MasterCard, Delta, Switch, Visa   Accommodation: 3 rooms, B&B £20 to £40*

SMARDEN   Kent   map 3

▲ *Bell Inn* 🍺 ❦

Bell Lane, Smarden TN27 8PW   TEL: (01233) 770283
off A274, 7m SW of Charing

This early sixteenth-century former blacksmith's forge is full of atmosphere and clearly appeals to many as it frequently gets very busy – a fact that the young, energetic and cheerful staff seem to take in their stride. It also appeals to young people, who are attracted, perhaps, by the simple cooking and very generous portions. The beers may also be a draw because the pub has a healthy mixture of well-known regional ales such as Shepherd Neame Masterbrew and Morland Old Speckled Hen, and less common beers like Harveys Sussex Pale Ale, and Rother Valley Level Best. The pub has a rambling layout, with various bars, which are either flagged or brick floored, log-burning fires, and lit candles in old wine bottles. Whether or not the provision of milk on draught pulls in the punters is a moot point. Chips with everything is the theme in the kitchen and they accompany steak, gammon and pineapple, chicken, scampi and sausages; these are frequently served with peas. Other offerings include jacket potatoes and pizzas, and more adventurous dishes include moules marinière, roast duck and curries. Puddings might be apple crumble and chocolate crunch cake, but waffles and cherries in kirsch is the pub's speciality. The wine list features two or three guest wines each month, plus a dozen by the glass and half a dozen bottles including a champagne. SAMPLE DISHES: garlic mushrooms £3.25; steak and kidney pudding £6; treacle pudding £2.75.

Open *11.30 to 3, 6 to 11, Sun 12 to 3, 7 to 10.30; closed 25 Dec; bar food 12 to 2 (2.30 Sat and Sun), 6.30 to 10*
Details *Children welcome in family room   Car park   Garden   No smoking in one bar/restaurant   Background music and jukebox   Dogs welcome   Amex, Delta, MasterCard, Visa, Switch   Accommodation: 4 rooms, B&B £20 to £42*

SMART'S HILL   Kent   map 3

Bottle House Inn

Smart's Hill, Penshurst TN11 8ET   TEL: (01892) 870306
off B2188, 1m S of Penshurst

Built as a farm dwelling in 1492, the pub was converted into an ale and cider house of unknown name in 1808, acquiring its current title only in 1938 when refurbishment uncovered a stash of unusual bottles. These may have been hoarded by the lady ghost who is supposed to stalk the house. The pub is approached via a raised patio and garden, which lends the white-fronted, tiled building a jolly, rustic air. One reporter commented that 'they have obviously got the formula right to be able to pull in customers on a Thursday night when the rain was blowing sideways.' One menu operates in both the bar and the dining-room, and with around 16 starters and 30-plus main courses there is plenty of choice. Cooking is modern British pub, where traditional dishes receive some imaginative touches: so garlic breaded mushrooms come with chilli oil, and fried whitebait is spiced up with a jalapeño, garlic and ginger dip. Those of a spicy disposition can bypass the steaks, beef Wellington and minted lamb and opt for chargrilled Cajun chicken or spicy chicken chimichanga with sour cream and cheese. Fishwise, the more traditional-minded could opt for skate wing with lemon butter, capers and parsley, while others might try Thai fish-cakes with chilli jam or fresh king prawns in filo pastry with hoisin sauce. There are vegetarian and children's menus, and puddings such as amaretti and cherry torte are listed on a blackboard. The pub serves local Larkins Ale as well as Harveys from Sussex and Young's from South London, and a 50-strong wine list features local bottles from Penshurst and

Chiddingstone. SAMPLE DISHES: Pekinese crab claws with red onion and coriander dip £5; calf's liver with bubble and squeak and caramelised onion gravy £12; wild mushroom and aubergine balti £8.

Open *11 to 3 (winter 2.30), 6 to 11, Sun 12 to 3, 7 to 10.30; closed 25 Dec; bar food and restaurant 12 to 2, 6.30 to 10, Sun 12 to 2, 7 to 9.45*
Details *Children welcome   Car park   Garden and patio   No smoking in dining-room   Background music   No dogs in dining-room   MasterCard, Switch, Visa*

Spotted Dog Inn
Smart's Hill TN11 8EE   TEL: (01892) 870253   **VIEWS**

This whitewashed pub lies down from the road and you approach through a pretty cottagey garden, with wonderful views across the valley on offer at the back. At the main door a sign tells walkers to remove their boots or cover them with plastic bags (provided in a dispenser). Once inside, in your stockinged feet, you will find a mixed clientele enjoying the open fires, low ceilings, quarry tiled and oak wood floors, velvet curtains and wooden panelled walls. The welcome is warm, the service chatty and efficient, and the atmosphere is enhanced by candlelit tables in the evening. Menus are arranged on a number of blackboards, with one for starters, three for main courses, one for pudding, one for ice-creams and one just for ciders. The beers served are a range of regional ales, King & Barnes Sussex, Adnams, Eldridge Pope Royal Oak and Greene King Abbott Ale; in addition there is a selection of bottled lagers from around the world. The wine list covers the world and offers 5 by the glass; place your order with the landlord once you have chosen from the extensive selection. Chicken breasts seem to be a house speciality arriving in a variety of guises; spicy Mexican with rice and salad; Cajun spiced; honey and mustard; lemon and garlic or yoghurt and almonds, not to mention regularly changing curries. Vegetarian dishes change too and may include Thai stuffed peppers with bulgar wheat, coriander and lime, or a tomato, mozzarella, basil and avocado plait. Puddings are equally extensive, with jam roly poly and fruit cobblers being a bit of a departure from the norm. SAMPLE DISHES: taramasalata and pitta bread £4; rabbit and pistachio nut pie £8; spotted dick £3.50.

Open *11.45 (10.30 Mon) to 2.45, 6 to 11 (10.30 Sun and Mon); closed 25 and 26 Dec; bar food and restaurant 12 to 2.15 (3 Sun and bank hol Mons), 7 to 9.15*
Details *Children welcome in dining-room   Car park   Garden and patio   Background music   No dogs   Amex, Delta, MasterCard, Switch, Visa*

SNAPE   Suffolk   map 6

▲ *Crown Inn* ♀ ❦

Main Street, Snape IP17 1SL   TEL: (01728) 688324
off A1094, on way to Snape Maltings

This 500-year old archetypal East Anglian pub not only caters for
annual visitors to the Aldeburgh Festival, but also for the locals.
Inside it has brick floors, beamed ceilings, and a little alcove with a
double Suffolk settee. Fish, not surprisingly, features heavily on the
menu and vegetables are grown organically. Blackboard menus offer
dishes available throughout the inn. The cooking is noted for its
tendency to draw on global influences – typical dishes might be sauté
pigeon breasts with bacon and parsnip chips, crayfish tails with
mango and orange dressing, fillet of sea bass with lettuce wrap or
calf's liver in marsala sauce. Reporters have enjoyed sun-dried
tomato and mozzarella crostini and butternut squash soup to start,
followed by wild boar steak, with a gamey flavour, served on a bed
of mash, and tender confit of duck with stir-fried vegetables. The
pub is tied to Adnams, which naturally supplies the beers, and the
70-bottle wine list also comes from their range, with eight by the
glass kept by the Verre de Vin system. SAMPLE DISHES: Andalusian
gazpacho soup £2.25; salmon and fresh herb fish-cakes with home-
made lime tartare sauce £7.50; home-made pavé of chocolate £3.75.

Open *12 to 3, 6 to 11, Sun 12 to 3, 7 to 10.30; closed 25 Dec and eve 26
Dec; bar food and restaurant 12 to 2, 7 to 9*
Details *Children over 14 only   Car park   Wheelchair access (also WC)
Garden and patio   No smoking in restaurant   No dogs   MasterCard, Switch,
Visa   Accommodation: 3 rooms, B&B £35 to £50*

SNETTISHAM   Norfolk   map 6

▲ *Rose & Crown* ❦

Old Church Road, Snettisham PE31 7LX   TEL: (01485) 540099
*off A149, 4m S of Hunstanton; pub is off main road through village
by the cross*

Being a foodie pub that is children friendly makes the Rose & Crown
a bit of an odd fish. The walled garden has a large kids' play area
with cargo nets, climbing frames and an aviary. The inside of this
fourteenth-century inn is a little too spick and span to truly bring out
its antiquity, but the layout is labyrinthine enough to satisfy you of
its age. A new chef, Martin Lyon, who has cooked with Prue Leith,
joined Anthony Goodrich and Julie Jennings in 1998 and now puts

together the menu which changes weekly. As the pub is a stone's throw from the sea, fish is a bit of a speciality and is delivered daily; look for it on the specials board. The rest of the menu is on the blackboard too. On offer are dishes that are a little different without being too over-ambitious or fancy. So goats' cheese will come with chorizo, and crab with lemon mascarpone. Both these could be starters or mains on a menu that is available throughout the pub. Grilled calf's liver comes on tarragon mash, and baked salmon comes with crispy fried leeks in orange sauce. Beers from local brewers Woodforde's sit next to those from Adnams, Bass and Shepherd Neame on the bar. The wine list, provided by Adnams, offers 11 by the glass. SAMPLE DISHES: warm muffin and poached egg with cheese sauce and crispy Parma ham £4.25; chargrilled lamb steaks with braised red cabbage £8.25; pasta salad with tarragon, roasted vegetables and cashew-nuts £4.50/£6.50.

Open *11 to 11, Sun 12 to 10.30; bar food 12 to 2, 6 to 9 (2.15 summer, 9.30 Fri and Sat); restaurant 12 to 2, 6 to 9.30*
Details *Children welcome in family room   Car park   Wheelchair access Garden and patio   No smoking in 1 bar   No music   Dogs welcome by arrangement   Delta, MasterCard, Switch, Visa   Accommodation: 3 rooms, B&B £40 to £55*

SOUTH GODSTONE   **Surrey**   **map 3**

Fox and Hounds

South Godstone RH1 8LY   TEL: (01342) 893474
off A22 at South Godstone, follow signs for Godstone farm; pub is ³⁄₄m from farm, ½m from railway bridge

The core of this attractive brick-and-tile-hung pub dates from the fourteenth century, though it has many seventeenth-century additions. The bar is furnished with ancient-looking settles and is warmed in winter by a wood-burning stove, and beyond it, up a short flight of steps, is a pleasant dining-room. Though the emphasis here is on food, the bar is reserved for drinking in the evening. Locally sourced produce features strongly on the short menu. There may be chilled melon and smoked duck breast, or home-made broadbean and rosemary soup to start, perhaps followed by local sausages with mash, leek and Stilton pie, or fillet of plaice with dill sauce. A slight affectation of the menu is that home-made fish-cakes are not £4, they are 'four pounds', grilled sardines are 'four pounds fifty pence', and steak, ale and mushroom pie will cost you 'seven pounds', but the food is none the less reckoned to be good value. Sweets range from fresh fruit to meringue chocolate crème brûlée. The pub is owned by Greene King, which supplies their usual beers, IPA and Abbott, and the conventionally priced wine list is strong on France, Spain and Australia. SAMPLE DISHES: spinach, avocado and crispy bacon salad £5; liver and bacon £6; apple and blackberry crumble £4.

Open *11 to 3, 6 to 11, Sun 12 to 3, 7 to 10.30; bar food L only 12 to 2, restaurant all week L 12 to 2, Wed to Sat D 7 to 9*
Details *Children welcome in dining-room   Car park   Garden   Background music   No dogs in restaurant   Delta, MasterCard, Switch, Visa*

SOUTH LEIGH   Oxfordshire   map 2

▲ *Mason Arms*

South Leigh OX8 6XN   TEL: (01993) 702485
off A40, 3m SE of Witney

This splendid fifteenth-century thatched pub in superb gardens is not likely to be popular with anyone with children, a dog or a mobile phone in tow (all banned), or indeed vegetarians, or anyone who dislikes smoke, or is keeping to a modest budget; but a great many others will relish its essence of times past. For 'Gerry Stonhill's Individual Mason Arms' is a lovingly maintained 'establishment for eating, drinking and smoking', as characterful as they come. The setting evokes that of a gentlemen's club, faces lit by candlelight, the walls dark with hessian, rugs on the flagstones, fires blazing in the huge inglenooks, nice paintings and prints on the walls, motoring tomes, old cigar boxes and wine bottles. Good quality and no fuss is the maxim behind the food, which is 'served with great charm': Mr Baxter's potted shrimps, wild smoked salmon, asparagus, Angus steaks, local game (perhaps spit-roast venison), lamb and plum casserole, or crispy boned duck done with orange and Grand Marnier or apple. If you choose sea bass or lemon sole, say, a vast fish will be brought to you for inspection before it is cooked. Chips are hand cut and vegetables are also excellent. Classy puddings may simply be the best of strawberries. The Ind Coope Burton is drawn directly from the barrel, while the exclusively French wine list concentrates on Champagne, Bordeaux and Burgundy; whiskies and cognacs are out in force. Dylan Thomas was living at the village manor-house while working on *Under Milk Wood* and Wesley preached his first sermon in the twelfth-century church. SAMPLE DISHES: rough liver pâté £6; whole lemon sole £13; French apple tart £5.

Open *Tue to Sat 11.30 to 3, 6.30 to 11.30, Sun 12 to 3; bar food Tue to Sat 12.30 to 2.30, Sun 12.30 to 3*
Details *No children   Car park   Patio   No music   No dogs   Amex Accommodation: 2 rooms, B&B £35 to £50*

Millbrook Inn

South Pool TQ7 2RW   TEL: (01548) 531581
1½m S of A379 at Frogmore, SE of Kingsbridge

An idyllic setting adds much to this cosy white-painted inn on one of
the Kingsbridge estuary's picturesque tidal tentacles. Indeed, the
vagaries of the tides may even affect the opening hours. Inside, three
small rooms awash with china ducks, horsebrasses, clay pipes and
sporting trophies create a welcoming atmosphere. Young and
friendly staff are drafted in as seasonal helpers, for this part of the
world gets very busy in the holiday season. Food is varied and
appetising, comprising of home-made soups, fresh fish and traditional puddings. You could start, for instance, with smoked salmon
and dill pâté, then enjoy halibut au poivre or Scottish sirloin in a
cream, brandy and mushroom sauce and finish with treacle tart (all
puddings come with clotted cream). Beers like Ruddles and
Tanglefoot are on draught, and there is Heron Farm cider as well as
a few simple wines. SAMPLE DISHES: crab and sweetcorn chowder
£2.50; lobster and avocado salad £9; sticky toffee pudding £3.

Open *summer 11 to 3, 5 to 11, winter 12 to 2.30, 6 to 11; bar food 12 to 2,
7 to 9*
Details *Children welcome in family room   Wheelchair access   Garden and
patio   No music   No dogs   No cards*

Swan Inn

Southrop GL7 3NU   TEL: (01367) 850205
2m off A361 Lechlade to Burford road

This Swan has made her nest within a giant creeper which turns a
brilliant red in autumn. The L-shaped building is in the old style,
where 'public' and 'saloon' bars are not connected. The public bar
serves beer lovers and a contingent of skittles players, while the
remainder of the pub is turned over to an 'above-average' food operation, with an emphasis on quality ingredients, and 'mature, involved
and observant' service. Staff are knowledgeable about both the food
and the wines offered. The menu is confidently short; regular dishes
include smoked haddock and prawns in a creamy sauce, and locally
smoked salmon in dill, horseradish and mustard sauce. Puddings
change daily and home-made ice-creams are a speciality and an
opportunity for experimentation: try the pear and cinnamon flavour,

or the toffee, hazelnut and Southern Comfort. The serious business of skittles-playing is lubricated with the infrequently seen Morland Original, as well as guest ales from some of the better-known West Country independents like Cottage, Wood and Archers. On the compact wine list there is, according to one reporter, 'hardly a boring bottle to be seen', and only champagne is over £20. SAMPLE DISHES: blinis with taramasalata and guacamole £3.50; Southrop beef Wellington £11.25; rich chocolate and brandy mousse £3.

Open *12 to 3, 7 to 11, Sun 12 to 3; closed 25 Dec; bar food and restaurant 12 to 2, 7 to 9.30*
Details *Children welcome   No-smoking area   No music   Dogs welcome Amex, Delta, MasterCard, Switch, Visa*

SOUTH STOKE   Oxfordshire   map 2

Perch & Pike

South Stoke RG8 0JS   TEL: (01491) 872415
off B4009, 1m N of Goring

Good food and a pleasant setting, inside and out, make this 300-year-old pub not far from the Thames a popular watering-hole. An imaginative use of ingredients marks the kitchen out from the ordinary, and the chef changes the short menu in order to capitalise on seasonal ingredients every two months. Autumnal cuisine will match rustic fish-cakes with anchovy crème fraîche or brown shrimps in spiced butter with quails' eggs. Beef, mushroom and herb dumpling stew cooked in a Brakspear ale sounds suitably warming, as do chargrilled pork and sage sausages with cider and apple gravy. Vegetarians will find macaroni cheese with leeks, onions and sun-dried tomatoes similarly heartening. There are imaginative sweets in among the sticky toffee puddings – banana and caramel crumble, for example. This Brakspear pub serves the brewery's Pale Ale and Special, and a 20-strong wine list offers wine in half-bottles and by the glass, with different choices in each category. SAMPLE DISHES: pan-fried chicken liver crostini with black olives and capers £4.25; chargrilled lamb chump chop with a minty pea purée £11; bread-and-butter pudding £4.50.

Open *12 to 2.30, 6 to 11, Sun 12 to 2.30; closed 25 Dec and eve 26 Dec; bar food 12 to 2, 7 to 9, Sun 12 to 2*
Details *Children welcome in bar eating area   Car park   Wheelchair access Patio   No smoking in dining area   No music   Dogs welcome   MasterCard, Switch, Visa*

Use the maps at the centre of the Guide to plan your trip.

SOUTH ZEAL   Devon   map 1

▲ *Oxenham Arms*

South Zeal EX20 2JT   TEL: (01837) 840244
off A30, 4m E of Okehampton

Inquire about the history of the Oxenham Arms, and the friendly
and enthusiastic staff may well whisk you off on a tour of this Grade
II listed building. It mostly dates from the late-sixteenth century,
though it is believed that the earliest parts are twelfth-century, and in
the lounge bar can be seen a prehistoric standing-stone, around
which the pub was built. It is, in the words of one reporter, 'hugely
atmospheric'. The lunchtime blackboard menu is fairly traditional
and simple, offering salads and sandwiches alongside main dishes
like fish pie or chicken stir-fry, while evening choices are more
varied. Puddings are home-made offerings such as cherry and
almond frangipane, or lemon and lime cheesecake. As befits a house
of this antiquity, the beers are served direct from casks behind the
bar, and come from the local Princetown brewery. The wine list runs
to 40-plus bins, including some very good burgundies. SAMPLE
DISHES: Oxenham pork and liver pâté with salad and toast £3.25;
Oxenham steak, kidney, Guinness and mushroom pie £6.25; home-
made fruit pie with clotted cream £2.50.

Open *11 to 2.30, 6 to 11, Sun 12 to 2.30, 7 to 10.30; bar food and
restaurant 12 to 2, 7 to 9.30*
Details *Children welcome in family room and dining-room   Car park
Wheelchair access   Garden and patio   No smoking in family room
Occasional background music   No dogs in dining-room   Amex, Delta, Diners,
MasterCard, Switch, Visa   Accommodation: 8 rooms, B&B £40 to £60*

SPARSHOLT   Hampshire   map 2

Plough

Sparsholt SO21 2NW   TEL: (01962) 776353
off B3049, 1½m W of Winchester

'Very much a dining pub', reports one visitor to this farmhouse-
turned-pub, which attracts quite a business clientele from nearby
Winchester. You sit on benches at big old tables, under beams
garlanded with hops, or in the peaceful large garden in summer. Old
prints and bottles, decorative plates on bare brick walls, a log fire in
one of the bars – this is the setting for a civilised meal. All the menus
are blackboard specials, some of the dishes spicy and modern (such
as Cajun chicken pasta and Thai vegetable curry), some reassuringly

traditional (herby sausage and mash, lamb's liver and bacon). Fish in a creamy sauce could well be an option, such as salmon in a lemon and dill sauce, or monkfish tails with a cucumber and chive version. On a separate dessert board are likely to be listed the same mix of new and old – perhaps mulled fruits with granita ice or a treacle suet pudding. This is a Wadworth pub, with IPA and 6X on handpump; these are joined by SummerSault and one guest beer. Malt whiskies are many and varied and five wines come by the glass. Service is punctilious and pleasant. SAMPLE DISHES: chicken liver parfait £5; wild mushroom and new potato Stroganov £6; Eve's pudding £3.25.

Open *11 to 3, 6 to 11, Sun 12 to 3, 6 to 10.30; closed 25 Dec; bar food 12 to 2, 6 to 9 (8.30 Sun and Mon, 9.30 Fri and Sat)*
Details *Car park   Wheelchair access (also WC)   Garden and patio   No-smoking area   No music   Dogs welcome on a lead   Delta, MasterCard, Switch, Visa*

STANDLAKE   Oxfordshire   map 2

Bell ✿✿

21 High Street, Standlake OX8 7RH
TEL: (01865) 300784
off A415, 5m SE of Witney

This half-timbered, custard coloured, 300-year-old inn offers highly rated modern British pub cooking, with touches of the Mediterranean and Fiji thrown in (the landlady is Fijian). There is a handkerchief of lawn at the front with a few trestle tables, and inside there is a very tiny bar, all very domestic and relaxed with a very unpubby interior, mostly in shades of green and gold. The black-board bar lunch menu lists around 17 items and is not divided into starters and main courses, though there is a more formal evening restaurant menu, which may well feature several of the same dishes. The range takes in pea and ham soup, black pudding with bacon and fried apples, Malaysian-style chicken curry, which comes with home-made chutneys, and Scottish mussels steamed with Thai red curry spices. Pickled oranges make an unusual accompaniment to duck breast, and pan-fried avocado with shallots, smoked bacon, wine and cream is certainly a bit different. The Fijian influence might make itself felt in kokoda, a traditional dish of marlin marinated in lime, coconut and chilli. Puddings might include white chocolate cheese-cake or more exotic pineapple baked in rum served with coconut ice-cream. Morland Old Speckled Hen is augmented by guests from the major regionals and the wine list is a good, well-kept selection with ten available by the glass. SAMPLE DISHES: doorstep sandwiches £3.50;

pan-fried tiger prawns with tomatoes, chilli, garlic and fresh coriander with rice £8.50; chocolate, cinnamon and prune pudding £4.

Open *all week 12 to 3, Tue to Sat 6 to 11, Sun 7 to 10.30; closed 25 Dec
eve, 1 Jan L; bar food Tue to Sat L only 12 to 2.30, Sun 12 to 2, bank hol Sun
and Mon 12 to 2, 7 to 9; restaurant Sun L 12 to 2, Tue to Sat D 6.30 to 9.30*
Details *Children welcome in eating areas Car park Wheelchair access to bar
(also WC) Garden No-smoking area in restaurant Background music No
dogs in eating areas Delta, MasterCard, Switch, Visa*

STANFORD DINGLEY　　Berkshire　　map 2

Old Boot Inn

Stanford Dingley RG7 6LT　TEL: (01189) 744292
off A4, 5m SW of Pangbourne

It may be 200 years old but it is a well-heeled sort of boot in a well-
heeled part of the world. Everything is just so inside the white-
painted brick building which houses one big and comfortable
beamed bar as well as a locals' snug. The specials board is notably
strong on fish dishes – such as salmon and crab wrapped in a vine
leaf with lime and ginger – for anyone not tempted by slow-cooked
ham hock in a cider and apple gravy, lamb's liver, kidneys and black
pudding, or chicken, leek and Stilton pie. Chargrilled aubergine, leek
and asparagus pancakes, and baked mushrooms with ricotta cheese,
spinach and basmati rice make tempting vegetarian numbers. Heaps
of fresh vegetables come as standard. A home-made pudding would
be a good reason to linger by the large inglenook or outside in the
well-tended garden that sports a dovecote and a wishing-well: how
to choose between treacle tart and Belgian chocolate terrine, or
blackberry and apple crumble and another half-dozen? Guest beers
at this freehouse usually include a local one alongside the
Brakspear's, and various ciders are on offer too. SAMPLE DISHES: cod
in beer batter £8; beef and venison casserole with herb dumpling £8;
banoffi pie £3.50.

Open *11 to 3, 6 to 11; bar food and restaurant 11 to 2.15, 7 to 9.30*
Details *Children welcome Car park Wheelchair access Garden and patio
No smoking in conservatory No music Dogs welcome Delta, MasterCard,
Switch, Visa*

*Report forms are at the back of the book; write a letter if you prefer,
or email your pub report to guidereports@which.co.uk.*

▲ *Carpenters Arms*

Stanton Wick, nr Pensford BS39 4BX   TEL: (01761) 490202
off A368, ½m W of junction with A37 Bristol to Shepton Mallet road

This pub is in a row of attractive low-roofed former miners' cottages
converted into a picturesque inn on a quiet road. A mass of colour
from flowerbeds and an abundance of hanging baskets on every wall
makes the Carpenters Arms a vivid sight in summer. Inside the long,
wide bar and lounge area serves as the pub side of the enterprise,
with a small snug alongside and a dining area known as Coopers
Parlour for bar meals. There is also a large beamed restaurant and
the inn has a dozen rooms in an adjoining annexe. The interior is
pleasant; the old stone walls are adorned with prints and small wall
lights and the wide sills of the many windows have a collection of
blue and white Chinese-style vases. Furniture is neat and tidy and
there is no music (apart from the pianist on Friday and Saturday
evenings) or machines. Starters double as light meals; smoked trout
mousse is offset with a tangy prune and mango chutney and a salad
of asparagus, grapefruit, artichoke hearts and pine kernels with lime
and orange dressing is an original dish in anyone's book. Fishy
starters may be potted crab and prawns with fresh herbs on summer
leaves, or spicy tiger prawns with coriander, tomato, mushrooms and
red onions. More hearty fare includes the catch of the day, and
indeed the stir-fry of the day. Spanish omelette curiously does not
appear on many pub menus, nor does bubble and squeak, in this
instance accompanying chargrilled loin of pork. The pub serves
Butcombe Bitter and Bass as well as two guests, and a 60-strong wine
list offers a half dozen named selections by the glass. SAMPLE DISHES:
smoked fillet of duck and chicken salad with crispy bacon £4.75;
scampi tails, chips and peas £6.75; sticky toffee pudding £2.75.

Open *11 to 11, Sun 12 to 10.30; bar food 12 to 2, 7 to 10; restaurant all
week 12 to 2, Tue to Sat 7 to 10*
Details *Car park   Wheelchair access   Garden   Live music on Fri and Sat eve
Dogs welcome in bar area only   Amex, Diners, MasterCard, Switch, Visa
Accommodation: 12 rooms, B&B £52.50 to £69.50*

▲ *Fox & Hounds*

Starbotton BD23 5HY   TEL: (01756) 760269
on B6160, 16m N of Skipton

This charming building, which has been a pub for the last 160 of its 400 years, enjoys a beautiful setting in the heart of walking country. The unpretentious flagstone-floored, oak-beamed interior is decorated with a collection of plates and jugs and a 'sturdy mix' of furnishings. In summer there is outdoor seating and in winter you can warm yourself before the open fire, provided you do not disturb the serious business of dominoes. James McFadyen looks after the cellar, stocking Theakston ales, augmented in the summer with guest beers, while wife Hilary does the cooking. Ploughman's and starters come with freshly home-baked bread, while at lunch-time there are knapsack-friendly French sticks, as well as Yorkshire pud with onions, mince and gravy. In the evening a small number of extra dishes are added, such as baked salmon with a herb crust and creamy dill sauce, or peppered venison steak with a port, lemon and redcurrant sauce. Puddings are home-made – Yorkshire hot wine pudding is a speciality. There are also around 56 malt whiskies on offer and three wines by the glass. SAMPLE DISHES: cream of onion soup £2.25; chicken, ham and mushroom crumble £7; brown sugar chestnut meringues £2.50.

Open *all week 11.30 to 3, Tue to Sat 6.30 to 11, Sun 7 to 10.30; closed early Jan to mid-Feb; bar food 12 to 2, 7 to 9*
Details *Children welcome in dining-room   Car park   Wheelchair access Patio   No smoking in eating area   Background music   No dogs   Delta, MasterCard, Switch, Visa   Accommodation: 2 rooms, B&B £35 to £50*

▲ *Sea Trout*

Staverton TQ9 6PA   TEL: (01803) 762274
off A385, 2m N of Totnes

A name like this needs some explanation: it was called the Church House Inn until a former landlord caught an exceptionally large sea trout in the nearby River Dart. Stuffed fish are now a feature of the décor. The fifteenth-century inn has over the years extended into adjoining cottages and a smart accommodation extension. The feel is of respectability rather than age, though there are some suitably cosy corners in which to tuck oneself away. Service by hosts Andrew and

Pym Mogford and their staff is informative, approachable and generous. Not surprisingly, fish is a bit of a speciality but done in a
homely, unfussy style. Whole grilled Brixham plaice, local trout or
lemon sole will be served with chips and peas, and the pub's own
pork sausages come with chips and salad. For more interesting dishes
bypass the printed menu and go for the specials board, where you
may find half a grilled guinea-fowl with port and orange sauce, or
grilled Torbay scallops with cheese and tomato sauce. For the
savoury-toothed, West Country cheeses are an alternative to
Salcombe dairy ice-cream, or Bakewell tart. Andrew stocks beers
from Cotleigh as well as Bass, Wadworth 6X and Dartmoor Bitter,
plus there is always a guest. The wine list strongly favours the whites.
SAMPLE DISHES: avocado with Stilton £2.75; seafood platter £7;
mango sorbet £2.75.

Open *11 to 3, 6 to 11, Sun 12 to 3, 7 to 11; bar food 12 to 2, 7 to 9.45;*
restaurant Mon to Sat D only 7 to 9.45
Details *Children welcome in bar eating area   Car park   Garden and patio*
No smoking in restaurant   Jukebox   Dogs welcome   Amex, Delta,
MasterCard, Switch, Visa   Accommodation: 10 rooms, £43 to £68

STEDHAM   West Sussex   map 3

Hamilton Arms ☻

School Lane, Stedham GU29 0NZ
TEL: (01730) 812555
off A272, 2m W of Midhurst

The Hamilton Arms is a taste of old Siam in Sussex, with waitresses
in traditional Thai costume, various Thai artefacts and a restaurant
called Nava Thai, and must rank as one of the first in the recent
colonisation of English pubs by Thai cooking. Nor do the owners
miss a trick: food is available to take away, they run the local village
shop at the back of the pub and inside there is a selection of Thai
foods and spices for those whose taste buds have been set alight by
the cooking. The owners are on the ball on the beer front too. Not
only do they sell Chaing Thai beer, but they also offer Ballard's Best,
Fuller's London Pride, Gales HSB and Courage Best to please the
real ale crowd, and the wine list is pretty well chosen too. The menu
is illustrated with mouth-watering pictures and dishes are based on
the Thai styles of red and green curry, noodles, sesame and ginger
with varying combinations of chicken, beef or pork. Mixed starters
(called Titbits) contain things like spring rolls, dim-sum, crispy
wuntuns etc. For the unadventurous, scampi, sausage and eggs, burgers and pies are also available, plus a selection of sandwiches. SAMPLE
DISHES: Thai salad with egg and peanut sauce £4; roast duck with

light sesame sauce and pickled ginger on rice £6.25; coconut ice-cream £2.25.

Open *Tue to Sat 11 to 3, 6 to 11, Sun 12 to 3, 7 to 10.30; bar food Tue to Sun 12 to 2.30, 6 to 10.30 (9.30 Sun)*
Details *Children welcome in eating areas Car park Wheelchair access (also WC) Garden and patio No smoking in restaurant Background music Dogs welcome on a lead in bar only MasterCard, Switch, Visa*

STIFFKEY   Norfolk   map 6

▲ *Red Lion* 🍺

44 Wells Road, Stiffkey NR23 1AJ
TEL: (01328) 830552
on A149, 4m E of Wells-next-the-Sea

Three cheers for a real old-fashioned pub which keeps locals and visiting birdwatchers and walkers happy in its simplicity, friendliness and policy of using local ingredients and serving only local beers. The car park may be massive, but once you enter the series of small bars you can revel in this brick and flint pub's unspoilt qualities: tiled floors, worn but comfortable seating, upright piano, log fire crackling in the inglenook. The blackboard menu offers some proper rustic cooking that reflects both the sea as well as Norfolk's flat sweeping fields full of game: thus expect grilled whole plaice or lemon sole, deep-fried Blakeney whitebait, moules marinière, roast stuffed pheasant breast, and samphire, asparagus and strawberries – too bad if you turn up in the wrong season. One visitor was delighted by a huge, steaming helping of Norfolk game casserole full of pheasant and rabbit, in a rich terracotta-coloured wine-based sauce. Vegetables are sensibly plain. They run to sandwiches on Saturdays and during school holidays. Do not be afraid to ask for tea, coffee and hot chocolate if you want to throw off the chill of the marshes before moving on to the serious East Anglian stuff: Woodforde's Wherry from the barrel, Adnams Southwold Bitter, Elgood's Golden Newt or Greene King Abbott Ale. Wines, including ten by the glass, are from Adnams too. SAMPLE DISHES: wild mushroom soup £3.50; Stiffkey fish pie £6.50; apple pie and cinnamon ice-cream £3.

Open *11 to 3, 6 (7 in winter) to 11; bar food 12 to 2, 7 to 9 (6.30 to 9 during school hols)*
Details *Children welcome Car park Wheelchair access (also WC) Garden and patio No-smoking area Live music Dogs welcome Delta, MasterCard, Switch, Visa Accommodation: 2 rooms, B&B £30 to £50*

STILTON   Cambridgeshire   map 6

▲ *Bell Inn*

Great North Road, Stilton PE7 3RA   TEL: (01733) 241066
off A1, 6m SW of Peterborough

The Bell Inn is hard to miss; its splendid sign, which is an exact
replica of the sixteenth-century original, weighs just short of three
tonnes and extends far out into the street. Guests have included Dick
Turpin, Lord Byron, Clark Gable and Joe Louis, though many
present-day visitors are there for the business conference facilities of
the hotel. The Bell's historical connection with Stilton cheese – it
was sold here to travellers on the Great North Road during the
1720s – is very much in evidence. The bar menu will nearly always
commence with Stilton and celery soup, and if this is your first time,
so should you. Naturally the ploughman's is a Stilton ploughman's,
but Stilton paté is also on offer, and the eponymous cheese will also
appear in glazes and sauces. For those whose prefer not to indulge in
the cheese, other starters include Scottish smoked salmon with
capers, shallots and brown bread, or a carpaccio of beef with garlic
croûtes. Main courses might be tagliatelle cooked with fresh sage,
mushrooms and double cream, or salmon fillet topped with cod
mousse and Parmesan crust, while Stilton lovers can choose chicken
suprême with Stilton and cider sauce. Puddings are listed on a daily-
changing board. On tap are Tetley Bitter, Marston's Pedigree and
Jeffrey Hudson Bitter from Oakham Ales, and an international wine
list has a number of house wines at under £10; ten wines are served
by the glass. SAMPLE DISHES: home-made paté with onion relish and
crusty bread £2.75; pan-fried calf's liver with mash and lime jus
£9.75; steak and egg sandwich on ciabatta £5.75.

Open *12 to 2.30, 6 to 11, Sun 12 to 3, 7 to 10.30; closed 25 Dec; bar food
and restaurant 12 to 2 (exc restaurant Sat L), 6.30 to 9.30, Sun 12 to 2, 7
to 9*
Details *Car park   Garden and patio   No-smoking areas   Background music
No dogs   Amex, Delta, Diners, MasterCard, Switch, Visa   Accommodation:
19 rooms, B&B £49 to £107*

STOCKLAND   Devon   map 2

▲ *Kings Arms Inn* ❦

Stockland EX14 9BS   TEL: (01404) 881361
*signposted from A30 Chard to Honiton road, or from A35 take Shute
garage exit W of Axminster*

Although it is at the centre of this small East Devon village, at night
the only lights to be seen are those of the pub. The entrance to this
long, thatched, whitewashed building is impressive – a long flagstoned walkway passing under a tall porch which stands alone, as if
leading to a churchyard. Go through wide doors opening on to a hall
housing an old GPO phone box, now painted grey, and proceed to
the bars at the end. The public bar comprises three rooms: the bar
proper, a games room and another resembling a sitting-room. The
cosy lounge is divided by an ancient oak screen and has a traditional
atmosphere. A large inglenook fireplace dominates one half, with a
table on either side – prime seating on a cold night. The clientele is a
mixture of a young set drinking in the public bar and a slightly older
set eating in the lounge. An extensive blackboard bar menu (available
at lunch-time only) is displayed in the lounge and might offer starters
such as delicately flavoured celeriac and salmon soup, Denhay
sausages, or seafood bisque and Brie in filo, and main courses of king
prawn brochette, venison medallions, or even fillet of ostrich. For
vegetarians there is mushroom Stroganov, vegetable curry or a pasta
dish. A pudding menu offers an enticing and definitely above-average
selection, such as apricot and frangipane strudel, or Grand Marnier
soufflé glacé. The pub serves John Smith's Best, Marston's Pedigree,
Exmoor and Otter Ales. The wine list and selection of liqueurs, malts
and cigars is unashamedly self-indulgent; ten wines are available by
the glass and a tobacco list ranges from Havana cigars to snuff.
SAMPLE DISHES: devilled whitebait £3.50; lamb Siciliano £9.50;
crêpes Suzette £3.50.

Open *12 to 3, 6.30 to 11, Sun 12 to 3, 7 to 10.30; 25 Dec 11 to 1 (drinks
only) bar food Mon to Sat 12 to 1.45; restaurant Mon to Sat 12 to 1.45, 6.30
to 9*
Details *Children welcome in bar eating area and in restaurant if over 12   Car
park   Wheelchair access (also WC)   Garden and patio   Background and live
music   Dogs welcome exc in eating areas   Delta, MasterCard, Switch, Visa
Accommodation: 3 rooms, B&B £25 to £40*

---

*Many pubs have separate restaurants with very different menus. These
have not been inspected. A recommendation for the pub/bar food does
not necessarily imply that the restaurant is also recommended.*

STOGUMBER   Somerset   map 2

▲ *White Horse*

Stogumber TA4 3TA   TEL: (01984) 656277
off A358, 4m SE of Watchet

The White Horse is a traditional village local offering good beers
and reasonable food. This white painted village centre pub is part of
a row of Victorian cottages and it retains an ambience from that era.
The interior consists of a single, fairly large bar with a counter at one
end and ample seating at the other. The furniture is a mix of red
upholstered banquettes, polished dark wood tables and captain's
chairs. Cask conditioned beers in the form of ales from the Cotleigh
and Otter breweries are on offer and, during summer, Lane's cider is
available. One or two interesting dishes stand out from the daily
specials board – mixed meat kebabs and Cajun gammon, for example. Starters on the printed menu are likely to feature reasonably
priced fare such as egg mayonnaise, or deep-fried mushrooms; main
courses might be trout with almonds, or minted lamb chops as well
as some sausage, beans and chip type grub and a range of sandwiches
and ploughman's. Home-made puddings include solidly traditional
choices of ice-creams, peach melba, crème caramel and treacle tart. A
short basic wine list starts with house wines at £5. SAMPLE DISHES:
soup of the day £1.80; chicken with peaches £6; walnut tart and
cream £2.

Open *11 to 2.30, 6 to 11, Sun 12 to 3, 7 to 10.30; bar food 11 (12 Sun) to
2, 6 (7 Sun) to 10*
Details *Children welcome in family room   Car park   Wheelchair access (also
WC)   Garden   Background music   Dogs welcome in bar only   MasterCard,
Switch, Visa   Accommodation: 2 rooms, B&B £40*

STOKE-BY-NAYLAND   Suffolk   map 6

▲ *Angel Inn* ✿

Polstead Street, Stoke-by-Nayland CO6 4SA   TEL: (01206) 263245
on B1068, 5m SW of Hadleigh

Set in the Dedham Vale conservation area, the very attractive Angel
Inn has been providing travellers with food and drink since the
sixteenth century. Seats on the pretty patio with flower-filled tubs are
provided for summer drinking, while the virtually open-plan interior,
with only standing timbers for dividers, has Elizabethan beams and
exposed brickwork, lots of tables, fresh flowers and log fires in
winter. The same menu is served throughout, but there is a cover

charge for eating in the Well Room, where tables need to be reserved. It describes itself as 'a restaurant within a pub', but with the same daily-changing blackboard menu throughout, the Angel's only other concession to pubbiness is a ploughman's at lunch-time; otherwise, starters might be soup, griddled fresh sardines, steamed mussels, or tomato and feta cheese salad. Main-course choices could be griddled haddock, skate wing or plaice, honey-glazed rack of lamb, ballottine of duckling with cassis sauce, or vegetable filo parcels. Puddings might include brown bread ice-cream, steamed apple pudding or raspberry bavarois. Imaginative touches raise the food above the usual pub standard, with a well-considered use of herbs and spices; a starter of locally smoked cod's roe with a tartlet of garlic and horseradish confit, accompanied by a good salad of mixed leaves and fresh bread, was particularly commended. Service has been described as 'pleasant, efficient and extremely courteous'. Beers come from Greene King and Adnams, plus guests such as Fuller's London Pride and local Nethergate Umber from Clare. The lengthy wine list covers the world, has four half-bottles, but the only glasses on offer are the two house wines. SAMPLE DISHES: deep-fried Cambozola £4.50; suprême of chicken filled with Brie and coated with crushed hazelnuts £9.25; dark chocolate ganache gâteau £3.50.

Open *11 to 2.30, 6 to 11, Sun 12 to 3, 7 to 10.30; closed 25 and 26 Dec; bar food 12 to 2, 6.30 to 9, Sun 12 to 2.30, 7 to 9; restaurant 12 to 2, 7 to 9* **Details** *No children   Car park   Wheelchair access   Patio   No smoking in 1 room   No music   No dogs   Amex, Delta, Diners, MasterCard, Switch, Visa Accommodation: 6 rooms, B&B £47.50 to £61*

STOKE DOYLE   Northamptonshire   **map 6**

▲ *Shuckburgh Arms*   NEW ENTRY
Stoke Doyle PE8 5TG   TEL: (01832) 272339
2m SW of Oundle

Not to be confused with a pub of the same name in the nearby village of Southwick, this Shuckburgh Arms is a seventeenth-century, ivy-covered stone building, looking as though it is about to fall over backwards. Only a stone's throw from a lovely old church and over-looking acres of farmland, it is a friendly pub serving excellent soul-warming food, a fine pint and a decent glass of wine. During term time it is likely to be full of parents and teachers from nearby Oundle school, hoping they will not bump into any sixth formers; during the holidays it is reclaimed by the locals. The main body of the pub is not particularly stylish, but the pleasant games room has traditional Northamptonshire skittle tables and lovely old settees. Cooking is solid: a combination of regular pub fare like garlic mushrooms, or pâté and their own particular specials like sausage Creole or Stoke smokies (smoked haddock with mushrooms and tomato, topped with grilled cheese). A lighter snack menu is available at lunch-time and it is advisable to pre-book in the evening, as the starters tend to run out early. Mains include some pub stalwarts, such as gammon steak with pineapple, and scampi tails, but these are joined by casseroles like lamb in mead, ginger and tomatoes, or kangaroo in white and ginger wines with fennel, plus a daily-changing special. Puddings are fairly standard – cheesecake or spotted dick, for example – but there is always a special pudding of the day. The pub looks after its Greene King IPA, and guest beers which change every few weeks, and a decent wine list offers some very quaffable house wines. SAMPLE DISHES: devilled kidneys £4.25; pork casseroled in cider, pineapple, ginger and rosemary £7.25; chocolate fudge cake £3.25.

Open *12 to 3, 7 to 11 (10.30 Sun); closed 25 Dec; bar food 12 to 2, 7 to 9*
Details *Children welcome in dining-room and games room   Car park*
Wheelchair access (also WC)   Garden   No smoking in dining-room   No
music   Amex, Delta, MasterCard, Switch, Visa   Accommodation: 5 rooms,
B&B £30 to £50

STOKE HOLY CROSS   Norfolk   map 6

Wildebeest Arms

Norwich Road, Stoke Holy Cross NR14 8QJ   TEL: (01508) 492497
from Norwich take A140 Ipswich road; directly after roundabout take left turn signposted Stoke Holy Cross

The Wildebeest is an establishment which, in one inspector's opinion, still 'has to decide whether it is a wine bar, bistro, local, disco, or restaurant.' Another said that in the '60s she might have called it hippy, referring to its idiosyncratic African theme, heavily prominent, with spears, face masks and bongo drums giving a very ethnic feel to a building that was only a few years ago known as the Red Lion. Good food at excellent value is what gives the pub something to shout about, though many *Guide* readers will need to be warned that shouting may be *de rigueur* as you compete with loud music throughout what is essentially an open plan eating and drinking area. Start with Cajun spiced chicken with a pineapple and lime salsa, or glazed mushroom, spinach and basil lasagne with pine-nuts and mascarpone cheese that could equally be chosen as a main course. Full-blown mains might include rump of lamb with a ragoût of sweet potatoes, Puy lentils and shallots, flavoured with thyme; or charred salmon with grilled vegetables, rocket leaves and a yellow pepper and basil dressing. The modern style continues into puddings like banana, Bourbon and honeycomb parfait with vanilla sauce, or a savoury Welsh rarebit on granary toast with onion chutney. A lengthy wine list offers a variety of wines at a variety of prices to suit tyros and the educated alike, while beers run just to Adnams Best and John Smith's. SAMPLE DISHES: chargrilled tuna with French beans and candied hazelnuts £5.50; breast of Barbary duck with spinach, Jerusalem artichokes, bacon and Madeira glaze £12; sticky toffee pudding with pecan toffee sauce £4.

Open *12 to 3, 6 to 11, Sun 12 to 3, 7 to 10.30; bar food and restaurant 12 to 2, 7 to 10, Sun 12.30 to 2.30, 7 to 9.30*
Details *Children welcome   Car park   Wheelchair access (also WC)   Garden No-smoking area in dining-room   Background music   No dogs   Amex, Delta, Diners, MasterCard, Switch, Visa*

STOKE ROW   Oxfordshire   map 2

Crooked Billet

Newlands Lane, Stoke Row RG9 5PU
TEL: (01491) 681048
off B481 Reading to Nettlebed road, 5m W of Henley-on-Thames

LOCAL PRODUCE

A pub/restaurant without a bar would not normally get past the editor, but you must consider that when the Crooked Billet was built in 1642, it would not have had a bar then either. Beer today is served as it was in the days of Charles I, direct from the cask in the cellar; though whether proprietor Paul Clerehugh likes to think of himself as a 'pot boy' is another matter. The pub's classic country cottage appearance has won it numerous TV and advert backdrops. Inside is equally rustic, with low beams and inglenook fireplace, hop bine adorned windows, a clutter of organised chaos and wine bottles and racks absolutely everywhere – 'it's not smart by any means', wrote one. It is primarily an eating pub and great effort is taken to obtain local produce for dishes that may turn out to have global influences. Honey comes from the hives in the rambling pub garden; meat is smoked on the premises; bread is baked with flour from ancient Mapledurham mill; and a local farm provides organic meat and dairy produce. Gourmet evenings celebrate ingredients gathered from a ten-mile radius.

The jokily illustrated menus change weekly. Thai crab cakes with avocado butter may top the bill one week; chilled Ogen melon with Parma ham and pink peppercorn dressing the next. Alsace hors d'oeuvre of spicy Kesselstall and chorizo style sausage may give way to a selection of Italian salamis, or you might find provençale tomatoes with black pepper, oil and basil. Domestic ingredients also get international treatments as in Scottish salmon with a Parmesan crust and chilli scented olive oil. The pudding menu recommends Chiltern

Valley dessert wine as an accompaniment to white chocolate and vanilla fudge cheesecake with honey ice-cream, or orange and Grand Marnier mousse cake. The beer so laboriously carried upstairs is Brakspear's Best Bitter, and an extensive wine list is as global as the menu and as chaotically laid out as the pub itself. SAMPLE DISHES: Indian-spiced white crab meat with cucumber and crème fraîche salad and caviare £7; free-range chicken breast stuffed with green pesto and cream cheese £12; French-style lemon tart with mango sorbet £6.

Open *12 to 2.30, 7 to 10, Sun 12 to 10; bar food 12 to 2.30, 7 to 10, Sun 12 to 10*
Details *Children welcome   Car park   Garden   Background music   No dogs MasterCard, Visa*

STOUGHTON   West Sussex   map 3

Hare and Hounds 🍺

Stoughton PO18 9JQ   TEL: (01705) 631433
off B2147 at Walderton, 5m NW of Chichester

'No flashy eatery but a pub in tune with its surroundings' is the drift of one accolade for this brick and flint pub on a quiet country road. Chickens peck around the terrace tables, and a garden at the back is an agreeable spot for surveying the South Downs. Inside, the pub is compact, comfortable and well-cared-for, with beams, brick walls and blackboards a plenty. Beers have long been a draw here, with six beers always on handpump, including regularly changing guests; there might, for example, be Timothy Taylor Landord, Gale's HSB, Harveys, Young's, Ballard's Wassail and Ringwood. Wines run to 30 on a well-rounded list, with four available by the glass. Foodwise, skilful hands prepare nicely old-fashioned snacks and unfussy main meals, adding half a dozen specials to the standards, such as finely flavoured Italian marrow bake. Game maintains quite a presence in season, with venison in sausages or a pie, and pheasant in a casserole. Fishy choices might be smoked mackerel pâté, crispy cod's roe, or grilled Mediterranean prawns with salad. Shepherd's pie and half a roast chicken are other safe bets. Leave room for light treacle sponge or 'properly dense' spotted dick, and leave time to visit the village's Saxon and Romanesque church with its especially fine font. SAMPLE DISHES: game soup £3.50; cheese and onion flan with salad £5; fruit crumble £3.

Open *11 to 11, Sun 12 to 10.30; bar food 11 to 2, 6 to 10*
Details *Children welcome   Car park   Wheelchair access (also male WC) Garden and patio   Occasional background and live music   Dogs welcome Amex, Delta, MasterCard, Switch, Visa*

STOW BARDOLPH   Norfolk   map 6

Hare Arms

Stow Bardolph PE34 3HT   TEL: (01366) 382229
off A10, 2m N of Downham Market

When a couple have been running a pub for over 20 years, two
things can be deduced. First, they are good at what they do and,
second, they enjoy doing it. This is the case at the Hare Arms. The
pub was built during the Napoleonic war, and takes its name from
the local landowners, the Hare family, whose ancestor Sir Nicholas
bought the freedom of the Hundred of Clackclose in 1553. King's
Lynn is only nine miles distant and town and country meet at this
affable hostelry. If you sit outside the creeper-clad inn, expect to
share the environs with the doves and peacocks who regard the pub
as home. Bar food is traditional and the printed menu is beefed up
with blackboard specials, with the emphasis very much on home
cooking. Pâté and game pie are prepared on the premises. Cheese
and vegetable Wellington is this particular pub's unusual dish, and
chicken breast wrapped in bacon with a whisky sauce is also out of
the ordinary. Children have their own menu of the beans and
nuggets variety, and there is an above-average vegetarian selection. A
more expensive *carte* and set-price menus are available in the restaurant in the evening. Beers are delivered by pub owners Greene King,
and the short wine list is competent rather than exciting. SAMPLE
DISHES: pint of prawns £5.75; 10oz grilled gammon sandwich and
fries £6; banoffi pie £3.25.

Open *10.30 to 2.30, 6 to 11, Sun 12 to 2.30, 7 to 10.30; closed 25 and 26
Dec; bar food 12 to 2, 7 to 10; restaurant Mon to Sat 7.30 to 9.30*
Details *Children welcome in conservatory   Car park   Wheelchair access
Garden and patio   No smoking in conservatory and only after 10pm in
restaurant   No music   No dogs   Delta, MasterCard, Switch, Visa*

STOW-ON-THE-WOLD   Gloucestershire   map 5

Queens Head

Market Square, Stow-on-the-Wold GL54 1AB
TEL: (01451) 830563
at junction of A429, A436 and A424, 8m W of Chipping Norton

Set in the middle of the busy town of Stow – which means parking
problems – this heavily beamed and flagstoned pub has Turkey
carpets, high-backed settles, log fires, horsey prints, and exposed
stonework in the front lounge. The tiny courtyard garden at the

back has room for only two large tables for summer drinking. The simple menu offers soup, sandwiches (lunch-time only), pâté, jacket potatoes, omelettes or sausages as starters. If main dishes of lasagne, steak and kidney or cottage pies, or macaroni cheese do not fit the bill, take a look at the daily-changing specials board. Puddings range from treacle sponge to fruit crumble and apple and blackberry pie. Beers come from the local Donnington brewery and four wines are offered by the glass. SAMPLE DISHES: pork and chive sausage £2.75; chicken and leek pie £6; chocolate pudding £2.50.

Open *11 to 3, 6 to 11 (Sat 6.30), Sun 12 to 2.30, 7 to 10.30; bar food (exc Sun and D Mon) 12 to 2, 6 (Sat 6.30) to 9*
Details *Children welcome in bar eating area   Wheelchair access   Garden Background music   Dogs welcome   MasterCard, Visa*

STRINESDALE   **Greater Manchester**   **map 8**

Roebuck Inn

Strinesdale OL4 3RB   TEL: (0161) 624 7819
from Oldham take A62 Huddersfield road, then left on to A672 Ripponden road, then right after 1m on to Turf Pit Lane; follow for 1m

---

Although close to the centre of Oldham, this white-painted family-run pub is in open country, with views down to the town. The pleasant interior consists of one large room, plus a separate dining-room, all decorated in dusky pink, with red ceilings, wooden tables, red covered banquettes, photos and drawings on the walls and fireplaces filled with artificial flowers. Excellent-value set-price two- and three-course meals offer two or three choices per course. Otherwise choose from the long *carte* which typically offer soup, prawn platter, egg mayonnaise, salads, ploughman's and pâté. Daily specials might be wild boar and garlic sausages on a bed of black pudding mash, or casserole of pork fillet and apricots; fish dishes could be seafood tagliatelle, grilled lemon sole, or fillet of sea bass with green-lipped mussels. More meaty offerings could be roast rack of lamb; steak, kidney and ale pudding or roast duck with Grand Marnier sauce; a daily vegetarian choice is always on the menu. Finish with apple and cinnamon pancakes, mango and peach cheesecake, or meringue nest with dark chocolate sauce. Service has been described as 'very pleasant and efficient from everyone'. Boddingtons, Whitbread and local Oldham beers are on draught and an affordable list of some 36 wines has a small selection by the glass. SAMPLE DISHES: seafood salad £4.25; veal à la crème £9.25; jam roly-poly £2.50.

Open *12 to 3, 5 to 11, Sun 12 to 10.30; bar food and restaurant 12 to 2.30, 5 to 9.45, Sun 12 to 9.30*
Details *Children welcome in eating areas   Car park   Wheelchair access (also WC)   Garden   No smoking area   Background music   Dogs welcome in bar only   Amex, Delta, MasterCard, Switch, Visa*

SUMMERHOUSE   Co Durham   map 10

Raby Hunt Inn

Summerhouse DL2 3UD   TEL: (01325) 374604
on B6279, 6m NW of Darlington

After 22 years at this simple stone freehouse well placed for Raby Castle, the Allisons understandably see no reason to alter their approach. The pub's recipe for success consists of offering at least two real ales on handpump, more at weekends, such as Theakston Black Bull or John Smith's Magnet, and a short wine list with four by the glass, plus simple food at lunch-time only, in congenial, unfancy surroundings. The food is superb value, starting with burgers and sandwiches all under £2, and with everything else under £5. This buys you good home-cooking such as Cumberland pie (shepherd's pie with cheese on top), steak braised with beer and mushrooms, chicken breast in a leek and bacon sauce, a salad (such as poached salmon, pork, quiche), and always a roast of the day. Hot meals come with four vegetables as well as ratatouille and a choice of potatoes. If that does not sound quite enough, add on a soup or pâté as a starter, and a perfectly pubby pud, such as jam sponge and custard, peach melba or sticky toffee pudding. SAMPLE DISHES: pâté with toast £2.50; game pie £4.50; lemon meringue pie £2.

Open *11.30 to 3, 6.30 to 11, Sun 12 to 3, 7 to 10.30; bar food Mon to Sat 11.30 to 2*
Details *Children welcome   Car park   Wheelchair access   Garden and patio No music   Dogs welcome   No cards*

SUTTON BASSETT   Northamptonshire   map 5

Queens Head ▮ ❧

Main Street, Sutton Bassett LE16 8HP   TEL: (01858) 463530
on B644, 3m NE of Market Harborough

This is a freehouse – and how. Ruddles County and Greene King Abbot reign at the white-painted roadside local, but visiting beers from microbreweries up and down the land have stretched to four figures since the enthusiastic and friendly Powells started this caper in 1994. That could well hold the clue to the name of another beer, Up 1000, from the Grainstore Brewery. Depending on when you visit you might also happen upon Dylans, Old Speckled Hen and, for a right old knees-up, Waggledance. Do not feel, however, that these bars, cosy with open fires and an array of copper pans, are just a club for beer-bellies: energy is also invested in the wine list, which is approachable, fairly priced and wide-ranging; nine examples can be had by the glass. English country wines are another draw, such as damson or birch (dry), rhubarb or cowslip (medium), and orange or redcurrant (sweet). Freshly prepared and simple food is likely to appeal to a broad range of tastes, and the printed menus come anno-tated with symbols for 'healthy eating' and 'suitable for vegetarians'. At its simplest you could go for a home-made soup, a jacket potato or toasted sandwich; huge club sandwiches, such as Bassett Beefy (a minute steak served in crusty bread with onions, mushrooms and chips), sound heartening. Broccoli and leek hotpot, gammon with mustard and mozzarella, lasagne and fresh scampi will all get votes, and if you still cannot decide, look at the blackboard. The simplest options are not available on Friday and Saturday evenings; then, and at Sunday lunch-time, the olde-worlde crisp-clothed upstairs restau-rant comes into its own. Puddings might be a brandy-snap basket filled with chocolate mousse and pistachio ice-cream or a cheesecake of some sort. SAMPLE DISHES: chicken Caesar salad £3.50; coq au vin £7; summer fruit meringue pie £3.25.

Open *11.45 to 2.30 (3 Sun), 6 to 11 (10.30 Sun); closed 25 Dec; bar food 12 to 2, 7 to 9.30 (10 Fri and Sat); restaurant Fri and Sat 7 to 9.30, Sun 12 to 2* **Details** *Children welcome Car park Patio No-smoking area Background music No dogs MasterCard, Visa*

SUTTON   Cheshire   **map 8**

▲ *Sutton Hall*

Bullocks Lane, Sutton SK11 0HE   TEL: (01260) 253211
off A523, 2m S of Macclesfield

The part black-and-white hall, some of whose gnarled and knotted beams have seen one thousand years of history, houses a splendid atmospheric pub. Oak panelling, exposed stonework, flagstones, leaded windows and two huge open fireplaces – one guarded by a suit of armour – who could want for another ounce of character? Regulars clearly do not take this one-off for granted, and newcomers too feel instantly at ease. The Bradshaws' printed bar menu, supple-mented by a typed list of specials, is a mixture of the traditional and the less traditional: French onion soup, beef curry, lasagne, grilled lamb cutlets on the one hand, branching out to pan-fried Dovedale potato cake with garlic mayonnaise, or halibut with basil cream sauce on the other. A hot pudding appears on the specials list most days. Sunday lunch is a traditional roast. Fifty or so malts are a significant draw, but then so are the well-kept Bass and Marston's Bitter and a procession of guest beers, perhaps enjoyed at a table on the tree-sheltered lawn. The Hall has its own-label French house wines by the glass, plus a list of over 40 others by the bottle. Further attractions for overnight visitors are the library and well-appointed four-poster rooms. SAMPLE DISHES: deep-dried Camembert £4; locally dressed crab salad £7.50; ginger sponge with crème Anglaise £2.

Open *No 11 to 11, Sun 12 to 4, 7 to 10.30; bar food and restaurant 12 to 2.30 (2 Sun), 7 to 10*
Details *No children   Car park   Wheelchair access (also WC)   Garden and patio   Background music   Dogs welcome in bedrooms only   Amex, Delta, Diners, MasterCard, Switch, Visa   Accommodation: 10 rooms, B&B £75 to £90*

SUTTON GAULT   Cambridgeshire   map 6

▲ *Anchor Inn* ✿ 🍺 🍇

Sutton Gault CB6 2BD   TEL: (01353) 778537
off B1381 Sutton to Earith road, 6m W of Ely

New staff at the Anchor Inn have helped Robin and Heather Moore boost its activities and its reputation as one of Cambridgeshire's better food pubs. Keeley Moyle, who runs front-of-house, and husband Geoff, who leads the kitchen team, have come with stints at acclaimed London restaurants Le Pont de la Tour and Mezzo. They are adding to Robin and Heather's enthusiasm for preserving rare breeds by thinking of new ways to serve them up. The inland Anchor was built in 1650 on the banks of the 'Hundred Foot Drain', as the New Bedford River is known, to cater for the needs of the men conscripted by the Earl of Bedford to drain the fens, and served the boatmen who worked these newly created waterways. It still has a historic feel; wonky floors illustrate the difficulties of building on a marsh, and the area is still wet enough in winter for it to be an important RSPB reserve.

The menu changes daily depending on availability of fresh produce and has been described as 'simple, but careful home cooking, that doesn't try to be more than it is'. Unfussy cooking might deliver locally smoked salmon with a fennel and lemon mayonnaise, or button mushrooms in cream and garlic au gratin. The passion for rare breeds may show itself in Norfolk Horn lamb noisettes with potato rösti and redcurrant sauce, or Portland lamb, served with celeriac mash and rosemary and garlic sauce. Wild boar is often on the menu, either fricasseed or in a cassoulet. Another house speciality is English cheese – Lincolnshire Poacher from Louth, or Beenleigh Blue from Totnes, for example – which you order at the start so it can warm to the proper temperature by the time it is brought to your table. Alternatively, for the sweet of tooth there is tarte au citron, or fresh fruit meringue. Good-value two-course lunch menus are available most weekdays, though not in December or on bank holiday Mondays. Real ales come from Elgood's as well as local microbreweries such as Nethergate, Leyland and City of Cambridge. The wine list (supplemented by four to six monthly-changing special offers) is extensive, with over 100 bins including a couple of English bottles, and some good-quality vintages that should go well with the cheese. There's a page of half-bottles, and eight wines are offered by the glass. SAMPLE DISHES: grilled dates wrapped in bacon on a mustard sauce £5; breast of guinea-fowl with wild mushroom sauce £12; chocolate and brandy pot with a shortbread biscuit £4.25.

Open *12 to 3, 7 to 11, Sun 7 to 10.30; bar food all week L 12 to 2, Sun to Fri D 7 (6.45 Sat) to 9 (9.30 Sat)*
Details *Children welcome in 2 rooms   Car park   Wheelchair access (also WC)   Patio   No smoking in 3 rooms   No music   No dogs   Amex, Delta, MasterCard, Switch, Visa   Accommodation: 2 rooms, B&B £50 to £82.50*

SUTTON-ON-THE-FOREST   North Yorkshire map 9

Rose & Crown Inn 🍇

Main Street, Sutton-on-the-Forest YO6 1DP   TEL: (01347) 810351
on B1363, 8m N of York

This whitewashed, ivy-clad pub is very much an eating place. It has an olde-worlde décor with low ceilings, comfortable armchairs and cushioned wooden banquettes. The food is displayed on two blackboards – 'regulars' and 'specials'. The former offers home-made soup with a roll, chicken livers in Madeira and mushroom croustade, fresh seafood salad, fillet steak in red wine sauce, ham and eggs, bangers and chive mash or lamb cutlets. Fish choices might be monkfish in a white wine sauce, grilled halibut or king scallops and bacon. Sandwiches and light dishes such as smoked salmon and scrambled egg or Welsh rarebit are available from Tuesday to Saturday, at lunch-time only. Desserts might be bread-and-butter pudding, cornet of autumn fruits, chocolate nut sundae or sticky toffee meringue. Theakston Best is on draught, and there is an excellent selection of wines by the bottle, with 12 by the glass. SAMPLE DISHES: creamed mushroom and smoked salmon brioche £4; smoked duck in port wine sauce £13; white chocolate cheesecake £4.

Open *Tue to Sat 11 to 2.30, 6 to 11, Sun 11 to 3; bar food and restaurant
Tue to Sat 11 to 2.30, 6 to 9.30, Sun L only 11 to 2.30*
Details *Children welcome   Car park   Wheelchair access   Garden   No
smoking in dining-room   Background music   No dogs   Delta, MasterCard,
Switch, Visa*

SWAN BOTTOM   Buckinghamshire   map 3

Old Swan

Swan Bottom HP16 9NU   TEL: (01494) 837239
off A413, between Great Missenden and Wendover, just N of The Lee

This sixteenth-century pub is set in the countryside of the Chilterns
and has a large, pretty garden for summer eating, with a play area
for children. The inter-connecting rooms have very low beams,
wooden floors and photos and prints on the walls. Weekday
lunchtime bar snacks include soup of the day, sandwiches and
ploughman's, plus daily specials of moules marinière, casseroles or
steak and kidney pie. Food is served only in the restaurant in the
evening, but it is still possible to have just a starter and a pudding.
Dishes on offer might be a starter of avocado, prawn and bacon
salad, with main dishes of cod fish-cakes, smoked fish platter, roast
rack of local lamb on a bed of wild mushrooms, roast partridge or
fillet steak; vegetarian choices are always available. Desserts could be
fresh fruit brûlée or apple crumble. Beers come from the local
Brakspear brewery or Adnams, and there is also Stowford Press
cider. Around 20 wines are offered, with six half-bottles and six by
the glass. SAMPLE DISHES: chicken liver pâté £3.75; Swan fish pie
£.75; hazelnut meringue £2.75.

Open *Mon to Fri 12 to 3, 6 to 11, Sat and Sun 12 to 11; closed 25 Dec; bar
food and restaurant 12 to 2, 6.30 to 9*
Details *Children welcome   Car park   Wheelchair access (also WC)   Garden
and patio   No-smoking area in restaurant   No music   Dogs welcome on a
lead in bar only   Delta, MasterCard, Visa*

SWANTON MORLEY   Norfolk   map 6

▲ *Darby's*   NEW ENTRY

THAI

Swanton Morley NR20 4JT   TEL: (01362) 637647

Here is a tale with a cheery ending. In 1988 one of the remaining
village pubs in Swanton Morley closed and local farmer John Carrick
decided that this was not a good thing, so he converted two deserted

farm cottages into what is now Darby's. It proved so successful that the other pub reopened. Despite looking as if it is as old as the hills, Darby's is among Britain's younger country pubs. Inside, there is lots of farming memorabilia, a photographic record on one wall charts the transformation of the cottages into the pub, and bar stools are made out of old tractor seats with folded sacking as covers. The pub has a very friendly atmosphere and a genuine welcome. Daily specials appear on the blackboard, while bar food consists of a mixture of traditional English pub food – scampi and chips, steaks, jacket potatoes and the like – and a separate Thai menu, which goes way beyond the currently fashionable green curry. So ginger chicken, seafood homok (seafood with coconut and Thai curry paste), and prawn with cashew-nuts will tempt those who fancy something a bit out of the ordinary. Home-made sweets are of the bread-and-butter pudding variety. Hall & Woodhouse Tanglefoot is the only non-Anglian beer on the bar, sitting next to Adnams Broadside, Woodeforde's Wherry and Greene King IPA and Abbott Ale; a small wine list is supplied by Adnams. SAMPLE DISHES: tomato skins £2.25; cod in batter £6; spotted dick £2.50.

Open *Mon to Fri 11 to 2, 6 to 11, Sat 11 to 11, Sun 12 to 3, 7 to 10.30; bar food 12 to 1.45, 6.30 to 9.45 (Sat all day in summer)*
Details *Children welcome   Car park   Wheelchair access (also WC)   Garden and patio   No smoking in restaurant   Background music   Dogs welcome MasterCard, Switch, Visa   Accommodation: 8 rooms, B&B £15 to £49*

TANGLEY   **Hampshire**   map 2

▲ *Fox Inn* 🍇

Tangley SP11 0RU   TEL: (01264) 730276
off A343, 5m NW of Andover

A classic rural freehouse deep in Hampshire lanes, this cosy place appeals to a wide clientele. There is not much elbow room in its two small, low-ceilinged bars, but customers of all ages find their way to it even in the most dismal weather. A genuine, solicitous welcome and 'some of the lowest prices I've seen for years' are two of its main assets. Besides being very well kept ('bags of character without gimmicks'), it also offers a highly respectable range of food on its bar and restaurant menus – helpings are notably generous. Bar food might include firecracker prawns with salad, chilli beef on rice or lamb and apricot curry, while the restaurant menu runs to more ambitious main courses such as grilled salmon in watercress sauce, pork tenderloin flamed in calvados, or breast of chicken in a prawn and sherry sauce. Sweets are home-made and of the sticky toffee variety. Resident beers are Courage Best, Royal Oak and Theakston, but the main focus is on the wine list, with around two dozen choices, and with a red and white representative from most countries and eight by the glass. SAMPLE DISHES: fresh sardines £2; steak and kidney pie £5.50; banoffi pie £2.50.

Open *12 to 3, 6 to 11, Sun 12 to 3, 7 to 10.30; closed 25 Dec and eve 26 Dec; bar food and restaurant 12 to 2, 6 (7 Sun) to 9.30*
Details *Children welcome   Car park   Wheelchair access (also WC)   Patio No smoking in restaurant   No music   Dogs welcome exc in dining-rooms Delta, MasterCard, Switch, Visa   Accommodation: 1 room, B&B £40*

TARRANT MONKTON   Dorset   map 2

▲ *Langton Arms* 🍺

Tarrant Monkton DT11 8RX   TEL: (01258) 830225
on Tarrant Valley thoroughfare, ½m off A354, 4m NE of Blandford Forum

This seventeenth-century thatched pub is situated in a peaceful village in the heart of the unspoilt Tarrant Valley. Plenty of flowers decorate the outside, and the garden is kitted out with tables and chairs, as well as an adventure play area for children. Inside, the skittle alley becomes a family room at lunch-time, when children can partake of their own menu of fish fingers, chicken nuggets, sausages and chips all set out buffet-style. In the front rooms are tiled floors, window seats, low beams and – in the main bar – an inglenook. The usual offerings of filled baguettes or soup are supplemented by blackboard main courses of venison pie, fresh salmon in a dill sauce, or perhaps breast of chicken in a red wine and bacon sauce. More elaborate dishes are offered in the restaurant, along the lines of warm salad of stir-fried oriental duck, roast tenderloin of pork, and sirloin of beef braised in ale. For pudding lovers there is home-made chocolate cake, treacle tart and cream, or plum and almond flan. Among the five regularly changing real ales on handpump might be Cotleigh Barn Owl Bitter, or Ringwood Old Thumper and Summer Madness. The good wine list offers nine by the glass. SAMPLE DISHES: home-made faggots £5.75; pigeon breasts in a red wine sauce £6.75; profiteroles £3.

Open *11.30 to 11, Sun 12 to 10.30; bar food 11.30 to 2.30, 6 to 9.30, Sun 12 to 3, 6 to 9.30; restaurant Sun L 12 to 2, Mon to Sat D 7 to 9*
Details *Children welcome in family room and restaurant   Car park Wheelchair access (also WC)   Garden   No smoking in family room or restaurant   Background music; jukebox   No dogs in main bar or family room MasterCard, Switch, Visa   Accommodation: 6 rooms, B&B £45 to £60*

TEMPLE GRAFTON   Warwickshire   map 5

▲ *Blue Boar*

Temple Grafton B49 6NR   TEL: (01789) 750010
off A46, 3m W of Stratford-upon-Avon

The oldest part of this stone inn dates from the 1600s, although the first landlord was not recorded until 1776; the current one is appropriately named Mr Brew. The rambling interior is arranged around a central bar, with a restaurant at the back. Plenty of beams, a glass-covered well and two open fires, plus bench seating and stools, make the pub a popular place with business people from Stratford, tourists on the Shakespeare trail and walkers. The standard printed bar menu offers pub favourites like soup, pâté, prawn cocktail and steak and ale pie, while the blackboard might list pan-fried lambs' liver, chicken curry, vegetarian bake or deep-fried lobster tails. Some of the specials also crop up on the restaurant menu. Desserts might be banana crunch, apple strudel or chocolate mousse. Sunday lunch has both a set-price menu and a *carte* and always includes a couple of roasts. Beers come from Hook Norton, Theakston, Courage and Morland. An extensive wine list has eight half-bottles and offers house wines by the small or large carafe. SAMPLE DISHES: Thai-spiced crab-cake £5; beef Stroganov with rice £7; chocolate whisky pudding £3.

Open *11.30 to 3, 5.30 to 11.30 (winter from 6), Sat and Sun 11.30 to 11.30; bar food and restaurant 12 to 2.30, 6 to 10, Sun 12 to 3, 6.30 to 9.30*
Details *Children welcome   Car park   Wheelchair access   Patio   No-smoking area   No music   Guide dogs only   Amex, Delta, Diners, MasterCard, Switch, Visa   Accommodation: 11 rooms, B&B £40 to £60*

TESTCOMBE   Hampshire   map 2

Mayfly

Testcombe SO20 6AZ   TEL: (01264) 860283
on A3057, between Stockbridge and Andover

Sore-footed walkers along the Test Way are happy to rest awhile at the Mayfly and enjoy its fine riverside setting: early birds will grab the picnic benches outside and the window seats in the non-smoking conservatory. Indeed, the pub opens daily at 10am for non-alcoholic sales. The décor of this low-beamed, early-nineteenth-century farmhouse celebrates the Test's reputation as a superb trout river. The pub can get very busy, but staff stay friendly as they serve food buffet-style – probably the most effective way to cope with demand.

Diners queuing at the food counter will have plenty of time to make their selections from the extensive range of cheeses, of which the pub is proud. Flowers, Wadworth 6X and Morland Old Speckled Hen are available to wash down the hot dish of the day or help-yourself salads, and home-made treacle tart. Alternatively, around eight wines are available by the glass. SAMPLE DISHES: cheese selection £4.25; chicken tandoori £6.25; maple and walnut tart £3.

Open *11am to 11pm, Sun 12 to 10.30; bar food 11.30 to 9*
Details *Children welcome in conservatory   Car park   Garden and patio   No smoking in conservatory   Background music   Dogs welcome   MasterCard, Switch, Visa*

THELBRIDGE   Devon   map 1

▲ *Thelbridge Cross Inn*

Thelbridge EX17 4SQ   TEL: (01884) 860316
off B3137 from Tiverton, before Witheridge, take left fork on to B3042 for 2m

This isolated former coaching-inn and cider house is 'run like a tight ship' by the landlord, assisted by young and helpful staff, 'all without the aid of any fruit machines, pool table or noisy jukebox'. The place is popular with those touring Dartmoor and Exmoor or following the Tarka Trail; the Lorna Doone stagecoach stops off here. What visitors find is a modernised inn with smart hotel accommodation; the main beamed bar is open-plan with comfortable sofas and armchairs grouped round the log fire; cartwheels, local photos up to the time of the Great War and framed foreign banknotes are the decorative themes. The bar food is 'fresh and honest', with nothing la-di-da. This might mean thickly sliced home-cooked ham in good brown bread for a lunchtime sandwich, or a decent vegetable and chicken soup, and a light cheesecake-like banoffi pie with clotted cream. Blackboard specials might include a roast, steak and kidney pie, beef curry, or cottage pie, while typical puddings could be banana split or sticky walnut pudding. Alongside about 50 malt whiskies, local Down St Mary wines and Butcombe Bitter, Bass and Morland Old Speckled Hen are joined by a summer guest beer and a 'festive' winter one. SAMPLE DISHES: smoked fish platter £3.75; roast beef and Yorkshire pudding £5.25; strawberry pavlova £2.75.

Open *11.30 to 3, 6.30 to 11, Sun 12 to 3, 7 to 10.30; closed 26 Dec; bar food and restaurant 12 to 2, 7 to 9*
Details *Children welcome in eating areas   Car park   Wheelchair access Garden   No smoking in restaurant   Background music   No dogs   Amex, Delta, Diners, MasterCard, Switch, Visa   Accommodation: 8 rooms, B&B £35 to £50*

THORGANBY   North Yorkshire   map 9

▲ *Jefferson Arms* `NEW ENTRY`

Thorganby YO4 6DB   TEL: (01904) 448316
3m N off A163, 5m S of York

A useful find in the rather nondescript territory between York and
the Humber estuary, the Jefferson Arms struck recent visitors as an
'incredibly homely and friendly place, where everyone seems to
know everyone else and everyone is chatty'. In this part of Yorkshire,
it can hardly have been the mountainous terrain which attracted
Swiss-born Adolf Rapp to forsake his native land. His English wife
Margaret, resident in Switzerland for over twenty years, may have
had more to do with their decision to take over this genuine old
village local in 1997. In any event, the Rapps seem to have settled
quickly into this highly traditional part of the English countryside,
like ducks to water, and now contribute much to Thorganby's social
life. Swiss ways, however, are by no means entirely abandoned; classic rösti dishes feature prominently on the restaurant menu available
throughout the pub. The Swiss penchant for mingling fruit and
creamy sauces with savoury main courses shines through Zürich-style
veal and pork steak 'Walliser'. Other foreign exotica include ostrich
burgers, salmon carpaccio and Greek salads, though there is plenty
of plain fare like steaks and fried fish too. Beer drinkers can enjoy a
good range of real ales including Black Sheep and John Smith's, but
wine is a special interest, as revealed by the shortish but carefully
chosen and enthusiastically annotated list of bottles, plus several
'value for money' house wines by the glass. Selby Abbey and the
Yorkshire Air Museum are nearby attractions. SAMPLE DISHES: yellow
pea soup with bacon £2.80; rösti with salmon and herbs £5; mocha
parfait £2.50.

Open *Tue to Sat 12 to 3, 6 to 11, Sun 12 to 10.30; bar food and restaurant
Tue to Sun 12 to 2.30, 6.30 to 9*
Details *Children welcome in conservatory   Car park   Wheelchair access
No smoking in restaurant   Background music   Dogs welcome   Delta,
MasterCard, Switch, Visa   Accommodation: 3 rooms, B&B £35 to £55*

THORNHAM   Norfolk   map 6

▲ *Lifeboat Inn*   NEW ENTRY

Ship Lane, Thornham PE36 6LT   TEL: (01485) 512236
on A149, 6m from Hunstanton

This sixteenth-century smugglers' inn is on the edge of the village of
Thornham, with nothing but the fields between it and the sea. It is a
sprawling, white-painted brick and stone building comprising bars,
restaurant and accommodation. A huge archway reflects a series of
architectural styles. There is also a children's adventure playground,
and a lovely walled garden with outside tables. The pub part is quite
atmospheric – with lots of beams and standing timbers, tiled floors,
log fires, horse brasses, ships' lamps, some nautical and farming bric-
à-brac suspended from the ceiling, a mad assortment of dark and
wood chairs, carved benches, fireplace and panelling. The restaurant
at the end boasts white cloths and candles, and there is a vine-
covered conservatory, very light and airy, that looks on to the walled
garden. This is a good family pub and is also popular with walkers.
The menu makes a big thing of fish. A specials board offers oven-
baked sea bass with Chardonnay and saffron cream, new potatoes
and vegetables, or maybe prime cuts of salmon cooked in a chive
butter sauce in a pastry basket with salad. Mussels are made a fuss of,
and are served up in a variety of styles. Otherwise, there might be
leek and cauliflower soup, roast duck breast with orange and apricot
sauce, or cheese and chive omelette with chips and salad. The
printed menu runs through pâté, ploughman's, steaks, burgers and
traditional fish and chips. Local pheasant casseroled in ale with field
mushrooms, shallots and herbs comes as a huge portion. Set-price
two- and three-course menus are served in the restaurant in the
evening. Beers on handpump include Adnams, Greene King and
Woodforde's; a short wine list has around two dozen bottles. SAMPLE
DISHES: half a dozen Brancaster oysters £5.75; medallions of monkfish £9.75; banoffi pie £3.

Open *11 (12 Sun) to 11; bar food 12 to 2.30, 6 to 9.30; restaurant D only 7
to 10*
Details *Children welcome   Car park   Wheelchair access (also WC)   Garden
No smoking in bedrooms   No dogs in restaurant   MasterCard, Switch, Visa
Accommodation: 12 rooms, B&B £48 to £74*

🍺 *indicates a pub serving exceptional draught beers.*

🍷 *indicates a pub serving better-than-average wine.*

Ring O'Bells ❦

212 Hill Top Road, Thornton BD13 3QL   TEL: (01274) 832296
just off B6145, 3m W of Bradford

Although Ann and Clive Preston have been successful in their efforts
to win the Ring O'Bells a reputation for its food, it retains a fairly
pubby atmosphere, no doubt due to the well-kept selection of Black
Sheep Bitter and Theakston beers. Despite a number of whimsical
names for dishes – Italian Job, Dogger Bank, or Naughty But Nice,
for example – food is taken seriously and the menu is eclectic, extensive and modern. The daily specials board might include roasted
belly of pork on butternut squash, or grilled swordfish steak on a
sauce of ginger wine and plum. The reasonably priced wine list runs
to over 100 bins and 'Clive and the team' have clearly enjoyed the
research involved in putting it together. There is a good choice of
dessert wines and half-bottles, as well as ten wines available by the
glass. Enthusiastic staff share the proprietors' pride in the establishment, and over-enthusiastic diners may well appreciate the separate
'slimmers' menu'. SAMPLE DISHES: cream of smoked salmon soup with
lemon and thyme £3; roast chump of lamb on caramelised red onion
and tomato purée £12; shortcake biscuits with raspberry and mango
mousse £3.50.

Open *11.30 to 4, 5.30 to 11, Sun 11.30 to 4, 6.30 to 10; closed 25 Dec; bar
food and restaurant 12 to 2, 5.30 (6.30 Sat and Sun) to 9.30*
Details *Children welcome   Car park   Wheelchair access (also WC)   Patio
No smoking in restaurant   Background music   No dogs   Delta, MasterCard,
Switch, Visa*

▲ *Buck Inn*

Thornton Watlass HG4 4AH   TEL: (01677) 422461
off B6268 midway between Masham and Bedale

Overlooking the village green, the Buck Inn is right in the centre of
one of North Yorkshire's prettiest villages. The local-stone building
contains a very traditional interior, with upholstered wall settles and
a real log fire, which perhaps provides some solace to customers
denied the sight of cricket on the green in winter. The lunch menu
features typical pub dishes such as Whitby haddock with chips, and
mushroom rarebit. The evening menu is more lavish, but still traditional, with an emphasis on fresh local produce. With Wensleydale

on the doorstep, cheese features in the cooking, as in Wensleydale and ale on toast topped with bacon, and the pub has won an award for its ploughman's. A feature at Sunday lunch-times is live jazz. Beers include Black Sheep, Theakston, Tetley and John Smith's plus a guest ale from a local independent such as Cropton, Durham or Hambleton. There is also a selection of over 40 malt whiskies and a 20-bin wine list. SAMPLE DISHES: cheese and ale soup £2.50; beef and beer curry £6.50; bread-and-butter pudding £4.25.

Open *Mon to Fri 11 to 3, 6 to 11, Sat 11am to 11pm, Sun 12 to 3.30, 6.30 to 10.30; closed 25 Dec; bar food and restaurant 12 to 2, 6.30 to 9.30 (2.30 Sun)*
Details *Children welcome   Car park   Wheelchair access (also WC)   Garden No smoking in restaurant   Live music   No dogs   Amex, Delta, Diners, MasterCard, Switch, Visa   Accommodation: 7 rooms, B&B £34 to £48*

THORPE LANGTON   Leicestershire   map 5

Bakers Arms   NEW ENTRY

Thorpe Langton LE16 7TS   TEL: (01858) 545201
off B6047, 4m N of Market Harborough

Here is a delightful sixteenth-century thatched cottage in the village centre, oozing period charm with its ancient walls and low beamed ceilings in several intimate rooms, especially the cosy no-smoking snugs. It is all beautifully kitted out with large pine tables, antique pews, settles and country chairs, open fires, terracotta walls and rugs on the floors – all in all a relaxing place in which to enjoy excellent food. Beer drinkers are not particularly well catered for: they have the choice of Tetley or nothing, and virtually all the tables are given over to dining, but the place is still undeniably a pub. Well-heeled customers choose meals from the daily-changing blackboards, which are full of well-presented modern dishes that display an imaginative use of fresh ingredients. Fish and vegetarian dishes are usually in abundance, such as baked salmon rösti with avocado and lemon salsa – 'excellent flavour combinations' – and mushroom and horseradish soup. Or choose fillet steak with spring onion and Stilton sauce, or beautifully presented monkfish with Parmesan crust, served with well-cooked vegetables. There is a good list of decent wines, including six by the glass. SAMPLE DISHES: confit of duck on Puy lentils £4.25; lamb shank with colcannon £8.50; pavlova with summer berries £3.50.

Open *Tue to Sun L 12 to 2 (3 Sun), Tue to Sat eve 6.30 to 11; bar food 12 to 2, 6.30 to 9.30*
Details *No children   Car park   Wheelchair access   Garden   No-smoking areas   Live music at Fri D   No dogs   Amex, Delta, MasterCard, Switch, Visa*

Bull

Dunster Mill Lane, Three Legged Cross TN5 7HH
TEL: (01580) 200586
*take Three Legged Cross road signposted in centre of Ticehurst,
off B2099*

This brick and tile-hung pub, with tiny-paned glass windows, is
based around a Wealden Hall house built between 1385 and 1425,
and later extended. It is set in a pretty garden with two *pétanque*
pitches and a weekend bouncy castle. The interior has sturdy black
beams, exposed stonework and flagstone floors, with plenty of
tables, benches and chairs; the more modern restaurant is decorated in light pine. The bar menu offers the usual staples of filled
baguettes, ploughman's and soup, as well as more exotic starters
such as pan-fried frogs' legs or quails' eggs served with crudités.
Main courses could be fresh whole plaice, estouffade de boeuf, coq
au vin or bouillabaisse – the pub stresses that everything is freshly
prepared on the premises. Puddings are of the sticky toffee and
bread-and-butter variety, plus banoffi pie and 'hokey pokey ice-
cream'. The restaurant menu is only slightly more elaborate, with
all main courses priced under £10. Beers come from Harveys of
Lewes and Worthingtons. A short and attractive wine list offers
three house wines by the glass and bottle. SAMPLE DISHES: barbecued spare ribs £3.75; rogan josh with onion bhaji and naan bread
£5.50; chocolate marquise £3.25.

Open *11 to 3, 6 to 11, Sun 12 to 3, 7 to 10.30; closed Mon D in winter, 25
Dec; bar food and restaurant all week L 12 to 2.30, Tue to Sat D 7 to 9.30*
Details *Children welcome   Car park   Wheelchair access (also WC)   Garden
No pipes in restaurant   Live music   Dogs welcome on a lead   Delta,
MasterCard, Switch, Visa*

Old Hall Inn

Threshfield, Grassington BD23 5HB   TEL: (01756) 752441
on B6265, 1m W of Grassington

Value for money at lunch, and avant-garde in the evening, is how Ian
and Amanda Taylor choose to present the Old Hall Inn to the world.
Threshfield is a tiny Dales village, not far from Skipton, and the pub
stands back slightly from the village proper. A large bar replete with

stained glass window with the legend 'Old Hall' sets the tone for this traditionally furnished pub with conservatory extension. Young, polite service will convey dishes chosen from a blackboard, which may well list ham and Stilton stuffed fresh mushrooms, or grilled Brie, perhaps followed by steak and mushroom pie, pan-fried lambs' liver, or braised lamb with lemon and garlic. In the evening you could choose between a venison steak on a bed of garlic mash in shallot and red wine sauce or a fresh seafood medley in a cream sauce. Polish it all off with rich stout cake topped with lashings of chocolate sauce or a selection of home-made cheeses. Beers from the owner's namesake include Timothy Taylor Landlord, Best Bitter and Golden Best. Four wines are available by the glass. Accommodation run by the pub is not integral but is adjacent. SAMPLE DISHES: chilled Ogen melon stuffed with champagne sorbet £4.50; jumbo fish and chips £6.50; orange sponge with compote of peaches in Amaretto £3.

Open *Tue to Sun (and bank hol Mons) 11.30 to 3, 6 to 11 (10.30 Sun); bar food and restaurant Tue to Sun (and bank hol Mons) 12 to 2 (2.30 Sun), 6 to 9 (Sun eve from May to Sept only)*
Details *Children welcome in family room   Car park   Wheelchair access (also WC)   Garden and patio   Background music   MasterCard, Switch, Visa*

TILLINGTON   West Sussex   map 3

▲ *Horse Guards Inn* 🅰 🍇

Upperton Road, Tillington GU28 9AF   TEL: (01798) 342332
just off A272, 1m W of Petworth

This pretty, whitewashed 300-year-old inn stands opposite the 800-year-old village church. Originally three cottages, it has a secluded garden for summer eating, with good views to the South Downs. Inside is a series of rooms described as 'quaint, but very well maintained and comfortable', with exposed stripped beams, pine panelling, open fires and hunting prints. Very much a dining pub – booking is advisable in the evening – it offers imaginative, but not cheap food, although bar snacks such as sandwiches and ploughman's are available. Starters might be French onion soup, moules, pan-fried mushrooms or oeuf en cocotte, followed by baked haddock fillet crumble, casserole of rabbit, tagliatelle carbonara or Thai-style stir-fry of mixed vegetables. In the evening, dishes such as spicy crab linguine, roast Aylesbury duck and whole grilled Lemon sole make an appearance; Sunday lunch specials include a choice of roasts plus Selsey lobster or dressed crab au gratin. Desserts might be summer pudding, crème brûlée, tiramisù or Bakewell tart. Badger Best and local Ballards Best are the beers on offer, while the slightly pricey list

of some 40 wines offers ten by the glass. SAMPLE DISHES: Caesar salad
£4.75; chicken curry with rice £7.25; chocolate temptation £4.

Open *11 to 3, 6 to 11, Sun 12 to 3, 7 to 10.30; closed 25 Dec; bar food 12
to 2 (12.30 to 2.30 Sun), 7 to 10*
Details *Children welcome at lunch-time only   Garden   No music   Amex,
Delta, Diners, MasterCard, Switch, Visa   Accommodation: 3 rooms, B&B £62
to £65*

TIRRIL   Cumbria   map 10

▲ *Queens Head*

Tirril CA10 2JF   TEL: (01768) 863219
on B5320, 2m S of Penrith

The Queens Head is a long-fronted, white-painted Grade II listed
building, situated between Pooley Bridge and Penrith. Built around
1719, it was once owned by William Wordsworth, and a debenture
signed by him to that effect is on display. Inside, it has very low-
beamed ceilings and plenty of English oak about. The bar snacks
menu offers baguettes, jacket potatoes and pitta breads stuffed with
various fillings, and several pasta options, with England and Italy
meeting in the midst of a Cumberland penne. Main courses include
Gammon steak 'viking', which means it comes with paprika and
melted Cheddar cheese, and there are also Mexican beef enchilladas.
The wine list, which includes a selection of English country fruit
wines from Lindisfarne, points out that nearly all wines listed are
from private or family-run estates. Four regular real ales are supplemented by a frequently changing guest. In August they hold a beer
and sausage festival. SAMPLE DISHES: cheddar and cranberry parcels
£3; lambs' liver and bacon £6.75; steamed syrup sponge £2.50.

Open *Mon to Fri 12 to 3, 6 to 11, Sat 12 to 11, Sun 12 to 10.30; bar food
and restaurant 12 to 2, 6 to 9.30*
Details *Children welcome   Car park   Patio   No-smoking area in restaurant
Live music   Dogs welcome in bar only   Amex, Delta, MasterCard, Switch,
Visa   Accommodation: 7 rooms, B&B £30 to £45*

TOLLARD ROYAL   Wiltshire   map 2

▲ *King John Inn* 🍺 [NEW ENTRY]

Tollard Royal SP5 5PS   TEL: (01725) 516207
on B3081 (off A354), 14m SW of Salisbury

An unassuming ivy-clad, brick building dating from 1859 and built
to supply the refreshment needs of the workers at the Tollard Royal
iron foundry, the pub is nowadays well placed to perform a similar
function for those exploring the nearby ancient forests and
Cranborne Chase, which brought King John here for the sport of
kings – hence the pub's name. A homely, simply furnished bar area,
with wall bench seating and cushioned chairs around a mix of tables,
opens into a small dining area tucked away on one side. This village
inn offers good-value home-cooked food, with simple but freshly
prepared dishes. Ploughman's are a speciality and come with a range
of cheeses from Cornish Yarg to Somerset Brie, or local ham.
Blackboard menus offer cauliflower and blue cheese soup, fresh
pasta with chicken and tarragon sauce, fish pie, or grilled trout.
Puddings are along the lines of crème caramel, lemon and elderflower syllabub or treacle tart. In addition to the *carte*, set-price
meals are available on Friday and Saturday evenings and might
include mussels in garlic butter followed by roast partridge with
celeriac purée; a roast main course is always available on the Sunday
lunch menu. The short wine list is reasonably priced, while real ales
are sourced locally from Smiles, Oakhill and Stonehenge Ales
(formerly Bunces). SAMPLE DISHES: feta and olive salad £4; spicy
Mexican pork £5; squidgy chocolate log £3.

Open *12 (11 Sat) to 2.30, 6.30 to 11, Sun 12 to 2.30, 7 to 10.30; closed 25
Dec, 26 Dec and 1 Jan eves; bar food and restaurant 12 to 2, 7 to 9 (9.30 Fri
and Sat, 8.30 Sun)*
Details *No children   Car park   Wheelchair access   Garden   No smoking in
restaurant   No music   Dogs welcome exc in restaurant   Amex, Delta,
MasterCard, Switch, Visa   Accommodation: 3 rooms, B&B £34 to £50.*

TORCROSS   Devon   map 1

Start Bay Inn

Torcross TQ7 2TQ   TEL: (01548) 580553
on A379 Dartmouth to Kingsbridge coast road

In summer queues start to form outside this sixteenth-century
thatched pub on Slapton Sands even before it opens. The crowds
come mainly for the enormous portions of fish and chips: in fact, the
pub thrives on this quintessentially English institution, and is in

effect part pub, part 'chippy', with décor kept simple and sauces served in plastic sachets. Starters invariably focus on seafood, and include the likes of deep-fried squid, and giant prawns in garlic butter, while non-fish main-course dishes tend to be of the gammon and pineapple variety, and snacks such as ploughman's and jacket potatoes are also available. But fish is the main thing here: check out the specials blackboard for what has been caught that day. Children have their own menu. To drink, there is Heron Valley local farm-house cider in addition to Bass and Flowers Original. The very reasonably priced wine list has a fair selection from around the world – including England – with six wines available by the glass. Those venturing beyond the beach might want to visit the nature reserve at Slapton Ley. SAMPLE DISHES: crab cocktail £3.75: large battered cod £5.25; treacle sponge pudding £2.75.

Open *winter 11.30 to 2.30, 6 to 11, Sun 12 to 2.30, 6 to 10.30; summer and school hols 11.30 to 11, Sun 12 to 10.30; closed 25 Dec evening; bar food 11.30 to 2 (2.15 summer), 6 to 9.30 (10 summer), Sun 12 to 2, 6 to 9 (all day summer)* **Details** *Children welcome in family room   Car park   Patio   No smoking in children's room and 1 area in bar   Jukebox   Dogs welcome on a lead   No cards*

T R E B U R L E Y   Cornwall   **map 1**

Springer Spaniel ✿

Treburley PL15 9NS   TEL: (01579) 370424
on A388 halfway between Launceston and Callington

They take food very seriously in this solid, squat-looking roadside pub. The main bar is dominated by a wood-burning stove with a huge settle snuggling up to it. Two other bars are similarly decorated with prints of a country nature, giving the place a comfortable ambience. An indicator of the Spaniel's popularity, one reader tells us, is that it is necessary to book a fortnight in advance to get a table on a Saturday night. The licensees are keen to stress that they employ three chefs plus a separate chef for preparing vegetables, many of which they grow themselves. Much use, in fact, is made of local supplies generally, and everything except bread and ice-cream, we are told, is made on the premises. Bar food includes a sound, reasonably priced selection of sandwiches and salads, and pleasingly simple dishes such as cold roast beef with home-made pickles and chips. Also available in the bar are starters and pies from the pub's restaurant menu: terrine of duck livers, soused Orkney herrings, and venison and game pie, for example. For the sweet-toothed there is fresh-fruit pavlova, bread-and-butter pudding, or imaginative ice-creams. The New World makes a strong showing on the concise wine list, which features four pudding wines; three wines are sold by the small or large glass. On tap are St Austell Dartmoor Best and

HSD, and there is an extensive selection of whiskies, liqueurs, sherries and ports. SAMPLE DISHES: macaroni cheese £4; kidneys in Meaux mustard with rice £9; spotted dick £3.25.

Open *11 to 3, 5.30 to 11, Sun 12 to 3, 7 to 10.30; closed 4 days over Christmas; bar food and restaurant 12 to 2, 6.30 to 9*
Details *Children welcome in family room and dining-room   Car park Wheelchair access   Garden   No smoking in dining-room until after 10pm No music   No dogs in dining-room   Delta, MasterCard, Switch, Visa*

TREGADILLET   Cornwall   map 1

▲ *Eliot Arms*

Tregadillet PL15 7EU   TEL: (01566) 772051
off A30, 2m W of Launceston

The pub actually has two names – Eliot Arms and Square & Compass – owing to its long and rather convoluted history. In fact, time can be whatever you want it to be here, depending on which of the 70-odd clocks, including half a dozen grandfathers, you consult. But you are likely to lose track of time, anyway, examining possibly the largest collection of snuffboxes in the world, all the advertising junk, sepia postcards, cigarette cards, books and, in one of the bars in particular, a mass of horse brasses. Candlesticks, china and books are crammed into all the nooks and crannies. The tables and chairs themselves, antique settles and chaises longues among them, will also catch the eye. While you wait for your food to be cooked, you could potter round these cosy rooms, musing on the pub's history (as coaching-inn, smithy, then masonic lodge, where former French prisoners released from Dartmoor Prison after the Napoleonic Wars would meet), with a pint of St Austell HSD, Dartmoor Best, or Marston's Pedigree in hand. Others will prefer Countryman Scrumpy, one of eight wines sold by the glass, or indeed one of a dozen malt whiskies. It won't be hard to find something appealing from four pages of printed menu, perhaps a home-made special such as vegetable moussaka, salads, chargrills, something smoked on the premises, or various ploughman's, open sandwiches and basket meals. But the blackboard might have taken your fancy first, with turkey and leek pie, whole sole with lemon and parsley butter, or a hot winter pud with Cornish cream. SAMPLE DISHES: open gammon steak sandwich topped with cheese £4.50; fisherman's crunch £6; half a home-smoked chicken with barbecue sauce and coleslaw £8.

Open *11 to 3, 6 to 11, Sun 12 to 2.30, 7 to 10.30; bar food 12 to 2 (1.45 Sun), 7 to 9.30*
Details *Children welcome in family room   Car park   Wheelchair access Patio   Background music   Dogs welcome in 1 bar only   Delta, MasterCard, Switch, Visa   Accommodation: 2 rooms, B&B £20 to £50*

Plough

Taylors Lane, Trottiscliffe ME19 5DR   TEL: (01732) 822233
off M20 junction 2, between A20 and A227, 2m S of
Culverstone Green

This 500-year-old, weatherboarded inn is a popular family destination, not least because Trosley Country Park is nearby. Expect fun
rather than huge sophistication. A short bar menu offers soup of the
'moment' rather than soup of the day, which is suggestive of some
spontaneity in the kitchen; other starters are also refreshingly different. Peeled prawns poached in chilli and garlic butter is tempting and
alliterative, and grilled goats' cheese is served with home-made chutney. Ploughman's and jumbo rolls aside, the main dishes are all on
the specials board, which may offer ribeye steaks, fresh salmon fillets
in a variety of sauces, or home-made meat curries that take their
influence from Thailand, India and even Arabia. Many of the
puddings, such as bread-and-butter or marmalade sponge, are
prepared by a local pensioner. Peter Humphrey sells a most un-
Kentish range of ales, including Adnams, Wadworth 6X, Flowers
and Fuller's, and a cheerful wine list is guaranteed not to stretch the
pocket. SAMPLE DISHES: smoked fillet of trout with horseradish
£3.50; curry of the day £5; profiteroles £2.50.

Open *11.30 to 11; bar food 11.30 to 2, 6 to 9.30*
Details *Children welcome in bar eating area   Car park   Wheelchair access*
Patio   Background and live music   No dogs   Delta, MasterCard, Switch, Visa

▲ *Queens Head Hotel*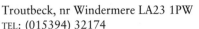

Troutbeck, nr Windermere LA23 1PW
TEL: (015394) 32174
at start of Kirkstone Pass, 2½m from junction of A591 and A592

This seventeenth-century coaching-inn in the Troutbeck valley lies at
the bottom of the Kirkstone Pass in magnificent scenery, with stunning
views from the front terrace. The rambling interior has a wealth of
beams, carved settles, sturdy tables, open fires and interesting old local
photographs. A surely unique feature is the carved four-poster bed
which forms part of the serving counter. The same enticing menu is
served in the bar and upstairs evening restaurant and is awash with
late-twentieth-century notions of seared this on a bed of that, lavished
with something else and set on a compote of thingamijig. Filled
baguettes are served at lunch-time only; otherwise, start with soup,

mussels or a warm salad of feta cheese, caramelised rhubarb and apricots with a chilli dressing. Main courses might be steak, ale and mushroom cobbler, or rack of Lakeland lamb with parsnip and sweet potato rösti, with desirable fish choices of salmon, tuna or bream; vegetarians are offered a lentil and chickpea boudin and a platter of roasted vegetables. Children have their own grown-up-sounding menu – none of your turkey dinosaurs here. Puddings might be blackberry parfait, brûlée of the day, or spiced oat cookies with cranachan and raspberry compote (those that stay overnight can wake up to devilled kidneys on home-made crumpets). Beers are an excellent choice from Tetley and Boddingtons as well as Mitchell's Lancaster Bomber, and Coniston Bluebird and Old Man. The 20-bottle wine list is made up of attractive wines but only three house wines can be had by the glass. SAMPLE DISHES: pan-fried chicken livers £5; braised shank of English lamb £9.50; bread-and-butter pudding with an apricot glaze £3.50.

Open *11 to 11, Sun 12 to 10.30; closed 25 Dec; bar food 12 to 2.30, 6.30 to 9; restaurant all week D only 6.30 to 9*
Details *Children welcome Car park Wheelchair access Patio No-smoking areas Background music Dogs welcome Delta, MasterCard, Switch, Visa Accommodation: 9 rooms, B&B £40 to £75*

TUCKENHAY Devon   map 1

▲ *Maltsters' Arms* [NEW ENTRY]

Bow Creek, Tuckenhay TQ9 7EQ TEL: (01803) 732350
off A381, 2½m S of Totnes

Denise and Quentin Thwaites took over the Maltsters' Arms in late 1997 after ten years running a pub on the Thames at Richmond. They have re-introduced a concept that is so traditional as to be almost totally forgotten: the pub as village store. All those things that you only ever seem to need at night – plasters, aspirin, toothbrushes, fuses, torches, matches, stamps and, of course, Sevruga caviare – are all available from the pub. That other vital item, beer, is also provided in abundance. Dartmoor IPA is always on, as is a Blackawton ale, and in their first year the Thwaites have managed to sell over 60 different guests, as well as local Ruddy Turnstone cider. Narrow stone stairs lead up to the bar, which contains an an informal restaurant area. Further on is a snug, with a small log-burning fire and just two long trestle tables, making sharing a must. The pub is decked out with red-painted wood-strip walls, bare scrubbed floorboards, a collection of pewter tankards, and large framed prints of the battle of Waterloo; there is even a picture screwed to the ceiling.

The menu warns that prices for fish and game dishes will fluctuate with the market. So do not necessarily expect to pay the same for your pigeon breasts with kumquats and orange curaçao, or game terrine and winter berry relish, on different days. And that goes for your wild boar, juniper and cranberry pie, venison steak with redcurrant and Madeira glaze, or pot-roasted woodcock with sloe gin and winter vegetables. The children's menu is headed 'real food for children'; not a nugget in sight, just dishes like pan-fried chicken breast, and meatballs in tomato sauce. The pub has regular barbecues, and food is served on the quayside of Bow Creek. A short wine list has a couple of English bottles and dessert wines, and sports one or two superior selections and plenty of good drinking by the glass. Floodlit at night, Bow Creek is an ideal place for spotting rare birds. SAMPLE DISHES: melon with wild smoked venison £5; turkey and bacon pie £7.50; red fruit bread-and-butter pudding £4.

Open *summer 11 to 11, Sun 12 to 10.30, winter Mon to Fri 11 to 2.30, 6 to 11, Sat 11 to 11, Sun 12 to 10.30; closed for food 25 Dec, bar open 12 to 2; bar food and restaurant 12 to 3 (2 winter), 6.30 to 9.30 (9 winter), snacks all day Sat and in summer*
Details *Children welcome in bar eating area   Car park   Wheelchair access Garden and patio   Live music   Dogs welcome   MasterCard, Switch, Visa Accommodation: 4 rooms, B&B £40 to £85*

TURVILLE   Buckinghamshire   map 3

Bull and Butcher

Turville RG9 6QU   TEL: (01491) 638283
between B480 and B482, 5m N of Henley-on-Thames

This small seventeenth-century black-and-white timbered pub is set in a Chilterns village that has featured in both *The Vicar of Dibley* and *Chitty Chitty Bang Bang*. Just by the thirteenth-century church, the front lawn has tables, chairs and fruit trees, and barbecues are occasionally held on summer weekends. Inside, beams from captured Spanish Armada ships provide extra counter space for drinking. Food is cooked to order and includes an eclectic mix: start perhaps with tapas, stir-fried calamares, black pudding, or potted prawns, followed by scallops with lemon grass and garlic, steak Wellington, roast Barbary duck or fillet of venison. A reporter described roast neck of lamb with red wine sauce as 'first class with excellent vegetables'. Vegetarians have the choice of a vegetable crêpe, or a pasta dish, while desserts might be treacle and nut, or lemon tart. A range of Brakspear beers is offered, plus Weston's Old Rosie cider. A list of three-dozen wines includes 22 by the glass. SAMPLE DISHES: roast goats' cheese £6; calf's liver and bacon £15; tarte au citron £3.50.

Open *11 to 3, 6 (6.30 Sat) to 11, Sun 12 to 3, 7 to 10.30; bar food Tue to Sun L 12 to 2 (2.30 Sat and Sun), Tue to Sat D 7 to 9.45*
Details *Children welcome in bar eating area   Car park   Garden   No music Dogs welcome   Delta, MasterCard, Switch, Visa*

ULVERSTON   Cumbria   map 8

▲ *Bay Horse Hotel* ✿

Canal Foot, Ulverston LA12 9EL   TEL: (01229) 583972
*off A590, 8m NE of Barrow-in-Furness, take Canal Foot turn in
Ulverston, then next signed left turn following lane to pub*

A renowned dining destination on the Cumbrian coast, this well-
run small hotel ('more a restaurant-with-rooms') has a good pubby
atmosphere in a traditional bar and is well worth the uninspiring
drive through a huge Glaxo factory complex to get there. This
seventeenth-century inn is located on the shores of the Leven estuary with fine views across Morecambe Bay to the Lancashire and
Cumbrian fells. Formerly a staging-post for coaches that crossed
the sands of Morecambe Bay, it is a beautiful spot on a clear day,
and the views are best appreciated from the terrace of the pub
while indulging in a long, refreshing drink. The traditional
Lakeland pub interior has old beams, gleaming brassware, attractive armchairs, comfortable padded wall bench seating, plenty of
plates and an open fire. Very much an evening destination, with
its attractive conservatory dining-room, it draws a discerning,
well-heeled clientele who come for the imaginative restaurant
food.

The bar menu (lunch-times only) is supplemented by a blackboard
of daily specials. Cheese and herb pâté is a classic dish from Robert
Lyons's days at Miller Howe in Windermere, and tomato and
orange salad with garlic and herb bread is another example of his
imaginative style; sandwiches are also available. Main courses are
likely to be layers of cooked ham, pear and Stilton baked in a cheese
and chive pastry; a large field mushroom filled with caramelised
apricots and shallots baked with a Cheddar cheese and grain
mustard topping; or pan-fried strips of chicken, leeks and button
mushrooms on a bed of savoury rice with sweet-and-sour sauce.
Various pickles and chutneys are home-made, as are the desserts,
which might be poached pears with butterscotch sauce or chocolate
Drambuie terrine; or try a cheese platter with home-made biscuits
and soda bread. Theakston Best, Morland Old Speckled Hen,
Ruddles County, Marston's Pedigree and Courage Directors are on
handpump and, there is a well-chosen list of wines from around the
world, with six house wines available by the bottle or glass. SAMPLE
DISHES: button mushrooms in a tomato, cream and brandy sauce on
a peanut butter croûton £5.75; minced beef, red chilli peppers,
spring onions and ginger glazed with honey, calvados and raspberry
vinegar £8.75; fresh raspberry and frangelico crème brûlée with
vanilla butter biscuits £5.

Open *11 to 11, Sun 12 to 10.30; bar food Tue to Sun L 12 to 2; restaurant Tue to Sat 12 to 1.30, 7.30 for 8 (1 sitting)*
Details *Children welcome in bar eating area   Car park   Garden   No smoking in restaurant   Background music   Dogs welcome in bedrooms only MasterCard, Switch, Visa   Accommodation: 7 rooms, B&B £85 to £160*

UPTON   Nottinghamshire   map 5

French Horn   NEW ENTRY

Upton NG23 5ST   TEL: (01636) 812394
on Southwell to Newark road, 5m from Newark

This eighteenth-century former farmhouse in the centre of an attractive village, noted for its church and Upton House (NT), is a popular
dining pub offering an extensive range of food. There is a comfortable and welcoming single front bar, a boon for travellers as food
(not the full menu) is served all day. Some dishes, such as creamy
tuna pasta bake, gammon steak and other typically pubby things, are
available in the bar only, but you can sit anywhere to enjoy pan-fried
queenies with deep-fried leeks and a Pernod cream sauce, or prawns
in a Caesar salad as starters. From there you could choose poached
halibut steak in a Thai curry sauce, one of the fishy daily specials, or
a pork fillet wrapped in bacon with an apple and brandy sauce,
before moving into the sweets or cheeses. This Ward's pub offers
beers from parent company Vaux – Sampson and Waggledance – as
well as Ward's Thorne and Superior. There is also short wine list
that you will find printed at the foot of the menu, and nine or ten
wines by the glass are listed on a blackboard. SAMPLE DISHES: mushrooms stuffed with Stilton £3.25; chicken stir-fry with cashew-nuts
£6.25; profiteroles £3.

Open *11 to 11 (Sun 12 to 10.30); closed 25 Dec eve; bar food and restaurant 12 to 2, 6 to 9.30 (a restricted menu operates from 2 to 6)*
Details *Children welcome if eating   Car park   Garden   No-smoking area Background music   Guide dogs only   Delta, MasterCard, Switch, Visa*

UPTON BISHOP   Herefordshire   map 5

Moody Cow

Crow Hill, Upton Bishop HR9 7TT   TEL: (01989) 780470
at crossroads of B4224 and B4221, 4m NE of Ross-on-Wye

Carrying on happily in the successful style he has been creating at the
Moody Cow since 1993, James Lloyd offers fresh food at good

value, given the portions, in a fun bistro/pub environment. You would be wise to book a table on Thursdays (live jazz night) and over the weekend as it can be pretty busy; and you may have to wait even longer for your food, which is all cooked to order. Starters can be taken as mains, so 'start', in the most literal sense only, with a basket of melon with peeled prawns – a house speciality – or pan-fried sardines in garlic butter and served on a bed of tomato slices, swimming in garlic butter, and then move on, figuratively, to breast of chicken stuffed with Stilton and wrapped in bacon, or fillet of beef stuffed with garlic and Brie in a brandy and mushroom sauce, or steamed fillet of salmon with a chive sauce, all served with vegetables and potatoes. They urge you to ask for the lighter bar menu if all this is too much. Ample puddings are of the bread-and-butter pudding and banoffi pie variety. The pub serves Flowers IPA, Smiles Best, Wadworth 6X and Boddingtons; only the three house wines are available by the glass. SAMPLE DISHES: duck liver terrine with apricot chutney £4.50; sauté lamb's liver with bacon and mushrooms £10; bread-and-butter pudding £3.

Open *12 to 2.30, 6.30 to 11, Sun 12 to 3, 7 to 10.30; bar food and restaurant 12 to 2, 6.30 to 9.30*
Details *Children welcome in eating areas   Car park   Wheelchair access Patio   No smoking in restaurant   Background and live music   No dogs Amex, Delta, Diners, MasterCard, Switch, Visa*

WADDESDON   **Buckinghamshire**   map 3

▲ *Five Arrows Hotel*

Waddesdon HP18 0JE   TEL: (01296) 651727
on A41 between Bicester and Aylesbury

The five arrows refer to the sons of Meyer Amschel Rothschild (the founder of the dynasty), who were sent to establish major banking houses across Europe. The Grade II listed building was built by Baron Ferdinand de Rothschild in 1887 as part of his Waddesdon estate and was erected, as was common with building projects of the time, to cater for the artisans constructing the rest of the manor – a way of clawing back some of their wages. It is one of the most interesting buildings in the village, being half-timbered with fine chimneys and wrought ironwork. It is still owned by the Rothschilds and, within, you will find artefacts of Waddesdon from the Baron Ferdinand era. A pleasant terrace and lovely gardens are available for summer drinking.

As befitting its ownership, this is an upmarket establishment offering modern cooking with some imaginative touches; note that food is available only at lunch-time, and not on Sunday. Deep-fried artichoke hearts on a bed of rocket would be a typical starter from a regularly changing menu. From there you could move on to an imaginative crisp filo parcel of mousseline of Waddesdon pheasant with a champagne sauce, and then to hazelnut meringue with a grain chocolate sauce. Trendy touches come in the form of field mushrooms with sun-dried tomatoes and dolcellate and there is a bit of name dropping in the Boodles apricot and orange trifle with a mirabelle eau-de-vie. Wines are all good vintages, yet surprisingly reasonably priced. There is also a selection from the Rothschild vinyards, in particular a 1984 Ch. Mouton Rothschild at £80. Beers are from Adnams and Fuller's. SAMPLE DISHES: brandied chicken liver parfait with an orange confit £5.50; Cajun blackened salmon with smoked potato wedges and a remoulade sauce £8.50; treacle, orange and cinnamon tart £4.25.

Open *11 to 3, 6 to 11, Sun 12 to 3, 7 to 10.30; Mon to Sat bar food and restaurant L only 12 to 2.15*
Details *Children welcome   Car park   Wheelchair access (also WC)   Garden and patio   No smoking in restaurant   Background music   No dogs MasterCard, Switch, Visa   Accommodation: 6 rooms, B&B £60 to £75*

WADENHOE   Northamptonshire   map 6

▲ *King's Head*

Church Street, Wadenhoe PE8 5ST   TEL: (01832) 720024
2m off A605 between Oundle and Thrapston

Set in one of Northamptonshire's most picturesque villages, the King's Head, with its stone and thatch construction, does its fair share to add to the local ambience. It is owned by the Wadenhoe Trust, which has worked closely with the licensees to preserve the pub, which dates back to 1662. Drinkers head for the atmospheric twin bars with their oak beams and open fires; one bar is oak-floored and the other is laid with quarry tiles. For those wanting to drink al fresco, there is a sheltered courtyard and a paddock bordering the River Nene. Diners may choose between the lounge bar or the non-smoking dining-room, and select from the regularly changing printed menu favourites as steak and kidney casserole with herb suet dumplings, and bread-and-butter pudding. The lunch menu is simpler, offering ploughman's and Welsh-rarebit-style fare. The 80-strong wine list tends to favour Old World wines, with a respectable number available in half-bottles or by the glass. For beer drinkers, ales from Adnams plus Marston's Pedigree are on draught. The pub is on the Nene Way and nearby attractions include Fotheringhay, Rockingham Castle and Elton Hall. SAMPLE DISHES: herb mousse on tomato and basil sauce £4.25; salmon roasted with olive oil, tomatoes and courgettes £9.75; pasta al forno £7.

Open *Tue to Sun 12 to 3, Mon to Sat 7 (6 summer and Fri and Sat winter) to 11 (10.30 Sun); bar food and restaurant Tue to Sun 12 to 2, Tue to Sat 7 to 9*
Details *Children welcome in eating areas   Car park   Wheelchair access (also WC)   Garden and patio   No smoking in restaurant   No music   Dogs welcome in public bar   MasterCard, Visa   Accommodation: 2 rooms £35 to £50*

WALBERSWICK   Suffolk   map 6

▲ *Bell Inn*

Ferry Road, Walberswick IP18 6TN   TEL: (01502) 723109
on B1387, off A12, S of Southwold

Any aficionado of this part of Suffolk knows what to expect of a pub, and as an Adnams tied house, the Bell is all too happy to oblige with a splendid glass of ale. Walberswick is a loveable village, and only the most determinedly resentful would accuse it of being over-gentrified. Certainly, though, it is a regular weekend bolt-hole, and in this village-green location patrons may well include metropolitan refugees of an artistic bent. If this bothers you, down another glass and stroll outside to admire the views of neighbouring Southwold beyond the River Blyth. The Bell is a genuinely antique but sympathetically extended hostelry, upgraded greatly by licensee Sue Ireland Cutting, and unpretentiously furnished in rustic style. The food is given much thought, and tables are arranged in all the bars as well as an overflow dining-room. The printed menu is terse and basic, offering various fish platters, ploughman's lunches and sandwiches. Children have a few suggestions too. For more interesting daily specials, consult the chalkboard – it is tricky to read from the far side of the bar, but not to be missed. A 'huge bowl of superb, minestrone-style soup [which] couldn't have been bettered' was praised on a recent inspection, along with good vegetables and 'super-crisp salad'. Helpings are described as 'gargantuan', prices good value, and service 'friendly, efficient and prompt'. Aside from Adnams 'in perfect condition', on offer are 20 or so inexpensive but interesting wines (half a dozen by the glass and a good range of half-bottles too). SAMPLE DISHES: Stilton and celery soup £2.50; gammon, spinach and cheese bake £6; vanilla terrine with blackcurrant coulis £3.

Open *11 to 3, 6 to 11, Sat and school summer hols 11 to 11, Sun 12 to 10.30; closed eves 25 and 26; bar food and restaurant 12 to 2, 6 to 9; no food Sun eve in winter*
Details *Children welcome in eating areas and games room   Car park Wheelchair access (also WC)   Garden   No smoking in restaurant   No music Dogs welcome   MasterCard, Switch, Visa   Accommodation: 5 rooms, B&B £40 to £100*

WAMBROOK   Somerset   map 2

▲ *Cotley Inn*

Wambrook TA20 3EN   TEL: (01460) 62348
off A30, just W of Chard

Under the same management for over a decade, this rural pub has a quiet, reliable air. Though apparently off the beaten track, and a little tricky to find (especially at night), Wambrook is not at all far from the major holiday routes to the south-west. From the outside, the inn is a long stone building with smallish windows rather like a typical Somerset farm. Inside, it is reassuringly cosy with log fires and plush buttoned banquettes; a flagstoned bowling alley lies to one side. The menu offers 'something for everyone', as a recent inspection confirmed, and the promise 'We do not do fast food, but good food as fast as possible' augurs well for freshness and quality. Menus (chalked and printed) offer a wide choice of 'small eats' (devilled kidneys on toast or a Brie filo with a fruit sauce), 'big meaty eats' (steaks, chops and grills), 'big fishy eats' (seafood gratin or whole king prawns), plus omelettes and vegetarian dishes. There is a snack menu and blackboard specials too. Drinks include Otter and Flowers real ales, and over a dozen easy-drinking wines at reasonable prices, including four by the glass. SAMPLE DISHES: lambs' kidneys in port and cream £3.75; trout stuffed with prawns and cucumber £9; Somerset apple cake £2.50.

Open *11 (12 Sun) to 3, 7 to 11; bar food and restaurant 12 to 2.30, 7 to 9.30*
Details *Children welcome   Car park   Garden   No smoking in restaurant No music   Dogs in bar only   Delta, MasterCard, Switch, Visa Accommodation: 2 rooms, B&B £29 to £41*

WARDLOW MIRES   Derbyshire   map 8

Three Stags Heads 🍺

Wardlow Mires SK17 8RW   TEL: (01298) 872268
at junction of B6465 and A623, 2m E of Tideswell

Pat and Geoff Fuller explain that since their modest stone cottage freehouse in prime walking and pot-holing country is rather isolated, and since they are committed to serving freshly cooked food, they may decide not to open the pub on some weekday evenings during the winter months. Too bad if you make the journey specially, so you would be advised to phone if the weather is at all dodgy. Those fortunate enough to gain entry will find two rustic rooms, and some wonderful decisions to make on the beer front. Shall it be

Springhead Best Bitter, or the Abbeydale Brewery's Matins or Last Rites direct from the cask, or the occasional guest? On the menu, too, are some difficult choices (and before you read further, note that food is available only in the evening except Mondays and at Saturday and Sunday lunch-times), with everything home-made apart from a few good-quality gâteaux. A hearty soup may be just the job to reinvigorate anyone who has spent an active Peak District sort of a day. To follow there might be a curry of spinach with either lamb or chickpeas, a leek and Stilton hotpot, pigeon breasts or other game in season. Puddings also tend to follow the season, such as autumnal plum crumble. SAMPLE DISHES: hummus £2.50; rabbit in mustard and herb sauce £7.50; apple and mincemeat pie £2.50.

Open *Tue to Fri 7 to 11, Sat and Sun 12 to 11 (winter opening times may vary); bar food Sat and Sun L 12.30 to 3, Tue to Sun D 7.30 to 9.30*
Details *No children   Car park   Occasional live music on weekends   Dogs welcome   No cards*

WARHAM ALL SAINTS   Norfolk   map 6

▲ *Three Horseshoes* 🍺

Bridge Street, Warham All Saints NR23 1NL
TEL: (01328) 710547
off A149 or B1105, 2m SE of Wells-next-the-Sea

OLD ENGLISH

Warham is a pretty village of flint cottages slightly inland from the North Norfolk coast: an area popular with walkers, birdwatchers and fishermen. The pub is a long, split-level, flint building, whose first recorded appearance as an alehouse was in 1725. Its gas-lit interior has stone floors, scrubbed wooden tables, an open fireplace, and on a quiet afternoon your reverie will be broken only by the gentle ticking of the grandfather clock. Beers, which are the pub's strong point, are served through a hole-in-the-wall bar direct from cask. Woodforde's Wherry, Polly's Folly from tiny Norfolk microbrewery Buffy's, and Greene King IPA are on tap, while for drivers there is home-made lemonade. Food is traditional pub grub, with a printed menu supplemented by daily blackboard specials. Pies – best eaten with a spoon – are a speciality: there's head forester's pie for vegetarians (mushrooms and mixed nuts cooked in elderberry wine), or perhaps poacher's game pie for meat eaters. Snacks and light meals are also available, and puddings such as Bakewell tart and spotted dick are chalked up on a board. Lending interest to the basic wine list is a range of Lurgashall Winery English country wines, including Silver Birch. Not far from the pub can be found Warham Camp, an Iron Age fort, and Warham Marsh, one of Europe's largest salt marshes. SAMPLE DISHES: mackerel pot £3.50; beef, walnut and Stilton pie £7.25; lemon drizzle tart £2.50.

Open *11.30 to 2.30, 6 to 11, Sun 12 to 3, 6 to 10.30; bar food 12 to 1.55, 6.30 to 8.25 (6.30 to 8.55 Fri and Sat)*
Details *Children welcome in family room and dining-room   Car park Wheelchair access (also WC)   Garden   No smoking in 1 room at meal times Live music Sat nights   Dogs welcome   No cards   Accommodation: 5 rooms, B&B £20 to £48*

W A S S   North Yorkshire   map 9

▲ *Wombwell Arms* ✿ ▯ ❀

Wass YO61 4BE   TEL: (01347) 868280
off A19 to Coxwold, then follow signs for 2m to Ampleforth and Wass

---

When nearly a decade ago Alan and Lynda Evans took over this eighteenth-century inn, part of which was formerly a granary, they spent a great deal of effort turning it into one of the best eating pubs in the region. The four connecting rooms are done out in stripped pine furniture and Laura Ashley fittings, and the main bar features an open log fire. The menu changes frequently and is written up on blackboards. Lunchtime fare is sandwiches and snacks, such as warm salad of chargrilled chicken with pesto, plus a small selection of reasonably priced main dishes. The evening menu runs to around eight main courses. Service is described as 'consistently excellent and unobtrusive'. The well-kept beers include Timothy Taylor Landlord, Black Sheep Bitter and a guest from a Yorkshire independent. There is also a small selection of malt whiskies and a confident but changing wine list includes two wines of the month and at least seven wines by the glass. SAMPLE DISHES: smoked haddock with Welsh rarebit dressing £5.75; guinea-fowl with port, cream and mushroom sauce £8.75; caramelised rice-pudding £3.25.

Open *Tue to Sat 12 to 2.30, 7 to 11, Sun 12 to 3, 7 to 10.30; closed Sun eve winter; bar food 12 to 2, 7 to 9 (9.30 Fri and Sat)*
Details *Children welcome in family room   Car park   Wheelchair access   No smoking in some rooms   No music   No dogs   Delta, MasterCard, Switch, Visa   Accommodation: 2 rooms, B&B £29.50 to £49*

WATH-IN-NIDDERDALE   North Yorkshire   map 8

▲ *Sportsman's Arms* ✿

Wath-in-Nidderdale HG3 5PP   TEL: (01423) 711306
off B6265, 2m NW of Pateley Bridge

The Sportsman's Arms is hard to miss as it is the largest building in
Wath-in-Nidderdale. Its pubby exterior does not prepare you for
what is quite a formal establishment inside. The bar is kept toasty
warm by a roaring open fire and the bar walls are adorned with
fishing rods, sporting prints of gun dogs and other country sports
regalia. Tables are plain and candlelit, but once you have ordered
they are laid by young staff who impress with their degree of
knowledge of the menu and their unpretentious air. One reporter
was quite taken aback by their casual confidence. 'Scarborough
woof, sir, that is a firm fish, taken about one mile off the
Scarborough coast, not a flat fish, quite chunky....' Perhaps the
service left an impression, for the same visitor reported that he ate
'the best pub meal I have had in a very long time'.

Fish is the order of the day. The same menu operates in the bar
and restaurant and in addition to the half-dozen starters and mains
listed there is a daily specials board featuring a similar quantity of
dishes. The cooking aims to take good ingredients and allow the
freshness to speak for itself, so fish dishes are likely to be simply
cooked. The specials board might read as follows: chicken liver
terrine, moules marinière, mushrooms in garlic with bacon,
smoked chicken with salad, cod rarebit, halibut with prawns and
tomatoes, monkfish pancake, pheasant with bacon and mushrooms,
or lemon sole Grenoblaise. Soups are something of a house speciality: tomato and orange or carrot and coriander, perhaps. The other
dish for which the pub is famous is summer pudding, which has
been described as 'the best in the UK and possibly the world'. For
beer drinkers there are Theakston Best, John Smith's and Younger's
Scotch. There is a short wine list in the bar, with four available by
the glass, but the extensive restauarant list can also be requested.
SAMPLE DISHES: locally smoked Scottish salmon on rösti potatoes
with sour cream and chives £5; baked Scarborough woof in a garlic
and mustard crust with tomato and caper butter £8.75; Sportman's
summer pudding £3.75.

Open *12 to 2.30, 7 to 11 (10.30 Sun); bar food and restaurant 12 to 2, 7 to
9; closed 25 Dec*
Details *Children welcome   Car park   Wheelchair access (also WC)   Garden
No smoking in restaurant   Background music   No dogs   Delta, MasterCard,
Switch, Visa   Accommodation: 12 rooms, B&B £45 to £110*

WATTON-AT-STONE Hertfordshire map 3

George & Dragon

High Street, Watton-at-Stone SG14 3TA TEL: (01920) 830285
on A602, 5m SE of Stevenage

This pink-washed, half-timbered pub cuts a dash on the main street
of the village of Watton-at-Stone. Recent reporters describe it as 'just
what a tourist is looking for in old pub interiors' – a well-rounded
amalgam of polished copper and brass, blackened beams, oak tables,
Windsor chairs, hunting prints, etc. Fires blaze in chilly weather, the
tables are smartly laid with fresh flowers, and the service is courteous. This part of Hertfordshire is an affluent area; the food is ambitious and pricing is geared to well-heeled patrons, including local
business folk, though the Millionaire's and Billionaire's Buns (steak
sandwiches) are a slight exaggeration. Standards of cooking are high
and the choice is varied. A printed menu includes half a dozen
starters (the house special is smoked haddock with a tomato
concasse) and about twice as many main courses, for example fresh
salmon fillet with tarragon stuffing or roast breast of duck.
Sandwiches and lighter dishes are on offer too. Blackboard specials
are more elaborate (Mediterranean king prawns grilled with garlic
butter or half a local pheasant pot-roasted in red wine and cranberry
sauce). There is a knowingly annotated wine list ('I'm sure that Oz
Clarke would be delighted to know that I entirely agree with him,'
exclaims one description), with only a few of the 20 choices scraping
under the £10 barrier, plus several house wines by the glass or
carafe. Beer drinkers have a choice of Greene King IPA and Abbot
ales, plus 'big name' stouts, lagers and ciders. Whisky fans are
catered for too. SAMPLE DISHES: fresh mussels in white wine, garlic
and cream £4.75; lamb's liver and bacon pan-fried with Madeira and
mushroom sauce £7.25; chocolate mousse £2.75.

Open *11 to 2.30, 6 to 11, Sat 11 to 11, Sun 12 to 3, 7 to 10.30; closed 25
and eve 26 Dec; bar food and restaurant all week 12 to 2, Mon to Sat 7 to 10*
Details *Children welcome in eating areas   Car park   Garden and patio   No
smoking in 1 dining-room   No music   No dogs   Amex, Delta, Diners,
MasterCard, Switch, Visa*

WENLOCK EDGE   Shropshire   map 5

▲ *Wenlock Edge Inn*

Hilltop, Wenlock Edge TF13 6DJ   TEL: (01746) 785678
on B4371, 4½m S of Much Wenlock

The Waring family make this a very special pub through their total
lack of pretension, and a family-run pub it certainly is. There are
Warings in the kitchen and Warings behind the bar. The pub is an
isolated, rough stone building on a very narrow B road that traverses
the ridge which is Wenlock Edge, and offers stupendous views.
There are two entrance porches – one per bar – a very small, rough-
stone patio with plants in old beer casks and just one trestle table.
The interior is small and traditional. Two bars, which share the bar
counter between them, are separated by a door; one is graced by
very plain wooden tables and chairs, the other has the best feature of
the place – a giant cast-iron stove of the type that burns anything at
all. The style of cooking is very traditional and very simple, and
sauces are often based on fruit and alcohol. Raw materials are good
quality, and beef is not only local, but also organically raised. The
menu appears on light boards rather than blackboards, but changes
rarely. Where frozen fish is used, it is indicated on the menu. Start
with bradan rost – hot-smoked salmon, served warm with a little
salad and a home-made organic wholemeal roll and butter – or try
sliced mushrooms in a creamy garlic and sherry sauce, and follow
with venison pie, Hereford chicken or Shrewsbury lamb. For
pudding you could tuck into a rich chocolate roulade, queen of
puddings, or raspberry and apple crumble. The Warings take great
care over their beers and serve Hobson's Best and Town Crier, plus
an occasional guest. The 30-strong wine list majors on France, but
also has representatives from around the world: four wines are available by the glass. SAMPLE DISHES: cream of asparagus soup £2.75;
chicken, bacon and asparagus gratin £7; blackcurrant and apple tart
£3.25.

Open *Tue to Sun 11.30 (12 Sun) to 2.30, all week 6.30 to 11; closed 2
weeks Nov, 24 to 26 Dec; bar food and restaurant Tue to Sun 12 to 2, 7
to 9*
Details *Car park   Patio   No smoking in dining-room   No music   Dogs in
public bar only   Amex, Delta, MasterCard, Switch, Visa   Accommodation: 3
rooms, B&B £45 to £70*

▲ *The Crown Inn*

Wentnor SY9 5EE   TEL: (01588) 650613
off A489, 6m NE of Bishop's Castle

This seventeenth-century white pub is in the village centre and has a
small garden and patio, with lots of flower-filled tubs in summer.
The feel of the pub is 'very cosy, like a nice friend's living-room'.
Welsh dressers with Portmeirion china, and lots of curtains everywhere reinforce the domesticity. The menu is short and traditional,
with fresh home-made soup, or perhaps prawn and cucumber salad,
setting the tone. A reporter was tempted by the Shrewsbury-style
lamb chops which came accompanied by a tangy lemon, redcurrant
and mushroom sauce: 'delicious' was the verdict. Ocean crumble is a
collection of smoked seafood, white fish and prawns with a cheesy
wholemeal breadcrumb topping. There is an above-average range of
vegetarian dishes – a medley of vegetables in spicy tomato chilli
sauce, say – and all the puddings are prepared on the premises.
Bread-and-butter pudding comes in regular style or chocolate
flavoured, and all sweets come with custard, fresh cream or ice-
cream. The beer list keeps a balance between established brands –
Morland Old Speckled Hen and Worthington – and beers from local
brewers Wood and Hobsons. The wine list offers a short, 13-bottle
selection, plus a 'Connoisseurs selection' of five more expensive
bottles and four champagnes and sparkling wines. SAMPLE DISHES:
smoked trout fillets with horseradish sauce £4; chicken Caesar
£8.50; pecan cheesecake £3.

Open *12 to 3, 7 to 11 (10.30 Sun); bar food and restaurant 12 to 2, 7 to 9;
no food 25 Dec*
Details *Children welcome   Car park   Wheelchair access   Garden and patio
No smoking in restaurant   Background music   MasterCard, Switch, Visa
Accommodation: 4 rooms, B&B £25 to £53*

▲ *Ye Olde Salutation Inn* ❦

Market Pitch, Weobley HR4 8SJ   TEL: (01544) 318443
*just off A4112 Leominster to Brecon road, in village centre,
12m NW of Hereford*

This 500-year-old black-and-white timber-framed former ale and
ciderhouse is situated near the 900-year-old church in a medieval
village. The adjoining cottage offers well-appointed bedrooms, and

there is a patio with tables, chairs and umbrellas for summer eating. Inside, the public bar has fruit machines and other games, while the comfortable main lounge has a wealth of beams, standing timbers and an inglenook fireplace. At lunch-time choose from a variety of ploughman's or filled baguettes; bar menu starters might be soup, pâté, deep-fried Brie wedges, or sauté of chicken livers, followed by steak and stout pie, fillet of cod, or pan-fried lamb cutlets. The separate Oak Room restaurant offers more sophisticated dishes, such as feuilleté of wild mushrooms, or ravioli of chicken mousse, with main courses of braised half-guinea-fowl, saddle of venison or seasonal fish of the day; vegetarians have their own menu. Bread-and-butter pudding and dark chocolate mousse are typical meal endings. Local Leominster guest brews augment the usual beers on offer, Hook Norton Best and Fuller's London Pride. There are seven wines by the glass plus a very extensive round-the-world list of bottles, all at reasonable prices – a separate fine-wine list rises to £300 for a 1987 Ch. Petrus Pomerol. SAMPLE DISHES: savoury pancake £4.25; medallions of pork with a port and Stilton sauce £7.25; Bramley apple tart £4.

Open *11 to 11, Sun 12 to 10.30; closed 25 Dec; bar food 12 to 2, 7 to 9.30; restaurant Tue to Sat 12 to 2, 7 to 9*
Details *Children welcome in bar eating area   Car park   Wheelchair access Patio   No smoking area in lounge bar; no smoking in restaurant   No music Dogs welcome in public bar only   Amex, Delta, Diners, MasterCard, Switch, Visa   Accommodation: 5 rooms, B&B £40 to £70*

WEST BEXINGTON   **Dorset**   **map 2**

▲ *Manor Hotel*

Beach Road, West Bexington DT2 9DF
TEL: (01308) 897616
on B3157, 3m NW of Abbotsbury

SEASIDE

The Manor is a hotel, but its cellar bar is sufficiently pubby to bring in a pub-seeking clientele. The original building was constructed as a manor-house in the eleventh century, and is mentioned in the Domesday Book. Outside, there are 'stunning' views of Chesil Beach while, inside, drinkers and diners have a choice of the dark, traditional bar or the lighter, airier conservatory. Fish is a feature, and manifests itself in any number of guises: Mediterranean fish soup, crab and asparagus pancake, or lobster thermidor. Meat-eaters might find air-dried ham and exotic fruits a tempting starter, before settling on cottage pie, bangers and mash, or rabbit casserole. A separate restaurant offers two- or three-course set meals that might include crab-cakes with chilli dressing, followed by roast breast of pheasant with wild boar sausage, and sweets from the trolley. This privately owned establishment sells beers from the Thomas Hardy Brewery. There is an extensive wine list, but only house wines are available by the glass. SAMPLE DISHES: shell-on prawns with garlic butter £7; lemon sole £11; crème brûlée £3.75.

Open *11 to 11; closed 25 Dec eve; bar food 12 to 2, 6.30 to 10; restaurant 12 to 1.30, 7 to 9.30*
Details *Children welcome   Car park   Garden   No smoking in conservatory Background music   Dogs welcome   Amex, Diners, MasterCard, Switch, Visa Accommodation: 13 rooms, B&B £52 to £95*

WEST CAMEL   Somerset   map 2

▲ *Walnut Tree*

Fore Street, West Camel BA22 7QF   TEL: (01935) 851292
off A303, between Sparkford and Ilchester

'Sunday lunch for four: excellent seafood tagliatelle with plenty of things fishy; steak and kidney pie with a big puff of pastry on good meat and first-class gravy; moist turkey, again with excellent gravy; and very fresh and crunchy garlicky salad with king prawns.' This sums up the pub's capabilities well. It does indeed major on fish and seafood, offering six daily choices on a blackboard, perhaps halibut with a buttery prawn and mushroom sauce, or salmon with prawns and cucumber. Sauces are another hallmark: non-fish eaters may be pleased by filo parcel of Cheddar with onion compote and tomato and basil sauce, or chicken breast wrapped in bacon with a creamy asparagus sauce. Puddings are home-made, with some unusual numbers among them, such as white and dark chocolate cups with Tia Maria sauce. Bass and Butcombe Bitter on draught or 30 wines, five of them by the glass, are the liquid accompaniments. Two miles from both the Fleet Air Arm Museum and the Sparkford Motor Museum, the pub has been renovated and considerably extended, its furniture and furnishings now modern and comfortable. Some of the well-kitted-out flowery bedrooms are on the ground floor. SAMPLE DISHES: crab gâteau £4.50; tuna fillet in cream and pepper sauce £11; mango mousse £3.

Open *11 to 2, 6.30 to 11; closed Sun eve in winter; bar food and restaurant 12 to 2, 7 to 9.30 (exc Sun D)*
Details *Children welcome in eating area of bar   Car park   Wheelchair access Garden and patio   No smoking in dining-room   Background music   Guide dogs only   Amex, Delta, Diners, MasterCard, Switch, Visa   Accommodation: 7 rooms, B&B £46 to £80*

WEST ILSLEY   Berkshire   map 2

Harrow Inn ❀   NEW ENTRY

West Ilsley RG20 7AR   TEL: (01635) 281260
1½m off A34, 10m N of Newbury

Scott Hunter and Emily Hawes took over this Morland pub in
November 1996, just too late to be included as a main entry in the
last edition, though feedback since then suggests promotion from
'Out and About' is well deserved. The whitewashed, roadhouse-style
inn has three separate garden areas, with outside eating areas for fine
days. Opposite is the village cricket pitch and duck pond, and
beyond are fields of sheep. Inside the well-lit bar are light wood
tables and dark wood chairs, and the walls are decorated with horsey
prints, notably Derby winners, reflecting the importance of horse
training in the area. The 'first-class cooking' is a mix of bar snacks
(not available in the evening) and more expensive specials, several
available as either starters or mains, and the menu is sensibly short.
The blackboard might tempt you to start with seafood bisque, or
grilled goats' cheese on walnut salad. Dishes like onion tart and
potato salad, or smoked chicken, orange and avocado salad can be
first or second courses. Full main courses may include monkfish tail
served on artichoke mash, salmon in lime vinaigrette, or sea bass
with mussel casserole. Braised lamb shank arrives pinkish and the
meat falls off the bone. Mindful, perhaps, of the birds on the pond,
duck makes frequent appearances on the menu – oven roast on wild
mushrooms, possibly, or breast and confit leg surrounded by shallots
in a wine sauce. Morland ales are served, and the wine list offers ten
very reasonably priced wines by the glass. SAMPLE DISHES: chicken
liver parfait and home-made chutney £3.50; fillet of halibut with
lemon and parsley butter £10; chocolate brownies £4.

Open *11 to 3, 6 to 11, Sun 12 to 4, 7 to 10.30; bar food all week L 12 to
1.50, Mon to Sat D 7 to 8.50*
Details *Children welcome   Wheelchair access (also WC)   Garden   No
smoking in dining-room   No music   Dogs welcome   Delta, MasterCard,
Switch, Visa*

WESTLETON   Suffolk   map 6

▲ *Crown*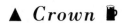

Westleton IP17 3AD   TEL: (01728) 648777
on B1125, 8m N of Saxmundham

This former coaching-inn at the hub of the attractive village of
Westleton presents a fairly plain frontage to the world, which disguises
a quite extensive building with a traditional bar, as well as a restaurant
and lounge, plus accommodation, making it convenient for visits to
nearby Snape Maltings or Minsmere RSPB reserve. The bar walls are
almost obscured by a plethora of prints, photos and ancient farm
implements. Shove ha'penny and ninepins are available for aficionados. At the rear are landscaped gardens designed by Chelsea Flower
Show gold medallists Blooms of Bressingham. The lengthy bar lunch
menu is reasonably priced and portions have been described as
'gargantuan'. House specialities include 'knaves on horseback' – pâté-
stuffed mushrooms with bacon – and home-made soups and ice-cream,
but the emphasis is on locally caught fish, such as grilled oak-smoked
haddock in garlic butter. In the evenings, the more formal restaurant
menu takes priority and bar food may not be available. Beer drinkers
will be pleased to note that an impressive tally of six real ales is on
offer. Southwold being only seven miles distant, Adnams is a permanent feature; the other five ales change regularly. There is also a
whisky list with over 100 malts and superior blends, and the extensive,
80-bottle wine list includes 12 half-bottles and six wines by the glass.
SAMPLE DISHES: sea-fish thermidor £3.50; steamed fillet of turbot £14;
home-made chocolate, orange and Cointreau ice-cream £3.25.

Open *11 to 11; closed eve 25 and 26 Dec; bar food and restaurant 12 to
2.15, 7 to 9.30*
Details *Children welcome in dining-room   Car park   Wheelchair access (also
WC)   Garden and patio   No-smoking area   Background music   Dogs
welcome in bar   Amex, Delta, Diners, MasterCard, Switch, Visa
Accommodation: 19 rooms, B&B £58.50 to £109.50*

WESTON TURVILLE   Buckinghamshire   map 3

Chequers Inn

35 Church Lane, Weston Turville HP22 5SJ   TEL: (01296) 613298
*from A41 midway between Aylesbury and Tring, take B4544 then
Bates Lane and Church Lane*

Set in a quiet lane, this cream-washed pub has a pretty front patio
with tables and umbrellas. The interior has an attractive flagstoned
floor and flint walls, with beams and a large fireplace. Friendly

service creates a pleasant atmosphere. The blackboard bar menu offers soup, pâté, or warm chicken salad for starters, plus light meals of lasagne, scampi, prawns or moussaka. More substantial main courses could be half a shoulder of lamb, beef and ale pie or a steak sandwich. Daily fresh fish might be sea bass, tuna or lobster. Puddings range from strawberry charlotte to fresh fruit salad or summer pudding. The separate, more expensive restaurant has an extensive *carte*, as well as a three-course table d'hôte menu. On tap are Adnams, Wadworth 6X, and Fuller's London Pride, plus a monthly-changing guest ale – plus Inches cider. Wines by the glass are offered from bottles displayed on the counter. SAMPLE DISHES: whitebait with granary bread £4.50; lamb hotpot £7; tarte Tatin £2.50.

Open *Tue to Sat L 12 to 3, Mon to Sat eve 6 to 11, Sun 12 to 3, 7 to 10.30; closed bank hols; bar food and restaurant Tue to Sun L 12 to 2, all week D (exc restaurant Mon) 7 to 9.30*
Details *Children welcome   Car park   Wheelchair access   Background music Guide dogs only   Amex, Delta, MasterCard, Switch, Visa*

WEST WYCOMBE   Buckinghamshire   map 3

▲ *George & Dragon*

High Street, West Wycombe HP14 3AB   TEL: (01494) 464414
on A40, 3m W of High Wycombe

This Grade II listed Tudor coaching-inn is on the village main street, with an old cobbled yard at the back for summer drinking. Inside there are blackened beams, Windsor chairs, window seats and red painted walls. A printed menu of regular dishes such as soup, chicken goujons or potted Stilton to start, followed by steak and kidney pudding, beef Wellington or various steaks from the chargrill is supplemented by blackboard specials. These might be grilled goats'-cheese salad, pancakes, whole grilled plaice or salmon and broccoli pie. A seafood platter starter was commended for the lavishness of its lobster, prawns, shrimps and smoked salmon. A banoffi crumble dessert was also praised; otherwise, head for treacle tart, spotted dick or caramel rice-pudding. Beers come from Courage, plus two guest beers, and the wine list is strong on half-bottles, although only the house Reynier is available by the glass. SAMPLE DISHES: spicy Cajun chicken wings £4.50; chicken chasseur £7.50; apple and sultana strudel £3.

Open *11 to 2.30, 5.30 to 11, Sun 12 to 3, 7 to 10.30; bar food 12 to 2, 6 to 9.30, Sun 12 to 2.15, 7 to 9*
Details *Children welcome in family room   Car park   Wheelchair access (also WC)   Garden   No smoking in family room   No music   Dogs welcome Amex, Delta, Diners, MasterCard, Switch, Visa   Accommodation: 8 rooms, B&B £56 to £66*

White Horse

Rede Road, Whepstead IP29 4SS   TEL: (01284) 735542
just off B1066, 4m SW of Bury St Edmunds

This heartily traditional white-painted old pub in a classic Suffolk village has an unusual flavour inside. Landlady Mrs Woolf hails from Mauritius, and her adventurous cooking features pan-fried dishes with exotic sauces and home-made curries for tastes that stray far beyond sirloin steaks with chips – though these are available in generous, well-prepared portions too. Starters are limited to garlic bread, and mostly-cold puddings spring few surprises, but the daily-changing chalkboard main-course specials are well worth investigating. Friendly, courteous staff dispense food at well-spaced bar tables with minimum delay. A pool table provides alternative amusement in a neighbouring bar for non-diners. Greene King beers are the mainstay in this tied house, regularly stocked IPA, Abbot and Triumph ales being augmented by seasonal specials such as Captain Christmas. Blackboard suggestions supplement a printed wine list, but only a couple come by the glass. An orchard garden makes an appealing retreat on fine days, perhaps before or after a visit to the strikingly designed National Trust property of Ickworth just up the road. SAMPLE DISHES: pan-fried halibut with mango sauce £6.25; Thai green curry £5; salmon Stroganov £5.50.

Open *11.30 to 3, 6.30 to 11.30, Sun 12 to 3, 7 to 10.30; bar food 11.30 to 2, 6.30 to 9.30*
Details *No children under 5   Car park   Wheelchair access   Garden   No music   No dogs   No cards*

Red House ✿ ▮

Whitchurch RG28 7LH   TEL: (01256) 895558
on A34 between Basingstoke and Andover

This enterprising establishment goes from strength to strength, mostly on the basis of Shannon Wells's accomplished modern cooking. Understandably, its well-run blend of casual chic appeals to a youngish, affluent crowd, and the place fairly buzzes with activity. Speciality menus feature from time to time – you might encounter an Italian pasta night or a Mediterranean night, and prospective customers are exhorted to 'book early to avoid disappointment'. If you do find a table, disappointment is rare, with such a well-presented, wisely manageable menu, plus blackboard specials. Start with crab and cream cheese lasagne or, perhaps, monkfish salad with watercress and bacon, and move on to smoked haddock with asparagus and soft eggs or seared duck breast with grilled pineapple and honey. Finish with 'well-presented' puddings like chocolate terrine, tiramisù or apple crumble. Vegetarians are catered for, and bread is freshly baked each day. Food tends to be served in the separately entered lounge-bar/restaurant areas of voguish mirrorglass and beechwood flooring, rather than in the more traditionally rustic public bar with its inglenook fireplace and flagstones. Drinkers get a decent choice of real ales (Theakston XB, Cheriton Brewhouse's Pots Ale or the award-winning Itchen Valley Godfathers). Wines circuit the globe at reasonable prices, with around half a dozen house wines by the glass. SAMPLE DISHES: monkfish, bacon and watercress salad £5; asparagus and wild mushroom pancakes with Brie fondue £6.25; pecan pie £2.50.

Open *11 to 3, 6 to 11, Sun 12 to 3, 7 to 10.30; bar food and restaurant 12 to 2, 4.30 (7 Sun) to 9.30*
Details *Car park   Wheelchair access   Garden and patio   No smoking in restaurant   Background and live music   Dogs welcome in public bar only MasterCard, Switch, Visa*

WHITEWELL   Lancashire   map 8

▲ *Inn at Whitewell* 🍇

Whitewell, Forest of Bowland BB7 3AT
TEL: (01200) 448222
off B6243 Clitheroe to Longridge road, 6m NW of Clitheroe

An art gallery, wine merchant and shirtmaker all share the premises of this large and sprawling inn owned by the Duchy of Lancaster, which is not so much at Whitewell but *is* Whitewell. Richard Bowman has been the long-suffering landlord here, overseeing a largely family business (which is why he describes himself as long-suffering) and providing a wide selection of food and drink for well over 20 years. The inn itself dates back to the 1300s in its oldest parts and was once the home of the 'Keeper of the Foret' (the royal hunting ground). Shooting parties regularly rub shoulders with those who come to enjoy the five miles of salmon, trout and sea trout fishing on the banks of the River Hodder, and guests can fish from the pub grounds. Late starters can choose from a bar lunch menu which offers a trio of fish-cakes, haddock Welsh rarebit, Whitewell fish pie – the pub's 'signature' dish – and roast breast of guinea-fowl, as well as sandwiches and salads, which are missing from the otherwise similar evening bar menu. The restaurant menu offers a short selection with lots of British and Irish produce. The wine list reflects theinn's other occupation as wine merchants – Bowland Forest Vintners –

and all bottles are available to take away. It neatly dissects France into well-represented regions and gives Australia prominence in the New World. For bitter drinkers Boddingtons and Marston's Pedigree are available. SAMPLE DISHES: crispy belly pork with a spinach salad and chilli dressing £4.75; grilled Norfolk kipper £6.50; home-made ice-cream £3.75.

Open *10 to 3, 6 to 11, Sun 12 to 3, 7 to 11; bar food and restaurant 12 to 2, 7.30 to 9.30*
Details *Children welcome   Car park   Wheelchair access (also WC)   Garden   No music   No dogs in dining-room   Amex, Diners, MasterCard, Switch, Visa   Accommodation: 15 rooms, B&B £53 to £108*

WHITNEY   Herefordshire   map 5

▲ *Rhydspence Inn*
Whitney HR3 6EU   TEL: (01497) 831262
off A438 Hereford to Brecon road, 4m E of Hay-on-Wye

This fourteenth-century drovers' inn once had 140 acres of its own land to accommodate the livestock whose owners were catered for by the inn, before setting off on the Black Ox Trail into England. Today this half-timbered, tile-roofed pub sits in rather smaller grounds, and the stream at the bottom of the garden marks the boundary between England and Wales. The two bars are both situated in the older part of the inn and look suitably traditional, and in a later extension there is also a dining-room, the domain of Pam Glover, whose husband Peter is the other half of the team. From the bar menu you could choose from a selection of salads (with prawns, gravad lax or cold meats); go abroad with tagliatelle carbonara, or Thai chicken curry; or stay at home with steak and kidney pie, or organic Devon sausages with creamed potato and mustard sauce. The dining-room menu might offer starters of seared scallops, or chicken liver pâté, followed by main courses like Hereford fillet steak with pepper sauce, rack of Welsh lamb, or roast Aylesbury duck with orange and Grand Marnier sauce. Ice-cream is all made on the premises. Real ales are supplied by Bass, Robinsons and Ansells and the inn also serves Dunkerton cider. The mainly Old World wine list includes around ten half-bottles, but only three by the glass, a couple of English wines and a bin-end list. SAMPLE DISHES: seafood platter £9; grilled rainbow trout with mushroom, thyme and white wine sauce £9; whimberry pie £4.50.

Open *11 to 2.30, 7 to 11, Sun 12 to 2.30, 7 to 11; closed 25 Dec; bar food and restaurant 11 to 2, 7 to 9.30, Sun 12 to 2, 7 to 9.30*
Details *Children welcome in eating areas   Car park   Wheelchair access   Garden and patio   No smoking in dining-room   No music   No dogs   Amex, Delta, MasterCard, Switch, Visa   Accommodation: 7 rooms, B&B £33 to £75*

WHITTLESFORD   Cambridgeshire   **map 6**

Tickell Arms

Whittlesford CB2 4NZ   TEL: (01223) 833128
off A505, or M11 junction 6, 7m S of Cambridge

Ed Fischer has run this quirky freehouse for 20 years now, and regulars have got used to his little ways at this pleasant country pub set in a well-heeled village. It is easy to drive past the blue and white gothic villa that looks very much like a private house, hidden from the road as it is by large overgrown shrubs. There are cardinal red flagstones in one bar, rugs in the other, and the whole has a relaxed, cluttered look reminiscent of 'antique shop décor'. Background classical music adds to the overall flamboyance. If you are a smoker you'll be allowed in the conservatory only or the gorgeous gardens. The menu does not stray too far from pub staples – omelettes, prawn cocktail, sandwiches, but also scrambled egg and smoked salmon – and enthusiasm rather than talent defines the cooking. Blackboard specials take in mushroom gratinée, stuffed duck leg in red wine sauce and strips of pork with a sherry cream sauce, with Belgian chocolate torte for pudding. The pub serves Adnams and Greene King Abbot, and eight to nine wines from a list of 30 to 40 bottles are available by the glass. SAMPLE DISHES: seafood gratinée £4.75; lamb in a Madeira sauce £9; mixed fruit crumble £3.50.

Open *Tue to Sun 11 to 2.30, 7 to 11, Sun 12 to 3, 7 to 10.30; bar food and restaurant Tue to Sun 12 to 2.30, 7 to 10*
Details *Children welcome   Car park   Wheelchair access   Garden and patio   No smoking exc in conservatory   Background music   Dogs welcome on a lead   Delta, MasterCard, Switch, Visa*

WHITWELL   Rutland   **map 6**

▲ *Noel Arms*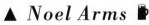

Whitwell LE15 8BW   TEL: (01780) 460334
on A406, 4m E of Oakham

It is easy to miss this much extended pub, which is set back from the main road up a narrow driveway. Being only half a mile from Rutland Water, it is a popular watering-hole for fishermen and sailors. There are two distinct halves to the pub. The original thatched building houses the tiny village bar which is traditionally furnished and has a relaxing atmosphere, ideal for drinkers. The stone extension to the rear is where you'll find the comfortable, spacious, open-plan lounge bar and the pine-furnished dining-room. The menu changes with the seasons and is enhanced by fish specials on a board. Wok-fried prawns seared in chilli oil and a honey and curry dressing, or smoked duck breast on pink grapefruit salad give some idea of the style, which is certainly not just traditional pub grub, though things like steak and kidney pie or cod and chips do still appear. You could also start with an 'all day breakfast salad', or a rich game terrine with juniper berries and gin, while idiosyncratic main courses might include a saucy cabbage cake with sunblush tomatoes and mozzarella served on a tomato and basil broth, or roast baby chicken with apricot and sausage-meat stuffing. Puddings, however, revert to type, with crème brûlée and brandy-snap basket as typical examples. The pub serves Marston's Pedigree, Hook Norton, Courage Best as well as Grainstore Gold from Oakham and Robin a Tiptoe from the John O'Gaunt brewery, while a 35-strong wine list is reasonably priced and offers a good range, with seven by the glass. SAMPLE DISHES: roast vegetable tartlet £4.25; grilled sea bass £10.50; hazelnut and strawberry gâteau £3.75.

Open *11 to 11, Sun 12 to 10.30; bar food and restaurant 12 to 3, 7 to 10*
Details *Children welcome in eating areas   Car park   Wheelchair access (also WC)   Garden and patio   Background music   No dogs in eating areas   Delta, MasterCard, Switch, Visa   Accommodation: 8 rooms, B&B £45 to £60*

WIDECOMBE IN THE MOOR   Devon   map 1

Old Inn

Widecombe in the Moor TQ13 7TA   TEL: (01364) 621207
from Bovey Tracey take Haytor road and continue to Widecombe in the Moor, 5m NW of Ashburton

Set high up on the moors, this quaint old pub stands in the centre of the moorland village made famous by song. It stands next to the handsome church dubbed the 'Cathedral of the Moor'. Inside the inn, rough stone walls and cosy, firelit rooms of dark wood and crimson plush make this fourteenth-century building warmly inviting. It is a popular venue for parties and celebrations, so tables are best booked in advance if you are dining. Lengthy printed menus cater for conservative tastes, running from soups, pâtés, and potato-skin starters, through steaks and grills to ice-creams, but there is also innovative cooking. Regular house specialities include lamb in gin sauce or pan-fried duck breast. Choices for vegetarians are usually a celery and nut roast or a bean casserole. Separately listed 'monthly star specials' might be seared salmon fillet with a lobster and prawn sauce, or a pork steak with Bramley apples and bacon in a Stilton and port sauce. If that is not enough, check the blackboards for fresh inspiration among daily casseroles and luscious speciality desserts. Nearly 40 wines are available, with six by the glass. Real ales include

Websters Green Label or Theakston XB, and Gray's Farm Cider is on offer too. SAMPLE DISHES: haggis with neeps and tatties £3.50; spicy pork chops £7.75; zabaglione trifle £3.25.

Open *summer 11 to 3, 6 to 11 (10.30 Sun), winter 11 to 2.30, 7 to 11 (10.30 Sun); bar food 11 to 2.30, 6.30 (7 winter) to 10*
Details *Children welcome in dining-room   Car park   Wheelchair access (also WC)   Garden and patio   Background music   Dogs welcome   Delta, MasterCard, Switch, Visa*

WINCLE   Cheshire   map 8

Ship Inn

Wincle SK11 0QE   TEL: (01260) 227217
1m S of A54, between Congleton and Buxton, 5m SE of Macclesfield

---

New licensees in the summer of 1998, Steven and Sally Simpson, haven't made many changes to this inn, which will please the many walkers and others who like to organise their days out round a visit to the tiny rural sandstone pub on a hill in the Lower Pennines. Muddy boots are not a problem in the simply furnished back bar or the raised garden that looks out over rolling countryside; or you can enjoy the neat and comfortable main green bar – homely with a coal fire, old pub tables and hunting prints on the thick stone walls. No games or Muzak impinge on the traditional pub atmosphere. The Simpsons are also keeping the menu style: hearty, home-cooked, fresh local produce. Everything changes daily depending on what has been bought; you could strike lucky with haddock or crab delivered from Grimsby on Wednesdays. The day's soup might be Scotch broth or curried apple and parsnip; to follow there might be a casserole or a curry, grilled local trout sautéd in garlic butter, a beef or gammon steak, or fritto misto with garlic mayonnaise. A handful of attractive-sounding puddings is likely to include a steamed pudding and a sundae. Boddingtons from the cask is joined by two or three guest ales each week, perhaps York Brewery's Stonewall, Goose Eye Bitter, Whim's Hartington Bitter or Adnams; or you might fancy some Stowford Press cider or a wine from the regularly reviewed list of approachable and varied wines. SAMPLE DISHES: spinach and ricotta filo parcels £3.50; haddock and prawn puff-pastry pie £6.25; bilberry and apple pie £2.50.

Open *12 to 3, 7 to 11, Sun 11 to 3, 7 to 10.30 (all day bank hol weekends); bar food 12 to 2.30, 7 to 9.30*
Details *Children welcome in family room and dining-room   Car park Garden and patio   Smoking in lounge area only   No music   Dogs welcome in tap rooms only   No cards*

Brickmakers Arms

Chertsey Road, Windlesham GU20 6HT   TEL: (01276) 472267
on B386 Bagshot to Sunnydale road

This red-brick pub is not far from Wentworth and Sunningdale golf courses, and less than a mile from Windlesham village. A pleasant garden with colourful flowers has wooden bench tables, and there is a secluded vine-covered area with marble-topped tables on old treadle sewing machine bases, just outside the back entrance into the bar. Inside is cosy with dark wooden tables and chairs, an L-shaped bar, and a separate restaurant which also has its own outside summer eating area. The printed bar menu is supplemented by daily specials and a two-course, limited-choice set menu for under £10. Dishes can also be ordered from the restaurant menu, except at very busy times. Smoked haddock kedgeree with poached eggs is a staple, as are ciabatta breads offered with a selection of fillings: from crispy bacon and egg to three different cheeses. Other main dishes might be steak and kidney pie, salad niçoise or baked field mushrooms with spinach and Camembert, while the restaurant menu takes in a good range of fish dishes. Desserts range from crème brûlée to ice-creams and sorbets. Service can be slow when the pub gets busy. Beers on offer include Courage Best, Fuller's London Pride and bitters from Brakspear and Hall & Woodhouse. Six wines by the glass are available from the bar, and the full list is a good selection from around the world. SAMPLE DISHES: moules à la crème £5; salmon and saffron fish-cakes on a chive cream sauce £8; baked banana with chocolate sauce £4.

Open *11.30 to 3, 5 to 11, Sun 12 to 4, 7 to 10.30; bar food and restaurant all week 12 to 2.25, Mon to Sat 6 to 9.55*
Details *Children over 5 welcome in dining-room   Car park   Wheelchair access (also WC)   Garden and patio   No-smoking area in dining-room Occasional live music   Dogs welcome in bar   Amex, Delta, Diners, MasterCard, Switch, Visa*

▲ *Sun Inn* ❀

PLOUGHMAN'S

Winforton HR3 6EA   TEL: (01544) 327677
on A438 Hereford to Brecon road, 6m S of Kington

Light, bright and welcoming – much as one would expect from a sun – and on a quiet main road at the entrance to a tiny village in the superb scenery of the Welsh borders lies this whitewashed inn run by

Brian and Wendy Hibbard for 15 years. The open stone lounge area is full of equestrian paraphernalia, while the dining area is done out in more of a country farmhouse style. Wendy Hibbard has won for the pub a reputation for exceptional cooking which is faithful to Welsh tradition but which also plucks from the rest of the world. So, for instance, Mamgu's cawl ('grandmother's broth') sits on the blackboard next to hot spicy Singapore prawns, while another starter, Camembert filo parcels with elderflower and gooseberry sauce, exemplifies the imagination Mrs Hibbard injects into her cooking and food-matching. A house speciality need not be complicated: here ploughman's, for example, is a generous plate of at least six English and Welsh cheeses with all sorts of the pub's own pickles and chutneys, a simple twist that many another pub would do well to copy. Main dishes might include, on the traditional side, Ludlow lamb casseroled with redcurrants, apples and English herbs, and, looking to influences beyond these shores, vine leaves with a filling of wild rice, apricots, raisins and spices, served on a bed of cumin and coriander couscous. Desserts are just as imaginative: greengage and frangipane tart with real custard, and summer berries brûlée are scrumptious variations on popular favourites. The pub serves beers from Hook Norton, Wadworth and Brains, as well as a selection of Belgian and German bottled beers. Four wines are available by the glass. SAMPLE DISHES: chicken, coriander and mango salad £5; fantail of Norfolk duck breast with a quince and orange sauce £12; terrine of three chocolates on a raspberry coulis £4.

Open *Wed to Mon 11 to 3, 6 to 11; bar food and restaurant 12 to 2, 6.45 to 9.30*
Details *Children welcome in bar eating area   Car park   Wheelchair access (also WC)   Garden   Occasional background music   No dogs   No cards Accommodation: 3 rooms: B&B £30 to £58*

WING   Rutland   map 6

▲ *King's Arms*

Top Street, Wing LE15 8SE   TEL: (01572) 737634
off A47, 4m SE of Oakham

Located near Rutland Water, this seventeenth-century Grade II listed inn has a large lawned garden with tables and chairs, and a children's play area. The oldest part is the King's bar with its beams and flagstone floor and an open fire. There is also a comfortable restaurant, created from an old barn, set out with white and pink tablecloths and oil lamps on the tables. Bar food includes filled baguettes, ploughman's and pasta of the day, as well as more substantial dishes such as fish stew and steak and kidney pudding. A more ambitious à la carte menu, available throughout the inn, might offer lobster bisque, or smoked venison with melon, grapefruit and citrus sauce to start, followed by roasted chicken suprême, or a mixed grill of fish. Vegetarians might tuck into roasted aubergine and peppers with cashew-nut pilaf, or stir-fry of seasonal vegetables on egg noodles. For those with room for dessert, there is dark and white chocolate terrine, or walnut and maple steamed pudding. Ruddles Best and Bateman XB are supplemented by a guest beer, and a reasonably priced wine list offers nine by the glass; there is also an interesting selection of whiskies. SAMPLE DISHES: wild mushroom fricassee £4.50; chicken breast marinated in Chinese spices £6.50; lemon and ginger cheesecake £3.25.

Open *summer 11 to 11, Sun 11 to 10.30, winter 11 to 3, 6.30 to 11, Sun 11 to 3, 6.30 to 10.30; bar food and restaurant all week L 12 to 2, Sun to Fri D 6.30 to 9.30 (9 winter)*
Details *Children welcome   Car park   Wheelchair access   Garden and patio No smoking in restaurant   Background and live music   No dogs   Amex, Delta, MasterCard, Switch, Visa   Accommodation: 7 rooms, B&B £35 to £100*

WINGFIELD   Suffolk   map 6

De La Pole Arms 🍺 NEW ENTRY

FISH

Wingfield IP21 5RA   TEL: (01379) 384545
off B1118 Framlingham to Diss road, just N of Stradbroke

'What a find in this remote and lovely part of North Suffolk!' was how one reporter described this buttermilk-coloured, superbly restored seventeenth-century pub. Located in a very peaceful spot directly opposite the church, it is owned by St Peter's Brewery, which also owns the Cornwallis Arms in Brome (see entry). Within, an eclectic mix of stripped-wood tables and chairs, tiled floor, beamed ceiling, log burning stoves and candles sets the scene. This is a food-orientated country pub, with an upmarket feel to the place. Both in the bar and separate restaurant the focus is on fish: from the bar menu choose De La Pole fish-cakes, Mediterranean cod steak crumble, or the boatman's lunch (smoked mackerel and horseradish pâté with smoked salmon, rollmop herring and shell-on Atlantic prawns). House specialities include fish and chips, made with St Peter's wheat beer batter and with chunky home-made chips; salmon and prawn suet pudding (which had one reporter's husband drooling over the memory it for days); and one of the seafood bowls – prawns, perhaps, or mixed seafood with half a lobster – served with crusty bread. Crispy filled baguettes are also served at lunch-time, and the separate restaurant menu offers more expensive items such as an open tartlet of chicken livers followed by roasted fillet of red mullet. The pub serves the full range of St Peter's draught ales, as well as their distinctive bottles for taking away. The wine list is shorter than at the Cornwallis Arms, with only five by the glass, including a local Oakhill white. SAMPLE DISHES: chicken and bacon terrine £5; caramelised pan-fried pork steak £7.25; hot chocolate brownies £3.25.

Open *11 to 3, 6 to 11, Sun 12 to 10.30; closed eve 25 Dec; bar food and restaurant 12 to 2 (2.30 Sun), 7 to 9 (9.30 Fri and Sat)*
Details *Children welcome   Car park   Wheelchair access (also WC)   Garden No smoking in restaurant   Background music   Dogs welcome   Delta, MasterCard, Switch, Visa*

W I N S F O R D   Somerset   map 1

▲ *Royal Oak Inn*

Winsford, Exmoor National Park TA24 7JE
TEL: (01643) 851455
off A396, 5m N of Dulverton

This is one of the most eye-catching pubs you are ever likely to come across, its thatching impeccable over ancient creamy walls, and with just the right number of hanging baskets. The village too is calendar fodder. Inside, the place has a smart, almost clubby feel, with genial, chatty service. The pink-clothed restaurant serves fixed-price three-course meals, while simpler food is served in the bars – both with open fireplaces and oak beams, one cosy with tartan stools and chairs, the other furnished with pine booth seating. Snacks are stylish and unaffected, though with little for vegetarians. Sandwiches – perhaps home-cooked ham with mustard, or chicken with lemon, spring onion and mayonnaise – come with salad and crisps. Open sandwiches are actually croissants. A steak sandwich with mush-rooms and tomatoes or a baked potato filled with ham, parsley, smoked cheese and onion sound fine, while soup, perhaps home-made mushroom, or smooth chicken liver pâté with generous salad and flavoursome vinaigrette would be other good choices. For some-thing a bit more substantial, grilled plaice or pan-fried lamb cutlets are possibilities, or look at the dishes of the day. Home-made sweets such as chocolate truffle cake or glazed lemon tart come from the restaurant's trolley. Prices are very reasonable, given the upmarket feel to the place. Interestingly, the bar has its own succinct and appealing wine list; three wines are offered by the glass. For beers the pub offers Exmoor Ale and Spitfire as well as Flowers Original and IPA. SAMPLE DISHES: hot peppered mackerel ploughman's £5; beef, ale and mushroom pie £8; grape crème brûlée £3.

Open *11 to 3, 6 to 11, Sun 11 to 3, 6 to 10.30; bar food and restaurant 12 to 2, 6.30 to 9 (9.30 summer)*
Details *Children welcome in bar eating area   Car park   Wheelchair access (also WC)   Garden   No music   Dogs welcome   Amex, Diners, MasterCard, Switch, Visa   Accommodation: 14 rooms, B&B £75 to £125*

WINTERTON-ON-SEA   **Norfolk**   map 6

▲ *Fishermans Return* 🍺

The Lane, Winterton-on-Sea NR29 4BN   TEL: (01493) 393305
on B1159, 8m N of Great Yarmouth

This seventeenth-century, brick and flint pub – a conversion of a row of fishermen's cottages – has managed to retain its integrity. A low-ceilinged lounge with open woodburner, leather seats, old prints and photos radiates nostalgia, while a spacious public bar offers church pew seating. Exceptional beers and above-average food, as well as the pub's setting near the beach, are the obvious attractions. Beers are sourced from local independents: Adnams beers make frequent appearances, as do those from Woodforde's, and Scott's of Lowestoft. Other guests are predominantly East Anglian. Also on offer is the St Peter's range of bottled beers from Bungay in Suffolk. The printed menu offers simple, well-done pub food: fish pie, chilli con carne, battered cod, or burgers. More enticing offerings on the daily specials board will, naturally, feature fish dishes such as fresh plaice fillet in caper and mushroom sauce, or monkfish coated in mild curry sauce. There is a modest selection of wines chosen by the hosts, all decently priced; three wines come by the glass. SAMPLE DISHES: moules marinière £4; lamb in lime and coriander on basmati rice £7.25; baked raspberry cheesecake £2.50.

Open *Mon to Fri 11 to 2.30, 6.30 to 11, Sat 11 to 11, Sun 12 to 10.30; closed 25 Dec eve; bar food 12 to 2, 6.30 to 9.30*
Details *Children welcome in family room and dining-room   Car park Garden and patio   No smoking in 1 bar and family room   Background music; jukebox in family room   Dogs welcome   Amex, Delta, MasterCard, Switch, Visa   Accommodation: 3 rooms, B&B £30 to £50*

If you disagree with any assessment made in the Guide, write to tell us why – The Which? Guide to Country Pubs, FREEPOST, 2 Marylebone Road, London NW1 1YN.

Freemasons Arms

8 Vicarage Fold, Wiswell BB7 9DF   TEL: (01254) 822218
1m off A680 near Whalley

This homely freehouse is tucked away along an unmade lane in the middle of a tiny village (pronounced wize-well) at the foot of Pendle Hill. It was originally three cottages, one of which was was a freemasons' lodge, and you can still see the joins. Brass, beams, copper-topped tables and comfortable benches are the setting in the neat bar and old taproom; the upper dining area is more formal. To this pleasant place come regulars a plenty for fresh, honest home cooking with few frills. For starters from the printed menu, or blackboard specials, how about spinach pancake, local black pudding with mustard sauce, or tiger prawns in filo pastry? Main courses likewise are appetisingly simple, calling on fine meat and local fish: decent-sized salmon fish-cakes with a creamy parsley sauce, grilled plaice with home-made tartare sauce or roast rack of pork with apple and cranberry sauce. Puddings, if you get that far, might be summer pudding, Mississippi mud pie or lemon meringue pie. Jennings Bitter and Cumberland Ale are the beers, and the pub has made malt whiskies another reason to return, with 66 to try. A short wine list offers four by the glass. SAMPLE DISHES: baked stuffed tomatoes £4; steak and kidney pie £6.75; caramel meringue with toffee sauce £3.

Open *Wed to Sun 12 to 3, 6.30 to 11; bar food and restaurant Wed to Sun 12 to 2 (2.30 Sun), 6.30 to 9.30 (Sun 6 to 9)*
Details *Children welcome in dining-room   Patio (summer only)   Background music   No dogs   Delta, MasterCard, Switch, Visa*

Dorset Arms

Withyham TN7 4BD   TEL: (01892) 770278
on B2110, 2m E of Hartfield

This family-run black and white tile-hung pub was originally an open hall farmhouse, and coming upon the great log fire in the bar with its ancient Sussex oak floor you might imagine yourself back in the fifteenth century. The pub is set back from the road on the green in the centre of a small village close to the edge of Ashdown Forest, and is girt about with window boxes and hops in summer; it would be pleasant to sit outside at the picnic tables. As well as the crowded public bar, there is a carpeted lounge with small round tables, velvet upholstered settles and chairs, and a separate restaurant, its massive beams another reminder of the pub's early days. Many visitors will wish for no more than a lunchtime sandwich, jacket potato or ploughman's, but other dishes available as both hot lunches and light suppers include soup, crispy mushrooms, half a pint of prawns, and sausages, ham and fish served with chips. A separate specials board carries dishes such as a half-shoulder of lamb, ratatouille bake, mushroom Stroganov, toad-in-the-hole and fish pie, while puddings range from fresh fruit salad to meringuey confections. Sunday lunch is a traditional roast, with a few other options. Handpulled beers are seasonal brews from Harveys of Lewes, and a 25-bottle wine list – lacking in vintages – has three house wines available by the half-litre or litre carafe. SAMPLE DISHES: smoked salmon with brown bread £4; gammon steak with pineapple and chips £6.75; deep-filled lemon tart £3.

Open *11.30 to 3, 5.30 to 11, Sat 11 to 3, 6 to 11; bar food and restaurant 12 to 2, Tue to Sat 7.30 to 9, light snacks Sun evening in summer*
Details *No children   Car park   Garden and patio   Background music   Dogs welcome in bar only   Amex, Delta, Diners, MasterCard, Switch, Visa*

WOOBURN COMMON   **Buckinghamshire**   **map 3**

▲ *Chequers Inn* ♥ ❦

Kiln Lane, Wooburn Common HP10 0JQ   TEL: (01628) 529575
just S of M50 junction 2

Lovers of beams will be in heaven in the Chequers. This handsome Tudor brick inn is stuffed with them. This 'superb all-rounder' – hotel, pub, conference centre – is perpetually packed with a well-heeled late-20s and 30s clientele. The décor is truly eclectic: a stuffed fish in a case, car rally photos, and pictures of horseracing and the like all help set the tone, along with settees, small tables, and fairly tightly packed benches and stools. There is a blackboard menu in the bar and a printed set-price menu and *carte* in the restaurant. On the blackboard you will find sandwiches, ploughman's, a daily soup – cream of vegetable with coconut and croûtons, perhaps – and more complex dishes like twin breast of pheasant with orange and juniper berry sauce, or seared collops of monkfish with cashew-nuts in a light oyster sauce with crisp vegetables. Your Scotch sirloin steak will arrive perfectly timed, cooked as desired, in a well-made boursin and red wine sauce, and accompanied by enjoyable just-cooked vegetables. Desserts might include chocolate fudge cake with pecan and toffee sauce, or fresh raspberry and meringue flan. The more up-market restaurant menus offer dishes such as smoked breast of duck on mango and mixed leaves with an oriental sauce, followed by mignons of pork fillet with a Stilton stuffing, or a trio of roasted local game birds with redcurrant and orange sauce. Marston's Pedigree is the ever-present ale, but visitors might include Fuller's London Pride, or Marlow's Smuggler, and a full wine list offers an excellent choice, with around 20 above-average wines by the glass, including champagne. During summer the sunken garden plays host to barbecues. SAMPLE DISHES: cream of asparagus soup £3; fresh steamed mussels £9; tiramisù £3.

Open *10 to 11, Sun 12 to 10.30; bar food and restaurant 12 to 2.30, 7 to 9.30*

Details *Children welcome in bar eating area   Car park   Garden   Background music   No dogs   Delta, MasterCard, Switch, Visa   Accommodation: 17 rooms, B&B £72.50 to £92.50*

WOODBOROUGH   Wiltshire

Seven Stars 🍇 ☐ NEW ENTRY

Bottlesford, Woodborough SN9 6LU
TEL: (01672) 851325
off A345 at mini-roundabout at North Newnton; follow signs for Woodborough then Bottlesford

The Seven Stars is a lovely old thatched pub adorned with creepers and climbing roses beside a narrow lane in the Vale of Pewsey. It is as off the beaten track as it is possible to be, but is worth seeking out for if nothing else its splendid gardens within nine acres of grounds, with views towards the Uffington White Horse. A cobbled front entrance leads to a fine rambling interior, complete with beams, black oak panelling, quarry-tiled floor, brick fireplace with open log fire and mix of antique settles and pine furnishings. At the back is the dining-room decked out in gingham tablecloths and fresh flowers. Philippe Cheminade (co-owner with Kate Lister) describes the pub as 'a little bit of France in Wiltshire'. France is indeed very much on the menu, and not just the albeit desirable clichés of French onion soup, frogs' legs and escargots bourguignonne. Britanny seafood platters are the house speciality, while other dishes waiting to be tried are Seven Stars bouillabaisse and fillet of pork with apricots and armagnac. Game tends to be a winter feature and fresh fish and shellfish a summer one. The pub serves Dorset Best and Wadworth 6X as well as beers from the local micro-brewery Stonehenge, and locally produced organic cider will go well with this style of food. The 42-strong wine list, well-annotated, acknowledges the presence of viniculture outside France, though only French wines are available by the glass (two sizes). SAMPLE DISHES: Brittany fish soup £3.75; wild rabbit casserole £9; raspberry crème brûlée £4.

Open *Tue to Sun 12 to 3, Tue to Sat 6 to 11; also open Mon bank hols L; bar food and restaurant 12 to 2, 7 to 9.30*
Details *Children welcome in restaurant   Car park   Wheelchair access (also WC)   Garden   No-smoking area made available on request   Background music   Dogs welcome by arrangement   Delta, MasterCard, Switch, Visa*

W O O D H I L L   Somerset   **map 2**

▲ *Rose and Crown*

Woodhill, Stoke St Gregory TA3 6EW   TEL: (01823) 490296
between A361 and A378, 8m E of Taunton, via North Curry

Hard to find behind a high hedge deep in the Somerset Levels, and 'nothing special outside' apart from a lovely sheltered garden, this 300-year-old cottage-turned-pub undergoes an almost magical transformation as you cross the threshold. Inside is a maze of dark and dimly lit low rooms, the 'nicotine yellow' walls covered with old prints, photos and posters. Locals gossip with the enthusiastic landlady and landlord, while others plot and plan in the table booths. 'One gets a strong impression of what country pubs were like before electricity,' mused a reporter. The bar menu goes in for lots of grills, such as lamb cutlets, steaks, or lemon sole, served with quantities of vegetables. Half a roast chicken or a seafood platter would be other possibilities in an unfussy selection, supplemented at lunch-time by soups, salads, granary sandwiches and a few other lighter items. Note that prices are more expensive in the evening, but traditional Sunday lunch is good value. West Country brews include Exmoor Ale, Withycutter, Thomas Hardy and Royal Oak, alongside Old Rascal and Dry Blackthorn ciders. SAMPLE DISHES: grilled kidneys and bacon £6/£7.25; scrumpy chicken £6/£7.25; raspberry pavlova £2.50.

Open *11 to 3, 7 to 11, Sun 12 to 3, 7 to 10.30; bar food and restaurant 12.30 to 2, 7 to 9.45*
Details *Children welcome   Car park   Wheelchair access   Garden and patio   No-smoking area   Background music   Well-behaved dogs welcome in bar   Delta, MasterCard, Switch, Visa   Accommodation: 3 rooms, B&B £25 to £50*

WOODSTOCK Oxfordshire map 3

▲ *Feathers Hotel* ☻ [NEW ENTRY]
Market Street, Woodstock OX20 1SX   TEL: (01993) 812291

This attractive old inn is in the centre of a pleasant country town alongside Blenheim Palace and its park. The L-shaped flagstoned bar area has a large gas-fuelled flame fire which provides a focal point for both rooms, while the restaurant has low ceilings and a yellow and blue décor, making an appealing setting for meals. It has a shady rear courtyard for drinks and bar meals in fine weather. This is a fairly high-powered eating establishment which impresses inspectors and reporters. The bar menu (not available in the evenings on Saturday and Sunday) might offer as starters a risotto of rocket, rouille and olive salsa, or a confit of tomato and fresh Parmesan crostini. This might be followed by salmon fish-cakes with a mustard hollandaise, or avocado, bacon and poached egg salad with new potatoes, and, to finish, steamed lemon pudding, chocolate and hazelnut brownie, or a selection of British and French cheeses. The restaurant, with Mark Treasure as chef, has both a *carte* and set-price menus offering dishes such as duck terrine with toasted brioche or salmon cannelloni followed by roast partridge with foie gras and cep sauce, or braised shoulder shank of lamb with crushed potato and olive salsa, and finishing with an apricot délice. Wadworth 6X is the only ale on offer, and a lengthy, rather pricey wine list has plenty of half-bottles but only four by the glass. SAMPLE DISHES: red pepper soup with basil £4; sausage and mash, thyme and deep-fried cabbage £8.50; apple and cinnamon fritters £4.25.

Open *11 to 3, 6 to 11, Sun 12 to 3, 7 to 10.30; closed eve 25 Dec; bar food and restaurant 12.30 to 2.15, 7.30 to 9.15 (no bar food Sat and Sun D)*
Details *Children welcome in eating areas   Garden   No smoking in restaurant   Background music   Amex, Delta, Diners, MasterCard, Switch, Visa   Accommodation: 22 rooms, B&B £99 to £275*

WOOLHOPE Herefordshire map 5

▲ *Butchers Arms*
Woolhope HR1 4RF   TEL: (01432) 860281
off B4224, 7m SE of Hereford

This very pretty black and white, half-timbered pub is just outside the village in an isolated, hilly and very rural setting surrounded by orchards, vineyards, hop gardens, and good walking country. The fourteenth-century house has very low beams, even by old pub standards, so mind your head. It has been under new ownership since early 1998, and now three chefs are employed to run the kitchen, turning out a menu of pub staples such as gratinated garlic mushrooms, or leek and hazelnut terrine, followed by lasagne, venison sausage with mash, chicken curry, or 'Woolhope Pie', made with local wild rabbit braised in Stowford Press cider. There is also a specials board, which might feature deep-fried vegetables with a blue cheese dip, or egg mayonnaise with asparagus and anchovies, followed, perhaps, by délice of salmon on a bed of seaweed with warm pesto sauce, or chicken kebabs stuffed with cream cheese, chives and garlic. Puddings feature things like mixed fruit cheesecake, or seasonal fruit crumbles. Hook Norton Old Hooky and Wadworth 6X are on draught along with Stowford Press cider. SAMPLE DISHES: goujons of plaice with tartare sauce $5; rump steak with mushrooms and onions £9; chocolate brandy mousse in a chocolate cup £3.50.

Open *11.30 to 3, 6.30 to 11, Sun 12 to 3, 7 to 10.30; bar food and restaurant 12 to 2, 6.30 to 9.30 (10 Fri and Sat)*
Details *Children welcome in bar eating area   Car park   Wheelchair access (also WC)   Garden and patio   No smoking in restaurant   No music   No dogs No cards   Accommodation: 2 rooms, B&B £30 to £39*

Crown Inn
Woolhope HR1 4QP   TEL: (01432) 860468

Set in the middle of the village, next to the church, is this substantial old stone pub, now rendered and cream coloured. Inside, the dining area has an informal appearance, with pine furniture, while the bar has red velvet banquette seating. The menu runs to not far short of 100 items, so there is bound to be something to suit everyone. It is divided into sections, which should help make choosing easier. Start with solidly traditional curried egg mayonnaise, home-made crabcakes, or devilled whitebait, followed by home-made fish pie, liver and bacon casserole in Yorkshire pudding, beef bourguignon, or perhaps faggots in onion gravy. There is even a lengthy vegetarian selection, offering cashew-nut moussaka, or perhaps chestnut, onion and apple pie with Cumberland sauce. Children are also catered for, and puddings typically include banoffi pie, or treacle tart and custard. Only a handful of real ales is served, including Hook Norton Best and Smiles Best, as well as guests which may often come from the Wye Valley brewery in nearby Hereford. The wine list is extensive and offers a good range, with four by the glass. SAMPLE DISHES: bacon and cheese crumpet £4; turkey and ham vol-au-vent £6.50; profiteroles £3.

Open *12 to 2.30, 6.30 (7 in winter) to 11, Sun 12 to 2.30, 7 to 10.30; closed eves 25 and 26 Dec; bar food and restaurant 12 to 2, 6.30 to 10*
Details *Children welcome   Car park   Wheelchair access (also WC)   Garden and patio   No smoking in dining-room   Background music   Guide dogs only Delta, MasterCard, Switch, Visa*

WOOLLEY MOOR   Derbyshire   map 5

White Horse Inn 🍺

Badger Lane, Woolley Moor DE55 6FG   TEL: (01246) 590319
on W side of Ogston Reservoir, off B6014, between Matlock and Stretton

This low stone building in this middle-of-nowhere village of Woolley Moor is an above-average eating and drinking operation. Taking the latter business first, the White Horse has got its thinking just about right. It offers a well-known standard – Bass – as a regular brew and then rotates four guests, taking care to offer three of varying strengths, possibly Hook Norton Best Bitter, Black Sheep Special and Bateman XXXB (in rising order of strength), and then always a fourth dark beer, for example Jennings Sneck Lifter. Five beers are about the most a good pub operation can serve while maintaining quality. On the food side, straightforward starters might be pâtés, prawn cocktail, garlic mushrooms or potato skins, while main courses are of the shepherd's pie and chilli con carne variety. There are also salads, jacket potatoes and more substantial dishes on the daily-changing specials board: roast loin of pork with damson and juniper sauce, rosemary and chilli lamb casserole, or fresh salmon asparagus fricassee, perhaps. Children have their own menu running to sausages, beefburgers, fishfingers and the like, all served with chips and beans or salad. Puddings might be chocolate and brandy mousse, lemon and ginger crunch pie, or sticky toffee. On the short wine wine list are some reasonably priced offerings, and two reds and one white of the week. SAMPLE DISHES: cauliflower cheese £2; gammon, pineapple, chips and salad £4.75; citrus mousse with a lime and vodka coulis £2.50.

Open *11.30 to 2.30 (3 Sat), 6 to 11, Sun 12 to 10.30; closed 25 and 26 Dec; bar food and restaurant 11.45 to 2, 6 to 9, Sun 12 to 8.30*
Details *Children welcome in eating areas   Car park   Wheelchair access (also WC)   Garden   No smoking in 2 dining-rooms   Background music   Dogs welcome in bar only   No cards*

The Guide is totally independent, accepts no free hospitality and carries no advertising.

▲ *Kings Head*

Chapel Hill, Wootton OX20 1DX

TEL: (01993) 811340

take Wootton turn-off 1m N of Woodstock

Wootton is about as far from the sea as it is possible to get in the UK, so one trusts that the fish, very much the house speciality, takes less time to arrive from the coast than would have been the case when this neat honey-coloured stone building was erected. The menu is the same whether you eat in the bar or the restaurant – a simple one during the day and an elaborate one in the evening. The house style is modern Mediterranean, so for lunch kick off with a salad of marinated anchovies, a simple dish that really should appear on more pub menus. Move on to a charred fillet of turbot or sea bass with parsley pesto, or a modern olive and pancetta confit of corn-fed chicken with couscous. Allow a little extra time to digest the evening menu as each dish is accompanied by an essay. Try muscovado and lime-cured Scottish salmon or another Mediterranean-inspired dish, roasted trio of tomatoes (served with goats' cheese). From there you could learn that nori steamed fillet of salmon has 'attitude' or five-pepper roasted cutlets of lamb are 'elegant'. Puddings are of the type that separates the chefs from the cooks, even down to the fascination that chefs seem to have with white chocolate. Ruddles Best Bitter, Wadworth 6X and Marston's Pedigree are on handpump and some ten wines are available by the glass. Woodstock and Blenheim Palace are both nearby. SAMPLE DISHES: parfait of fois gras £6; sea-salted and steamed fillets of sea bass £16; délice of finest white chocolate £4.75.

Open *11 to 11, Sun 12 to 10.30; bar food and restaurant 12 to 2, 7 to 9.30*
Details *Children welcome in eating areas   Car park   Wheelchair access (also WC)   Garden   No smoking in restaurant or part of lounge   No music   Guide dogs only   Delta, MasterCard, Switch, Visa   Accommodation: 3 rooms, B&B £54 to £90*

▲ *Royal Oak* ❧

Wootton Rivers SN8 4NQ   TEL: (01672) 810322
off A346, 3m NE of Pewsey

Down a very narrow road, the picture-postcard sixteenth-century Royal Oak is in the centre of a thatched Wiltshire village near the Kennet & Avon Canal. A pretty patio garden has white chairs, tables and umbrellas. Inside, the bar area is a wealth of low beams, settles and armchairs, and although there is a separate dining-room, the same menu is available throughout the pub. Ploughman's, filled warm ciabattas and sandwiches are available only at lunch-time; otherwise, choose from soup, pâté, avocado with prawns or baked goats' cheese. Basket meals offer chicken, scampi or sausages, while children get fishfingers or chicken nuggets with chips. Main courses include a good variety of salads, steaks of various kinds, chicken dishes, plus an excellent selection of fish from Cornwall. Sherry trifle, or figs with cream, might be a good way to finish off a meal. Beers are from Boddington and Wadworth, with assorted guest ales on tap. The extensive, worldwide wine list offers eight to ten by the glass, and also many cognacs, armagnacs, liqueurs and whiskies. SAMPLE DISHES: Cornish crab soup £3.50; steak and ale pie £7.50; hot chocolate fudge cake £3.

Open *10.30 to 3.30, 6 to 11.30; bar food and restaurant 12 to 2 (2.30 Sun), 6.45 to 9.30*
Details *Children welcome in bar eating area   Car park   Wheelchair access Garden and patio   No cigars in restaurant   Jukebox   Dogs welcome on a lead Amex, Delta, Diners, MasterCard, Switch, Visa   Accommodation: 5 rooms, B&B £20 to £50*

YARMOUTH   Isle of Wight   map **2**

▲ *King's Head*   NEW ENTRY

Quay Street, Yarmouth PO41 0PB   TEL: (01983) 760351

If you arrive on the ferry from Lymington, you can recover your land legs with a short stroll to the King's Head. It's one of the first buildings you come to as you head towards the heart of Yarmouth, considered rather generously by the islanders as a town rather than a village. The exterior of the premises is in keeping with the ancient history of the town and it is likely that more than one of the garrison of the sixteenth-century fort just across the road popped in for a stiffener before guard duty. Robert and Michelle Jackson are happy to welcome families throughout the pub, which is suffused with the sounds of mellow jazz around its spacious bar areas. The chalkboard menu contains, as one would hope, plenty of fish, and dishes ranging from the fancy – scallops wrapped in bacon with king prawns on a kebab – to the plain and simple – steak and Guinness pie. A reporter was impressed by his stunningly fresh piece of brill served in a lemon and white wine sauce, followed by a light fruits-of-the forest cheesecake. Pizzas, chargrilled steaks and burgers are also available, and the specials board offers items like sea bass in orange and ginger sauce, or beef Wellington in a wild mushroom sauce. Children have their own menu and meals can also be taken in a comfortable wood-floored dining-room adjoining the bar. Beers on draught include Flowers Original, Bass and Boddingtons, and three house wines are offered by the glass. SAMPLE DISHES: crab au gratin £4.50; Cajun chicken breast with roast peppers and onions £8.25; home-made apple crumble £3.25.

Open *11 to 11, Sun 12 to 10.30; bar food 12 to 2.30, 6.30 to 9.30*
Details *Children welcome　Wheelchair access　Garden and patio　No-smoking area　Background music　Dogs welcome　Delta, MasterCard, Switch, Visa　Accommodation: 3 rooms, B&B £30 to £40*

YATTENDON　　Berkshire　　　　　　　　　　map 2

▲ *Royal Oak* 😋😋 🍇

The Square, Yattendon RG18 0UG　　TEL: (01635) 201325
off B4009, 5m W of Pangbourne

The pub sign, half obscured by climbing foliage, depicts a crown in an oak tree, indicating that the pub takes its name from Charles II – though it was Oliver Cromwell not Charles II who stayed at the inn, on the eve of the battle of Newbury. This particularly well-heeled corner of the Home Counties is not short of good eating places and many a fine pub in the area has been 'lost' – that is, lost its pubby roots to become a full-fledged restaurant. Fortunately, the Royal Oak is not one of them, as it is still possible to sit and drink here. There are three open-plan, wood-panelled rooms for informal eating, plus a dining-room proper that is done out in cheery yellows with floral pictures. Booking is recommended, even to eat in the bar, as the place can get extremely busy.

Chef Robbie Macrae was once a sous-chef under Marco Pierre White, and the influence is apparent in his cooking today. Foie gras and chicken liver parfait with onion marmalade and brioche could easily come (one might think) from Marco's Criterion Brasserie in London, the difference here is that you can eat it in the bar. Gazpacho is served with pickled sardines and crème fraîche, and chargrilled swordfish with crushed new potatoes and pesto is very attractively presented – a thinnish slab of succulent white fish with griddle marks, on top of crushed new potatoes. End it all with an 'adult' dessert of liqueur-infused chocolate fudge pudding with pistachio ice-cream. The separate set-price three-course restaurant menu has even more exotic dishes such as a mosaic of game with redcurrant dressing and tomato compote, and casserole of rabbit with roasted salsify and fondant new potato. For beer drinkers only well-kept Fuller's London Pride and local West Berkshire Good Old Boy are on offer. The wine list, however, tells a rather different story. If you always have wanted to spend £140 on a 1985 Ch. Pichon Longueville, Comtesse de Lalande, 2me Cru Classé, then this is the place to come. For those on a more modest budget, probably one of the very decent ten wines by the glass, ranging from £2.50 to £3.50, would better suit. SAMPLE DISHES: tian of a Cornish crab with avocado and pink grapefruit £6.75; sauté bream served with a squid risotto and bouillabaise jus £12.50; soup of fresh berries with vanilla ice-cream £4.50.

Open *12 to 3, 6 to 11 (10.30 Sun); bar food 12 to 2, 7 to 9.30 (10 Fri and Sat); restaurant Tue to Fri and Sun L 12 to 2, Mon to Sat D 7 to 10*
Details *Children welcome in bar eating area   Car park   Garden   No smoking in restaurant   Background music   Dogs welcome   Amex, Delta, Diners, MasterCard, Switch, Visa   Accommodation: 5 rooms, room only £95 to £125*

YEALAND CONYERS   Lancashire   **map 8**

New Inn 🍺 🍇

40 Yealand Road, Yealand Conyers LA5 9SJ
TEL: (01524) 732938
off A6, 2m N of Carnforth

PUDDINGS

This typical village pub serving locals and travellers alike is in good order with interesting, if a bit pricey, food, courteous service and fine ale. Operated by Ian and Annette Dutton, who also run Miller Howe Café in Windermere (and who were formerly at the highly regarded Miller Howe restaurant), the pub is very much at the heart of the straggling North Lancashire village, and is easily spotted at night thanks to its fairy lights twinkling along the side of the lane. Two of the three rooms are set as a formal restaurant, while the third and largest is the bar, with blazing fire, photographs of 'how it used to be', plates and farm implements. Lighting is subdued, with candles in wine bottles, and dried hops cover the ceiling beams – the place has a timeless quality. The highly individual menu is available in both bar and restaurant with, unusually, the blackboard offering lighter dishes as well as plenty of vegetarian options. That day's soup comes with sticky treacle and sultana bread, or you could have bobotie pot, a South African dish of spiced minced lamb under a brandied egg custard. Main courses are of the 'flashed under the grill' variety and come in round dishes accompanied by a large jacket potato straight from the oven. Caribbean pork comes with an intense tomato sauce liberally finished with pineapple and toasted coconut slivers; Cumberland sausage swims in a very creamy, crunchy and lightly herbed onion sauce.

Puddings are a sheer indulgence – generous helpings with masses of cream. Sticky toffee pudding with butterscotch sauce is light and flavoursome and, as for chocolate, peanut, cherry and date slice, worry about the calories another day. An unusual range of beers includes Hartleys Mild and XB, Old Tom and Robinson's Best, and a formal wine list of not quite 70 bottles, including the odd half, is geographically organised and comes with some useful summaries. Leighton Hall, famous as the home of the furniture-making Gillow family, is a couple of miles away. SAMPLE DISHES: chicken, orange and liver gâteau £5; oven-baked ham with sugar and spices £9; chocolate wheatmeal slice with warm butterscotch sauce £3.50.

Open *summer 11 to 11, winter Mon to Fri 11 to 3, 5.30 to 11, Sun all year and Easter 11 to 11; bar food and restaurant 11 to 2.30, 5.30 to 9.30 (Easter and summer school hols all day)*
Details *Children welcome   Car park   Garden   No smoking in restaurant Background music   Guide dogs only   Delta, MasterCard, Switch, Visa*

S·C·O·T·L·A·N·D

APPLECROSS   Highland   map 11

▲ *Applecross Inn*

Shore Street, Applecross IV54 8LR
TEL: (01520) 744262
off A896, 18m W of Loch Carron

Visitors are drawn here by the enticing combination of the seafood
dishes that are the Inn's hallmarks, and the setting. To get to
Applecross, you need to cross Bealach na Bar, the highest mountain
pass in Britain – rising over 2,000 feet in six miles – to be rewarded
on a clear day by spectacular views of Raasay and Skye, Ben Nevis
and the Cairngorms. Plenty take that journey, crowding into the
busy bar and tiny dining-room for dressed crab salad, oysters, or
squat lobster done in a cocktail or a curry or fried in garlic butter, or
perhaps a special suggested by the day's catch. Burgers – venison,
beef and vegetarian versions – are alternative snacks, along with
macaroni cheese, vegetable samosas and chicken breast in leek and
blue cheese sauce. Everything is locally harvested or grown, including herbs, vegetables and soft fruits. Banana split and hot chocolate
fudge cake are also Applecross staples. Children can ask for their
own menu or scaled-down versions of the bar menu. Tables need to
be reserved for the fixed-price three-course dinners in the restaurant.
Depending on the mood or hour (in the summer the pub is open all
day), you can choose tea, coffee or hot chocolate; in terms of alcohol, McEwans 80/- or Theakston Best are the beers, alongside a
score of wines, 50 malt whiskies, and Scottish bottled ales such as
Grozet gooseberry lager and Fraoch heather ale. SAMPLE DISHES:
smoked salmon platter £5; queen scallops in a creamy mushroom
sauce £7.50; raspberry cranachan £2.50.

Open *summer 11 to 11.30, Sun 12 to 11, winter 12 to 2.30, 5 to 11, Sun 12
to 7; closed 25 Dec, 1 Jan; bar food 12 to 9 (no food after 2.30 Nov to
March); restaurant D only 6 to 8.30*
Details *Children welcome   Car park   Wheelchair access   Garden and patio
No smoking in dining-room   Live music; jukebox   No dogs in dining-room
Delta, MasterCard, Visa   Accommodation: 5 rooms, B&B £25 to £55*

▲ *Galley of Lorne*

Ardfern PA31 8QN   TEL: (01852) 500284
on B8002, reached from A816 N of Lochgilphead

Ardfern is a yachtsman's hideaway on the shore of Loch Craignish, on the west coast of Argyll, and the Galley of Lorne is what they come ashore for. The name may hark back to the far-off days when this coastline was haunted by the fast-sailing craft of the island chiefs, but the pub is a good deal more modern than that, by and large an expanded croft house. The Galley Bar lies at its heart – something of a cavernous shed-like place, but one where wet wellies and oilskins would never be an embarrassment. There's a good fire to dry out by, over which the day's offerings are chalked up on a blackboard. Most of these are staple bar food, but the garlic mushrooms, spaghetti, or pies are supplemented by local seafood, and these are the obvious things to choose – local langoustines, Islay scallops or battered sole fillet, for example. Light options – ploughman's, soup and open sandwiches – are available at lunch-time, and children have their own menu. The atmosphere is jovial and chatty, and in season you can expect a good deal of nautical banter. No real ales are served, but there is a short wine list and a good selection of malt whiskies. SAMPLE DISHES: haggis with cream and whisky £3.25; halibut steak £13.50; orange and Cointreau cheesecake £3.25.

Open *summer 11am to midnight, Sun noon to midnight, winter 11 to 11, Sun 12 to 11; closed 25 Dec; bar food 12 to 2, 6 to 9 (8 in winter); restaurant Easter to Nov 12 to 2, 6 to 9*
Details *Children welcome in bar eating area   Car park   Wheelchair access (also WC)   Garden   Background music   Dogs welcome   MasterCard, Switch, Visa   Accommodation: 7 rooms, B&B £39 to £77*

▲ *Harbour Inn*

The Square, Bowmore, Isle of Islay PA43 7JR   TEL: (01496) 810330

Local produce is very much the theme at the Harbour Inn – that means both fresh produce, such as beef, lamb and venison from Islay and Jura and daily-landed fish, and the complete set of malt whiskies produced on Islay. Scott Chance is proprietor and chef. He cooks breakfasts, lunches and evening meals, as well as finding time to converse with visitors and residents. The dining-room offers brilliant views across cobalt-blue waters towards the profile of a reclining woman that is Jura. There is a certain overlap between the lunch and evening menus, though lunch is generally lighter and less expensive. Seafood features, especially shellfish, but so do meats from the grill. Loch Gruinart oysters are a regular on the menu in season, while half a fresh local lobster would make a filling lunchtime main course. Fans of local produce might opt for the unpretentiously served Islay lamb cutlets. Puddings are reasonably priced: rich Drambuie cream with crushed almond praline perhaps, or steamed apple and toffee sponge with custard. The wine list in the restaurant runs to 50 bins; four wines are available by the glass. Real ales on offer are McEwan 60/- and 80/-. SAMPLE DISHES: salad of lardons, croûtons and Parmesan cheese £3; stir-fried Lagavulin scallops and leeks in Muscat sauce £8.75; plum grits with iced whisky parfait £3.75.

Open *all week 11am (12 Sun) to 1am; closed 25 Dec and 1 Jan; bar food and restaurant Mon to Sat L 12 to 2.30, all week D 7 to 9*
Details *Children welcome in dining-room Wheelchair access Patio No smoking in restaurant No music Dogs welcome Amex, Delta, MasterCard, Switch, Visa Accommodation: 5 rooms, B&B £35 to £65*

BRIG O'TURK   Stirling   **map 11**

Byre Inn

Brig o'Turk FK17 8HT   TEL: (01877) 376292
on A821, between Callander and Aberfoyle

As its name suggests, this tiny Victorian inn was converted from an eighteenth-century stone cow byre. Set in a very secluded spot, it is open only from Friday to Sunday during the winter (all week except Tuesday in summer). The main bar is beamed, with a welcoming log fire, prints and photos on the walls, and old pews and comfortable chairs. The separate dining area is at the back, and a garden with tables under umbrellas provides space for summer eating. The bar menu may tempt with soup of the day, deep-fried haggis, pâté or barbecued chicken wings to start, followed by steak, wild game casserole with garlic croûtons or haddock baked with prawns in a lobster sauce. Vegetarian offerings might be warm French onion tart, vegetable gratin or pasta. Desserts are of the sticky toffee, 'death by chocolate cake' and lemon meringue pie variety, and include various ice-creams. More elaborate dishes in the evening could be pan-fried pigeon breast or roast venison in a red wine and redcurrant jus with fondant potatoes, finishing off with 'Highland Fling' crêpes enveloping summer berries laced with whisky and cream. Among a selection of liqueur coffees are Gaelic and Calypso. A range of Scottish 'craft beers' (with pine, heather and gooseberry flavours) supplements beers from Maclay. The 19-bottle wine list offers three by the glass. SAMPLE DISHES: soup of the day £2.25; Cumberland sausage wheel with crispy straw potatoes £7.25; fruits of the forest bread-and-butter pudding £4.

Open *summer Wed to Mon and winter Fri to Sun 12 (12.30 Sun) to 12 (11 in winter); bar food L 12 to 2.30, D (not on Sat) 6.30 to 9*
Details *Children welcome   Car park   Wheelchair access (also WC)   Garden   No smoking in restaurant   Background and live music   No dogs   Delta, MasterCard, Switch, Visa*

CANONBIE   Dumfries & Galloway   map 11

▲ *Riverside Inn*

Canonbie DG14 0UX   TEL: (013873) 71295
just off A47, 6m S of Langholm

With its broad frontage, whitewashed walls and flagpole before the front door, this seventeenth-century inn has something of the appearance of a colonial outpost. Inside, the décor is bright and homely. The split-level bar is on the left of the main entrance and has an open fire, stuffed birds, knick-knacks and a modern stone serving bar with a wooden top. Dedication to fresh ingredients simply prepared is the kitchen's philosophy, allowing the quality of the produce to do most of the work. The daily-changing menu – frequently the same in bar and dining-room – is short but diverse enough to offer plenty of appeal. Soups are something of a house speciality – beetroot, cream of Stilton, Scotch broth, or leek and parsnips perhaps. Pâtés come in the form of guinea-fowl terrine, chicken liver parfait, or ballottine of duck, and the smoked fish version makes frequent appearances. Air-dried Cambrian ham is another popular ingredient. Fish dishes may include Aga-roasted cod with Cheddar and red onion crust, or sea bass with ginger, sherry and spring onions. Scottish chargrilled rib eye steak will appeal to trenchermen, as will lamb's liver, bacon and onions. A popular pudding is home-made brown sugar meringue, or you might find marmalade bread-and-butter pudding. An extensive wine list supplied by Adnams includes a comprehensive range of well-chosen bottles. For beer drinkers, Yates's Bitter and Caledonian IPA are on handpump. SAMPLE DISHES: fresh langoustines and crevettes £6; casserole of roe deer in Guinness with vegetables £8; ginger syllabub £3.25.

Open *11 to 2.30, 6.30 to 11; closed Feb; bar food and restaurant all week L 12 to 2, Tue to Sat D 7 to 9*
Details *Children welcome   Car park   Wheelchair access   Garden   No smoking in dining-room and 1 area in bar   No music   No dogs in public rooms   Delta, MasterCard, Switch, Visa   Accommodation: 7 rooms, B&B £55 to £85*

CLACHAN **Argyll & Bute**   map 11

▲ *Tigh an Truish*

Clachan Seil, Isle of Seil PA34 4QZ   TEL: (01852) 300242
on B844, 12m S of Oban

Having to juggle beer pumps and petrol pumps is a possibly unique job description, but such is the requirement at this eighteenth-century whitewashed stone pub on an island peninsula of moor and woodland. You may therefore have a bit of a wait for your McEwan 80/-, guest beer or modestly priced glass of wine, but you can always stroll out to admire the graceful arch of the Atlantic Bridge that links Seil to the mainland south of Oban. Also decorative is the real wooden bar with its corner seat, but the pub goes in for few other adornments apart from a dartboard and a blackboard listing the day's menu. The style is down-to-earth and home-made, the ingredients local, with chocolate puddle pudding with Mars Bar sauce being the eyebrow-raiser. Beforehand, you might have started with a big mug of soup, moules marinière or smoked salmon, then progressed to lasagne, spicy bean casserole, beef Stroganov, steak and oyster pie or seafood risotto, enjoyed in a chatty and leisurely atmosphere. SAMPLE DISHES: home-made pâté £3.25; squat lobster curry and rice £5.50; syrup sponge £2.

Open *summer 11am (12.30 Sun) to 11.30pm, winter 11 (12.30 Sun) to 2.30, 5 to 11.30; closed 25 Dec and 1 Jan; bar food and restaurant 12 (12.30 Sun) to 2.15, 6 to 8.30*
Details *Children welcome in dining-room   Car park   Wheelchair access Garden and patio   No smoking in 1 room   Background music   No dogs in bedrooms   No cards   Accommodation: 2 rooms, B&B £40*

COMRIE **Perthshire & Kinross**   map 11

Deil's Cauldron

27 Dundas Street, Comrie PH6 2LN   **SCOTTISH**
TEL: (01764) 670352
on A85 Perth to Crianlarich road

This listed building stands at the edge of the village of Comrie at the entrance to Glen Lednock, which offers beautiful walks through beech and pine forests up to Lord Melville's monument, a wildlife centre and, of course, the Deil's Cauldron waterfall from which the inn takes its name. The small, low-ceilinged building features a tiny bar serving Belhaven Best and St Andrew's Ale, as well as a comfortable seating area and a small restaurant. The printed menus continue to offer solidly Scottish food: at lunch after a bowl of home-made soup, or a plate of smoked Tay salmon, you can tuck into 'The Great Chieftain O' the Pudding Race' (haggis), served with 'bashed neeps and chappit tatties', or perhaps 'The Poacher's Pouch' (vol-au-vent with filling of the day). On the very short evening menu sauté langoustines with herbs are a more exotic alternative to avocado salad as a starter, and the presence of Aberdeen Angus steak (cooked pink unless requested otherwise) as a main-course option is no surprise. The wine list is surprisingly long – 28 bottles – given the brevity of the menus, and balances well-chosen Old and New World bins. Three house wines are available by the glass, and nine half-bottles are listed, including two dessert wines. SAMPLE DISHES: Deil's own paté with Cumberland sauce and oatcakes £4; fillet of herring in oatmeal, cooked in butter with cider and apple sauce £5.50; ginger sponge and custard £2.50.

Open *Wed to Sat 12 to 2.30, 6 to 11, Sun 12.30 to 2.30, 7 to 11; closed Christmas and New Year; bar food 12 to 2.30, 7 to 9 (best to check bar food times in winter)*
Details *Children welcome in eating areas   Garden   No smoking in dining-room   No music   Guide dogs only   Delta, MasterCard, Switch, Visa*

CROMARTY   Highland

map 11

▲ *Royal Hotel*

Marine Terrace, Cromarty IV11 8YN
TEL: (01381) 600217
from Inverness cross Kessock Bridge, follow signs for Cromarty for approx 17m

SEASIDE

Albert, a 'local worthy', gathers molluscs from the beach across the road from the Royal Hotel, which is why they appear on the menu as 'mussels Albert'. Scottish fare dominates the cooking at this three-storey black and white painted house, and local history is very much the theme of the décor. The printed menu shows imagination and variety. Crêpes are a speciality – the filling of the Cromarty seafood version varies depending on the contents of the local catch – and there are grills and pasta dishes. It is worthwhile checking out the specials board for, perhaps, Orkney herrings in sherry, whole trout, or chicken in spicy tomato sauce. Belhaven is the only beer worthy of mention, but there is a 30-plus selection of malt whiskies to compensate. The pub's accommodation makes it a suitable base for exploration of Black Isle and Firth of Cromarty, which is famous for its colony of bottlenose dolphins. SAMPLE DISHES: deep-fried haggis balls in Drambuie sauce £4; fisherman's pie £7; granny's apple pie £3.

Open *11 to 11; bar food and restaurant Mon to Fri 12 to 2, 6 to 9, weekends 12 to 2.30. 6 to 9.30*
Details *Children welcome   Car park   Wheelchair access (also WC)   Garden Background and live music; jukebox   Dogs welcome in bar only   Amex, Delta, MasterCard, Switch, Visa   Accommodation: 10 rooms, B&B £30 to £60*

DRYMEN   Stirling   map 11

Clachan Inn

2 Main Street, Drymen G63 0BP   TEL: (01360) 660824
off A811, 20m W of Stirling

As one of the oldest pubs in Scotland, the Clachan is proudly kept as a traditional hostelry, with ales still the focus of the place. Belhaven Best and St Andrew's Ale, and Deuchars IPA from Caledonian are the handpumped beers in question, but there are also a few wines by the bottle, carafe or glass. A separate restaurant operates under the same roof, but by way of straightforward and comforting bar food you are likely to find burgers, fried fish, jumbo sausages or baked potatoes with a variety of fillings, including haggis. Vegetarians are decently catered for – perhaps with vegetable pakora, broccoli quiche or vegetable lasagne – while meat-eaters may home in on half a roast chicken, rack of lamb, or steaks, which come plain or with pesto, pâté, haggis, or Cajun and Creole spices. Main meals come with chips or baked potatoes and salad. Forest fruit trifle, sticky toffee meringue and apple pie are typical sweets, with a daily steamed pudding – nice with various coffees or tea. SAMPLE DISHES: marinated herring £3; fillet of salmon £8; cheesecake £3.25.

Open *11am to midnight, Sun 12.30 to 11.30; closed 25 Dec and 1 Jan; bar food and restaurant 12 (12.30 Sun) to 4, 6 to 10*
Details *Children welcome in dining-room   Wheelchair access (also WC) Background music   Dogs on a lead welcome in bar only   MasterCard, Switch, Visa*

Old Rectory 🍇

West Quality Street, Dysart KY1 2TE   TEL: (01592) 651211
off A955 Methil road, N of Kirkaldy

'This is the sort of pub ones dreams of finding,' writes a reporter: 'clean, warm, efficient, friendly with real quality food at staggeringly low prices.' Located in what was once a major port on the Fife, the pub was built by a wealthy local merchant in 1771. The road it is on was known at the time as Quality Street because of its popularity with the local well-to-do, and the building was originally known as Rectory House, although no clergymen lived there until 90 years after it was built. Today it retains its Georgian splendour and one or two interesting features – in particular a now-sealed aperture once used to pass food and drink to persons outside. Inside, there are odd plates and books and a collection of old Romeo y Julieta cigar boxes among the low beams. The small bar is definitely not of the propping up variety, and there is a restaurant at rear. The pub's main attraction is its good-value food. At lunch-time nothing is more than £5.50 and a separate bar menu operates in the evening as well as a *carte*.

Start with haggis Drambuie 'the Old Rectory Way', or perhaps smoked mackerel mousse. In the evening you could choose between a hot prawn bisque or a 'You think it up, we'll make it' omelette. Snails à la bourgignonne are for the more adventurous, and there is a hot oil cauldron offering deep-fried mushrooms, onion rings, Camembert and Brie. Lunchtime main courses centre round a cold buffet, though you can have venison casserole or smoked ham shank, and evening specials are likely to include a lemon chicken risotto, or steak and vegetable red wine casserole. Puddings are among the cheapest you will ever see – try sticky toffee with butterscotch sauce or bread-and-butter with custard. The pub serves no real ale – but this is Scotland – and a 70-strong wine list offers a world-wide selection with ten by the glass. SAMPLE DISHES: potted beef £2; spaghetti bolognaise £4.75; treacle sponge with ginger sauce £1.50.

Open *Tue to Sat 12 to 3, 7 to 12, Sun 12.30 to 4; closed 1 week mid-Jan, 2 weeks mid-Oct; bar food and restaurant 12 to 2 (3 Sun), 7 to 9.30*
Details *Children welcome in eating areas   Car park   Wheelchair access (also WC)   Garden   No music   Guide dogs only   Amex, Delta, MasterCard, Switch, Visa*

The Guide is totally independent, accepts no free hospitality and carries no advertising.

Food mentioned in the entries is available in the bar, although it may be possible to eat in a dining-room.

EAGLESFIELD   Dumfries & Galloway   map 11

▲ *Courtyard*

Eaglesfield DG11 3PQ   TEL: (01461) 500215
off A74, 3m E of Ecclefechan

In the heart of Thomas Carlyle country (not far from his birthplace
at Ecclefechan) and just south of Burns country, this pub is handy for
visiting Gretna Green, and as a stopping point for travellers heading
north to the Highlands. There is a relaxed and welcoming front bar
where preprandial drinks can be enjoyed before one goes through to
another room for bar meals or to the restaurant with its own menu.
Licensee Michael Mason's preferred style of cooking is strong on
sauces and fruit and has an inventive streak – pear with strawberries
and tarragon mayonnaise is a starter you may not see elsewhere.
Chicken with a fruity curry sauce manages to combine the two influences, and side salads may well have mango hidden among the
leaves. Puddings are home-made. Theakston beers are the only real
ales served and the wine list is almost exclusively from the New
World. SAMPLE DISHES: smoked venison and salmon duet £3.50; fillet
of pork with grain mustard sauce £7.75; chocolate roulade £2.50.

Open *Tue to Sun 12 to 2.30, all week 6.30 to 12; bar food and restaurant 12
to 2, 7 to 8.30*
Details *Children welcome   Car park   Wheelchair access (also WC)   Garden
No smoking in restaurant   Background music   Dogs welcome   MasterCard,
Visa   Accommodation: 3 rooms, B&B £21 to £40*

EDDLESTON   Borders   map 11

▲ *Horseshoe Inn*

Eddleston EH45 8QP   TEL: (01721) 730225
on A703, 4m N of Peebles

Originally a blacksmith's forge, this low, whitewashed building is in
a tiny village, yet only 20 minutes' drive from Edinburgh. The interior has two spacious and comfortable rooms, one of which has an
interesting circular window and is attractively decorated with anvils
and horseshoes in the fireplace, plus shelves containing china dogs,
porcelain and dried flowers. There are two longish menus, one for
lunch and one for dinner, with quite a bit of overlap. Both feature
starters such as home-made soup, pâté, and fish-cakes with a lemon
and coriander sauce, and main courses ('house favourites') like
'Smiddy' lasagne, scampi, and steak and ale pie. In the evening more
expensive main dishes also feature: scampi thermidor, lamb chasseur,

or fanned fillet of chateaubriand (for two people), for example.
Main courses come with potatoes or rice, although vegetables must
be ordered separately. Salads are always available, and sandwiches at
lunch-time. A selection of ice-creams includes 'Horseshoe Surprise' –
honey and drambuie with raspberries and cream and a honey
topping; other desserts might be Caledonian creams, cheesecakes or
pavlovas. Real ales from the cask are on offer in the summer, with
beers on tap in the winter from Broughton, while four wines come
by the glass. SAMPLE DISHES: black pudding and apple with onion
marmalade £3.75; smoked gammon steak £6.75; banoffi pie £3.

Open *12 to 3, 5.30 to 11.30; closed 25 Dec; bar food and restaurant Mon to
Sat 12.30 to 2.30, 6 to 9.30, Sun 12.30 to 9.30*
Details *Children welcome   Car park   Wheelchair access (also WC)   Garden
No-smoking area in bar; no smoking in restaurant before 9pm   Background
music   Dogs welcome   Amex, Delta, Diners, MasterCard, Switch, Visa
Accommodation: 8 rooms, B&B £25 to £50*

ELIE   Fife   map 11

Ship Inn

The Toft, Elie KY9 1DT   TEL: (01333) 330246
on A917, 5m W of Anstruther

An odd sort of a place is the Ship Inn, especially if you are Scottish.
For a start they play cricket on the beach at low tide, but yet this is
not the Caribbean where you might expect to find such a scene, or
England where cricket is a fact of life. Rugby matches are held too,
but the tide can be relied on to return the pitch to good bowling
order. Summertime sees jazz festivals, beer festivals and barbecues, in
or outside the pub, and the garden enjoys fine views of the beach,
bay and pier for the more sedentary-minded. Richard and Jill Philip
have run the pub since 1989 and have built up a well-oiled operation, which can get quite busy in summer, with customers drawn
not only by the sight of men in whites battling against the tide, but
also by the many nearby golf courses, watersports centre and other
attractions such as Lady Anstruther's Bathing Tower and Deep Sea
World. The menu will include starters such as seafood hors d'oeuvre
and Parisienne melon, and main courses will tempt you with Ship
Inn fruits de mer – an assemblage of halibut, lemon sole, king prawns
and smoked salmon poached in white wine and cream sauce. Finish
with a pudding of the sticky toffee/banoffi variety and toast the
cricket team from a short wine list with one or two intelligent
choices or, indeed, in Belhaven 80/- or Best, or Theakston Best.
SAMPLE DISHES: king prawns in garlic butter £4.50; penne pasta with
mussels and prawns £7; fresh fruit pavlova £3.50

Open *Mon to Thur 11am to midnight, Fri and Sat 11am to 1am, Sun 12.30 to midnight; closed 25 Dec; bar food and restaurant Mon to Sat 12 to 2, 6 to 9 (9.30 Fri and Sat), Sun 12.30 to 2.30, 6 to 9*
Details *Children welcome in bar eating area   Wheelchair access (also WC) Garden   No music   No dogs in restaurant   Delta, MasterCard, Switch, Visa*

GLENDEVON   **Perthshire & Kinross**   map 11

▲ *Tormaukin Hotel* 🅦 🍺 🍇

Glendevon FK14 7JY   TEL: (01259) 781252
on A823, 6m SE of Auchterarder

Located in an idyllic setting in the Ochil Hills, on the attractive road to Auchterarder, this eighteenth-century drovers' inn is typical of those large whitewashed Highland pubs that seem to appear from nowhere around a bend on an isolated road. The bar menu has all the usual elements in place, plus some interesting variations on a theme. Crispy fried tattie skins demonstrate that potato wedges do not just belong in 'surf and turf' pubs, and goat's-cheese pâté neatly rolls two popular starters into one. Haggis makes an appearance with medallions of fillet steak, and there are a number of exotic treatments such as Cajun pork with couscous, and breast of chicken with red Thai curry sauce. Vegetarian dishes include a vegetable paella, as well as creamed leek and tarragon crêpes. Salads are suitably modern: feta cheese and olives, marinated in basil and garlic, or smoked chicken and apricots bound in crème fraîche. There is a separate children's menu, and desserts, with delights like layered banana and toffee pudding, should appeal to children of all ages. A more expensive à la carte menu features in the restaurant during the evenings. Scottish hotels are not noted for the quality of their ales, but the Tormaukin is an exception, serving Waverley and Bitter & Twisted from the Harviestoun Brewery in Dollar, as well as Burton ale. A wine list dominated by France contains some formidable vintages, as well as some excellent half-bottles. SAMPLE DISHES: seasonal salad leaves with bacon and avocado £3.75; crispy duck legs with an orange glaze £9; strawberry pavlova £3.50.

Open *11 to 11, Sun 12 to 11; closed 10 days in Jan; bar food 12 to 2, 5.30 to 9.30, Sun 12 to 9.30; restaurant 6.30 to 9.30*
Details *Children welcome   Car park   Wheelchair access (also WC)   Patio Background and live music   Dogs by arrangement only   Amex, Delta, MasterCard, Switch, Visa   Accommodation: 10 rooms, B&B £50 to £75*

Assessments of wine in pubs are based largely on what is available in the bar. Many pubs also have full restaurant wine lists.

▲ *Glenelg Inn*

Glenelg, by Kyle of Lochalsh IV40 8JR   TEL: (01599) 522273
at head of Sound of Sleat, off A87 at Loch Duich

Glenelg lies on the mainland at the closest point to Skye; island
drovers used to bring their cattle over at the nearby Kylerhea
narrows. Dr Johnson and Mr Boswell visited the inn in 1773 and had
a thoroughly bleak time of it, finding no meat, milk, bread, eggs or
wine, and enduring a damp, dirty and smelly room. The inn cannot
have been much fun for local Jacobites either, being right next door
to the Hanoverian Barracks of Bernera. Now the barracks are in ruins
and the inn has undergone a sea change. Staying guests are offered
'uncluttered homeliness' from a cultured and thoughtful host; those
turning up for just a bar meal can lunch on locally smoked salmon,
deep-fried mushrooms, baked potatoes or hoagies (rolls) with various
fillings, soups, stews and elegant puddings (in the evening more
formal meals are served in the separate dining-room). You sit on
upturned wooden fish boxes by an enormous log fire, and soon get
drawn into the ceilidh atmosphere: some of Scotland's finest fiddlers
and folk singers may be there. Whiskies, some cask-strength, are the
inn's speciality, and Christopher Main has put together a short and
attractive wine list, though with only one by the glass. Real ales are
absent, but a pot of tea or coffee with scones and cakes may be just as
welcome after a day's walking, climbing, pony-trekking, seal-watching
or boating amid superb mountain and loch scenery. SAMPLE DISHES:
prawn and salmon terrine £3.50; fish pie £6; pear clafoutis £3.

Open *summer 12 to 2.30, 5 to 11 (12 Sat, 11.30 Sun), winter Sat L 12 to
2.30, all week eve 5 to 11; bar food 12 to 2.30, restaurant from 7.30*
Details *Children welcome   Car park   Wheelchair access (also WC)   Garden
Background and live music   Dogs welcome on a lead; no dogs in restaurant
MasterCard, Switch, Visa   Accommodation: 6 rooms, B&B £28 to £80*

Waterside 🍺

1–5 Nungate, Waterside EH41 4AT
TEL: (01620) 825674
off A1, 16m E of Edinburgh

Located beside a river and opposite the historic church in the oldest
part of Haddington, this pub/bistro offers fantastic views of the river
and ancient churchyard. Inside, it is low-ceilinged, quite dark and
cluttered, but welcoming, with a long bar and tables located along

the window side of the room, which gives everyone a good view. To the rear is another dining-room, without the views, and there is a restaurant upstairs. The late '70s and '80s style of the bar menu remains in evidence, and lovers of devilled whitebait and deep-fried Brie with redcurrant jelly will be happy to learn that the bar menu has made little effort to enter the '90s (though mysteriously in the restaurant deep-fried Brie comes with mango chutney). Plenty of fish courses feature: start with kipper and fresh herb mousse, grilled monkfish with garlic and lemon butter, or smoked salmon and prawn pancake, before moving on to fresh salmon and nectarine salad, deep-fried scampi tails, or goujons of sole. Alternatively, start off with deep-fried haggis in whisky sauce, or salad of chicken and crispy bacon and then settle for chicken, beef or prawn curry with rice, gammon and pineapple, or escalope of pork and pepper sauce. Puddings are solidly traditional. The bar serves Belhaven 80/-, Deuchars IPA, Timothy Taylor Landlord and Wadworth 6X, and in addition to the extensive wine list there is a large selection of whiskies. SAMPLE DISHES: fresh mussels, served as requested £4; poached sole fillets 'pescador' £7; sticky toffee pudding £2.75.

Open *11.30 to 2.30, 5 to 11, Sun 12.30 to 11; bar food 12 to 2, 5.30 to 10, Sun 12.30 to 10; restaurant 12 to 2, 6.30 to 10*
Details *Children welcome   Car park   Wheelchair access   Garden   No-smoking area   No music   No dogs   Amex, Delta, Diners, MasterCard, Switch, Visa*

HOWGATE   Midlothian   map 11

The Howgate   NEW ENTRY

Howgate EH26 8PY   TEL: (01968) 670000
on A6094 Leadburn to Auchendinny road, 1½m SE of Penicuik

Set by the main road, though miraculously free from traffic noise, the Howgate is a newly refurbished row of farmworkers' cottages. The interior is very stylishly designed with simple clean lines, and is quite bright with blue carpet, an open fire and simple wooden tables. There is a bar, bistro and restaurant although distinctions are blurred and you can eat from the same menu anywhere. Clientele are a mix of locals from Penicuik and Edinburgh residents, some of whom come via the pub's courtesy bus. The menu, which changes every five or six weeks, comprises traditional fare, mixed with some nice modern touches and rotates some common themes. Thus among starters will usually be a risotto, fish-cakes and something with pastry. Main courses may include flavoursome and meaty venison sausage with onion gravy and grain mustard; beef steak pie; chicken with a black pudding sauce and polenta; penne pasta with a tomato and basil sauce; or lamb shank with mashed potato and cabbage with a good, rich, stocky gravy. Desserts are individual variations on popular favourites: mango cheesecake, for example, or a rich chocolate mousse pie, studded with mini marshmallows. Accompany your meal with a pint of Belhaven Best or a selection from the extensive wine list, which includes four wines by the glass. SAMPLE DISHES: creamy garlic mushrooms in a puff pastry case £3.50; chargrilled ostrich burger with all the trimmings £6; banoffi pie with ice-cream £3.

Open *Tue to Sun 11 to 2.30, 6 to 11; closed 25 Dec, 1 Jan; bar food and restaurant 12 to 2.30, 6 to 10*
Details *Children welcome　Car park　Wheelchair access (also WC)　Garden Background music　No dogs　Amex, Delta, Diners, MasterCard, Switch, Visa*

INNERLEITHEN　　**Borders**　　　　　　　　**map 11**

▲ *Traquair Arms* 🍺

Traquair Road, Innerleithen EH44 6PD
TEL: (01896) 830229
off A72, 6m SE of Peebles

HOME BREW

The Traquair Arms Hotel is a traditional Victorian medium-sized hotel just off the main street in the small textile-based town of Innerleithen. The bar area is pleasant, complete with a real fire and a tank full of fish (not for eating), and to the rear is a larger, more formal dining area. Clientele are predominantly locals and visiting fishermen keen to try their hand at catching salmon on the Tweed. The menu should be praised for its wide selection of vegetarian options, even offering two daily soups, one meat stock based, the other not, and prices are reasonable. Battered and nicely seasoned mushrooms come with a flavoursome garlic mayonnaise; lamb chops arrive pink if so requested and with very good chips; while steaks make their appearance in all shapes and sizes and have been certified by the Aberdeen Angus Society as being from genuine Aberdeen Angus grass-fed herds. Choose either a sirloin or a fillet, select the size you want, and then decide to have it done chasseur, au poivre, Diane, or in garlic butter. Fish lovers could try a Finnan savoury – a house original made with Scottish smoked salmon, onions, Ayrshire Cheddar cheese and double cream. Mussels cooked with potatoes, spicy sausage, garlic, stock, sherry and cumin seeds make an unusual alternative. Consult the separate menu for sweets and a selection of Scottish cheeses. If you have the time, visit the Traquair House Brewery some hundred yards distant, where the Bear Ale served in the pub is brewed; Broughton Greenmantle is also on tap. Also see the famous Bear Gates, which have not opened since Bonnie Prince

Charlie passed through them and will not open until a Stuart regains the throne. SAMPLE DISHES: citrus salad £4.25; Traquair steak parfait £ 6.50; cranachan £3.

Open *11 to 11, Sun 12 to 11; closed 25 Dec, 1 and 2 Jan; bar food and restaurant 12 to 9*
Details *Children welcome   Car park   Wheelchair access   Garden and patio Background music   Dogs welcome   Amex, Delta, Diners, MasterCard, Switch, Visa   Accommodation: 10 rooms, B&B £45 to £58*

KILBERRY   Argyll & Bute   map 11

▲ *Kilberry Inn*

Kilberry PA29 6YD   TEL: (01880) 770223
on B8024, between Lochgilphead and Tarbert

'Persistence rewarded' ought to be the motto of the Kilberry Inn, for this isolated outpost of good cooking is to be found exactly halfway around a 16-mile single-track detour from the main Lochgilphead to Tarbert road, and it takes a good deal of time to get to it. Kath and John Leadbeater's pub may have started life catering to tourists travelling this scenic Kilberry road, but for many, it has become a reason in itself to take the detour, for it is doubtful if you will find such a varied range of good home cooking anywhere else for quite some miles. A low-slung, red-roofed building, the Kilberry looks more like a country post office, and only a roadside blackboard and a suspiciously well-used parking area opposite alert you to its real character. Inside, liberal quantities of blackboards draw your attention to the day's offerings. These include not only the staple hot and cold foods – pâtés, beef in beer, venison, or sausage pie – but a range of home-baked breads and jars of jams, chutneys and other preserves. The same bountiful approach goes into the puddings, with cheesecakes in abundance, shortbreads and apple pies. No real beers are served – blame the remote location – but some interesting bottled ales are on hand, including Old Jock, Fraoch Heather, Black Douglas, Greenmantle and The Ghille Oatmeal Stout, as well as a good selection of malt whiskies. Wines range from around £9 to £20 per bottle, and three are available by the glass. SAMPLE DISHES: leek and oak-smoked haddock bake £4.75; Aberdeen Angus steak cooked in red wine with Stilton £14.50; malt whisky and oatmeal ice-cream with raspberries £4.75.

Open *11 to 2, 5 to 10; closed mid-Oct to Easter; bar food Mon to Sat 12.15 to 1.45, 6.30 to 8.45*
Details *Well-behaved children welcome in family room   Car park   No smoking in family room   No music   No dogs   Delta, MasterCard, Switch, Visa   Accommodation: 2 rooms, B&B £39 to £67*

Lade Inn 🍺

Trossachs Road, Kilmahog FK17 8HD   TEL: (01877) 330152
on A281 at junction with A84, 1m N of Callander

On a snowy day the inn looks especially smashing, and within you can see snow- (and unsnow-) covered pictures of it behind the small bar. The pine-panelled interior is small, clean and bright, offering something of an oasis in this remote setting. The pub serves a regularly changing selection of four or five Scottish beers, including Orkney Red MacGregor and Broughton Greenmantle, as well as the heather ale Fraoch, a throwback to the days before hops were available this far north. Food is pub grub with a Scottish touch and a fair dollop of local ingredients. Naturally, the cuts of beef are Scottish, and both Angus sirloin and 'Tartan' chicken are stuffed with haggis, which is also served on its own with tatties and neeps. Venison comes in the form of sausages, or roast haunch from Perthshire in a red wine sauce. There is a range of sandwiches and jacket potatoes at lunch-times, and children have their own menu. Puddings are posted on the board opposite the bar. The wine list is short with some New World offerings; three wines come by the glass. SAMPLE DISHES: marinated herring in sweet dill sauce £3.50; game casserole £7.50; treacle sponge £3.

Open *summer 12 to 11, Sun 12.30 to 11, winter 12.30 to 3, 5.30 to 11, Sun 12.30 to 11; closed 1 Jan; bar food 12 to 2.30 (3.15 Sun), 5.30 to 9*
Details *Children welcome in bar eating area; no children under 16 after 9pm Car park   Wheelchair access (also WC)   Garden   No-smoking area Background and live music   Dogs welcome in bar area only   MasterCard, Switch, Visa*

▲ *Cuilfail Hotel*

Kilmelford PA34 4XA   TEL: (01852) 200274
on A816 at head of Loch Melfort, 12m S of Oban

The creeper-covered stone building of the Cuilfail is the most substantial house in Kilmelford, a tiny hamlet, tucked in a hollow of the Argyll hills. On a gloomy day, it can look an unlikely spot to find some excellent food and a cheery bar, but once you have penetrated the rather cavernous reception area, and been ushered to the bar by landlord David Birrell, the atmosphere changes. Lined with bare stone, and warmed by a crackling wood fire, the bar is a home-from-home, especially on a dreich, drizzly west coast day.

Tables are well spaced out around the walls and in odd corners, and the bar is not over-obtrusive. Whatever is best from the local suppliers goes on to the menu, which frequently changes. In summer the 'Tartan Puffer' restaurant offers a separate menu, though items from this can also be selected in the bar. Deep-fried haggis balls appear alongside warm prawn tails and black pudding salad for starters, while main courses range from roast chicken to scallops, venison medallions in warm Cumberland sauce, and steak. One real ale is provided for beer drinkers, along with a list of three dozen wines. Over 700 malt whisky miniatures are also on display, and some rare old bottles, including a 60-year-old Macallan valued at £12,000 (not for sale). SAMPLE DISHES: local mussels and bacon kebab £4.25; saddle of venison £8; barbecued seafood platter £14.

Open *summer 11 to 11, winter 12 to 2.30, 6 to 11; bar food and restaurant 12 to 2.30, 6.30 to 9.30*
Details *Children welcome in bar eating area   Car park   Wheelchair access (also WC)   Garden   Background and live music   Dogs welcome MasterCard, Switch, Visa   Accommodation: 14 rooms, B&B £20 to £70*

KINNESSWOOD   Perthshire & Kinross   map 11

▲ *Lomond Country Inn*
Kinnesswood KY13 7HN   TEL: (01592) 840253
on A911, 4m SE of Milnathort

Situated on the slopes of the Lomond Hills, this Victorian inn enjoys views over Loch Leven towards the island castle where Mary Queen of Scots was imprisoned. Though it is the centre of the village, there are fields to the rear of the pub. The atmosphere is relaxed, and it is 'definitely a locals' pub as well as a place to eat'. The lunch bar menu offers the likes of warm smoked mackerel salad with whisky dressing to start, followed by a selection of salads, omelettes, pasta, curries or pies. Puddings range from raspberry cranachan to chocolate fudge cake, sticky toffee pudding or rhubarb crumble. The good-value, set-price 'Scottish menu' might open with soup or deep-fried haggis followed by lamb chops or Tay salmon, and finish with clootie dumpling; a more expensive *carte* includes venison steak, baked monkfish tail or roast pigeon. Beers come from Jennings and Marston's, and the long wine list is strong in the New World and offers three house wines by the bottle or glass. Nearby Vane Farm RSPB Nature Reserve is particularly popular with children. SAMPLE DISHES: Cullen skink £2.75; seafood pancake with Parmesan £5.50; apple pie £3.50.

Open *all week 11 to 11; bar food and restaurant Mon to Fri 12 to 2.30, 6 to 9, Sat and Sun 12 to 9*
Details *Children welcome　Car park　Wheelchair access (also WC)
Garden　No-smoking area　No music　Dogs welcome in bar only　Amex, Delta, Diners, MasterCard, Switch, Visa　Accommodation: 12 rooms, B&B £40 to £70*

KIPPEN　　Stirling　　　　　　　　　　map 11

▲ *Cross Keys*

Main Street, Kippen FK8 3DN　　TEL: (01786) 870293
on B822, 10m W of Stirling

The 'kingdom' of Kippen in the heart of Stirlingshire is little more than a main street running up a hillside. In the centre of the village the Cross Keys, which dates back to 1703, presents a welcoming face to the street. Inside, this welcome is confirmed by Angus and Sandra Watt, whose establishment has a very family-run feel, and service is friendly and attentive, even when busy. The same reasonably priced menu is available at lunch and dinner, typically offering bramble and port liver pâté, lamb stovies with crusty bread, and Kashmiri chicken with naan. Puddings are all home-made and include ubiquitous favourites like clootie dumpling and bread-and-butter-pudding. Smaller portions for children and OAPs are available. Beers include Greenmantle Ale from Broughton Brewery in the Borders and there are four wines available by the glass. The more formal Vine Restaurant takes its name from the famous Kippen Vine. Planted here in 1891, it grew to become the largest vine in the world under glass. It stretched for 300 feet in length and prior to its demise in 1964 was producing around 2,000 bunches of Gros Colman grapes a year. SAMPLE DISHES: mushrooms and garlic mayonnaise £2.50; chicken korma £5.75; banana fritters £2.

Open *Mon to Fri 12 to 2.30, 5.30 to 11 (12 Fri), Sat 12 to 2.30, 5.15 to 12, Sun 12.30 to 11; closed 25 Dec eve, 1 Jan; bar food 12 to 2, 5.30 to 9.30, Sun 12.30 to 2, 5.15 to 9.30; restaurant all week D only 7 to 8.45*
Details *Children welcome in family room　Car park　Wheelchair access (also WC)　Garden　No pipes or cigars while food is served　Background music; jukebox　Dogs welcome　Delta, MasterCard, Switch, Visa　Accommodation: 3 rooms, B&B £19.50 to £39*

If you visit any pubs that you think should appear in the Guide, write to tell us – The Which? Guide to Country Pubs, FREEPOST, 2 Marylebone Road, London NW1 1YN.

KYLESKU   Highland   map 11

▲ *Kylesku Hotel* 🍇

Kylesku IV27 4HW   TEL: (01971) 502231
*on A894, at S side of old ferry crossing, by new bridge linking
Ullapool and Kylkestrome*

Only open from March to the end of October, this small hotel in a
fishing hamlet is worth visiting for the wonderful views over Loch
Glencoul alone. The low, croft-type whitewashed building contains
two rooms, one a wood-panelled dining-room, and draws in tourists
and locals alike. Although the emphasis in the restaurant is French –
chef/patron Marcel Klein hails originally from Alsace – snacks in the
bar are traditional, e.g. soup, venison terrine or mussels to start,
followed by haddock and chips, scampi, various chicken dishes or
steak. Daily blackboard specials might be home-cured smoked
salmon, or lobsters from the loch, while desserts range from fruit
crumbles and bread-and-butter pudding to banoffi gâteau. Set-price
two- and three-course meals are available in the restaurant and run
to baked mussels in puff pastry with lobster sauce, grilled ribeye
steak with Café de Paris butter, or grilled jumbo langoustine with
garlic mayonnaise. Beers are not an inspired selection, but rare malt
whiskies and a wonderful wine list go some way to compensate for
the lack of ales. Although mainly French, the list has bottles from
around the world, including seven house wines from five different
countries, and ten wines are offered by the glass. SAMPLE DISHES:
soup of the day £2.25; chicken tikka with savoury rice £7; chocolate torte £2.50.

Open *11 to 11; closed Nov to Feb; bar food and restaurant 11.30 to 2.30,
5.30 to 9.45*
Details *Children welcome   Car park   Wheelchair access (also WC)   Garden
No smoking in restaurant   Background music   Dogs welcome   MasterCard,
Switch, Visa   Accommodation: 8 rooms, B&B £25 to £70*

LIMEKILNS   Fife   map 11

Ship Inn 🍺

Halketts Hall, Limekilns KY11 3HJ   TEL: (01383) 872247
on N bank of Firth of Forth, 2m W of Inverkeithing

The Ship Inn 'looks like it has been a fisherman's pub for ever',
wrote one enthusiast. The pub offers fine views over the Firth of
Forth to the bridges downstream, and the parklands of Hopetoun
and the House of the Binns across the water. Inside are plenty of

shipping memorabilia, but done in an ungimmicky fashion. The overall feel is one of genuineness in ingredients, welcome, service and value. Beers – though not wines – are taken seriously here: on draught are Belhaven 80/-, St Andrew's and IPA, plus a guest. The very reasonably priced menu – nothing is more than £5 – offers 'good, honest value', presenting unambitious cooking (at lunch-time only) that does not pretend otherwise. Lobster bisque, or soup of the day, tops the bill, while main courses include fisherman's pie, scampi, and gammon and pineapple. Side orders of chips have been pronounced 'admirably non-greasy'. For the chipped-out, there is a selection of 'rice platters', including mushroom Stroganov, chicken Madras, and vegetable curry, and to finish things off is sticky toffee pudding or perhaps apple sponge. SAMPLE DISHES: hot and spicy chicken dips £2.75; home-made chilli £4.75; ginger sponge pudding with lemon sauce £1.75.

Open *11 to 11 (12 Thur to Sun); bar food L only Mon to Fri 12 to 2, Sat and Sun 12.30 to 2.30*
Details *Children welcome   Wheelchair access (also WC)   Garden   No-smoking area   Background and live music   Dogs welcome   Amex, Delta, MasterCard, Switch, Visa*

LOCH CLUANIE   **Highland**   map 11

▲ *Cluanie Inn*   WHISKY

Loch Cluanie IV3 6YW   TEL: (01320) 340238
on A87, between Loch Ness and Skye ferry, at W end of Loch Cluanie

It was in a cave above Cluanie that Bonnie Prince Charlie took refuge for several days after his escape from Skye, protected by 'the seven men of Glen Moriston', despite a massive ransom on his head. But such is the remoteness of this place, the nearest habitation a couple of miles away, that you are hardly surprised his hiding-place remained undiscovered. The squat whitewashed inn, cosily furnished, has been cosseting travellers to this area of outstanding beauty for over 100 years. Walkers and climbers are happy to tuck into simple, sustaining food, whether home-made soup, lasagne, steak and ale pie, chicken korma or mushroom Stroganov – or a baked potato with a filling of haggis or grated Orkney Cheddar. Alternatively, you could assemble your own salad from the salad bar, or ask for a lunchtime sandwich, such as smoked salmon with West Highland Crowdie cheese. A slightly more formal three-course menu is served in the restaurant. For beer drinkers there is McEwan 80/- and Gillespie's Malt Stout, and for whisky drinkers more than 40 malts, which are probably the best relaxant for tired muscles. SAMPLE

DISHES: game pâté with oatcakes £3.50; Aberdeen Angus mince and tatties £5; sticky toffee pudding £3.

Open *11 to 11; bar food and restaurant 12 to 2.30, 6 to 8.30*
Details *Children welcome   Car park   Wheelchair access (also WC)   Garden and patio   Background and live music   Dogs welcome   Amex, MasterCard, Switch, Visa   Accommodation: 13 rooms, B&B £30 to £44*

MELROSE   Borders   map 11

▲ *Burts Hotel* 🍇

The Square, Melrose TD6 9PN   TEL: (01896) 822285
on A6091, midway between Galashiels and St Boswells

This whitewashed hotel, a listed building in a picturesque eighteenth-century Borders village, was originally built in 1722 as a house for a local dignitary, and has since been carefully extended. The lounge bar has a blazing log fire in winter, and the hotel's garden is available for summer drinking. Lunch and supper menus are served in the bar. Starters of turkey parfait, quail galantine or pan-fried salmon fish-cakes may be followed by warm salad of black pudding with wild mushrooms, deep-fried goujons of chicken, a pasta dish or freshly crumbed scampi tails, plus a choice of Aberdeen Angus steaks; a fish special might be seared fillet of grey mullet on a niçoise salad. Finish with apricot clafoutis, Selkirk bannock pudding, or rich chocolate tart. A set-price menu operates in the separate restaurant offering items such as galantine of duck followed by duet of rabbit and pigeon or medallions of beef fillet. Beers are 80/- and Sandy Hunter's Traditional Ale from Belhaven, and malt whiskies run to some 80 choices. An extensive wine list covers the world and is particularly strong on well-chosen half-bottles. SAMPLE DISHES: Greek salad with feta cheese £4; fried fillet of haddock £5.75; glazed crème Chilboust £4.

Open *12 to 2.30, 5 to 11; closed 26 Dec; bar food and restaurant 12 to 2, 6 to 9.30*
Details *Children welcome   Car park   Wheelchair access   Garden   No music Dogs welcome   Amex, Delta, Diners, MasterCard, Switch, Visa Accommodation: 20 rooms, B&B £48 to £100*

MINNIGAFF   Dumfries & Galloway   map 11

▲ *Creebridge House Hotel* ❦

Minnigaff DG8 6NP   TEL: (01671) 402121
off A75, just N of Newton Stewart

White-chimneyed Creebridge House is an attractive stone building in
three acres of gardens and woodland and was once the residence of
the Earls of Galloway. It feels most like a country hotel, targeting
itself at business people, golfers and anglers; but Bridges Brasserie,
the pub bit of the Walker family operation, is more down to earth.
You still find the 'collages' and 'chiffonades' that doll up the separate
Garden Restaurant menu, but beneath the fancy descriptions are
some attractive cooked-to-order bar meals, not least among the
lunchtime sandwiches. Filo parcels of wild mushrooms and North
Atlantic prawn cocktail will have their adherents, while among main
courses the kitchen turns its hand to pretty well anything, whether
sweet chilli vegetable stir-fry in the vegetarian section, or deep-fried
cod with home-made tartare sauce, sea bass on fennel, medallions of
venison, balti chicken curry, or chargrilled steaks in half a dozen
tempting ways. Lamb is a particularly strong suit. Sweets range from
banoffi pie and Cream o' Galloway ice-cream to citrus lemon tart
and iced raspberry parfait. Sunday lunch is a carvery meal. If Scottish
drinks such as the malt whiskies and Orkney Dark Island fail to
tempt, you could opt for Black Sheep, Tetley or Marston's Pedigree.
The wine list roams the world to come up with some imaginative
finds by glass or bottle. SAMPLE DISHES: Caesar salad £3.50; roast loin
of lamb with basil mousse and sweetbreads £9.75; terrine of chocolate mousses £2.75.

Open *12 to 2.30, 6 to 11.30; closed 26 Dec; bar food 12 to 2, 6 to 9 (10
Sat); restaurant April to Oct D only 7 to 9*
Details *Children welcome in bar eating area   Car park   Wheelchair access
(also WC)   Garden   No smoking in restaurant   Background music   No dogs
in eating areas   Amex, Delta, MasterCard, Switch, Visa   Accommodation: 19
rooms, B&B £45 to £85*

NETHERLEY   Aberdeenshire   map 11

▲ *Lairhillock Inn*

Netherley AB39 3QS   TEL: (01569) 730001   **LOCAL PRODUCE**
on B979, 4m S of Peterculter

Lying just outside Stonehaven, a quiet resort and dormitory town of
Aberdeen, the Lairhillock Inn aims to offer something for everyone. A
new conservatory with fine views caters well for families, and there's

a snug as well as a more formal restaurant with a gallery. The focus of the pub, however, is the bar, traditionally furnished and with a splendid central-hooded open log fire. The versatility and international approach of the kitchen are demonstrated by such dishes as baked avocado and Gruyère with a wild mushroom sauce, chicken suprême with wild mushroom sauce on tagliatelle, or grilled steaks or venison escalopes. Other imaginative starters and main courses are stir-fry of monkfish and king prawns, gambas créole and a curry of the day. But the kitchen does not turn its back on Scotland – far from it. Chicken écossais (with a haggis stuffing), baked local cod, Highland lasagne based on venison and wild boar (and more wild mushrooms), and the interesting-sounding black pudding in a crispy herb and sesame crust have all made appearances on the menu. Lighter bites at lunch-time are ploughman's and salad-filled half-baguette, and sticky toffee pudding and cheesecake are among the sweets. As all the food is cooked to order it would be unwise to visit if you are in a hurry. Ales at this free-house include Directors, Boddingtons, Flowers and McEwans 80/-, plus a guest beer. Malt whiskies are thick on the ground, and the wine list concentrates on grapes from France and Germany, with other palatable bottles from Spain, Italy, Australia and California. Five wines can be bought by the glass. SAMPLE DISHES: cullen skink £3.75; braised duck legs £8; banana butterscotch sundae £4.

Open *12 to 2.30, 5 to 11(midnight Fri and Sat), Sun 12 to 2.30, 6.30 to 11; closed 25 and 26 Dec, 1 and 2 Jan; bar food 12 to 1.45, 6 to 9.15 (10 Fri and Sat); restaurant Sun L 12 to 1.45, all week D 7 to 9*
Details *Children welcome in dining-room   Car park   Wheelchair access (also WC)   Garden and patio   Background and live music   Dogs welcome in snug bar   Amex, Delta, Diners, MasterCard, Switch, Visa   Accommodation: 2 rooms, B&B £65*

PLOCKTON   Highland   map 11

▲ *Plockton Inn*   NEW ENTRY

Innes Street, Plockton IV52 8TW   LOCAL PRODUCE
TEL: (01599) 544222
off A87, 5m NE of Kyle of Lochalsh

Good fresh fish is the thing at this friendly west coast pub, 100 yards up from the harbour, with its typical colour scheme of cream, tartan and maroon in the two bars. They also smoke their own fish so from the printed menu or the blackboard you could choose queenie scallops in bacon, cream and garlic, smoky fish-cakes with tartare sauce, 'chunky and substantial' west coast fish soup, gravadlax cured with dill and brandy, or haddock or scampi with chips. 'Plockton prawns' are actually langoustines and are served either hot with garlic butter or cold with garlic mayonnaise, and either whole or just tails for even better value. Meat and game broaden the choice: pork steak with honey and mustard sauce, medallions of venison with port sauce, and haggis (traditional or vegetarian) and clapshot (neeps and tatties) served with the pub's own pickled beetroot. Soups also come in vegetable- , fish- or meat-based forms, with excellent brown bread; there are sandwiches too. Most of the items on the menu can be ordered as starters or main courses. Sweets – of the sticky toffee pudding variety – are home-made. There's a separate restaurant, but curling up by a log fire with a pint of one of the Caledonian brewery's range of ales, or indeed Grozet (gooseberry beer) or Fraoch (heather ale), sounds more the ticket. SAMPLE DISHES: mussels in white wine, onions and butter £3.75/£6; grilled Mediterranean vegetable medley £3.25/£6; jacket potato with salmon and herby mayonnaise £3.

Open *Mon to Fri 11am to 1am, Sat 11 to 11.30, Sun 12.30 to 11; bar food 12 to 2.30, 5.30 to 10 (9 winter); restaurant 12 to 2.30, 5.30 to 10 (9 winter)* **Details** *Children welcome   Car park   Wheelchair access (also WC)   Garden and patio   No smoking in restaurant   Background and live music   Dogs welcome   Delta, MasterCard, Switch, Visa   Accommodation: 6 rooms, B&B £26 to £58*

PORTPATRICK   **Dumfries & Galloway**   map 11

▲ *Crown*

9 North Crescent, Portpatrick DG9 8SX
TEL: (01776) 810261
off A77, 6m SW of Stranraer

Situated in the picturesque fishing village of Portpatrick, the Crown is a handsome three-storey building, white-painted with blue window frames, looking out over the harbour towards Ireland. If you venture beyond the pub's cosy confines, you will discover a cool-toned bistro and non-smoking conservatory, and beautifully refurbished cottagey bedrooms. But the pub is the thing here, for all the world like a smugglers' haunt, its two bars smoky from wood and tobacco and with a fire blazing in winter. Depending on your preferences, you can pick from more than 70 malt whiskies, Scrumpy Jack cider, an extensive wine list, and Theakston Best, and McEwan's 70/- and 80/- on draught. The bar menu sticks to plain, toasted or open sandwiches, and basket snacks with chips, such as scampi, scallops or cheeseburger; also afternoon teas. The bistro menu is more expensive but the quality is high, with stylish starters such as scallops wrapped in bacon, and pâté served with whisky marmalade and oatcakes, and main courses like Portavogie cod in beer batter with tomato sauce, collops of venison, and steaks with various sauces. Salads also look enticing, such as Dublin Bay prawns, and roast Galloway beef. Peach Pavlova with raspberry sauce, and apple and toffee flan, would make pleasant ends to a fine meal. SAMPLE DISHES: trio of smoked fish with gooseberry sauce £5; baked ragoût of monkfish tails £10; strawberry shortbread £3.25.

Open *11 to 11.30, Sun 12 to 11.30; closed 25 Dec; bar food 12 to 2.30, 6 to 10; snacks and afternoon tea 2.30 to 6*
Details *Children welcome   Car park   Garden   No-smoking area Background and live music   Dogs welcome   Amex, MasterCard, Switch, Visa Accommodation: 12 rooms, B&B £36 to £48*

R A T H O   Edinburgh   map 11

Bridge Inn

27 Baird Road, Ratho EH28 8RA
TEL: (0131) 333 1320/1251
off M8 and A8, 8m W of Edinburgh; follow signs for Edinburgh Canal Centre from Newbridge roundabout; pub is alongside canal

Ronnie Rusack has been growing his canal enterprise since 1971. To date it consists of the Edinburgh Canal Centre, a fleet of four craft including two luxury narrowboats fitted up for dinner dances and weddings, and a children's pirate area, with a hotel complex at Ratho and a pub/restaurant a cruise away, both planned as part of Rusack's Millennium Line. At the heart of it is the Bridge (not forgetting the visitor centre), which looks directly on to the Union Canal. The pub was originally a farmhouse, but became a staging post for passenger boats as the canal developed. A snack in the Pop Inn, as the bar is known, might consist of just a jacket potato, a brown bread sandwich or the Hungry Bargee's Lunch (aka ploughman's). For a fuller meal, without going the whole hog in the separate à la carte dining-room, you could start with soup, duck liver pâté or sauté mushrooms in a korma sauce with rice. Carry on in international mode with Cantonese stir-fried vegetables with noodles or Yorkshire pudding with chicken tikka masala – but plain tastes will also be pleased by fresh fillet of haddock, a high-quality beefburger or cold seafood platter. If it has not got cream, ice-cream or chocolate in it, it probably will not feature on the sweets menu. Beers are Belhaven 80/- and IPA, plus 80/- and Deuchars IPA from Caledonian, while wines are various but anonymous. They are proud of their service here, with commendations on display for their approach to families and disabled guests. SAMPLE DISHES: poached salmon with lemon mayonnaise £5; hot spicy jalapeños £6.50; knickerbocker glory £3.50.

Open *Mon to Thur 12 to 11, Fri and Sat 11am to midnight, Sun 12.30 to 11; closed 25 Dec eve, 26 Dec, 1 Jan; bar food Mon to Sat 12 to 9, Sun 12.30 to 8; restaurant Mon to Sat 12 to 2, 6.30 to 9, Sun L only 12.30 to 2*
Details *Children welcome in bar eating area   Car park   Wheelchair access (also WC)   Garden and patio   No-smoking area   Background music   Guide dogs only   Amex, Delta, Diners, MasterCard, Switch, Visa*

STRACHUR   Argyll & Bute   map 11

▲ *Creggans Inn*

Strachur PA27 8BX   TEL: (01369) 860279
on A185, to N of village

For years, this was Sir Fitzroy Maclean's pub, and part of its appeal was the personality of its soldier-scholar owner. His larger-than-life character still seems to infect the place with a cheery bonhomie, and lingers on in the numerous photographs which decorate the dining-room, showing the numerous celebrities who made a point of coming here – often as not engaged on a film set in the surrounding rugged countryside. Only five miles or so from the main Glasgow-Campbeltown road, Creggans Inn makes a great lunch stop. It is not a spectacular building, just a small, white-painted house overlooking the waters of Loch Fyne. MacPhunn's bar is the heart of the inn – a smart, cool place with wood panelling, comfortable chairs and a fire. Another fire blazes in the dining-room, where bar food and more elaborate offerings are served. The home-made fish-cakes are a necessary experience, bearing little resemblance to the off-the-shelf supermarket varieties. The surrounding hills and waters provide more first-class ingredients for the kitchen – mussels and oysters from local growers, venison off the Maclean estate and fish from the Oban boats. Service is cheerful and prompt, and the whole outfit runs like clockwork. To supplement the food, there is a good cellar and a fair range of malt whiskies, including one bottled for MacPhunn himself. SAMPLE DISHES: tomato and mozzarella salad £3.75; calf's liver with bubble and squeak £6.75; apple crumble with clotted cream £3.

Open *11am to 1am, Sun noon to 1am; bar food 12 to 2.30, 6 to 9; restaurant D only 7 to 9*
Details *Children welcome in bar eating area   Car park   Patio   No smoking in restaurant   Live music and jukebox   No dogs in eating areas   Amex, Delta, Diners, MasterCard, Switch, Visa   Accommodation: 19 rooms, B&B £48 to £115*

SWINTON   Borders   map 11

▲ *Wheatsheaf Hotel* ❀

Main Street, Swinton TD11 3JJ   TEL: (01890) 860257
on A6112, Coldstream to Duns road

Chef and proprietor Alan Reid and his wife Julie continue to provide
cooking, service and an atmosphere that are difficult to beat.
Although the Wheatsheaf began as a pub and remains a focal drinking venue for the village, the restaurant side of the business has blos-
somed. Its reputation extends over a fair stretch of the countryside,
so it is advisable to book if you intend to eat. The place is sensitively
and tastefully decorated; the bar exudes a warm Scottish welcome
and the dining-room has a Scandinavian air. 'An oasis in a culinary
desert,' wrote one reporter.

The menu is lengthy, with a further extensive list of daily specials,
and the cooking is confident and imaginative. Lunchtime specials
take in such dishes as baked eggs florentine and deep-fried cheese, a
British (Teviotdale) rather than a French cheese at that. Tomato and
crayfish bisque is a novel starter, as is warm wild wood pigeon with
black pudding and Savoy cabbage. Cleanse your palate with an elderflower champagne sorbet, before perhaps selecting a chargrilled
Scotch fillet with parsley butter, suprême of halibut with a couscous
crumble on a lemon butter sauce, or roast Gressingham duckling in a
peach liqueur sauce. Finish it all off with a difficult choice from the
dessert menu: iced strawberry shortcake melts in the mouth and
summer pudding has been highly commended. Beer lovers can enjoy
Calders 70/- and Caledonian 80/-, both traditional styles, and
Broughton Bramling Cross, a new style with a single-variety hop
noted for its blackcurrant notes. Those who prefer wine will find a
comprehensive list that will pander to the tastes of the knowledgeable; six wines are available by the glass. SAMPLE DISHES: marinated
herring fillets with Madeira £4.25; local ostrich fillet in a red wine
and bramble sauce £13; warm glazed chocolate tart £4.25.

Open Tue to Sun 11 to 2.30, 6 to 11 (10.30 Sun); closed Sun eve from Nov
to Mar, 2 weeks mid-July and 2 weeks mid-Oct; bar food and restaurant Tue
to Sun 12 to 2 (2.15 restaurant), 6 to 9 (9.30 restaurant)
Details Children welcome in bar eating area   Car park   Wheelchair access
Garden   No smoking in dining-rooms   No music   Dogs welcome in
bedrooms only   Delta, MasterCard, Switch, Visa   Accommodation: 6
bedrooms £36 to £100

Many pubs have separate restaurants with very different menus. These
have not been inspected. A recommendation for the pub/bar food does
not necessarily imply that the restaurant is also recommended.

TAYVALLICH   **Argyll & Bute**   map 11

Tayvallich Inn

Tayvallich PA31 8PL   TEL: (01546) 870282
on B8025, off B841, reached from A816 N of Lochgilphead

Tayvallich is one of the prettiest villages in Argyll, benefiting from a
perfect semi-circular bay, which fills with holidaying yachts in summer.
It is a long way from anywhere, at the end of its own lonely road, but
this is part of the appeal of the place. It is an unusual spot to find a
pub of such quality as the Tayvallich, but the inn has built its reputation on its food, and draws its own trade. From the outside, it looks
little more than a large croft house, fronting Loch Sween on the edge
of the village, but it turns out to be spacious enough inside, with two
separate bars, plenty of eating space and terrific views through the
large picture windows. Sensibly, the bar menu makes the most of local
produce, especially fish. The shellfish in mussels marinière come from
a little farther up the loch and the salmon is smoked locally. Even the
baked goats' cheese is likely to be from one of the Argyll smallhold-
ings. Hot seafood pie and a variety of steaks round off the bar menu.
Many of the same ingredients, cooked in ambitious ways, appear in
the restaurant. A short but interesting wine list and a good range of
whiskies compensate for the rather ordinary beers. SAMPLE DISHES:
mushrooms with black pudding and potato scone £4.75; seafood
hotpot £14.50; Cajun salmon with black butter £10.

Open *summer 11am to midnight (1am Fri and Sat), winter 12 to 2.30, 6 to
11; closed 25 Dec, 1 Jan; bar food and restaurant 12 to 2, 6 to 9*
Details *Children welcome in eating areas   Car park   Wheelchair access
Garden   No smoking in conservatory during meals   No music   Dogs
welcome   Delta, MasterCard, Switch, Visa*

WEEM   **Perthshire & Kinross**   map 11

▲ *Ailean Chraggan*

Weem PH15 2LD   TEL: (01887) 820346
on B846, ½m N of Aberfeldy

This small hotel overlooks the Tay to the hills beyond and is in easy
reach of Lochs Tummel and Rannoch. There are two terraces and a
garden for summer eating, while the interior has been re-decorated in
autumnal colours and is comfortably furnished with banquettes;
photographs of local scenes taken by the landlord hang on the walls.
The same menu is served throughout and the emphasis is on local
ingredients: Loch Etive mussels, Luing prawns, Tay salmon, beef,

game and home-grown vegetables. Snacks such as soup, pâté, mussels or Cullen skink are always available, while more substantial dishes could be chicken breast with a peppercorn sauce, venison steak or beef fillet Stroganov with rice. Sunday lunch adds a roast such as Scottish beef with Yorkshire pudding, and children have their own 'Waggon' menu with pizza, sausages and fish fingers. Desserts range from lemon mousse to hazelnut and passion-fruit roulade. No real ales are stocked, but there is a good selection of bottled beers, a range of malt whiskies and an extensive wine list offering a good number of half-bottles and six wines by the glass. SAMPLE DISHES: shrimp cocktail £4; pork fillet with Dijon mustard sauce £9.75; cinnamon brûlée £3.50.

Open *11 to 11, Sun 12.30 to 11; closed 25 and 26 Dec, 1 and 2 Jan; bar food and restaurant 12 to 2, 6 to 9.30 (8.30 winter)*
Details *Children welcome   Car park   Wheelchair access   Garden and patio Background   No dogs in dining areas   Delta, MasterCard, Switch, Visa Accommodation: 5 rooms, B&B £30 to £70*

W E S T R U T H E R   Borders   map 11

Old Thistle Inn

Westruther TD3 6NE   TEL: (01578) 740275
from A697, between Lauder and Greenlaw, take B6456

'A charming unspoilt building' is how one reporter saw the Old Thistle, a whitewashed Victorian terraced cottage at the heart of the remote moorland village of Westruther, not far from the border. Its olde worlde bar is warmed by a coal fire, and food is served in the slightly more formal dining-room or in an adjoining 'snook', but note the unusual opening hours. At weekends, the menu offers sandwiches, soup, sausages, lasagne or fish and chips, but the weekday evening menu is also available on request. This offers additional starters of garlic mushrooms and prawn cocktail followed by pan-fried chicken breast, gammon steak, scampi and salads. Aberdeen Angus steaks come as sirloin, fillet or rib-eye in different weights, served with a side salad and chips or baked potatoes. Finish with ice-creams, which range from Belgian chocolate to rum and raisin, or sticky toffee apple fudge cake, or cheese and biscuits. Beers come from Tennents, and four of the nine wines are offered by the glass. Although the pub has no car park, there is off-street parking in the village. SAMPLE DISHES: garlic mushrooms £2.50; pan-fried Scottish butterfly salmon fillet £10.50; chocolate fudge cake £2.50.

Open *Mon to Fri 5 to 11, Sat and Sun 12.30 to 11; bar food Mon to Fri 6 to 9.30, Sat and Sun 12.30 to 9.30*
Details *Children welcome in dining-room   Wheelchair access (also WC) Patio   No music   No dogs in eating areas   No cards*

W·A·L·E·S

ABERDOVEY   Gwynedd   map 7

▲ *Penhelig Arms Hotel* ♀ ❦

Aberdovey LL35 0LT   TEL: (01654) 767215
on A493 Tywyn to Machynlleth road, opposite Penhelig station

This early-eighteenth-century inn by the harbour on the main road at
the southern end of this charming village was originally known as Y
Dafarn Fach (the Little Inn) and today still looks sufficiently modest
from the exterior that no one would guess there is a comfortable bar
and restaurant inside. In fine weather it is possible to sit outside on
the tiny patio behind the harbour wall. The bar, which is divided
into two areas, is rather cramped, but authentically old and characterful, with wood-panelled walls, beams, settles, pictures of sailing
boats, seafaring memorabilia and a shelf full of toby jugs behind the
serving bar. Bar food comes from the same kitchen as the well-
respected restaurant – indeed, the same menu is available in both bar
and restaurant at lunch, while separate menus are offered in each in
the evening – with simpler presentation in the bar.

Prices are very reasonable, especially the soup starter, which may
be something on the lines of potato, broccoli and walnut. Melon
with prosciutto ham caters for those who like simple flavours, and
pear with lemon sorbet and honey vinaigrette reminds us that not all
starters need be savoury. The bar menu is appropriately fishy in the
main courses, though the fish can wear disguises: mixed fish goujons
are deep fried with tartare sauce, hake fillet is under a prawn and
cheese sauce. Meat eaters might be tempted by a chicken breast fillet
coated in tomato sauce, cardamom and ginger. Pears in fudge sauce
is an unusual pudding, treacle tart more familiar. There is an
extensive range of mainstream real ales – Adnams, Bass, Greene King
Abbot Ale, Wadworth 6X and Brains SA – as well as a guest.
Landlord Robert Hughes used to work in the wine trade and has
produced a well-annotated list of bottles from around the world; a
good selection of half-bottles and 14 by the glass make for good
drinking. SAMPLE DISHES: avocado and crab £5.50; bream baked with
herbs, peppers, garlic and white wine £8; summer pudding £2.75.

Open *11 to 3.30, 5.30 to 11, Sun 12 to 3.30, 7 to 10.30; closed 25 Dec; bar
food and restaurant 12 to 2, 7 to 9*
Details *Children welcome in eating areas   Car park   Garden   No smoking in
restaurant   No music   No dogs in restaurant   Delta, MasterCard, Switch,
Visa   Accommodation: 10 rooms, B&B £39 to £78*

---

*Report forms are at the back of the book; write a letter if you prefer,
or email your pub report to guidereports@which.co.uk.*

*The Guide is totally independent, accepts no free hospitality and
carries no advertising.*

AFON-WEN   Flintshire   map 7

Pwll Gwyn

Denbigh Road, Afon-Wen CH7 5UB   TEL: (01352) 720227
off A541, 10m NW of Mold

Externally, Pwll Gwyn is not what you would call a handsome edifice in a winsome setting, though a few flowers outside lend a dash of colour. Originally built as a dower house, it became a coaching-inn in the early 1820s, and the present façade was built in the early 1900s by the Chester Brewery when it was an upmarket hotel. 'It's not the sort of place you'd drop in to if you didn't know.' On the inside, however, it is a different story, and the pub was deemed by one to be 'everything it ought to be'. A large inglenook in the bar area, old photographs, horse brasses, pewter mugs and beams all create a warm and friendly ambience.

The cooking is another plus: it produces well-executed, thoughtful pub food with one or two highlights. Smoked mussels served in a light cream sauce topped with smoked cheese got top marks from an inspector, and 'extremely good' game pie comes filled with pheasant, pigeon, rabbit, hare and wild boar all cooked in red wine and tucked under light puff pastry. Vegetarians have a fair selection, too, and at lunch-times there is an extra omelette and 'hot butty baguette' menu, while an à la carte menu operates in the restaurant on Friday and Saturday evenings. Occasional special evenings might feature dishes from around the world. Puddings can be of the alcoholic sort – chocolate brandy truffle, or mint chocolate meringue with crème de menthe, for example – though traditionalists might opt for bread-and-butter pudding. Service is very friendly and fuss-free. Wines are not a strong point. Beers are well kept, though not particularly adventurous for what is now a free house; Tetley Bitter features as a regular along with two guests. SAMPLE DISHES: scallop and prawn bake £4.10; chicken Casanova £7.75; rice-pudding £1.50.

Open *Mon to Fri 12 to 2, 7 to 11, Sat and Sun 12 to 3, 6 to 11 (10.30 Sun); opening hours may vary in winter; closed 26 Dec and 1 Jan; bar food Mon to Fri 12 to 2, 7 to 9.30, Sat and Sun 6.30 to 9.45 (all day Sun in summer)*
Details *Children welcome   Car park   Wheelchair access (also WC)   Garden No smoking in 1 dining-room   Background music   Guide dogs only   Amex, Delta, MasterCard, Switch, Visa*

The details under the text are taken from questionnaires that have been filled in by the pubs that feature in the book.

After the main section of the Guide is the special 'Out and about' section listing additional pubs that are well worth a visit. Reports on these entries are most welcome.

▲ Ty Gwyn Hotel

Betws-y-Coed LL24 0SG   TEL: (01690) 710383
on outskirts of village, at junction of A5 and A470 by
Waterloo Bridge

Much is made of the strategic location of this attractive, flower-decked coaching-inn on the outskirts of town. 'Gateway to Snowdonia,' trumpets the local tourist literature, and views over the Conwy valley are a strong selling point. A family-run enterprise, Ty Gwyn has a homely atmosphere, much reinforced by antique furnishings and an amiable clutter of knick-knacks on every available surface in the two bars ('a kind of granny parlour,' notes one visitor). Menus are wide-ranging and eclectic, where crowd-pleasers like lasagne and cottage pie rub shoulders with more exotic fare like kangaroo fillet in Coonawarra wine jus. Somewhere between these gastronomic poles lies a solid hinterland of local dishes like Conwy salmon or oven-baked Welsh lamb. The chef's own recommendations show a penchant for seafood – 'a whole fresh wee salmon', perhaps. A restaurant is open for dinner and Sunday lunch. Service is prompt, cheerful and unpretentious. Wherever you eat, there's a decent wine list available, strong on New World suggestions, with some interesting-sounding half-bottles and three wines by the glass. Beers include Flowers Original and Boddingtons Bitter. SAMPLE DISHES: port and hazelnut pâté £3.50; mushroom and nut fettucini £6; grilled mullet with king prawns and garlic butter £9.

Open *12 to 2, 7 to 9.30 (9 in winter); closed Mon to Wed in Jan; bar food 12 to 2, 7 to 9; restaurant all week D 7 to 9, Sun L 12 to 2*
Details *Children welcome   Car park   Wheelchair access   No-smoking area in restaurant   Background music   No dogs in eating areas   Delta, MasterCard, Switch, Visa   Accommodation: 15 rooms, B&B £17 to £90*

Halfway House

Bontddu LL40 2UE   TEL: (01341) 430635
on A496, between Barmouth and Dolgellau

Bontddu, meaning Black Bridge, is a tiny village set near the Mawddach Estuary in Snowdonia National Park. The pub is located next door to the Clogau gold mine, famous for providing the metal used in royal wedding rings. This tall, half-timbered building dates from the eighteenth century but has a very Tudor feel about it. The clientele is a mixture of locals and walkers, and all are assured a friendly greeting. A printed menu is padded out with one or two daily specials. The cooking is good, sustaining pub fare with one or two nice touches like vegetarian karachi, or hazelnut and orange terrine with spicy tomato sauce, from an above-average choice of vegetarian dishes. Prices are very reasonable with all starters less than £5. Start with deep-fried baby sweetcorn with a lemon dip and follow with a strongly recommended lamb and mint lasagne. Specials include home-made pies and baltis, and there are fish dishes and ploughman's as well as a selection of Welsh cheeses. A short wine list is strong on Australian bottles and, again, is reasonably priced. The pub also serves Marston's Pedigree and Thwaites Bitter. SAMPLE DISHES: sweet-and-sour mushrooms with melted Welsh cheese £4; home-baked cider ham with double egg £5.75; steamed butterscotch pudding £2.50.

Open *12 to 3, 6 to 11, Sun 12 to 3, 6 to 10.30; bar food 12 to 2, 7 to 9*
Details *Children welcome in eating areas   Car park   Garden and patio Background and live music   Guide dogs only   MasterCard, Switch, Visa*

B R E C O N   **Powys**   **map 4**

▲ *George Hotel*

George Street, Brecon LD3 7LD   TEL: (01874) 623421/2

This old town centre hotel is a cheery place with open fires, light wood fittings and furniture, copper-topped bar tables and colourful leafy tablecloths in the restaurant. Certainly the place is well situated for shoppers and visitors on livestock market day, the Jazz Festival and anything else in this busy rural town. The all-day 'just a snack' menu, also available in the restaurant until 6pm, offers a dozen items along the lines of filled jacket spuds and pancakes, salads, ploughman's, curry and lasagne – all reasonably priced. The choice continues with another all-day menu of six starters and a dozen main courses, plus a selection of grills. There may be pies – chicken and ham, or steak and mushroom – Welsh lamb and mint sausage, rabbit casserole, or salmon with orange and mustard sauce. A further menu with evening specials has more elaborate starters, including a trio of fish mousses, sole bonne femme, and chicken and ham parcels. Overwhelmed with choice, you can mix and match the menus. Salmon Shantie to start is generous, tasty, with plenty of fresh fish. Lamb Reform is an old-fashioned dish of breaded cutlets on a sweet sauce. The pudding menu makes interesting reading: home-made lavender sorbet and cinnamon pear samosa must be pretty rare. Alternatively, there is a selection of Welsh cheeses. This is another freehouse serving the usual suspects: Morland Old Speckled Hen,

Greene King Abbot Ale, Tetley's and Burton. A fair selection of
wines includes some good drinking. SAMPLE DISHES: tarragon chicken
pancake £4; pork in cider sauce £5.75; brandy bananas £3.50.

Open *11 to 11, Sun 12 to 10.30; bar food and restaurant 11 (12 Sun) to 10*
Details *Children welcome   Wheelchair access (also WC)   Patio   No smoking
in restaurant   Background music   Guide dogs only   Delta, MasterCard,
Switch, Visa   Accommodation: 8 rooms, B&B £35 to £85*

BWLCH-Y-CIBAU   Powys   map 7

Stumble Inn

Bwlch-y-cibau SY22 5LL   TEL: (01691) 648860
on A490, 3m SE of Llanfyllin

Situated in a rural farming village in the heart of mid-Wales, the
Stumble Inn is an attractive old borders-style stone building opposite
the church with a large lawn where people sit out on mild evenings.
Inside, the atmosphere is very much of the village local, with dark
wooden beams, white walls hung with brasses and saddlery, a few
paintings and dried flowers. The pub is run by Ashley and Sian Potts:
he oversees the kitchen while she looks after front-of-house. Since
the last edition of the *Guide*, a new oak-floored restaurant has been
added, offering a monthly-changing menu that might produce dishes
such as venison medallions and Toulouse sausage in a wild
mushroom cream sauce, or Parisian chicken. Bar snacks on the
printed menu might run to baguettes and ploughman's, but can also
satisfy heartier appetites with Cajun chicken, a ten-ounce rump steak
or perhaps grilled haddock in a saffron and prawn cream sauce. In
terms of interest it's best to shift up a notch for the daily blackboard
specials: swordfish with Cajun spices and lime dressing, or rib eye of
steak with Café de Paris butter. Children have their own mini-menu
of the chicken nuggets and beefburger variety. Tetley Bitter is on
handpump, and the greatly expanded wine list features a good, fairly
priced selection from around the world; four house wines are sold
by the glass. SAMPLE DISHES: chicken liver pâté £4.25; creamy prawn
curry £8.25; chocolate, whisky and hazelnut mousse £3.

Open *Tue to Sat 11 to 3, 6 to 11, Sun 12 to 3, 7 to 10.30; bar food and
restaurant Tue to Sun 12 to 2, 6 (7 Sun) to 9*
Details *Children welcome in eating area of bar before 9pm   Car park
Wheelchair access to restaurant   Garden and patio   No-smoking areas
Background and live music   No dogs   Delta, MasterCard, Switch, Visa*

Use the maps at the centre of the Guide to plan your trip.

▲ *Bryn Tyrch Hotel*

Capel Curig LL24 0EL   TEL: (01690) 720223
on A5, 5m W of Betwys-y-Coed

If you are puzzled by the boar motif which recurs at this plain, white-painted inn, a little translation may be in order. Apparently, Bryn Tyrch means 'Boar's Hill'. There are not too many wild boars in the heart of Snowdonia these days, but it is certainly the kind of rugged, mountainous terrain where you might expect to find them. What you will often find are keen walkers, climbers, fishing folk, geology students and outdoor enthusiasts of all types: it often makes for a lively, convivial atmosphere. Unsurprisingly, the interior boasts no superfluous decorative frills: sturdy wooden furnishings kit out its two bars (one with pool table and dartboard), and the Caffi Bryn dining area. The enterprising menu immediately suggests an alternative slant; it boldly claims 'the most outstanding range of vegan and vegetarian meals in North Wales', though there is some carnivorous fare too. All corners of the globe are plundered for culinary influences: there are Mexican fajitas and beer-battered mushrooms in teriyaki sauce, as well as Italian and Greek specialities such as ciabatta and halloumi. At tea-time you can home in on more local bara brith (Welsh fruit loaf) or a Caerphilly Welsh rarebit. Bryn Tyrch offers a fine range of special teas and coffees, along with several real ales – Flowers IPA, Worthington, Castle Eden – and a short, good-value wine list is 'eminently quaffable'. SAMPLE DISHES: zucchini dippers with spicy tomato sauce £3.60; stir-fried tamari, ginger and garlic free-range chicken £9; vegan scrunchy syrup tart £3.

Open *all week 12 to 11; closed 25 Dec; bar food 12 to 9.30*
Details *Children welcome in eating areas   Car park   Garden   No smoking in dining-room   No music   No dogs in eating areas   MasterCard, Switch, Visa Accommodation: 15 rooms, B&B £25 to £49*

▲ *Carew Inn* 🍺

Carew SA70 8SL   TEL: (01646) 651267
off A477, 4m E of Pembroke

This imposing stone building overlooks the Carew River and a tidal watermill (open on summer afternoons) in one direction, and towards the somewhat austere ruins of Carew Castle in the other. A tented terrace provides an outdoor eating area and the large garden has a children's play area. There is live music on Thursday evenings and on Sundays during the summer school holidays, when a barbecue is also in operation. Inside are three separate eating areas, including an upstairs dining-room. The public bar has a dartboard, and beams, rustic settles and local prints on the walls make for a pleasant ambience. Those wanting a light bite will find sandwiches, ploughman's and filled baguettes available at lunch-time and, at both lunch and in the evening, deep-fried Camembert, mussels or garlic mushrooms. Heftier appetites might want to tuck in to steak, scampi, chilli con carne or seafood pie and end things sweetly with Bakewell tart, syrup sponge or chocolate gâteau. Children have their own menu. Beers on offer include Worthington, Buckley's Reverend James or Dorothy Goodbody's from the Wye Valley Brewery; a short, reasonably priced wine list offers three by the glass. SAMPLE DISHES: prawn cocktail £3; tarragon and lime chicken £7; fruit crumble £2.25.

Open *summer 11 to 11, winter Mon to Fri 11.30 to 2.30, 4.30 to 11, Sat 11 to 11, Sun 11.30 to 3, 7 to 10.30; closed 25 Dec; bar food summer 12 to 2.30, 6 to 9.30, winter 12 to 2, 7 to 9*
Details *Children welcome in eating areas   Car park   Wheelchair access (also WC)   Garden and patio   No smoking area in dining-room   Background and live music   Dogs welcome in bar only   MasterCard, Switch, Visa
Accommodation: 1 room, B&B £15 to £25*

CLYTHA   **Monmouthshire**   **map 2**

▲ *Clytha Arms* 🍺 🍇

Clytha NP7 9BW   TEL: (01873) 840206
off old Abergavenny to Raglan road, S of A40, 6m E of Abergavenny

This pub, set in its own grounds, is a former dower house and looks like it. Andrew and Beverley Canning have run it since 1988 and have been careful not to forget that it is a pub as well as a restaurant. It is a whitewashed building adorned with lots of flowers, plants and hanging baskets; an attractive veranda with seating overlooks a landscape that is almost 'parkland' in appearance. Inside are window seats, posters, mirrors, china and knick-knacks, bar skittles and shove ha'penny, and a wood-burning stove in a large fireplace provides a pleasant, welcoming warmth. The smaller lounge is similarly decorated but with slightly more comfortable furnishings. Choose from either the bar or restaurant menu; both are topped up with specials. The former is full of good ideas: croque monsieur, for example, bacon, laverbread and cockles, or wild boar sausages and potato pancakes. There are more 'regular' dishes too – crab and avocado salad, or black pudding with fried apple and cider sauce – but further refined touches come in the form of smoked salmon and scrambled egg, or duck cassoulet. There is an extensive range of puddings, again a dash above the ordinary – ginger syllabub, perhaps, or lime and mascarpone tart with pecan and caramel ice-cream. The pub takes care of its beers; Hook Norton and Bass appear to be fairly regular, some other larger brands change occasionally, and there are some more frequently rotating guests. An extensive wine list, divided into regions, has plenty of vintages and half-bottles, as well as an above-average number by the glass. SAMPLE DISHES: salmon burger with tarragon mayonniase £6; grilled queen scallops and salad £7; Sauternes cream and spiced prunes £3.50.

Open *Mon to Fri 12 to 3.30, 6 to 11, Sat 12 to 11, Sun 12 to 4, 7 to 10.30; closed 25 Dec eve; bar food Mon to Sat L 12.30 to 2.30, Tue to Fri D 7 to 9.30; restaurant Tue to Sun 12.30 to 2.30, 7 to 9.30*
Details *Children welcome   Car park   Wheelchair access   Garden and patio No smoking in dining-room   Occasional background and live music   No dogs MasterCard, Switch, Visa   Accommodation: 3 rooms, B&B £45 to £70*

CREIGIAU   Cardiff   map 4

Caesar's Arms ✿

Cardiff Road, Creigiau CF4 8NN TEL: (01222) 890486   **FISH**
2m N of M4 junction 33

'In a nutshell, what you see is what you get,' wrote one reporter. Looking a bit like a golf club, this old, white-stone country house has a huge, modern extension which encompasses the dining-room. However, there is still a pubby atmosphere in the big lounge and smaller side areas, and although this is largely a food pub, people still go there just for a drink. Booking is advisable and you need to know the system. Once you have been allocated a table, choose your meal from the produce on show – fish is a speciality – at the row of refrigerated counters. Prices are attached and further information is displayed on huge blackboards overhead; once you have picked out your future meal it is whisked away to the kitchen for preparation.

Food is presented with light French and Spanish touches, with lots of tomato-based sauces. Starters might take in provençale fish soup, game terrine with Cumberland sauce, Bajan fish-cakes, or asparagus hollandaise. Specials change twice a day and the large selection of fish normally on offer ranges from salmon and local wild trout to monkfish, halibut and lobster. Also on display are steaks and kebabs and various cuts of game, and even the puddings – among them mille-feuilles, citrus cheesecake or raspberry pavlova – can be viewed. For beer drinkers there is Hancocks HB and Welsh Bitter, and a lengthy wine list chalked on blackboards above the food counters is strong on France and Spain; nine wines are served by the glass. If your table gives you a view of the open kitchen, you can watch the progress of your food from cold counter to chef, to waiter and on to you. SAMPLE DISHES: mussels provençale £4; sea bass in rock salt £12 per lb; strawberry mille-feuille £3.50.

Open *all week 12 to 3, Mon to Sat 6 to 10.30; closed 25 Dec, 26 Dec eve; bar food and restaurant 12 to 2.30, 7 to 10.30*
Details *Children welcome   Car park   Wheelchair access (also WC)   Garden and patio   Background music   Guide dogs only   Amex, Delta, Diners, MasterCard, Switch, Visa*

CRICKHOWELL   Powys   map 4

▲ *Bear Hotel* ✿ ❦

Crickhowell NP8 1BW   TEL: (01873) 810408
on A40, 6m NW of Abergavenny

This former coaching-inn, dating from 1432, has a long-standing reputation for character and a good table. The Hindmarshes have been consistent in their drive for good quality, and considering the quantity of food they turn out they do it very well. An aura of pleasantness pervades within, augmented by half-timbering, flagstone floors, antique furniture and open fires. Pleasantness comes on the plate, too, where you will find skilfully presented, well-rendered versions of Caesar salad, thick-sliced home-cured beef with a roast pepper salad and lemon oil, or smoked mackerel pâté with horseradish. The more peckish among you can move on to fresh gnocchi in a tomato and basil sauce with melted Parmesan, home-made faggots and peas, or braised back of Welsh lamb. For those hankering after something with an imaginative touch, there is Morocco-spiced lamb, chicken satay, or goats' cheese and fried onion pie. A fine way to end would be home-made ginger ice-cream in a brandy-snap 'barrel', or lemon crunch pie – or choose from the good selection of Welsh cheeses. Beers on offer are Bass and Ruddles Best and County. The extensive, well-balanced wine list groups bins by style and includes five half-bottles. Ten wines are available by the glass. SAMPLE DISHES: chicken liver parfait £4.95; salmon fish-cakes with salad and sauté potatoes £6.75; warm orange pancakes £3.50.

Open *10 to 3, 6 to 11, Sun 12 to 3, 7 to 10.30; bar food and restaurant 12 to 2, 6 to 10, Sun 12 to 2, 5 to 9.30*
Details *Children welcome in family room   Car park   Wheelchair access (also WC)   Garden   No-smoking area in bar   Background music   Dogs welcome Amex, MasterCard, Switch, Visa   Accommodation: 34 rooms, B&B £45 to £110*

Nantyffin Cider Mill Inn ✿ 🍺 🍇

Brecon Road, Crickhowell NP8 1SG
TEL: (01873) 810775

LOCAL PRODUCE

1½m W of Crickhowell at junction of A40 and A479

The Nantyffin has won acclaim and a loyal following for what the owners are trying to do – which is, in their own words, to try to develop the British pub 'along the lines of a French bistro, serving quality fresh food, accessible to all, in a relaxed and informal atmosphere'. In this they appear to have succeeded without falling into the trap of ceasing to be a pub. Just outside Crickhowell, the sixteenth-century building was originally a drovers' inn, and has lovely views of the River Usk and mountains beyond. The dining area is an old stone barn built on two levels, with high ceilings, brown beams and small, 'arrow slit' windows. By the kitchen is a massive wine rack.

The emphasis – apart from modern, inventive cooking – is on the use of local produce. A family-run farm provides organic vegetables, and local meat and seasonal ingredients feature strongly. Bar and restaurant menus are available throughout the pub, and there are specials as well as a separate early-evening menu. The inventiveness of the kitchen can be seen in dishes like starters of Moroccan filo parcels filled with fresh spinach, soft cheese and merguez sausage served with toasted-sesame dressing, or deep-fried spicy Thai fish-cakes with noodles and coriander coconut broth. Local venison comes on to the menu in winter, wrapped in coppa, with caper and mint sauce. Local lamb could appear on the specials list with a chorizo and herb crust, or seared calf's liver could be served with a shallot sauce, foie gras and mash. Home-made ices are a speciality made with cream supplied from a local Jersey herd, or you could finish with banana pavlova with toffee sauce. Three real ales, mainly from the larger regionals, and three ciders are always on tap. Drivers might want to try the home-made lemonade. The wine list is notable for concentrating exclusively on North and South America, apart from an errant bottle from Australia and some New Zealand fizz, and presents a good choice at fairly reasonable prices; five house wines start at £9.95, or £2 a glass. SAMPLE DISHES: open ravioli with home-smoked chicken and truffle cream sauce £5.50; chargrilled loin of pork with onion rings, mustard pearl barley risotto and Madeira wine dressing £11; whimberry ice-cream £3.75.

Open *Tue to Sat 12 to 2.30, 6 to 11, Sun 12 to 3.30, 7 to 10.30; closed 1 week Nov, 2 weeks Jan, and Tue in winter; bar food and restaurant Tue to Sun 12 to 2.30, 6.30 (7 Sun) to 9.45*
Details *Children welcome   Car park   Wheelchair access (also WC)   Garden No smoking in restaurant   No music   Dogs welcome   Amex, Delta, MasterCard, Switch, Visa*

▲ *Farmers Arms*   [NEW ENTRY]

Cwmdu NP8 1RU   TEL: (01874) 730464
on A479, 4m NW of Crickhowell

LOCAL PRODUCE

Andrew Lawrence and Sue Brown have been licensees at the Farmers Arms since the end of 1997, both coming from the Blue Anchor at East Aberthaw (see entry on next page), where Andrew had been head chef for seven years. The enthusiastic couple have smartened up this old village pub on the edge of the Black Mountains, in good walking country, and are offering 'fresh, interesting and good-value home-cooked food'. Change is coming slowly, but gradually they are attracting a varied dining clientele, from locals to farmers who 'emerge from the hills at weekends'. Menus are on regularly changing blackboards. At lunch-time expect to see lasagne, ham, egg and chips, steak and kidney pie, or whole plaice with dill and lemon butter sauce. In the evening find spinach and Stilton tart, roast rack of local lamb, or baked salmon fillet topped with prawns. Venison comes from a local farm and meat is supplied by a butcher who knows which farm each cut comes from, which perhaps explains why the pub is so popular with farmers. International touches show up as well: pan-fried duck breast with plum and hoisin sauce, or a Welsh rump steak with Cajun spices. Puddings are likely to be along the lines of raspberry cheesecake on a muesli base, or apple and plum crumble. The pub serves Wadworth 6X plus a guest from one of the local independent brewers, while the wine list is short but varied. SAMPLE DISHES: smoked mackerel pâté with gooseberry chutney £2.75; faggots with mushy peas and onion gravy £5.25; lemon tart on raspberry coulis £3.25.

Open *summer Mon to Fri 11 to 3, 6 to 11, Sat 11 to 11, Sun 12 to 4, 7 to 10.30, winter Mon and Tue eve only 6 to 11, Wed to Sat 11 to 3, 6 to 11, Sun 12 to 4, 7 to 10.30; bar food and restaurant 12 to 2.30, 7 to 9.30 (all day bank hols)*
Details *Children welcome in eating areas   Car park   Wheelchair access Garden   No smoking in restaurant   Background music   Dogs welcome in bar only   Delta, MasterCard, Switch, Visa   Accommodation: 3 rooms, B&B £20 to £40*

Blue Anchor Inn 🍺

East Aberthaw CF62 3DD   TEL: (01446) 750329
off B4265, between St Athan and Barry

'A veritable warren of cosy little rooms, bars and lounges' set under a low, grey thatch which curves around upper floor windows, and with creepers clinging to its weathered stone walls, the Blue Anchor is wonderfully atmospheric. A wide selection of beers includes well-known brands such as Wadworth 6X, Flowers IPA, Theakston Old Peculier and Marston's Pedigree, plus a frequently changing guest from one of Britain's many microbreweries. The reasonably priced bar menu offers 'good basic, robust home cooking' along the lines of avocado vinaigrette, peppered rump steak, jacket potatoes and sand-wiches, plus daily specials on the blackboard, while the restaurant menu presents more ambitious fare such as Cornish crab-cakes, or baked fillet of monkfish. House wine comes from Stowells and the list runs to around 40 bins. SAMPLE DISHES: sauté garlic mushrooms £3; fresh pasta with sweet red peppers, cheese and wild mushroom and cream sauce £5.25; milk chocolate marquise £2.50.

Open *11 to 11, Sun 11 to 10.30; bar food Mon to Sat L 12 to 2, Mon to Fri D 6 to 8; restaurant Sun L 12.30 to 2.30, Mon to Sat D 7 to 9.30*
Details *Children welcome   Car park   Patio   Background and live music; jukebox   Dogs welcome in bar only   Delta, MasterCard, Switch, Visa*

Queen's Head ✿

Glanwydden LL31 9JP   TEL: (01492) 546570
just off B5115 Colwyn Bay to Llandudno road

PUDDINGS

'Probably the best pub grub in Wales' is how one reporter summed up the Queen's Head, which she also found to be 'warm, friendly, effi-cient and great value'. Externally, the rather plain building has had a bit of face-lift – the Queen now has rosy cheeks. On the inside, comfortable red-cushioned benches and a 'very effective' wood-burning stove inside a stone chimney breast set the scene for some first-class cooking. A well-schooled team of waitresses keep the crowds happy with a stream of hot and cold appetisers, open rolls, salads, as well as pasta, fish and vegetarian dishes, and evening steaks. Many choices are based on local ingredients, such as Welsh smoked mush-rooms with hollandaise and smoked applewood cheese, and braised Welsh Black beef in a wild mushroom and garlic sauce, but the main emphasis is on quality seafood. Simple grilled fillet of plaice topped with sauté prawns and almonds is superbly fresh, delivering 'the taste of the sea', while seafood platter – a chef's special – proves to be much more than its description might indicate, and includes crab, king prawns, shrimp, smoked salmon and trout, green-lipped mussels, local Conwy mussels and smoked haddock, all set out with rocket, celery and fresh redcurrants. The locals know to leave room for one of the excellent-value cold desserts or hot puddings: from 'light and crunchy' blackberry cheesecake, and crème brûlée, to bread-and-butter pudding, and treacle tart. If that really is not your bag, perhaps a plate of cheeses, including Stilton and local Pencarreg with biscuits and port, would fit the bill. Thirty or so wines, many around the £10 mark, are good partners for the food, or you could stick to Tetley, Burton or Benskins, or whatever the guest beer is that week. SAMPLE DISHES: smoked breast of goose with kiwi fruit £4.35; trio of local fish served with couscous £12; chocolate brandy trifle £2.75.

Open *11 to 3, 6 to 11; closed 25 Dec; bar food 12 to 2, 6 to 9*
Details *No children under 7   Car park   Garden   No-smoking area*
Background music   Guide dogs only   MasterCard, Switch, Visa

HAY-ON-WYE   Powys   **map 4**

▲ *Old Black Lion*

26 Lion Street, Hay-on-Wye HR3 5AD   TEL: (01497) 820841

This lion is very old – over 700 years old, in fact – and takes its name from the old Lion Gate entrance to this historic border town, which is famous as 'the second-hand book centre of the world'. Cromwell reputedly stayed here during the siege of Loyalist stronghold Hay Castle, and the pub's restaurant is named after him, while the main bar is named after Richard the Lionheart. The low-beamed ceiling, wooden chairs and settles, and candlelit tables create a subdued, intimate atmosphere. There is a bar menu, a separate restaurant menu and a specials board, but you can eat from any menu anywhere throughout the pub. Returning Crusaders brought back with them exotic food and spices, but even King Richard did not get far east enough to account for the satays, stir-fries and curries (both Indian and Thai) that appear alongside more traditional dishes. Goat's-cheese salad vies for attention with stir-fried prawns, while cod Mornay competes with tempura-battered plaice. The restaurant menu is more expensive and features slightly more complex dishes with less of an oriental influence: main courses are more likely to be mille-feuille of sole and smoked salmon, or medallions of beef. The sweet menu is the same throughout and changes regularly to rotate some individual creations: lemon posset with hazelnut and almond praline, or apple and mango parfait with caramel coulis. The extensive main wine list is strong on the New – and very new – World: those tempted by Chinese stir-fried chicken may find a bottle of Tsingtao Riesling the ideal accompaniment. It is backed up by a special restaurant selection chosen by Tanners, which includes 12 half-bottles, and a blackboard of bin-ends. House wines are available by the carafe. The house beer is brewed by Wye Valley brewery; Wadworth 6X and Boddingtons are alternatives. SAMPLE DISHES: smoked loin of boar with spicy pepper dressing £5.50; Thai beef curry £9; treacle tart with walnuts and ginger and walnut ice-cream £4.

Open *11 to 11, Sun 11 to 10.30; bar food and restaurant 12 to 2.30, 7 to 9.30*
Details *Children welcome   Car park   Wheelchair access   Garden and patio*
No smoking in restaurant   No music   Dogs welcome   Amex, Delta,
MasterCard, Visa   Accommodation: 10 rooms, B&B £28 to £47.90

LAMPHEY   Pembrokeshire   map 4

Dial Inn

The Ridgeway, Lamphey SA71 5NU   TEL: (01646) 672426
just off A4139 Tenby to Pembroke road

Close to the ruins of the Bishop's Palace at Lamphey, this plain, white-painted inn was formerly the dower house to Lamphey Court. It has a welcoming and homely interior, simply decorated with various plants and china on the walls and in recessed cabinets, with an unusual mural of the palace taking centre stage over the fireplace. The menu focuses on freshly prepared home-cooked food. Interesting typed menus are supplemented by blackboard dishes featuring fresh local fish. Guacamole salad is a novel starter, as is diced melon and mandarin with ginger, redcurrant and port sauce. Main courses are sometimes novel too: perhaps pheasant breast wrapped in smoked bacon and pan-fried with almond flakes and whisky, or tournedos of Welsh beef with caramelised shallots and Madeira sauce. For dessert there might be lemon or strawberry meringue, or apple pie. Real ales offered are Hancock's HB, Worthington Best and Bass, and eight wines are available by the glass. SAMPLE DISHES: chicken liver and pork terrine with autumn plum chutney £4.25; wild mushrooms and field mushrooms with cream, Stilton and garlic sauce topped with puff pastry £8; ginger and chocolate cheesecake £3.

Open *11 to 3, 6 to 11, Sun 11 to 3, 7 to 10.30; bar food and restaurant all week L 12 to 2, Mon to Sat D 7 to 9*
Details *Children welcome   Car park   Wheelchair access   Garden   No smoking in restaurant   Background and live music   No dogs   Amex, Delta, MasterCard, Switch, Visa*

LITTLE HAVEN   Pembrokeshire   map 4

Swan Inn

Point Road, Little Haven SA62 3UL   TEL: (01437) 781256
off B4341, 6m W of Haverfordwest

In the words of one reporter, the Swan 'must be one of the better places to eat along this stretch of coastline', with many of the other 'resort' pubs offering basic pub grub for the bucket-and-spade brigade. The Swan stands out among its competitors for its position by the sea wall and for the simple but fresh food it serves, notably crab, organic steak and Welsh cawl (lamb stew). The pub is homely and welcoming, with two interconnecting rooms, both carpeted and featuring a mix of high-backed settles, pine and oak tables, stripped stonework, open fires and numerous prints. Sought after window tables offer the best view. Local produce on the menu includes the aforementioned crab, either dressed or in a bake, as well as lamb, salmon and lobster. The pub serves Worthington Best, Bass and Wadworth 6X, as well as four wines by the glass. SAMPLE DISHES: grilled sardines, spinach and egg £5; ham salad £6; Irish coffee meringue gâteau £3.

Open *11.30 to 3 (2.30 winter), 6 (7 winter) to 11, Sun 12 to 3, 7 to 10.30;*
closed 25 Dec eve; bar food all week L 12 to 2, Wed to Sat D 7 to 9;
restaurant Wed to Sat (Thur to Sat in winter) D only 7 to 9
Details *No children   Patio   No music   Clean dogs welcome on a lead   No cards*

LLANARMON DYFFRYN CEIRIOG   Wrexham map 7

▲ West Arms

Llanarmon Dyffryn Ceiriog LL20 7LD
TEL: (01691) 600665
off A5 Langollen to Oswestry road at Chirk, then
follow B4500 for 11m

It is a long way to go to get to the West Arms, situated in the remote and pretty Ceiriog Valley, but your arrival at the pub is consolation for the effort. Llanarmon is an archetypal estate village and country-house parties still shoot grouse locally. The West, as it is known, is an ideal place for guns to rest, and non-shooters staying over will find a full range of activities available, from walking, mountain biking and pony trekking to golfing, fishing and canoeing. There are so many interesting features around that a small guidebook to the interior of the pub might be appropriate: vast inglenooks, slate-flagged floors and timber work which is ebony hard with age. The oak mantelpiece in the lounge bar is decorated with shiny brassware and carriage lamps. In the same room is a large canopied and enclosed seat which may have been a confessional originating from one of the Cistercian abbeys that once flourished in the area. There are old mantel shelves behind the bar, and lovely antiques are used everyday throughout the hotel. The predominating colour scheme, warm pink and green stone and chintzy chair covers, is a great success with visitors, as is the airy and stylish conservatory overlooking gardens with a mountain backdrop beyond.

Blackboard specials indicate a healthy preference for fresh fish, despite the inland location. Smoked haddock in a white wine cheese sauce on a bed of tagliatelle is described as 'absolutely delicious', with 'meltingly fresh' fish oak-smoked to subtle perfection; while diced ham, mushroom, spinach and garlic pancake is 'most enjoyable'. The bar menu offers ploughman's and pâtés, but there is also chicken tikka, or rabbit and apricot terrine. Local Ceiriog trout and local lamb chops appear among the main dishes, as does stir-fried pork with hoisin sauce and 'rainbow' vegetables, and a tasty sounding vegetarian option would be button mushrooms, tofu and mixed nuts in a herb cream sauce served in a giant Yorkshire pud. On the real ale front the pub serves only Flowers IPA and Boddingtons, and the extensive wine list is largely supplied by Tanners. SAMPLE DISHES: smoked trout salad £5.50; lemon and tarragon chicken breast with basmati rice £6.75; white chocolate cheesecake £2.75.

Open *11 to 11; bar food and restaurant 12 to 2.30, 6.30 to 9.30*
Details *Children welcome   Car park   Wheelchair access (also WC)   Garden   No smoking in dining-room   Background and live music   Well-behaved dogs welcome   Delta, MasterCard, Switch, Visa   Accommodation: 15 rooms, B&B £40 to £80*

LLANDINAM   **Powys**   map 4

▲ *Lion Hotel*   NEW ENTRY

Llandinam SY17 5BY   TEL: (01686) 688233
on A470 in the centre of the village, 8m SW of
Newtown, 6m N of Llanidloes

Llandinam is a small, pretty village, the home of the famous Davies family – mine owners and philanthropists – who brought the railways and electric lighting to Wales. The Lion is a red-brick building on the roadside, with a garden and a meadow extending to the banks of the upper Severn. Outside tables make it a pleasant scene in summer. Inside there is a public bar with oak tables, fireplace, beams and a country atmosphere, while the lounge bar has a 1970s feel, with fixed seating, pub tables and plain carpet. The restaurant, which overlooks the meadow and river, has more oak tables, captain's chairs, slate place mats and whitewashed walls. The same menus are available throughout, offering 'homely Montgomeryshire fare'. At lunch expect casseroles, hotpots and even curries, while the evening menu has a lot of 'standard stuff' – Brussels pâté, plaice goujons, prawn cocktail, deep-fried mushrooms and soup – all very reasonably priced. Main dishes are a mix of steaks, gammon, lamb chops, trout. Twice-baked Welsh rarebit soufflé comes sizzling in a square pie dish, crunchy-topped with a creamy light cheese bubbling all round. From the board, lamb hotpot contains generous chunks of lamb, slowly cooked with vegetables in a rich red wine sauce. Puddings are displayed in a fridge: gâteaux plus lighter options such as orange syllabub, and more unusual things like piña colada cheesecake. One reporter 'eulogised at length' over the apple crumble. The wine list from Tanners has about 20 bins from France and the New World at very reasonable prices, but beer is limited to Tetley. Service from the family is courteous and efficient. SAMPLE DISHES: honeydew melon with raspberry coulis £3.25; mushroom Stroganov £6; orange and Grand Marnier pannacotta £2.75.

Open *12 to 3, 6.30 to 11, Sun 12 to 3, 7 to 10.30; closed 25 Dec; bar food and restaurant 12 to 2.15, 6.30 to 9.30, Sun 12 to 2.15, 7 to 9*
Details *Children welcome in eating areas   Car park   Wheelchair access (also WC)   Garden and patio   No smoking in restaurant   Background music; jukebox   Guide dogs only   Delta, MasterCard, Switch, Visa Accommodation: 4 rooms, B&B £28 to £50*

LLANDWROG   **Gwynedd**   map 7

▲ *Harp Inn* 🍺

ACTIVITIES

Llandwrog LL54 5SY   TEL: (01286) 831071
off A499, 5m SW of Caernarfon

The Ty'n Llan, also known as the Harp, is a squat, stolid old North Wales stone building at the centre of a small village a mile from the beach. Inside, you are likely to find a busy scene, with locals mingling with residents taking advantage of the inn's organised walking holidays. Food, as you might imagine, is hearty and sustaining for people who have spent the day working up considerable appetites, and though simple it is accurately cooked, of good quality and value, and – most importantly of all – is served piping hot to the table. Smooth chef's pâté has good flavour, and home-made soup of the day could well be a walker's choice. Battered cod, scampi, and fish-cakes come with chips and peas, and for the really hungry are steaks, home-made pies or casseroles. Or perhaps choose chicken and leek pie and chips, chicken and mango curry with rice, or chilli con carne. Welsh lamb chops come pink and garnished with grilled tomatoes and mushrooms, vegetables are correctly cooked, and one reporter enjoyed a nutty-flavoured mature autumn lamb with a herby savour. Puddings might include apple pie or gâteaux, and there is also a selection of Welsh cheeses on offer. The beers on sale have changed considerably since the last edition of the *Guide* owing to the habit of small breweries to go out of business – at inspection the available beers were Bitter and Fusilier from Plassey, Cutlass from Harviestoun, Dick Turpin from Coach House, and Rev James from Brains. They also have a range of 30 cold-banishing malts, as well as a short wine list which includes their own-label Welsh wine. SAMPLE DISHES: chicken wings with spicy dip £4.50; Aberdeen Angus steak with tomato, onion rings, mushrooms and chips £11.75; crêpes suzettes with orange and brandy sauce £2.75.

Open *summer Mon 6 to 11, Tue to Sun 12 to 11, winter Tue to Sun 12 to 3, all week 6 to 11; bar food and restaurant Tue to Sun 12 to 2, 6.30 to 8.30 (9 Fri and Sat)*
Details *Children welcome in dining-room and family room   Car park Wheelchair access (also WC)   Garden and patio   No smoking in restaurant Background music; jukebox   No dogs in restaurant   Delta, MasterCard, Switch, Visa   Accommodation: 4 rooms, B&B £17 to £22*

LLANFIHANGEL NANT MELAN   **Powys**   map 4

▲ *Red Lion Inn* 😀 😀

Llanfihangel nant Melan LD8 2TN
TEL: (01544) 350220
on A44 Rhayader to Kington road, 3m W of New Radnor

The welcome offered by the Johns family warms the simple interior of this roadside pub, which has gathered quite a following for accomplished cooking at 'unbelievably low prices'. Chef Gareth Johns has built his reputation on resolute use of local produce and seasonal ingredients, and writes that 'my philosophy here is very simple: find the best, freshest produce around, do as little as necessary to it as well as I possibly can, and sell it at the best price I can afford to'. It is a formula that seems to be working, as affirmed by reports from readers who appreciate the pub's unpretentious presentation and simple commitment to quality and individual service. The menu changes daily and is written up on a blackboard, although some popular items, such as toasted Pencarreg goats' cheese, are fixtures. Starters might include chicken liver pâté, or smoked salmon, followed by much-praised peppered duck breast, or maybe seafood casserole, and to finish, chocolate truffle or a selection of well-kept Welsh cheeses. Diners can choose to sit in either the bar or the plainer conservatory (which overlooks the road). Note that the pub is open only evenings and Sunday lunchtime. The solitary beer is Hook Norton Best Bitter, while a shortish wine list is also noted for its exceptional value; five wines are available by the glass. SAMPLE DISHES: home-made parsnip and apple soup £3; Brecon venison with red wine and chocolate sauce £10: cappuccino mousse £3.

Open *7 (6.30 Sat) to 11, Sun 12 to 2, 7 to 10.30; closed 26 Dec, 1 week Nov and Tue in winter; bar food Mon to Sat D only 7 to 9 (9.30 Sat), Sun 12 to 2, 7 to 9*
Details *Children welcome   Car park   Garden   No smoking in 1 dining-room No music   Dogs welcome in bar area and garden   Delta, MasterCard, Switch, Visa   Accommodation: 3 rooms, B&B £20 to £40*

LLANGATTOCK   **Powys**   map 4

Vine Tree Inn

The Legar, Llangattock NP8 1HG   TEL: (01873) 810514
off A40, SW of Crickhowell

Situated beside the River Usk, the Vine Tree has been formed from a row of low, pink-painted cottages, is fronted by picnic benches and a fine magnolia tree, and is popular with walkers along the Monmouth & Brecon Canal. There is a traditional, no-frills feel about the interior, with its exposed stonework, wall bench seating, cosy alcoves and brass artefacts, and open fires in winter. This is very much a dining pub, with a huge blackboard menu by the bar, which runs the whole gamut from traditional pub options – pâtés, pies, steaks and casseroles – to more adventurous offerings such as monkfish in a Pernod and leek sauce, and chicken stuffed with prawns, wrapped in bacon and served in a seafood sauce. Vegetarians, too, have a fair choice, with pasta, a nut roast or vegetable bake as likely options. Available at lunch-time are ploughman's, filled baguettes, cottage and fish pies; Sunday lunch is a roast. If you've room for pudding, you might go for rhubarb crumble, or perhaps Jamaican pancakes or apple pie. Service is both 'friendly' and 'well organised'. Beers come from Boddingtons, Wadworth and SP Sporting Ales, while the mainly French 30-bottle wine list is very reasonably priced and offers four by the glass, half-litre or bottle. SAMPLE DISHES: stockpot soup £2.25; venison casserole £10; cherry strudel £2.75.

Open *12 to 3.30, 6 to 11, Sun 12 to 3.30, 7 to 10.30; bar food 12 to 3, 6 to 10*
Details *Children welcome   Car park   Wheelchair access (also WC)   Patio   No music   No dogs   Delta, Diners, MasterCard, Switch, Visa*

LLANGYBI   Monmouthshire   map 4

▲ *White Hart*

Llangybi NP5 1NP   TEL: (01633) 450258
just off A449, between Newport and Usk.

Most pubs come with some interesting baggage, but this one in the Vale of Usk can boast over eight centuries of history. Built by Cistercian monks, it was subsequently demanded as part of Jane Seymour's dowry by Henry VIII. Those fired up by even older events will realise that Caerleon, which garrisoned some 5,500 men, women and children as part of a Roman legion which was in the process of subjugating the local Silurian population, is a few miles down the road. Flash forward 2,000 years and you find a traditional whitewashed and slate-roofed freehouse in a secluded village offering Wadworth 6X, Hancock's HB and Bass as well as some modestly priced basic wines. The beamed bar is spacious, the décor of the ladderback chair and horse brass type; open fires make for a cosy atmosphere, and service is friendly and informal. Lunch is the time for quick bites: a jacket potato, a hot dog or a toasted sandwich, say. If you are feeling a bit more peckish than that or are visiting in the evening, expect hefty helpings of steaks and chicken breasts in various ways, lasagne or curry, with chips, rice or potatoes and enormous salads. Vegetarians may be pleasantly surprised by, for instance, mushroom, broccoli and leek pancakes or roasted cashew-nut roulade with cider and sage sauce. Sweets are largely 'toffee this and that', sorbets and sundaes. SAMPLE DISHES: black pudding with mustard sauce £2.75; mushroom Stroganov £5.50; duck breast with brandy and pepper sauce £8.

Open *Mon to Fri 11.30 to 3.30, 6 to 11, Sat 11.30 to 11, Sun 12 to 4, 7 to 10.30; bar food and restaurant 12 to 2.30, 7 to 10 (no food 25 Dec)*
Details *Children welcome   Car park   Wheelchair access (also WC)   Patio   Background music   No dogs   MasterCard, Visa   Accommodation: 2 rooms, B&B £25 to £40*

LLANGYNIDR   Powys   map 4

Coach & Horses   [NEW ENTRY]

Llangynidr NP8 1LS   TEL: (01874) 730245
off B4558, 4m W of Crickhowell

Situated on the edge of a village in the Usk Valley, surrounded by the
Black Mountains and the Brecon Beacons, this simply furnished
traditional Welsh inn enjoys a scenic location by the restored
Monmouth and Brecon Canal with its towpath walks and narrowboats. The garden (across the road from the pub) is right on the bank
of the canal and is where the boats tie up. The interior is down-to-
earth and with no frills. There is a small public bar with the usual
games and pool table, and a spacious, open-plan lounge with a
comfortable bar area with banquette seating, a couple of small sofas
and an open fire. A 'light bites' menu offers the likes of fish-cakes,
chicken curry, cod, cottage pie and faggots, most of which come
with chips and peas, while the extensive main menu takes in just
about anything from melon and tangerine cocktail to frogs legs in
garlic butter; from lasagne to pork Napoleon, sirloin steak chasseur
and chicken Mathis (marinated chicken breasts flambéd in
Benedictine). One experienced pub reporter commented, 'It seems
plenty of effort goes into sourcing local ingredients and it is evident
that food is home-made.' Bass and HB are on draught, plus one
guest. SAMPLE DISHES: asparagus 'Meridiana' £4.75; fillet of Cornish
plaice £9; tiramisù £3.75.

Open *11 to 11, Sun 12 to 10.30; bar food and restaurant 12 to 2, 6.30 to 10*
Details *Children welcome   Car park   Wheelchair access (also WC)   Garden
and patio   No-smoking area   Background music   Dogs welcome   Amex,
Delta, MasterCard, Switch, Visa*

LLANGYNWYD   Bridgend   map 4

Old House

Llangynwyd CF34 9SB   TEL: (01656) 733310
off A4063, 2m S of Maesteg

The Old House is almost always crowded. Its warm welcome, cosy
atmosphere and busy young waitresses create a setting that is,
thought one reporter, 'obviously the focal point of the local
community – most of them seem to be there'. Dating back to 1147,
the thatched building, with a stone Celtic cross outside, lays claim to
being one of the oldest licensed premises in Wales. It is one of the
last places in the Principality still to respect the annual tradition of

Mari Lywd, and has associations with the poet Wil Hopkin and the story of the 'Maid of Cefn Ydfa'. The restaurant is housed in what was once the first non-conformist chapel in the Llynfi Valley, dated 1840. The thick walls keep the pub cool in summer and warm in winter, and the decorations – lots of antiques and bric-à-brac – are designed to remind visitors of what life used to be like in the Welsh valleys. It is a popular place to eat and offers an extensive menu of generously portioned dishes. Start with melon and prawns (cold) or seafood mix (hot), before moving up to main courses like lasagne verdi, or beef curry. The fresh fish section of the menu might include pan-fried hake tail, and there is a range of steaks and grills, as well as children's, slimmers' and vegetarian options. Puddings change daily and are selected from the trolley. On handpump are Flowers Original and IPA, Brains Bitter and Worthington Bitter, and the wine list offers a single choice each from a large selection of wine styles and regions. In addition, the pub claims to offer over 350 whiskies, including a Welsh one. SAMPLE DISHES: whitebait £2.75; ham in parsley sauce £6; banana split £2.25.

Open *11 to 11; bar food and restaurant 11 to 2.30, 5 to 10, Sun 11 to 10*
Details *Children welcome in dining-room   Car park   Wheelchair access (also WC)   Garden and patio   No-smoking area   Background music   No dogs Amex, Delta, MasterCard, Switch, Visa*

LLANVAPLEY   **Monmouthshire**   **map 2**

Red Hart 🍺

Llanvapley NP7 8SN   TEL: (01600) 780227
on B4233, 4m E of Abergavenny

Although on the main Abergavenny to Monmouth road, this family-run, whitewashed pub is a good example of a country inn, with its extensive garden looking out over rolling countryside. The interior consists of a bar area with beams and exposed stone walls, a lower room with a pool table, and a dining-room converted from a seventeenth-century cider press. The menu features an unusual selection of dishes from around the world. Start with deep-fried king prawns, Thai-style fish-cakes, or assorted dim-sum. Main courses might be Greek-style fish casserole, three-mustard pork Stroganov, jambalaya (New Orleans paella), chargrilled gammon, or Mediterranean chicken. Vegetarians get the choice of lasagne, vegetable Stroganov, chilli, or aubergine and mozzarella bake. An excellent selection of desserts offers Mississippi mud pie, treacle sponge and custard, lemon crunch with cream, or ice-creams. Traditional Sunday lunch is good value. Real ales all come from the Cottage Brewing Company in Somerset with railway-themed names, such as Western Glory,

Golden Arrow or Goldrush. A short wine list of bottles from around the world includes Monmouthshire wines from Offa's Vineyard; three wines are available by the glass. SAMPLE DISHES: whitebait £4.50; Texas chilli £7; apple pie and custard £3.

Open *Mon and Wed to Sat 12 to 3, Mon to Sat 6 to 11, Sun 12 to 3, 7 to 10.30; bar food and restaurant Wed to Mon L 12 to 2 (3 Sun), Mon to Sat D 7 to 9.30*
Details *Children welcome   Car park   Wheelchair access   Garden   No smoking in restaurant   Background music   No dogs in restaurant   No cards*

LLANVIHANGEL CRUCORNEY   Monmouthshire   map 4

▲ *Skirrid Mountain Inn*

HISTORY

Llanvihangel Crucorney NP7 8DH
TEL: (01873) 890258
off A465 Hereford to Abergavenny road, 4½m N of Abergavenny

Without doubt the Skirrid Inn is a national treasure. Claimed to be the oldest inn in Wales and one of the oldest in Britain, it can be traced back to 1110 when James Crowther was hanged from a beam at the inn for stealing sheep. Space precludes a detailed resumé of the Skirrid's colourful history, which takes in Owain Glyndwr, the Monmouth Rebellion and a gruesome tally of over 180 hangings, the last in the seventeenth century, and, like the first, for the crime of sheep-stealing. A regularly changing menu is strong on traditional cooking and local produce, and typical dishes are local Dexter roast beef, and Crucorney trout. Because it is an Ushers house, beers offered are Ushers Best, Founders and seasonal brews, plus bottled 1824 Particular Ale. The wine list takes in a breadth of styles, and house wines are 'own label'. Should you visit, do ask why there is a bale of hay suspended from the ceiling. SAMPLE DISHES: home-made cawl (lamb stew) £3.50; alehouse pie £7.50; Judge Jefferries pudding £2.75.

Open *summer 11 to 11, Sun 12 to 10.30, winter 11 to 3, 6 to 11, Sun 7 to 10.30; bar food and restaurant all week L 12 to 2, Mon to Sat D 7 to 9*
Details *Children welcome   Car park   Garden and patio   No music   No dogs in restaurant   No cards   Accommodation: 2 rooms, B&B £35 to £79*

All details are as accurate as possible at the time of going to press, but pubs often change hands, and it is wise to check beforehand by telephone anything that is particularly important to you.

If a pub has a special point of interest, this is indicated by a 'flashed' word or phrase at the top right of the entry.

▲ *Bell Inn*

Llanyre LD1 6DY   TEL: (01597) 823959
just off A3081, 1m W of Llandrindod Wells

In the seventeenth and eighteenth centuries drovers used to pass by
through the hills above Llandrindod Wells on the way from west
Wales to the cattle markets at Hereford and Gloucester. The grey-
stone Bell is still an inn, though much modernised over the years,
and now with eleven bedrooms and a restaurant. In the modern bar,
with its plush wall bench seating and simple furniture, the landlord
(new since the last edition of the *Guide*) has plumped for traditional
dishes, many of which would have pleased those drovers: 'creamy
home-made soup, thick with vegetables' and lamb hotpot, crammed
with lean and tender meat in a rich tomato-based sauce – 'a meal in
itself', quite apart from the warm crusty bread. Other 'lite bites' and
'not such lite bites' require no leaps of faith either, whether jacket
potatoes, spicy potato wedges, garlic bread in various guises, sandwiches, toasties, or summer salads in the first category, or braised
liver, leeks and onions, curry of the day, scampi, or cod in batter in
the second. The blackboard may come up with other suggestions.
You can also eat on the patio, pretty with pots and pergola. Service
is quick and friendly. Beers are Bass and Hancocks HB, also
Worthington and All Bright; six wines are available by the glass.
SAMPLE DISHES: spicy potato wedges with dips £3; turkey and ham
pie £6.25; baked Alaska £3.

Open *11 to 4, 6 to 11, Sun 12 to 4, 7 to 10.30; bar food and restaurant 12
to 2, 6.30 to 9.30, Sun 12 to 2, 7 to 9*
Details *Children welcome   Car park   Wheelchair access (also WC)   Garden
No smoking in restaurant   Background music   Dogs in bedrooms only
Delta, MasterCard, Switch, Visa   Accommodation: 9 rooms, B&B £37 to £63*

▲ *Griffin Inn* ❦

Llyswen LD3 0UR   TEL: (01874) 754241
on A470 Builth Wells to Brecon road

The Griffin Inn could almost be the Triffid Inn in that this fifteenth-
century sporting inn in the upper Wye Valley is gradually disap-
pearing beneath the foliage of a giant creeper. The bar is on two
levels with a log fire in each. The lower level has a quarry tile
floor and pine tables, while the upper level is carpeted and has a

high-backed settle of character, dark tables and comfortable chairs.
There are beams, bare stone walls and interesting pictures on the
walls, and a number of reporters have commented on the spotless
housekeeping. The pub also draws comment for its atmosphere: a
combination of setting and service. It is very much a family-run
affair, Richard and Di Stockton having been there since 1983. The
pub is twinned with Auberge 'La Diege' in the French Lot Valley,
which explains why the menu is a fusion of English ingredients with
modern French presentation.

This is very much a food pub. Eat at the bar at lunch-time, or
either there or in the restaurant in the evening, when a different
menu operates. On arrival you are informed of any likely delay in
the kitchen, which is an efficient touch. Marinated fish and meat in
raspberry vinegar on mixed leaves is almost enough to be a main
course; home-made pâtés and terrines are fresh and fully flavoured;
'Salad of the Auberge' is a direct import from their twin establishment. Lunchtime cooking is traditional in style, so liver and
bacon, or cottage pie, will make an appearance, whereas evening
meals are more likely to be braised Hereford beef in claret and
garlic, or chargrilled Welsh salmon with pesto and basil. Real ales
come from Crown Buckley, Tomos Watkin and Wye Valley, and the
wine list is comprehensive with a good range of house wines at
reasonable prices, all available by the glass, backed up with a French-
dominated list. SAMPLE DISHES: warm salad of Penclawdd cockles and
laverbread £5; slow roast crispy duck in autumn berry jus £13:
whimberry crumble £3.25.

Open *12 to 3, 7 to 11, Sun 12 to 3, 7 to 10.30; 25 and 26 Dec; bar food
Mon to Sat 12 to 2, 7 to 9; restaurant Sun L 12 to 2, Mon to Sat D 7 to 9*
Details *Children welcome   Car park   Wheelchair access (also WC)   Patio
No smoking in dining-room   No music   Dogs welcome   Amex, Delta, Diners,
MasterCard, Switch, Visa   Accommodation: 7 rooms, B&B £40 to £80*

M A E N T W R O G   **Gwynedd**   **map 7**

▲ *Grapes Hotel* 🍺

Maentwrog LL41 4HN   TEL: (01766) 590365
off A496, 5m S of Blaenau Ffestiniog

This welcoming Grade II-listed, seventeenth-century coaching-inn,
popular with locals and visitors to the Snowdonia National Park, in
which it is situated, dominates the main street in the village. It is
reputedly the best-known pub for many miles and boasts two ghosts:
an old lady in Victorian clothes below stairs and a piano player on
the residents' landing. As they say, 'We've never figured out how
they got the piano up there.' George Barrow called the pub the

Marntwrog Inn in his book *Wild Wales* , and both Lillie Langtry and
Lloyd George took tea there (though not together). This is a
drinkers' pub and satisfies its customers with a solid 30-strong list of
rotating guest ales as well as Bass, Young's, Morland Old Speckled
Hen and Whoosh from Tomos Watkin. A good bar menu offers food
that is slightly out of the ordinary, such as Stroganov, fajitas, korma
masala, and cannelloni. On a separate menu you'll find puddings,
salads, sandwiches and children's portions. The wine list is honestly
pubby: short, well-priced and with enough cabernets, chardonnays
and sauvignons to satisfy the popular palate. SAMPLE DISHES: salmon
strips in honey, dill and mustard £5.25; lamb dopiaza £6.75; treacle
sponge £2.25.

Open *11 to 11, Sun 11 to 10.30; bar food Mon to Fri 12 to 2.15, 6 to 9.30,
Sat and Sun 12 to 9.30; restaurant Thur to Sat D only 7 to 10*
Details *Children welcome in family room   Car park   Wheelchair access (also
WC)   Patio   No smoking in dining-room   Jukebox   Dogs welcome in public
bar   Amex, Delta, Diners, MasterCard, Switch, Visa   Accommodation: 8
rooms, B&B £28 to £55*

MARFORD   Wrexham   map 7

▲ *Trevor Arms Hotel*
Marford LL12 8TA   TEL: (01244) 570436

Situated next door to a nature reserve and conveniently placed for
Chester, this early-nineteenth-century coaching-inn still provides the
essential services of an old inn – food and shelter for travellers.
Good, uncomplicated pub fare is served up at good value for money.
The light-snacks menu features garlic mushrooms, barbecue spare
ribs, sauté king prawns and lasagne. Salads and omelettes are also
available, as are a range of chargrilled steaks, priced the same in both
bar and restaurant. More ambitious courses come in the shape of
medallions of pork with caramelised apples with cider and chive
sauce, or grilled halibut steak marinated in lime and honey with a
pink grapefruit and a wholegrain mustard sauce. Ask the waitress
what sweets are on offer and she will guide you through a list of
gâteaux, ice-creams and cheesecakes. The pub serves an eclectic
range of real ales: Greenall's, Tetley's, Caledonian 80/-, Cocker
Hoop and Gales IPA; and a two-page wine list features no bottles
over £10 (except champagne). SAMPLE DISHES: tomato and basil soup
with soured cream £1.75; baked rack of lamb with garlic and
rosemary crust and a redcurrant-in-wine jus £9.75; baked Alaska £3.

Open *11 to 11, Sun 12 to 10.30; bar food and restaurant 11 to 9.30, 11 to
9.30*

Details *Children welcome in eating areas and family room   Car park
Wheelchair access (also WC)   Garden   No smoking in restaurant
Background music   No dogs   Amex, Delta, MasterCard, Switch, Visa
Accommodation: 30 rooms, B&B £31 to £50*

PEMBROKE FERRY   **Pembrokeshire**   **map 4**

Ferry Inn

WATERSIDE

Pembroke Ferry SA72 6UD   TEL: (01646) 682947
off A477, N of Pembroke at southern end of Cleddau Bridge

The Ferry acquired new captains in late 1997, Colin and Sarah
Williams, who seem keen to maintain the pub's tradition of serving
fresh local fish in a good pubby environment. The creeper-clad
building stands by the rippling tidal waters of Pembroke Ferry, right
under the Cleddau Bridge, affording splendid views of the bustling
activity on the estuary and al fresco seating on the waterside terrace.
Inside is a good pubby bar with a welcoming coal fire, friendly
atmosphere and interesting collection of local photographs and
nautical memorabilia. The bar menu is reasonably priced and is of
the prawn cocktail, gammon steak, pineapple and chips school.
There are some more modern touches too: crispy fried clams with
crunchy salad or nachos and spicy tomato salsa, followed perhaps by
lamb kebabs, marinated in honey and mint. You could have a prawn
salad as a main course, or from the specials board pick freshly caught
cod, plaice, brill, lemon sole, or sea bass, all usually accompanied by
chips. Apple pie type sweets are also on the same board. On tap is a
range of Bass beers, including Worthington and Hancock's HB,
while a baker's-dozen-long wine list is supplied by James Willis wine
merchants. SAMPLE DISHES: breaded mushrooms in garlic sauce £2.75;
salmon en croûte with hollandaise sauce £6.50; chocolate fudge cake
£2.50.

Open *11.30 to 2.45, 6.30 (7 Mon) to 11, Sun 12 to 2.45, 7 to 10.30; bar
food and restaurant 12 to 2, 7 to 10 (9 Sun)*
Details *Children welcome in eating areas   Car park   Patio   Background
music   No dogs   Delta, MasterCard, Switch, Visa*

Boat Inn

Long Lane, Penallt NP5 4AJ   TEL: (01600) 712615
*just across the footbridge from Redbrook (car park off A466
Monmouth to Chepstow road in Redbrook)*

The Boat Inn has a glorious setting only yards away from the River
Wye (and, occasionally, *in* the River Wye). Not only is the view of
the river superb, but you can sit in the steeply sloping garden
alongside and watch the water cascade down the escarpment, or, in
winter, gaze at the huge icicles. All year long, therefore, this is an
attractive location for the 350-year-old stone pub, much frequented
by walkers and ramblers. Inside, it is quite plain – with a quarry-tiled
floor, stone walls and minimal decoration – except for lots of printed
information about the community of Redbrook and a photographic
record of local floods through the years. Yet cold it is not, thanks to
the old wood-burning stove, the warm welcome and, especially in
summer, the sheer numbers who come here (best to arrive early).
  Service is 'efficient, helpful and very friendly', and the cooking is
based on fresh ingredients, rendered with a touch of flair. A printed
menu is at the core, backed up by a few daily specials. You could
start with a well-flavoured home-made (and usually vegetarian) soup
such as pumpkin and carrot, served with 'an enormous doorstep' of
granary bread, or opt for bacon and Stilton melt en croûte. For a
main course, there are hotpots, pies such as Brie and haddock, and
shepherd's (made with sesame mash), curries – chicken, three vegetarian versions, lamb Madras, and beef and onion – or perhaps try
turkey and tomato crumble. There are jacket potatoes for snackers,
and the children's menu includes lamb-burger on potato waffle
among more usual choices. The wine list is short, offering just four
bottles (three also available by the glass), although the beer board
widens this a tad with its selection of English country wines. Real ale
is the house's forte, with casks mounted in full view behind the bar.
Theakston Old Peculier is a regular, with a further seven to ten
guests such as Oakhill Mendip Gold, Cotleigh Old Buzzard and
Hook Norton Old Hooky, which change as each cask finishes.
Tintern Abbey and Offa's Dyke are both close by. SAMPLE DISHES:
chicken liver pâté £2.50; Greek-style moussaka £5.25; rum and
raisin sponge cake £2.50.

Open *Mon to Fri 11 to 3, 6 to 11, Sat 11 to 11, Sun 12 to 10.30; bar food
Mon to Fri 12 to 2.30, 6 to 9.30, Sat and Sun 12 to 9.30*
Details *Children welcome   Car park   Garden and patio   Live music Tue and
Thurs eve   Dogs welcome   Delta, MasterCard, Switch, Visa*

Use the maps at the centre of the Guide to plan your trip.

PONTARDDULAIS   Swansea   **map 4**

▲ *Fountain Inn*   NEW ENTRY

111 Bolgoed Road, Pontarddulais SA4 1JP   TEL: (01792) 882501

The Fountain Inn is at the eastern end of the village of Pontarddulais, which is on the Western outskirts of Swansea. It is a long roadside building, cream with black timbers and hanging baskets. Inside, it is timber and brick, adorned with mining memorabilia depicting Graig Merthyr colliery – original props, miners' lamps and boots, knee pads, explosions pouches, and the inevitable miners' pick and shovel. On Wednesday night Pontarddulais male-voice choir drink after their weekly practice, which continues here until late into the night. Chef Alan Johns arrived in mid-1998 and seems intent on building trade and expanding the repertoire (the pub's, that is, not the choir's). The menu changes monthly and is supplemented at lunch by excellent-value blackboard specials. Bar meals take in boiled ham and parsley sauce, chicken curry, or steak and ale pie, while on the main à la carte menu you might find cawl (traditional Welsh lamb and vegetable broth), or warm slivers of smoked duck breast on a bed of mixed leaves with orange sauce, followed by haunch of venison in Madeira and mushroom sauce, salmon stuffed with lemon spinach and baked in filo pastry, or pistachio and coriander parcels with tomato and black olive sauce. Desserts – perhaps bread-and-butter pudding or (in summer) strawberry and white chocolate terrine – change daily, and there is a Welsh cheese board alternative. The pub serves Tomos Watkin's Whoosh, Buckley's Best Bitter, Worthington Dark and Best, and offers a wine list with plenty of cheaper New World selections and slightly more expensive French vintages. SAMPLE DISHES: mushrooms stuffed with leek crumble £3.50; grilled lemon sole with parsley butter £9.25; crème brûlée £3.

Open *12 to 3.30, 6 to 11, Sun 12 to 3.30, 6 to 10.30; bar food and restaurant 12 to 2.30, 6.30 to 9.30*
Details *Children welcome   Car park   Wheelchair access (also WC)   Garden No-smoking area in restaurant   Background music   No dogs   Amex, Delta, MasterCard, Switch, Visa   Accommodation: 10 rooms, B&B £20 to £48*

PORTHGAIN   Pembrokeshire   map 4

Sloop Inn   NEW ENTRY

Porthgain SA62 5BN   TEL: (01348) 831449
off A487, 4m W of Mathry

Located by the harbour in a tiny hamlet on a very scenic and popular stretch of the Pembrokeshire coast, the Sloop can be very busy in summer. The long, low building, a pub since 1743, resembles a row of workers' cottages – which it probably once was – and is fronted by Welsh slate patios hung with lobster pots, lines and floats. It has a strong maritime flavour, enhanced by relics from the ship Carowna, which was wrecked off Porthgain in 1859. Around the pub, tables for eating are named after vessels from HMS Hood to the Lusitania. In the main dining area there is a counter for self-service salads and food orders. As is common with many resort pubs, the main menu selection is rather long, but it is clear that the Sloop makes sound strides towards producing a fair amount of home-cooked dishes, including making good use of local fish and seafood. Blackboard main courses range from macaroni and seafood bake with Llangloffan cheese, to steak, kidney and mushroom pie, and 'Angry Dog' burger (topped with onions, cheese, mayonnaise and American-style mustard), and moves on to Mexican chilli, broccoli and tomato bake, and 'dragon's fire' chicken curry. At night the restaurant-style menu extends to include pâté or garlic mushrooms, moules marinière, and local sea bass, as well as dogfish thermidor, and Welsh lamb leg steaks. Puddings are of the jam roly-poly and banoffi pie variety. The pub serves Worthington Best, Brains SA and Felinfoel Double Dragon. SAMPLE DISHES: seafood pancake £4.25; trout with almond butter £7.50; Bakewell tart £3.

Open *11 to 11, Sun 12 to 1.45, 6 to 10.30; bar food and restaurant 12 to 2.30, 6 to 9.30*
Details *Children welcome before 9.30   Car park   Patio   No-smoking area in dining area   Background music   No dogs   No cards*

PWLLGLOYW   Powys   map 4

Seland Newydd ✿

Pwllgloyw LD3 9PY   TEL: (01874) 690282
on B4520, 4m N of Brecon

It is *de rigeur* when describing this pub to point out that the name is Welsh for New Zealand, where hostess Freya Harvey hails from. That aside, it is a foodie pub that has not fallen into the trap of

forgetting its pub origins. The décor is as ruddy a pink as the faces of
the local farmers who may well be propping up the bar. Freya's
husband Maynard is chef, and his cooking is often technically ambitious. Carrot, honey and ginger soup has 'real texture and taste',
asparagus and tomato mousse is delicately layered. You may be
offered raspberry sorbet between courses, before tucking into collops
of monkfish with green mustard and brioche crust and mussel, white
wine and dill sauce, or roast rack of lamb served with a Welsh faggot
and soubise sauce. Cheesecake may be flavoured with bitter coffee
and Baileys, while dark chocolate and coconut torte is doused in
Malibu. Wines provide more interest than the beers, and the list, not
surprisingly, focuses on New Zealand – maps of the country's wine
regions are a nice touch. SAMPLE DISHES: roulade of laverbread and
cream cheese with gazpacho dressing £4.25; blackened salmon with
oriental sauce £11.50; glazed lemon tart with iced lime parfait £4.

Open *11 to 3, 6 to 11, Sun 11 to 3, 6 to 10.30; bar food 12 to 2, 6.30 to 9*
Details *Children welcome   Car park   Wheelchair access   Garden*
Background music   Dogs welcome   Delta, MasterCard, Switch, Visa

---

RED WHARF BAY   Isle of Anglesey   map 7

Ship Inn

Red Wharf Bay LL75 8RJ   TEL: (01248) 852568
off A5025, 6m N of Menai Bridge

This whitewashed sixteenth-century pub, enlivened with hanging
flower baskets and parasols, is right down on the beach at Red
Wharf Bay on the Isle of Anglesey, and the terrace with its tables and
chairs is an ideal place to have a bite and just enjoy the view. Inside,
a stone bar faces the entrance, flanked on either side by a spacious
room with a shelf of toby jugs and hunting cartoons. In winter there
are open fires and during the day the dining-room becomes a no-
smoking family room. The pub attracts a fair-sized crowd during the
summer so it is advisable to arrive early. Menus change regularly but
dishes you are likely to find will include dressed crab, or smoked
duck with balsamic vinegar dressing. Your duck might grow into a
mallard – or braised mallard in red wine at any rate. Braised half-
shoulder of lamb with redcurrant and rosemary, or pan-fried ostrich
steak with three-pepper au poivre sauce, might be other options.
Since fish are living a few yards from the front door, there is no
reason to suppose they should not drop in occasionally. On any day
a red mullet might be visiting, or a whole grilled plaice, even a
peppered monkfish. Puddings are just slightly out of the ordinary –
lemon mousse gâteau or pecan pie – and this freehouse takes a good
range of Carlsberg-Tetley brews: Burton Ale, Tetley Bitter and Dark

Mild, Friary Meux and a guest. Six wines are sold by the glass. SAMPLE DISHES: feta cheese and black olive salad £4.50; paupiettes of beef fillet £14; toffee crunch pie £2.75.

Open *summer 11 to 11, winter Mon to Fri 11 to 3.30, 7 to 11, Sat 11 to 11, Sun 12 to 10.30; bar food summer 12 to 9.30, winter 12 to 2.30, 7 to 9.30; restaurant Fri and Sat 7 to 9.30*
Details *Children welcome in eating areas   Car park   Wheelchair access Garden and patio   No-smoking rooms   Background music   No dogs   Delta, MasterCard, Switch, Visa*

R O S E B U S H   Pembrokeshire   map 4

Tafarn Newydd ❀ 🍺 🍇
Rosebush SA66 7RA   TEL: (01437) 532542
on B4313, 8m SE of Fishguard

Tafarn Newydd means 'New Tavern' – a relative term, since the pub probably dates back well over three hundred years. At various stages in its history it has served as a coaching-inn on the road from Haverfordwest to Cardigan, and later as a substantial farmhouse. Though the original site is old, the present building is something of a phoenix, sympathetically recreated from the ashes of a disastrous fire in the 1970s. The former *raison d'être* of the place remains: it is a flagstoned no-nonsense country pub with real ales and folk music, a dartboard in the bar and an informal atmosphere. Do not expect fast food or heel-clicking service here, especially when they are busy. Furnishings are eclectic, and the clientele casually attired. Under Diana Richards's regime, there is a strong emphasis on the kitchen, which offers an interesting range of country-style cooking with some exotic touches. Local ingredients like Welsh beef and good regional cheeses may rub shoulders with Korean pork patties or Basque-style vegetable risotto, and one regular thought his smoked halibut with fennel demonstrated how 'brilliant' the kitchen is with fish. Thirty-plus wines on the helpfully annotated list provide superior drinking from Old and New Worlds; six wines are available by the glass. Beers too are a draw, with Wye Valley Bitter on tap, plus a host of guest beers, as well as bottled wheat beers. Single malts are available too. SAMPLE DISHES: crostini of cockles and bacon with laver sauce £5; fillet of dab with cream and cider £8.50; plum clafoutis £3.75.

Open *summer 12 to 11, Sun 12 to 10.30, winter Mon and Wed to Sat 12 to 11, Sun 12 to 3; closed 25 Dec, 2nd and 3rd week Jan; bar food 12 to 2, 7 to 9, Sun 12.30 to 2*
Details *Children welcome   Car park   Patio   No smoking in dining-room Background and live music   No dogs   Delta, MasterCard, Switch, Visa*

RUTHIN   Denbighshire   map 7

▲ *Ye Olde Anchor*

Rhos Street, Ruthin LL15 1DX   TEL: (01824) 702813
at junction of A525 and A494

Despite the image conjured up by anything called 'Ye Olde', the
Anchor succeeds on the strength of its food. In terms of décor, it
lives up to its name: beams, copper, brass, stoves, inglenooks,
copper-topped tables, photographs of old Ruthin, and a couple of
shotguns over the fireplace as a reminder to tardy drinkers. Service,
however, is extremely friendly and, as one reporter noted, the staff
are obviously proud of the place. A member of staff is sent daily to
market to fetch the fish, so dishes may vary, with the exception of
scampi and scallops which are regularly available, sautéd in butter,
onions and garlic and then flambéd in brandy. To start, there may be
mushrooms au poivre, or devilled lambs' kidneys, while the main-
course speciality is steak done various ways, such as a 'carpet bag'
version (stuffed with mushrooms and chestnuts), and chateaubriand
for those dining in pairs; otherwise there may be chicken Boursin,
and vegetarians might opt for hazelnut roast or mushroom
Stroganov. Puddings are old favourites – chocolate fudge cake, for
example – plus one or two novelties, such as 'Jamaican crunch', or
watermelon ice-cream. Note that bar food is served lunch-times
only, although a separate restaurant operates both at lunch and in
the evenings, offering dishes such as pan-fried lemon sole with an
avocado and prawn mousse, and roast breast of duck marinated in
apple juice. On tap are Bass, Hancock's HB and guest ales. Only the
house wine is served in the bar, but a fuller list from Tanners is
available in the restaurant. SAMPLE DISHES: chicken satay £4.75;
Indonesian pork £12.50; tiramasù £4.

Open *12 to 2.30, 5.30 to 11, Sun 12 to 2.30, 7 to 10.30; bar food all week L
only 12 to 2; restaurant 12 to 2.30, 7 to 9.30*
Details *Children welcome in restaurant and lounge bar   Car park
Wheelchair access (also WC)   Garden   No smoking in restaurant
Background music   Dogs welcome   Amex, Delta, Diners, MasterCard, Switch,
Visa   Accommodation: 14 rooms, room only £33 to £48*

Kinmel Arms ❦   NEW ENTRY

St George LL22 9BP   TEL: (01745) 832207
off A55, 2m SE of Abergele

Situated in the small village of St George, the pub overlooks the
North Wales strip of lowland that reaches far to the west. With its
North Wales grey-slate exterior and small leaded windows, the
building has been refurbished within to make a large lounge bar with
conservatory extension to the left and a more traditional public bar
to the right. It is pleasantly and simply decorated with white walls,
green curtains and swags. Service is pleasant and efficient; one
reporter was happy to find 'a lovely barmaid of the sort I knew in
my youth and thought had long since disappeared'. Chef/patron
Gary Edwards, with more than 20 years' cooking experience under
his belt, runs the kitchen, producing an à la carte and table d'hôte
menu for the restaurant, as well as an extensive bar menu and a
blackboard of daily specials.

Cooking is well balanced, offering a range of light starters: classic
dishes such as black pudding with apple, chicken liver pâté, and
smoked haddock tartlet, or more modern options such as spiced
chicken kebabs. Main courses mostly follow similarly classic lines with
modern touches – chilli noodles, chargrilled vegetables or balsamic
onions – and smoked salmon comes from their own smokery. The
range covers anything from gammon steak with egg and chips, to
chicken salazar, and specials from lasagne, or local venison casserole,
to rogan josh. Sweets are of the apple pie and ice-cream, or chocolate
torte with chocolate sauce variety. The wine list is split into a house
selection, sommelier's selections and connoisseur's selection, with
some good bottles lurking in there; beer drinkers can expect Marston's
Bitter and Thwaites Best on draught. SAMPLE DISHES: Caesar salad
£3.50; garlic mushroom pasta bake £5.50; strawberry meringue £3.

Open *12 to 3, 7 to 11, Sun 12 to 3, 7 to 10.30; bar food and restaurant 12
to 2, 7 to 9.30 (no food Mon D Oct to Feb, or L 25 Dec)*
Details *Children welcome   Car park   Wheelchair access   Garden and patio
No smoking in restaurant   Background music   Dogs welcome in tap room
only   Delta, MasterCard, Switch, Visa*

---

*Prices quoted in an entry are based on information supplied by the
pub, rounded up to the nearest 25 pence. These prices may have
changed since publication and are meant only as a guide.*

*All details are as accurate as possible at the time of going to press, but
pubs often change hands, and it is wise to check beforehand by
telephone anything that is particularly important to you.*

ST HILARY   Vale of Glamorgan   map 4

Bush Inn

St Hilary CF71 7DP   TEL: (01446) 772745
off A48 Cardiff to Bridgend road

This long-fronted, thatched sixteenth-century pub is perpetually busy, having built up a reputation for good-value, simple dishes that are 'just a little different from basic pub grub'. The overall atmosphere is one of age, but without being twee or old-fashioned. Unadorned, thick stone walls with wide windows, low beams and a large open fireplace make an attractive setting for the ghost of highwayman Ianto Ffranc, who, hanged for his crimes, reputedly haunts the pub. The printed menu is supplemented by half a dozen or so specials. Orders are taken by waitresses who will serve you your Welsh rarebit, laverbread and bacon, or French onion soup, followed perhaps by chicken curry and rice, steak and ale pie, or trout with bacon. More expensive dishes feature on the restaurant menu, which is available in the bar during the evenings and which might run to medallions of pork Normandy, or rack of Welsh lamb. Bass, Hancock's HB, Worthington Bitter and Morland Old Speckled Hen are all available to wash down your meals. Wines span the globe; four are available by the glass, and there are nine half-bottles. SAMPLE DISHES: spinach and cheese crêpe £3; cod grilled with butter with a tomato sauce £4.25; banoffi pie £2.75.

Open *11 to 11, Sun 12 to 10.30; closed 25 Dec eve; bar food and restaurant all week L 12 to 2.30 (3 Sun), Mon to Sat D 7 to 9.30*
Details *Children welcome in eating areas   Car park   Wheelchair access (also WC)   Garden and patio   Background music   No dogs   Delta, MasterCard, Switch, Visa*

SOLVA   Pembrokeshire   map 4

Cambrian Inn

Main Street, Solva SA62 6UU   TEL: (01437) 721210
off A487, 3m W of St David's

'Welsh' and 'home-made', with lots of Italian influences, sum up the essence of the cooking at this inn at the bottom of a steep hill near Pembrokeshire's westernmost point. You can eat in any of the pub's three rooms, and although bar food is available at lunch-time and in the evening, certain things are restricted to one or other period: jacket potatoes and sandwiches (perhaps toasted) at lunch, and some of the Welsh fish and lamb specialities in the evening, for instance.

From the printed bar menu salmon fish-cakes, vegetable lasagne or pancake, and fried whitebait would be attractive choices, while in the evening garlic mushrooms, 'tender and outstanding' cig oen caerfili (Welsh lamb stuffed with leek, herbs and Caerphilly cheese) and chicken Cordon Bleu have been singled out for praise. The blackboard might add to the difficulties of choosing, in the shape of Cambrian fish terrine, fish chowder and chicken cacciatora. Desserts are locally made ice-creamy concoctions, raspberry meringue with amaretto, orange and amaretto bread-and-butter pudding – here again it would be hard not to dither. You may have to wait while your food is cooked, but service is helpful and friendly. Worthington Best and Marston's Pedigree are usually on handpump; wines are serviceable from an anonymous list. SAMPLE DISHES: cawl £4; Welsh black steak with red wine and mushrooms £12; lemon brûlée £2.75.

Open *summer 11.30 to 3, 6.30 to 11, winter 12 to 2.30, 7 to 11; closed 25 and 26 Dec; bar food and restaurant 12 to 2, 7 to 10*
Details *Car park   Wheelchair access (also WC)   Patio   Background music Guide dogs only   No cards*

STACKPOLE   **Pembrokeshire**   **map 4**

Armstrong Arms

Jasons Corner, Stackpole SA71 5DF   TEL: (01646) 672324
off B4319, 3m S of Pembroke

'Two sixteenth-century stone cottages with great potential in super location': thus thought a local builder by the name of Armstrong who in the early 1990s realised that potential by turning them into a pub. It lies in part of the National Trust's Stackpole Estate, which includes part of the Pembrokeshire coastal path. Now a friendly mother-and-daughter team, Margaret and Valerie Westmore, run the pub, with Maria happily inherited from the previous incumbents to make the puddings – 'banoffi pie is our bestseller'. The menus include plenty of local produce and take into account the walkers at lunch-time and the well-heeled evening crowd. Lunch dishes are simple and sustaining: lasagne and garlic bread, or smoked haddock with Welsh rarebit; while in the evening you could go for beef, Guinness and mushroom pie, say, or local fish, maybe in the form of a fish platter, simply treated Tenby plaice, or 'generous, juicy and piquant' monkfish tails with sundried tomato sauce, served with good vegetables. Vegetarians are well catered for. The locals tend to drink their Charles Wells Bombardier, Buckley's Best or Reverend James in the Quay bar, while meals are served efficiently in the pretty garden or in the rambling series of beamed cottagey rooms furnished with modern pine. The wine list is short but appropriate, and whisky is quite a thing here. (Do not confuse Stackpole with Cheriton, otherwise known as Stackpole Elidor, which is just up the road.) SAMPLE DISHES: poached Teifi salmon with lemon and lime hollandaise £7.50; rack of Welsh lamb with port, cranberry and orange sauce £9; tiramisù £3.25.

Open *summer 10 to 5.30, 6.30 to 11, winter 11 to 3.30, 7 to 11; bar food 12 to 2.30, 7 (6.30 in summer) to 9.30*
Details *Children welcome in eating areas and family room   Car park Wheelchair access (also WC)   Garden   Background music   No dogs in restaurant   MasterCard, Switch, Visa*

TYN-Y-GROES   Conwy   map 7

▲ *Groes Hotel*   NEW ENTRY

Tyn-y-Groes LL32 8TN   TEL: (01492) 650545
4m S of Conwy; from mini-roundabout at Conwy Castle take B5106 towards Trefriw for 2m

---

The Groes lays claim to being the 'first licensed house' in Wales, dating back to 1573, and although refurbishment has made it look very modern it still has the ambience of a very old pub. Set back from the road, the pristine building enjoys views of the Conwy estuary and flood plains to the east and Snowdonia to the west. Inside, it is well turned out with polished brasses and copper, an inglenook with a huge slate beam and a wood-burning fire. There is a printed bar menu but see if any of the chef's specials or the catch of the day appeal before placing your order at the bar.

The cooking takes its influence from 'traditional British and Welsh dishes enhanced by continental tastes'. Lamb from the salt marshes of the Conwy Valley, pheasant and game from nearby estates, Welsh beef, and farm-cured hams are all regulars on the inn's menu. Fish and seafood is caught locally – there is Conwy crab and plaice, wild salmon, oysters and mussels. Ice-cream is home-made with free-range eggs and cream. The Welsh seem particularly proud of their cheese at present and the Groes is no exception: try a starter selection of Welsh cheeses with pickle and crusty bread. A reporter's roast beef came as one hefty slab, with gravy, roast and new potatoes and a light, crisp Yorkshire pudding. Other bar menu main courses are equally traditional: steak and kidney pot with thyme dumplings, or Anglesey gammon with eggs and big chips. There is also a separate restaurant offering a table d'hote menu. The pub serves Bank's Bitter and Marston's Pedigree. The wine list is an international selection of around two dozen bottles, plus a handful of half-bottles, and six wines by the glass. SAMPLE DISHES: grilled fillets of Manx kipper with smoked bacon and brown bread £5.50; two salmon fish-cakes, fresh and smoked salmon with home-made tartare sauce £6.75; fresh fruit pavlova £3.25.

Open *12 to 3, 6.30 to 11; bar food 12 to 2 (2.15 Sun), 6.30 to 9*
Details *Children welcome in family room   Car park   Wheelchair access (also WC)   Garden and patio   No smoking in conservatory   Background music Guide dogs only   Amex, Delta, Diners, MasterCard, Switch, Visa Accommodation: 14 rooms, B&B £63 to £104*

WOLF'S CASTLE   Pembrokeshire   **map 4**

▲ *The Wolfe* ❧   NEW ENTRY

Wolf's Castle SA62 5LS   TEL: (01437) 741662
on A40, 7m S of Fishguard

This neat horseshoe-shaped pub, set about a patio seating area, has been attracting attention since Gianni and Jackie di Lorenzo took over in summer 1998. Refurbishment under way as the *Guide* went to press prevents more detailed description of the bar, but three dining-rooms to the side and rear have individual themes. Choose to eat in the Hunting Lodge, the Victorian Room or the Italian Conservatory. The di Lorenzos offer a friendly welcome to a fairly well-heeled clientele who appreciate extra touches like home-made bread and superior coffee. Menus change twice daily, at lunch and dinner. A lunchtime starter might be country terrine of chicken liver, pork and duck, or Welsh cheeses with salad and chutney. In the evening you might start with a selection of sliced meats, or a sweet potato and blue cheese brûlée, and proceed with seared venison steak, fish of the day, suprême of guinea-fowl filled with leeks and walnuts served on red onion and red wine piquant sauce, or a vegetarian dish of the day. If you are extra hungry you could have a pan-fried Welsh Black sirloin steak at either session. There are also frequent themed evenings – seafood or Thai, perhaps. Puddings are home-made, but you may prefer a further selection of local cheeses. Worthington is the only regular draught ale, though there is an additional guest that changes once a month. The wide-ranging wine list has a particularly good Italian selection, six French and Australian half-bottles, and eight wines by the glass. SAMPLE DISHES: chilled melon on fruit purées with fresh fruit and sorbet £4; roast grouse with shallot sauce and redcurrant jelly £15; warm coconut pie £3.50.

Open *11 to 3, 6 to 11; closed mid-Jan to mid-Feb, Sun eve and Mon in winter; bar food and restaurant Tue to Sun L 12 to 2, all week D 7 to 9*
Details *Children welcome in eating areas   Car park   Wheelchair access (also WC)   Garden and patio   No smoking in restaurant   Background music and occasional live music   Well-behaved dogs welcome on a lead   Delta, MasterCard, Switch, Visa   Accommodation: 2 rooms, B&B £25 to £40*

OUT AND ABOUT

OUT AND ABOUT

Country pubs have all kinds of attractions, and people use them for all kinds of reasons. Pubs in 'Out and About' are a mixed bag, but each has some special quality that makes it well worth visiting.

Some of the pubs listed here are superlative outlets for real ale; others have fascinating history and architecture. There are hostelries close to public gardens, castles, rivers and canals; walkers, bird-watchers, climbers and fishermen will also find plenty of establishments serving their own interests. Many places are also excellent family venues, and some may offer decent accommodation.

Most of these pubs serve food, although that is not the main reason for their inclusion in 'Out and About'. Food is often incidental to the proceedings, and some places provide only limited snacks; a few serve no food at all.

Pubs are listed on the basis of readers' recommendations, backed up in many cases by inspectors' reports. Further feedback on these places is most welcome.

ENGLAND

Staffordshire   map 5

Bagot Arms

Bagot Street,
Abbots Bromley WS15 3EG
TEL: (01283) 840371
on B5104, 6m W of Uttoxeter
This imposing, black and white painted
Marston's pub has theme nights about
once a month, including murder-
mystery evenings and cuisine-of-the-
world nights. There is a newly
refurbished games room with
traditional pub games, and a broad
menu offers everything from steak
burgers to specials like chicken tikka
masala and sweet-and-sour pork.
Open *12 to 2.30, 5.30 to 11, Sun 12
to 3, 7 to 10.30*

Dorset   map 2

Ilchester Arms

Market Street, Abbotsbury DT3 4JR
TEL: (01305) 871243
on B3157, 9m W of Weymouth
A very handsome stone building with a
Romanesque crest over a bricked-up
entrance. The pub has recently become
part of the Greenalls empire and offers
their own Bitter, as well as Bass and
Flowers ales. A reasonably priced bar
menu has dishes of the prawn cocktail
or beef and ale pie variety.
Open *11 to 11, Sun 12 to 10.30*

Buckinghamshire   map 3

Old Thatched Inn

Adstock MK18 2JN
TEL: (01296) 712584
off A413, 8m SW of Milton Keynes
A pretty, whitewashed, creeper-clad,
thatched pub dating from the
seventeenth century and enjoying a
tranquil location near Buckingham. It is
handy for visitors to Stowe Gardens,
Claydon House (National Trust) and
Silverstone. Some interesting dishes
appear on the printed menu, and beer

drinkers can enjoy Hook Norton and
Morrells.
Open *12 to 3, 6 to 11, Sun 12 to 3, 7
to 10.30*

Cumbria   map 10

New Crown

Ainstable CA4 9QQ
TEL: (01768) 896273
*take A6 from M6 junction 41, follow
signs to Armathwaite, then 2m to
Ainstable*
Set in the heart of the unspoilt Eden
Valley, this traditional family-run inn is
handy for such attractions as the
Roman Garrison at Birdoswald,
Carlisle Cathedral and Castle, Tullie
House Museum and the Lake District.
Tetley is the only ale on offer, but a
short list of mainly New World wines
compensates.
Open *11 to 11, Sun 12 to 10.30*

Suffolk   map 6

Ye Olde Cross Keys Inn

Crabbe Street, Aldeburgh IP15 5BN
TEL: (01728) 452637
on A1094, 8m E of A12
This pub in the heart of Adnams
territory offers their beers as an ideal
temperature regulator in summer,
when you can quench your thirst after
coming off the beach. In winter relax in
front of the fire with such fare as
devilled whitebait, Dover sole, or fish
in beer batter and chips.
Open *summer 11am to 11.30pm,
winter 1 to 3, 5.30 to 11.30*

South Gloucestershire   map 2

Bowl Inn

16 Church Road,
Lower Almondsbury BS32 4DT
TEL: (01454) 612757
on A38, 7m N of Bristol
An historic inn with origins as a monk's
hostel in 1146, and a pub since the
sixteenth century. The present building
was used as a courthouse by Sheriffs
trying to suppress the supporters of the

Duke of Monmouth, and the pub is said to be haunted. It takes its name from its location on the edge of the Severn Estuary. Bar meals are available all day and range from soup to burgers, steaks, salads or pasta dishes; more expensive meals are available in Lilies restaurant.

Open *11 to 3, 5 (6 Sat) to 11, Sun 12 to 4, 7 to 10.30*

ALSTON

Cumbria   map 10

Turk's Head

Market Place, Alston CA9 3HS
TEL: (01434) 381148
at junction of A686/A689/B6277, 16m NE of Penrith

The Turk's Head is a small narrow building, part of a terrace of commercial premises overlooking the square in what is reputedly the highest market town in England, not far off the Pennine Way. Daily specials are advertised on a blackboard outside the pub and a cheerful fire blazes in winter at the far end of the lounge. The pub serves Higson's and Boddingtons and, in the summertime, Theakston too.

Open *11 to 4, 6.30 to 11, Sun 12 to 4, 7 to 10.30*

ALVESTON

Warwickshire   map 5

Ferry Inn

Ferry Lane, Alveston CV37 7QX
TEL: (01789) 269883
off B4056, between Stratford-upon-Avon and Wellsbourne

There has been a change of ownership at the Ferry since the last edition of the *Guide*, but it remains a popular destination for people having a day out from Stratford and for visitors to the National Trust property Charlecote Park. Greene King Abbot Ale, Flowers IPA, Hook Norton and Bass are all served at this Whitbread pub.

Open *11 to 2.30, 6 to 11, Sun 12 to 2.30, 7 to 10.30*

AMERSHAM

Buckinghamshire   map 3

Kings Arms

30 High Street,
Old Amersham HP7 0DJ
TEL: (01494) 726333

Dating from the 1450s and extended in the eighteenth century with a Georgian frontage, this pub shows no concessions to modernity, with its solid beams, open fires and the like. It takes its food seriously and gives the impression to some that it would rather be a restaurant. Has a fair share of loyal fans.

Open *11 to11, Sun 12 to 10.30*

ANICK

Northumberland   map 10

Rat Inn

Anick NE46 4LN
TEL: (01434) 602814
just N of A69, 1½m NE of Hexham

This pub was called the Board Inn for many years, but was known locally as the Rat even then. Whatever the name, there has been an inn in this Saxon village for centuries. It offers a comprehensive selection of ales, including Theakston Black Bull, Charles Wells Bombardier and Morland Old Speckled Hen, backed by a value for money bar menu.

Open *11 to 3, 6 to 11, Sun 11 to 3, 7 to 10.30*

APPLEBY

Cumbria   map 10

Tufton Arms

Market Square, Appleby CA16 6XA
TEL: (017683) 51593

This Victorian coaching-inn is now a comfortable hotel in the centre of this small country town and is, thankfully, family run. It still has a drop-in bar and bar menu to qualify it as a *Guide* entry, and unlike the majority of British hotels, it actually knows what real ale is – its own house ale is served alongside Theakston and Tetley, and there is a decent wine list.

Open *11 to 11, Sun 12 to 3, 7 to 10.30*

APPLETON ROEBUCK

North Yorkshire   map 9

Shoulder of Mutton

Chapel Green,
Appleton Roebuck YO23 7DP
TEL: (01904) 744227
3m SE of A64 Leeds to York road, turn off at Colton Lane End
Samuel Smith's Brewery is one of the few still delivering beer in wooden casks, and the Shoulder of Mutton is a good place to try Tadcaster's finest. The 13-bottle wine list contains nothing over £10, and both bar snack and restaurant menus are exceptional value for money.
Open *11 to 3, 6.30 to 11, Sun 12 to 3, 7 to 10.30*

ARNCLIFFE

North Yorkshire   map 8

Falcon

Arncliffe BD23 5QE
TEL: (01756) 770205
off B6160, 7m NW of Grassington
Younger's Scotch Bitter is served straight out of the barrel into a jug in this small, family inn which is ideally situated for walking and touring in the Dales. It has its own private fishing on the River Skirfare, and offers a very simple bar menu at lunch-time only.
Open *12 to 3, 6.30 (9 winter) to 11*

ASHBURNHAM

East Sussex   map 3

Ashtree Inn

Ashburnham TN33 9NX
TEL: (01424) 892104
just off B2204 (off A271), 4m W of Battle
One gets the feeling of stepping back in time when visiting this pub, according to one visitor who was impressed by the traditional and unspoilt nature of the place. The pub is owned by the Ashburnham Estate, which may explain its unspoilt aspect. It serves Harveys Bitter, Wadworth 6X and Morland Old Speckled Hen as well as a short handwritten menu of confident, hearty dishes.
Open *summer 12 to 4, 7 to 11, winter 12 to 3.30, 7 to 10.30*

ASHBY ST LEDGERS

Northamptonshire   map 5

Olde Coach House Inn

Ashby St Ledgers CV23 8UN
TEL: (01788) 890349
off A361, 4m N of Daventry
Deserving its entry for its attractive, creeper-clad building, proximity to Althorp House and the M1, and its excellent range of 11 real ales, most of which change regularly, this pub has recently been taken over by the Tom Hoskins brewery company of Leicester.
Open *12 to 2.30, 6 to 11, Sun 12 to 3, 7 to 10.30*

ASHENDON

Buckinghamshire   map 2

Gatehangers Inn

Ashendon HP18 0HE
TEL: (01296) 651296
off A41, midway between Bicester and Aylesbury
In the summer it is enjoyable to sit on the small patio garden picnic tables and enjoy the views from this sixteenth-century inn, which was once the local magistrate's court. Under new ownership since mid-1998; reports please.
Open *12 to 3, 6 to 11*

ASHLEWORTH

Gloucestershire   map 5

Boat Inn

The Quay, Ashleworth GL19 4HZ
TEL: (01452) 700272
off A417, 5m N of Gloucester
This delightful waterside pub has been in the Jelf family for over 400 years and there is plenty of history to be enjoyed. Beer and cider are tapped from casks behind the bar, and good West Country ales from the likes of Wye Valley, Arkell's, Oakhill and RCH are to be enjoyed in idyllic surroundings.
Open *11 to 2.30 (3 Sat), 6 to 11, Sun 12 to 3, 7 to 10.30; closed Wed L in winter*

AYOT ST LAWRENCE

Hertfordshire   map 3

Brocket Arms

Ayot St Lawrence AL6 9BJ
TEL: (01438) 820250
off B656/B651, 2m W of Welwyn
Set in a lovely historic village within
easy reach of London, this fourteenth-
century inn retains many traditional
features – an inglenook fireplace, low
oak beams and a walled garden. It is
reputedly haunted by a priest who was
hanged here during the Reformation.
Good-value pub food and beers from
Adnams, plus guest ales, are served.
Open *all week 11 to 11*

BADBY

Northamptonshire   map 5

Windmill

Main Street, Badby NN11 3AN
TEL: (01327) 702363
*on A361 Daventry to Banbury road, 2m
S of Daventry*
This is a thriving country pub and
hotel, successfully catering for
conferences and hotel guests, with a
good pubby bar filled with local
drinkers and diners. It has plenty of
charm and character, and is handy for
walkers on the Knightley and Nene
Ways, and visitors to Althorp House
and National Trust-owned Canons
Ashby.
Open *11.30 to 3, 5.30 to 11*

BARBON

Cumbria   map 8

Barbon Inn

Barbon LA6 2LJ
TEL: (01524) 276233
just off A683, 3m N of Kirkby Lonsdale
Theakston Best and a wine list with an
Aussie accent are the key features at
this seventeenth-century coaching-inn
situated in prime walking country
between the Dales and Lake District.
The bar menu offers traditional pub
grub, with some interesting things like
bacon and mushroom baguette.
Open *12 to 3, 6.30 to 11, Sun 12 to 3,
7 to 11*

BARHAM

Suffolk   map 6

Sorrel Horse

Barham IP6 0PG
TEL: (01473) 830327
off A14 at Claydon, 5m N of Ipswich
Spotlessly clean pub offering well-kept
ales from Tolly Cobbold and a range of
menus which may well focus on the
cuisine of a particular country.
Cooking is competent and this large
pub has a popular local following. If
you are lucky you may turn up on quiz
night.
Open *Mon to Fri 11 to 3, 5 to 11, Sat
11 to 4, 6.30 to 11, Sun 12 to 3, 7 to
10.30*

BARLEY

Hertfordshire   map 3

Fox & Hounds

High Street, Barley SG8 8HU
TEL: (01763) 848459
off B1039, 3m SE of Royston
The village of Barley is pretty with
thatched cottages set in winding lanes.
The pub sits on a bend in the road and
is notable for its old-fashioned pub sign
which extends right across to the other
side. Inside, it has a relaxed and
friendly atmosphere. New owners are
serving a good range of beers, but the
kitchen regime is yet to be assessed.
Reports please.
Open *11 to 3, 6 to 11, Sun 12 to 3, 7
to 10.30*

BARTHOMLEY

Cheshire   map 5

White Lion

Barthomley CW2 5PG
TEL: (01270) 882242
*off Alsager road, from M6 junction 16,
4m SE of Crewe*
A timeless seventeenth-century black-
and-white thatched building, standing
beside the original cobbled cart track in
the heart of the village. The unspoilt
interior oozes period charm. It is popular
with walkers, cyclists and lunch-time
visitors, who can refresh themselves with
Burtonwood Bitter, Buccaneer Bitter,
James Forhaw's and Top Hat, all from
the Burtonwood Brewery.

Open *11.30 to 11 (Thur 5 to 11), Sun 12 to 10.30*

BARTON

Warwickshire   map 5

Cottage of Content
15 Welford Road, Barton B50 4NP
TEL: (01789) 772279
off A439, just S of Bidford-on-Avon
The house speciality of this unusually named pub is espetada – cubes of beef marinated in herbs and wine then grilled on a large skewer. For vegetarians the house special is a rather original Stilton and Guinness pâté. Drink beers from Theakston, Flowers or Courage.

Open *11 to 2.30, 6 to 11, Sun 12 to 3, 7 to 10.30*

BECK HOLE

North Yorkshire   map 9

Birch Hall
Beck Hole YO22 5LE
TEL: (01947) 896245
off A169, 2m S of Grosmont
Beers and butties make the Birch Hall worth a visit. It is run by a brother and sister team who offer a selection of bottle-conditioned beers from Cropton brewery and other local independents, as well as Theakston Black Bull, Black Sheep Bitter, and ales from the Black Dog brewery in Whitby. A Beckhole Butty is a wedge of their special bread filled with ham, cheese or pâté. A great pub.

Open *summer 11 to 11, Sun 12 to 10.30, winter 11 to 3, 7 to 11, Sun 12 to 3, 7 to 10.30*

BECKLEY

Oxfordshire   map 2

Abingdon Arms
High Street, Beckley OX3 9UU
TEL: (01865) 351311
off B4027, 5m NE of Oxford
Enthusiastic new owners took over just before the *Guide* went to press, promising to give equal importance to eating and drinking, and to make this traditional stone pub 'an asset to the community'. Beers on offer are Hook Norton plus a guest. Reports please.

Open *11.30 to 2.30, 6.30 to 11, Sun 12 to 2.30, 8 to 10.30*

BERKSWELL

West Midlands   map 5

Bear Inn
Spencers Lane, Berkswell CV7 7BB
TEL: (01676) 533202
off A452, 6m W of Coventry
A busy but friendly atmosphere operates at this popular Chef & Brewer pub in a pretty village. Despite its imposing size it is quite cosy, with traditional fittings despite a recent renovation.

Open *11 to 11, Sun 12 to 10.30*

BERRYNARBOR

Devon   map 1

Ye Olde Globe
Berrynarbor EX34 9SG
TEL: (01271) 882465
off A399, 4m E of Ilfracombe
An interesting pub for antiques and curios, it was first licensed in 1675 having been converted from a row of cottages that are believed to date from around 1280. The standard menu features good vegetarian options, and a childrens' section. The unusual décor in the lounge alone makes the pub worth a visit.

Open *11.30 to 2.30, 6 (7 in winter) to 11, Sun 12 to 2.30, 7 to 10.30*

BEST BEECH

East Sussex   map 3

Best Beech Inn
Mayfield Lane, Best Beech TN5 6JH
TEL: (01892) 782046
on B2100, midway between Mark Cross and Wadhurst
Parts of the inn date back to 1680, but recent refurbishment is more in keeping with its largely Victorian character. Adnams, Harveys and Fuller's beers are served, along with a moderately priced wine list and a traditional menu. New owners took over shortly before the *Guide* went to press.

Open *Tue to Sun 11.30 to 2.30, all week 6 to 11*

BETCHWORTH

Surrey   map 3

Dolphin

The Street, Betchworth RH3 7DW
TEL: (01737) 842288
*off A25, 2m W of Reigate, in centre of
Betchworth*
This sixteenth-century pub overlooking
a working blacksmith's forge has tables
out front and a terrace at the rear. This
is a Young's pub (a rare creature
outside London) but there is not much
space for mere enjoyment of their well-
kept beers. In the main dining area you
can enjoy a variety of dishes with big
portions and small prices.
Open *Mon to Fri 11 to 3.30, 5.30 to
11, Sat and Sun 11 to 11*

BEWDLEY

Worcestershire   map 5

Little Packhorse

High Street, Bewdley DY12 2DH
TEL: (01299) 403762
3m W of Kidderminster
'This place is a treasure,' wrote one
visitor to this fifteenth-century pub,
with its eccentrically decorated, tiny
interior. Beers are from Ushers and the
pub also offers a short menu of things
like minted lamb and tattie pie, and
'poultry, pig and fungi' pie.
Open *Mon to Fri 11.30 to 3, 6 to 11,
Sat 11 to 11, Sun 12 to 10.30*

BILDESTON

Suffolk   map 6

Crown

104 High Street, Bildeston IP7 7EB
TEL: (01449) 740510
*just off B1115/B1708, 4m NW of
Hadleigh*
This attractive fifteenth-century timber-
framed pub on the village high street
serves a strictly Suffolk range of beers
including Adnams, Nethergate and
Tolly Cobbold, and a good range of
wines. In addition to the restaurant
menu it also offers bar food such as
salads, omelettes, three-tier club
sandwiches and steaks.
Open *11 to 2.30, 6 to 11, Sun 12 to 3,
7 to 10.30*

BLACKAWTON

Devon   map 1

Normandy Arms

Chapel Street, Blackawton TQ9 7BN
TEL: (01803) 712316
*off A381 and B3207, 5m W of
Dartmouth*
Named after Operation Tiger – the
Normandy D-Day-landing practice
exercise, which took place along the
nearby sands – this attractive pub dates
back to the fifteenth century and, with
accommodation, is an ideal base for a
range of activities from bird-watching
on Slapton Sands to sea-fishing or river
trips. In the evening, wash the sea salt
from your throat with Blackawton
Brewery ales or one of another 44
guests on rotation.
Open *Sun to Fri 12 to 2.30, 7 to 11
(10.30 Sun), Sat 12 to 11*

BLACKMORE END

Essex   map 3

Bull

Blackmore End CM7 4DD
TEL: (01371) 851037
*between A1017 and B1053, 6m N of
Braintree*
Under new ownership since late 1998,
this neat, long, single-storey building
has a fairly sizeable garden for fair-
weather eating in a setting just outside
the village, surrounded by fields.
Serving Greene King IPA, Adnams Best
and a guest beer, it also offers fairly
classy-sounding dishes like smoked
salmon mousse with gravad lax salad
and sirloin of beef with port and Stilton
crust in red wine. Reports please.
Open *12 to 3, 7 to 11, Sun 12 to 2.30,
7 to 10.30*

BLAISDON

Gloucestershire   map 5

Red Hart

Blaisdon GL17 0AH
TEL: (01452) 830477
off A4136, 2m from Huntley
Tame rare breed pigs live in the
'gorgeous' garden of this roadside inn
in a small hamlet on the edge of the
Forest of Dean. Ales are the main
attraction: a permanent selection of

Hook Norton Best, Tetley, Chandos Gold from the Moor Brewing Co, Deuchars IPA and Our Ken from Cottage is augmented by three guest beers, perhaps including Hop Back Summer Lightning.
Open *11.30 to 3, 6 to 11, Sun 12 to 3.30, 7 to 10.30*

BLAKENEY

Norfolk   map 6
King's Arms
Westgate Street,
Blakeney NR25 7NQ
TEL: (01263) 740341
on A149, 5m W of Holt
The date 1760, picked out in dark tiles on the roof of this Grade II listed pub, refers to its inception as a freehouse. Good real ales and a short menu that makes good use of local produce, plus the inglenook fireplace, beer garden and accommodation, all make this north Norfolk pub well worth a visit.
Open *10.30 to 11, Sun 12 to 10.30*

BLETCHINGLEY

Surrey   map 3
Prince Albert
Outwood Road,
Bletchingley RH1 4LR
TEL: (01883) 743257
on A25, 2m W of Godstone
A late-fifteenth/early-sixteenth-century red-brick house, set diagonally at the bottom of the main street. At the rear is a pretty garden. Inside, it is totally unmodernised, a basic pub food menu offers filled baguettes, jacket potatoes, ploughman's and the like, and beers come from Brewery on Sea, including some house beers.
Open *11 to 3, 5.30 to 11, Sun 12 to 4, 7 to 10.30*

William IV
Little Common Lane,
Bletchingley RH1 4QF
TEL: (01883) 743278
A local pub serving good real ales such as Harveys, Young's, Fuller's and local microbrewery brew Pilgrim's Progress. The pub is also expanding its food operation and an extensive menu serves up home-prepared pizzas as well as grills, steaks and daily specials.
Open *11 to 3, 6 to 11, Sun 12 to 3, 7 to 10.30*

BLICKLING

Norfolk   map 6
Buckinghamshire Arms
Blickling NR11 6NF
TEL: (01263) 732133
off B1354, from A140, 2m NW of Aylsham
Built in 1693 for guests and servants of Blicking Hall, it is known locally as the Bucks. The kitchen prides itself on using only fresh local produce wherever possible. Seafood features strongly on a menu which offers confident, modern British cooking. Real ales come from Woodforde's, Adnams and Reepham, plus a regular guest.
Open *summer all week 12 to 11, winter 12 to 3, 6 to 11, Sun 12 to 3, 7 to 10.30*

BODICOTE

Oxfordshire   map 5
Plough
Bodicote OX15 4BZ
TEL: (01295) 262327
just off A4260, 2m S of Banbury
Real ales are the draw at this long-standing family-run pub, home of the Bodicote Brewery, which serves their range of four beers – Bitter, No. 9, Porter and Triple X. Food ranges from sandwiches to steaks, with joints, casseroles and vegetarian options between. Bodicote House is among nearby attractions.
Open *11 to 2.30, 5.45 to 11, Sun 12 to 2.30, 7 to 11*

BOTTOM-OF-THE-OVEN

Cheshire   map 7

Stanley Arms

Bottom-of-the-Oven,
Macclesfield Forest SK11 0AR
TEL: (01260) 252414
*just S of A537, between Buxton and
Macclesfield*
Situated in a bizarrely named village,
this Marston's pub offers their basic
range of ales and some fairly traditional
English pub grub of the deep-fried Brie,
chicken Kiev, scampi and steak au
poivre variety.
Open *Mon to Fri 12 to 3, 5.30 to 11,
Sat and Sun 12 to 11.30 (10.30 Sun)*

BOURTON

Dorset   map 2

White Lion Inn

High Street, Bourton SP8 5AT
TEL: (01747) 840866
just off A303, 4m E of Wincanton
Popular for its well-kept real ales –
Courage Directors, Ushers Best and
Wadworth 6X – this 200-year-old
coaching-inn is known locally as the
Bush, best explained by the fact that
the Bush is the pub's restaurant.
Open *12 to 3, 5 to 11, Sun 12 to
10.30*

BOUTH

Cumbria   map 8

White Hart Inn

Bouth LA12 8JB
TEL: (01229) 861229
off A590, 4m NE of Ulverston
Under new ownership since mid-1998,
the White Hart offers a short menu of
traditional pub fare mixed with lighter
Mediterranean dishes, all backed by an
impressive range of real ales and well-
chosen guests.
Open *Wed to Sun 12 to 2.30, all week
6 to 11*

BOWLAND BRIDGE

Cumbria   map 8

Hare & Hounds Inn

Bowland Bridge LA11 6NN
TEL: (015395) 68333
off A5074, 8m S of Windermere

Run by former international footballer
Peter Thompson and his wife since
1982, this place is more of a country
hotel-style inn, but it has a pubby
lounge and it is possible to drop in for
a drink or a bar meal. A reasonably
priced menu is on offer and there are
plenty of nearby attractions.
Open *summer 11 to 11 (10.30 Sun),
winter 11 to 3, 6 to 11 (10.30 Sun)*

BOWNESS-ON-WINDERMERE

Cumbria   map 8

Hole in't Wall

Bowness-on-Windermere LA23 3DH
TEL: (01539) 443488
*on A5074, on E shore of Lake
Windermere*
History and literary links galore at this
lovely old pub with a warm, welcoming
interior crammed with intriguing
flotsam and jetsam. Champion wrestler
Will Longmire was landlord here in the
1800s. Best visited outside the tourist
season, when the Hartley's and
Robinson's ales can be enjoyed in peace
and quiet.
Open *11 to 11, Sun 11 to 10.30*

BRADFIELD

South Yorkshire   map 8

Strines Inn

Mortimer Road, Bradfield S6 6JE
TEL: (0114) 285 1247
*2m off A57 (not in village), 6m NW of
Sheffield*
This handsome stone pub was
originally built as a manor-house for
the Worral family in 1275, but most of
the building dates from the 1550s. A
simple ale selection includes Marston's
Pedigree, Flowers Original and
Morland Old Speckled Hen, to
complement the bar menu of grills,
baltis and salads.
Open *summer all week 10.30am to
11pm, winter Mon to Fri 10.30 to 3, 7
to 11, Sat and Sun 10.30 to 11*

BRANCASTER STAITHE

Norfolk   map 6

Jolly Sailors

Main Road,
Brancaster Staithe PE31 8BJ
TEL: (01485) 210314

on A149, between Hunstanton and
Wells-next-the-Sea

A very straightforward place on the
main coast road, popular with sailing
types and the boat builders next door.
It is a down-to-earth place ('children,
dogs and wellies very welcome'),
serving food all day from 8am,
including a popular all-day breakfast.
Wash it down with a large selection of
real ales including Greene King IPA
and Abbot, Woodforde's Wherry and
Nelson's Revenge, Adnams Broadside
and Boddingtons Bitter.

Open *8 to 11, Sun 8 to 10.30*

White Horse

Brancaster Staithe PE31 8BW
TEL: (01485) 210262

This recently renovated pub,
overlooking Brancaster saltmarshes,
was due to be a main entry but changed
licensees as the *Guide* was about to go
to press, too late for re-inspection. It is
to be hoped that the promise being
shown at this airy yet traditionally
furnished pub continues. Reports
please.

Open *11 to 3, 6 (7 in winter) to 11,*
Sun 12 to 3, 7 to 10.30

BREDON

Worcestershire   map 5

Fox & Hounds

Church Street, Bredon GL20 7LA
TEL: (01684) 772377

from M5 junction 9, follow signs
Tewkesbury then take B480 to Bredon

The Fox & Hounds is in danger of
becoming more of a restaurant than a
pub, but still serves a decent selection
of beers. Comprising two distinct but
linked buildings, the pub is very much a
feature of the village. The menu is
modern and occasionally ambitious.

Open *12 to 2.30, 6 (6.30 in winter) to*
11, Sun 12 to 2.30, 6 to 10.30

BRETFORTON

Worcestershire   map 5

Fleece Inn

The Cross, Bretforton WR11 5SE
TEL: (01386) 831173

on B4035, 4m E of Evesham

Under new ownership since early 1998
but encouragingly selling a good range
of ales from breweries as diverse as
Uley, Hook Norton and Highgate. It
also offers simple pub fare of the
gammon steak and chicken and leek pie
variety.

Open *Mon to Fri 11 to 3, 6 to 11, Sat*
11 to 11, Sun 12 to 3, 6 to 10.30

BRINDLE

Lancashire   map 8

Cavendish Arms

Sandy Lane, Brindle PR6 8NG
TEL: (01254) 852912

on B5256 between Leyland and
Blackburn

Children are welcome in the dining
areas at this seventeenth-century inn in
an equally ancient Lancashire village.
Burtonwood ales and changing guests
are strictly for the adults, however. The
house speciality is Cavendish fish pie.

Open *11 to 3, 5.30 to 11, Sun 12 to 3,*
7 to 10.30

BROAD CAMPDEN

Gloucestershire   map 5

Bakers Arms

Broad Campden GL55 6UR
TEL: (01386) 840515

off B4081, 1m SE of Chipping
Campden

This appealing creeper-clad Cotswold
stone pub offers first-rate beers such as
Timothy Taylor Landlord, Exmoor
Gold and Marston's Bitter, and never
fewer than six are on offer. A
blackboard menu lists traditional pub
fare such as liver and onion, coq au vin,
fish pie.

Open *11.30 to 2.30, 6 to 11, Sun*
11.30 to 3, 7 to 10.30

BROADWAY

Worcestershire   map 5

Crown and Trumpet

Church Street, Broadway WR12
7AE
TEL: (01386) 853202

*off High Street (A44), on Snowshill
road*

A seventeenth-century Cotswold stone
pub with some quirky touches such as
an occasional asparagus menu, a pub
quiz with a difference – a cross
between a quiz and bingo – and beers
from the Stanway Brewery, as well as
the regular Whitbread portfolio, on top
of a menu of home-made dishes.

Open *11 to 3, 5 to 11, Sun 12 to 3.30,
5.30 to 11*

BROCKHAM

Surrey   map 3

Royal Oak

Brockham Green,
Brockham RH3 7JS
TEL: (01737) 843241

just off A25, 2m E of Dorking

A popular summertime venue, focusing
on a broad range of real ales from a
variety of regional brewers, such as
Harveys, Fuller's, Wadworth, Gale's
and Greene King, as well as their own
house bitter. A modest wine list
complements a simple bar menu of
pies, pasta dishes, seafood and grills.

Open *Mon to Fri 11.30 to 3, 5 to 11,
Sat 11 to 11, Sun 12 to 10.30*

BROCKTON

Shropshire   map 5

Feathers

Brockton TF13 6JR
TEL: (01746) 785202

on B4378, 5m SW of Much Wenlock

Not your average English pub at all,
but more an exuberantly decorated
Mediterranean tavern with washed
terracotta walls, garlands of grapes and
vines on the walls, and chock-a-block
with pots, flowers, curtains etc.
Cooking does not quite live up to
promise, but with Banks's Bitter and
Morrell's Bitter on offer it is certainly a
fun place to visit.

Open *Mon to Fri 6 to 11, Sat and Sun
11 to 11*

BROOM

Bedfordshire   map 6

Cock

23 High Street, Broom SG18 9NA
TEL: (01767) 314411

on B658, 2m SW of Biggleswade

Known locally as the 'pub with no bar',
since all the Greene King beers are
served directly from the cellar. There is
a snack menu served directly from the
kitchen, plus modern pub specials like
chicken balti and naan bread, filled
giant Yorkshire puddings or breast of
Cajun chicken.

Open *12 to 3, 6 to 11*

BURCOT

Oxfordshire   map 2

Chequers

Burcot OX14 3DP
TEL: (01865) 407771

on A415, 4½m E of Abingdon

Theme evenings – perhaps a 'grand pig
roast party' or a gourmet evening – are
a feature at the Chequers. Long-serving
landlord Michael Weeks serves
Brakspear, Wadworth 6X and Ruddles
and a 'small but neat' wine selection.

Open *11 to 2.30, 6 to 11, Sun 12 to 3,
7 to 10.30*

BURGH ISLAND

Devon   map 1

Pilchard Inn

Burgh Island TQ7 4BG
TEL: (01548) 810344

*island (opposite Bigbury-on-Sea)
signposted from A379 Modbury to
Kingsbridge road*

Burgh Island is famous for being cut off
twice a day as the sea inundates its
sandy causeway. You can still get there
before high tide, however, when its
tractor on stilts crosses the submerged
sands. If you are cut off for an hour or
two, drop in to the Pilchard for a
sandwich or a pasty.

Open *summer all week 11 (12 Sun) to
11, winter 11 (12 Sun) to 3, 7 to 11*

BURITON

Hampshire   map 2

Five Bells

High Street, Buriton GU31 5RX
TEL: (01730) 263584
off A3, 1m S of Petersfield
Dating from 1639 and named after the
bells of Buriton church, this is a
characterful pub set above the village
lane. Part of it was formerly a farriers.
It was bought by Hall & Woodhouse in
mid-1998 and serves their range of
ales, plus some guests like Ballards and
Mauldons. Reports please.
Open *11 to 2.30 (3 Fri and Sat), 5.30
to 11, Sun 12 to 3, 7 to 10.30*

BYWORTH

West Sussex   map 3

Black Horse

Byworth GU28 0HL
TEL: (01798) 342424
just S of Petworth, off A283
Beers like Fuller's London Pride and
Arundell Gold, as well as Nadder
Valley cider, are served at this unspoilt
country pub with a relaxed
atmosphere. The garden offers
stunning views over the South Downs,
and a fairly basic bar menu and a
separate traditional restaurant menu
are available.
Open *11 to 3, 6 to 11, Sun 12 to 3, 7
to 10.30*

CARDINGTON

Shropshire   map 5

Royal Oak

Cardington SY6 7JZ
TEL: (01694) 771266
off B4371, 4m E of Church Stretton
This 500-year-old village pub, not far
from Wenlock Edge, is strong on
Shropshire fare, whether it be beers
such as Wood's or Hobson's, or food
like 'Shropshire Fidget Pie' – the house
speciality – from a list of standard pub
grub and home-made desserts.
Open *Tue to Sun and bank hols 12 to
2.30, 7 to 11*

CAREY

Herefordshire   map 5

Cottage of Content

Carey HR2 6NG
TEL: (01432) 840242
*between A49 and B4224, 6m SE of
Hereford*
A single menu, featuring pie of the day
and seasonal fish, along with a choice
of Hook Norton Bitter and Weston's
Old Rosie cider, plus around 40
different malts, offers every prospect of
contentment at this 500-year-old,
whitewashed pub, found at the end of
winding lanes.
Open *12 to 2.30, 7 to 11, Sun 12 to
2.30, 7 to 10.30*

CASTLE ACRE

Norfolk   map 6

Ostrich Inn

Stocks Green, Castle Acre PE32 2AE
TEL: (01760) 755398
*just off A1065 Swaffham to Fakenham
road, 4m N of Swaffham*
This seventeenth-century coaching-inn
occupies a charming spot opposite the
tree-lined green in an historic and
attractive village on the Peddlers Way,
making it popular with walkers and
visitors to the ruins of the Cluniac
Priory and Castle. Greene King ales
and good-value food provide
sustenance.
Open *12 to 2.30, 7 to 11, Sun 12 to 3,
7 to 10.30*

CASTLE HEDINGHAM

Essex   map 3

Bell

10 James Street, Castle Hedingham
TEL: (01787) 460350
off B1058, 4m NW of Halstead
This pink coaching-inn serves an
impressive range of real ales from casks
ranged behind the bar, including
Greene King IPA and Abbot Ale,
Shepherd Neame Masterbrew and
Spitfire, as well as guests which might
come from local brewery Ridley's. Part
of the sixteenth-century wattle and
daub construction has been exposed
behind glass, and its series of small
inter-connecting rooms make it

popular with a young crowd also attracted by occasional live music.
Open *11.30 to 3, 6 to 11, Sun 12 to 3, 7 to 10.30*

CAULDON
Staffordshire   map 5
Yew Tree
Cauldon ST10 3EJ
TEL: (01538) 308348
off A523 Leek to Ashbourne road at Waterhouses, 6m NE of Cheadle
Alan East has run this pub since 1961, since when it has become not so much a pub as a museum of Victorian memorabilia. However, it still serves well-kept ales such as Bass, Burton Bridge and Ridley's Mild. Visitors flock to see the amazing collection of artefacts and to enjoy its unspoilt pub character.
Open *10 to 2.30, 6 to 11, Sun 12 to 3, 7 to 10.30*

CERNE ABBAS
Dorset   map 2
New Inn
14 Long Street,
Cerne Abbas DT2 7JF
TEL: (01300) 341274
on A352, 7m N of Dorchester
Visitors to the famous chalk figure, carved on a nearby hillside, can stop off in the village at this popular sixteenth-century watering-hole. Well-kept Hardy Country Bitter and Royal Oak are on tap at the bar, along with a guest ale. Accommodation is available.
Open *11 to 3, 6 to 11 (10.30 Sun)*

CHEDINGTON
Dorset   map 2
Winyard's Gap
Chedington DT8 3HY
TEL: (01935) 891244
on A356, between Crewkerne and Dorchester, at Winyard's Gap
This plain, white-painted pub, under new ownership since early 1998, enjoys a spectacular location on the edge of the Dorset Downs, offering far-reaching views into Somerset, which are best enjoyed from the front terrace on sunny days over a pint of Flowers

Original or Wadworth 6X. The pub offers a fairly standard bar menu.
Open *11 to 3.30, 6 to 11, Sun 12 to 2.30, 7 to 10.30*

CHERITON BISHOP
Devon   map 1
Old Thatch Inn
Cheriton Bishop EX6 6HJ
TEL: (01647) 24204
off A30, between Exeter and Okehampton, 6m SW of Crediton
This charmingly thatched sixteenth-century Grade II listed former coaching-inn serves a superior range of real ales from breweries such as Branscombe Vale, Princetown, Otter and Adnams, a straightforward bar menu, and a short, reasonably priced wine list.
Open *11.30 to 3, 6 to 11, Sun 12 to 3, 7 to 10.30*

CHIDDINGFOLD
Surrey   map 3
Crown Inn
The Green, Petworth Road, Chiddingfold GU8 4TX
TEL: (01428) 682255
on A283, 5m S of Milford
An inn of historical importance, dating back to 1285, this well-preserved timber-framed building has hosted many important visitors over the centuries. It is worth visiting for the wonderful décor alone, but you can enjoy the Hall & Woodhouse ales while you're there.
Open *11 to 11, Sun 12 to 10.30*

CHURCH HOUSES
North Yorkshire   map 9
Feversham Arms
Church Houses YO62 7LF
TEL: (01751) 433206
off A170, 7m N of Kirkbymoorside
A simple stone pub in the middle of nowhere, at the head of beautiful Farndale. Winding narrow lanes lead up the valley, presenting spectacular views, and there is the famous daffodil walk which attracts visitors in the spring. A homely main bar offers only

Tetley as refreshment, and a reasonably priced traditional bar menu.

Open *summer 10.30 to 3, 5.30 to 11, winter 12 to 2.30, 7 to 11*

CHURCHILL

N.W. Somerset   map 2

Crown Inn
The Batch, Churchill BS25 5PP
TEL: (01934) 852995
off A368, 3m S of Congresbury
Handy for the Wildlife Trust Reserve at Dolebury Warren, this little cottage pub on a hill at the foot of the Mendips serves its range of six to ten real ales straight from the cask. Bass apart, it concentrates admirably on regional independent brewers.

Open *Mon to Thur 11.30 to 3, 5.30 to 11, Fri and Sat 11 to 11, Sun 12 to 10.30*

COCKWOOD

Devon   map 1

Anchor
Cockwood EX6 8RA
TEL: (01626) 890203
off A379, on W side of River Exe estuary opposite Exmouth
The 200-yard trip from the mussel beds to the kitchen must be the only short thing about the Anchor. A lengthy wine list, fish cooked in a myriad of ways, including 12 ways with oysters and scallops and no fewer than 30 ways with mussels, leaves all others in the shade. Even treacle tart comes in more than one style.

Open *11 to 11, Sun 12 to 10.30*

CONDER GREEN

Lancashire   map 8

Stork Hotel
Conder Green LA2 0AN
TEL: (01524) 751234
This bird has worn a number of guises since 1660, when first reference to the alehouse is known. It does not take its name from its popularity with bird-watchers, visiting the nearly mudflats of the Lune Estuary, but rather from the coat of arms of the Starkies of Huntroyde, who acquired the local

estate in the 1880s. Traditional pub staples are on offer, plus daily specials and a children's menu. This is a good alehouse, favouring guest ales from small local breweries.

Open *11 to 11, Sun 12 to 10.30*

COOKHAM

Berkshire   map 3

Bel and the Dragon
High Street, Cookham SL6 9SO
TEL: (01628) 521263
on A4094, off A404 just N of Marlow
This fifteenth-century inn with wattle-and-daub walls takes its name from one of the books of the Apocrypha. It offers a modern, bistro-style menu with a wine list to match and beers from Brakspear and Marston's.

Open *summer 11 to 11, winter 11 to 3, 6 to 11*

CORFE CASTLE

Dorset   map 2

Fox Inn
West Street,
Corfe Castle BH20 5HD
TEL: (01929) 480449
An unpretentious, sixteenth-century village local, tucked away by the parish church, in this busy, touristy village noted for its castle ruins. The pub's main attractions are its sun-trap garden with apple trees and views of the castle, which make it an ideal place to sit and enjoy Gibbs Mew Bishop's Tipple, Greene King Abbot Ale, Hardy Royal Oak, Burton Ale and Wadworth 6X, all drawn directly from the cask.

Open *11 to 3 (2.30 in winter), 6.30 to 11, Sun 12 to 3, 7 to 10.30*

The Greyhound

The Square, Corfe Castle BH20 5EZ
TEL: (01929) 480205
on A351 in village centre
Originally two sixteenth-century
cottages plus the stables to the rear, this
historic old inn in a popular National
Trust village has a garden bordering the
moat of Castle Corfe and boasts fine
views of the Purbeck Hills. A lengthy
menu of chilli con carne, jumbo
haddock and fisherman's pie type fare
accompanies a brief selection of
Flowers Original, Boddingtons and
Poole Best Bitter.
Open *all week 11 to 11*

CORFTON

Shropshire   map 5

Sun Inn

Corfton SY7 9DF
TEL: (01584) 861239
on B4368, 4m E of Craven Arms
The pub has a constantly changing
range of around 150 real ales every
year which come exclusively from small
independent brewers, and they plan to
open their own Corvedale Brewery
later this year. Children are made very
welcome and have their own menu and
play area. The pub particularly stresses
its facilities for people with disabilities.
Open *11 to 2.30, 6 to 11, Sunday 12
to 3, 7 to 10.30, bank hol weekends 11
to 11*

COWBEECH

East Sussex   map 3

Merrie Harriers

Cowbeech BN27 4JQ
TEL: (01323) 833108
off A271, 4m NE of Hailsham
A straightforward white
weatherboarded pub in a growing
hamlet, the Merrie Harriers has a
slightly teashop air about it. A fairly
lengthy menu is on offer, and families
can enjoy the garden in summer.
Harveys Sussex Bitter is the only real
ale, but some acceptable wines are to
be found on the short list.
Open *11 to 2.30, 6 to 11, Sun 12 to 3,
7 to 10.30*

CRANBORNE

Dorset   map 2

Fleur de Lys

Wimborne Street,
Cranborne BH21 5PP
TEL: (01725) 517282
on B3078 in centre of Cranborne
This seventeenth-century inn is partly
hidden under a mass of ivy and
creepers. Famous guests have included
Hanging Judge Jeffreys, poet Rupert
Brooke (a verse he wrote here hangs
over the fireplace) and Thomas Hardy,
who visited whilst writing *Tess of the
D'Urbervilles*. Play shove ha'penny
while drinking Hall & Woodhouse
beers.
Open *11 to 3, 6.30 to 11, Sun 12 to 3,
7 to 10.30*

CRASTER

Northumberland   map 10

Jolly Fisherman

Craster NE66 3TR
TEL: (01665) 576218
off B1339, 6m NE of Alnwick
This harbourside pub offers incredibly
cheap snacks of the sandwich, soup and
burger variety. The selection of
seasonal beers includes Thorne Best
Bitter from Ward's, and guest beers
which change every six weeks.
Open *summer 11 to 11 (10.30 Sun),
winter 11 to 3, 6 to 11, Sun 12 to 3, 7
to 10.30*

CRAY

North Yorkshire   map 8

White Lion

Cray BD23 5JB
TEL: (01756) 760262
off B6160, 2m N of Buckden
A characterful stone-built former
drovers' inn, nestling beneath Buckden
Pike, 1,100 feet above sea level – the
highest pub in Wharfedale. It is
situated opposite a tumbling stream
and is very popular with walkers, who
can enjoy the game of ring the bull
while enjoying beers from Moorhouse
and the occasional pint of Rooster's.
Open *all week 11 to 11*

CROSCOMBE

Somerset   map 2

Bull Terrier

Croscombe BA5 3QJ
TEL: (01749) 343658
on A371, between Wells and Shepton Mallet
An historic old inn with accommodation, a variety of bars and a no-smoking family room. The pub recommends that you sharpen your appetite with a walk from the Bishop's Palace at Wells, after which you can tuck into hearty pub grub, or choose from an above-average range of vegan and vegetarian dishes.
Open *12 to 2.30, 7 to 11, Sun 12 to 2.30, 7 to 10.30*

DALWOOD

Devon   map 2

Tuckers Arms

Dalwood EX13 7EG
TEL: (01404) 881342
1m N of A35, between Honiton and Axminster
Dating back to the thirteenth century, this easy-to-miss, characterful longhouse has a thatched roof and a small 'court-yard' at the front. Service is friendly, and the massive collection of miniature spirits is impressive. Beers served are Flowers, and Otter Bitter and Ale.
Open *11 to 3, 6.30 to 11, Sun 12 to 3, 7 to 10.30*

DENT

Cumbria   map 8

Sun

Main Street, Dent LA10 5QL
TEL: (015396) 25208
in Dentdale, 4m SE of Sedbergh
Dent Brewery owns both the pubs in this chocolate box village. Martin Stafford ran the Sun before acquiring the George and Dragon just across the street. He also went on to set up Dent Brewery and Flying Firkin real ale wholesalers, who supply superb cask ales to several pubs in this guide, including the delightfully named Kamikaze Ale. A great village local with award-winning ales.
Open *11 to 11, Sun 12 to 10.30*

DITCHLING

East Sussex   map 3

Bull Hotel

2 High Street, Ditchling BN6 8TA
TEL: (01273) 843147
on B2112, midway between Haywards Heath and Brighton
Excellently kept beers, and a good number of them too, commend the Bull Hotel. It stands on the crossroads of this attractive village at the foot of the South Downs, full of antique shops and interesting old houses. A long, timbered bar with a traditional feel defines the ambience.
Open *11 to 11, Sun 12 to 10.30*

DOCKING

Norfolk   map 6

Pilgrims Reach

High Street, Docking
TEL: (01485) 518383
on B1153, 11m W of Fakenham
This solid building may lack decorative charm, but makes up with real warmth and a sincere welcome from the proprietors. Adnams provides the beers, while a standard bar menu is enhanced by blackboard specials which are strong on fish.
Open *12 to 2.30, 6 (7 winter) to 11 (11.30 Sat), Sun 12 to 3, 7 to 10.30*

DORCHESTER-ON-THAMES

Oxfordshire   map 2

George Hotel

25 High Street,
Dorchester-on-Thames OX10 7HH
TEL: (01865) 340404
on A423, 4m NW of Wallingford
This late-fifteenth-century coaching-inn with its timber-framed black and white structure, oak antiques, polished brass and interesting old prints and photos, has the potential to be a characterful English hostelry. Brakspear ales are on tap.
Open *11 to 11, Sun 11 to 10.30*

DORSTONE

Herefordshire   map 5

Pandy Inn

Dorstone HR3 6AN
TEL: (01981) 550273
*off B4348 Hay-on-Wye to Hereford
road, 5m E of Hay-on-Wye*
New owners took over just before the
Guide went to press – reports on the
new regime would be most welcome.
Dating from 1185, it was built to cater
for craftsmen building Dorstone
Church, and is surrounded by the
beautiful scenery of the Golden Valley.
Open *12 to 3, 7 to 11*

DREWSTEIGNTON

Devon   map 1

Drewe Arms

Drewsteignton EX6 6QN
TEL: (01647) 281224
2m S of A30, 8m W of Exeter
A long, low, thatched pub next to the
village church, separated from the road
by a small flower-covered wall. This
pub is famous as the house of Mable
Mudge, who, until she retired in 1994,
was Britain's oldest landlady. It is now
owned by Whitbread. An interesting
bar menu offers some idiosyncrasies
such as 'Devon Pork Tower', and the
brewery's beers are on tap.
Open *11 to 2.30, 6 to 11, Sun 12 to 3,
7 to 10.30*

EARL SOHAM

Suffolk   map 6

Victoria Inn

Earl Soham IP13 7RL
TEL: (01728) 685758
on A1120, 3m W of Framlingham
This pub is the brewery tap of the Earl
Soham brewery, which is on the
premises. Its beers include Victoria
Bitter, Albert Ale and Gannet Mild. A
menu of hearty, substantial pub grub is
also offered.
Open *11.30 to 3, 5.30 to 11, Sun 12
to 3, 7 to 10.30*

EAST BERGHOLT

Essex   map 3

Kings Head

Burnt Oak, East Bergholt CO7 6TL
TEL: (01206) 298190
off B1070, follow signs to Flatford Mill
Enjoying a picturesque setting in the
heart of Constable Country with a
lovely garden, this pub serves Greene
King IPA, Flowers Original, Wadworth
6X and guest from the Pubmaster
Tapster's Choice, which changes every
two weeks.
Open *12 to 3, 6.30 to 11, Sun 12 to 3,
7 to 10.30*

EASTBRIDGE

Suffolk   map 6

Eels Foot

Eastbridge IP16 4SN
TEL: (01728) 830154
off B1122, 2m N of Leiston
A twitchers' pub where you will find
both watchers and warders from
Minsmere RSPB Reserve swapping
stories with walkers and
holidaymakers. 'Adnamshire' this
certainly is, and the brewery's full
range is on tap, but there is also
Bateman's Dark Mild. The bar menu
offers standard pub fare.
Open *summer Mon to Fri 11 to 3, 6 to
11, Sat 11 to 11, Sun 12 to 10.30;
winter all week 11 to 3, 7 to 11 (10.30
Sun)*

EASTGATE

Norfolk   map 6

Ratcatchers Inn

Easton Way, Eastgate NR10 4HA
TEL: (01603) 871430
*10m NW of Norwich off B1149 Holt
road, 1m SE of Cawston*
Under new management since late
1998, this pub has a lengthy menu with
something for everyone – a
comprehensive list of interesting
vegetarian dishes, home-made pies,
fresh seafood, and curries and stir-fries.
There is also a 50-strong wine list, and
real ales from Adnams and Bass.
Reports please.
Open *12 to 2.30, 6 to 11, Sun 12 to 3,
7 to 10.30*

EAST HENDRED

Oxfordshire   map 2

Plough

Orchard Lane,
East Hendred OX12 8JW
TEL: (01235) 833213
*off A417 Wantage to Streatley road, 4m
E of Wantage*
A splendid rear garden, festooned with
flowers in summer, and offering a
football play area, makes this a popular
family attraction. The pub enjoys an
attractive village location and you will
find some good real ales from brewery
owners Morland.
Open *11 to 3, 6 to 11*

EAST ILSLEY

Berkshire   map 2

Crown & Horns

East Ilsley RG20 7LH
TEL: (01635) 281545
just off A34, 9m N of Newbury
Situated in the racing village of East
Ilsley and five minutes' walk from the
Ridgeway path, this pub offers a short
selection of wines and real ales from
the well-known regionals, and the
menu is full of tried-and-tested
favourites. It also has a skittle alley.
Open *11 to 11, Sun 12 to 10.30*

EAST KNOYLE

Wiltshire   map 2

Fox and Hounds

The Green, East Knoyle SP3 6BN
TEL: (01747) 830573
off A350, 5m N of Shaftesbury
A hard to find, good real ale pub that
started life in the late-fifteenth century
as a row of three cottages. This
attractive white-painted and thatched
pub enjoys a stunning setting with fine
views across the Blackmore Vale. No
fewer than six real ales are on at any
time, with Wadworth 6X, Fuller's
London Pride and Smiles Golden Bitter
on permanently.
Open *11 to 2.30, 6 to 11, Sun 12 to 3,
7 to 10.30*

EAST LYNG

Somerset   map 2

Rose & Crown

East Lyng TA3 5AU
TEL: (01823) 698235
on A361, 5m NE of Taunton
A white-painted front gives way at the
back to red brick and a lovely flower-
filled garden. This is a well-maintained
village pub, solid, comfortable and
spick-and-span. A massive inglenook
fills one wall and racing prints and
magazines set a rural tone in which to
enjoy simple pub food or Butcombe
Bitter.
Open *11 to 2.30, 6.30 to 11, Sun 12
to 3, 7 to 10.30*

EAST PRAWLE

Devon   map 1

Pig's Nose Inn

East Prawle TQ7 2BY
TEL: (01548) 511209
off A379, 1m NE of Prawle Point
This unusually named inn also shares
the distinction of being the most
southerly pub in Devon. Overlooking
Lannacombe Bay, it is popular with
walkers and bird-watchers, who can
add their own observations to the
landlord's 'bird log' over a pint of
Wadworth 6X.
Open *summer 11 to 3, 5 to 11, winter
12 to 2, 6 to 11*

EFFINGHAM

Surrey   map 3

Plough

Orestan Lane, Effingham KT24 5SW
TEL: (01372) 458121
*½m N of A246 Guildford to
Leatherhead road, signposted Effingham
junction*
This large white and red-brick pub
offers good-value, fresh food and good
ales in comfortable surroundings. Beers
are supplied by Young's of
Wandsworth and the menu offers
meals like potato soup, steak and
kidney pie or open smoked salmon and
prawn sandwiches.
Open *11 to 3, 6 to 11, Sun 12 to 3, 7
to 10.30*

EXTON

Rutland   map 6

Fox and Hounds

The Green, Exton LE15 8AP
TEL: (01572) 812403
2m off A606, between Stamford and
Oakham
This 300-year-old creeper-clad inn is
handy for Rutland Water. It serves
beers from Bateman's, Greene King,
Sam Smith's and Morland, and wines
from Eldridge Pope. Accommodation is
available and children are welcome.
Sunday lunch is a traditional roast.
Open *11 to 3, 6.30 to 11, Sun 12 to 3,*
7 to 10.30

FALSTONE

Northumberland   map 10

Blackcock Inn

Falstone NE48 1AA
TEL: (01434) 240200
off B3620, 8m W of Bellingham
This freehouse has been under new
ownership since summer 1998. Bar
food is traditional stuff, while the
restaurant menu looks promising, with
some interesting-sounding dishes and
good vegetarian options. Five real ales
are offered. Reports please.
Open *11 to 11*

FARTHINGSTONE

Northamptonshire   map 5

Kings Arms

Farthingstone NN12 8EZ
TEL: (01206) 822425
off A5, 5m SE of Daventry
The Kings Arms enjoys a village
location in peaceful countryside close
to the National Trust owned Canons
Ashby. It offers a friendly welcome and
a good range of well-kept real ales,
which, excepting Hook Norton Old
Hooky, vary regularly. Food service
was restricted as the *Guide* went to
press, but this may change. Reports
please.
Open *Sat and Sun 12 to 3, all week 7*
to 11

FEERING

Essex   map 3

Sun Inn

Feering, nr Witham CO5 9NH
TEL: (01376) 570442
off A12, 5m NE of Witham
Five handpumps and up to 20 different
ales per week make the Sun something
of a real ale Mecca. This historic
sixteenth-century mansion house insists
it is a pub which sells food, and it has a
wide repertoire of bar menu dishes
which rotate, including plenty of
home-made soups.
Open *11 to 3, 6 to 11*

FEN DRAYTON

Cambridgeshire   map 6

Three Tuns

High Street, Fen Drayton CB4 5SJ
TEL: (01954) 230242
off A14, 7m SE of Huntingdon, in
centre of village
This fifteenth-century building,
'modernised' in the late sixteenth
century, is believed to have originally
been the guildhall of this typical
Fenland village. These days it is a
Greene King pub, serving Abbot and
IPA as well as the brewery's new brew
Triumph. The interior contains lots of
dark beams, horse brasses and a stone
fireplace, and the whole effect is very
pleasing.
Open *11 to 2.30, 6.30 to 11, Sun 12*
to 2.30, 7 to 10.30

FITZHEAD

Somerset   map 2

Fitzhead Inn

Fitzhead TA4 3JP
TEL: (01823) 400667
off B3227, 2m N of Milverton
The archway to the side of the pub
gives the place a touch of the air of a
Caribbean buccaneers hideout at this
Somerset pub. Under new ownership
since mid-1998, it is still a bit of an
unknown quantity, but offers a
respectable range of West Country ales
from independent brewers. Reports
please.
Open *12 to 2.30, 7 to 11*

FOOLOW

Derbyshire   map 8

Bulls Head

Foolow S32 5QR
TEL: (01433) 630873
off A623 Chapel-en-le-Frith to
Chesterfield road, 3m E of Tideswell
This long, well-kept, white-painted inn
is tucked away in a beautiful moorland
village, opposite the duck pond. It
affords good views, is well placed for
walkers and, with accommodation, is a
good base from which to explore the
Peak District. Return to base to sample
a first-rate selection of real ales.
Open *Tue to Sat and bank hols 12 to*
2.30, 7 to 11, Sun 12 to 3

FORD

Gloucestershire   map 5

Plough Inn

Ford GL54 5RU
TEL: (01386) 584215
on B4077, 4m E of Winchcombe
Comfortable accommodation, a lengthy
menu and a relaxed, friendly atmosphere marks this solid, Cotswold-stone
pub as out of the ordinary. Under a
new licensee since October 1998, this
Donnington Brewery pub serves their
Best and Special. Reports please.
Open *11 to 11*

FORD

Wiltshire   map 2

White Hart

Ford SN14 8RP
TEL: (01249) 782213
on A420, 5m W of Chippenham
Situated by the Bybrook River, this
sixteenth-century pub is an
atmospheric and fairly slick operation.
It was recently taken over by Lionheart
Inns, and the new team's style has yet
to emerge. A range of major beer
brands like Bass, Marston's Pedigree,
Wadworth 6X and Fuller's London
Pride are served, as well as regional
brands like Smiles Bitter and Badger
Tanglefoot. Reports please.
Open *11 to 3, 5.30 to 11, Sun 12 to 3,*
7 to 10.30

FORDCOMBE

Kent   map 3

Chafford Arms

Spring Hill, Fordcombe TN3 0SA
TEL: (01892) 740267
on B2188, off A264 East Grinstead to
Tunbridge Wells road, 4m W of
Tunbridge Wells
A very imposing, tile-hung building
that is smothered in flowers, with
colour everywhere, all year round.
Catering for visitors to Hever Castle
and Penshurst Place, this pub has an
old-fashioned atmosphere. Larkins
Bitter, Bass and Chafford cider are
available to drink alongside a
comprehensive and reasonably priced
menu.
Open *11 to 2.30, 6.30 to 11, Sun 12*
to 4, 7 to 10.30

FORTY GREEN

Buckinghamshire   map 3

Royal Standard of England

Forty Green HP9 1XT
TEL: (01494) 673382
off B474 out of Beaconsfield at Knotty
Green
This 900-year-old inn, previously
called the Ship, was given its unique
name in 1660 by Charles II in gratitude
after it served as a Royalist head-
quarters during the civil war. It is also
the original home of Owd Roger (now
brewed by Marston's), a strong ale
whose recipe was handed down from
landlord to landlord for over 300
years.
Open *11 to 3, 5.30 to 11, Sun 12 to 3,*
7 to 10.30

FRISTON

Suffolk   map 6

Old Chequers

Aldeburgh Road, Friston IP17 1NP
TEL: (01728) 688270
just off B1121, 3m SE of Saxmundham
David Grimwood is still landlord,
although the pub has now been taken
over by the Old English Pub Company.
Adnams Best and Old (in winter) and
Greene King IPA are on offer for
drinkers, but food is the main business.
The emphasis is on lunch, a hot buffet

of seven dishes accompanied by seasonal vegetables, while dinner is a more formal affair. The wine list is the company standard. Reports please.

Open *11.30 to 2.30, 6.30 to 11, Sun 12 to 2, 8 to 10.30*

FULLER STREET

Essex   map 3

Square & Compasses

Fuller Street CM3 2BB
TEL: (01245) 361477
off A131 or A12, 5m W of Witham
A very rural pub in the centre of a small hamlet, so hard to find that you deserve a pint of Ridley's IPA or the guest ale on offer as a reward. Surrounded by fields, this pleasant pub has flower baskets and a rear garden and is popular with locals and ramblers. Hearty country cooking.

Open *11.30 to 3, 6.30 (7 winter) to 11, Sun 12 to 3, 6.30 to 10.30*

GARRIGILL

Cumbria   map 10

George & Dragon

Garrigill CA9 3DS
TEL: (01434) 381293
Originally serving the needs of the local zinc and lead miners, the George & Dragon now caters to the needs of walkers and visitors to the area, whether they come there to tackle Cross Fell (2,930ft) or the many castles, museums and tourist attractions in the area. Expect to find a simple bar menu and regularly changing beers.

Open *12 to 3 (4 winter), 6 (7 winter) to 11, Sun 12 to 3, 7 to 10.30*

GEDNEY

Lincolnshire   map 6

Old Black Lion

Chapelgate, Gedney PE12 0BJ
TEL: (01406) 363767
just off A17, 1m W of Long Sutton
A traditional bar menu with some modern touches like Cajun chicken and stuffed peppers is one of the reasons behind the popularity of this Fenland pub. Beers served include Draught Bass and changing guests.

Open *12 to 2.30, 7 to 11, Sun 12 to 3, 7 to 10.30*

GESTINGTHORPE

Essex   map 3

Pheasant

Gestingthorpe CO9 3AX
TEL: (01787) 461196
off B1058, from A131, 4m SW of Sudbury
Well-kept, interesting beers and a menu that includes some interesting-sounding dishes mark this out as a pub that has the right idea, Expect Pope's Traditional, Adnams Best, and Green King IPA or Abbot Ale.

Open *11 to 3, 6 to 11, Sun 12 to 3, 7 to 10.30*

GODALMING

Surrey   map 3

Ram Cider House

Catteshall Lane,
Godalming GU7 1LW
TEL: (01483) 421093
take Catteshall Road off A3100 Guildford to Godalming road, then second left after Farncombe boathouse; turn immediately right, then left
This sixteenth-century wattle-and-daub building of significant constructional technique sits in a peaceful hollow surrounded by an old English cider-apple orchard, with a stream flowing through it. It has an impressive range of some 30 different ciders, as well as three real ales. Food is of the baked potato, sandwich or ham and chips variety.

Open *11 to 11, Sun 12 to 10.30*

GODMANSTONE

Dorset   map 2

Smith's Arms

Godmanstone DT2 7AQ
TEL: (01300) 341236
on A352, 4m N of Dorchester
This converted fifteenth-century smithy is very probably England's smallest pub, and as such is a popular stop on the tourist route. Its size means there is only room for one ale, Ringwood Best. Long-standing landlord John Foster

retired shortly before the *Guide* went to press. Reports please.
Open *11 to 3, 6 to 11; closed Jan*

GRATELEY

Hampshire   map 2

Plough Inn

Grateley SP11 8JR
TEL: (01264) 889221
off B3084, 6m SW of Andover
'Chips with everything and very much in the realms of pub grub,' but the brownie points are won for the children's adventure area and a large family room overlooking the garden and play area.
Open *12 to 2.30, 6 to 11, Sun 12 to 3, 7 to 10.30*

GREAT BARRINGTON

Gloucestershire   map 5

Fox Inn

Great Barrington OX18 4TR
TEL: (01451) 844385
off A40, 3m W of Burford
The Fox stands on the banks of the River Windrush, and it is possible to sit outside and enjoy the views at all times thanks to newly fitted gas heaters in the garden. If it becomes too inclement, the skittles alley should provide sufficient diversion, as should the beers from the Donnington Brewery.
Open *11 to 11, Sun 12 to 10.30*

GREAT LANGDALE

Cumbria   map 8

Old Dungeon Ghyll Hotel

Great Langdale LA22 9JY
TEL: (015394) 37272
on B5343, 6m from Skelwith Bridge on A593
Set in truly impressive countryside, this is one of the highest pubs in the country, sitting at the foot of the dramatic Langdale Pike. Theakston Old Peculier, Yates Bitter and Jennings Bitter are on offer to accompany a bar menu that is hearty and sustaining.
Open *11 to 11, Sun 12 to 10.30*

GREAT OFFLEY

Hertfordshire   map 3

Green Man

Great Offley SG5 3AR
TEL: (01462) 768256
off A505, midway between Luton and Hitchin
An attractive, child-friendly Chef & Brewer pub, dating from the sixteenth century. Recent refurbishment has made more space for eating – just as well, as it tends to get packed, especially at weekends. The quality of the food has improved of late, even if the selection of beers is rather dull. The house speciality is the 'hot hob' – half a baguette with a choice of fillings, served with chips.
Open *11 to 11, Sun 12 to 10.30*

GUNNISLAKE

Cornwall   map 1

Rising Sun

Calstock Road,
Gunnislake PL18 9BX
TEL: (01822) 832201
just off A390, between Tavistock and Callington
A splendid little pub dating from the seventeenth century; all higgledy-piggledy, with terraced gardens and small rooms opening off each other, decorated with a collection of chamber pots hanging from the ceiling and a range of eclectic clutter. Beers are a pull here, in particular Cornish beers like St Austell Tinners, Sharp's Cornish Coaster and Skinner's, as well as interlopers like Otter and Bass.
Open *11 to 3, 5 to 11, Sun 12 to 3, 7 to 10.30*

HALSTEAD

Leicestershire   map 5

Salisbury Arms

Oakham Road, Halstead LE7 9DJ
TEL: (01162) 597333
off B6047, 8m S of Melton Mowbray
An isolated rural pub extended during the summer months and Christmas period with huge marquees to house the wedding parties and conferences that they clearly set out to attract. The

'Tilton Hilton', as the pub is styled, serves Bass and Adnams Broadside.

Open *Tue to Sat 11.30 to 3, 6.30 to 11, Sun 12 to 3*

HAPPISBURGH

Norfolk   map 6

Hill House

Happisburgh NR12 0PW
TEL: (01692) 650004
on B1159, 6m E of North Walsham
A white-fronted, oddly handsome pub with a walled garden at the rear, offering views of the church steeple. Scott's Blues & Bloater and Shepherd Neame Spitfire are regular cast members to support cameo appearances by guest ales. The pub has a simple bar menu and a more extensive separate restaurant menu.

Open *Mon to Fri 12 to 2.30, 7 to 11 (all day in summer), Sat 12 to 11, Sun 12 to 10.30*

HARBERTON

Devon   map 1

Church House Inn

Harberton TQ9 7SF
TEL: (01803) 863707
off A381 Totnes to Kingsbridge road, 2½m S of Totnes
Built around 1100 to house masons working on the church next door, the inn then became a Chantry House for monks. It then remained a church-owned property until 1950, when a fine medieval oak screen was uncovered as well as other original features. There is an exciting range of beers and the pub's Portuguese chef frequently injects his native cuisine into the menu.

Open *12 to 3, 6 to 11, Sun 12 to 3.30, 7 to 10.30*

HARRIETSHAM

Kent   map 3

Ringlestone Inn

Ringlestone Road,
Harrietsham ME17 1EX
TEL: (01622) 859900
off A20, 3m NE of Harrietsham, take B2163 N signposted Sittingbourne, turn right towards Doddington at crossroads by water-tower after Hollingbourne
A sixteenth-century former monks' hospice which became an alehouse after the Reformation. Beer is still a serious matter at this popular pub, which is likely to be very busy. Casks behind the bar dispense Ringlestone Bitter, Marston's Pedigree and Adnams, among others.

Open *12 to 3, 6 to 11, Sun 12 to 3, 7 to 10.30 (Sat and Sun 11 to 11 25 Dec)*

HARRINGWORTH

Northamptonshire   map 6

White Swan

Seaton Road,
Harringworth NN17 3AT
TEL: (01572) 747543
off B672, 6m N of Corby
An attractive stone inn in a picturesque village in the Welland Valley, this pub is a handy B&B and stopping-off point for Rockingham Castle, Kirby Hall and the historic towns of Uppingham and Oakham. The neighbourhood also offers good local walks through Rockingham Forest and the Welland Valley.

Open *11.30 to 2.30, 6.30 to 11, Sun 12 to 3, 7 to 10.30*

HARTFIELD

East Sussex   map 3

Anchor Inn

Church Street, Hartfield TN7 4AG
TEL: (01892) 770424
village on junction of B2026 and B2110, 6m SE of East Grinstead
This mock Tudor pub on a hill, near the village church, offers a first-rate selection of ales, including Harveys Best, Fuller's London Pride, Bass and Wadworth 6X, as well as a respectably short menu, which includes some nice touches like omelette Arnold Bennett and Californian grilled cod.

Open *11 to 11, Sun 12 to 10.30*

HASCOMBE

Surrey   map 3

White Horse

Hascombe GU8 4JA
TEL: (01483) 208258
on B2130, 3m SE of Godalming
Handy for the National Trust
Arboretum at Winkworth, this busy pub
serves well-prepared pub food along the
lines of potato skins, jacket potato with
chilli, and gammon, pineapple and
chips. A good wine list makes up for a
rather dull selection of real ales.
Open *Mon to Fri 11 to 3, 5.30 to 11,
Sat 11 to 11, Sun 12 to 10.30*

HEATH

West Yorkshire   map 9

Kings Arms

Heath Common, Heath WF1 5SL
TEL: (01924) 377527
*from A638 between Wakefield and
Crofton take A655, then turning to
Heath and Kirkthorpe*
Built in the early 1700s and set in 100
acres of commom grassland, the Kings
Arms became a pub in 1841. A pint of
Clark's Bitter or Timothy Taylor
Landlord is a worthy reward for a brisk
walk across the heath.
Open *11.30 to 3, 5.30 to 11, Sun 12
to 10.30*

HEBDEN BRIDGE

West Yorkshire   map 8

Hare and Hounds

Hebden Bridge HX7 8TN
TEL: (01422) 842671
*off A6033 Hebden Bridge to Keighley
road at Pecket Well, signposted Old
Town, then 1m*
Notable for its spectacular views and
the full range of Timothy Taylor beers
in tip-top condition, this simple but
friendly rural village local offers basic
Yorkshire fare of the shepherd's pie
and filled Yorkshire pudding variety.
No food is available on Monday and
Tuesday.
Open *summer Wed to Sun 12 to 2, all
week 7 to 11, winter Fri to Sun 12 to 2,
7 to 11*

HELFORD

Cornwall   map 1

Shipwrights Arms

Helford TR12 6JX
TEL: (01326) 231235
*take A3038 from Helston towards
Lizard, join B3293 for Coverack, turn
left for St Martin's and follow signs for
Helford*
Situated on the south side of the River
Helford, the pub is well known for its
attractive setting, child-friendly
atmosphere and riverbank moorings
which make it a popular place to tie up
for a while and enjoy a pint of Castle
Eden or Flowers IPA. Note no food is
served Monday evenings.
Open *11 to 2.30, 6 to 11 (10.30 in
winter), Sun 12 to 2.30, 7 to 10.30*

HELSTON

Cornwall   map 1

Blue Anchor

50 Coinagehall Street,
Helston TR13 8EX
TEL: (01326) 562821
off A394, 15m SW of Truro
A pub spoken of in hushed tones by ale
lovers, being perhaps the oldest pub in
Britain to brew its own beer. It dates
back to the early fifteenth century,
when it was a monks' rest home, and
became a tavern when the monasteries
were dissolved. Over the centuries it
has served a variety of clientele, from
the local gentry to tin miners.
Open *11 to 11, Sun 12 to 10.30*

HERMITAGE

West Sussex   map 3

Sussex Brewery

36 Main Road,
Hermitage PO10 8AU
TEL: (01243) 371533
on A259, just out of Emsworth towards Chichester
Known as the sausage pub, this inn offers a variety of platters combining a huge selection of 'gourmet' sausages, from ostrich to Moroccan lamb, from Aberdeen beef to pork and apricot, all washed down with ales from Hall & Woodhouse, Timothy Taylor, Young's and guests.
Open *11 (11.30 Sun) to 12 (1 Thur to Sat)*

HOFF

Cumbria   map 10

New Inn

Hoff CA16 6TA
TEL: (017683) 51317
B6260, 2m S of Appleby
A reliable family pub that draws lots of locals. Much of the cooking is good home-produced stuff – ham salad, Cumberland sausage and the like – with consistently huge portions. It is run by Angela Taylor and her two grown-up children, who create a relaxed atmosphere, and they will be happy to serve you a pint of Black Sheep Bitter or Tetley.
Open *summer 12 to 3, 6 to 11, winter Sun to Thur 12 to 2, 7 to 11, Fri and Sat 12 to 2, 6 to 11*

HOLBETON

Devon   map 1

Mildmay Colours

Holbeton PL8 1NA
TEL: (01752) 830248
off A379 Plymouth to Modbury road, 1m after National Shire Horse Centre, signposted Mothecombe and Holbeton
Built as a local manor-house in 1617, this pub has a very horsey theme, though the inspiration is National Hunt, rather than the National Shire Horse Centre, which is nearby. The menu of pub staples is divided into racing-themed sections, and the house beer is sold alongside a guest ale.
Open *11 to 3, 6 to 11*

HOLYPORT

Berkshire   map 3

Belgian Arms

Holyport SL6 2JR
TEL: (01628) 634468
off M4, 2m S of Maidenhead
Located in a little lane off the village green, this attractive village local was known as the Eagle until German prisoners held nearby during World War I took to saluting the pub sign. It is a friendly local pub, especially useful as a staging-post for travellers on the M4.
Open *Mon to Fri 11 to 3, 5.30 to 11, Sat 11 to 3, 6 (7 in winter) to 11, Sun 12 to 3, 7 to 10.30*

HOLYWELL

Cambridgeshire   map 6

Old Ferry Boat Inn

Holywell PE17 3TG
TEL: (01480) 463227
off A1123, 2m E of St Ives
A contender for the much disputed title 'England's Oldest Inn'; records indicate that liquor was first served here in AD 560. It grew up on the site of an important river crossing and still has the right to run a ferry, but prefers instead to sell guest ales from the major regionals and offer a short, modern pub menu.
Open *11 to 3, 6 to 11, Sun 11 to 3, 7 to 10.30*

HOOK NORTON

Oxfordshire   map 5

Pear Tree

Scotland End,
Hook Norton OX15 5NU
TEL: (01608) 737482
off A361, 5m NE of Chipping Norton
Very much the brewery tap of the Hook Norton Brewery and a good place to sample all five of its beers after a brewery visit. Bar food includes soups with crusty bread, jacket potatoes and the house special Hooky casserole (beef

cooked in their own ale), but the ales are the main attraction.

Open *11.30 to 3, 6 to 11, Sat 11 to 11, Sun 12 to 4, 7 to 10.30*

HOPE

Derbyshire   map 8

Poachers Arms

Castleton Road, Hope S30 2RD
TEL: (01433) 620380

on A625, between Chapel-en-le-Frith and Hathersage

Along with a standard selection of ales, a lengthy and interesting bar snacks menu is the draw here, ranging from a half-pint of prawns to walnut and spinach canelloni, or rabbit casserole. There are also standard dishes like gammon and eggs, plus more unusual ones like tortellini pugliese.

Open *12 to 3.30, 6 to 11, Sun 12 to 3, 7 to 10.30*

HORSEBRIDGE

Devon   map 1

Royal Inn

Horsebridge PL19 8PJ
TEL: (01822) 870214

off A384, 5m W of Tavistock

This 500-year-old inn is home to the Horsebridge Brewery, which turns out Tanner, Heller and Right Royal for consumption in the bar, along with some guests. The wine list includes plenty of country wines from Moorland. The bar menu offers chilli cheese tortillas and cod and chips type fare. Children are welcome at lunchtime only.

Open *11.30 (12 in winter) to 3, 6 (7 in winter) to 11, Sun 12 to 3, 7 to 10.30*

HORSEY

Norfolk   map 6

Nelson Head

Beach Road, Horsey NR29 4AD
TEL: (01493) 393378

off B1159, 9m NE of Acle

Unpretentious 400-year-old pub tucked down a narrow lane near the coast, an ideal retreat for walkers and bird-watchers exploring the windswept delights of Horsey Mere and the North Norfolk footpath. Two neat bars serve Woodforde's ales for supping in front of the fire.

Open *11 to 2.30, 6 (7 winter) to 11, Sun 12 to 3, 7 to 10.30*

HUNDON

Suffolk   map 6

Plough Inn

Hundon CO10 8DT
TEL: (01440) 786789

off A143, 2m N of Haverhill, take right turn to Kedington, then 1m towards Hundon

The Plough enjoys pleasant sweeping views across gently rolling downs from its hilltop location, and offers warm, comfortable accommodation and cosy bars in which to enjoy Greene King Abbott Ale and Adnams Bitter, plus weekly guest beers.

Open *summer 11 to 3, 5 to 11, Sun 12 to 3, 7 to 10.30, winter 12 to 2.30, 6 to 11, Sun 12 to 3, 7 to 10.30*

HURLEY

Berkshire   map 2

Dew Drop

Batts Green, Hurley SL6 6RB
TEL: (01628) 824327

take Honey Lane off A423, a little outside Hurley between Maidenhead and Henley-on-Thames, continue past council houses and through farm until wood, turn right at T-junction on to smaller lane; inn is a few hundred yards on right

A rustic-looking Brakspear inn with outside tables serving the full range of the brewery's ales, and simple pub staples of sandwiches, ploughman's and jacket potatoes. More substantial dishes are steaks, venison casserole, chicken tikka masala, or rabbit and gammon pie in winter, salmon and asparagus quiche in summer.

Open *12 to 3, 6 to 11, Sun 12 to 3, 7 to 10.30*

ICKLESHAM

East Sussex   map 3

Queens Head

Parsonage Lane,
Icklesham TN36 4BL
TEL: (01424) 814552
*just off A259 Hastings to Rye road, 2m
W of Winchelsea*
Built in 1632, the pub is pretty difficult
to miss since 'Queens Head' is picked
out in slates on the roof. It serves an
impressive range of real ales, focusing
mainly on local(ish) independents such
as Old Forge, Swale, Rother Valley and
Woodforde's, all accompanied by a
snacks and steaks type menu.
Open *summer 11 to 3, 6 to 11, winter
12 to 5, 7 to 10.30*

INGLEBY

Derbyshire   map 5

John Thompson

Ingleby DE73 1HW
TEL: (01332) 862469
off A514, 3m NW of Melbourne
Named after its landlord of 30 years'
standing, who also brews his own beers
on the premises, this pub offers good
home-cooked food in simple, pubby
surroundings. The roast beef and
Yorkshire pud comes in for frequent
praise.
Open *10.30 to 2.30, 7 to 11, Sun 12
to 2.30, 7 to 10.30*

INGS

Cumbria   map 9

Watermill

Ings LA8 9PY
TEL: (01539) 821309
just off A591, 2m E of Windermere
No juke box, pool table or fruit
machines at this attractive stone pub,
covered in red creeper on one side. In
addition to good home-cooking, the
pub offers Theakston Best and Old
Peculier, Coniston Bluebird, Black
Sheep Special, Jennings Cumberland
and Lees Moonraker all the time, and
guests such as Dent, Moorhouse's, Hop
Back, Hesket Newmarket, Kelham
Island and many others.
Open *12 to 2.30, 6 to 11, Sun 12 to 3,
7 to 10.30*

INKBERROW

Worcestershire   map 5

Old Bull

Inkberrow WR7 4DZ
TEL: (01386) 792428
*off A422, Worcester to Stratford-upon-
Avon road, 5m W of Alcester*
Wadworth 6X, Flowers Original and
Boddingtons are served here, but you
almost might expect to get a pint of
Shires, for this ramshackle half-
timbered pub is also known as the Bull,
home of Sid and Kathy Perks in *The
Archers*. You might be joined by
members of the cast enjoying dishes
from a short blackboard selection.
Open *11 to 11*

KELD

North Yorkshire   map 8

Tan Hill Inn

Keld DL11 6EP
TEL: (01833) 628246
off B6270 at Keld, then 4m N
Famous as the highest inn in the UK,
this pub on the Pennine Way offers a
welcome break for walkers. Countless
stories tell of people being snowed in
for days, and of guests holding the beer
lines in their hands to thaw them. Black
Sheep and Theakston ales and basic
sustaining food are offered. The pub
has no mains electricity and relies on a
generator for power.
Open *all week 11 to 11 (may close
early in winter)*

KERSEY

Suffolk   map 6

Bell Inn

The Street, Kersey IP7 6DY
TEL: (01473) 823229
1m W of A1141, 2m NW of Hadleigh
It may be seafood week when you drop
in to the Bell Inn, so try lobster bisque
or green-lip mussels. If not, try spring
lamb samosa with mango chutney, or
deep-fried goujons of plaice,
accompanied by Shepherd Neame
Spitfire or Charles Wells Bombardier.
Open *summer 11 to 11, Sun 12 to 5, 7
to 10.30, winter 11 to 3, 7 to 11, Sun
12 to 5, 7 to 10.30*

KINGSAND

Cornwall   map 1

Halfway House Inn

Fore Street, Kingsand,
Cawsand PL10 1NA
TEL: (01752) 822279
just off B3247 at Cawsand Bay, 1m SE of Millbrook
Situated on the Cornwall coastal path, just 30 yards from the beach, this pub specialises in fish dishes with some interesting wines, and a bar menu offering deep-fried whitebait, grilled sardines and fishy dailies all washed down with Sharp's Doom Bar as well as Bass, Boddingtons and Flowers.
Open *12 to 3, 7 to 11 (10.30 Sun)*

KINGSBRIDGE

Devon   map 1

Crabshell Inn

Embankment Road,
Kingsbridge TQ7 1JZ
TEL: (01548) 852345
off A381, 8m SW of Totnes
The Crabshell was built as a watering-hole for the sailors that moored at the quayside and is older than it looks. There is still free mooring for customers and al fresco diners can take advantage of the estuary views. Menus are, unsurprisingly, fishy, and in addition to an extensive wine list the pub serves Bass, Flowers IPA and the pub's own house ale.
Open *11 to 11*

KNIPTON

Leicestershire   map 5

Red House

Croxton Road, Knipton NG32 1RH
TEL: (01476) 870352
off A607, 6m SW of Grantham
The Red House has been taken over by new owners who plan to invest heavily in refurbishment. The pub is situated on the Belvoir Castle estate, owned by the Duke of Rutland, and initial indications are that things under the new regime are moving rapidly in the right direction. A more aristocratic approach to the ales would also help. Reports please.
Open *summer 11 to 11, Sun 7 to 10.30, winter 11.30 to 3 (exc Wed), 6 to 11, Sun 7 to 10.30*

LACOCK

Wiltshire   map 2

Red Lion

1 High Street, Lacock SN15 2LQ
TEL: (01249) 730456
on A350, 3m S of Chippenham
This Wadworth pub is a large red-brick building dominating the end of the main street of this beautiful National Trust-owned village of medieval cottages. Offering real fires and real ales, friendly service and an 'olde English' ambience, it has almost all the elements for a great English pub.
Open *11.30 (12 Sun) to 11*

LANGLEY

Cheshire   map 8

Leather's Smithy

Clarke Lane, Langley SK11 0NE
TEL: (01260) 252313
off A523, 2m SE of Macclesfield, 1¼m from village towards Macclesfield Forest
Formerly a smithy owned by William Leather, who gained a licence in 1821, it overlooks Rudgegate Reservoir and is popular with walkers and fishermen attracted by the beautiful surrounding countryside. Other attractions are whiskies and real ales like Banks's Bitter, Morrell's Varsity, Camerons Strongarm and Marston's Pedigree.
Open *12 to 3, 7 to 11, Sun 12 to 10.30*

LANREATH

Cornwall   map 1

Punch Bowl Inn

Lanreath PL13 2NX
TEL: (01503) 220218
off B3359, 5m NW of Looe
Change is in the air at this pub with accommodation: a new restaurant is scheduled for April 1999 and a new bar menu was under wraps as we went to press. The 'new' regime (since 1996) is clearly keen to make improvements and, with Bass and Sharp's Doom Bar on the bar counter, is building on a solid foundation. Reports please.
Open *summer 11 to 11 (10.30 Sun), winter 12 to 3, 6.30 to 11 (10.30 Sun)*

LAPWORTH

Warwickshire   map 5

Navigation Inn
Old Warwick Road,
Lapworth BN4 6NA
TEL: (01564) 783337
on B4439, 1m SE of Hockley Heath
Creeper-clad pub dating from the mid-
eighteenth century. An excellent
position by the Grand Union Canal
makes it popular in summer, when the
splendid back terrace and canalside
garden provide ideal venues for things
artistic, including jazz, Morris dancing
and theatre.
Open *11 to 2.30, 5.30 to 11, Sun 12
to 11.30*

LINWOOD

Hampshire   map 2

High Corner Inn
Linwood
TEL: (01425) 473973
off A338/A371, 7m NE of Ringwood
Set in seven acres of secluded
woodland in the heart of the New
Forest, this early eighteenth-century
inn is reached at the end of a long
gravel track. Offering accommodation,
as well as ales from the Hampshire
Brewery, Wadworth 6X and Fuller's
London Pride, the inn is a good place
to get away from it all.
Open *summer 11 to 11, winter 11.30
to 2.30, 7 to 10.30 (6.30 to 11 Fri), Sat
and Sun 11 to 11*

LITTLE HADHAM

Hertfordshire   map 3

Nags Head
The Ford, Little Hadham SG11 2AX
TEL: (01279) 771555
*between B1004 and A120, 3m W of
Bishop's Stortford*
Cottage-style pub with a superior
selection of fish dishes. As well as
interesting wines, it offers the full
range of brewery owner Greene King's
ales, including XX Dark Mild, IPA and
Abbot Ale, as well as the seasonal
specials.
Open *11 to 2.30, 6 to 11, Sun 12 to 3,
7 to 10.30*

LITTLE HAMPDEN

Buckinghamshire   map 3

Rising Sun
Little Hampden HP16 9PS
TEL: (01494) 488393
*from Great Missenden take road
signposted Rignall and Butler's Cross;
after 2m take turn marked 'Little
Hampden only'*
Expect to find several pairs of muddy
walking boots outside the front door of
this popular walkers' pub. Blackboard
menus list the day's offerings in the
bar, and there is a separate restaurant
for more formal occasions. Beers from
Adnams, Brakspear and Marston's can
be enjoyed in the garden on sunny
days.
Open *Tue to Sat 11.30 to 3, 6.30 to
11, Sun 12 to 3*

LITTLEHEMPSTON

Devon   map 1

Tally Ho!
Littlehempston TQ9 6NF
TEL: (01803) 862316
off A381, 2m NE of Totnes
A long, dark, atmospheric fourteenth-
century pub with rooms, serving brews
from the Teignworthy and Dartmoor
breweries in front of the fire in winter,
and on the patio in summer. It also
offers an extensive bar menu, with
desserts chalked up on 'Naughty Boards'.
Open *12 to 3, 6 to 11, Sun 12 to 3, 7
to 10.30*

LITTLE LONGSTONE

Derbyshire   map 8

Packhorse Inn
Little Longstone DE45 1NN
TEL: (01629) 640471
off B6465, 2m NW of Bakewell
Built in the sixteenth century as a
miner's cottage before becoming an inn
in 1787, this unspoilt stone-built village
local is set in the heart of the Peak
District National Park. It has long been
a favourite of walkers trekking the
Monsal Trail. Full of old-fashioned
charm, it has a rustic taproom and new
tenants have done little to alter its
traditional atmosphere. Marston's
beers are on offer.

Open *11 to 3.30 (2.30 in winter), 5 to 11, Sun 12 to 3, 7 to 10.30*

LITTLE STRETTON

Shropshire   map 5

Ragleth Inn

Ludlow Road,
Little Stretton SY6 6RB
TEL: (01694) 722711
on B4370, off A49, just SW of Church Stretton
The Ragleth, built in 1663, nestles at the foot of the Long Mynd Mountain in a well-maintained village near Shrewsbury. Traditional food in a traditional setting is the aim, so no surprises on the menu, just good home-cooked fare supported by a decent wine list and beers from Hobsons of Kidderminster, Theakston and Morland.
Open *12 to 2.30 (3 Sat), 6 to 11, Sun 12 to 10.30*

LLANYBLODWEL

Shropshire   map 5

Horseshoe

Llanyblodwel SY10 8NQ
TEL: (01691) 828969
just off B4396, 5m SW of Oswestry
A tiny pub with a roadside/riverside setting, offering views of hillsides rising up behind the river. Inside, a darkish atmosphere prevails owing to the blackened beams and unusually low ceilings, but the general air is friendly. There is a long, ambitious menu, and beers come from Marston's and Banks's.
Open *11.30 to 3, 6.30 to 11*

LONG PRESTON

North Yorkshire   map 8

Maypole Inn

Long Preston BD23 4PH
TEL: (01729) 840219
on A65 Skipton to Settle road
No prizes for guessing where the name comes from – the maypole in question stands on the village green in front of this handsome pub, which was first licensed in 1695. Good ales on offer include Alesman from the Worth brewery, and an extensive, interesting

bar menu is backed up with daily specials.
Open *Mon to Fri 11 to 3, 6 to 11, Sat 11 to 11, Sun 12 to 10.30*

LOW CATTON

East Riding of Yorkshire   map 9

Gold Cup

Low Catton YO41 1EA
TEL: (01759) 371354
off A166, just S of Stamford Bridge
Ryedale Vintners of Malton supply a value-for-money selection of wines, and the bar menu may start with chicken drumsticks and follow with ham salad, sirloin steak, breaded scampi, or roast beef and Yorkshire pudding. Puddings might include banoffi pie, or lemon roulade, and Tetley and John Smith's are available on the beer front.
Open *12 to 2.30 (not Mon), Sat and Sun 12 to 11 (10.30 Sun)*

LOWER ASHTON

Devon   map 1

Manor Inn

Lower Ashton EX6 7QL
TEL: (01647) 252304
from A38 S of Exeter, take B3193 towards Christow, signposted on right after 5m
Ales from some of the best West Country independent brewers, like Princetown, RCH and Teignworthy are the big pull at this freehouse, which has racked up well over one thousand guest ales in its lifetime. Local farm cider is also on offer, and there are always plenty of choices on the blackboard menus, including at least three vegetarian options.
Open *Tue to Fri and bank hol Mons 12 to 2.30, 6 to 11, Sat 12 to 2.30, 7 to 11, Sun 12 to 2.30, 7 to 10.30*

LOWER PEOVER

Cheshire   map 7

Bells of Peover
The Cobbles,
Lower Peover WA16 9PZ
Tel: (01565) 722269
on B5081, 6m E of Northwich
The bar is the core of the operation at
this pretty pub in the heart of the
Cheshire stockbroker belt, but the
crowds also come for the food. With its
roaring fire and informal dining area,
this is a typically English pub serving
well-kept Greenalls ales.
Open *Mon to Fri 11.30 to 3, 5.30 to
11, Sat 11 to 11, Sun 12 to 10.30*

LOWICK

Northamptonshire   map 6

Snooty Fox
Main Street, Lowick NN14 3BS
Tel: (01832) 733434
just off A6116, 2m NW of Thrapston
A typical east Northamptonshire stone
pub with ancient tiled roof and solid
appearance. It displays its wares on a
series of blackboards surrounding the
stone fireplace with its wood-burning
grate. Basic pub fare such as filled
baguettes, lasagne, duck in orange
glaze, and the obligatory steaks, are
accompanied by ales from Adnams,
Everards, Woods and Batemans, and
there is a rotating guest. Champagne
and six other wines are available by the
glass from the list.
Open *12 to 3, 6.30 to 11, Sun 12 to 3,
6.30 to 10.30*

LOW NEWTON-BY-THE-SEA

Northumberland   map 10

Ship
Low Newton-by-the-Sea NE66 3EL
Tel: (01665) 576262
off B1340, 2m N of Embleton
This is still an honest-to-goodness local
pub-cum-village shop in a National
Trust-owned row of cottages, in a small
town by the sea. New owners were
taking over as the *Guide* went to press.
Reports please.
Open *11 to 11, Sun 12 to 3, 7 to
10.30 (Sun 12 to 10.30)*

LUGWARDINE

Herefordshire   map 5

Crown & Anchor
Cotts Lane, Lugwardine HR1 4AB
Tel: (01432) 851303
off A438, 3m E of Hereford
A nice, traditional, old-fashioned pub,
with unpretentious décor in a rabbit
warren of rooms and a very impressive
giant hearth with log fire. There is a
well-tended little patio garden and the
overall effect is one of an unspoilt pub.
Simple pub cooking is on offer.
Open *11.30 to 11, Sun 12 to 10.30*

LYNMOUTH

Devon   map 1

Rising Sun Hotel
Harbourside, Lynmouth EX35 6EQ
Tel: (01598) 753223
on A39, 9m W of Porlock
A prime setting by the harbour in this
Devon fishing village is one of the main
attractions for visitors to this thatched,
fourteenth-century smugglers' inn. It
has bedrooms, good ales, above-
average wines by the glass, reasonably
priced and modern bar food and a
short but confident restaurant menu.
Open *summer 11 to 3, 5.30 to 11, Sun
12 to 2, 6 to 10.30, winter 11 to 2.30,
6.30 to 11, Sun 12 to 2, 6.30 to 10.30*

MALHAM

North Yorkshire   map 8

Buck Inn
Malham BD23 4DA
Tel: (01729) 830317
off A65, 5m E of Settle
At the centre of the village, this
handsome, red, ivy-clad stone inn is a
family-run affair offering
accommodation as well as a lengthy
menu of hearty grub, with plenty of
choices of pâtés, steaks, fish dishes and,
in particular, pasta, rice and vegetarian
dishes. It also serves the big three
Yorkshire brews – Theakston, Black
Sheep and Timothy Taylor Landlord.
Open *summer 11 to 11, Sun 12 to
10.30, winter 11 to 3, 6 to 11, Sun 12
to 10.30*

MARSWORTH

Buckinghamshire   map 3

Red Lion

90 Vicarage Road,
Marsworth HP23 4LU
TEL: (01296) 668366
off B489, 2m N of Tring
A popular waterside pub situated by
Bridge 130 on the Grand Union Canal,
with a clientele made up of narrowboat
enthusiasts plus walkers and bird-
watchers drawn by nearby Tring
Reservoir. The pub supplements
Fuller's London Pride and Tetley with
guests and its own house bitter, and
offers hearty pub fare.
Open *Mon to Fri 11 to 3, 6 to 11, Sat
11 to 11, Sun 12 to 10.30*

MARTYR'S GREEN

Surrey   map 3

Black Swan

Old Lane,
Martyr's Green KT11 1NG
TEL: (01932) 862364
off M25 and A3, 2m SW of Cobham
This creeper-clad brick-built pub is
popularly known as the 'mucky duck'
(see the alternative pub sign for an
explanation), and it can be found on a
country crossroads between Ockham
and Cobham. Popular with families and
walkers, it serves no fewer than 14 real
ales all year and food is available all
day. Check out the big butty board.
Open *11 to 11, Sun 12 to 10.30*

MATFEN

Northumberland   map 10

Black Bull

Matfen NE20 0RP
TEL: (01661) 886330
off A68 or B3618, 5m NE of Corbridge
Having been head chef at the Black
Bull for ten years, Clive Wood has now
completely taken over the food side of
things at this 200-year-old stone pub.
The bar menu still has a traditional
feel, while the restaurant menu shows
ambitions. Drink Theakston beers.
Reports please.
Open *Mon to Fri 11 to 3, 6 to 11, Sat
and Sun 12 to 11*

MAYFIELD

East Sussex   map 3

Rose & Crown Inn

Fletching Street,
Mayfield TN20 6TE
TEL: (01435) 872200
This pretty, white, weatherboarded inn
with a sizeable front terrace started life
as a coaching-inn in the sixteenth
century. It serves Harveys Best, Greene
King Abbot Ale and Morland Old
Speckled Hen, and offers a short wine
list. Bar food might be grilled goats'
cheese or scallop and saffron mousse,
followed by roast chump of lamb or
pan-fried fillet of salmon. New owners
in 1998, so more reports please.
Open *11 to 3, 5.30 to 11, Sun 12 to 3,
7 to 10.30*

MEAVY

Devon   map 1

Royal Oak Inn

Meavy PL20 6PJ
TEL: (01822) 852944
*off A386/B3212 at Yelverton, SW of
Burrator Reservoir*
This parish council-owned pub offers
beers ranging from Cornish Rebellion
Bitter to draught Bass, a wine list from
ever expanding drink wholesalers Beer
Seller, and a moderately priced menu
that is strong on chilli, fish pies and
lasagne type dishes, with daily specials
in a similar vein.
Open *11.30 to 3, 6.30 to 11, Sun 12
to 3, 7 to 10.30*

MENITHWOOD

Worcestershire   map 5

Cross Keys

Menithwood WR6 6UB
TEL: (01584) 881425
*between A443 Tenbury Wells to
Worcester road and B4202 Clows Top
to Abberley road*
The Cross Keys claims to be the 'best
pub in Menithwood', but how many
competitors does it have? Possibly not
many, but it does have a reputation for
good hot and cold sandwiches, washed
down with Marston's beers and guests.
Open *Mon to Fri 11 to 3, 6 to 11, Sat
11 to 11, Sun 12 to 3, 7 to 10.30*

MEYSEY HAMPTON

Gloucestershire   map 2

Masons Arms

High Street,
Meysey Hampton GL7 5JT
TEL: (01285) 850164
off A417, 1½m W of Fairford
This seventeenth-century inn with
accommodation is situated on the
southern edge of the Cotswolds, just
beside the village green. A good
selection of real ales with frequently
changing guests is backed up by a menu
which shows promise in the form of
spicy turkey goujons, hot Cajun
chicken salad, pork medallions, herb
trout and above-average vegetarian
options.
Open *11.30 to 3 (2.30 winter), 6 to
11, Sun 12 to 4, 7 to 10.30*

MICHELDEVER

Hampshire   map 2

Dever Arms

Winchester Road,
Micheldever SO21 3DG
TEL: (01962) 774339
off A33, 6m N of Winchester
A child-friendly Marston's pub serving
Best and Pedigree as well as the Head
Brewer's Choice range of ales, which
changes fortnightly. An interesting
blackboard menu might offer quail's
egg salad, mussels, pork in Dijon
mustard, chicken in white wine, and
rice-pudding.
Open *12 to 3, 6 to 11, Sun 12 to 3, 7
to 10.30*

MILTON BRYAN

Bedfordshire   map 3

Red Lion

South End,
Milton Bryan MK17 9HS
TEL: (01525) 210044
An attractive brick-built pub tucked
away in a peaceful old village close to
Woburn Abbey and its safari park. It
offers a welcoming, relaxing and
spotlessly maintained interior, with
large rugs on the modern floors and a
mix of sturdy furnishings, with plenty
of beams and exposed brickwork. This

Marston's pub offers a range of that
brewery's beers.
Open *11 to 3 (4 Sat), 6 to 11, Sun 12
to 4, 7 to 11*

MORWENSTOW

Cornwall   map 1

Bush Inn

Morwenstow EX23 9SR
TEL: (01288) 331242
*3m W of A39, between Bude and
Clovelly, 6m N of Bude*
In winter Morwenstow feels about as
remote as you can get, but visitors
come in summer to see the village's
Celtic fort and the National Trust's
smallest property, Hawker's Hut. The
Bush is one of Britain's oldest pubs,
with parts dating back to AD 950 when
it is thought to have been a chapel for Celtic
hermits. Today it is similarly no-frills,
with heavy beams, rough stone floors
and log-burning fires.
Open *12 to 3, 7 to 11*

MUCH WENLOCK

Shropshire   map 5

George & Dragon

2 High Street,
Much Wenlock TF13 6AA
TEL: (01952) 727312
*on A458, between Shrewsbury and
Bridgnorth, 8m NW of Bridgnorth*
Under new ownership since summer
1998, the George & Dragon promises
change more than anything. Licensee
Barry Blakeman sounds enterprising
and is full of ideas. One to watch.
Open *12 to 2.30, 6 to 11, Sun 12 to
2.30, 7 to 10.30*

Talbot Inn

High Street,
Much Wenlock TF13 6AA
TEL: (01952) 727077
This half-timbered pub has been an inn
since 1360, and James II stayed here in
1687. It offers much more history
besides, as well as an extensive menu of
traditional pub fare, and opens early
for morning coffee.
Open *9 to 3, 6.15 to 11 (10 winter),
Sun 12 to 2, 7 to 10.30*

NAUNTON

Gloucestershire   map 5

Black Horse

Naunton GL54 3AD
TEL: (01451) 850565
off B4068, 5m W of Stow-on-the-Wold
Another pub in new hands, the Black
Horse shows promising signs in a menu
that takes in home-made celery and
Stilton soup, rollmop herring, and
traditional main courses, with extra
specials like fresh fillet of salmon in
saffron sauce. Beers from owners
Donnington brewery, and a very
reasonably priced New World wine list,
may excite your curiosity. Reports
please.
Open *11.30 to 3, 6 to 11, Sun 12 to 3,
7 to 10.30*

NEAR SAWREY

Cumbria   map 8

Tower Bank Arms

Near Sawrey LA22 0LF
TEL: (015394) 36334
on B5285, 2m SE of Hawkshead
The Tower Bank is the small country
inn that appears in Beatrix Potter's *The
Tale of Jemima Puddleduck*, and it can
be found next door to Hill Top, her
former home. The inn owns fishing
rights on local lakes and is a superb
outdoor activities pub. Good northern
beers such as Theakston and Coniston,
plus guests and a selection of superior
Belgian bottled beers, and a hearty
menu mark this out as worth a visit.
Open *11 to 3, 5.30 (6 winter) to 11,
Sun 12 to 3, 7 to 10.30*

NESSCLIFFE

Shropshire   map 7

Old Three Pigeons

Nesscliffe SY4 1DB
TEL: (01743) 741279
on A5, 8m NW of Shrewsbury
This ancient, low-beamed pub, dating
from 1405, offers a regularly changing
seasonal menu that focuses on fish and
local produce. Beers change every
week, so you will never find the same
selection twice.
Open *11 to 3, 5 (6 winter) to 11*

NETHER HEAGE

Derbyshire   map 7

Spanker Inn

20 Spanker Lane,
Nether Heage DE56 2AT
TEL: (01773) 853222
off A6, 3m W of Ripley
An unusual-looking pub built of large
stone blocks and half-timbering just
below the eaves. Wednesday night is
steak night and at other times a carvery
operates, as well as a lunch menu
offering traditional pub grub and old-
fashioned puddings like sherry trifle
gâteau. Vaux Samson is the only real
ale available.
Open *11 to 3.30, 7 (6 Wed) to 11, Sun
12 to 3.30, 7 to 10.30*

NEWTON

Cambridgeshire   map 6

Queens Head

Newton CB2 5PG
TEL: (01223) 870436
on B1368, 6m S of Cambridge
Landlord David Short has been at the
Queens Head since 1962 and has built
up a solid business offering Adnams
ales, winter beers in season and a
simple menu of sandwiches and soup of
the day. This must be one of very few
pubs where you can get toast with beef
dripping.
Open *11.30 to 2.30, 6 to 11, Sun 12
to 2, 7 to 10.30*

NORTH WOOTTON

Dorset   map 2

Three Elms

North Wootton DT9 5JW
TEL: (01935) 812881
*on A3030 Sherborne to Sturminster
Newton road, 2m SE of Sherborne*
A pretty stone pub enjoying a lofty
setting with fine views over the
Blackhorse Vale. It offers a fine range
of ales with regularly changing guests
and a cheerfully cluttered interior fully
adorned with pumpclips of previous
guest ales and a collection of over
1,000 Matchbox model cars, all neatly
arranged in wall cabinets.
Open *11 to 2.30, 6.30 (6 Fri and Sat)
to 11, Sun 12 to 3, 7 to 10.30*

NUNNEY

Somerset   map 2

George

11 Church Street,
Nunney BA11 4LW
TEL: (01373) 836458
off A361, 2m SW of Frome
A seventeenth-century coaching-inn
made notorious by Hanging Judge
Jeffreys, who used a room at the
George as a courthouse for his Bloody
Assizes, when the condemned were
taken out and hanged in the pub
garden. Today the only thing hanging
is likely to be game, though the pub
menu primarily concentrates on fish
dishes.
Open *11.30 to 4, 6 to 11, Sun 12.30
to 4, 6.30 to 10.30*

OMBERSLEY

Worcestershire   map 5

Crown & Sandys Arms

Ombersley WR9 0EW
TEL: (01905) 620252
*off A449 Worcester to Kidderminster
road, 4m W of Droitwich*
Remodeled in 1810 by the
Marchioness of Downshire, to give it a
striking and unique appearance, this
seventeenth-century pub appears much
older inside than out. Enjoy a
characteristic fireside seat as well as a
changing range of draught ales,
primarily from West Country
independent brewers, and a wine list by
Tanners.
Open *10.30 to 3, 5.30 to 11, Sun 12
to 3, 7 to 10.30*

ONECOTE

Staffordshire   map 5

Jervis Arms

Onecote ST13 7RU
TEL: (01538) 304206
*on B5053, 1m off A523 Leek to
Ashbourne road, 4m E of Leek*
A simple, tidy, cream-painted
seventeenth-century inn on the banks
of the River Hamps in the Peak
District, offering a riverside beer
garden, and family rooms. A fairly
plain menu has something for
everyone, and two weekly-changing

guest ales complement regulars like
Bass, Pedigree and Stones Bitter.
Open *11 to 3, 7 (6 Sat) to 11, Sun 12
to 10.30*

ORFORD

Suffolk   map 6

Jolly Sailor

Quay Street, Orford IP12 2NU
TEL: (01394) 450243
on B1084, 9m E of Woodbridge
An unassuming Adnams pub, once
popular with smugglers. The usual
range of the brewery's beers are on
offer along with its seasonal ales. A
short bar menu features local fish and
chips, alongside other pub food staples.
The bar has no facilities for children.
Open *11.30 to 2.30, 7 to 11, Sun 12
to 2.45, 7 to 10.30*

OSWALDKIRK

North Yorkshire   map 9

Malt Shovel

Oswaldkirk Y06 5XT
TEL: (01439) 788461
on B1363, 4m S of Helmsley
A substantial seventeenth-century stone
village pub worth seeking out for its
characterful interior and superbly kept
Samuel Smith's OBB. Close to the
Yorkshire moors, the building has been
in its time a manor-house, a busy
coaching-inn and latterly a Grade II
listed property. The Hambleton Hills,
Ampleforth College, Nunnington Hall
and Rievaulx Abbey are nearby.
Open *11.30 to 3, 6.30 to 11, Sun 12
to 10.30*

OVING

West Sussex   map 3

Gribble Inn

Gribble Lane, Oving PO20 6BP
TEL: (01243) 786893
off A259, 4m E of Chichester
Home of the Gribble Brewery since
1987, the pub has been taken over by
Hall & Woodhouse but still continues
to sell the full range of seven Gribble
Ales. This rose-covered pub is a pretty
but unusual combination of red brick

and thatch and offers a confident and competent modern pub menu.

Open *summer 11 to 11, Sun 12 to 3, 7 to 10.30, winter 11 to 3, 5 to 11, Sun 12 to 3, 7 to 10.30*

OWSLEBURY

Hampshire   map 2

Ship Inn
Owslebury SO21 1LT
TEL: (01962) 777358
off A33/A272, 4m S of Winchester
This thatched village pub is owned by Marston's and offers the brewery's usual range of ales plus a guest which changes every two weeks, but also an extensive and ambitious menu.

Open *11 to 3, 6 to 11 (Sat 11 to 11 in summer), Sun 12 to 10.30*

PAGLESHAM

Essex   map 3

Plough & Sail
East End, Paglesham SS4 2EQ
TEL: (01702) 258242
off B1013, 4m E of Rochford
Fish predominates on the menu at this 400-year-old weatherboarded pub, which has been run by the Oliver family for over 35 years. Oysters are still on the menu, though they no longer come from the local beds, but from nearby West Mersea instead. The beer range has expanded to include Flowers IPA, Morland Old Speckled Hen, and a guest beer – perhaps Charles Wells Bombardier or Fuller's London Pride.

Open *11.30 to 2.30, 7 to 11, Sun 12 to 3, 7 to 10.30*

PEACEMARSH

Dorset   map 2

Dolphin Inn
Peacemarsh SP8 4HB
TEL: (01747) 822758
on B3092, N of Gillingham
This Hall & Woodhouse pub opposite the fire station offers the brewery's usual beers, as well as dishes such as fanned avocado with bacon and melted Camembert, peacemaker pie and Tanglefoot pudding.

Open *11 to 3, 6 to 11, Sun 12 to 4, 6 to 10.30*

PELDON

Essex   map 3

Peldon Rose
Mersea Road, Peldon CO55 7QJ
TEL: (01206) 735248
off B1025, 5m S of Colchester
This large 600-year-old half-timbered inn is ideally suited for visitors to the many wildlife sites in the area, which include Cudmore Country Park and Ray Island. A range of guest beers as well as regular Adnams, Wadworth 6X and Flowers IPA will quench the thirst of walkers, bird-watchers and fishermen.

Open *11 to 3, 5.30 to 11, Sun 12 to 3, 7 to 10.30 (all day summer)*

PELYNT

Cornwall   map 1

Jubilee Inn
Pelynt PL13 2JZ
TEL: (01503) 220312
on B3359, 3m NW of Looe
Formerly the Axe, this pub had a name change in 1887 to celebrate Queen Victoria's Golden Jubilee. This sixteenth-century pub offers food and accommodation in very handsome surroundings, as well as Bass and St Austell Trelawney's Pride.

Open *Mon to Fri 11 to 3, 6 to 11, Sat 11 to 11, Sun 12 to 10.30*

PENELWEY

Cornwall   map 1

Punch Bowl & Ladle

Penelewey TR3 6QY
TEL: (01872) 862237
*on B3249 (off A39 at Playing Place),
3m S of Truro*
The Punch Bowl is a cream-painted,
thatched and much extended roadside
pub with lots of standing timbers
within. The mood is set by low
lighting, various cosy rooms filled with
well-stuffed sofas, armchairs, books
piled on windowsills, knick-knacks and
farm implements. This Greenalls pub
serves Bass, Sharp's Doom Bar, Flowers
Original and Tetley.
Open *11 to 3, 5.30 to 11, Sun 12 to 3,
6 to 10.30*

PHILLACK

Cornwall   map 1

Bucket of Blood Inn

Phillack TR27 5AE
TEL: (01736) 752378
off A30, across the canal, N of Hayle
It is worth a visit just to discover the
origins of the legend behind this St
Austell pub's gory name, but also worth
visiting to meet Rose Shackleton, who
has run it since 1972. Drinkers are
offered cask ciders as well as cask ales,
and a menu (plus specials board) that
always includes at least two curries and
four vegetarian options.
Open *11 to 2.30 (3 Sat), 6 to 11, Sun
12 to 4, 7 to 10.30*

PHILLEIGH

Cornwall   map 1

Roseland Inn

Philleigh TR2 5NB
TEL: (01872) 580254
off B3289, 4m NE of St Mawes
This white, pebbledash, cottagey pub
has a narrow garden at the front and
real log fires inside, plus friendly staff
creating a very welcoming atmosphere.
It is all rounded off with a selection of
beers like Sharp's Doom Bar, Morland
Old Speckled Hen, Bass and Marston's
Pedigree.
Open *summer 11 to 11, winter 11 to
3, 6 to 11*

PIERCEBRIDGE

Co Durham   map 10

George Hotel

Piercebridge DL2 3SW
TEL: (01325) 374576
just off A67, 5m W of Darlington
An old coaching-inn set on the banks of
the River Tees and famous for the
Grandfather Clock that 'stopped short,
never to go again when the old man
died'. Very well appointed with a
thriving function business. Black Sheep
Bitter and Theakston Black Bull are on
draught and a good range of pubby
food is available.
Open *11 to 11*

PILLATON

Cornwall   map 1

Weary Friar

Pillaton PL12 6QS
TEL: (01579) 350238
*2m W of A38, between Saltash and
Callington*
This twelfth-century inn lies next to the
church of St Odolphus in typically
Cornish countryside. Dartmoor,
Bodmin Moor and the delights of
Cornwall and Devon are all accessible
from the Weary Friar, and the weary
traveller will be happy to find
refreshment in Dartmoor Best Bitter,
Greene King Abbot Ale and Butcombe
Bitter.
Open *12 to 11, Sun 12 to 10.30*

PILSLEY

Derbyshire   map 8

Devonshire Arms

Pilsley DE45 1UL
TEL: (01246) 583258
off B6048, 2m NE of Bakewell
Owned by the Chatsworth estate, and
only a mile from Chatsworth House,
this seventeenth-century inn is notable
for its good-quality beers from
Batemans, Mansfield and others, and
for a good local atmosphere. If you are
the energetic sort, put your boots on
for the landlord's walk, which takes in
a host of local attractions.
Open *11.30 to 3, 7 to 11*

PIN MILL

Suffolk   map 6

Butt & Oyster

Pin Mill IP9 1JW
TEL: (01473) 780764
off B1456, 5m SE of Ipswich
Tolly Cobbold beers, and plenty of
them, are kept by Dick and Brenda
Mainwaring, who have run the Butt &
Oyster for over 15 years. They have
made it a very popular site, taking
advantage of its views over the Orwell
Estuary. The nautical feel of the scenes
below are replicated in the bar, which
is decorated with modern ships and
maritime photographs.
Open *summer 11 to 11, Sun 12 to
10.30, winter Mon to Fri 11 to 3, 7 to
11, Sat 11 to 11, Sun 12 to 10.30*

PITTINGTON

Co Durham   map 10

Blacksmiths Arms

Low Pittington DH6 1BJ
TEL: 0191 3720287
off A1(M)/A690, 4m NE of Durham
Situated on the edge of a site of special
scientific interest, this characterful pub
is popular with lovers of the outdoor
life. A variety of guest ales are offered
and the bar menu of pub staples is very
good value.
Open *12 to 11, Sun 12 to 3, 7 to
10.30*

PITTON

Wiltshire   map 2

Silver Plough

White Hill, Pitton SP5 1DU
TEL: (01722) 712266
on A30, 5m E of Salisbury
Now owned by Woodhouse Inns, this
striking pub in a delightful village
setting, offers a good range of bar food
from soup to glazed breast of duck,
plus sandwiches, ploughman's and
omelettes. A range of English fruit
wines is available by the glass.
Open *11 to 3, 6 to 11, Sun 12 to 3, 7
to 10.30*

PLUMLEY

Cheshire   map 7

Smoker

Plumley WA16 0TY
TEL: (01565) 722338
off A556, 3m SW of Knutsford
'This inn was privileged to serve the
subjects of Queen Elizabeth I and is still
open,' proclaims the pub's literature.
Near to the National Trust's Tatton
Park, it has a traditional interior with
lots of copper and brass, oak panelling
and real flowers, and serves a menu of
contemporary British pub food.
Open *11 to 3, 5.30 to 11, Sun 12 to 3,
7 to 10.30*

POLPERRO

Cornwall   map 1

Blue Peter

The Quay, Polperro PL13 2QZ
TEL: (01503) 272743
on A387, 3m SW of Looe
There is no food on offer at the Blue
Peter, which is a solid drinking pub,
but customers can bring in their own
cold food, including shellfish bought
from the stalls on the quay outside. 'A
super pub with a smashing
atmosphere'. Well-kept beers come
from St Austell and Sharp's breweries,
with plenty of guests.
Open *11 to 11, Sun 12 to 10.30*

POSTBRIDGE

Devon   map 1

Warren House Inn

Postbridge PL20 6TA
TEL: (01822) 880208
*on B3212, between Postbridge and
Moretonhampstead*
Wonderful views over Dartmoor are
the draw here. A new restaurant was
under construction as the *Guide* went
to press, so we shall watch with interest
to see how the changes affect the bar
food. The pub serves Butcombe Bitter,
Tanglefoot and Bishop's Tipple.
Reports please.
Open *summer 11 to 11, Sun 12 to
10.30, winter Mon to Fri 11 to 3, Sat
11 to 11, Sun 12 to 10.30*

POYNINGS

West Sussex   map 3

Royal Oak Inn

The Street, Poynings BN45 7AQ
TEL: (01273) 857389
off A281, 6m NW of Brighton
Under the same ownership as the Bull
Hotel at Ditchling (see Out and About
entry), this very square, white building
with trailing plants offers a varying
range of beers, perhaps including Bass
and Morland Old Speckled Hen, plus a
bar menu of things like bangers and
mash and Scotch fillet steak, with
simple daily specials like grilled lemon
sole and pork loin steaks in mustard.
Open *11 to 11, Sun 12 to 10.30*

RAMSBURY

Wiltshire   map 2

Bell

The Square, Ramsbury SN8 2PE
TEL: (01672) 520230
off A4192, 6m E of Marlborough
Set in a charming village, the Bell came
under new ownership in September
1998, and seemed to be shifting the
emphasis of its food operation towards
the restaurant. The bar menu is a short
selection of sandwiches and
ploughman's, with one or two more
substantial dishes like pie of the day,
while the restaurant menu is modern
'bistro' style. A broad range of regional
real ales should appeal to all.
Open *12 to 3, 6 to 11, Sun 12 to 3, 7
to 10.30*

REEDHAM

Norfolk   map 6

Reedham Ferry Inn

Reedham NR13 3HA
TEL: (01493) 700429
off B1140, 6m S of Acle
The Archer family have run this
Norfolk Broads pub for 50 years,
operating a winning formula of
offering East Anglian ales such as
Adnams and Woodforde's, plus one
local mild. This seventeenth-century
building next to the chain ferry over
the River Yare is handy for the

Strumpshaw bird sanctuary and the
Steam Engine Collection.
Open *11 to 3, 6.30 (7 winter) to 11,
Sun 12 to 10.30*

RIBCHESTER

Lancashire   map 8

White Bull

Church Street, Ribchester PR3 3XP
TEL: (01254) 878303
on B6245, 5m N of Blackburn
A pillared stone building with a horse
mounting block out front, the
eighteenth-century White Bull in the
heart of the Ribble Valley is a useful
resting place for those visiting the
Roman museum or ancient bath house
in the village. This Whitbread pub sells
the brewery's usual ale portfolio and a
bar menu of pubby food.
Open *11.30 to 3, 6.30 to 11, Sun 12
to 10.30*

RINGMER

East Sussex   map 3

Cock Inn

Uckfield Road, Ringmer BN8 5EX
TEL: (01273) 812040
just off A26, 2m NE of Lewes
An unpretentious country house which
is comfortable and welcoming, offering
eating in the simple bar and rooms
beyond, or outside where there are an
enormous number of tables. The menu
has been described as a 'long, eclectic
set of Euro nosh and trad English'; a
good range of beers from Harveys, plus
Flowers Original and Marston's
Pedigree, completes the picture.
Open *11 to 3, 6 to 11, Sun 12 to 3, 7
to 10.30*

RINGSTEAD

Norfolk   map 6

Gin Trap Inn

High Street, Ringstead PE36 5JU
TEL: (01485) 525264
off A149, 2m E of Hunstanton
Enjoying a peaceful village setting, this
attractive seventeenth-century
coaching-inn is a popular destination
for holidaymakers staying at nearby
Hunstanton and a welcome watering-

hole for hikers trudging the Peddar's Way. The pub serves Adnams and Woodforde's ales, while the menu takes dishes like lasagne, ham and gammon and gives them a variety of treatments.

Open *11.30 to 2.30, 6.30 (7 in winter) to 11, Sun 11.30 to 2.30, 7 to 10.30*

ROBIN HOOD'S BAY

North Yorkshire   map 9

Laurel Inn

New Road,
Robin Hood's Bay YO22 4SE
TEL: (01947) 880400
at end of B1447 (off A171), 5m SE of Whitby
Set in a lovely village of red-roofed cottages and whitewashed houses which tumble down to the sea at Robin Hood's Bay, this tiny pub is a good spot to enjoy a pint of Marston's or Theakston Old Peculier over a game of dominoes, darts or cribbage. An interesting feature is the bar, which is carved from solid rock.

Open *12 to 11, Sun 12 to 10.30*

ROKE

Oxfordshire   map 2

Home Sweet Home

Roke OX10 6JD
TEL: (01491) 838249
signposted 'Home Sweet Home' off B4009, between Benson and Watlington
A partly thatched pub in a pretty row of former cottages dating from the sixteenth century. Inside, there is a good beamed bar with a central open fireplace, standing timbers, armchairs and sofas. While the choice of real ales is short, the number of dishes on the menu is huge.

Open *11 to 3, 6 to 11, Sun 11 to 3*

ROMALDKIRK

Co Durham   map 10

Kirk Inn

Romaldkirk DL12 9ED
TEL: (01833) 650260
Once upon a time there were thousands of pubs like this: tiny, one-room affairs, offering a small selection of local ales – though usually from just one brewery rather than the several supported here. The pub is a focus for the community, doubling as the local post office by day, and offering quizzes every fortnight, as well as a substantial menu.

Open *12 to 2.30, 6 to 11, Sun 12 to 3, 7 to 10.30; closed Mon and Tue L in winter*

ROTHERWICK

Hampshire   map 2

Coach and Horses

The Street, Rotherwick RG27 9BG
TEL: (01256) 762542
off B3349/A30/A33, 2m NW of Hook
This 300-year-old building was one of Hall & Woodhouse's first Hampshire acquisitions. A good range of real ales is on offer, including Badger Tanglefoot, Dorset Best and IPA, Gribbles, Black Adder, Reg's Tipple and Dick Turpin's ales. A basic pub menu offers baguettes, baked potatoes, soups and more substantial dishes such as grilled steaks, gammon and chicken.

Open *11 to 11, Sun 12 to10.30*

ROTHWELL

Lincolnshire   map 9

Nickerson Arms

Rothwell LN7 6AZ
TEL: (01472) 371300
off B1225, 2m SE of Caister
Well off the beaten track in a sleepy little hamlet, this long, low pub 'of indeterminate age' has an old-fashioned feel to it, though extensions have been added over the years. A straightforward menu is enhanced by some interesting dishes, with a 'carvery' Sunday lunch. Drink Batemans XXXB, Mansfield Riding or Marston's Pedigree.

Open *12 to 3, 7 to 11, Sun 12 to 3, 7 to 10.30*

RYE

East Sussex   map 3
Mermaid Inn
Mermaid Street, Rye TN31 7EY
TEL: (01797) 223065
This historic inn claims to date back to
1156, and was once a popular haunt of
smugglers. Beams, open fires, and
leaded windows mean it really looks
the part. Marston's Pedigree, Morland
Old Speckled Hen and John Smith's
are served in the bar.
Open *11 to 11, Sun 12 to 10.30*

ST AGNES

Isles of Scilly   map 1
Turk's Head
St Agnes TR22 0PL
TEL: (01720) 422434
*take boat or helicopter from Penzance
to St Mary's, then boat to St Agnes*
This nineteenth-century slate-roofed
cottage is decorated in a maritime
theme, reflecting its location
overlooking the harbour on this tiny
island, which is very popular with
wildlife watchers. The bar lunch menu
offers light meals, sandwiches and
jacket potatoes, while dinner is more
substantial pub fare. One room is
available for guests.
Open *11 to 11, Sun 12 to 10.30*

ST BREWARD

Cornwall   map 1
Old Inn
St Breward PL30 4PP
TEL: (01208) 850711
off B3266, 4m S of Camelford
The highest inn in Cornwall is a
handsome whitewashed building next
to the village church. Apart from
Ruddles County and Bass, they serve
Sharp's Doom Bar and Special from the
local independent brewery, as well as
an interesting and thoughtful wine list
and confident and varied menu. **Open**
12 to 3, 6 (7 Sun) to 11

ST EWE

Cornwall   map 1
Crown Inn
St Ewe PL26 6EY
TEL: (01726) 843322
*between B3287 and B3273, 5m SW of
St Austell*
A charmingly flower-festooned pub
with hydrangeas and climbing roses in
the borders and geraniums in the
hanging baskets on the first floor; it
also boasts a pretty sheltered garden. A
St Austell brewery pub, it serves its
range of ales as well as a bar menu of
pub staples.
Open *11 to 3 (2.30 in winter), 6 to 11,
Sun 12 to 2.30, 7 to 10.30*

ST JUST

Cornwall   map 1
Star Inn
Fore Street, St Just TR19 7LL
TEL: (01736) 788767
on A3071/B3306, 4m N of Land's End
'A great pub', serving good Tinners ale
from casks behind the bar. The pub is
always full of genuine locals in a
relatively tourist-free spot, and it has a
lively atmosphere. It serves real cider in
the summer and a pasty and sandwich
menu all year round.
Open *summer 11 to 11, Sun 12 to
10.30, winter Mon to Thur 11 to 3, Fri
and Sat 11 to 11, Sun 12 to 10.30*

SAPPERTON

Gloucestershire   map 4
Daneway Inn
Sapperton GL7 6LN
TEL: (01285) 760297
off A419, 5m W of Cirencester
This whitewashed, rural-looking pub is
a Wadworth managed house and offers
the brewery's beers plus Adnams Bitter.
The bar menu features a special hot
bap plate, popular with walkers, as well
as things like Cumberland sausage,
gammon steaks, chicken tikka masala
and some good vegetarian options.
Open *summer 11 to 2.30 (5 Sat), 6.30
to 11, Sun 12 to 5, 7 to 10.30, winter
Mon to Fri 11 to 2.30, 6.30 to 11, Sat
11 to 3, Sun 12 to 3*

SCAWTON

North Yorkshire   map 9

Hare Inn

Scawton YO7 2HG
TEL: (01845) 597289
off A170, 4m W of Helmsley
Graham Raine and Heather Jones took
over this cluttered, eccentric, cottagey
pub in late 1998. Blackboard menus
suspended over a wood-burning stove
show promise, with a range of
ambitious and interesting options, such
as crab pasty, or roast pork knuckle
with spiced baked apple. Black Sheep,
Timothy Taylor Landlord and Vaux
Sampson are on tap. Reports please.
Open *Tue to Sun 12 to 3, Mon to Sat
6.30 to 11*

SCOLE

Norfolk   map 6

Scole Inn

Norwich Road, Scole IP21 4DR
TEL: (01379) 740481
on A140, 2m E of Diss
A wonderfully atmospheric Grade I
listed building full of authentic
features, the Scole Inn was built in
1655 as a coaching-inn. It was famous
for its sign, the largest in England,
which extended right across the street.
Modern cooking and daily specials
complement the Adnams Bitter.
Open *11 to 11, Sun 12 to 10.30*

SEEND CLEEVE

Wiltshire   map 2

Barge Inn

Seend Cleeve SN12 6QB
TEL: (01380) 828230
*between A361 and A365, 5m W of
Devizes*
An eccentric canalside pub which takes
the 'rose and castle' style of
narrowboat decoration and crosses it
with a healthy strain of Romany Gypsy.
Dishes on the menu take their name
from waterway life, and the large
garden/mooring area means the pub
will get busy in summer.
Open *11 to 2.30, 6 to 11, Sun 11 to 4,
6 to 10.30*

SHAMLEY GREEN

Surrey   map 3

Red Lion Inn

Shamley Green GU5 0UB
TEL: (01483) 892202
on B2128, 4m SE of Guildford
A neat, white-painted pub opposite the
village green. A range of approved ales
from the Pubmaster list are served in
the bar – Young's Bitter, Flowers
Original and Greene King Abbott Ale –
and the wine list has expanded.
Separate bar and restaurant menus
operate, the former strong on
toasties/sandwiches, 'jackets' and
salads. The restaurant menu shows
traditional influences.
Open *all week 11 to 11*

SHARDLOW

Derbyshire   map 5

Malt Shovel

The Wharf, Shardlow DE72 2HG
TEL: (01332) 799763
off A6, 6m SE of Derby
Plagued by a mischief-making ghost
named Humphrey, this converted
malthouse on the Trent & Mersey
canal is a popular and lively spot
during summer. It plays host to a canal
theatre company and jazz bands who
entertain the boaters, walkers, cyclists
and families stopping for a pint or two
of Marston's ales.
Open *11 to 11, Sun 12 to 4, 7 to
10.30*

SHAVE CROSS

Dorset   map 2

Shave Cross Inn

Shave Cross DT6 6HW
TEL: (01308) 868358
*off B3165, in Marshwood Vale, 5m NW
of Bridport*
This fourteenth-century cob-and-flint-
built inn was reputedly the last staging-
post on the pilgrim route to the shrine
of St Witta at Whitchurch Canon-
icorum. The name comes from the fact
that monks would have their tonsures
shaved here. The pub serves good West
County ales and, in summer, local
cider.
Open *Tue to Sun and bank hols 12 to
3 (2.30 winter), 7 to 11*

SHEEPSCOMBE

Gloucestershire   map 2

Butchers Arms

Sheepscombe GL6 7RH
TEL: (01452) 812113
*off A46 Cheltenham to Stroud road, 2m
E of Painswick*
Set in the heart of *Cider with Rosie*
country, the Butchers Arms, dating
from around 1670, is on National
Trust land in the middle of the
stunning, rolling Stroud Valley. The
bar serves above-average ales – Hook
Norton Best, Archers Best and Uley
Old Spot – as well as an interesting bar
menu, including such dishes as
ratatouille taco shells, and smoky pork
pot casserole, and offers a wine list that
includes several English Country
Wines.
Open *11 to 3 (2.30 in winter), 6 (6.30
in winter) to 11, Sun 12 to 3, 7 to
10.30*

SHENINGTON

Oxfordshire   map 5

Bell

Shennington OX15 6NQ
TEL: (01295) 670274
off A422, 6m W of Banbury
This solidly built pub, dates from the
eighteenth century and is somewhat off
the beaten track. Clearly popular with
a local clientele, it turns out
competently prepared dishes such as

deep-fried Brie, lamb and mint
casserole, and duck in port and
blackberries. Hook Norton and
Boddingtons are the beers and there is
a short wine list.
Open *12 to 2.30, 6.30 (7 Sun) to 11*

SHIPTON-UNDER-WYCHWOOD

Oxfordshire   map 5

Shaven Crown Hotel

High Street,
Shipton-under-Wychwood OX7 6BP
TEL: (01993) 830330
on A361, 4m NE of Burford
The name refers to a monk's tonsure,
and this attractive honey-coloured
stone pub dates back to the fourteenth
century, when it was a monks' hospice
for Bruern Abbey. Inside and out it has
the feel of a manor-house. Hook
Norton and Hardy beers are served in
the bar along with a short menu of
standard pub food.
Open *12 to 2.30, 5 to 11*

SHRALEYBROOK

Staffordshire   map 5

Rising Sun

Knowle Bank Road,
Shraleybrook ST7 8DS
TEL: (01782) 720600
Charles I and Executioner ales are
brewed on the premises at this good
real ale house. A further four or five
beers are offered, changing as casks are
exhausted, which means that they
might get through 20 different brews in
a week – a clue that this can be a fairly
busy pub.
Open *Mon to Thur 11.30 to 3.30, 6 to
11, Fri and Sat 11.30 to 11, Sun 11.30
to 10.30*

SHUSTOKE

Warwickshire   map 5

Griffin

Shustoke B46 2LB
TEL: (01675) 481205
on B4114, 2½m E of Coleshill
Home of the Church End Brewery, the
Griffin sells its own ales as well as
those of the Exmoor Brewery and
popular national brands like Marston's
Pedigree and Theakstons Old Peculier.

Fruit wines are also on offer, and simple grub like steak cobs, club sandwiches and steak and ale pie are all reasonably priced.

Open *12 to 2.30, 7 to 11, Sun 12 to 2.30, 7 to 10.30*

SIXPENNY HANDLEY

Dorset   map 2

Roebuck

High Street,
Sixpenny Handley SP5 5NR
TEL: (01725) 552002
on B3081, 1m off A354 between Salisbury and Blandford Forum
New owners John and Ann Fury took over in mid-1998 and look keen to continue providing good locally produced real ales from the Ringwood Brewery, supplemented with other local independent brews like Hop Back.

Open *summer 11 to 11, Sun 12 to 10.30, winter 11 to 3, 6 to 11*

SMARDEN

Kent   map 3

Chequers Inn

Smarden TN27 8QA
TEL: (01233) 770217
off A28/A274, 7m W of Charing
This fourteenth-century weather-boarded inn with *en suite* accommodation offers a bistro-style menu which focuses on fish. Beers offered include Fuller's London Pride, Young's Special, draught Bass, Rother Valley Level Best and Morland Old Speckled Hen. A number of golf courses are in easy reach.

Open *11 to 2.30, 6 to 11, Sun 12 to 3, 6.45 to 10.30*

SNAPE

Suffolk   map 6

Golden Key

Priory Road, Snape IP17 1SG
TEL: (01728) 688510
just off B1069, 3m S of Saxmundham
Adnams' longest-standing tenants have served enough years between them to have fine-tuned their business to the requirements of the visitors to

Aldeburgh and the Snape Maltings. Enjoy some good, popular bar food and, if you are early enough, snatch the curved settle for the best seating.

Open *11 to 3, 6 to 11, Sun 12 to 3, 7 to 10.30*

SOUTH DALTON

East Riding of Yorkshire   map 9

Pipe and Glass Inn

West End, South Dalton HU17 7PN
TEL: (01430) 810246
off A1079/A164, 6m E of Market Weighton
This family-run country inn set in the heart of the Yorkshire Wolds offers a straightforward but interesting bar menu of things like black pudding, feta and bacon salad, duck and orange pie, and herb pancakes filled with roast vegetables. Theakston Best and McEwan's 80/- are on tap to wash it all down.

Open *Mon to Fri 12 to 2.30, 7 to 11 (10.30 in winter), Sat and Sun 12 to 3, 7 to 11; closed Sun eve Jan and Feb*

SOUTH WOODCHESTER

Gloucestershire   map 2

Ram Inn

Station Road,
South Woodchester GL5 5EL
TEL: (01453) 873329
off A46, 2m S of Stroud
This freehouse serves an eclectic range of beers, including Stones Bitter, Woodforde's Wherry and Archers Best. Daily specials may well feature smoked salmon pâté, filled baguettes, chargrilled shark steak with mustard sauce, or chicken jalfrezi with poppadums and rice. Finish with jam roly-poly.

Open *11 to 11, Sun 12 to 10.30*

SPELDHURST

Kent   map 3

George & Dragon

Speldhurst TN3 0NN
TEL: (01892) 863125
*between A26 and A264, 2m NW of
Tunbridge Wells*
This striking black and white timbered
pub, set directly opposite the church,
was built around a thirteenth-century
Wealden hall, with the most modern
bits dating from the sixteenth and
seventeenth centuries. There is a
massive log-burning inglenook and an
impressive iron fire-back dated 1604.
Open *11 to 11, Sun 12 to 10.30*

SPREYTON

Devon   map 1

Tom Cobley Tavern

Spreyton EX17 5AL
TEL: (01647) 231314
*off B3219 (from A30), 7m E of
Okehampton*
Set on the northern edge of Dartmoor,
this traditional alehouse serves Cotleigh
Tawny Bitter, Bass, a selection of malt
whiskies and a respectable selection of
wines, as well as down-to-earth home-
made bar snacks.
Open *Tue to Sat 12 to 2, 6 to 11, Sun
12 to 2, 7 to 10.30; closed L in winter*

SPROTBROUGH

South Yorkshire   map 9

Boat Inn

Nursery Lane,
Sprotbrough DN5 7NB
TEL: (01302) 857188
just off A1(M), 3m W of Doncaster
This characterful old inn with a
courtyard, built in 1652, was made
famous as the house in which Sir
Walter Scott wrote *Ivanhoe*. This
Scottish & Newcastle pub serves a
fairly standard range of beers but offers
some interesting bar food, such as
halibut meunière, and swordfish bonne
femme.
Open *Mon to Thur 11 to 3, 6 to 11,
Fri to Sun 11 to 11*

STALISFIELD GREEN

Kent   map 3

Plough

Stalisfield Green ME13 0HY
TEL: (01795) 890256
off M20/A20, 8m NW of Ashford
This fifteenth-century freehouse is set
in the gently rolling hills of the North
Downs with green fields as far as the
eye can see. A comfortable Kentish-
style pub, the Plough serves Adnams,
Wadworth 6X and Flowers IPA. A
pubby menu offers some interesting
vegetarian options.
Open *12 to 3, 7 to 11 (10.30 Sun)*

STAPLE FITZPAINE

Somerset   map 2

Greyhound Inn

Staple Fitzpaine
TEL: (01823) 480227
*between A358 and B3170, 5m SE of
Taunton*
The Greyhound was bought in late
1998 by Lionheart Inns, and the style
of the new regime had yet to emerge at
the time of going to press. If it remains
up to previous standards, the pub is
worth a visit for its location and
character. Reports please.
Open *12 to 11, Sun 12 to 10.30*

STEEPLE ASTON

Oxfordshire   map 5

Red Lion

South Street,
Steeple Aston OX6 3RY
TEL: (01869) 340225
*just off A4260, or B4030, 4m S of
Deddington*
Not easy to find, but a stalwart none
the less, this tiny pub offers food only
at lunch-time, and is, in reality, little
more than a longish narrow room.
There is plenty of clutter, a big fire on
an open hearth, and its slightly worn
character gives it the aspect of a
favourite jacket. An old friend of a pub.
Open *11 to 3, 6 to 11, Sun 12 to 3, 7
to 10.30*

STEYNING

West Sussex   map 3

Star Inn

130 High Street,
Steyning BN44 3RD
TEL: (01903) 813078
*just off A283, 5m NW of
Shoreham-by-Sea*
A child-friendly pub with spacious
garden and a family room. The
extensive bar menu offers a range of
traditional pub grub, and beers include
King & Barnes Sussex. Intriguingly, the
pub is home to something called the
Bald Headed Club.
Open *11 to 2, 5.30 to 11, Sat 11 to
11, Sun 12 to 3.30, 7 to 10.30*

STOKE BRUERNE

Northamptonshire   map 5

Boat

Stoke Bruerne NN12 7SB
TEL: (01604) 862428
just W of A508, 4m E of Towcester
Run by the Woodward family since
1877, this canalside pub is very much
one of the main features of Stoke
Bruerne, a village much focused on the
Grand Union Canal. The pub can get
very busy, but if you are there early
enough you might get a prime seat to
enjoy one of the several real ales on
offer while watching people just
messing about on boats.
Open *summer all week 11 to 11,
winter Mon to Fri 11 to 3, 6 to 11, Fri
to Sun 11 to 11*

STOKENHAM

Devon   map 1

Tradesmans Arms

Stokenham TQ7 2SZ
TEL: (01548) 580313
*off A379 Kingsbridge to Dartmouth
road, 5m E of Kingsbridge*
A fun pub with a jovial landlord. The
popular and busy bar is a small, cosy,
split-level room with alcove seating and
a log-burning stove. It offers a good
selection of regularly changing ales,
and a menu of traditional bar food.
Open *summer all week 12 to 3, 7 to
11 (10.30 Sun), winter all week 12.30
to 2.30, Fri and Sat 7 to 11*

STONE STREET

Kent   map 3

Padwell Arms

Stone Street TN15 0LQ
TEL: (01732) 761532
off A25, 3m E of Sevenoaks
According to the landlord the food is
an 'adjunct' to the beer, though reports
indicate that the food itself is pretty
good at this rural pub that attracts
locals, walkers, and horseriders. They
no doubt come to enjoy the seven real
ales that are always on – as many as a
dozen served within a week – plus two
real ciders. More reports please.
Open *12 to 3, 6 to 11, Sun 12 to 3, 7
to 10.30*

SUSWORTH

Lincolnshire   map 9

Jenny Wren

Main Street, Susworth DN17 3AS
TEL: (01724) 784000
off A519, 3m W of Scotter
This striking building was already a
pub when renamed the White Horse in
1716, and has always played an
important role for this inland port on
the River Trent. Over the years it has
performed many functions, but now
has settled down to the provision of
well-kept real ales and an interesting
bar menu.
Open *12 to 3, 5 to 11, Sun 12 to 3, 7
to 10.30*

TENTERDEN

Kent   map 3

William Caxton

West Cross, Tenterden TN30 6JR
TEL: (01580) 763142
on A28, 10m SW of Ashford
A large white-painted and tile-hung
Shepherd Neame pub, with some
forecourt seating facing the main road.
The menu includes a large range of pub
food starting with sandwiches and
baguettes, and covering the whole
gamut from fish and chips, garlic
prawns and lasagne to steak and
Guinness pie, and steaks with all the
trimmings.
Open *11 to 3, 5 to 11, Sat 11 to 11*

THOMPSON

Norfolk map 6

Chequers Inn

Griston Road, Thompson IP24 1PX
TEL: (01953) 483360

1m off A1075, 3m S of Watton
A long and narrow sixteenth-century
village inn with an impressive thatch
descending to almost head height. It
offers Adnams Best, Wolf Best and
Fuller's London Pride to the thirsty,
and an interesting bar menu of light
bites and grills, and a daily specials
board which may feature pigeon
breasts, calf's liver or halibut steak and
a variety of home-made desserts.
Open *11.30 to 2.30, 6.30 to 11, Sun
12 to 3, 7 to 10.30*

THURGARTON

Nottinghamshire map 5

Red Lion

Southwell Road,
Thurgarton NG14 7GP
TEL: (01636) 830351

on A612, 3m S of Southwell
Originally a fourteenth-century monks'
alehouse, the pub is notorious for the
murder of its elderly landlady Sarah
Ellen Clark by her niece in 1936; the
gory details are on show behind the
bar. But they are unlikely to put you
off enjoying your beef and Guinness
casserole or sweet-and-sour chicken, or
maybe one of the vegetarian choices or
cold dishes. Wash it down with a pint
of Mansfield Bitter or Old Baily.
Open *Mon to Fri 11.30 to 2.30, 6.30
to 11, Sat 11.30 to 11, Sun 12 to 10.30*

TICHBORNE

Hampshire map 2

Tichborne Arms

Tichborne SO24 0NA
TEL: (01962) 733760

off A31/B3046, 2m SW of Alresford
In a modern red-brick building,
wearing a thatched top-knot in order to
fit in with the rest of the village, the
Tichborne Arms is situated in the
pretty Test Valley. A lovely large
garden at the rear is a good place from
which to enjoy the surroundings, some
well-kept beers, including Flowers and

Wadworth 6X, and a range of country
wines and wines by the glass. Friendly
welcome.
Open *11.30 to 2.30, 6 to 11, Sun 12
to 3, 7 to 10.30*

TILLINGHAM

Essex map 3

Cap & Feathers

South Street, Tillingham CM8 7TH
TEL: (01621) 779212

*off B1021, 5m NE of Burnham-on-
Crouch*
A rare creature indeed is the Cap and
Feathers – a pub owned by one of
Britain's independent brewers, in this
case Essex-based Crouch Vale, whose
beers are stocked, as well as Hook
Norton. This weatherboarded pub
shows promise, and its confident-
sounding menu warrants a further
look. Reports please.
Open *11.30 to 3.30, 6 to 11, Sun 12
to 4, 7 to 10.30*

TIVETSHALL ST MARY

Norfolk map 6

Old Ram

Ipswich Road,
Tivetshall St Mary NR15 2DE
TEL: (01379) 676794

on A140, S of Norwich
This large roadside pub, decorated in
striking colours, is a handy stopping-off
place and is very popular. It offers an
extensive bar menu all day with
something for everyone; beers are from
Adnams and Woodforde's.
Open *11 to 11, Sun 12 to 11*

TOOT HILL

Essex map 3

Green Man

Toot Hill CM5 9SD
TEL: (01992) 522255

*off A414, between North Weald and
Chipping Ongar*
This pub lives up to its name – it is
partly covered in ivy – and offers a
modern-sounding monthly-changing
menu which is supplemented by daily
specials. Wine is very much the thing
here: as well as an extensive list, there
are monthly wine-tasting sessions. Beer

drinkers are offered Crouch Vale IPA, Marston's Pedigree and a weekly-changing guest.

Open *11 to 3, 6 to 11, Sun 12 to 3, 7 to 10.30*

TOPSHAM

Devon   map 1

Bridge

Topsham EX3 0QQ
TEL: (01392) 873862

2¼m from M5 junction 30; follow signs for Sidmouth, after 400 metres turn right at roundabout to A376 Exmouth road, then follow signs to Topsham

A building has been on this site since at least 1086, and the pub itself is still largely sixteenth century. The Cheffers family who run the pub have been there since 1897 and, as is fitting in an old brewhouse, the present-day Cheffers maintain the tradition of promoting real ales. Around ten are normally on offer, including well-known national brands and local brews.

Open *12 to 2, 6 (7 Sun) to 10.30 (11 Fri and Sat)*

TRESCO

Isles of Scilly   map 1

New Inn

Tresco TR24 0DQ
TEL: (01720) 422844

take the ferry or helicopter from Penzance

The inn is very much a key part of the life of Tresco, the second largest of the Scilly Isles. Not surprisingly, the pub has a strong nautical theme and is an ideal spot to learn about what the Isles have to offer – it has even produced its own guide to the island. A decent selection of real ales on offer includes Flowers IPA and Original, Castle Eden and St Austell Bosun's Bitter.

Open *11 to 11, Sun 12 to 3, 6 to 11*

TRUDOXHILL

Somerset   map 2

White Hart

Trudoxhill BA11 5DP
TEL: (01373) 836324

1m off A361 Frome to Shepton Mallet road

This creeper-clad seventeenth-century stone village pub was formerly a coaching-inn and is better known today as the home of the Ash Vine Brewery. The brewery has now moved to larger premises, but its beers – such as Challenger, Black Bess Porter and Hop & Glory – are still available here.

Open *11 to 3, 6 to 11, Sun 12 to 3, 6 to 10.30*

TURVEY

Bedfordshire   map 6

Three Cranes

High Street, Turvey MK43 8EP
TEL: (01234) 881305

on A428, 7m W of Bedford

This 300-year old inn in a picturesque village has a friendly atmosphere and offers typical pub grub of bangers and mash, garlic mushrooms, steak and ale pie, plus more expensive items such as a mixed grill of sirloin steak. Real ales, plus a 30-bottle wine list, are available.

Open *11 to 2.30, 6 to 11, Sun 12 to 3, 7 to 10.30*

UPTON GREY

Hampshire   map 2

Hoddington Arms

Upton Grey RG25 2RL
TEL: (01256) 862371

off B3349, 4m SE of Basingstoke

A big garden with a children's play area is a plus at this roadside pub. Inside, the décor is simple, as is the menu of 'stalwart' pub food. It is a Morland pub, serving the brewery's ales plus Bass and Flowers Original.

Open *11 to 2.30, 6 to 11, Sun 12 to 2.30, 7 to 10.30 (Sat 11.30)*

VENTNOR

Isle of Wight   map 2

Spyglass Inn

The Esplanade, Ventnor PO38 1JX
TEL: (01983) 855338

'Well-behaved dogs on leads and
muddy boots welcome,' says the blurb
at the Spyglass, prompting one to
consider perhaps that well-behaved
dogs would wear only clean boots.
Good sea views can be enjoyed from
this nautically decorated large pub
which offers live entertainment most
evenings as well as Ventor Golden,
Dorset Best and Tanglefoot ales on tap.
A menu of pub staples makes a feature
of locally caught seafood.

Open *summer all week 10.30 to 11,
winter Mon to Fri 10.30 to 3, 6.30 to
11, Sat 12 to 11, Sun 12 to 10.30*

WALCOTE

Leicestershire   map 5

Black Horse

Lutterworth Road,
Walcote LE17 4JU
TEL: (01455) 552684

on A427, 1m E of M1 junction 20
Thai cooking and good cask-
conditioned beers are what recommend
the Black Horse to *Guide* readers.
Lovers of Kaeng Phad, Prik Khing and
Phat Nam Mann Hoy, as well as
Hoskins, Hook Norton and whatever
guest happens to be on will be happy.

Open *Wed to Thur 12 to 2, Mon to
Thur 7 to 11, Fri 12 to 2, 5.30 to 11,
Sat 6.30 to 11, Sun 12 to 10.30*

WARBLETON

East Sussex   map 3

War-Bill-in-Tun

Warbleton TN21 9BD
TEL: (01435) 830636

*off B2096, 4m S of Heathfield, opposite
village church*
An old inn in a village full of history.
Its name is, in all probability, a pun on
the village name, though a more
interesting story relates it to an episode
in the civil war. Harveys aside, the pub
offers WSB and Ironmaster Bitter, both
house brews, plus a fair wine list and

an extensive menu, strong on seafood
salads.

Open *11 to 3, 6.15 to 11, Sun 12 to 3,
7 to 10.30*

WASDALE HEAD

Cumbria   map 8

Wasdale Head Inn

Wasdale Head CA20 1EX
TEL: (019467) 26229

*off A595, between Gosforth and
Holmbrook; follow the signs for 8m*
Wasdale is one of Lakeland's most
remote and unspoilt valleys, and this
whitewashed inn is dwarfed by the
peaks rising dramatically behind it. The
pub is a popular centre for rock-
climbing, walking and mountaineering,
and the energetically inclined can slake
their thirst with an impressive range of
around eight real ales, including two
house beers and a range of malt
whiskies.

Open *11 to 11 (10 winter), Sun 12.30
to 10.30*

WATLINGTON

Oxfordshire   map 2

Chequers

Love Lane, Watlington OX9 5RA
TEL: (01491) 612874

*take B4009 from M40 junction 6 and
turn right down Love Lane just before
Watlington, signposted Icknield School*
A rambling old pub, handy for visitors
to the town, boasting a summer garden
and vine-covered conservatory. There
is a fairly cosy and welcoming interior
in which to enjoy the beers from owner
Brakspear brewery, as well as
interesting-sounding dishes like
Polynesian chicken, veal chop
valdostano and Mexican sliced beef.

Open *11.30 to 2.30, 6 to 11, Sun 12
to 3, 7 to 10.30*

WELL

Hampshire   map 2

Chequers Inn

Well RG29 1TL
TEL: (01256) 862605

*off A31 at Bentley, 5m SW of Farnham;
follow signs for Well and Long Sutton*

Set on the edge of a tiny village beside a peaceful lane, deep in the heart of unspoilt Hampshire countryside, this sixteenth-century pub has an amazing vine-covered front patio and pergola. Hall & Woodhouse beers are served, and the daily-changing blackboard menu is strong on fish.
Open *Mon to Fri 11 to 3, 6 to 11, Sat 11 to 11, Sun 12 to 10.30*

WEST HUNTSPILL

Somerset   map 2

Crossways Inn

Withy Road,
West Huntspill TA9 3RA
TEL: (01278) 783756
on A38, 3m S of Burnham-on-Sea
Licensees of over 25 years' standing, Michael Ronca and Tony Eyles run a good real ale pub and a popular food operation. Flowers IPA and Original and Thomas Hardy Royal Oak are always on tap, but expect also to find guests from such breweries as RCH and Butcombe.
Open *10.30 to 3, 5.30 (6 Sat) to 11, Sun 12 to 3, 7 to 10.30*

WEST TANFIELD

North Yorkshire   map 9

Bull Inn

Church Street,
West Tanfield HG4 5JQ
TEL: (01677) 470678
on A6108 Ripon to Masham road
Built in the seventeenth century on the banks of the River Ure, the pub has a lovely riverside garden where barbecues take place in summer. A chips with everything menu is available and three of the four Yorkshire big real ales are on offer – Theakston, Tetley and Black Sheep – and there is a short wine list.
Open *11 to 11, Sun 12 to 10.30*

WEST WITTON

North Yorkshire   map 8

Wensleydale Heifer

West Witton DL8 4LS
TEL: (01969) 622322
on A684 Leyburn to Hawes road

Built in 1631, this attractive coaching-inn is situated in the heart of picturesque Wensleydale. The bar/bistro offers a mix of traditional and modern dishes. There is also a list of lunchtime bar snacks, and a separate restaurant. The usual Yorkshire ales play second fiddle to the long wine list.
Open *10am to 11pm*

WIDDOP

West Yorkshire   map 7

Pack Horse Inn

Widdop HX7 7AT
TEL: (01422) 842803
on unclassified road across Widdop Moor from Hebden Bridge to Colne, 6m NW of Hebden Bridge
Standing 1,000 feet above sea level on an old trading route used by packhorse drivers, this pub dates from the early seventeenth century. It has been substantially modernised over the years but retains a pleasant pubby feel, and serves Thwaites Bitter, Morland Old Speckled Hen, Theakston XB, Black Sheep Bitter, and over 130 malt whiskies to help dispel the cold.
Open *12 to 2.30, 7 to 11, Sun 12 to 3, 7 to 10.30*

WIDECOMBE IN THE MOOR

Devon   map 1

Rugglestone Inn

Widecombe in the Moor TQ13 7TF
TEL: (01364) 621327
off A38, 5m NW of Ashburton
A short walk from the centre of this pretty village, this cosy inn offers local real ales straight from the barrel. Butcombe Bitter and Dartmoor Best as well as local farm cider accompany home-cooked fare: beef and stout stew, roast Mediterranean vegetable and pasta bake, and steak and kidney pie will nearly always be on the specials list.
Open *11.30 to 2.30, 6 (7 winter) to 11, Sun 11 to 3, 6 to 10.30*

WILDBOARCLOUGH

Cheshire   map 8

Crag Inn

Wildboarclough SK11 0BD
TEL: (01260) 227239
off A54, 5m SE of Macclesfield
A very friendly and informative host,
plus a pleasant atmosphere enhanced
by an open fire, horse brasses and
beams, makes this pub an inviting place
in which to enjoy your Boddingtons,
Tetley or Bass. If you have come after a
day of Peak District walking, be sure to
remove your muddy boots before
entering. No food on Sunday evening
or Monday.
Open *12 to 3, 7 to 11*

WISTANSTOW

Shropshire   map 5

Plough

Wistanstow SY7 8DG
TEL: (01588) 673251
*off A49 Church Stretton to Ludlow
road, 2m N of Craven Arms*
The original tap of the Wood Brewery,
which is at the rear, this pub in a one-
street village in the fold of a valley
serves the brewery's full range of beers,
including the popular Shropshire Lad.
It also offers seasonal brews and a
number of visiting ales from other
microbreweries; brewery tours can be
arranged.
Open *12 to 3, 7 to 11*

WIVENHOE

Essex   map 3

Black Buoy Inn

Black Buoy Hill,
Wivenhoe CO7 9BS
TEL: (01206) 822425
*take B1028 (off A133 1½m E of
Colchester); in Wivenhoe turn left at
the church into East Street, pub is
200yds on right*
Standards seem to be on the up at this
Pubmaster-operated house, situated
hard by the River Colne. A traditional
interior and jovial service are to be
found here along with a decent range
of ales, including Greene King IPA and
Abbot Ale, Flowers, IPA, plus guests,

while the lengthy bar menu is strong on
chargrilling and has a balti section.
Open *11.30 to 2.30, 6.30 to 11, Sun
12 to 3, 7 to 10.30*

WOLTERTON

Norfolk   map 6

Saracen's Head

Wolterton NR11 7LX
TEL: (01263) 768909
*off A140 Aylsham to Cromer road,
through Erpingham and Calthorpe*
Self-styled as 'North Norfolk's Lost
Inn', this idiosyncratic pub in the style
of a Tuscan farmhouse is bustling with
a fun atmosphere. An above-average
wine list is supplied by Adnams, and
Adnams Bitter and a guest brew are
always on draught.
Open *11 to 3 (3.30 in winter), 6 to 11,
Sun 12 to 3, 7 to 10.30*

WOODBASTWICK

Norfolk   map 6

Fur & Feather Inn

Slad Lane,
Woodbastwick NR13 6HQ
TEL: (01603) 720003
1½m N of B1140, 8m NE of Norwich
This thatched pub in the midst of the
Norfolk Broads doubles as the brewery
tap for Woodforde's brewery, which is
next door. The pub must be one of the
very few that offers the entire range of
eight Woodforde's beers; they even
appear in the Woodforde's pie.
Open *summer 11 to 3, 6 to 11, Sun 12
to 3, 7 to 10.30, winter 12 to 2.30, 6
to 11, Sun 12 to 3, 7 to 10.30*

WORTH

Somerset   map 2

Pheasant

Worth BA5 1LQ
TEL: (01749) 672355
on B3139, 3m W of Wells
New landlord Craig D'Ovidio took
over in summer 1998 and promises an
interesting menu with dishes such as
warm salad of turkey, bacon and
honey, and stuffed pheasant with
cranberries. The pub serves Buckley's

Bitter and Bass. One to watch – reports please.

Open *Mon to Fri 11.30 to 3, 5 to 11, Sat 11 to 11, Sun 12 to 10.30*

WRENINGHAM
Norfolk   map 6
Bird in Hand
Church Road,
Wreningham NR16 1BH
TEL: (01508) 489438
off B1113, 5m S of Norwich
This large, red-brick pub offers good choice in all departments: a frequently changing bar menu, plus daily specials, and a separate restaurant menu, as well as a decent selection of wines, and a wide range of real ales, including seasonal guests.

Open *11.30 to 3, 5.30 (6 in winter) to 11, Sun 12 to 3, 6 to 10.30*

YANWATH
Cumbria   map 10
Gate
Yanwath CA10 2LF
TEL: (01768) 862386
from A6 turn right onto B5320 Pooley Bridge road after Eamont Bridge
A typical roadside Lakeland pub offering good-value food. In the centre of the hamlet of Yanwath, the Gate, like many pubs in the region, has a central entrance into a single low-ceilinged bar. Try perhaps a superior black pudding and a novel bread-and-butter pudding made with french bread; portions are generous.

Open *12 to 3, 6 to 11, Sun 12 to 2.30, 7 to 11*

YARDE DOWN
Devon   map 1
Poltimore Arms
Yarde Down EX36 3HA
TEL: (01598) 710381
take Blackmoorgate Road off A361 for 1m, then follow signs for Simonsbath for 4m
This charming old pub on the edge of Exmoor enjoys a lovely situation and is a favourite of friendly locals. Good real ales include Cotleigh Tawny and a regularly changing guest, and bar food

might include a half-pint of prawns or even a prawn curry with poppadoms.

Open *12 to 2.30, 6.30 to 11, Sun 12 to 2.30, 7 to 10.30*

SCOTLAND

BRIDGE OF CALLY
Perthshire & Kinross   map 11
Bridge of Cally Hotel
Bridge of Cally PH10 7JJ
TEL: (01250) 886231
on A93, 6m N of Blairgowrie
A house for the hungry, catering as it does for a mix of skiers, walkers, anglers and other outdoor types. If they rack up a thirst there is no real ale to slake it, but a respectable wine list compensates, and a hearty menu featuring local fish and game will restore the weary.

Open *11 to 11, Sun 12 to 10.30*

BROUGHTY FERRY
Dundee   map 11
Fisherman's Tavern
10–14 Fort Street,
Broughty Ferry DD5 2AD
TEL: (01382) 775941
off A930 (shore road)
In summer you can sit outside this seventeenth-century listed fisherman's cottage in the pavement café. This is a first-rate real ale pub specialising in the best of Scottish brewing. It also offers cask-strength malt whiskies and a bar menu strong on the local staple catch – haddock – as well as baltis, pies and salads.

Open *11 to 12 (1 Fri and Sat), Sun 12.30 to 12*

CLOVENFORDS

Borders   map 11

Clovenfords Hotel
1 Vine Street, Clovenfords TD1 3LU
TEL: (01896) 850203
on A72, 3m W of Galashiels
The hotel is set in the centre of a small
Borders village, complete with a statue
of Sir Walter Scott. Inside is a plain
lounge with an open fireplace and
pictures of local castles and rivers. The
pub sells Caledonian 80/- as a regular
ale plus occasionally changing guests,
and offers a menu likely to feature local
game such as venison and pheasant, as
well as sea trout and salmon.
Open *11 to 12, Sun 12 to 12*

COLONSAY

Argyll & Bute   map 11

Isle of Colonsay Hotel
Colonsay PA61 7YP
TEL: (01951) 200316
2hrs 15mins by ferry from Oban
A place to really get away from it all –
the ferry to the mainland visits only
three times a week. Claude and
Christine Reysenn took over the hotel
in the summer of 1998 and are
concentrating on building a daily-
changing menu based on fresh produce.
Reports please.
Open *12 to 2.30, 7 to 1am*

DERVAIG

Argyll & Bute   map 11

Bellachroy Hotel
Dervaig, Isle of Mull PA75 6QW
TEL: (01688) 400314
on B8073, 5m W of Tobermory
Beautiful views, loch, river and sea
fishing, excursions to the bird
sanctuaries of the Treshnish Islands and
the legendary island of Staffa (where
Fingal's Cave can be found) all make
this hotel an ideal place in which to
rest and revitalise.
Open *summer all week noon to 1am,
winter Mon to Fri 12 to 2.30, 5 to 1,
Sat and Sun noon to 1am*

GLENCOE

Highland   map 11

Clachaig Inn
Glencoe PA39 4HX
TEL: (01855) 811252
*just off A82, Crianlarich to Fort
William road*
A good real ale pub in a poor real ale
part of the world. At any time there are
six beers on offer, though Arrols 80/-
and Fraoch Heather Ale are permanent
fixtures. This pub in the heart of
Glencoe doubles as a mountain rescue
centre, with some of Scotland's highest
peaks forming the background scenery.
Open *Mon to Thur 11 to 11, Fri 11am
to midnight, Sat 11am to 11.30pm, Sun
12.30 to 11*

HALBEATH

Fife   map 11

Hideaway
Kingseat Road, Halbeath KY12 0UB
TEL: (01383) 725474
on A907, 2m E of Dunfermline
Newly constructed accommodation, an
extensive bar menu and superior ales
like Orkney Dark Island and Calder's
70/- mark the Hideaway out from the
run of the mill.
Open *11 to 2.30, 5 to 11, Sun 12.30
to 11*

ISLE OF WHITHORN

Dumfries & Galloway   map 9

Steam Packet
Harbour Row,
Isle of Whithorn DG8 8HZ
TEL: (01988) 500334
off A750, 12m S of Wigtown
A quayside location and a broad range
of food from snacks to restaurant
meals, backed by some fine real ales
and reasonably priced house wines,
makes the Steam Packet worth seeking
out. Menus give plenty of choice, and
include several good Scottish dishes
and daily specials.
Open *summer all week 11 to 11,
winter Mon to Thur 11 to 2.30, 6 to
11, Fri to Sun 11 to 11*

KIPPFORD

Dumfries & Galloway   map 9

Anchor Hotel

Kippford DG5 4LN
TEL: (01556) 620205
off A710, 4m S of Dalbeattie
A good menu, good beers and friendly
staff, is how one visitor summed up the
attractions of this large white pub,
overlooking the yachting marina. There
are plenty of fishy and vegetarian
offerings, and ales from Theakston and
Boddingtons.
Open *summer all week 11am to
midnight, winter Mon to Fri 11 to 3, 6
to 11, Sat and Sun 11 to 11*

KIRKTON OF GLENISLA

Angus   map 11

Glenisla Hotel

Kirkton of Glenisla PH11 8PH
TEL: (01575) 582223
*from Alyth head N on B954, turn left
on to B951, follow signs*
This seventeenth-century coaching-inn,
has long been a focal point for
travellers. The pub has an interesting
history and an equally interesting
selection of real ales from the
Aberdeenshire Brewery, plus a fair
selection of malts, a competent wine
list and an imaginative menu.
Open *summer Mon to Thur 11 to 11,
Fri and Sat 11 to 11.45, Sun 12 to 11,
winter Mon to Fri 11 to 2.30, 6 to 11,
Sat and Sun 12 to 11*

LINLITHGOW

West Lothian   map 11

Four Marys

65 High Street,
Linlithgow EH49 7ED
TEL: (01506) 842171
One of the top real ale pubs in Scotland
with a faultless line-up of almost
exclusively Scottish real ales – a feat
that only a few years ago would not
have been possible. Belhaven,
Caledonian and Deuchars are all well
represented, as are small Scottish
independents Orkney and Harviestoun.
Open *Mon to Wed 11 to 11, Thur to
Sat 11 to 11.45, Sun 12.30 to 11*

LOCH ECK

Argyll & Bute   map 11

Coylet Inn

Loch Eck PA23 8SG
TEL: (01369) 84426
*on A815, 9m N of Dunoon, at S end of
loch*
Richard Adams has run this family-
owned inn on the banks of Loch Eck
since 1969. Hire boats and fishing
permits are available from the pub, as
are Duechars IPA, McEwans 80/- and
one guest ale per week. Food is basic
pub grub.
Open *11 to 2.30, 5 to 11 (12 Fri and
Sat), Sun 12.30 to 2.30, 6.30 to 11*

PENNAN

Aberdeenshire   map 11

Pennan Inn

Pennan AB43 6JB
TEL: (01346) 561201
*on B9031, between Banff and
Fraserburgh*
The setting in a pretty fishing village
with stunning sea views and
possibilities of seeing puffins, eider
duck, gannets, seals and dolphins make
this seaside pub a popular tourist
destination. Belhaven Best is the only
ale on offer, and the good-value bar
menu plays second fiddle to a more
extensive restaurant operation.
Open *summer all week 11am to
midnight, winter Mon to Fri 11 to 2.30,
5 to 10.30, Sat and Sun 11 to 10.30*

ST MARY'S LOCH

Borders   map 11
Tibbie Shiels Inn
St Mary's Loch TD7 5LH
TEL: (01750) 42231
100yds off A708, 13m W of Selkirk
This eighteenth-century inn, named
after local widow Isabella Shiels, is
located amid spectacular hills and
enjoys breathtaking views. Described
by one as 'like the Lake District but
better because there's nobody about'.
Good Scottish ales from Broughton and
Belhaven are on offer as well as good
Scottish fare like Yarrow trout, or pâté
and oatcakes.
Open *Mon to Thur 11 to 11, Fri and
Sat 11am to midnight, Sun 12.30 to 11*

SHIELDAIG

Highland   map 11
Tigh an Eilean Hotel
Shieldaig IV54 8XN
TEL: (01520) 755251
*on A896, midway between Kinlochewe
and Strathcarron*
The 'House of the Island' is on the
edge of the sea at the centre of this
unspoilt little fishing village in the
Torridon Hills. Bar food is simple –
spicy lobster cocktail, Sheildaig crab
salad, or haggis, neeps and tatties. Most
rooms have views of the sea with the
National Trust Island of Pine in the
foreground.
Open *summer 11 to 11, Sun 12.30 to
2.30, winter Mon to Fri 11 to 2.30, 5
to 11, Sat 11 to 11*

SOUTH QUEENSFERRY

Edinburgh   map 11
Hawes Inn
Newhalls Road,
South Queensferry EH30 9TA
TEL: (0131) 331 1990
*on A904, off M9, S side of Forth Road
Bridge*
This is the inn made famous by Robert
Louis Stevenson, who chose it for the
scene of the kidnapping of young
David Balfour by his ruthless uncle
Ebenezer. Today, in the shadow of the
Forth Bridge, the pub trades on its
Stevenson and Walter Scott

associations, and the menu plays on the
Kidnapped theme. The pub serves
Burton PA, Deuchars IPA and
Caledonian 80/-.
Open *11 to 11 (midnight Mon to Fri
during Edinburgh festival), Sun 12
to 11*

STROMNESS

Orkney   map 11
Ferry Inn
John Street, Stromness,
Orkney KW16 3AA
TEL: (01856) 850280
*take the ferry from Aberdeen or
Scrabster*
This recently modernised inn is situated
centrally by the harbour area of the
picturesque town of Stromness with its
winding, narrow, paved and cobbled
streets. From the lane one can view the
harbour and beyond it the former
wartime naval base of Scapa Flow. The
well-respected Orkney Ale is on tap
and a sustaining bar menu is strong on
fish.
Open *11am to midnight (1am Thur to
Sat), Sun 11.30am to midnight*

WALES

ABERGORLECH

Carmarthenshire   map 4
Black Lion
Abergorlech SA32 7SN
TEL: (01558) 685271
on B4310, S of Llansawel
A sound village pub which has its roots
in the sixteenth century and has
managed to retain most of its authentic
character. The bar is unspoilt, with
black beams and a flagstone floor.
Worthington Best is the only ale, but it
seems to satisfy the largely Welsh-
speaking clientele. Anglers should note
that the owners have fishing rights on a
stretch of the Cothi River, which flows
past the pub.
Open *11.30 to 3, 7 to 11, Sun 12 to
3.30, 7 to 10.30*

ALLTWEN

Neath Port Talbot · map 4

Butchers Arms

Alltwen Hill, Alltwen SA8 3BP
TEL: (01792) 863100
on A474, 1m SE of Pontardawe
The owners of this pub, situated
halfway up a hill overlooking the
Swansea valley, offer not only a warm
welcome but also over 100 different
real ales every year, with around half a
dozen on at any time. There are also
more than 40 malt whiskies.
Open *12 to 3, 6.30 to 11, Sun 12 to 3,
7 to 10.30*

BEAUMARIS

Isle of Anglesey · map 7

Ye Olde Bulls Head

Castle Street LL58 8BH
TEL: (01248) 810329
This Grade II listed building dates back
to 1472 and was rebuilt in 1617.
Cromwell's troops commandeered the
pub in 1645 while laying siege to
nearby Beaumaris Castle. The inn
boasts the largest door in the British
Isles, and there is a ducking stool in the
bar. A new brasserie has recently been
constructed, so the new food operation
will be one to watch. The pub serves
Bass and Worthington plus one guest
and has an 180-bin wine list. Reports
please.
Open *11 to 11, Sun 12 to 10.30*

BODFARI

Denbighshire · map 7

Dinorben Arms

Bodfari LL16 4DA
TEL: (01745) 710309
off A55, 4m NE of Denbigh
The present Dinorben Arms is dated
1640, though the origins of the inn are
believed to be much earlier.
Smorgasbord, buffets and the
'carverboard' are the food specialities,
and over 160 different malt whiskies
and a private wine cellar compete with
a real ale selection comprising Tetley
and two guests.
Open *12 to 3.30, 6 to 12, Sun 12 to
10.30*

CADOLE

Flintshire · map 7

We Three Loggerheads

Cadole CH7 5PG
TEL: (01352) 810337
on A494 Ruthin road, 2m SW of Mold
This 250-year-old pub is a popular
destination for families visiting
Loggerheads Country Park and offers a
very child-friendly environment. Food
is listed on a printed menu and on
blackboards which feature specials such
as mussels, nut Wellington, or steak
and kidney pudding. Drink draught
Bass.
Open *summer 11 to 11, Sun 12 to
10.30, winter 11 to 3, 6 to 11, Sun 12
to 3, 7 to 10.30*

CILGERRAN

Pembrokeshire · map 4

Pendre Inn

High Street, Cilgerran SA43 2SL
TEL: (01239) 614223
off A478, 3m S of Cardigan
The inn claims to date back to the
fourteenth century. It is a freehouse
built of cream-painted local stone and
has a beer garden at the rear. Inside, a
minuscule bar, with one stone wall,
tongue-and-grove panelled walls and
beams, offers a fair range of locally
produced ales, and the whole place has
a low-key atmosphere of unspoilt
charm.
Open *Mon to Thur 11 to 2.30, 6 to
11, Fri to Sun 11 to 11 (Sun 11 to
2.30, 7 to 10.30 in winter)*

GRESFORD

Wrexham   map 7

Pant yr Ochain
Old Wrexham Road,
Gresford LL12 8TY
TEL: (01978) 853525
This beautiful old building has been
described as a cross between a
conservatory and a library. Every
available inch of wall space is crammed
with pictures or books and lots of
World War II photos. The pub offers
an ambitious menu and beers from
Whitbread and the local Plassey
Brewery.
Open *12 to 11, Sun 12 to 10.30*

HOWEY

Powys   map 4

Drovers Arms
Howey LD1 5PT
TEL: (01597) 822508
off A483, 1m S of Llandrindod Wells
Choose whichever side of this
operation most appeals to you:
drinking (Drover's Ale from Woods of
Wistanstow, selected Welsh ales); or
dining (Welsh lamb and home-cooked
food provided exclusively by local
suppliers).
Open *12 to 2.30 (exc Tues), 7 to 11
(10.30 Sun)*

HUNDLETON

Pembrokeshire   map 4

Speculation Inn
Hundleton SA71 5RU
TEL: (01646) 661306
*at junction of B4320/B4319 at
Pembroke, follow Texaco and power
station signs*
A pub since 1730, and in the current
family ownership since 1915, this
simple roadside hostelry is a good
example of the traditional local pub.
Felinfoel Drouble Dragon, Dragon
Bitter and Dragon Dark are on offer, as
is a short menu of bar snacks all priced
under £3.
Open *12 to 3 (2 in winter), 6 to 11,
Sun 12 to 3, 7 to 10.30*

LIBANUS

Powys   map 4

Tai'r Bull Inn
Libanus LD3 8EL
TEL: (01874) 625849
on A470, 3m SW of Brecon
Start climbing the towering peak of
Pen-y-Fen from right outside the front
door of this austere looking pub-cum-
B&B. Its tiny windows are a reminder
that things can get chilly up here at one
of the highest pubs in Wales, set in the
heart of the Brecon Beacons. The inn
serves solid pub grub and beers from
Whitbread.
Open *12 (6 Mon) to 11, Sun 12 to
10.30*

LLANDDAROG

Carmarthenshire   map 4

Butchers Arms
Llanddarog SA32 8NS
TEL: (01267) 275330
off A48, 5m E of Carmarthen
A well-kept, flower-festooned pub run
by friendly staff serving locally brewed
Felinfoel ales, traditional dishes such as
pan-fried cockles with laverbread and
bacon, as well as more adventurous
ones like smoked mackerel with
gooseberry sauce.
Open *summer 11 to 3, 5.30 to 11, Sun
7 to 10.30, winter 11.30 to 3, 6 to 11,
Sun 7 to 10.30*

White Hart Inn
Llanddarog SA32 8NT
TEL: (01267) 275395
off A48, 5m SE of Carmarthen
This is an interesting, cheerful village
pub with lots of character, and a
friendly welcome. The attractive old
stone building is adorned with flowers
in hanging tubs and has a beautiful
thatched roof; sit at picnic tables
outside to enjoy fine views over open
countryside.
Open *11.30 to 3, 6.30 to 12, Sun 12
to 3, 7 to 10.30*

LLANHENNOCK

Monmouthshire   map 4

Wheatsheaf Inn

Llanhennock HP6 1LT
TEL: (01633) 420468
off B4236, 2m N of Caerleon
At the top of the hill which winds
through the tiny village, this pub is an
old white, L-shaped stone farmhouse
with tables and chairs in the front
garden. Although in no way appearing
modernised, it is spick-and-span and
you can be assured of a warm welcome
from Mrs Powell and her team. All the
dishes are home-cooked and portions
are gargantuan. Wash the food down
with well-kept pints of Bass and
Worthington, plus one guest ale.
Open *summer 11 to 11, Sun 12 to 3, 7
to 10.30, winter 11 to 3, 5 to 11, Sun
12 to 3, 7 to 10.30*

LLANTHONY

Monmouthshire   map 4

Llanthony Priory

Llanthony NP7 7NN
TEL: (01873) 890487
on B4423, 9m N of Abergavenny
This higgledy-piggledy inn, formerly
the Abbey Hotel, can be found in a
startlingly beautiful setting 'like no
other I have seen', among wonderful
trees and with mountains all around. It
is built into a ruined twelfth-century
Augustinian abbey, and is a tumble-
down place of old lichen-covered
stone. Inside the bar is a vaulted crypt –
very atmospheric – where you can
drink Bass and Wadworth 6X.
Open *summer Mon to Fri 11 to 3, 6 to
11, Sat 11 to 11, Sun 12 to 10.30,
winter Fri 6 to 11, Sat 11 to 11, Sun 12
to 4*

LLOWES

Powys   map 4

Radnor Arms

Llowes HR3 5JA
TEL: (01497) 847460
*on A438 Brecon to Hereford road,
between Glasbury and Clyro, 2m W of
Hay-on-Wye*

Good wine is the big plus at the
Radnor Arms, which offers a long list
comprising a variety of regions,
countries and prices. Felinfoel is on
offer for ale lovers, and the bar menu
has one or two interesting options, like
Cantonese prawns or marinated
chicken breast. No facilities for young
children.
Open *Tue to Sun and bank hols 11 to
2.30, 6.30 to 10.30*

LLWYNDAFYDD

Ceredigion   map 4

Crown

Llwyndafydd SA44 6BU
TEL: (01545) 560396
*off A487 at Synod Inn, take A486
signposted for New Quay, turn left at
Cross Inn*
This 200-year-old pub enjoys a lovely
setting in a wooded valley near the
National Trust cliffs at New Quay. The
bar menu makes good use of local fish,
while a good wine list and a selection
of malt whiskies support Flowers IPA
and Original, Boddingtons, Wadworth
6X and numerous guest ales.
Open *12 to 3, 5.30 (6 in winter) to 11,
Sun 12 to 3, 6 to 10.30*

MONTGOMERY

Powys   map 4

Dragon

Montgomery SY15 6PA
TEL: (01686) 668359
*on B4385, 3m E of A483 Newtown to
Welshpool road*
A good range of sandwiches is available
at the Dragon, alongside a bar menu of
things like grilled peppered mackerel or
Yorkshire pudding with steak and
kidney in stout; there is also a separate
restaurant menu. Wash down a roast
pork and apple sandwich or a jumbo
sausage sandwich with a pint of
Wood's Bitter.
Open *11 to 11, Sun 12 to 3, 7 to
10.30*

NEVERN

Pembrokeshire   map 4

Trewern Arms

Nevern SA42 0NB
TEL: (01239) 820395
on B4582, 2m E of Newport
A picturesque, ivy-clad, sixteenth-
century inn situated in its own grounds
on the banks of the River Nevern. Ideal
for historians and ramblers: visitors
should stop by the eleventh-century
church with its Celtic Cross and
famous 'Bleeding Yew Tree' before
returning to the pub to enjoying a pint
of Castle Eden or Flowers.
Open *11 to 3, 6 to 11, Sun 12 to 3, 7
to 10.30*

OLD RADNOR

Powys   map 4

Harp Inn

Old Radnor LD8 2RH
TEL: (01544) 350655
*off A44, between New Radnor and
Kington*
One handpump belongs to Hancock's
HB and the other to whatever guest is
on offer. The bar menu covers a wide
range from filled baguettes to orange
and mozzarella salad. This 500-year-
old inn is a good place to rest after
exploring Offa's Dyke, Radnor Forest
and the Welsh Marches.
Open *Mon to Fri 6 to 11, Sat and Sun
12 to 3, 6 to 11*

OLDWALLS

Swansea   map 4

Greyhound Inn

Oldwalls SA3 1HA
TEL: (01792) 391027 and 390146
off B4295/B4271, just W of Llanrhidian
Child-friendly pub enjoying a superb
location across from Cefn Bryn hill
and Arthur's stone, the majesty of
which is best appreciated over a pint
of one of the real ales on tap – usually
two or three guests as well as Bass,
Marston's Pedigree, Bullmastiff Bitter
and others.
Open *all week 11 to 11*

REYNOLDSTON

Swansea   map 4

King Arthur

Higher Green,
Reynoldston SA3 1AD
TEL: (01792) 391099
Set in a beautiful location on Cefn Bryn
in the centre of the Gower Peninsula,
the King Arthur enjoys superb views of
grassland to the front and woodland to
the rear. This seventeenth-century pub
is great for families who can arrive by
car or on horseback and tie up at the
hitching pole. Both horse and rider can
refresh themselves with Bass,
Worthington, Brains or Felinfoel
Double Dragon, though the hearty
menu is not suited to horses.
Open *11 (12 in winter) to 11, Sun 11
to 10.30*

RHYD-DDU

Gwynedd   map 7

Cwellyn Arms

Rhyd-Ddu LL54 6TL
TEL: (01766) 890321
*on A4085, between Caernarfon and
Beddgelert*
A useful bolt-hole in this magnificent
Snowdonia wilderness. Its extensive
menu of bar food staples is aimed at
hungry passers-by who can enjoy the
lovely views while having a beer with
an unusual name, such as Plassey's
CWRW Tudno and Dragon's Breath or
Brains Reverend James.
Open *11 to 11, Sun 12 to 10.30*

ST DOGMAELS

Pembrokeshire   map 4

Ferry Inn

St Dogmaels SA43 3LF
TEL: (01239) 615172
on B4546, 1m W of Cardigan
An attractive waterside inn offering
Wadworth 6X, Brains Reverend James,
and Shepherd Neame Bishop's Finger
as well as guests from Welsh breweries.
It also serves a short, basic bar menu of
the usual staples, plus a selection of
specials with the emphasis on a local
ingredients; there is also a children's
menu.

Open *12 to 3 (2.30 in winter), 6 (7 in winter) to 11*

TALYBONT

Powys   map 4

Star

Talybont LD3 7YX
TEL: (01874) 676635
½m off A40, 6m SE of Brecon
Simple pub grub and an exceptional range of real ales draw people to the Star. No fewer than ten handpumps dispense a constantly changing selection, featuring a range of ales from major regionals and top-notch independents.

Open *Mon to Fri 11 to 3, 6 to 11, Sat 11 to 11, Sun 12 to 10.30*

TREMEIRCHION

Denbighshire   map 7

Salusbury Arms

Tremeirchion LL17 0UN
TEL: (01745) 710262
off A55 at Rhualt, on B5429, 5m N of Denbigh
This fourteenth-century coaching-inn offers a very reasonably priced decent wine list, a very creditable vegetarian menu, a children's menu and separate bar and restaurant menus. At lunchtime it is likely to feature baps, sandwiches and jacket potatoes with a few hot dishes such as pork chop and apple sauce, and in the evening there are plenty of steaks. No food on Sunday evening or Mondays.

Open *Tue to Sat 12 to 3, 7 to 11, Sun 12 to 3, 7 to 10.30*

INDEX OF ENTRIES

Index of main entries

Report form

To *The Which? Guide to Country Pubs,*
FREEPOST, 2 Marylebone Road, London NW1 4DF

PUB NAME ⸺⸺⸺⸺⸺⸺⸺⸺⸺⸺⸺

Address ⸺⸺⸺⸺⸺⸺⸺⸺⸺⸺⸺

⸺⸺⸺⸺⸺⸺⸺⸺ Telephone ⸺⸺⸺

Date of visit ⸺⸺⸺⸺⸺⸺⸺⸺⸺⸺

From my personal experience this establishment should be
(please tick)

main entry ☐   'Out and About' entry ☐   excluded ☐

Please describe what you ate and drank (with prices, if known), and
give details of location, service, atmosphere etc.

My meal for ___ people cost £____ Value for money? yes ☐   no ☐

I am not connected in any way with the management or proprietors.

Name and address (BLOCK CAPITALS) _____

_____

_____

Signed _____

Report form

To *The Which? Guide to Country Pubs,*
FREEPOST, 2 Marylebone Road, London NW1 4DF

PUB NAME ⸺⸺⸺⸺⸺⸺⸺⸺⸺⸺

Address ⸺⸺⸺⸺⸺⸺⸺⸺⸺⸺

⸺⸺⸺⸺⸺⸺⸺⸺ Telephone ⸺⸺⸺

Date of visit ⸺⸺⸺⸺⸺⸺⸺⸺⸺

From my personal experience this establishment should be
(please tick)

main entry ☐   'Out and About' entry ☐   excluded ☐

Please describe what you ate and drank (with prices, if known), and
give details of location, service, atmosphere etc.

Please turn over

My meal for ___ people cost £____ Value for money? yes ❑ no ❑

I am not connected in any way with the management or proprietors.

Name and address (BLOCK CAPITALS) _____

_____

_____

Signed _____

Report form

To *The Which? Guide to Country Pubs,*
FREEPOST, 2 Marylebone Road, London NW1 4DF

PUB NAME ⎯⎯⎯⎯⎯⎯⎯⎯⎯⎯⎯⎯⎯⎯⎯⎯⎯⎯⎯

Address ⎯⎯⎯⎯⎯⎯⎯⎯⎯⎯⎯⎯⎯⎯⎯⎯⎯⎯⎯

⎯⎯⎯⎯⎯⎯⎯⎯⎯⎯⎯⎯⎯⎯⎯⎯ Telephone ⎯⎯⎯⎯⎯

Date of visit ⎯⎯⎯⎯⎯⎯⎯⎯⎯⎯⎯⎯⎯⎯⎯⎯⎯

From my personal experience this establishment should be
(please tick)

main entry ☐   'Out and About' entry ☐   excluded ☐

Please describe what you ate and drank (with prices, if known), and
give details of location, service, atmosphere etc.

Please turn over

My meal for ___ people cost £____ Value for money? yes ❏   no ❏

I am not connected in any way with the management or proprietors.

Name and address (BLOCK CAPITALS) _____

_____

_____

Signed _____

Report form Pub 4

To *The Which? Guide to Country Pubs*,
FREEPOST, 2 Marylebone Road, London NW1 4DF

PUB NAME _____

Address _____

_____ Telephone _____

Date of visit _____

From my personal experience this establishment should be
(please tick)

main entry ☐   'Out and About' entry ☐   excluded ☐

Please describe what you ate and drank (with prices, if known), and
give details of location, service, atmosphere etc.

Please turn over

My meal for ___ people cost £____ Value for money? yes ☐   no ☐

I am not connected in any way with the management or proprietors.

Name and address (BLOCK CAPITALS) _____

_____

_____

Signed _____

Report form

To *The Which? Guide to Country Pubs,*
FREEPOST, 2 Marylebone Road, London NW1 4DF

PUB NAME —————————————————————————————

Address ———————————————————————————————

————————————————————————— Telephone ——————

Date of visit ————————————————————————————

From my personal experience this establishment should be
(please tick)

main entry ☐   'Out and About' entry ☐   excluded ☐

Please describe what you ate and drank (with prices, if known), and
give details of location, service, atmosphere etc.

Please turn over

My meal for ___ people cost £___ Value for money? yes ☐   no ☐

I am not connected in any way with the management or proprietors.

Name and address (BLOCK CAPITALS) _____

_____

_____

Signed _____

To *The Which? Guide to Country Pubs,*
FREEPOST, 2 Marylebone Road, London NW1 4DF

PUB NAME ————————————————————————

Address ————————————————————————

———————————————————————— Telephone ——————

Date of visit ————————————————————————

From my personal experience this establishment should be
(please tick)

main entry ☐   'Out and About' entry ☐   excluded ☐

Please describe what you ate and drank (with prices, if known), and
give details of location, service, atmosphere etc.

Please turn over

My meal for ___ people cost £____ Value for money? yes ❏   no ❏

I am not connected in any way with the management or proprietors.

Name and address (BLOCK CAPITALS) _____

_____

_____

Signed _____

Report form

Pub 4

To *The Which? Guide to Country Pubs,*
FREEPOST, 2 Marylebone Road, London NW1 4DF

PUB NAME —————————————————————————

Address —————————————————————————

————————————————————— Telephone ——————

Date of visit —————————————————————————

From my personal experience this establishment should be
(please tick)

main entry ☐   'Out and About' entry ☐   excluded ☐

Please describe what you ate and drank (with prices, if known), and
give details of location, service, atmosphere etc.

My meal for ___ people cost £____ Value for money? yes ❏   no ❏

I am not connected in any way with the management or proprietors.

Name and address (BLOCK CAPITALS) _____

_____

_____

Signed _____